MAKE

WORLDS

Willy Louis Jeanne De Smedt

The Book For Our Time!

The Revelation of John

READABLE TO THE CONGREGATION

ISBN 9791220143981
First edition: November 2023

The Book For Our Time!

Notes from the Translator

While rummaging through the contents of a stairway cupboard during spring cleaning, I came across a very old and dilapidated book with the title: "HET BOEK VOOR ONZE TIJD" (The Book for Our Time), written in Dutch by Friedrich Wilhelm Schwartz in 1872. The book was about the Revelation of John. Being very interested in the return of our Lord Jesus Christ, I immediately began to read the book.

As I read along, I became more and more excited and developed a longing to impart the knowledge and wisdom found in this book to all who would be interested. I studied the book diligently for over 40 years, checking each reference in the Bible, and researching Church and world history books to ascertain the validity of the illuminating and often unknown facts revealed in this amazing book. During this time many predictions came into fulfilment before my very eyes. This resulted in my being strongly convinced that the writer had been inspired by the Holy Spirit, and, since his main reference source was the Bible, and his historical facts could be found all over, I decided to translate this wonderful book into the English language for the future.

I adhered to the original text in Dutch as much as possible, and did so for the first six periods, except for the final date in the Chronology of Revelation on page 13, where 100 years could be added since the book was originally written in 1872. As I proceeded with the translation, I decided to divide the work into two volumes: Volume I dealing with the past (six periods) and Volume II dealing with the seventh period, the recent past, the present and the future.

May the earnest reader derive much joy and understanding at the clear and simple explanations of the imagery and prophetic language of the Book of Revelation, and, as I did, may he diligently confirm the explanation of the meaning of each word by referring to the given texts in the Bible.

"Blessed is he that readeth, and they that hear the words of this prophecy, and keep those things which are written therein: for the time is at hand." (Rev 1:3.)

The Translator

FOREWORD

This work was first published in 1872. Soon sold out and as a result of many enquiries, a second publication seemed called for. Because the year 1872 was so remarkable in relation to the Revelation of John, this work was republished without alterations. However, at the end, the reader will find a short summary of what transpired since 1872 in relation to the subsequent fulfilment of Revelation. We experience very exciting times and it is of great interest for all to know what will happen in the near future so that we can shun evil and choose that which is good.

The word of Jesus also applies to our time: "And *now I have told you before it come to pass, that, when it is come to pass, ye might believe.*" (John 14:29)

The Author

VOLUME ONE

The Past

PROLOGUE

And now I have told you before it come to pass, that, when it is come to pass, ye might believe JESUS.
John 14:29.

And he said, Unto you it is given to know the mysteries of the kingdom of God: But to others in parables; that seeing they might not understand JESUS.
Luke 8:10.

The Revelation of John, to be read to the congregation

A very promising title! Will the book give what its title promises?

After all that was already written about the Revelation, is it possible to write something that is new and important?

After reading just a few sentences further, the Christian reader will, we hope, immediately admit, that the book can give what its title promises. He will admit that he gains a totally new insight in the Revelation, and that with this key, the closed book, as the Revelation of John, regardless of all given interpretations, is still called today, can also be opened and its contents be understood even by a simple layperson.

Indeed, it is high time! The Lord Jesus gave His Revelation to His servants, to show them, what would happen (Rev 1:1.) and the most detailed and by far the greatest part concerns our time.

Daily we see more and more of the predicted events developing. If the Revelation must be understood by the Lord's servants, then it must be now, while we live in the time for which the Lord seems to have given His Revelation, because He depicted this time in such particular detail, and this specifically in order to warn His servants against the seduction of the great falling away, strengthen them in faith in Him and to preserve them in His Name.

The mysteries of the kingdom of God are not revealed to the wise of this world but to the pure in hart. (Luke 10:21) such as the servants of the Lord must be. And, should the simple servants of God, to whom the Revelation is given, understand it clearly, then the Revelation must also be simple, which it is.

That so many incomprehensible books have been written about the so-called incomprehensible Revelation, that men searched so far away, what was to be found so near, and that this interpretation was not found long ago, will remain as much of a mystery to the reader as it was for us once we gained the correct insight into the Revelation.

In order to immediately understand that the way we pursued, can be the only way to the correct interpretation of the predictions contained in this book, we will show by means of a few words how we, as simple servants of God, arrived at our conclusions.

Having read much, though not all, that is written about the Revelation, we found no satisfying agreement amongst the interpreters. They all diverged too far from each other, some spiritualized things too much, others took things up materially or carnally; everywhere too much depended on human reasoning, and everything went too high and too deep to be understood by simple servants of the Lord. Above all, the interpretations were often distorted and fashioned according to the rigid pattern of church and world history. With much reasoning one could try to fit one to the other, but never without often having the lines of the picture and examples diverging and crossing each other.

How else could it be? When one and the same image or vision from Revelation, was taken by different interpreters to apply to totally different happenings and situations, which sometimes occurred hundreds of years apart from each other. This experience caused many to shun the Revelation and to put it aside as incomprehensible.

However, we must admit, that although some prophesies and visions were interpreted quite well by a few writers (i.e. Auberlen), we never found a consequent, continuous interpretation, which, because of its clarity, simplicity and sense, and an irresistible overwhelming power of persuasion, offered an immediate feeling to the Christian mind of being the truth and the only one.

In despair over so much uncertainty, but yet longing to understand, what the Lord wanted to say to His servants, we asked for what could not be found with men from Him, from His Word, the Holy Scripture, and found it therein. This is the secret, the only true key to the Revelation, whereby it becomes understandable even to the simplest. What follows shows how!

The Revelation is given in imagery language and visions, like the prophesies of the Old Testament.

The Lord Jesus himself points to it in Rev 1:20, when He himself interprets the first image: "The mystery of the **seven stars**, which thou sawest in my right hand, and the **seven candlesticks**. The **seven stars** are the **seven angels** of the churches: and the **seven candlesticks** which thou sawest are the **seven churches**". Likewise, further on, we find in Rev 17:12: "The **ten horns** which thou sawest are **ten kings**" and in verse 15, "The **waters** which thou sawest are **nations**" and in verse 18, "The

woman which thou sawest is that **great city**", as well as Rev 19:8: "The **white linen** is the **righteousness of saints**".[1]

We see that the interpretation of some of the images in Revelation is explained by the Revelation itself. All interpreters of Revelation agree **so far**. **Why not further?**

What could be closer at hand, than to seek the meaning of the rest of the images, not explained in the Revelation, in the other books of the Holy Scriptures, especially in the prophecies of the Old Testament and in the parables of the Lord Jesus, (Matt 13:3, 10, 11). Indeed, the Lord himself often explained the meaning of His parables, (Matt 13:18–23, 36–43); as also did some of the prophets of the Old Testament, (Isaiah 9–14). What could be nearer at hand, we ask again, than the supposition that the Holy Spirit, who inspired the word of God and also this Revelation to the holy men of God, (2 Tim 3:16) and thus uttered His prophesies in figurative language and parables, speaking as it were, **a unique and personal language**, **remaining consequent enough** in the use of images, ensuring thereby that the meaning of the imagery in Revelation can be tracked down.

The repetition of so many words, images, expressions, even half and whole sentences from the prophecies of the Old Testament, should have been noticed earlier already. [2]

If it would seem, therefore, that through the consequent application of this principle, the Revelation should contain clearly understandable sentences and that its predictions had resulted in a clear, exact and indisputable fulfilment in the past centuries, then the meaning of the yet unfulfilled prophesies and visions concerning the future would also, by the same token, become clearly understandable, and thus, **the only true way to understand Revelation**, **and its only true interpretation would have been found.**

All previous attempts at interpretation were undertaken with the key of human wisdom. This one, taken from God's Word, would at least be a divine key.

---

[1] With these indications Christ Jesus not only once and for all discounted all the opponents of figurative (Allegorical) interpretations of the Revelation, but also gave the direction, in which its meaning and interpretation should be looked at.

[2] Vitringa correctly wrote: "In this one book (The Revelation.) everything is accumulated which is recommended in exceptional power or beauty, in the prophetic writings of the Old Testament.

At least a trial in this direction was worth it; the reward would be great if successful. – We have tried and succeeded beyond all prayers and expectations.

An indescribable joyous surprise often took hold of us, when, as if by magic, within a few moments, an image or an obscure word was revealed in plain language and its meaning proved to be the only true one as meant by Jesus himself, thrusting itself upon our heart with the undeniable power of truth. The interested reader of this work will often also experience this joyous surprise, when God's Word concerning the dark depths of Revelation suddenly shout out loud: "There is light.", and will often of his own volition say, concerning our assurance which was hard to believe, that we indeed did not promise too much with this work, but remained well below the truth with our promise.

Because of the originality of the solutions along this way, we could not take over anything from other writers, but the Revelation unfolded to a **completely new**, yet easily understood **prophetic picture of the history of the striving and victorious Church of Christ.**

All the unexplainable and natural wonders, which one has to accept, crumble completely by this method, and are solved by God's Word in the most simple and natural way, becoming understandable for everyone.

We do not know whether an explanation such as ours was ever published. To us, at least, this is totally unknown.

Even though some interpreters came *somewhat* close to it, we are still of the opinion to be able to answer this question in the negative, because, would it had been given, we would not have had to look for another.

Some parts of this work could easily be highlighted more intensively and more proof from the holy Scriptures could be added to it.

We do not claim it to be perfect; on the contrary: but nothing more than a powerful sketch in highlights. But on the whole, we trust, that the Christian reader will accept this interpretation as the true one, and that the controversy concerning the meaning of the Revelation is herewith resolved. With all humbleness, we believe we may consider this to be certain. An obstacle offers itself to good understanding of the Revelation, when one views it from the standpoint of a specific confession held by church associations or denominations, (Protestant or Roman).

On the contrary, seeing that God's Word must never be tested according to one confession, but rather that each confession should be tested according to God's Word, promotes as much as possible a universal point of view. We find this point of view promoted in the apostolic creed: "I believe in a holy universal Christian Church." The Revelation is not given to any particular church but encompasses the whole congregation, which the Son of God gathers to himself from the whole of the human race, to protect and keep. It is given to all the people of the New Testament, the body of Christ. (1 Cor 12:27. Eph 1:22, 23.). What good or evil will occur therein in the course of the centuries is predicted in images and in the language of the Holy Spirit and is therefore given for the whole congregation of Jesus Christ, i.e.: to all believers, whom He ransomed by His Blood as His property, regardless from which earthly church denomination. What concerns the much-discussed construction of Revelation, if it was as complicated as Gärtner proposed in his *Morgenlicht van den Wereldsabbath,* (Amsterdam, H. de Hoogh, 1866), it would be incomprehensible to the simple servants of the Lord. Its construction is on the contrary very simple, easy to accept and to remember.

The first chapter is an introduction. Then, follows:

1st Part. The history of Christ's Church on earth, or the Striving Church. (Contained in chapters 2, 3, 6. 7:1–7, 8, 9, 10, 11, 12. 13. 14:6–20, 16, 17, 18. 19:11–21).

2nd Part. The Church of Christ in the Kingdom of Glory, or the Victorious Church. (Described in chapters 4, 5. 7:9–17. 11:15–19. 14:1–5. 15:2–4. 19:1–9, 20, 21. 22:1–5).

The first part was always the stumbling block to all interpreters and readers of Revelation.

It is in its composition the most difficult part of the whole of Revelation and yet extremely simple once one understands the figurative language of Revelation.

This part contains, first, the seven candlesticks or epistles (letters), then, the seven seals, followed by the seven trumpets, and finally, the seven vials, all mentioned in part 1.

Each of the four sub-divisions, candlesticks, seals, trumpets and vials predict the same periods of the history of the Church on Earth up to the Kingdom of Glory; each however deals with a different theme from history.

At the end of each of the four sub-divisions, the Church of Christ is described to us as being in the Kingdom of Glory, as mentioned in part 2.

The four parts, candlesticks, seals, trumpets, and vials, though described one after the other, actually begin at the same time and constantly and simultaneously remain next to each other, so that the first period of Christ's

Church on earth is described in the first candlestick, the first seal, the first trumpet and the first vial.

The second period is sketched in the second candlestick, the second seal, the second trumpet and the second vial, and, similarly up to the seventh period, in the seventh candlestick, the seventh seal, the seventh trumpet and the seventh vial.

Each period in the Revelation predicts the following:

In the candlestick: the light or spiritual life of the congregation.

In the seal:　　　the spiritual life of powers in church and state.

In the trumpet:　the condition and the effect of the Gospel preached.

In the vial:　　　the pouring out of the judgement of God.

The seven periods of Christ's church on earth now seem to be:

> The 1st period from 33 AD to 324 AD.
> The 2n period from 324 AD to 622 AD.
> The 3rd period from 622 AD to 914 AD.
> The 4th period from 914 AD to 1215 AD.
> The 5th period from 1215 AD to 1517 AD.
> The 6th period from 1517 AD to 1815 AD.
> The 7th period from 1815 AD to 2? AD.

The whole concept of the construction of Revelation now lies therein that the flow of the story is as follows: the Lord Jesus shows John, that the history of the Christian Church on earth up to His return will consist of *seven periods*, and sketches *firstly*, in the *seven Candlesticks*, how *the spiritual condition of the congregation* will be in the seven consecutive periods (Rev 2 & 3). (Rev 4. 6. 7:9–17. 15:2–4. 19:1–9. Rev 20. 21. 22:1–5).

Chronology of Church history in Revelation

For as much as it is presently fulfilled, **1893.**

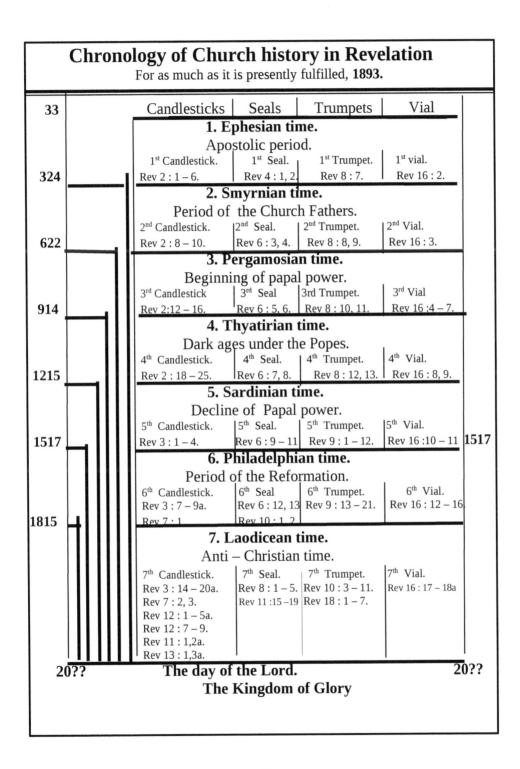

	Candlesticks	Seals	Trumpets	Vial
33				

1. Ephesian time.

Apostolic period.

1st Candlestick.	1st Seal.	1st Trumpet.	1st vial.
Rev 2 : 1 – 6.	Rev 4 : 1, 2.	Rev 8 : 7.	Rev 16 : 2.

324

2. Smyrnian time.

Period of the Church Fathers.

2nd Candlestick.	2nd Seal.	2nd Trumpet.	2nd Vial.
Rev 2 : 8 – 10.	Rev 6 : 3, 4.	Rev 8 : 8, 9.	Rev 16 : 3.

622

3. Pergamosian time.

Beginning of papal power.

3rd Candlestick	3rd Seal	3rd Trumpet.	3rd Vial
Rev 2:12 – 16.	Rev 6 : 5, 6.	Rev 8 : 10, 11.	Rev 16 :4 – 7.

914

4. Thyatirian time.

Dark ages under the Popes.

4th Candlestick.	4th Seal.	4th Trumpet.	4th Vial.
Rev 2 : 18 – 25.	Rev 6 : 7, 8.	Rev 8 : 12, 13.	Rev 16 : 8, 9.

1215

5. Sardinian time.

Decline of Papal power.

5th Candlestick.	5th Seal.	5th Trumpet.	5th Vial.
Rev 3 : 1 – 4.	Rev 6 : 9 – 11	Rev 9 : 1 – 12.	Rev 16 :10 – 11

1517 ... **1517**

6. Philadelphian time.

Period of the Reformation.

6th Candlestick.	6th Seal	6th Trumpet.	6th Vial.
Rev 3 : 7 – 9a.	Rev 6 : 12, 13	Rev 9 : 13 – 21.	Rev 16 : 12 – 16.
Rev 7 : 1	Rev 10 : 1, 2		

1815

7. Laodicean time.

Anti – Christian time.

7th Candlestick.	7th Seal.	7th Trumpet.	7th Vial.
Rev 3 : 14 – 20a.	Rev 8 : 1 – 5.	Rev 10 : 3 – 11.	Rev 16 : 17 – 18a
Rev 7 : 2, 3.	Rev 11 :15 –19	Rev 18 : 1 – 7.	
Rev 12 : 1 – 5a.			
Rev 12 : 7 – 9.			
Rev 11 : 1,2a.			
Rev 13 : 1,3a.			

20?? ... **The day of the Lord.** ... **20??**

The Kingdom of Glory

Thereafter the Lord Jesus once more begins with the first period to sketch the *condition and effect of the gospel preaching* during the seven periods, in the *seven Trumpets* (Rev 8:7 to Rev 14) and ends by predicting in the *seven Vials* (Rev 16 to 19) *the seven judgements* of God in each of the seven consecutive periods. Each period therefore consists of, 1 candlestick, 1 seal, 1 trumpet and 1 vial.

The flow of time shown in the chronology on page 13, concerning the already fulfilled part of Revelation, will make this evident.

We thus presently live in the seventh period, which is, in the Laodicean or anti-Christian period of the congregation, and under the seventh candlestick, the seventh seal, the seventh trumpet and the seventh vial, which already began its outpouring.

All this will become clear to the reader once the language of Revelation is understood.

According to this construction, as it becomes clear to us through the interpretation of its imagery, Revelation is really very simple, easy for everyone to understand and to remember, and up to the present, literally fulfilled in church history, as we will show in this work.

The plan is to discover for each period, the meaning of the images and visions in the candlestick, seal, trumpet, and vial, in God's Holy Word, and, with each unravelled image, indicate with only one word, its fulfilment in church history, in order to be better understood and easily remembered.

At the end of each period, we will translate the figurative language of the predictions in simple language (Paraphrase) and juxtapose the church history against it for as much as it already belongs to the past.

For this purpose, we will not write the church history ourselves, thereby avoiding suspicion, that we may write it to suit our interpretation of Revelation but will refer the reader to two generally well-known writers of church history, available in many hands, and published long before this interpretation of the Revelation of John. They are:

1.*Condensed chronological overview of the church history*, Mr W. van Loon, Amsterdam, H. Höveker, 1863.

2.*History of the Church of Christ Jesus, in connection with prophesies and Revelation,* translated from French by E. Guers. Amsterdam, H. M. Bremer. 1868.

The result which we will achieve is the end fulfilment of Revelation.

There is, however, another less important fulfilment: the foreshadowed, see the work by Guers mentioned above, in the prologue, pages 5–7, also called the *typical fulfilment*.

Such were for example, Isaac and Jacob, foreshadows or types of Jesus.

It cannot be denied that we see a foreshadowing of the already growing anti-Christian kingdom in Popedom and Mohamedanism.

Unbelief always reveals itself in the same, ever-recurring direction, which, through its repetition forms a certain pre-set pattern or type, wherein the final falling away is foreshadowed. This typical fulfilment is freely indicated by many writers like Guers. Our plan with this work is only to research with the reader the actual or end fulfilment of Revelation. Wherever necessary, we will bring to the attention the typical foreshadowed fulfilment, which is still considered by many to be the actual fulfilment. Of greater importance, we intend to show the similarity between the prophesies of Daniel and the Revelation, where applicable.

We can give the assurance and predict that, through this manner of research, we will come to highly noteworthy results, differing completely from other writers. Our wish is for the reader to find as much satisfaction and strengthening of faith in these pages, as we ourselves enjoyed in our research; a wish, we trust, that will find a measure of fulfilment when introduced to our readers who are interested in Christian truths. *Just as the Revelation receives its light from the Holy Scriptures, it in turn, throws a reciprocating and shining light upon many dark passages in God's Word, giving a clear answer to many, hereto unanswered questions and a wide insight into many mysteries.*

Because we actually live in the period (7th), which is described in particular detail in Revelation, which otherwise excels in shortness and power, indicating the high importance of this time,[3] that the Lord of the Church specifically wants to bring to notice these happenings, we propose, if God gives us life, strength and wisdom, to add a short postscript to our publication of this work, published in 1872, to show how we have progressed in the time table of history and Revelation, and which signs of the times have developed in fulfilment of prophecies.

Due to the sanctity and importance of this subject, we avoided all desire to show-off and sacrificed the striving after beauty, style or the reader's thanks.

A silent hope encouraged us throughout this work, namely, that, in God's hand, it could perhaps serve to convince many, who in all

---

[3] Such as for example: *"The wounded head."*, Rev 13:3, since the issuing of our proof-reading in 1871, *already half healed* and Rev 13 : 1 totally healed.

uprightness cannot believe the Christian truths, through the clear interpretation of these prophesies and their accurate fulfilment in Church and world history, that Christ, God's Son, truly is God, and that the testimony concerning himself, which He gave in the Holy Scriptures and in Revelation is true. When He came to this earth, the Lord confirmed His mission and godly power through signs and miracles, whereby many unbelievers became believers. Those who, today, twenty centuries later, do not believe in Him, will also not be convinced by the story of Jesus' miracles. They refuse categorically to believe the story as well as His testimony of himself. For them, however, Jesus also left this prophesy up until our days. Indeed, God himself and only He, can predict so accurately, what will occur in His Church in the following twenty centuries, and He, who as messenger of God, presents such a letter of credit, surely also earns credibility in what He testifies about His own personality and mission.

May then the Lord bless this poor attempt, to the honour of His never fully praised name and to the confirmation of His truth into the hearts of believers and unbelievers, give them ears to hear what the spirit sayeth to the congregation, enlightened eyes of the mind, and a receptive spirit, to understand what it was the Lord of the congregation wanted to reveal unto us through His old servant John on the Isle of Patmos.

For the enlightening texts, we made use of the state translation 1869. Ned. Bijbelgenootskap. Where we found a better form of the original text in the Lutherian or in the V.d. Palm translations, we used it a few times but indicated the source. Also, for the text in Revelation, we used those in the State translation, not because of its excellence, but so as not to offend the congregation with a totally new translation.

In some cases, we had to make use of better writings in the original, which relied on good sources. Now that the true meaning and fulfilment of the prophesies became known, some writings seemed completely impossible.

We had to discard many important exegetical and critical remarks, because we regarded them as less necessary for the congregation, and did not want to unnecessarily increase the scope of this work.

To theologians, these will become apparent to the spirit as a matter of course. Through this work, nevertheless, we resolved to open a new and important field of study and research and to restore the so often misunderstood Revelation to its elevated godly value. Only after reading the complete work can judgement about it be reached.

From the critics, we expect that they will be loyal and not be directed against our human faults and imperfections, which we acknowledge at the onset, not expanding on small issues, but only regarding the truth of the strict and consequent principle we applied; <u>The figurative language of the Holy Spirit in the biblical scriptures is the key to the Revelation of John</u>.

INTRODUCTION

> For I testify unto every man that heareth the words of
> the prophecy of this book, If any man shall add
> unto these things, God shall add unto him the
> plagues that are written in this book:
> And if any man shall take away from the words of the
> book of this prophecy, God shall take away his part
> out of the book of life, and out of the holy city, and
> from the things which are written in this book.
>
> Rev 22:18, 19.

The book of Revelation has always been the subject of much reflection. The interpretations, in part or more elaborate, given about this book during the course of the centuries are, therefore, also numerous and, especially in our time, many believers sit down to research through earnest study and prayers, to understand the deep mysteries of this highly important scripture, and to reveal it to the less developed masses in Christendom. As unbelievers boldly tear apart Revelation and reject and mock it as a Jewish fantasy or describe it as a controversial epistle of John against the apostleship of Paul, God creates a growing longing in the heart of his children, to hear, **what the spirit says to the congregation**.

The church of Christ nevertheless begins to feel in general, **that the end of present things is near**, and that the glorious day cannot be far away, on which the Lord and Bridegroom of the congregation shall soon come, to fulfil, all He promised her, will come to the fear of his enemies, but to the joy, of those who love him, to reveal before heaven and earth, that He truly is the Alpha and the Omega, the first and the last.

When, therefore, the congregation in its premonition and longing for the coming of the Lord takes His Revelation in hand, to test therein the signs of the times, and to compare them therein, many, if not all who want to understand this book, stumble each moment upon difficulties, which cause them to sigh from the dept of their soul: Oh! That a Phillip would come, who could interpret this scripture to me, so that I could know for certain what the Lord, through John, wants to teach and say to His congregation and also to me! If we could not, in all humbleness, arbour the well-founded confidence, to be to a small degree a Phillip to the reader, we would not have gone to all the trouble involved in compiling this work, which we undertook, not to attain praise or honour from men, but only, to impart the light given us in this scripture, as a teaching and comfort to our brothers and sisters in Christ, so that also the uninformed might obtain insight in the highly important things which the Lord wanted to say to the congregation, as well as to them.

For the testimony at the beginning of this book: **Holy is he who reads, and are they, who hear the words of this prophecy**, (Rev 1:3) always confirmed itself to the reading or hearing servants, even though the prophecies could only be understood in part.

How much more blissful would we be, should the full meaning of the predictions be imparted to us, and we could perceive their fulfilment before us. And this must not only be possible but not even be difficult. After all, the book begins by telling us, that it is: **The Revelation of Jesus Christ, which God gave him** (Rev 1:1). **A Revelation** is, therefore, given to John, and not an incomprehensible presentation of things, which no man can or would understand: for it is given with the purpose, **To show his servants the things which soon would happen;** in and to the church of Christ, and how these happenings would develop nigh and simultaneously with each other up to the time, when all ends, and the glorious work of Grace will be perfectly completed in the presence of heaven and earth.

It is self-evident that the servants were supposed to understand their Lord and God, for otherwise the Revelation would have been given in vain. After having conveyed the purpose of this book in the first three verses, follows the blessing and prayer of John in verses 4 to 8, with a most solemn and inimitably beautiful inner confession of his faith and his hope. We will learn to know the seven spirits of verse 4 as the powers of the Holy Spirit. In verses 4 and 5, John also testifies of his faith in God the Father, the Son and the Holy Spirit. Further explanations concerning these verses we deem unnecessary. In verse 9, the writer now gives the assurance, that he is the known John, the apostle banned to the isle of Patmos because of his faith, and begins to tell us in what manner he received this Revelation from Jesus Christ.

Three important questions present themselves when one wants to take a closer look at Revelation.

1.   **Why** was it given?
2.   **By whom** was it written?
3.   **When** was it given?

1. <u>**Why** was it given?</u> Revelation itself gives us the answer to the first question in its first verse: **to show** the servants of Jesus Christ, **the things which soon must come to pass.**

Since the kingdom of Jesus is not of this world (John 18:36), the contents of Revelation cannot be meant to imply the history of the kingdoms of this world or world history, but **the history of the kingdom of God**, which came to us with the coming of Jesus on earth, (Mark 1:15. Matt 22:28), and thus: **the history of the Christian** nations here **on earth** and **in the realm of glory**, or the **striving** and **victorious** church, the **kingdom of heaven**, as mentioned in Matt 3:2. 4:17. 10:7. 23:13 etc…

The kingdoms of this world can only be mentioned as far as they come into contact with and influence the kingdom of heaven, **the Church.** This work will indisputably show that it is the content of Revelation as proved by the many already fulfilled parts of the church's history.

2. By **whom** was it written? Till recently, it was almost undeniably certain: by the apostle John. Recent critics, however, later considered that it was not John who wrote it, but that another writer used his name to gain credence. The latest critics again return to the authorship by John. Our interpretation will indisputably reveal the truth of the last-named theory on totally different grounds. It will appear from the amazing outcome, that here, we are dealing with a **true Revelation of God**. Modern critics, after having learned to know its accurate fulfilment, will not ever be able to deny it without wilfully closing their eyes to the truth. And even though they would not acknowledge that this godly Revelation was given by the Holy Spirit, they will still have to concede, that on the whole a holy spirit confronts us. Therefore, only one choice remains: either God himself inspired this work in such a holy spirit, given to us by means of a liar and deceiver, who calls himself (Rev 1:9), the banned apostle John from Patmos, and then God himself would be an accomplice in the deception or the apostle John himself received this Revelation from God and wrote it down. From earlier times on, one mostly believed correctly the last to be true. The difference in style between the gospel, the epistles of John and Revelation lies therein, that, the first reflects the language and style of John, and the latter more the prophetic language and style of the Holy Spirit.

3. **When** was Revelation written, before or after the destruction of Jerusalem? Currently, it is generally accepted that it was before the destruction of Jerusalem, only because one considers the seals, trumpets and vials, as being fulfilled with the destruction of Jerusalem, and this last to be the main prediction of Revelation, but indeed, if it is a prophecy, then it must also be written before its fulfilment.

Actually, this question is irrelevant to the congregation. Revelation for all that, was not given to the Jews, neither to the Gentiles, but to the servants of Jesus Christ, to the Christian Church, and as such, did not have anything to do with the destruction of Jerusalem, but rather, with the resurrection of the Lord Jesus, the kingdom of Israel of the Old Testament had come to an end by God's standard.

There is thus also nothing in Revelation when one understands its language, which even remotely alludes to this terrible event.

When we consider that the Lord not only wants to show John the things still lying in the far future, but also those which would happen shortly, (Rev 1:1), and that John saw that which already was, (Rev 1:19) therefore also the already existing conditions then, Revelation not only describes the future, but also the present and, as we shall see, even partially the past. But then it ceases to be prophecy **or prediction** in relation to what already happened or was still at least ongoing!

Truly! We will learn to know Revelation, not only as a metaphorical prediction, concerning the fate of the Christian Church but, above all, (**and this the Christian reader must never lose sight of**), as containing in visions and images an indication to John and all later believers, of how the conditions in the Church would appear in the eyes of the Lord, His thoughts and views and His judgment concerning these conditions, in the consecutive periods of its existence. This is why John saw what already was. But then Revelation also begins with the establishing of the Church, the pouring out of the Holy Ghost, in the year 33 AD., and stands totally indifferent, whether it was given to John in 69, thus before the destruction of Jerusalem, or in 93, after the destruction. However, because John himself said, that he received it on the isle of Patmos, and was banned there during the second Christian persecution in 93, the last-mentioned date is considered to be correct, and since Revelation has nothing to do with the destruction of Jerusalem, all reason to argue about the date disappears. Furthermore, it is not accepted that, before the year 70, the congregations of Thyatira and Sardis already were in the condition that the Lord describes in chapters 2 and 3, and one cannot also ascribe exclusively a prophetic meaning to the letters to these congregations.

According to old historical records, John was the bishop of the congregation of Ephesus at the time of the second Christian persecution, which began under Emperor Domitian in 93. The apostle was admonished there by the Roman town clerk, to deny Christ and to refrain from preaching His Gospel. John is said to have answered with apostolic religious courage: *One must be more obedient to God than to man; therefore, I will also, neither deny Christ my God, neither cease to proclaim His name until I completed my ministry, which I received from God.* Thereupon the Town clerk had him thrown in a kettle of boiling oil, from which he emerged unharmed. After this miracle, the Town keeper did not dare torture or kill the holy man; but, in order not to leave the Emperor's command unexecuted, he banned him to Isle of Patmos, where John received from his Lord and Saviour, this Revelation whose mysterious depths, believers reflected upon for approximately twenty centuries, yet, whose true meaning would only be revealed in our time.

A prime requirement, to understand this book is, that, like John, one must be transposed **to the day of the Lord**.

Usually one understands by this, that it was a Sunday, when John, enlightened by the Holy Spirit, received this Revelation. This, to our understanding, is incorrect. Nowhere in the Holy Scriptures is **"The Day of the Lord"** meant to be a Sunday. When Paul wanted to speak about it, he did not say: **"On each day of the Lord"**, but: **"On each first day of the week"** each of you put something away, etc...(1 Cor 16:2, see also Acts 20:7.).

The day of the Lord, wherewith John, in the spirit was occupied, is **the great Day of the Lord**, of which the prophets of the Old Testament and Jesus himself in the Gospels, and the apostles in their epistles, etc... spoke with such emphasis, as the **future** of Christ.

To understand Sunday to be this day is of much later origin. According to the flesh, John was (verse 9) banned to the isle of Patmos, but in the spirit (verse 10) he was totally transposed to the great day of the future of the Lord, where he suddenly heard the voice of the Lord, and received this Revelation from Him.

If we now want to understand this correctly, we need:

1.   A somewhat similar measure of exaltation of the spirit above the carnality of this world, as that which John found himself in when he received this Revelation. The soul, however, filled with the things of this world, cannot possibly discern the things of the spirit; it has neither eye nor desire for it.

2.   A wide heart, such as the Lord's heart was. Even as He wants to be the Saviour of all believers, so must His servants also consider all Christians as His people, as people of the covenant, as subjects of the future kingdom of Glory. Whoever lacks this attitude or even is of the opinion, that the church denomination, the congregation or party, to which he belongs, is the only true church or the body of Christ, can never understand Revelation.

3.   We must hold fast to this concept, that John was transposed in the spirit to the end of the present dispensation, to the day of the Lord's future, and that the Lord allowed him to see, what would now happen to and in the

church from its inception till that day. Being in the spirit on the day of the Lord, John heard behind him a loud voice as from a trumpet saying: (verse 11) **"What you see, write in a book, and send it to the seven congregations, which are in Asia".**

Just as Paul was caught up to the third heaven, (2 Cor 12:2) John also was transposed. In the same spirit, he saw, not only the angel appointed to him (verse 1) who would accompany and inform him, but on turning around, he saw behind him the Son of God himself, who appeared to him, to now reveal unto His servant, that which He, in His state of humbleness, had not yet received as Revelation from the Father, (Mark 13:32) but in His glorified state at the right hand of God, could now reveal to His own, that they might know and proclaim, that which would occur in His Church until His second coming, His coming in Glory, yes, even what the true believers could expect and inherit at His glorious Return.

"And when I saw Him, I fell at his feet as dead" relates our grey apostle. No wonder, truly great was the majestic stature of the Son of Men, but yet how completely different was He now, from the days when He walked upon this earth as everyone's servant. **His eyes burned as a flame of fire, glowing like copper where His feet, the two-edged sharp sword from His mouth** threatened to destroy, and **His face** radiated **as** the sun, giving Him the appearance of a brilliance which no one could withstand (Jes 33:14). However, many reasons His enemies may have to fear Him, who received all power in heaven and on earth, and whose breath is enough, to kill the godless, His friends have no reason to tremble, for to them He is ever the same merciful Saviour, full of love and grace.

This He proved here once again to His servant, for he stretched out His right hand, to help him to his feet again, and said to him: **Fear not** for I did not come to kill you, but to let you know that **I am the first and the last**, the prince of life, and that **I have the keys of the realm of the departed (Hades) and of death**, and what you see, is not to frighten you, but as instruction concerning **that which now is, and that which shall happen hereafter**. Thus encouraged, John took pen in hand, and, with the same tranquillity and blissful peace, we now may take in hand what he wrote, when we, like John, also know and serve this Lord as our Lord, for then He lives, only that we should live with Him, and finally, saved from all tribulation and death, inherit the glory, which John was permitted to see, when he in a moment, saw the heavens open to him.

The figurative language of Revelation already occurs here, in the first chapter. The form in which John saw the Lord (verses 13-16), and the titles and power which the Lord allotted himself (verses 17–18) are not without great prophetic significance. The congregation must be the body of the Lord, He himself being its Head (1 Cor 12:27, Eph 1:22, 23). The form, in which the Lord revealed himself to John is a prophetic indication of the different ways and degrees to which the congregation of each period of the Church, would reflect and carry the likeness of its Head and Lord, for always, the congregation must conform to the image of the Son of God (Rom 8:29) and carry the image of the Lord from heaven (1 Cor 15:47–49). She did not actually do so equally in all periods, but more in one and less in another. At the beginning of each of the seven candlesticks or letters, we find again part of this description of the titles and powers of the Lord (Rev 2:1, 8, 12, 18. Rev 3:1, 7), there then will also be the right place for the interpretation of the figurative language, and its meaning for that period.

John saw the Lord, surrounded by **seven candlesticks**, and **in His right hand** there were **seven stars**. **The mystery of the candlesticks** represented, according to the Lord's own explanation (verse 20), **the seven congregations of Asia Minor** and **the seven stars their angels**, **bishops or teachers**, (Mal 3:1. 2:7. Mark 1:2, 3.) to each of whom a letter was subsequently directed.

Even to the superficial reader of Revelation, it must immediately become clear, that the number seven, throughout the whole book, takes on a special place. Here, at the beginning, we find seven candlesticks with seven stars; further on, a book with seven seals, then seven trumpets and finally once again seven vials. Since three is the symbolic number for God, four the number for the earth; the combination of both numbers, the number seven, is the completion of God's revelation on earth. **Furthermore, in the number seven lies hidden a succession**. In the Old Testament, seven years represented a complete time and seven times seven years, with the fiftieth as jubilee, again made out a time. Forty years or days, however, also form a time; this often appears in the scriptures as a time of tribulation or preparation. Forty times fifty give 2000 years, and these also make up a full time. Expressed in round numbers, the world was without law for 2000 years, for another 2000 years a part of humankind lived as a chosen people under the Old Covenant (Abraham) and for approximately 2000 years once more a part of humankind will live under the New Covenant (Christ) or under the Gospel. The last portion of 2000 years would be experienced by the Christians in seven consecutive periods.

If we divide these 2000 years by seven, we obtain approximately three hundred years for each period; and indeed, one finds in the history of the New Testament, from its beginning, the outpouring of the Holy Spirit, a highly important happening every three hundred years, whereby something new occurs in the history of Christ's Church on earth, something, so important to necessitate for the foregoing to become a completed period and for a new period to open itself to the Church of Christ. (See the chronological timetable on page 13 of the Introduction). Moreover, the 5th trumpet positively gives us a time of three hundred years for that 5th period. Three hundred years seems therefore to be a New Testament time.

If, however, the sixth period (6 times 300) ends at the start of the nineteenth century (1815), the seventh period would last until after 2100 in the twenty-first century, and we, therefore, are already living in the seventh period, while yet, as we shall see, the signs of the times and the fulfilment of the prophecies teach us, we are already very close to the end of the seventh or last time. This apparent contradiction is also fully solved by Revelation. There again we read in (Rev 10:6), at the end of the sixth trumpet and the sixth period, where they proceed to the seventh trumpet and the seventh period, the warning, that this last period would not last three hundred years. This indeed is the only but also conclusive interpretation of the solemn oath, which Christ, the angel of the Covenant, swears by the Almighty *"That there will be no more time, but that in the days of the voices of the seventh angel, when he shall sound the trumpet, the mysteries of God shall be fulfilled"*, and as we shall later see, this voice has already sounded; we live under the sound of the seventh trumpet: the gospel preached and its outcome, as it is predicted for this time.

The angel's warning, sworn to with such a solemn oath definitely applies to us and took place for our sake, who actually live in this last time, shortly before the end, that we should pay attention to the faithful and the true word of God (Rev 12:6), because the words of prophesies of this book, are not sealed up any longer, for "The time is at hand", (verse 10). Jesus comes soon and His reward is with Him to reward each one according to his works (verse 12). Therefore, those who have ears, hear, what the spirit has to say to the congregation.

Once the seven periods are completed, what will follow is a great time of peace, the jubilee year of the redeemed, the day of rest, which remains for God's people (Heb 4:9), the great kingdom of Glory, which is the ultimate goal of God's redeeming love, with which signs and descriptions, concludes the Revelation of John. We also find a foreshadowing of these seven periods, with their glorious conclusion, in the dispensation of the Old, as well as the shadow of the New Covenant, wherein the following sevenfold divisions are obvious.

The Old Covenant begins with Abraham, with whom God made the Covenant.

There we find:

1st. Period. Abraham, Isaac and Jacob, as strangers in Canaan.
2nd. Israel in Egypt.
3rd. Israel in the desert.
4th. Israel in Canaan under the Judges.
5th. Israel under the kings.
6th. Israel without inheritance in captivity in Babylon.
7th. Israel returns from Babylon, oppressed under the heathen and waiting for the coming of Christ.

In the end Christ appears; a small part of the people, who believed in Him as the awaited Messiah, are saved by Him and transposed in the kingdom of light; the majority however are scattered in spiritual darkness amongst the nations.

The serious reader will further still find many points of similarity, which, pointed out, would distract us too far from the goal. The seven candlesticks, or the seven letters to the congregations in Asia, definitely relate in the first instance to these seven congregations from the first Christian centuries: yet not these alone. Generally, it is felt, that these seven congregations also represent the whole Church; that, what is found or not found, happened or did not happen in these congregations, becomes a prophetic reflection of all that would happen to and in the Church in the course of the centuries; up to the return of Christ.

We trust, that the impressions created by our work and by the unravelling of the forthcoming images of the seven letters, will become a positive truth to the reader and that he shall see, how the Lord Jesus predicted there in the history of His Church, so that everyone who loves His appearing, should be able to derive therefrom, what would serve to their education, warning and encouragement, that which was, and is, and still is to be, and that all this follows each other in the same sequence as the seven epistles; so that in the Christian Church, after an Ephesian period, a Smyrnian period, thereafter, a Pergamosian period would follow, etc… until finally the Laodecian period, the last name of the seven congregations, would include the whole present dispensation.

One does not, however, accept that each period should close off with a sharp line, so that, whatever was in the first, should not be found in the second; but rather that they gradually flow into each other. Each consecutive period is prepared by the preceding one and flows forth from it, as the result of its origin.

What existed however in the one period, or came into being, retains its power and effect also throughout all the following periods, so that in the period of Smyrna, much of the Ephesian and in the Laodicean period something of the previous periods can be found.

During the time of the second candlestick, the first still shines, and as often as the next one alighted, the previous one still burnt on; similarly, the one trumpet still sounds when the sound of the next one is perceived and the woe of the one vial is still felt, when the next one is poured out. One can compare it with the building of a house. Each successive storey is only erected when the previous one is completed and serves as its foundation. Likewise, **something new reveals itself with each successive period** in the congregation, Church and Gospel preaching, **which did not exist in the previous periods**; the foregoing however also remains beside it, although with less power, continually, so that at the end of the Laodicean period, at its transition into the kingdom of Glory, all seven candlesticks are alight, all the seals are open, all the trumpets sound and all the vials are poured out.

Though the different periods in history are not separated from each other by a sharp line, at the boundaries of their transition, they always reveal a unique highly remarkable event, which indicates this transition, and whose date can be accepted as the end of the previous and the beginning of the next period. Each of the seven periods, therefore, carries the particular character of the Asian congregation, which is its image without totally erasing the characteristics of the former period.

The great exalted battle, between light and darkness, between good and evil, truth and lie, this battle, commenced at the beginning, is continued throughout all the periods in different ways and circumstances, until at the end, the striving Church emerges from the battle victoriously, and is glorified with her Lord and Master in the kingdom of truth and light.

The seven congregations are the seven candlesticks (Rev 1:20). We therefore have in the history of the Christian Church, from its beginning up to the future of Christ, seven periods; the last of which ends in the kingdom of Glory.

The seven candlesticks are followed by seven seals, thereafter seven trumpets and finally seven vials. These vials sketch everything, except glorious happenings, which can have no place after the seventh candlestick in the kingdom of Glory. So, we must place them earlier, but where?

Here, most of the interpreters of Revelation, if not all, lost track. Revelation itself contains enough indications, to also here show the way.

A superficial comparison of the six last trumpets with the six last vials already shows that the vials deal with the same matter as the trumpets, that the second vial corresponds with the second trumpet, the third with the third, etc... and that the pouring out of the vials does not occur at the conclusion of the trumpets but happens simultaneously. Compare for example: Rev 8:8, 9 with 16:3; Rev 8:10 with 16:4; Rev 8:12 with 16:8; Rev 9:1-12 with 16:10, 11; Rev 9:14 with 16:12; Rev 11:19 with 16:18–21. When one considers that at the conclusion of the candlesticks one has come to the kingdom of Glory, likewise, after the opening of the seals and so again and again, when the trumpets have sounded, and again when the vials have been poured out, always transported into the kingdom of Glory anew, the thought comes to mind, that here the same period of time is depicted four times, from Christ's coming on this earth till His return, but that the description, again and again, refers to a different topic of history. And so, it is! John could not see everything at the same time, and God, who is a God of order, therefore allowed him to read first, in the candlesticks, the history of the congregation, thereafter, in the seals, its spirituality, in the trumpets, its gospel preaching, and in the vials, His judgement of the Church and the world, as we have suggested in the chronology of the Church history on page 13, which will clearly be proven by the interpretation of the figurative language of each period.

The Lord chooses these four images in His Revelation: candlestick, seal, trumpet and vial, because:

1. The Church must be **a light** on earth; (Luke 11:33), it must radiate the light of the heavenly life, kindled in it by the Lord. The Lord made known to John how in the course of the centuries the Church would preserve and radiate this light, by means of the image of seven candlesticks; a candlestick after all, is a carrier of light, and the candlestick with seven branches, which stood in the tabernacle and which the high priest had to keep burning, also had this symbolic meaning of the light, which God would cause to shine in the midst of his people.

But, if the Church here on earth is a light.

2. ...It is also a **book**. It is the book or scroll, inscribed, not with pen and ink, but through the Spirit of the living God (2 Cor 3:2, 3). The church of Christ here on earth is the carrier and the guardian of the mysteries of God (1 Cor 4:1) and must declare His council and reveal His secrets to the nations. Consequently, after the Lord had revealed to John, in the seven candlesticks, how the light or godly life would fare in the Church, and walked with him through all seven periods up to where it ended in glory;

the future kingdom of Glory, He led him back again, to show him how the gospel would fare throughout the seven periods.

Then, John saw the book with **seven seals**, which no one was worthy to open (Rev 5:1–5) except the Lamb which was slain; and he saw the seals being broken one by one, and each broken seal opened a portion of the book (Scroll), and revealed, which truths and decrees the Lord of the congregation, through His servants in the churches, would reveal and proclaim to the world in each of the seven periods.

If the Church is a light and a book…

3.   …It is also a **fighting host** (Eph 6:10–17). The congregation of God here on earth has many and various enemies, who live by their own hearts, nesting secretly in the Church, or attacking it openly with united power, and they must be fought against and overcome, so that we should receive the crown, which the Lord prepared for us. John would also see the forthcoming struggle of the Church, and thus, the Lord transported him, when at the end of the seventh seal he again had come to the kingdom of Glory, back once more to the beginning, to show him, which enemies would stand out, and how the Church throughout all the centuries, would fight back and overcome. John then saw that the seven angels each received a trumpet, to call Gods warriors to battle.

For each of the seven periods, a trumpet was blown, and each trumpet sound had its own results because each period of the Church also had its own particular battle.

But if the Church on this earth, is a light, a book and a fighting host, finally…

4.   …It also is a **family** (2 Tim 2:20, 21); a community of brothers and sisters, children, born of God through the Holy Spirit. These children are often disobedient, self-righteous and quarrelsome children, who cause their Heavenly Father much trouble and sorrow, and force Him to constantly lift up His rod to make them feel His wrath.

His enemies, the world, in whose midst they live, also cause this family so much pain, that He must intervene with punishing justice, to save His own from the evil power; and to make His enemies know that he is God. This is why, from time to time, He must pour out His wrath on the Church and on the world, to purify His congregation and thus possibly bring to repentance or otherwise destroy His enemies. How and with what results this would happen in the course of the centuries, the Lord revealed to John in the judgements, which would strike the Church and the world in each of the seven periods.

And now John again saw from the beginning of the Christian Church, how the seven angels, with the seven golden vials, full of the wrath of God, who lives forever (Rev 15:7), poured out one vial upon the earth in each period. When the seventh vial was poured out, John saw himself once more transposed in the spirit to the entrance of the kingdom of Glory, this time not to once more have to go back, but finally to enter therein, to hear the hallelujah of the redeemed (Rev 21), to see the perfect victory of Christ and His own (Rev 20), and, in heavenly bliss, to walk in the new heaven and the new earth, where righteousness resides (Rev 21), there to worship in joyful ecstasy (Rev 22:8), Amen! Yes, come Lord Jesus! (Rev 22:20).

In this coherence of Revelation also lies hidden at the same time the natural order of treatment. It divides itself automatically into seven parts, being the seven periods of the earthly history of Christ's Church and, thereafter, as the eighth part, the kingdom of Glory.

Each of the seven periods again divides itself into four parts, in which the first would be dedicated to the interpretation of the candlestick, the second to that of the seal, the third to that of the trumpet and the fourth to that of the vial.

At the close of each period, we will compare the resolved and paraphrased prophesy against Church and world history.

Those interested can research this in ample detail in other works. We only wish to produce a work, which will also allow the simplest Christian reader to understand the book of Revelation.

Convinced as we are, that our work shall remain far below perfection, we wish to view it, as nothing more than a pointer, which will help other and more capable Bible interpreters to find the right track, to, after us, produce a more complete interpretation of this exalted subject, with more explicit reference to the fulfilment of His prophesies in the history of Christ's Church on earth. May the Lord accept this work only to His honour, bless it in the heart of our readers, so that, on the assurance of our great God and Redeemer: **The time is at hand; see: I come quickly**, they may answer with their whole heart: **Amen! Yes, come Lord Jesus! Amen!**

.

FIRST PERIOD

Ephesus

The Longing

(From 33 To 324)

FIRST PERIOD

Ephesus: *The Longing*

FROM

The Birth Of The Christian Church

TO

Its recognition as the State Church of The Roman Empire by Emperor Constantine, in 324 AD.

This first period thus spans the first three centuries of the Church, during which it expanded itself, under severe persecutions and oppression, over an important portion of the earth, until under the reign of Emperor Constantine the external struggle and persecution came to an end (323 AD.), followed by its public recognition as State Church (324 AD.).

In this period, **the first head of the beast**, (4th beast of Daniel: The Roman Empire), revealed itself.

This first head or Kingdom is **the first Heathen Roman Mountain.**
(Rev 17:9, 10)

FIRST PERIOD
Ephesian Time
Or
The Apostolic Period

1st Candlestick. Chapter 2,	1st Seal. Chapter 6,	Chapter 8,	1st Vial, Chapter 16,
Unto the angel of the church of Ephesus writes: These things saith he that holdeth the seven stars in his right hand, who walketh in the midst of the seven golden candlesticks; 2. I know thy works and thy labour, and thy patience, and how thou canst not bear them which are evil: and how thou hast tried them which say they are apostles, and are not, and hast found them liars. 3. And hast borne, and hast patience, and for my name's sake hast laboured, and hast not fainted 4 Nevertheless I have somewhat against thee because thou hast left thy first love. 5 Remember therefore from whence thou art fallen, and repent, and do the first works; or else I will come unto thee quickly, and will remove. thy candlestick out of his place, except thou repent. 6. But this thou hast, that thou hatest the deeds of the Nicolaitans, which I also hate. 7. He that hath an ear, let him hear what the Spirit saith unto the churches; To him that overcometh will I give to eat of the tree of life, which is in the midst of the paradise of God.	And I saw when the Lamb opened one of the seals, and I heard, as it were the noise of thunder, one of the four living creatures saying, Come and see. 2. And I saw, and behold a white horse: and he that sat on him had a bow: and a crown was given unto him: and he went forth conquering, and to conquer.	And the seven angels which had the seven trumpets prepared themselves to sound. 7.The first angel sounded, and there followed hail and fire mingled with blood, and they were cast upon the earth: and the third part of the trees was burnt up, and all green grass was burnt up.	And I heard a great voice out of the temple saying to the seven angels, Go your ways, and pour out the vials of the wrath of God upon the earth. 2. And the first went and poured out his vial upon the earth, and there fell a noisome and grievous sore upon the men which had the mark of the beast, and upon them which worshipped his image.

FIRST CANDLESTICK

or

THE LIGHT OR THE SPIRITUAL LIFE IN THE CONGREGATION

> I am the vine, ye are the branches: he that abideth
> in me, and I in him, bears much fruit
> John 15:5

Ephesus, Rev 2:1-7.

Ephesus, in former times was a blossoming town on the west coast of Asia Minor, renowned for its beautiful Temple dedicated to the goddess Diane (Acts 19:27–35), also counted as one of the seven wonders of the world. At the time of the apostles, it was a large town; today only an unsightly heap of ruins. In this town, Paul founded the largest Christian congregation in Asia Minor. Timothy was the bishop of this congregation; John, before his banning, also worked there after the remaining apostles had died and, according to tradition, he was buried there. It is, therefore, no wonder that a congregation led by bishops and men like Timothy, Paul and John stood solidly vested and rooted in the pure and upright Christian faith, of which Paul's letter to Ephesus, with its total approval, uplifting tone, neither reproaching nor reprimanding, is the best proof to us. (Compare it with the 1st to the Corinthians).

It is remarkable that the congregation of Ephesus is also the only one of the congregations mentioned in Revelation still in possession of an apostolic letter. This letter from Paul is, therefore, the best source from which we can learn to know the condition of the Ephesian congregation and is to us a standard and measuring rod of how a Christian congregation must live according to Jesus's precepts, requirements and institutions. This is especially so with respect to the prophetic meaning of the first candlestick, as pertaining to the condition of the Christian congregation during the first three centuries. For this reason, we can advise our reader to read Paul's letter to the Ephesians carefully, because it will clearly show how, during the latter periods, the Christian faith, love and life in the congregation of Christ increasingly deteriorated.

Also, even if the surmise of the theologians would be correct, that the letter to Ephesus was not only directed to this congregation alone but to a universal Epistle of which only one copy containing the name of Ephesus remains, even then this letter also becomes, yes, becomes even more a standard and measuring rod, of how a Christian congregation should stand in faith, hope, love and holy life.

About the meaning of the first candlestick for the original Ephesian congregation itself, we will not elaborate; enough has been written about it, and it is also of lesser immediate importance to us, since twenty centuries have already elapsed. Of this, as well as of the next candlesticks, we will apply the meaning of that which John had to write to the congregation, only in its prophetic historical sense on the different periods of the Church of Christ.

The seven candlesticks mean, as the Lord himself said (Rev 1:20), the seven congregations, and the seven stars, the seven angels of the congregations, or their bishops, (Overseers, Episcopes). The candlesticks and the stars therefore always *belong together*, which we will have to remember here and further on. Why did the Lord use images here, and further throughout the whole of Revelation, instead of naming things by their real names? Paul says it to us: "The prophecy is as a sign, not for the unbelievers, but for those who believe", (1 Cor. 14:22), and the Lord himself said, (Mark. 4:11, 12): "Unto you, it is given to know the mystery of the kingdom of God: but unto them that are without, all these things are done in parables: That seeing they may see and not perceive, and hearing they may hear, and not understand." Otherwise, these prophesies of Revelation could have had an effect on the acts of the godless and hindered the free will, the thoughts and desires of men as well as of world history.

Therefore, the Lord in His predictions also wanted to reveal things to His servants, which not everyone would understand. The mysteries of the kingdom of God are not for the godless and unbelievers: but to show to the servants of Christ "the things, which soon must happen" (Rev 1:1).

By representing the spiritual leaders in general by the metaphor of stars, the Lord indicates that they, as heavenly messengers, must radiate the light from heaven in the darkness upon the earth.

That the Lord names them angels, should remind the congregation, that her Head was glorified at the right hand of God in heaven and that they are His messengers to the congregation.

God the Father, nevertheless, is a spirit and has spiritual beings (Angels) in His service. The eternal Son of God however truly became man and, as the glorified godly man, has here on earth, besides angels, who as serving spirits surround His throne, also men as messengers and angels (Mal 2:7. Mal 3:1), sent by Him to His Church, to be active in His congregation; because, the preaching of the Gospel is not entrusted to angels, but unto men, as the messengers of the Lord on earth. For this reason, also the Lord held the seven stars, the angels of the congregations, in His right hand.

By representing the Ephesian and the other congregations as candlesticks, in whose midst He walked, the Lord indicated;

1. …that they, as carriers of their lamps, i.e.: their "spirituality", must serve as a light on earth; as such they were already foreshadowed in the Old Testament by the seven-branched candlestick with the oil lamps in the Tabernacle. But also…

2. …that not each congregation would reveal itself as a unit, but that all congregations together would form one body, with the Lord in its midst as its Head.

While the seven congregations in Asia-Minor, in prophetic meaning represent the whole Church of Christ until His return and as such, form a symbolic representation of the seven consecutive periods in the Church, the congregation of the Lord received, in what John had to write to it, as it where its last Canonical teaching, of how it would be tossed about in the severely agitated sea of nations; but also the last admonition to remain faithful to Him, until it would land in the destined haven of rest, in the kingdom of Glory. A deep and comforting meaning is given to all believers throughout all times, in the representation, which the Lord gives of himself, when:

Verse 1. **"He, that holdeth the seven stars in his right hand, who walketh in the midst of the seven golden candlesticks";** a clearer confirmation of the words He spoke to His servants earlier on earth: "He that heareth *you* heareth *me*." (Luke 10:16) and "I am with you always, even unto the end of the world." (Matt 28:20)

The Church will, as we shall see, in each of the seven consecutive periods of its history, reveal itself in the unique character of its foreshadowed congregation, already expressed and hidden in the *names* of the seven Asiatic congregations. Names are generally of great importance in the Holy Scripture, ever since the creation's history.

The names mostly express the essence of being, and also, where they are without any deeper meaning and purely accidentally given by men, God, in His guiding providence often knows how to use them for His purpose.

Ephesus means **longing and pleasing,** and this truly was the characteristic of the Ephesian congregation as well as of the first three centuries of the Church. She was full of *longing* not only to bring Jews and heathen to Christ, but also, to be presented to the Lord as a chaste virgin (2 Cor 11:2), and she had a deep and holy nostalgia for His promised return

45

in Glory, as the writings of these centuries strongly testify; therefore, the Lord found *pleasure* in her.

Ephesus, the largest City in Asia-Minor with its beautiful temple to Diana, the All-Mother, would, through its name and precedence over the other cities, be at the same time a metaphorical representation of the Church from the apostolic time, which, through her shining light, still shines unparalleled from the past up to our days. But the Church of the Ephesian apostolic period would also be and remain the All-Mother of all latter Christian churches, and throughout all the centuries believers would be found, who would regard the apostolic conditions and form of the Church as their ideal. How the Ephesian candlestick gave its light, is described in:

Verse 2: **"I know thy works**, says the Lord to the angel of the congregation, and through him to the congregation as a whole, **and thy labour, and thy patience and that thou canst not bear them which are evil.** They could still clearly recognise evil in the wicked and reject it.

The Lord also approves: **and thou hast tried them which say they are apostles and are not, and hast found them liars".** Paul already (2 Cor 11:3) said: "For such are false apostles, deceitful workers, transforming themselves into the apostles of Christ." Indeed, after the Lord had appointed His apostles during His life on earth, He later, through the Holy Spirit, called other men filled with faith into that ministry, i.e. Paul and Barnabas, (Acts 13:2, Acts 14:14); but when most of the apostles had already died, and the Lord gave no more true apostles to His Church, men forced themselves upon the congregation of that period, especially from Rome, who named themselves heirs to the chair of Peter and the apostles.

In this Ephesian period, the congregation tried them and found them to be liars, indeed, its light shone brightly enough, to recognise them as such.

The church of Rome however, adopted them in later centuries as apostles of Christ, as His Vicars, but by then the light on the candlestick was already quite dim.

Verse 3: **"And hast borne, and hast patience, and hast laboured, and hast not fainted".** Yes! The Church of the first three centuries had to suffer and struggle. With amazement, we still always look up to the courage of faith, which she revealed under all persecutions and oppressions, to the untiring labour, which she brought forth in preaching the Gospel to Jews and heathens.

With great accuracy the Lord could quite rightly prophetically testify: "I know thy works, and thy labour, and thy patience."

This sect, which was condemned everywhere, (Acts 28:22), with the bloody cross in her banner, which was to the Jews an aggravation and to the Greeks a foolishness, (1 Cor. 1:23), stood there, small and weak in herself, yet nevertheless, with feet shod in readiness for the Gospel, and burning with desire, to bring sinners to Jesus.

Though it was hard and tedious work, it did not require less effort, to keep the new converted for the Lord and to make them walk according to the Gospel. A single peek at the letters, written by the apostles to the newly established congregations, can convince us of how difficult it was to lead the carnally minded heathen to live by the Spirit and to cause the Jewish leaven of self-righteousness to yield by faith to the Gospel of Salvation. But, while the church of the first centuries loved the sinners, she hated evil, and this kept her from destruction, which assailed her from all sides.

Each candlestick, each seal, depicts to us the condition of the congregation and her servants, *especially*, as it appeared at the beginning of that period. From the trumpet and the vial, it becomes apparent, how this condition deteriorated in the course of that period, during the candlestick and the seal, and how, as they ended, the condition of the following period began. Therefore, the Lord already had, in this period, something to reproach His congregation about, namely:

Verse 4: **"Nevertheless I have somewhat against thee, because thou hast left thy first love",** not only the first fiery love for Him but also the love for the brethren. Even though the congregation hated (verse 6) them as enemies of Christ, and removed them from their midst, who, under the cover of a superficial Christendom, allowed the flesh with its lust to reign in their heart, yet the congregation had herself already left the first love for Christ, for, already in the second century, she had deviated from some of the original tenets and ministries of Christ, new religious orders had been introduced, the strife for spiritual dominion had already begun in the Church, and the sufferings for His name sake, the persecutions by heathen authorities, were already being bought-off by rich congregations and persons of means. Above all, the congregation then already began to lose her longing for the return of the Lord, which longing lived in her so ardently in the first century, as we can gather from the letters of the apostles.

The love for Christ fosters love for the brethren and where the first began to wane, the last must also diminish. We see this clearly in the different disputes and in the bitterness, which already arose in the second century of the Church, often concerning unimportant matters, while on the other hand, she sometimes dealt harshly with the weak brethren, who under the violent persecutions did not remain steadfast. This the Lord did not do, but said:

Verse 5: **"Remember therefore from whence thou art fallen, and repent, and do** again **the first works; or else I will come unto thee quickly** to judge, and not dim the light in you completely, but yet **remove thy candlestick out of his** exalted **place, except thou repent"**, because as the carrier of the true light of the Gospel, it can no more serve the purpose, for which I have appointed it.

Verse 6: **"But this thou hast, that thou hatest the deeds of the Nicolaitans, which I also hate".** Although the congregation had left her first love, she had not yet completely surrendered to the lusts of the flesh and had not yet fully left the way of the Gospel. Indeed, she could not suffer evil (verse 2) in her midst and also the Nicolatians [4] were rejected, considered not to belong to the congregation of Christ.

Verse 7: **"He that hath an ear, let him hear what the Spirit saith unto the churches; To him that** hears and **overcometh, will I give to eat of the tree of life, which is in the midst of the paradise of God".**

If she would repent, it must be to once again, in the first love, be able to say as Bride with the Spirit: "Come, Lord Jesus! Come soon!" and thus to overcome death and the Devil and to enter into God's paradise and to enjoy eating of the tree of life (Christ).

The Ephesian congregation, although worthy of the name *Longing and Pleasing* in the beginning of that period, did not remain in her first love for Christ and her longing for His return, nor in the good pleasure of the Lord. She still further distanced herself from Him and, instead of remaining the Bridal Congregation of Christ to fall in His arms at His return, the first Apostolic Church entrusted herself into the arms of Emperor Constantine (324 AD), to find rest and peace there, as the Church of Jesus Christ elevated to a State-church; forgetting that He once said: *"My Kingdom is not of this world"* (John 18:36).

---

[4] About Nicolas Ridderus said in his "Struggling Church", page 11, and he agreed with Clem: Alex: p 3, as follows: Nicolas taught the universality of women, in order to cause, the jalousie of men to be condemned. Moreover, he acknowledged, besides God, many spirits and powers, which one had to honour. This, according to his teaching, exonerated one from sin when eating offerings to Idols.

FIRST SEAL

or

THE SPIRITUAL LIFE OF THE POWERS IN THE CHURCH

> I send you forth as sheep in the
> midst of wolves.
> Matt 10:16.

Rev 6:1, 2.

One usually forms a wrong impression of the book or rather the scroll, described in Rev 5:1–7, which John saw in the right hand of Him who sat on the throne, a book, inscribed within and on the outside and sealed with seven seals.

Simple people might imagine a thick book, sealed with seven seals. In those days, however, one wrote on parchment pages of approximately one yard wide and several yards long, which was rolled up on a wooden rod. If the parchment was very long, a rod was attached at both ends, and as one read on, the bottom rod unrolled while the top rod took up the spent parchment. The parchments of the law in the Synagogues are still used in the same way today. One now usually imagines this scroll, with seven tightly knotted tapes on the side edge, tied along its length, each knot imprinted with a seal, and that the seven seals therefore stand in a straight line.

It would however be impossible, after opening the first, even after the opening of six seals, to unroll the scroll and take knowledge of its content. Only after breaking the last seal, would one be able, by unrolling, to read the first seal. This however is totally contrary to John's story. Whoever wants to understand this, should rather imagine that the seals were fastened to one of the sides of the end rod, so that with the parchment being 7 yards long, the rolled-up part of the parchment, pierced at each yard, had a cord attached to it, which was sealed at its end, so that at the opening of each seal, the scroll could only be unrolled as far as required to reveal the contents of that seal. Nevertheless, one should not imagine such visions from the Holy Spirit in an earthly natural form and try to interpret them in this way.

The sealed scroll was inscribed on both sides, within and on the outside, and in a rolled-up state, characters could therefore be seen on the outside, this is why John said written within and on the outside.

This described scroll is again the Church of the Lord. According to His omniscience, the Lord here once more wanted to give an insight in figurative language and visions, of what would happen in the Church of the New Testament, from the beginning to the end, for nearly 2000 years, in seven consecutive periods. As each seal was opened, John would see, in each newly opened portion of the scroll, what characteristic events would occur in the Church in each period, such as the reader will readily perceive with the interpretation of the figurative language. Before going over to the contents of the first seal, we must however become better acquainted with the persons and matters which appear at the opening of the seals, such as 1. The Lamb; 2. The book; 3. The seven seals and 4. The four living creatures. We will here only explain these last named superficially, as their true and actual interpretation can only follow when we treat Rev 4 &5.

1.The Lamb is Jesus Christ, of whom John the Baptist already said: behold the Lamb of God, which taketh away the sin of the world (John 1:29) and which Peter also (1Pet 1:19) called a Lamb without blemish; indeed, in (Isaiah 53:7) it was already predicted of Him: "as a lamb to the slaughter." (See Acts 8:32), where this prediction was also applied to the Saviour.

2. The book or the scroll. Zechariah also saw (Zach 5:1, 2) a scroll, a flying scroll, according to V.d. Palm, an unrolled scroll; according to Luther's translation a flying letter, all coming to the same thing. The angel in (verse 3) explains, that this scroll or letter is: "the curse that goeth forth over the face of the whole earth," so that (verse 4) it shall enter into the house of him that sweareth falsely by my name. The opened scroll is therefore the curse of the Lord or the Lord's decree against the ungodly. Likewise, in (Rev 5) the scroll is the decree of the Lord concerning His Church. Indeed, Paul describes the congregation (2 Cor 3:2, 3): "Ye are our epistle in Christ, ministered by us, (Paul), known and read by all men, written not with ink, but with the Spirit of the living God; in fleshly tables of the heart". The Church or Congregation is therefore this scroll or letter, written by the preaching of the Gospel, in the hearts of believers. The scroll therefore contains its future history or the decree of the Lord for His Church. On the outside of the scroll, everyone could see and read, how the life and conduct of the congregation was; what was written on the inside, was only legible to the believers, who understand the mysteries of the kingdom of God.

3. The book was sealed with seven seals. To be sealed with seals immediately acknowledges a secret. Hence, at the opening of each seal, a part of God's decree for His Church is revealed. The history of this Church

consists of seven periods. The seals are the angels or the Christian earthly kings with the "Priesthood" of the Church. Already in (Ezek 28:12), referring to the king of Tyrus, before he became high-minded, God spoke of him as: "a seal full of wisdom", (Luther Trans) or as the original text means: an imprint of the seal. In (Hagg 2:23), God says to Zerubbabel, in his role as type of Christ, and thus actually said to Christ, "I will make thee as a signet". The seal is an imprint of the signet ring, and the spiritual leadership, as the representative of Christ on earth, must display His image and imprint and thus form the seal.

4. In (Sol. Songs 5:14), it however says of Christ: "His hands are as gold (signet) rings". These hands on the body or the Church of Christ, where the ministries coming to the fore at the beginning, the apostolic and the prophetic ministry, and later the preachers of the Gospel or the teachers. (1 Cor 12:12, 15, 20–29). They, in turn, imprint their image upon the congregation, which therefore, except for her own spiritual life, also revealed the Royal Priesthood in each period of the Church.

The scroll, which is the congregation with the seals or the priesthood, in her consecutive strange conditions, thus together form the Church, and the scroll, sealed with the seven seals, is also the history of the Church of Jesus Christ, as it unravelled itself before the all-seeing eye of God from the outpouring of the Holy Spirit up to the return of the Lord. We still endeavour to record the fulfilment of Revelation, not at a given moment, when it is given, but from the beginning of the Christian Church. Indeed, the Lord showed John that which already was (Rev 1:19) and afterwards still would happen.

At the opening of each seal, the condition of the spiritual life of the powers in the Church is thus predicted, and, as from the second period, at the same time, that of the powers in the state or of the Christian kings. The interpretation of each seal and its fulfilment in history will reveal this to the reader.

5. The four living creatures, which are described in (Rev 4:6–8), are the same as those seen in (Ezek 1 and 10) and named Cherubim or bearers of salvation, also referred to as Seraphim or Principle in the kingdom (of God); on the other hand, in (Isaiah 6), have always been enigmatic beings. They were always considered to be the highest of the created beings, (which they also are), yet many divergent thoughts are further held concerning their specific significance and sphere of activity. While the usual translation as beasts is totally inapplicable and the original text, both in Ezekiel and John, refers to living creatures, we will forthwith refer to them shortly for singular Cherub and plural Cherubim.

Biblical research about their substance and meaning will only be accomplished successfully (Rev 4). Here it would distract us too much. For the present, as the result of this research, we can only state, as information, that they are the four ministries, visibly represented by angels, as exercised by Jesus Christ in His Salvation work; first personally and, after His ascension, by His chosen and called servants, ministries, who will also be represented by redeemed human beings in the kingdom of Glory. (Rev 5:8– 10. hast redeemed us). They are probably called Cherubim (Ezk 1) in their ministries as sent angels in God's work on earth, for the salvation of sinners; and Seraphim (Isaiah) in their task as worshipping Angels, corresponding to the double task of the servants of the Lord on earth; 1st.the edification of the House of the Lord, the Church or Congregation, which is the teaching service, and 2nd. the glorification of God or the worshipping service.

As the Redeemer of the sins of this world Jesus Christ was once slain as the Lamb of God and He obtained the eternal righteousness for all who believe in Him.

As our High Priest, He lives and prays for us and offers the incense of our prayers on the altar to God the Father. (Heb 4:14. Rev 5:8. Rev 8:3, 4).

But, as the Saviour and Redeemer of the world, He had to make His fulfilled Salvation work serve to the preservation of sinners and to lead them to the kingdom of God, through His commission on earth in the four ministries.

1st. He is the great Apostle of our calling, (Heb 3:1. Eph 2:20). His Apostolic ministry is represented by the first Cherub, (Rev 4:6, 7) in the likeness of the lion. (Ezek 1:10).

2nd. He is the great Shepherd and overseer of the souls. (Heb 13:20.1 - Pet 2:25. -1 Pet 5:4). His Shepherd Ministry is represented by the second Cherub, (Rev 4:7) in the likeness of a Calf or young Ox. (Ezek 1:10).

3rd. He is the great Evangelist or announcer of the Gospel, (Matt 11:5, Luke 4:18, 19, 43.). His Evangelist Ministry is represented by the third Cherub, whose face was like that of a Man.

4th. Finally, He is also the great Prophet. (Deut 18:15, 18, 19. Luke 24:19. Acts 3:22, 23.) and His Prophetic Ministry, from which the Revelation resulted, is represented by the fourth Cherub in the likeness of a flying Eagle.

These New Testamentary powers or ministries, which He himself fulfilled during His walk on earth, He later, after His Ascension, vested upon His servants in the congregation, giving each their talent and ministry, according as He wanted. In this sense Paul also said, (Eph 4:11, 12,) "And

He (Jesus Christ) gave some, apostles; and some, prophets; and some, evangelists; and some, pastors and teachers, for the perfecting of the saints, for the work of the ministry, for the edifying of the body of Christ." (The Congregation).

Should this interpretation not appear to be clear to the reader, one single well-known example from church history will clarify it completely. With the Reformation, the four main reformers, Luther, Melanchton, Calvin and Zwingli, formed, though differing here and there in minor areas of faith, in the main however, the re-erecting of the candlestick of the light of the Gospel, together forming a unity, a unity in Christ. They complemented each other. What the one lacked in talent, the other possessed. Through these four, in character so totally different men, Christ exercised His four ministries and was himself the Reformer in the reformers.

In the courageous, steadfast Luther, the apostle ministry was represented, or the sanctified courage and willpower of which the strong, courageous lion is the image. (First Cherub, Rev 4:7)

In the gentle, loving Melanchton we again find the shepherd ministry, or the sanctified feeling and patience, of which the active young ox (calf) is the image. (Second Cherub)

The thoughtful, hard-working Calvin shows us the Evangelist ministry, or the sanctified human understanding and comprehension, of which the clever face as a man is the image. (Third Cherub)

In the excited, fiery Zwingli we finally see the prophet ministry or the sanctified, high soaring power of imagination, of which the eagle, "who flies against the face of the sun" is the perfect image. (Fourth Cherub)

In the same manner, one will always see, not only in the reformers but also in each believing teacher, one of these four characters strongly coming to the fore, the religious courage, the meekness, the understanding or of the prophetic zeal.

That this notion is not totally arbitrary, or, perchance corresponds with the four characters of the reformers, is also apparent when, already since the first church fathers, and especially Irenaeus (approximately 200 AD) who saw the four Gospel writers,- who together also form a oneness, just as they together wrote a whole and complete Gospel, - represented and depicted as accompanied by these same living creatures from Revelation, from Isaiah and Ezekiel, whose characters again totally correspond with the strange drift of their books. In this manner the powerful Matthew, the Apostle, is represented by the lion, the bright Mark, the Evangelist, by the winged man next to him, the uplifting Shepherd Luke with the ox, and John, the Prophet of Revelation, with the Eagle, holding a pen in his beak.

(Augustine). Moreover, the full confirmation of this representation will become evident in the history of the Church, as predicted in the four first seals, whilst also with each one, the figurative language of the image of the Cherubim will be explained from Scripture. We can now proceed with the first seal.

The Lamb, Jesus Christ, opens (verse 1) the first seal and unrolls that portion of the scroll, to show John, how, during the first period of the Church, her condition, and what the priesthood's performance would be. The first of the four Cherubim, with the likeness of the lion, or the Apostle ministry, says there with the voice like thunder: "Come, and see". Jesus revealed on earth, was the lion out of the tribe of Juda. (Gen. 49:9, 10; Num. 24:17; Rev. 5:5). "Behold, the Lion of the tribe of Juda, the Root of David, hath prevailed to open the book, and to lose the seven seals". The lion is the image of royal power (Zeph. 3:3) and courage (Prov. 28:1), to perform a received commission (here the Apostle ministry) with firmness. Jesus, himself the Apostle of our calling, (Hebr. 3:1), but also the King of Kings, performed this spiritual Kingship through His apostles. "He that heareth you heareth me"; said the Lord to His apostles (Luke 10:16). Therefore, just as Jesus is the lion of the tribe of Juda, the Cherub likewise, bearing the image of the lion, is the representative of the Apostolic ministry, that of Jesus himself as well as of His ambassadors here on earth. This is also apparent from the following details.

John heard this Cherub say (verse 1): as it where the noise of thunder: "Come and see!". Thunder is the image of the voice of the Lord, and also of His Word spoken by His servants. (John 12:28, 29; Psalm 29:3; Rev. 10:4; Rev 19:6). The apostles spoke in their Apostolic ministry, not their own human words, but it was the Spirit of the Father which spoke in them, (Matt. 10:20). Who hears you, hears me, said Christ to them. James and John were surnamed Sons of Thunder by the Lord (Mark. 3:17). Only of the first Cherub it was said, that he spoke with a voice like thunder because this represented the Apostle ministry, which was present only in the first period.

The representative of that ministry spoke to John: "Come and see!" what will happen in this period.

Verse 2. And I saw, and behold a white horse, and he that sat on him had a bow. We have said, that the seal is the condition of the priesthood, and alluded to this already somewhat on page 49. Here it will become clearer. The contents of this first and of the three consecutive seals consist of the performance of the rider, who sits on the horse. What must we now understand by the horse and the rider? In (Zach. 10:3) we read: "For the

Lord of hosts hath visited his flock, the house of Judah, and hath made them as his godly horse in battle." The people of God or the Old Testament congregation is here represented as God's horse in battle. Similarly, the Lord says (Hosea 10:11): "I will make Ephraim to ride" and (Luke 10:16), "He that heareth you heareth me; and he that despised you despised me;" The Lord in His apostles or in the leaders of the congregation, is therefore the rider, guiding the horse, and the congregation is the horse, which carries the rider or the spiritual clergy. Also in (Zach.1:8–10 and Zach. 6:1–8), horses are seen by the prophet, of which the angel declares, (Zach 1:10) "These are those whom the Lord hath sent to walk to and from through the earth" and in (Zach. 6:8), "these have quieted my spirit in the country", also an image of the congregation in its missionary work. Likewise, we again see in (Rev. 19:11), the Lord himself, as the Rider seated on the white horse, or the congregation of those redeemed and made righteous by His blood. The rider, or the clergy, was thus seated on a white horse, the colour of righteousness, according to (Isaiah 1:18). It is, therefore, the Congregation in the first period, which is described as the white horse, as she stood there in the full strength of faith, equipped with the Holy Spirit and His gifts, having been freed from the power of the devil and of sin, washed white in the blood of the Lamb, but also ready, as a battle horse, to do battle against the violence of death and devils, and to deliver the poor and the lost souls from their power by the missionary work, the proclamation of the Gospel of grace to the Jews and to the heathens. Its white colour, or that of righteousness before God, wholly corresponds to the condition of the congregation, as we saw it described in the candlestick. The main character in the seal however is the rider, carried by the congregation which he steers, and we read, that he, who sat on it, had a bow. That this bow was not meant for a bloody purpose, is apparent, since the rider had no arrows, on or with the bow. The purpose of the bow was therefore of a spiritual nature and the bow thus an image, of which the Holy Scripture will give us the interpretation.

That the bow is a symbol of battle and a mark of a soldier, is well known, yet in (Jer 9:3) it says of the faithless, that "They bent their tongues like their bow for lies" and (Hos.7:16) "they are like a deceitful bow". The language or speech is therefore the bow, wherewith the faithless, through lies seek to reach their evil goals, but just as James said (James 3:9) "Therewith bless we God, even the Father; and therewith curse we men, which are made after the similitude of God.", so here it was the reverse, the tongue or speech was the bow, wherewith the apostles and their successors, as good soldiers of Jesus Christ, (2 Tim. 2:3) sought to attain their goal, i.e.

to free sinners from the power of the devil, and through the preaching of the Gospel, bring them to repentance and salvation, and to win them for the kingdom of God.

Even in figurative Language, the bow without an accompanying arrow would mean little towards the victory. The arrow was however of a spiritual, invisible nature. Indeed, Jesus Christ named himself (Isaiah. 49:2). "In His quiver hath He hid me", which the rider had to shoot with his bow in the heart of sinners, to kill the old man, and to cause the new man to rise in righteousness and holiness.

Thus equipped, the priestly ministry went out in the Apostolic time, as the rider on the white horse, conquering, and to conquer; he however received something else. We read: "And a crown was given to him". Which crown? The incorruptible crown of Glory (1 Cor. 9:25 and in 1 Peter 5:4) cannot be; this the servants of Christ will only receive on the day of the Lord.

We could also here think of an ornamental crown of wisdom, (Prov.4:7, 9) to be to the weak, weak, to the understanding, understanding, and to the foolish, foolish, in order to win the weak, wise and foolish for Christ. We will however do better by asking the apostles themselves, which crown they did receive, when they fought as soldiers of Christ and what they considered to be a crown.

Paul gives us an immediate answer on this; when he asks, (1 Tess 2:19, 20): "For what is our hope, or joy, or crown of rejoicing? Are not even ye in the presence of our Lord Jesus Christ at his coming? For ye are our glory and joy." And "Therefore my brethren dearly beloved and longed for, my joy and crown!" (Phil. 4:1). The redeemed souls, won for Christ as the inheritors of the eternal Glory, were thus the crown of the rider on the white horse. "And he went forth conquering, and to conquer". And they overcame, the spiritual riders of the first period of the Church, they overcame the devil and the powerful emperors of the Heathen Roman Empire; and their only weapon was God's word, the preaching of the Gospel, and their manner of battle was foreign, as yet unknown; they allowed themselves to be tortured and killed; they died on crosses and at the stake. Just like their great predecessor and Lord of hosts, who through his dying overcame death and hell, dying they also overcame the powers of darkness, the emperors of Rome. The death of the martyrs was the victory of the Church!

Oh! Had they only continued on that way! They had exchanged the corruptible for the incorruptible, (1 Cor.15:53, 54), and had entered heaven as the rider of the white horse, to meet the Heavenly Bridegroom. They however left this manner of battle. At the end of this period, going over to the second period of the Church, we see the white horse of the second period becoming red, red from blood, and the rider who, instead of having the bow of the Gospel as a weapon, is armed with a great sword. Alas! Not the sword of God's Word.

FIRST TRUMPET

or

THE CONDITION AND EFFECT OF

THE GOSPEL PREACHING

I am come to send fire on the earth

Luke 12:49.

Rev 8:2, 6, 7.

The images represented here, just as those in the other trumpets, already have the character of an impending judgment. It is not yet the full judgement, which is only to take place at the outpouring of the vials. The trumpet causes the earnest voice of God to be heard beforehand, to the sinners in the Church, as well as those in the world outside. The voice of the Lord, whether He speaks himself, personally or by means of men, His servants are described in many parts of the Scripture as the strident sound of a trumpet, as for instance at the law giving at Mount Sinai, (Exod. 19:16, 19. Exod 20:18.). The Lord himself said: (Isaiah 58:1) "Cry aloud, spare not, lift up thy voice like a trumpet, and show my people their transgression, and the house of Jacob their sins". And in (Zach. 9:14) "and the lord God shall blow the trumpet." In (Rev. 1:10), John describes the voice of the Son of God as a trumpet. Paul also teaches (1 Cor. 14:6–12), that when the Holy Spirit speaks through men, it is a distinctive trumpet sound, "because," he asks in verse 8, "if the trumpet give an uncertain sound, who shall prepare himself to the battle?" and from the battle against their enemies, to which the trumpet awoke the people of Israel, His image is transferred to the spiritual sphere. Indeed, what else is the Gospel preaching other than the trumpet, which awakes to the battle of light against darkness, of the servants of the Lord against those of Satan, of the kingdom of God against sin, death and the powers of hell.

The Lord Jesus promised His disciples, (Matt.10:19, 20), that it would not be them, who would speak, but it would be the Holy Spirit that would speak in them, and also said (Luke 10:16): "He that heareth you heareth me," which is the trumpet of Rev 1:10; and Paul wrote in (Rom. 15:18),

"For I will not dare to speak of any of those things which Christ hath not wrought by me", and in (2 Cor. 13:3): "Since ye seek proof of Christ speaking in me". If now, as we said, the voice of Christ, and the voice of the Holy Spirit are the sound of the trumpet, and both speak through sanctified and chosen men, which is self-evident, then these chosen and sanctified men, or all the servants of Christ who belong to one period of the Church, together form the angel of the Son of man (Rev 2:1), who blows the trumpet of Gospel preaching of that period. In this manner, each of the seven periods has its own angel and its own trumpet sound (Rev 8:2, 6).

The sound of the trumpet (currently, war bugle) in an army, does not only call its own people to the battle; it is also heard in the enemy camp, awakening them to defend and is therefore the cause of the beginning of the battle. In like manner the trumpet's Gospel preaching incites the enemy to the defence and to the battle against the confessors of the Christian teaching.

The outcome of this mutual battle and its consequences, both for the Church of Jesus Christ, as well as for her enemies, are described to us in prophetic language by the trumpet. We therefore named it; the condition and the effect of the Gospel preaching. John then saw:

Verse 2. "The seven angels which stood before God, that is, the clergy of each of the seven periods, and to them were given seven trumpets", the trumpets of the Gospel, such as they would occur in each of the seven periods.

Verse 6. "And the seven angels which had the seven trumpets prepared themselves to sound". The sound and the effect thereof are outlined to us with every trumpet sound.

Verse 7. "The first angel sounded, this is, according to the above explanation in other words: during the first period of the Church, or the first three hundred years, in which the Gospel was preached on earth, and as a result of the battle against lies and unbelief, awakened by it, hail and fire, mingled with blood, and they were cast upon the earth".

Here we meet four images, hail, fire, blood and earth, the meaning of which must be solved by the Holy Scripture.

1.Hail, everywhere in the Scripture, is used as the image of a destructive judgement, as it also has in nature, only a damaging and destructive, and not like lightning, thunder and snow, which have beneficial side effects.

In particular, hail is considered as the image of a destructive judgement of God over lies and unbelief (Exud 9:18–34. Isaiah 28:17. Hagg 2:17, 18. Psalm 78:47, 48. Psalm105:32).

There lies however still a deeper meaning: Hail consists of raindrops, which by falling through colder air layers freeze, and as hard bodies, come down and destroy everything which cannot offer them resistance.

The rain again is the image of the pouring out of the Holy Spirit, see (Heb. 6:4, 7) where the Christians who had received the Holy Spirit are compared to the earth, which absorbs the rain. Similarly, (Hosea 6:3. and Joel 2:23) describe the outpouring of the Holy Spirit at the beginning of the Christian Church the early, and at the end of the Church the latter rain. The rain drops however come forth out of the clouds, which in turn are the image of the Church, or the cloud of witnesses (Heb. 12:1), wherein the Spirit of God dwelleth (1Cor.3:16), who will guide it in all truth (John 16:13), and on which cloud, according to (Ezek. 1:4, 26. and Rev. 14:14) the Lord Jesus is seated. Therefore (Jude vs. 16), names the godless teachers: clouds without water, who thus do not contain the testimony of the Holy Spirit. The fire which Ezekiel sees in the cloud is also the fire of the Holy Spirit, which we will presently learn to know, or His testimony through the Gospel preaching; for it was not the apostles who were speaking, but the Spirit of the Father which spoke in them (Matt 10:20). The Scriptures above all often refers to rain and living water as the testimony of the Holy Spirit when God's Word is preached; i.e. (Deut. 32:1, 2), in the words of Moses: "O earth, the words of my mouth, my doctrine shall drop as the dew, as the small rain upon the tender herb" and in the words of Jesus, (John 4:10. John 7:37–39. Isaiah 45:8) gives us both images, clouds and rain, together as in verse 8: "Drop down, ye heavens, from above, and let the skies pour down righteousness: let the earth open, and let them bring forth salvation, and let righteousness spring up together".

It follows that this was salvation and righteousness, which the rain of the Holy Spirit had to bring forth out of the clouds of witnesses on the heathen earth. The spiritual atmosphere of heathenism, however, full of unbelief and worldliness and unprepared to bring forth life, which is from God, was too cold for the rain to impart fructification. The heathens rejected with loathing the Gospel which required sacrifice and self-denial. Notwithstanding however, the testimony of the Holy Spirit penetrated the heathen Romans, repelling the mist of unbelief, shaking the sleeping conscience, dethroning the idols, emptying the temples and paralysing the State administration by undermining the State religion.

The powerful Roman Empire was destroyed by the Gospel preaching. The scorned blessing became a curse. The mild rain of the Holy Spirit became a shattering hail to the heathen religion.

God does not allow himself to be ridiculed. "He gave them" according to (Psalm 105:32), "hail for rain".

Fire and Lightning are given two different meanings in the Scriptures. As holy fire, of zeal or enthusiasm, (Psalm 39:3. Psalm 79:5.) and in higher meaning as the fire of the Holy Spirit. (Jer. 23:29. Acts 2:3. Matt. 3:11. Luke 3:16.). Also the divine messengers appear in the form of lightning, (Matt. 28:) and as flames of fire, (Heb. 1:7). But also as the fire of wrath, or anger. (Deut. 32:22. Psalm 78:21. Psalm 89:46. Prov. 16:27. James 3:6. Ezek. 22:31.) Satan also shows himself as a bolt of lightning. (Luke 10:18).

This Fire with both meanings, which Jesus had come to kindle on earth (Luke 12:49), is also considered here. We have said, however, that the trumpet or war bugle not only calls its own army to battle but at the same time awakens the enemy to it. Likewise, must also the zeal for the preaching of the Gospel, wherewith the Christians of the first three centuries, in the power of the Holy Spirit, as divine messengers took to the field against heathen idolatry, awaken the anger and wrath of the heathen nations. "I am not come to bring peace, but a sword." (Matt. 10:34). The consequence was strife, not only on a spiritual level but also on the part of the heathen nations with weapons, wherewith the Christians had to exchange the fire of their religious zeal with death. Indeed:

3. Blood, in the Holy Scriptures, always represents the natural life, as well as the life of the body (Gen. 4:10. Lev. 17:14. Rev. 17:6. Rev 6:10), and as the natural life of the soul in the unrepentant state (Hebr. 12:4. Matt. 16:17). According to the text, blood here is the main matter, wherein the hail and the fire thrown upon the earth are revealed, and the heathen Roman nation is therefore the blood.

4. The earth means, according to (Isaiah 45:8. Jer. 6:19. Mica 1:2. Psalm 97:1. Dan. 7:17. Heb. 12:26), the existing social order of the time and the country, which is dealt with, and therefore here, the heathen Roman Empire, wherein the Gospel was preached.

Taking the images in their dual meaning together, John then saw in this image: that in the first period of the Church, the fire of the Holy Spirit and its testimony in the Gospel preaching (rain) would become a destructive judgement (hail) over the heathen Roman Empire (earth) and its religion (blood); that the holy fire of God's servants would do battle against the unholy fire of the heathen wrath and the hellish anger of Satan, and all this mixed with all the sinful tendencies of the unconverted flesh and blood of the heathen nations and the spilled blood of the witnesses of Jesus.

That this all happened, will not be unknown to the Christian reader. Already the pages of the New Testament show this clearly enough in the history of the first Christians; church and world history have also recorded their misfortunes and trials in those times for us.

The result of this trumpet sound of the Gospel preaching is reported to us in the last full sentence of this first trumpet.

And the third part of the earth was burnt up, and the third part of trees was burnt up, and all green grass was burnt up. That under the images of trees and grass we do not have to understand it to be the Christians, is already apparent therein, that the earth, from which the trees and grass come forth, is the heathen Roman Empire; they can therefore only be the heathen high ranking men (trees) and the common people (grass), which were planted and rooted in the Roman Empire. The trees are thus in the Holy Scripture the image of high-ranking men, and the grass the image of the common people. God allowed the high-minded king Nebuchadnezzar to see himself in the dream as a tree. (Dan 4:5, 11, 20–22. See also Ezek. 17:16, 24. and Ezek 31.). All flesh is grass, says (Isaiah 40:6). Peter takes over this image from Isaiah in (1 Pet. 1:24). The prophet Isaiah however adds this interpretation to this in verse 7: "Surely the people is grass".

In (Psalm 1:3 and Jer. 17:7, 8.) a believer, in (Psalm 37:35) the wicked are compared to a tree and similarly in verses 1, 2 the evildoers with grass and green herbs. Trees and grass are therefore used as the image of believing as well as of unbelieving people, simply and only to indicate their higher or lower station in society or in the kingdom of God. The grass of which John the Baptist spoke in the prophecy of (Isaiah 40:7, 8.) was not a Christian nation. Nebuchadnezzar was not a Christian but a heathen tree. In the first trumpet the trees and the grass, because they are planted and rooted in the heathen Roman Empire, are the distinguished and the common people of the heathen Empire.

Burning, in many instances in God's Word, is the image of the judgement of God over the wicked, i.e.: (Psalm 83:14. Isaiah 47:14. and in the words of John the Baptist and Jesus, Matt. 3:10, 12. Matt. 13:40. Rev. 18:8, 9), and thus here the undermining of the heathen Roman Empire caused by the victorious Gospel. Indeed, the third part of the earth or the Roman State is burned up, namely the third part of the high-ranking Romans, and all the grass or common people. We know that the Christian people were not destroyed, but the Romans, and that, at the end of this first trumpet, when the second period begins, all the grass is burned up by the Holy Spirit and by the Gospel into a Christian nation.

It is remarkable that the trees and especially the grass were not destroyed by the hail, which otherwise would suit the image perfectly; on the contrary, they were burned up by the fire, and it is clearly implied here, that it was not strictly a destruction or decline, but a weakening of the heathen Roman State power (earth), because many high placed Romans, and the nation in general, left the heathen temples and religion and went over to Christendom.

It was therefore the fire of the Holy Spirit and the redeeming zeal of the Christians out of this same trumpet of Gospel preaching, which burned them as heathen Romans, or consumed the heathenship in them, by convincing them of the errors and lies of their idolatry, and to cause them to be lost as heathen for heathen Rome. What we mean hereby will become clear, when we remember the appropriate saying of our days: "Turkey dies for lack of Turks", not because of a decrease in population, but through the melting away of original nationality, and the weakening of the Mohammedan's faith as a result of the enlightenment of our century.

The old heathen Rome likewise also died through the light of the Gospel preaching, from lack of old heathen Romans. This is already foretold in the prophecy of (Isaiah 40), where John the Baptist was commanded to preach, that (verses 7, 8) the grass, which truly is the nation, would wither or be burned by the fire of the Holy Spirit when the Spirit of the Lord and the Word of our God would blow therein with the coming of the Saviour.

That this is the meaning, becomes even more apparent from the details, that all the green, strong grass, and only the third part of the trees burned up. The being green of the grass is the indication of the yet-living faith in the nation and its trust in the truth of its heathen religion. This faith yet still alive in them (green, Luke 23:31) is consumed, and burned up by the works of the Holy Spirit.

The nation nevertheless, not bound by any great earthly interests in the existing order of things, is much more susceptible to such changes, also in the State's deeply encroaching revolution of morals, than the high-ranking persons, who as trees out of the earth received their food from the social order, too deeply rooted therein and bound to it by too many earthly bonds, than that they would not try with all their might to adhere to the existing order.

This is why only a third part of the trees were swept away by the Christian State's moral reform.

In this third there also lies another particular meaning. As we shall show in the next (2nd.) trumpet, where this word appears several times, it is not so much the numerical value, which is indicated thereby, but rather the susceptible part of those influenced by the Holy Spirit and the Gospel preaching, forming the purified third part (Zach. 13:8, 9).

But then, it is significant that the burning of the third part of the earth, the heathen Rome, indicates, that the preaching of the gospel has had a bettering, sanctifying effect on heathen Rome, and that the Christian Religious susceptible part of the high-ranking persons accepted it.

The fulfilment of the prophecy in this sense, becomes clear, when we reflect, that the last portion of the 1st trumpet sketches the effect of the hail and the fire and the blood, as it clearly comes to the fore at the end of that period, beginning the transition into the next. During the last persecution of the Christians however, Emperor Constantine Chlorus did everything in his power, to protect the Christians against the three other emperors.

Thus, during the first three centuries, the Gospel preaching had gradually exerted its healing and softening influence on the dreadful, iron-like (Dan. 7:7, 19, 23) Roman Empire, causing the Christian Religion to be accepted at the beginning of the next period as a State religion. That was the effect of the first trumpet and it still sounds throughout all times since those centuries, in the Gospel preaching to the heathen, in later years throughout all of Europe and a part of Asia, in our days even to the ends of the earth. And it always was and remains a destructive judgement for the heathen laws, morals and forms of government; still calling to battle between the holy and unholy fire; but yet also the hail and the fire mixed with the blood of the witnesses of Jesus.

In our opinion, there is still another particularity hidden in this trumpet While in the other trumpets, the opposing powers, believers and unbelievers, are shown as sharply separated from each other, John does not see this in the first trumpet, but only hail and fire mixed in blood. It appears therefore that this hail, fire and blood, had to do with both parties. From the fire, we have already seen this. In the Church's history of the first three centuries, we must therefore find the hail and the blood in Christendom itself.

Indeed it shows us that the rain from the clouds of witnesses, the pure teaching of Christ, began to deteriorate in the second and third century, losing its original warmth and love; that the love for Christ and the longing for His return began to cool of (Rev 2:4); that also in the Church of Jesus Christ, blood, or the lusts and aspirations of the natural, unrepented life, began to appear.

Through all this, the condition of the Church is gradually so altered, that in the second seal we see the congregation red from blood, and the spiritual rider armed with a great sword. The historical review at the end of the first period will clearly show this.

FIRST VIAL

or

THE JUDGEMENT OF GOD

> In the world ye shall have tribulation: but
> be of good cheer; I have overcome the world.
> John 16:33.

Rev 16:1, 2.

If it is a truth that with the first vial, we have to transpose ourselves once more to the first or the Ephesian period – and it IS true – then, we must first ask, which beast is meant here. John indeed does not describe it further in Rev 16, because he described it fully in Rev 13. If we remember that John, in the sequence in which he received the Revelation, had already learnt to know the beast in the seventh trumpet (Rev 13) and, after the seven trumpets were introduced to him, in that order, the Lord now lets him see the seven vials of His judgements in the seven periods of the Church. If John thus now sees in the 1st period and in the 1st vial the same beast appearing again, which he already saw in the 7th period and in the 7th trumpet, then it must also be one and the same beast, which already existed in the first period, and which appears again in the last period. This is then also the fourth beast of Daniel, or the Roman Empire, which already existed with Christ's coming on earth and would remain in existence until His return. (Dan. 7:3, 7, 17, 19, 23. Dan. 7:13, 14, 27)

This fourth beast was heathen till Emperor Constantine (AD 324), this heathen Roman Empire formed the first head or great Kingdom of the "beast", as we have mentioned in the title of this period on page 37 and will be dealt with at length in the 7th period. Ever since Emperor Constantine it became Christian. In the Christian persecutions by the heathen Rome, the beast revealed that it was (Rev 17:8), in the later persecutions by the Papal Rome, that it was, although it apparently was not, yet in the last days it will again come up from the bottomless pit as the fully revealed anti-Christian power; how? This, we will better understand in the seventh period.

Likewise, it will not be in vain to repeat here, that we have to see the Revelation, as a book given to the Christian Church, which does not predict world history, but only the history of Christendom, and especially its

Church history, and worldly happenings only for as far as they relate to its faith and religious confession. The Revelation is not given to the heathen, neither nor to the Jews, but to the servants or the Church of Christ, to show what would happen in and around it. (Rev 1:1-3.)

Verse 1. "And I heard a great voice out of the temple saying to the seven angels, Go your ways, and pour out the vials of the wrath of God upon the earth".

In chapter 15 it is mentioned, how the Lord, after in (chapter 14) the seventh trumpet has ended, shows John, in the seven vials, His judgement over the Church and the world in each of the seven periods. John names these vials (Rev. 15:1) the seven last plagues. This was inaccurately translated with the seven last plagues. This also caused the interpreters, again and again, to understand that these seven plagues swiftly followed one upon the other while, on the contrary, each was poured out in one of the seven periods. The original word (Eschata) means: "the outer boundary, the extreme end of something". Indeed, there cannot be seven outer borders or extreme ends to one matter or to one period; only one can be the extreme, and the power of the word therefore indicates positively, that each of the seven consecutive periods of the Church runs out in one of these end- or closing plagues, as the extreme boundary of that period, wherewith the wrath of God over that period ended. This linguistic remark will eventually totally be confirmed by the revealed interpretations and fulfilment.

The seven angels with the vials are here again the same priesthood of each of the seven periods, as the angels with the trumpets (page 58). In this image, they are indeed represented as the executors of God's judgement, where the Lord himself commanded them.

Vials are drinking vessels, such as were used in the old days, approximately what we presently name a beaker or a cup. In many places in the Bible, an image of a beaker or a drinking vessel is used, filled with the wrath of God, which the ungodly must drink from or which is poured out over them, i.e. (Psalm 11:6. Psalm 75:8. Isaiah 51:17, 22. Jer. 25:15, 27,28, 29. Zech. 12:2)

The prophets of the Old Testament had the mandate from God, to declare His wrath and judgement over Israel or to pour it out by fulfilling their ministry, and yet these same prophets also had to declare God's blessings and especially His promises.

The Lord Jesus himself was the messenger of Peace and Saviour, and yet He had, according to his ministry and sending, at the same time come into the world as a judge, to blind those who considered themselves to be spiritually seeing, yes, He at the same time spoke the loving words: "For

God so loved the world, that he gave His only begotten Son" (John 3:16), yet also God's judgement over Israel and Jerusalem (Matt 11:21–24. Luke 11:42–52. Luke 13:34, 35.). The Apostles Peter and Paul were similarly messengers of Peace and Angels of the Lord (page 41) and yet both did not only proclaim God's judgement over the wicked but also poured it out; Peter on Ananias, (Acts 5:5) and Paul on Elymas, the sorcerer (Acts 13:8–11). Paul in (2 Cor. 4:7. and 2 Tim. 2:20) described the people, believers and unbelievers, as vessels in the great House of God, vessels for domestic use, which also belong to the drinking vessels and cups. According to (Jer. 51:7 and Rev. 17:4–6), the people drinking from the cup are misled and become drunken and mad. The word or the instruction of the Lord to people, to proclaim God's judgement, is, therefore, the full cup or vial, full of the wrath of God, which must be poured out on one or more living generations. Thus is the lovely Gospel to one an odour of life to life, to another an odour of death to death. (2 Cor. 2:15–16).

The earth is already known to us from the first trumpet as the Roman State in that period. The people on this earth were the heathen, as opposed to the Christians in that Realm, who were not the people of that state, but the people of God.

Verse 2. And the first went and poured out his vial upon the earth, and there fell a noisome and grievous sore upon the men.

Grievous sores occur on the surface of the body and are mostly caused by impurities in the blood, which we have already know from the first trumpet as the natural life estranged from God. Already in the Old Testament grievous sores were God's judgement, on rebellion against Him, such as King Uzziah (2 Chron. 26:19–23) and also with Miriam (Num. 12: 10) who was punished with leprosy (Lev 13:2). In Church history, we do nowhere find that ever, at the testimony of the servants of Christ, similar illnesses broke out in a natural way, such as occurred in the Old Covenant, as seen happening with Elisha to Gehazi, (2 Kings 5:27). Consequently, we have to explain this evil and grievous sores to the people, brought forth at the proclamation of the Gospel, as spiritual sores.

In this sense, we also find this in (Isaiah 1:5, 6.) where it says of the falling away of Israel: "From the sole of the foot even unto the head there is no soundness in it; but wounds, and bruises, and putrefying sores".

Here it is probably not implied, that all individuals, (persons) forming the people of Israel, had wounds, bruises and putrefying sores, but the spiritual condition of the people of Israel, taken as a whole, is considered here. When Stephen proclaimed judgment to the Jews (Acts 7:54–57) they gnashed against him with their teeth, and this wrath, created by the testimony of

God, was the putrefying sore, which resulted, in that they united to kill Stephen. The natural man cannot bear the punishment of the Lord meted out by His servants; even when he sees his own guilt and unrighteousness, his heart is filled with revenge against God's messenger. Even as with the magicians of Egypt against Moses, the sores burst forth naturally, so it also happened with the Gospel Preaching in a spiritual way, and the hearts of the carnally inclined heathen in the Roman Empire were filled with wrath and revenge when the apostles and their helpers preached the unknown God unto them, and testified mightily against their immoral religion and the lewd idolatry of their poets, (Acts 17:22–32. Acts 19:23–28 and 34–37) for herein the heathen were nevertheless: "the men which had the mark (Seal) of the beast and which worshipped his image". This beast was the Roman Empire, or the fourth kingdom of (Dan. 7:7), which was in its highest development at the coming of Christ on earth. Since the Holy Scriptures nowhere gives us a solution, of what we should understand by the mark or the seal of the beast, history must reveal it to us. It becomes most important for us to learn to understand the mark and image of the beast, because in the 7th period, in which we live, and even in this century, probably even within a few years, the same mark will be enforced on the Christians again, and they will be forced to worship the same image, albeit in a modern form, or be liable to the worst persecution (Rev. 13:14–18. Rev 14:9–11. Rev. 15:2. Rev. 19: 20). Here already these wonderful texts, which were never yet understood, and whose absurd interpretations must cause the intelligent believer to loathe the Revelation, will appear in a totally different light to the reader, and possibly help to clarify their fulfilment as a completely natural matter.

History already mentions to us, that the slaves often carried the branding mark of their owners. In the spiritual sense, however, their masters, the heathen Roman citizens also carried the mark of the heathen Roman Empire, in which the State and State religion were narrowly connected to each other.

In general, the old nations, and particularly the Romans, held fast to the maintenance and the wellbeing of the State, being totally dependent on the worshipping of the Fatherland gods. The Christians, as confessors of a teaching, which forbid this worship, were thus not only criminal against the heathen religion, but also against the State, especially since these counted their departed leaders amongst their gods, and erected temples, altars and statues to them.

One could therefore not be a true Roman citizen, without accepting the State religion, even though some other cities, like Tarsus, rewarded its citizens, to a greater or lesser degree, with the privilege of Roman citizenship as a reward for faithfulness or services rendered to the State, whereby the Jew Saul was born a Roman citizen (Acts 21:39. Acts 22:25–28). This however did not give the right to vote, even less the qualification to a post as a civil servant, or to the ownership of a house in Rome, which was associated only with Roman Citizenship. This last was then also, for its further privileges, only available to strangers, (Acts 22:29) at a great price. (Acts 22:29).

If the heathen Roman State was the beast – then this mark of the beast existed in that Roman citizenship, or the registration document as Roman Citizen, which only the faithful followers of the national heathen religion could possess, and to which voting rights, the right to State officialdom, etc. was bound. When the Christian persecutions arose, the suspected Christian Romans were forced to curse Christ, and to sacrifice to the statues of the Emperor and to the idols, and, on refusing, were first stripped of their Roman citizenship and then tortured or killed. In this way, the well-known Town clerk Plinius of Bithynia had those who refused to offer the statues of the Emperor killed.

When King Nebuchadnezzar had his statue worshipped in (Dan 3:1–5), on pain of death on refusal (verse 6, 15) he declared the worshipping of that statue as a State religion in his kingdom.

The image of the beast, which the Romans worshipped is likewise the Religion of the beast, the heathen Roman State religion, even as also the Christian Church must be the image of Christ. (Rom. 8:29. Cor. 15:49). The heathen State Church was therefore also the image of the beast, and, the proof of the citizenship in that State, the mark, given by the beast to those who worshipped his image.

The idol-worshipping Romans were the people, who had the mark (citizenship) of the beast and who worshipped his image (State religion).

This beast, or the Roman Empire, persecuted the children of God; it was bloodthirsty against those, who did not have its mark or citizenship, who did not worship its image or State religion, who refused to bow before the statue of the emperor, or to honour the idols with incense, or to curse Christ. It was unbearable for the Roman Emperors and their State officials, that the Christians daily increased in numbers and became more powerful and that, if this trend continued, they would not only become superior in the empire but proud Rome would be overcome by the hated sect of the Nazarene, even without the use of the worldly sword. When they saw the heathen temples silent and abandoned, yes later even destroyed by the Christians, this plague of grievous sores reached its peak: the heathen religious and political sense of honour burst out in hefty opposition and revolt against the unknown God preached unto them, and in abominable persecutions of His people, as clearly attested by the sorrowful history of the Christian Church during the first three centuries.

But this vial would not only be poured out over the heathen, but also over the Christians, over those who, after being adopted as Children of God and having received the Holy Spirit, once more loved the world, worshipped the beast and carried his image, instead of the image and the likeness of the Son of God. And there were such, Alas! During the centuries. Paul named as such his fellow worker Demas (2 Tim 4:10). Luke mentions Simon the sorcerer (Act 8:9–24) who became a believer and was baptised and, according to tradition caused himself with his concubine Helena to be honoured as Aeons (heavenly beings). Church history also speaks of Macellius, bishop of the Roman congregation, who, at the beginning of the third century of this period still sacrificed to Jupiter.

It is of such as these that Paul wrote: "For it is impossible for those who were once enlightened, and having tasted of the heavenly gift, and were made partakers of the Holy Ghost, and have tasted the good word of God, and the powers of the world to come, if they shall fall away, to renew them again unto repentance: seeing they crucify to themselves the Son of God afresh, and put him to an open shame." (Heb 6:4–6) These remained therefore in their apostasy. The grievous sores of this vial were poured out over them, their souls totally opposed to God and His anointed. That these fallen away Christians became the bitterest enemies of the Christian Church is confirmed by the sad example of Julianus the fallen away, who unsuccessfully tried to revive heathendom, and, dying, called out: "Galilean! You have won." Concerning these Paul spoke the terrible words: "Let him be Anathema, Maran-atha". (1 Cor 6:22).

The period during which the first vial was poured out over those who had the mark of the beast, and who worshipped his image (State Religion), already lies in the past for many centuries. Also, five more periods of the Christian Church have come and gone since then, and we now find ourselves in the last or seventh period, the time when the beast or the anti-Christian state power again rises from the bottomless pit to seduce those living on earth (Rev 13:14) to its modern, unchristian religion. But also in our time, the seventh trumpet of the Revelation stands before us, with its terrible warning in a great voice (Rev 14:9–12): "If any man worships the beast and his image, and receive his mark in his forehead, or in his hand, the same shall drink of the wine of the wrath of God, which is poured out without mixture into the cup of His indignation: and shall be tormented with fire and brimstone in the presence of the holy angels, and in the presence of the Lamb: and the smoke of their torment ascended up for ever and ever; and they have no rest day nor night, who worship the beast and his image, and whosoever received the mark of his name. Here is the patience of the saints, here are they that keep the commandments of God and the faith of Jesus. Therefore, who hath ears, hear what the spirit also herein saith to the congregation".

SHORT OVERVIEW OF THE CHURCH HISTORY
OF
THE FIRST APOSTOLIC PERIOD

FROM 33 TO 324 AD.

In the introduction to this work we planned that, at the end of each period, after the explanation of the related candlestick, the seal, the trumpet and the vial, we would give a short overview of the Church history of that period literally borrowed from the stated writings of Mrs. Van Loon and E. Guers. In order to show this in its right perspective, we will always precede this with a translation of the candlestick, the seals, etc. from its imagery into normal language, such as we have solved from God's word. While we only draw from this source and not from human wisdom, we believe that in our respectful attempts, we do not make ourselves guilty of that which the Lord Jesus warned us against so earnestly at the end of the book of Revelation (Rev 22:18–19): adding to or taking away from the words of the prophecy of this book.

The first candlestick, therefore translated, reads as follows:

TRANSLATION OF THE FIRST CANDLESTICK

Rev 2:1–7.

1. Write to the bishop of the congregation and to all who long for my return and to my well-pleasing congregation of the first period of the Church: This says the Lord of the congregation, who sent her His (messengers), and remains with her to the end of the world.

2 I know your works of faith and of love and your zeal to spread my Gospel, and your patience under persecutions and torture, and that you cannot suffer so-called Christians among you, who do not walk in purity before me; also, that you have tried them who say they are sent by me as apostles, and yet did not stand in my truth, wherefore you found them liars.

3. And you have withstood all persecutions and suffered all torture and have worked for my name's sake for the conversion and preserving of so many sinners and did not become tired.

FULFILMENT IN THE HISTORY OF THE CHURCH

So far, these words concern the condition of the Congregation during the first century of the first period, up to the second century. Concerning the condition of faith and the life of faith of the Congregation during this time the harvest from the named writers is very scares. Actually, the general impression of the history of that time is so abundantly and favourably known among the Christians, that we should not have to say too much about it. Already they had to endure two persecutions. We agree wholeheartedly with Mr. Van Loon, who says on page 14 ad Aum 131:

> "Actually, the Christians never ceased to be persecuted, however, their condition always depended on the favour of the people and local authorities. Regardless of the severe persecutions the number of Christians constantly increased and formed a really considerable majority in the state. (Van Loon page 10).
> At this time the Church was under the cross (Guers page 14). The blood of her children flowed throughout the whole Roman Empire. A martyr for Jesus Christ, thrown in the arena is attacked by a leopard in the presence of a crowd of idol worshipers, and with one bite lies in a bath of his own blood while the crowd cries out with scornful derision: "He is being baptised in his blood.
> Yes! The Church is baptised in its blood. She is baptised with the baptism of sorrow, with the baptism of Jesus Christ in Gethsemane and on Golgotha".

The reader will excuse us for not giving further descriptions of all the other well-known pains, tortures and death sentences, which, with additional crucifixion and burning at the stake, the Congregation had to endure.

The first candlestick continues with the second century, up to now totally approvingly, but in verse 4, the prophecy of the Son of God becomes a warning and admonition.

> "But I have against you, that you now begin to forsake
> your first love for me and the brothers".

That at the end of the first century, the Church began to degenerate is shown to us in the five last candlesticks in their non-prophetic meaning as letters to the Congregation in Asia.

In the year 160 (Van Loon, page 15), the controversy between the East and Western Christians concerning the celebration of Pentecost (page 19) began, leading to much bitterness in the Church. Also briberies by the rich congregation and individuals against persecutions to heathen magistrates, the use of unethical weapons in the battle for the truth, such as supposititious and false books, etc... The belief in and the longing for the return of the Lord began to wane.

Therefore, the Son of God also said:

> 4.Remember therefore from whence you have fallen and strayed. Walk on the old way again, and again do the first works of love and righteousness. If you do not do so, I will not come to you as Bridegroom, but as Judge, and darken in you the light of the Gospel.
>
> 5.But this good you still have in you, that you dislike the sinful lusts of the flesh, and walk before the world in modesty and in holiness.
>
> 6.Whosoever has ears, let him hear what the Holy Spirit says to the Congregation of the first three centuries: who overcomes in the battle of faith, will have part in my Glory as a member of my body, and celebrate the holy communion of the wedding of the Lamb with me in the Kingdom of my Father.

Also the Chilianistic controversy says (Van Loon ,page 32) belongs to the quarrel of this (third) century; the more or less literal understanding of the so-called Thousand Year Kingdom, gave rise to much writing. Origen and his school spiritualised this matter away and Dionysius the Great even converted those of other opinion to this idea. Methodius and Lactantius tried in vain to rekindle the idea of Chilianism (Thousand Year Kingdom); the conversion of Constantine dimmed the need for a better and richer Glory and Salvation.

The name of this period; "Ephesus", (longing, pleasing), did not therefore reflect the whole truth. Even though we still look back with amazement at that period, the full blessing, the return of Christ to fetch His Bride, so that she after death, should immediately enter in Paradise and celebrate the holy Communion with Him (Rev 19:7–9), which blessing she did not receive. Although the Lord had explicitly promised it to her, she did not satisfy the conditions. She did not want to, but in the third century, as we shall see, she strayed more and more from the tenets of Christ, and the requirements of the Gospel, and consequently lost God's pleasure in her.

TRANSLATION OF THE FIRST SEAL

Rev 6:1, 2.

1.And when Christ Jesus opened the scroll of the first period of the history of the Church to me, I heard someone speaking to me from heaven saying: "See what Christ will achieve in His Apostle ministry through the testimony of His servants in the battle against the kingdom of darkness, and what will become of this Apostolic ministry.

1. And I saw the Congregation standing in Christ's full righteousness, and her priests in full godly armour and in the power of the Holy Spirit; and they went out to do battle against the Kingdom of darkness and overcame the powers of hell. And the many souls, whom they had won for Jesus, became an overcomer's crown for them.

———————

Van Loon, page 10: *"During the first century Christendom spread out across the whole Roman Empire. Spain and England claim to have received it from the Apostle Paul. Asia Minor was the focus of evangelisation, which spread to Europe, Africa and Asia".*

The activities of the Apostles except for what the book of Acts relates (up to 63 AD), are mostly unknown. Tradition, some of which deserves little credence, attributes that:

Peter died in Rome.

Matthew worked in Ethiopia (Abyssinia) with the chamberlain of Candace.

Mark evangelised Egypt.

Andreas journeyed to Scythe and died a martyr in Achaje.

Phillip of Bethsaida preached in Gallia and was killed in Hierapolis in Phrygia.

Bartholomew journeyed to India (others say Arabia) and was crucified in Albanopolis in Armenia.

Thomas Didymus brought the Gospel to Arabia, Persia, India yes even to Ceylon and established the so-called Christians of St Thomas along the coasts of Malabar.

James, the son of Alpheus worked in Spain.

Judas Thaddeus preached the Gospel in Arabia and Mesopotamia and died a martyr in Persia.

Matthias chose Macedonia and Simon Cananite worked in North Africa.

And page 9 Paul was beheaded (64-68) as a Roman citizen. The legend which once again deserves little credence, says that Peter was crucified upside down at the same time.

The fate of the apostle John has already been mentioned on (page 24). With the death of the apostles the Apostle ministry was lost to the Church.

About the second century Van Loon said, page 16:

"From the testimonies of Justinus Martyr, Irenaeus, Tertulianus, it appears that during this century Christendom not only spread across the Roman Empire, but also in the neighbouring countries, although the establishing of most Churches lies in darkness." And on page 19: "The Christian writers of this century mention clearly, that wonders, healings, exorcism of demons, raising of the dead, etc.…. still occurred quite often in the Church."

And then on page 26:

Although the borders of the Christian Church further expanded during the third century, it is not certain in which countries and amongst which nations followers of Christ could already be found. It is said that the North of Gallië, Germany, Scotland, The Gothic nations, who lived north of Thracia, and various areas of the Interland of Asia became more or less acquainted with Christendom. The hub of the congregation however remained actually in the Roman Empire; and page 33:

"The period (which lies behind us) was a time of great development and powerful efforts in the Church. During the persecutions, the Church established and spread itself in the Roman Empire and in all the adjacent countries. Notwithstanding the strife to expand externally, the Church has valiantly resisted the inner dissidents and heretics, and the many attempts which could already be noticed by the Church fathers to corrupt the teaching and the divine services, yet no specific heretical tenets were officially sanctioned. Also, the life of most of the leaders in the Church was on the whole holy and their walk of life irreproachable. It is even said that the extraordinary gifts of the Holy Ghost had not completely disappeared from the Church, and some miracles, though fewer than before still occurred.

TRANSLATION OF THE FIRST TRUMPET

<u>Rev 8:7.</u>

Through the preaching of the Gospel in the first three centuries strife developed between the influence of the Holy Spirit and that of Satan in the harts of the Heathen nations. The Gospel preaching has weakened the Roman Empire and Christendom replaces Heathendom, but at the expense of the lives of the witnesses of Jesus. A great part of the Heathens did convert to Christendom, but also brought with them their carnal mind in the Christian Church.

Since the trumpet is a warning and a preparation for the pouring out of the following vial, it follows that its fulfilment is understood to a great extend in the latter.

That the preaching of the Gospel in this period awoke the wrath and sense of vengeance in the Heathen and moved them to the most horrible persecution of the Christians, this battle of the Kingdom of Darkness against the Kingdom of Light will become more apparent from the first vial.

That the Christian Church despite all this, continually expanded and chased away the clouds of heathen superstition and unbelief, we have already seen.

After the death of the Apostle John early in the second century, the Church and the Gospel preaching already began to deviate from the apostolic form and its original purity; the great multitude of Heathen, who converted to Christianity, gradually brought with them something of their old carnal ideas into the Church.

Van Loon says on page 16:

"Despite the terrible persecutions, the number of Christians increased steadily and formed a very considerable minority. In the Church itself also various heresies and wrong practices began to develop, such as; the buying off from persecution by the rich congregations and individuals from the magistrates, the use of unethical weapons in the battle for the truth, such as supposititious and false books. Slowly a more elaborate hierarchy (priestly rule) crept in the Church", and page 27: "Increased power of the bishops, especially those in Rome, Alexandria and Antioch. Luxuries and carnal lusts, mixed with the celibacy amongst the clergy", and page 28: "The divine service becomes more cumbersome; prayers houses came into being and are decorated with statues; the preaching becomes longer and more elaborate, (much false taste therewith); the communion is celebrated with growing decorum, many acts in the Church are considered to be mysteries (hidden knowledge) forbidden to unbaptized. The baptism becomes more elaborate, preceded by exorcism, renouncing, followed by salving and laying on of hands, crowns and white robes."

Page 29: "The Heathen sciences also had a considerable impact on Christendom," and page 32: Concerning the heresy of Arius, (who teaches that God's Son is a creature, page 27) although this started at the end of this period, its history belongs so totally to the following period, that it will be more appropriate to speak about it then".

TRANSLATION OF THE FIRST VIAL

Rev 16:1, 2.

1.And in the first three centuries of the Christian Church, the preaching of the Gospel by the servants of the Lord has become a judgement over the Roman Empire, the idol-worshipping Romans and fallen away Christians completely rebelled against God and His anointed, and their hart hardened in unrighteousness against God the Lord.

That this rebellion ever more revealed itself in the persecutions of God's children, is proven in the whole of the history of Israel and Christendom.

With Guers (page 14) we find as the fulfilment of this prophecy of the Son of God the following:

"Let us, by the flickering light of the burning stakes, under the sound of her sighing and anxious cries follow the footsteps of the Holy Bride (The Church) of the Lord. During this period, she suffered ten great persecutions. Under Nero, who initiated the first (64 AD) our beloved brethren suffered the most horrible tortures. Domitianus, the instigator of the second general persecution (93 AD) committed the same horrible deeds. Under the first name, a martyr crown was obtained by the apostle Paul through the sword and Peter by crucifixion, while John was banned to the Island of Patmos by the latter, and there received the glorious Revelation of Jesus Christ which the Church admires and ponders about.

The third general persecution, under Trajanus (107AD), procured the palm of the martyr to Ignatius of Antioch, while the fourth had begun under Mark Aurelius, fifty years later (162 AD). At this time Polycarp, the noble bishop of Smyrna and student of John, died valiantly for the holy name of the Lord Jesus. Forced to insult Christ, he gave the remarkable answer; "I served Him already for eighty-six years and He never caused me any harm, why should I therefore blaspheme my King, who saved me?"

The six last General persecutions were not less horrifying than the former four. Satan, up to now calmly in possession of the Empire, was angry, when he saw everything slipping through his fingers and called therefore all the powers of hell to do battle against Jesus Christ, and the bloody scenes of

the first two centuries repeated themselves in the whole civilised world."
Page 16. Lactancius who lived at the end of this period said: "From the
East to the West the whole earth was flooded with blood". But Jesus was
with His Church, His beloved, in the furnace, which their persecutors, the
new Nabuchadnezer, had ignited. Yet a little sighing, yet a little suffering
and the Lord arises to deliver His own. On page 18: "The persecutors
already bragged that they had even eradicated the name of Christ when the
hand of the Lord suddenly heavily came down on them.   Constantine takes
over the reins of power (312 AD), the temples are destroyed and the
Christian Churches arise on the ruins; the Heathen powers and priests of
the false gods are repulsed or banned, to make room for the worshipers of
the Son of God."

"In the year 321, says Van Loon, pages 26 & 27, Emperor Licinius again
begins to plague the Christians, yet not openly for fear of Constantine. In
the war, which he undertook against them, he openly declares that his
victory will also be that of the old Roman idol worshippers, and the battle
becomes a true religious war. In 323 a renewed war began between
Licinius and Constantine due to the persecution of Christians by Licinius.
Licinius was defeated and fled to Asia. This was followed by the battle at
Chrysopolis, where Licinius abdicated and relinquished his title. His life is
temporarily spared. Martinianus is killed. Constantine is the sole Emperor
of the whole Roman Empire".

This ended the Roman persecution of the Christians.

"But, will the Church of Jesus Christ already be victorious? Will the
beautiful days, promised in the prophesy, already be at hand? - asks Guers,
page 19: and answers thereupon: "By no means. This is only preceding
and preparing for new storms. Satan has not lost his anger against Jesus
Christ. Up until now, he had mainly attacked the Church from the outside,
but henceforth he would endeavour to destroy her from the inside. Already
under the Heathen Rome, he began the work of darkness, which he would
later bring to its fullness. The Roman heathendom fell; Christendom
became the main religion of the State. Now the prince of the powers in the
air begins to hasten his hellish work, which could not have developed under
the cross and soon one will discover that the great religious revolution
under Constantine, although in more than one aspect good for the Gospel,
yet had in many other and important matters, the saddest results. In great
abundance, the door opened to all disorderliness. The disciples of Jesus
Christ, not called on to follow Him in sorrow and trials, now gave free reins

to their evil tendencies. High-mindedness and ambition, hate and discord simultaneously invaded the Church, while superstition and vice went hand in hand."

This concludes the first period of the Church of Jesus Christ on earth. The condition of the Church at the end of this period is such that, with the beginning of the next period, the horse or the Congregation is no longer whit but appears red, and the rider or spiritual leadership is not armed with the bow of the Gospel anymore, but with a great sword. The following period will teach us the meaning of those images.

END OF THE FIRST PERIOD

SECOND PERIOD

Smyrnian Time

The Period Of The Church Fathers

From 324 To 622

SECOND PERIOD

Smyrna: *The Bitterness*

FROM

The elevation of the Christian Church to the State Church of The Roman Empire

TO

The Beginning of Popedom and the Rise of Mohamed, 622 AD.

This second period thus spans the fourth, fifth and sixth centuries of the Church during which she, growing in respect and extent and not being subjected to heathen persecutions anymore, was however torn by internal quarrels, dissension and heresies and Christendom deteriorated and was lost in her more and more.

In this period the second head of the beast appears, (4th beast of Daniel: or the Christian-Roman Mountain).

(Rev 17 : 9, 10).

SECOND PERIOD

Smyrnian time

or

The Period of the Church Fathers

2nd Candlestick. Chapter 2,	2nd Seal. Chapter 6,	2nd Trumpet. Chapter 8,	2nd Vial, Chapter 16,
And unto the angel of the church of Smyrna write; These things saith the first and the last, which was dead, and is alive; 9. I know thy works, and tribulation, and poverty, (but thou art rich) and I know the blasphemy of them which say they are Jews and are not, but are the synagogue of Satan. 10. Fear none of these things which thou shalt suffer: behold, the devil shall cast some of you into prison, that ye may be tried; and ye shall have tribulation ten days: be thou faithful unto death, and I will give thee a crown of life. 11 He that hath an ear, let him hear what the Spirit saith unto the churches; He that overcometh shall not be hurt of the second death.	And when he had opened the second seal, I heard the second living creature say, Come and see. 4 And there went out another horse that was red: and power was given to him that sat thereon to take peace from the earth, and that they should kill one another: and there was given unto him a great sword.	And the second angel sounded, and as it were a great mountain burning with fire was cast into the sea: and the third part of the sea became blood; 9 And the third part of the creatures which were in the sea, and had life, died; and the third part of the ships were destroyed.	And the second angel poured out his vial upon the sea; and it became as the blood of a dead man: and every living soul died in the sea.

SECOND CANDLESTICK

or

THE LIGHT OR THE SPIRITUAL LIFE IN THE CONGREGATION

> My kingdom is not of this world: if my kingdom
> were of this world, then would my servants fight,
> that I should not be delivered to the Jews; but now
> is my kingdom is not from hence.
>
> John 18:36

Smyrna, Rev 2:8–11

Smyrna, a rich and prosperous commercial town in older times, still exists as such, though considerably dilapidated from former times. She still boasts of a Christian congregation and was formerly the seat of bishop Polycarp, who sealed his faith with his death at the stake in 167 AD. An eyewitness once told me: "Above the communion table in the Church of Smyrna is written; Be Faithful unto death, and I will give you the crown of life".

The name *Smyrna* means **Myrrh**, a preserving, aromatic yet bitter spice, a correct image of the Church of Christ, especially at the beginning of that period. This Congregation had to suffer severely during the Christian persecutions and, as a result, was reduced to poverty. The many Jews living there were the main instigators of these persecutions and the accusers of the Christians to the authorities. Thus did the Congregation there constantly live in mortal danger. This is why the Son of God comforts her in verse 8, calling himself *the first*, who also out of love came upon the earth, and died on the cross, but who was resurrected and ascended to heaven, and now forever watches over His faithful and prays for them. This John had to write as comfort to the Angel or bishop of the congregation and through him also to the Congregation so that she would remain steadfast in faith under all need and persecutions and received the crown of life. Just as this was necessary for the original Congregation of Smyrna, no less would it apply, in the prophetic meaning of this letter, for the second period of the Christian Church, from Constantine the Great to the rising of Popedom and Mohamed.

Jesus calls himself therefore **the first;** who not only as the word in the beginning was with God, (John 1:1), but also was manifested in the flesh here on earth in the first period of the Church.

So will He also return in glory in the last period, to be and remain the last, in the Kingdom of Glory as King of all Kings. If the Royal Priesthood was lost through sin in the first Adam, in the second Adam, the God-Man Jesus Christ, the Royal Priesthood, saved and sanctified, is revealed anew, and exactly in this period, Constantine the Great introduced the Christian Kingship on earth for the first time.

Christ, born as King (Luke 1:32, 33), also died as King on the cross (Matt 27:11, 37. John 19:15, 19–22). In the Congregation, which is the body, He became alive as King in this period, not only to be the Priest in the priests of the Church, but also the King of Christian kings, who, as a star amongst the stars and as angel amongst the angels, together with the priesthood had to form the light, which burned on the candlestick of the Congregation. If the king of Babel was a bright morning star in the sight of the Lord (Isaiah 14:12) and the king of Tyre (Ezek 28:12–16), an anointed Cherub or angel appointed by God before both became high-minded, how much more then will a Christian king, in whom Jesus wants to exercise His ministry as morning star, be a star amongst the stars, and an angel amongst the angels of the Son of Man. Therefore also: (*One must never lose sight of this*) as from the second period the kings formed, since they became Christian kings, together with the priests of the Church not only the light on the candlestick, but also the rider in the seal, the angel with the trumpet and the angel with the vial.

In the first period of the Church (The Ephesian), it became apparent, that the Church could also exist without the support of the worldly powers, flourish and increase even though the latter were hostile to her. It was clearly the intention of the Lord Jesus, that the spiritual leadership and the worldly powers should be vested in different persons under Him as invisible Head, until He himself, at His return in glory, would reunite the priestly and royal powers in His own hands.

The transition of royal power in the hands of Christians would *then* have been a blessing for the Christian people, if the kings had been the leaders of the people, such as the Lord named king Hezekiah, (2 King 20:5) and had they confined themselves to the protection of the Church, but above all, as simple members of the Congregation, having remained subservient to the spiritual powers in the Church; (such as Ambrosius, bishop of Milan, openly reprimanded Emperor Theodorus and forced him to do penance) and, on the other hand, that the spiritual leaders also would consider themselves subject to punishment for transgressions in worldly matters by the authorities. However, the aspiration and the strife to unite the worldly and spiritual powers into one person, which is not reserved for one person but only for the royal priest Jesus Christ in the Kingdom of Glory, which strife singly has brought about all further evil over Christ's Church. Because of this, from this period onward, a struggle began between Church and State for supremacy and now, the State was subjected to the Church, as in Popedom, and then again, the Church to the State, as in Protestantism. Please forgive us for our digression, which was highly necessary to the understanding of this and further periods.

Verse 9. **"I know thy works, and tribulation, and poverty, (but thou art rich)".** says the Lord to the Congregation of Smyrna. She let her light shine on the candlestick before men through her spiritual treasure of faith. Up to our time that light of the second candlestick still shines in the highly valued writings of the Church Fathers Athanasius, Ambrosius, John Chrysostomus, etc. Also, the acts of faith of Nice and of Athanasius come from this period. Precisely because of the religious zeal and battle for the Kingdom of God, the Church was later subjected to persecution and poverty. Though in the beginning of this period under Constantine she enjoyed honour and recognition, already after the fourth century this began to change, when, after the death of Constantine, his son Constantius came into power, and in his unbelief concerning the godliness of Christ, began to persecute the believers.

Although the Church of the Believers then again fell into outward poverty and diminished glory, she still remained rich in God, through the strong faith in His only begotten Son. The cause of this persecution lay in what the Lord names:

"The blasphemy of those who say they are Jews and are not, but are of the synagogue (school) of Satan." Though the original Smyrnian congregation had to suffer much at the hands of her natural enemies, rich and influential Jews who instigated the heathen authorities against her, whereby among many, the well-known bishop Polycarp died at the stake in 167, - also the second or Smyrnian period of the Church had to have Jews in the midst of Christendom, if the prophetic meaning of the letter to the Congregation of Smyrna has been fulfilled. Truly this is the case. In that period of the Church, the spiritual or Christian (venia, verbo) Jews appeared, who just like the Israelitic Jews in Smyrna, persecuted the believers in Christ of the second period.

Because just as the Jews, (John 5:18 and John 10:30–33) denied the godliness of Jesus, there also came amongst the Christians of that period, those who did not want to acknowledge the godliness of their Lord and Saviour, although He himself did not consider it as stealing[5] to be equal to God, (Phil 2:6). These were the Aryans of that period, whom we, therefore, call Jews. **Jew**, actually **Judah**, means: **Who praises God** (Gen 29:35) and in this meaning moreover lies hidden one of the wonderful prophetic mysteries, of which the Holy Scripture overflows.

With the beginning of that period, Aryanism originated in the Christian Church, or the teaching, that Jesus Christ, God's Son, was a creature, and also the rejection of the belief in one Triune God. Arius, presbyter (elder) in Alexandria, was the proclaimer of this unbelief, which, as also his followers, were named after him. In this rejection of the godliness of Jesus Christ, which they made out to be a *misrepresentation* and *dishonour* to a supreme Being, yes, an Idolatry, in this pretended glorification and recognition of the supreme God, they were Christ's predicted Jews, who, just as the descendants of Abraham, considered themselves the true worshippers, also being, that *they praised God but did not do so*, but were guilty of a great misunderstanding of the triune being of God, and especially of the godly being of their Lord and Saviour, God revealed in the flesh.

Therefore, the Lord also refers to them as **a school of Satan.** Satan means: **Opponent**, and from him emanates this teaching of opposition to God, wherewith he imprisons the souls through unbelief so that as a result of belief in the Godhead or any mediator of God or men, they should not be preserved for eternity.[6]

This teaching spread unbelievably quickly, not only in the Christian Church and Congregations, deacons, priests, bishops and Emperors, who even declared it a teaching of the State, but also immediately appealed to the recently converted Gothic nations.

That the true believers had to endure great persecutions and tribulation under these Christian Jews, especially when the Gothic-Aryan nation invaded the Southern states of Europe is well known. Therefore, the Lord comforts his own and says to them:

---

[5] To rob God of His honour, as a deed of accomplished evil, which word is used for it, never appears differently, than to represent such a deed as punishable.

[6] Should this explanation of the "Jews "appear somewhat far-fetched to the reader, then we must refer him to the 5th period, that of the Reformation, 1517 to 1815 AD, (Rev 3:7–13) where the Lord again predicts, verse 9; "Behold, I will make them of the Synagogue of Satan, which say they are Jews, and are not. "During the next three periods of the Roman Catholic Church 622 to 1517 AD, the teaching of Arius did not exist in the Church. After the Reformation it reappeared anew in Protestantism. If our explanation was not the true one, it would be a very strange coincidence.

Verse 10: "**Fear none of these things which thou shalt suffer**", as also the apostles, (Acts 14:22) "Confirming the souls of the disciples, and exhorting them to continue in faith, and that we must through much tribulation enter the kingdom of God."

This encouragement is also followed by the warning in verse 10, **"Behold the devil shall cast some of you into prison, that ye may be tried, and ye shall have tribulation 10 days",** -- that we should have to take this literally is doubtful, (Actually *a prison sentence of ten days* is of such a trifling nature, that the Revelation should mention it at all), and is not found in history. With imprisonment there cannot be any mention of overcoming by the prisoner, even if he is released, as it happens in verse 11.

Besides, here is no indication that the authorities, neither the spiritual leaders are the personal persecutors, but the devil, the *seducer*, the *father of lies*. **The imprisonment** occurred in the soulish life, **on a spiritual level**, which the rest of this candlestick attest to. David already prayed (Psalm 142:7) "Bring my soul out of *prison*". Paul says (Eph 4:8) that the Lord Jesus "led captivity captive", further he goes on to say (Rom 7:23) "and bringing me into captivity to the law (2 Cor 10:5), lead captive silly women, etc…all in a spiritual sense". When we therefore take into consideration, that it is the devil or seducer, who would take them as prisoners, then it is clear that it was a *spiritual temptation*, by which the devil would *imprison their souls*, so that they may be *tempted*, as verse 10 says. To this, the *persecution of ten days* completely fits in. Literally, or even as persecution of ten years never occurred as far as is known. Some wanted therefore to interpret it as ten consecutive persecutions, which the Christian congregations had to endure under the Roman Emperors. If it were so, this prediction would lose its prophetic meaning for the 2nd or Smyrnian period of the Church, as the persecutions had already come to an end in the 1st period. Over and above the historian writers, although not all, take as explanation ten different persecutions, counted according to the various Roman Emperors, under which they had taken place, but effectively they did not each evolve individually, into ten persecutions. They were much rather continuous series of persecutions with intermittent respites, than that the godly prophesy of Jesus Christ should have occurred beforehand according to human historical meaning.

In the concept of the image of a *"prison"* lies therefore also hidden, that the number ten here is a symbolic number. And this is so! **Ten** is the symbolic number of **the Kingdom of God.**

Seven is the number of God's revelation in men. **Three** is the absolute number of God. Taken together they form **ten**, but also therefore encompass the whole Kingdom of God on earth and in heaven, that is: the Kingdom of heaven. Thus, God gave Israel *ten commandments,* containing *all* the responsibilities to *God* and *men,* etc. Why more proof? The Lord Jesus says so himself: (Matt 25:1) "Then shall the Kingdom of Heaven be likened unto *ten* virgins, etc. Why not another number, if *ten* is not actually the symbolic number of the Kingdom of God? The tribulation of **ten days** is therefore a persecution of indefinite duration for the Kingdom of God or the faith. Translating again the 10th verse, Jesus says therein to His true believers, "Fear none of those things which thou shalt suffer, behold, the devil, the father of lies shall try to ensnare some of your souls, to hold them imprisoned and bound with his false teaching, yet fear not his temptation, I am with you till the end of days. You will have to suffer persecution for the sake of the Kingdom of God and for your faith, yet **remain steadfast unto death, and I will give you the crown of life.**" Apostle James also says (James 1:12) "Blessed is the man who endures the temptation, for when he is tried, he shall receive the crown of life, which the Lord hath promised to them, that love Him" and this is "the crown of righteousness" of which Paul says (2 Tim 4:8), "which the Lord, the righteous judge, reserved for them who keep the faith" - the incorruptible crown of glory of which (1 Pet 5:4) bears testimony.

The fulfilment of this prophecy to the Congregation of the second period is not difficult to find. The teaching of Arius which found such rapid favour with the many dissidents of the faith, which teaching, sponsored and supported by all the resources of Alexandrian Philosophy, and above all, finding a responsive echo in the unbelieving high-minded human heart, - this teaching must also have been a great temptation for the remaining steadfast believers. Being more understandable than the Bible - Apostolic view, which had remained in the Church up to now, it naturally had to make a deep impression on the souls of many faithful Christian spiritually imprisoning and binding them with its seducing idolatry. It became difficult to wrest themselves free from this, to bind themselves once more, with their whole heart to their Saviour and worship Him as God and Lord.

About the persecution for the Kingdom of God, which these steadfast believers of the Aryans had to suffer, both through the word and through the sword, we already have indicated through one word. We will find it again and explain it in greater detail in the seal of that period.

They, who under these temptations and persecutions of Satan and his followers, the Aryans, remained faithful to their Lord and Saviour, only they would receive the crown of Life.

The whole image of the spiritual prison, in which some souls would lie bound, is completed in the promise of:

Verse 11. **"He that overcometh shall not be hurt of the second death."** Overcoming is only possible, not in bodily imprisonment, but in spiritual temptation. What do we understand about *the second death*? The conclusion here once more indicated *a spiritual death*. In nature, however, only one death exists, in the spiritual sense there are actually two. The first was in Adam (Rom 5:15–19) through sin. From this, the merciful God graciously saved us through the rebirth in the Holy Baptismal Covenant as His children. Whosoever again loses this once-received privilege becomes prey to the second death.

The second death is, therefore, the horrible end of the unfaithful baptised, who do not value their adoption as children of God, and either did not come to repentance and faith in Jesus Christ or once having repented, once again went astray and again loved the world. Such are described by (Jude 12): "twice dead trees" and John says so movingly of them: (1 John 2:19) "They went out from us, but they were not of us; for if they had been of us, they would no doubt have continued with us." He that hath an ear, let him hear what the Spirit saith unto the Churches, warningly precedes this promise.

It is therefore not only to the congregation of Smyrna but to the Christians of all centuries, also to us, that this admonishing promise is directed to. Our Lord Jesus says (Matt 10:28), "And fear not them which kill the body, but are not able to kill the soul: but rather fear him which is able to destroy both soul and body in Hell." **The death of the soul**, or *the deprivation of the faith in Jesus Christ*, the only mediator of God and men, is, therefore, **the second**, **the eternal death**, because "Neither is there salvation in any other: for there is none other name under heaven given among men, whereby we must be saved." (Acts 4:12)

He who overcomes the temptation to fall away from faith, and remains in Christ his saviour, will not be hurt by the second death is the final promise of this second candlestick. If its light was considerably darkened in the following three periods, that of the Papal Church, with the period of the Reformation, the light of the second candlestick burned brightly again and shines forth, through our time, up to the return of Christ. The period of the Reformation, however, is mainly a repetition of the period of the Church-Fathers with all its sectarian disputes, with all its mutual strife and division between the confessors of the Christian faith. Also, the Jews or

Aryans, who deny the godliness of Christ, are not lacking in our time, on the contrary, their number are legion, and their understanding and teachings concerning the nature and personality of Jesus Christ, are even worse, than those of the Aryans of the second period. Where they still gave Jesus Christ a measure of godly honour, as the head of the Congregation, for the Aryans of our time He is no more than a prophet, a teacher, an Illuminate and a moral reformer, in line with Moses among the Jews, with Confucius among the Chinese, etc.

These Christian Jews of our time, or Deists (rhetorical religion, without revelation) are therefore also the anti-Christians (who are against Christ) of the end time; also there, where they still possess an outward appearance of godliness, but miss its inward life. Even the State again becomes anti-Christian, just as in the time of the Church-Fathers. In the few state documents still mentioning the name of God, we seek in vain for that of His holy child Jesus. Is the name of Jesus still mentioned in a state school, with the respect due to Him, who as: "Worthy is the Lamb that was slain to receive power, and riches, and wisdom, and strength, and honour, and glory, and blessing. ", as it is given to Him in heaven? (Rev 5:11–13). Is an official prayer, at the opening of one or other state school function or meeting, directed to God in the name of Jesus Christ, and supplicated from God in His name? If not, it is only because it is shameful to publicly mention the name of Jesus, it is an official transaction (amicable arrangement) with Aryanism, a more or less hidden public anti-Christian attitude, against which this candlestick warns us with so much emphasis, so that we should not be hurt of the second death.

Smyrna, or **Myrrh**, which is the name of the Congregation, this was the characteristic of Christendom of that period; the Church was not only sweet-smelling and preserving, through the faith which still existed in her, but also bitter as myrrh because her inward dissension and fierce strife, which kept the Christian faith awake, but harmed the mutual love. If the Church of the first period (Ephesus) was full of longing for the return of Christ, that of the second period had with her external prosperity and worldly lustre, lost all need for a better and higher salvation. Though her life of faith at the onset of that period was still strong, God had no more pleasure in her, to Him she had become bitter, as a result of her lack of love. The seal of that period will disclose this to us more clearly. But also, the trumpet and the vial will show us, how the Christian faith and life of the Church of that period deteriorated more and more.

SECOND SEAL

or

THE SPIRITUAL LIFE OF THE POWERS

IN THE CHURCH AND STATE

> Think not that I am come to send peace on earth:
> I came not to send peace, but a sword.
> Matt 10:34.

Rev 6:3–4.

Just as the second candlestick revealed to us that the Congregation of the second period was of inferior Christian quality than that of the first, the same occurrence is manifested in the spiritual powers and the powers of the State. Since with that period the kings have become Christians, the State powers together with the spiritual powers form the rider in the seal, as we have shown in the candlestick. If in the first seal the horse was white, the colour of righteousness, and the rider, armoured with the bow of the gospel, went out to preach: "Peace on earth, goodwill to all men", in the second seal less peaceful scenes are predicted for the Church of Christ.

The book or the scroll we already know as the Church in her development and history, whereof the powers in Church and State, as the seals, on being opened, bring in fulfilment the content or the decree of God for His Church in each period.

The **second Cherub**, who invites John: "Come **and see!**" is, according to (Rev 4:7) likened to a **calf** or **young ox**. (Ezek 1:10).

This second Cherub does not speak to John with the voice of thunder "come" because only the apostles in the first period were those who spake with voices like thunder.

It is again one of the four ministries, which Christ himself exercised on earth, and after His ascension, exercised in and through the preachers of the word, **the shepherd ministry**, namely of which the calf or **young ox**, as a symbol of **patient labouring**, is the image. [7]We find it as such already in

---

[7] This symbolic meaning of the ox does not often agree with our Western understanding, where one attributes totally different characteristics to the ox. Not only in Eastern

97

the golden calf, which Aaron and the people of Israel cast for themselves out of golden earrings and bracelets, while Moses was on the mountain for forty days, not so much to worship it as God, but as a mediator between God and men and to obtain help and comfort from it, in (Exod 32:4–8) while they expected to have to miss their shepherd and leader Moses. Similarly, Paul teaches us explicitly (1 Cor 9:9, 10. and 1Tim 5:17, 18.) that when the Lord causes it to be written in the laws of Moses; "Thou shalt not muzzle the ox", (Deut 25:4) this was not for the sake of the oxen, - does God also care for the oxen? he asks but for the sake of the shepherds and leaders of the Congregation, who, like the patient labouring ox, ploughed the Congregation and trashed the good seed from her. The **ox** is therefore also the image of the **shepherds** and **bishops** of the Congregation.   Jesus calls himself The *Good Shepherd* (John 10:11). Paul also calls Him (Heb 13:20) *The great Shepherd* of the sheep, and Peter *The chief Shepherd* (1 Peter 5:4). This, His Shepherd ministry, the great Shepherd and bishop of the souls (1 Peter 2:25) He still exercises in and through the ministration of the shepherds in His Congregation.

The question now arises, who does the Cherub with the likeness of the ox here invites John to see what would become of the spiritual leadership in this second period of the Church? The answer to this is that it was precisely this shepherd ministry of Jesus Christ, which He exercised in its purity and clarity through His servants in the first period of the Church with so much blessing for the Congregation, through the angels or bishops of the Congregation, by which she was protected against the wolves in sheep's clothing, this we say, precisely this glorious comfort and edification in Christ, this glorious work as a mediator ministry of Jesus Christ for the worried souls of the weak in faith or the sinners in the second period would deteriorate through the vehement disputes and mutual bitterness in Christendom. Therefore, the Cherub who represents *this* ministry of Christ says: "Come and see" what will become of this shepherd ministry in the 2nd period of the Church.

When the second seal, which would represent the history of the powers in the Christian Church and of the rapidly Christianizing State was opened, John said:

Verse 4. **"And there went out another horse that was red"**. The horse, as we already said in the explanation of the first seal, is the Congregation, yet separated from the spiritual leaders, who, from now on, together with the Christian kings, form the rider. The horse is actually no longer white

---

countries, but also still in many Western ones, where the domestic ox is the worker and provider for and of the family, one better understands the patient labour of the ox.

like that of the first period, but red. Do we have to understand that under this red colour, the Congregation was washed in the blood of Christ; and presented herself as such to the world? We do certainly have to understand it to be blood, for red is the colour of blood (Jes 63:2, 3) yet not the blood of Christ, since it makes pure and white (Jes 1:18. Rev 19:8). Actually, the first horse from the first period, which was purified by the blood of Jesus Christ and which stood in all His ordinances was white and not red, although her own natural blood flowed like rivers under the persecutions. Hence, the colour of the horse depicts the condition of the spiritual life in Christ in the Congregation. Besides, the horse of the second period was not painted or clothed in red, but red by nature. **Red** or **blood** therefore is the image of the **natural life**, bodily as well as spiritual, (1ˢᵗ trumpet), or the *life* in *sin* and *unrighteousness*. It follows that, the Son of God appeared to the prophet (Isaiah 63:2, 3) with red-stained clothes, because our sins and unrighteousness were heaped on Him. According to our prophecy, therefore, after the first three centuries, the Congregation would lose all patient love and her all-encompassing enduring faith under persecution and revert to the natural tendencies of the blood, high-mindedness, lust and strife, such as actually took place after the Church was freed from all persecutions under Constantine the Great, and came to worldly honour and greatness, and was recognised as State Church.

"And power was given to him that sat thereon, (the rider), **to take peace from the earth and that they should kill one another".** The rider, who guided the horse, is no longer only the spiritual leader, as in the first period, but now that the Christian religion in this period had become a State religion, *the powers in the State* or *the kings* together with the powers in the Church, or the spiritual leader, form from now on, not only together the rider, but also the whole seal, since it consists only of the actions of the rider. The earth in this period is no more the *heathen*, but the *Christian Roman State* with its *civic ordinances*, from which peace would be taken away.

It merits to be mentioned, that Constantine and his successors, as also later Charles the Great, bore the title of *Emperor* and not of king. The concept *king* is rooted in the holy Scriptures. It is of heavenly origin. Christ is the *King of Kings*. The concept *Emperor* = *Caesar* in comparison as embodied in an anti-term, Emperor, is used as historical term, (See also Luke 20:22–25), yet Christian idea.

Although in the holy Scriptures (Luke 2) and other texts the Scriptures name them, whom God vested with the highest political sovereignty: *Kings.*

(1 Peter 2:13) Already the title *Emperor* or *Caesar* is therefore, although often unconsciously, an anti-Christian concept.

Further enlightenment to the above is not required. It predicts one fact, that literally occurred in the history of the Church. We already mentioned it in the first candlestick, and the historical overview at the close of this period will further show us, how quickly in this period peace under the Christians was disturbed, through the Arian controversies and the Gothic emigrations, and - take note! – the prophecy says explicitly, *that they* would not kill their heathen enemies, but that the Christians *would kill one another*, and this had not happened yet. Instead of the *bow of the Gospel*, which the first rider carried, a great battle sword **was given** to **him**, (the kings and the spiritual leaders or the rider). This sword is not the two-edged sword of God's word and of Christ's teaching, (Rev 1:16. Rev 2:16. Eph 6:17) but **the worldly sword**, of which (Ezek 21:28) says: " The sword, the sword is drawn: for the *slaughter* it is furbished, to consume because of the glittering", but also the *sword* of embittering verbal disputes, mentioned in (Psalm 55:22):*Words* like *Naked swords* of them, who (Psalm 64:4) sharpen their *tongues* like a *sword* in the lively verbal disputes and controversial pamphlets between believers and the Aryans. Since the rider carries the sword, and the secular powers together with the spiritual leaders form the rider, the connection between the State powers and the Church leaders is indicated, as it occurred in this second period, and they did not carry the sword in vain (Rom 13:) in these religious conflicts about all sorts of teachings, as the history of that time so sadly attests. This is also why it was the second of the Cherubim, representing the shepherd ministry of Christ, who at the opening of this period had to say to John: "Come and see" how this ministry of Christian meekness and of patient labour, to bring the straying back on track, to uplift the weak, and to lead and feed all with shepherd-like faithfulness and love, how it would erupt in hate and strife.

SECOND TRUMPET

or

THE CONDITION AND EFFECT OF THE GOSPEL PREACHING

> And because iniquity shall abound, the love
> of many shall wax cold.
> Matt 24:12.

Rev 8:8, 9.

At the end of the 1ˢᵗ trumpet, we left the Church of Jesus Christ as she, elevated by Constantine to a State Church, is finding rest after all the revilement and humiliation, rose to honour and recognition; but yet the eternal Gospel, although still powerfully preached, is already not preached in its full purity anymore, like in the first century. In this condition, the first trumpet continues to sound in the Congregation, while now the second trumpet joins in next to it. (page 29). In order to form a good picture of this, we recognise that, from the first Gospel preaching (33 AD.) the Christian people and the Christian preachers increased in numbers throughout all the centuries. At the end of the first period, the Christian teachers split into two groups. The one continues to sound the trumpet of the Gospel preaching in the existing conditions, the other group elevates itself in its progressive deviation as the second trumpet next to it, and both continue to sound until the third adds itself to them, then later the fourth, etc

What the effect of this second trumpet sound was, what would occur under it, the prophecy teaches us:

Verse 8. **"And the second angel sounded.** This is therefore: through the Gospel preaching during the second period of the Church: **A great mountain burning with fire, was cast into the sea"**. We are faced with three images and just as many questions concerning the meaning of these few words:

1.   What is the **great mountain**? With the prophets, we find that a mountain represents a **powerful State** or **kingdom**, which, like a mountain rises above the great general sea of nations. In our days we would understand it to be *a mighty power* and hills the smaller powers.

This we find in the interpretation which Daniel, (Dan 2:18–23), through divine revelation, gave to king Nabucadnezar's dream, (Dan 2:35 and 44), clearly describing the *kingdom of Jesus Christ*, (The coming kingdom of peace and of glory) as the mountain formed of a stone (The cornerstone, Jesus Christ), and this kingdom would remain in all eternity, and would break up and destroy all the kingdoms." Isaiah also foretold the same in (Isa 2:2), "And it shall come to pass in the last days, that the *mountain* of the Lord's house shall be established in the top of the *mountains* and shall be exalted above the *hills*". Therefore, God the Father also said to (Isa 41:15): "Thou shalt thresh the *mountains* and beat them small, and shalt make the *hills* as chaff". We also find in (Jer 51:25) the Chaldean or *Babylonian kingdom* is named: "O destroying *mountain*", and the heathen nations in (Hab 3:6.) the everlasting mountains and perpetual hills of the earth.

2.   This mountain or this powerful nation **burns with fire**, which we already know from the 1st trumpet as the **holy fire** of the Holy Spirit, or the **unholy fire** of human, sinful lust. In this last meaning the mountain must have been a heathen nation or kingdom, in the first it could only have been the newly formed Christian Roman State, as the only one on earth, wherein the fire of the Holy Spirit could burn.

3.   This fiery burning mountain **is thrown into the sea**. This is the first time we encounter the **sea** as recognised by the many readers of Revelation as the well-known **sea of nations**. Except in (Rev 17) where in (verse 15) the *waters* which John saw, are said to be "peoples *and multitudes*", we find the image of the *sea* often used in Revelation to mean nations. In (Rev 13:1) for instance, one beast comes out of the *sea*, which the whole earth will worship according to verses 3, 4 and 8. A dragon rising from the sea, would not be worshipped by a modern enlightened generation, because, take good note, this beast will actually rise in our time and does not only already rises, but is already clearly visible, to those who know how to recognise it. Actually, we already learned to know it, in the 1st seal, as a power opposed to God, which rises according to (Rev 17:15) from the sea of nations. In the same sense, we also find the sea described in many passages in the Bible, eg: (Jer 51:42. Ezek 26:16. Jude 13. Dan 7:2, 3, 17), and especially in (Isaiah 17:12, 13); "Woe to the multitude of the many *people*, which make a noise like the noise of the *seas*; and to the rushing of *nations*, that make a rushing like the rushing of mighty *waters*!" The sea can therefore be the Christian sea of nations of that period or the heathen one.

History must thus provide an answer to the two questions, which according to this prophecy are possible, namely: Is the Christian nation, burning with the fire of the Holy Spirit, thrown down and extinguished in the heathen sea of nations, or on the contrary, a great heathen nation, burning with the fire of unholy lusts, thrown into the sea of nations?

History teaches us the latter.

Actually, with Emperor Constantine, at the beginning of this period, the Christian religion was elevated to a State religion, the heathen religion deteriorated gradually, and the heathen Romans were forced, although with reluctance, to cross over to the new State Church. This enforcement from Constantine and his successors to the incorporation of the heathen in Christendom and to the abolition of the heathen religion was the *sound of the second trumpet*. Through this, the Christian Church was totally corrupted. Christ had sent His Gospel messengers to convert Jews and heathen *through preaching*, to bring them to the faith and to preserve them for His Kingdom, but never meant, the opposite, to incorporate idolatrous heathendom by force into His body, His Congregation, which must be the temple of the living God. (John 18:36. 1 Cor 6:14–16). Since the trumpet sound did not answer to the Lord's intention, the trumpet itself becomes the vial of this period, and the spiritual leaders or the trumpet angel are also the angels with the vial, full of the wrath of God.

This *great*, **powerful Roman nation**, was therefore the **great mountain**, which, still **burning** with an unholy fire of heathen idolatry and from all sorts of sinful lusts and desires, as described by Paul in (Rom 1) is thrown into the Christian sea of nations. That this could not take place without highly adversely affecting the whole Christian people in its purity of faith and morals, and revealing the influence of the heathen ideology on the Christian teachings is readily suspected. The prophecy teaches us in abundance in the remainder of this verse:

"And the third part of the sea became blood". *Blood* we already know as the image of the *natural, sensual life,* such as reigned without God in the natural heathen or unconverted. It will thus also not be strange to us that the heathens incorporated into Christendom without Christian conviction and repentance only possessed the name and outward appearance of Christians, and their heart remained full of the old heathen sins and desires, without attaining redemption, which the Christian upright faith not only requires, but also achieves.

This especially is the reason for the blood-red colour of the second horse or of the Congregation of this period. She possessed this already at the beginning of this time, before even the heathens were incorporated into her; because having come to rest and earthly honour, she had already forgotten her unique calling, the calling of each Christian to carry the cross of sorrow and humiliation of Christ, and not to seek the things of this earth, but those things from above, where Christ is (Col 3:1); but through this incorporation of the heathens into Christendom, it deteriorated to even a greater degree. The angel, or the worldly and spiritual power in Christendom, who blew this second trumpet, is also actually the angel with the second vial. This deviating from the Lord's intentions caused this *blood* to become *a corpse*, as the second vial will teach us presently.

According to our prophecy, it is because of this victory of Christendom in body and spirit over the heathen religion, that *a third part* of the Christian people were brought back to the natural carnality (blood). That with this third part, something else is meant than a single numerical relation, we readily accept on good grounds. A similar example we already encountered in the number *ten* of this second candlestick. (Zach. 13:1, 2, 8,9) teaches us clearly, that at the return of our Lord Jesus Christ (verse 1), the idolatrous heathendom would expire (verse 2) and the Christian or new-testament people of God, **redeemed and sanctified as a third part** remnant (verses 8, 9). Three is the absolute number of God and the third person in the holy godly Being is the Holy Spirit. The third part is thus here also, just as in the first trumpet, that *sanctified part* of the Christian people susceptible to the influence of the *Holy Spirit* and *purified* by Him,[8] such as it existed in the first period of the Church. Lacking the indwelling of the Holy Spirit therefore as described in Scripture (1 Cor 3:16), brought back the former *third* or *sanctified* part of the Congregation, from her heavenly disposition to an earthly one, or blood. In her earthly rest and glory she also completely lost her longing for the return of the Lord. Consequently, the prophecy says:

That, **from the creatures in the sea of nations, who have life,** which is the life in God through Jesus Christ, **the third part** of those sanctified by the Holy Spirit, **died** in this period, and the **third part of the ships were destroyed**. The **ships** as transport across the sea, are the image of the **expansion of the Gospel in the heathen sea**. For Christ says: (Matt 13:47), "The kingdom of heaven is like unto a net, that was cast into the sea (of nations) and gathered of every kind." Likewise, the Lord says to His apostles: "I will make you fishers of men" (Matt 4:19, Mark 1:17).

When then the Gospel messengers and missionaries are the fishermen, the fishing vessels represent the missionary work. In this sense, we will clearly meet the ships again later in the 7th period of Revelation.

The trumpet is the condition and effect of the Gospel preaching. When then the preaching of the word, or the teaching in the second period of the

---

[8] Burnt. (1st Trumpet) Purified through the fire of the Holy Spirit. Zach 13:9.

Church, had lost its sanctified character, which according to this prophecy characterised it in the first period, and when it reverted to what this same Revelation called blood or worldly-mindedness, then it must inevitably result in that the Christian teaching with the preaching of the Gospel to the heathens would also be of the same kind, since it flowed from the same source than the Gospel preaching to the Congregation, and just like it, had lost its holy and God-pleasing character. In the destruction of the third part of the ships lies once more a proof, that by this third, a numerical value is not to be considered. In that case, then the prophecy would be proven wrong by history, since exactly in this second period of the Church the frontiers of Christendom expanded considerably. Where therefore this *third* part is not meant literally, the symbolic meaning *"holy and sanctified"* must take preference, and in this meaning, we will still often encounter it further on in Revelation.

Wherein now therefore existed the change in the Congregation, in the spirituality and in the Gospel teaching, which distinguished this second period from the first?

We have named this *period* in our chronology, that of the *Church Fathers*, we could just as well have named it that of the *Heretical Fathers*. With this period Christendom gradually began to lose its simple faith, which made it subservient to God's word and wanted to understand and declare, whereas God only expected believing acceptance. The heathen philosophy with its subtleties is drawn in to help, to explain, cripple and distort the mysteries of Christendom and its Bible teachings, through reason and to spread its sinful worldly light on it. The simple testimony of the Christians from the first period: "We believe to obtain salvation by the grace of our Lord Jesus Christ", became a controversy concerning all sorts of possible or impossible qualities of God, of Christ, etc., over all sorts of useless and impractical fine distinctions. In one word, in this period the Church was the fertile mother of countless false doctrines and countless heresies, some of which deeply affected the nature of the Church. Most statements and imaginations, which in later times of the Reformation and even still in our days, are sometimes presented as new, sparkling new insights are mostly nothing but warmed-up, garnished with a different scientific sauce, old heresies from this second period. We consider it totally useless, and it would be far outside the scope of this work to give the reader a list of all the heresies. Whoever is interested, can, to his heart's content, research it in the detailed Church history books, or find them in concrete form with our writer Mr. van Loon, in his overview of the second period, pages 53-58. See also article 9 of the reformed articles of faith.

With so many attacks, which the teaching of the Church experienced, it could not be avoided that faithful teachers had to stand up in her defence and apply all their acumen, scientific depths and biblical knowledge to fight against these heresies. The greatest and most famous amongst these defenders of the Christian teaching are known as Church Fathers, and, although one still stands amazed at their faith, zeal and knowledge, one also finds that even with them, already clear signs of deviation from the original Christian teaching, and that by many of them the seed of later degeneration into the Roman Catholic Church was already planted. We find a short overview of the Church Fathers with van Loon, pages 59–67.

Where now two such sharply defined parties stood against each other, the Christian love, the mutual uplifting and *the shepherd ministry* of Christ must necessarily go lost and had to make room for mutual bitterness and strife, which did not always end with words. Actually, the second rider "was given a great battle sword."

SECOND VIAL

or

THE JUDGEMENT OF GOD

Thou art an offence unto me, for thou savourest
not the things that be of God, but
those that be of men
Matt 16:23.

Rev 16:3.

After the previous explanations, this second vial needs little elaboration. The images are already known to us, as well as the condition of the Congregation and the spiritual powers. When both did not repent from their apostasy to the source of living waters, God gave them wholly over to the lusts of their hearts, **and the second angel poured out his vial**, full of the judgement of God over the Christian Sea of nations, **and it became as the blood of a dead man**. The angel with the vial is again the same power in Church and state, who sounded the trumpet. The 2nd trumpet, which did not comply with God's intentions, became a judgment vial for those, over whom it sounded. The sea was already blood, the horse and the Congregation were red from blood, yet it was only the still warm, natural blood of the carnal life, which strove against the Spirit.

Now this blood became **as from a dead man**, that is; *decaying* or totally subjected to sin **flesh and blood of a spiritually dead**. Indeed Christianity deteriorated more and more in faith and the correct understanding of Christian truth because of the aforementioned heresies of the spiritual leaders during this whole period, to become totally ready at the end of this time to accept Popedom, with all its human findings and superstitions. At the end of this period, when the vial was completely revealed, at the transition into the next period, as the Revelation teaches us, **every living soul died in the sea.** "For if ye live after the flesh, ye shall die," says Paul (Rom 8:13) not only the natural but also the spiritual death.

Just as little explanation of the words of this vial is required, just as little will we probably enlist immediate permission from the more developed reader, that approximately 600 years after Christ, all living souls had died in the sea of nations. One would want to claim, that under much corruption much upright faith was still to be found at the time, like with Gregorius I and others. Indeed, this is true, and in view of how we now stand with the explanation of the Revelation, it would be difficult for us to factually and clearly disagree with this claim. When, in the seventh period, at the end of the history of the Church of Christ on earth, we will have to give a short overview of her deterioration since the establishment of the Church, it will be easier for us to show, and to get the reader to agree, that the prophesy spoke total truth, when it said of the second period: *Every living soul died in the sea.* But with this the reader will temporarily be able to agree, that the Christian people, in which flowed blood as of a dead man could not in its entirety have life in them which is of God.

Here one must observe the difference between the first and second vial. The first is poured out by the angel or the spiritual leadership of the first period upon the *heathen Romans* because the sound of the first trumpet corresponded with the Lord's intention. The angel with the trumpet becomes to them the angel with the vial. They rebelled against God and killed his witnesses, but forfeited thereby the eternal salvation, which the Lord allowed to be presented to them through the gospel preaching. For their victims, death was no judgment of God's wrath, but an advance entry into God's paradise. The Christians longed to lay off their earthly tabernacle and to be with the Lord (2 Cor 5:1–8).

The second vial actually becomes, now that the sound of the second trumpet did not correspond to the Lord's intention, poured out over the Christian people. Her own spiritual leaders and kings or the angel with the second trumpet also becomes the angel with the second vial. The heathen impurity, brought into the Christian Church by the second trumpet angel, changes her first into blood, thereafter into blood as of a dead man.

SHORT OVERVIEW OF THE CHURCH HISTORY OF

THE SECOND PERIOD

FROM 324 TO 622 AD.

TRANSLATION OF SECOND CANDLESTICK

Rev 2:8–11

8. *Write to the bishops of the Congregation and to all who still believe, but yet not my well-pleasing Congregation of the second period of the Church. This says He, who came in humbleness to suffer and to die for you, but who is also risen and ascended to heaven, from where He shall return, to reign in eternity.*

9. *I know your powerful faith and your works and persecutions, your outward poverty and inward riches, but also the blasphemy of those, who say, that they worship God, and deny the Son, and are therefore a school of Satan, for no one comes to the father but by me.*

10. *Fear none of the temptations and persecutions, which you shall suffer. Behold the devil will tempt you with his false teaching, to ensnare your souls. You shall also be persecuted for the sake of the Kingdom of God, but be faithful unto death, and I will give you the crown of life eternal.*

11. *Who has ears, hear what the Holy Spirit predicts to the Congregation of the second three centuries. Who overcomes in this battle, will be saved from eternal perdition.*

FULFILMENT IN THE HISTORY OF THE CHURCH

With Van Loon, page 50, we read about this as follows:

"The borders of the Church expand, Christendom penetrates or obtains a solid foothold in Armenia, Liberia, Ethiopia, under the Saxsons in England, in Ireland and Scotland, under the Goths and the related tribes, who invaded western Europe. Heathendom disappeared from the Roman Empire, and also the nations, who assimilated with the former inhabitants (Goths) abandoned their idols and, at least outwardly, accepted Christendom. In the Roman Empire, the Church enjoys outwardly rest, in Persia she is repeatedly persecuted. The peace in the West is similarly disturbed in a violent manner through schisms and heresies, and the rulers, favouring one or the other party of the Church, persecute their subjects in the name of their particular Christian faith." And page 53; "This period is rich in heresies and especially in those, who deeply involve themselves in the nature of the Church, so that Her rejection or acceptance or even just tolerance is of the greatest meaning for the life of the Church in the following periods, and thus exert an important influence upon the worldly history."

"The most important is Aryanism. Arius, a presbyter in Alexandria, teaches that the Son of God is not eternal, also not created before the world. He gathers disciples. – Because Emperor Constantine joined this party, it obtained in approximately 356 AD an apparent total victory over the Orthodox." - page 54; "The Goths who originally accepted Aryanism, repeatedly persecute the Orthodox Church."

Guers, page 20, says about this period: "In the greatest measure the door to all disorderliness is opened. The disciples of Jesus Christ, not called, to follow Him under sorrow and pain anymore, give free reins to their evil tendencies. High-mindedness and honour, hate and discord simultaneously storm the Church, while superstition and vice go hand in hand."

TRANSLATION OF THE SECOND SEAL

Rev 6:3, 4.

3. *And when Christ opened the second period of the Church's history, I heard someone say: "Behold, how the shepherd ministry will come to an end in this period.*
4. *And the Congregation became carnal and worldly again, and the spiritual leaders and Christian kings do no longer preserve the*

peace in Christ; but heresies, schisms and bloody controversies divided the Church of Christ.

FULFILMENT IN THE HISTORY OF THE CHURCH

Van Loon says thereof, page 50:

"*Persecutions of the heretics by the secular powers, instigated by the Church, are launched. The Church favoured by the authorities, obtains more power, riches and recognition. The high spiritual leaders become gradually more demanding and new titles of honour and privileges are accorded to the most important bishops.*" – page 51; "*Strife between Rome and Constantinople for supremacy, is finally settled in favour of Rome. The growing influence of this bishop is favoured through various circumstances.*" – "*In this period, the famous Church Fathers flourished and victoriously exerted their faith and their knowledge in the battle against heresies, although already even with them clear traces of apostasy could be detected, in their teaching, discipline and practices, which gradually prepared the darkening of the middle ages.*"

TRANSLATION OF THE SECOND TRUMPET

Rev 8:9, 9.

8. *During the preaching of the gospel in the second period, the heathen Roman people were forced to accept the Christian religion but brought with them their carnal-mindedness in their Church, whereby the purity of the Christian people was lost.*
9. *Through this the Holy Spirit abandoned the Christian Church, the Christians again became spiritually dead, and also, the propagation of the gospel to the heathen thereby lost its holy character.*

FULFILMENT IN THE HISTORY OF THE CHURCH

About the gospel preaching or the teaching in this period, we find with Van Loon, page 52;

"*Fasting, prayer, vigils, reciting of psalms, etc... receive exceptional holiness, and, while the outward ceremonies in the Church steadily became more numerous and impressive, she lost more and more of the spiritual life.- The prayer houses became richer, more beautiful, and decorated with more statues, relics were visited and honoured, saints were not yet worshipped, but received a very ambiguous homage, feasts increased, also in honour of Mary, who gradually began to take a special place at the head of the saints and later next to Christ. Also in the teaching imaginations of purgatory, salving with oil, as spiritual medicine, private confessions, and especially the great difference between spiritual and secular laity gradually crept in, to bear ripe fruits in the following centuries."*

"The divine service lost more and more of its original simplicity; The sermons are very long in the East, flowery, theatrical and are applauded with hand clapping and the waving of cloths, in the West poorer and shorter. Each Church building has an altar, in the East only one, and in the West sometimes more. Numerous and expensive church paraphilia and tools, like the cup (for the communion), incense banners (for processions), etc... with paintings, bas-relief, gradually also statues, crucifixes etc.... are used in the services."

From Gruers, page 21; we still add the following:

"One seeks worldly glory and honour. Eloquent discussions replace the simple and artless teachings of the first century. Since one surpasses the idolaters in numbers, power and riches, one wants to outshine them also through pomp and ceremony in the divine service, and to bewitch their senses by listening to solemnities, and to spur them on to amazement, one allowed in the Church a multitude of practices which stem from heathen origin."

And page 23: *"The monk Pelagius, actually named Morgan, formed a new system, which was nothing else than Deism, hidden by the outward appearance of Christendom."*

"Man, said Pelagius, can be saved by the law just as well as by the gospel". There exists no original sin or inner decay. We can completely fulfil all the commandments of the law without God's help. What is called grace, is simply the natural freedom, wherewith we are all born, and the teaching from heaven, which shows us our responsibility, and by the example of Jesus, and through powerful admonitions, makes its fulfilment easy,"

"There is nothing new under the sun; so many heresies, which are presented to us in our time, as a result of research of highly enlightened science, is in essence nothing but, a straying from former time, and an old embellished heresy."

Page 22: *"Jesus, his love, His beloved blood, are not the only expectation of a corrupted multitude any more, henceforth one shall seek his salvation in fasting, in giving of alms, in strict observation of a self-righteous service, in manifold religious practices and in giving presents to Churches and Cloisters. Each day will bring a new superstition, unfaithfulness and heresies to the fore, each day will create a new church truth in order to promote a perfectly carnal-minded church government, which presently is Satan's strength among the Christians. This is in short, the history of the Church of the Lord during the second period of her struggle. Although apparently richer than during the first period, she is in fact poorer."*

TRANSLATION OF THE SECOND VIAL

<u>Rev 16:3.</u>

3. *The Powers in the Church and in the State in this period poured out God's judgement upon the Christian people, and it totally reverted to the natural life without God. All life from God died in her.*

FULFILMENT IN THE HISTORY OF THE CHURCH

The Church of Jesus Christ did not repent from her heresies, but continued on the way of perdition; therefore, God gave her over to the lusts and errors of the heart. The second vial of the Almighty is poured out upon her. Life that is of God, died in her. Carnal life thereby, not held in check anymore, took over completely: the sea of nations becomes as blood of a dead man. The general decay is not hindered by anything anymore; the souls lost for the kingdom of God, fall prey to the second death. The Church of Jesus Christ has been almost destroyed for several centuries.

Guers says of this time, page 35:

"Six centuries have already elapsed, three under heathen Roman Emperors, and three under rulers or Emperors who confessed Christendom. The first two periods of the struggling Church are past. Presently comes the third, wherein Mohamed and the man of sin reign. Heathen Rome was the forerunner of Christian Rome, Christian Rome was for its part the forerunner and vanguard of Papal Rome."

END OF THE SECOND PERIOD

THIRD PERIOD

PERGAMOS

Building the tower

FROM 622 TO 914 AD.

THIRD PERIOD

PERGAMOS: *Building The Tower*

FROM

The Beginning of Popedom and Mohammedism and Islam, 622 AD,

TO

The Dark Ages under Popedom and Islam, 914 AD.

This period covers the seventh, eighth and ninth Centuries. It started in the seventh century (622) with the rise of Popedom in the Western (Roman) and of Mohammedanism in the Eastern (Greek) countries, both not only tried to replace the Gospel with their carnal heresies, but both also wanted to unite the worldly with the spiritual powers in their own hand. It ends with the tenth century (914) when both had reached their goal.

In this period, **the third head of the beast**, (4th beast of Daniel: the Roman Empire), appeared.

This third head or Kingdom is **the third or the Christian Papal Mountain.** (Rev 17:9, 10).

THIRD PERIOD
PERGAMOSEAN TIME
or
THE BEGINNING OF PAPAL POWER

3rd **Candlestick.**	3rd **Seal.**	3rd **Trumpet.**	3rd **Vial,**
Chapter 2,	**Chapter 6,**	**Chapter 8,**	**Chapter 16,**
And to the angel of the church in Pergamos write; These things saith he which hath the sharp sword with two edges; 13. I know thy works, and where thou dwellest, even where Satan's seat is: and thou holdest fast my name, and hast not denied my faith, even in those days wherein Antipas was my faithful martyr, who was slain among you, where Satan dwelleth. 14. But I have a few things against thee because thou hast there them that hold the doctrine of Balaam, who taught Balac to cast a stumblingblock before the children of Israel, to eat things sacrificed unto idols, and to commit fornication. 15. So hast thou also them that hold the doctrine of the Nicolaitans, which things I hate. 16. Repent; or else I will come unto thee quickly, and will fight against them with the sword of my mouth. 17. He that hath an ear, let him hear what the Spirit saith unto the churches; To him that overcometh will I give to eat of the hidden manna, and will give him a white stone, and in the stone a new name written, which no man knoweth saving he that receiveth it.	And when he had opened the third seal, I heard the third living creature say, Come and see. And I beheld, and lo a black horse; and he that sat on him had a pair of balances in his hand. 6. And I heard a voice in the midst of the four beasts say, A measure of wheat for a penny, and three measures of barley for a penny; and see thou hurt not the oil and the wine.	And the third angel sounded, and there fell a great star from heaven, burning as it were a lamp, and it fell upon the third part of the rivers, and upon the fountains of waters; 11. And the name of the star is called Wormwood: and the third part of the waters became wormwood; and many men died of the waters, because they were made bitter.	And the third angel poured out his vial upon the rivers and fountains of waters, and they became blood. 5. And I heard the angel of the waters say, Thou art righteous, O Lord, which art, and wast, and shalt be, because thou hast judged thus. 6. For they have shed the blood of saints and prophets, and thou hast given them blood to drink; for they are worthy. 7. And I heard another out of the altar say, Even so, Lord God Almighty, true and righteous are thy judgements.

THIRD CANDLESTICK

or

THE LIGHT OR THE SPIRITUAL LIFE IN THE CONGREGATION.

> Woe unto the world because of offences! For it must
> needs be that offences come; but woe to that
> man by whom the offence cometh!
> Matt 18:7

PERGAMOS, Rev 2:12–17

Pergamos was the capital of the province Mysia, in Asia Minor and was renowned in those days for its great library and the invention of Parchment. It still boasts a small Christian Congregation in our time. The word **Pergamos** means a **high tower**; a prediction and image of their rising Popedom, *the tower* of the new *Babylon*. (Gen. 11:4). The borough of Troy was also named Pergamon.

The letter itself needs a little enlightenment and explanation. The **two-edged sword** (verse 12) which the Son of God has, (Rev 1:16): "and out of his mouth went a sharp two-edged sword"; is, according to (Heb. 4:12 and Eph. 6:17) the **Word of God**. The Lord introduces himself to the congregation of that time as: *"He which hath the sharp two-edged sword"* because the congregation of that period did not possess the sword anymore. And yet this sword of God's Word was so necessary to them, who lived, **where** (verse 13) **Satan's seat is**, to fight against his seduction. **Satan** means, as we have already seen in the second candlestick, **opponent of God**. We here not only have to think of Mohamed and his teaching but also of Popedom, notwithstanding that it had not yet come to its horrible later decadence. Even Peter already (Matt. 16:23), was called **Satan** by the Lord when he rebuked Him: "Be it far from Thee, Lord: this (suffering) shall not be unto Thee," and Popedom, which claims to sit on the Bishop throne of Peter, can also make claims to the title of *Satan*, for it is as if the Lord already *prophetically* judged it with the same word to Peter: "Get thee behind me, Satan: thou art an offence unto me: for thou savourest not the things that be of God, but those that be of men."

Also, in the warning, that the Lord gave Peter (Matt. 26:52 and John 18:11) concerning the use of the sword, a similar condemnation lay over Popedom, which exchanged the worldly sword for the sword of God's

Word, forgetting that Jesus had said "My Kingdom is not of this world." (John 18:36).

The congregation of Pergamos had not forgotten this and they **held fast to the name of Jesus Christ and had not denied their faith**, (verse 13), not even under the severe persecutions of the Christians, wherein **Antipas[9]**, the **faithful martyr** at Pergamos, died the martyr's death. That only *Antipas* is mentioned here by the Son of God, leads us to suspect that his **martyr's death** must have been extraordinary. According to the tradition during the Christian persecution, Antipas was placed in a copper ox (the well-known cow of Perillos) by Emperor Domitian in the year 98 and slowly roasted to death. Would Christian faith in our days be able to withstand such a test? And yet the prophecy warns them, who believe in Christ, with violent persecution: persecution so general and violent, that Jesus says of it (Matt. 24:21): *"For then shall be great tribulation, such as was not since the beginning of the world to this time, no, nor ever shall be."* And the time is at hand. Only God knows how near, in how few years, possibly even in this century.

Up to now, the letter to the Congregation of Pergamos is in an approving tone. Verse 14, however, contains the condemnation of Christ of the congregation. **"But I have a few things against thee because thou hast there them that hold the doctrine of Balaam,"** thus not that they did make themselves guilty of this, but that they suffered them in their midst, who degenerated into idolatry and estrangement from the true God. (harlot: Jer. 3:1) and *held the doctrine of Balaam*. **Bileam** (the Apostles Peter and Jude also named him, as well as here the Son of God, Balaam) means **"traitor"** and here is the true image (see Num. 31:16 and Num. 25) **of Popedom**, which is a false advisor and Prophet violate the truth of God and through human reasoning and fables seduced the Lord's Congregation to idolatry and drove them to ruin.

In this prophetic meaning of the letter for the third period, we see this realized in the collusion of the Christians in the Eastern Church with Islam and in the originating of the statue cult in the Western and Eastern Church. In the last named, it was already approved by the second council of Nice in the year 787; in the first named, after much strife, it was instituted only in the year 842 by Empress Theodora.

There were also in this period those who, according to verse 15, **held the doctrine of the Nicolaitans**, already discussed in the first candlestick (Rev. 2:6) and to which we further refer. That with Popedom worldliness

---

[9] Antipas means against all.

120

and all carnal lusts entered the Church, and that these repelled the Christian life of faith is well known from church history. There is however already a great difference between this period and the first or Ephesian one. There the Lord praised the congregation: *But this thou hast, that thou hatest the deeds of the Nicolaitans, which I also hate.* Here in the third period, the Congregation receives the admonition from the Lord, that they *suffered* the evil amongst them, and that there were amongst them those who *held the doctrine of the Nicolaitans*, which is: **adoration of** other **heavenly beings** next to the only God.

From this, the Son of God demands repentance (verse 16) or warns to fight against them with **the sword of His Mouth**. This is the sharp sword of which already in Isaiah the promised Messiah speaks against the unbelievers: "And He (the Lord) hath made my mouth like a sharp sword" (Isa. 49:2).

Whomsoever **overcometh** the temptations of the throne of Satan, (verse 17) the Lord promises to **give to eat of the hidden manna**, and that is the "bread from heaven" (John 6:31, 49, 58) not as your fathers did eat manna, and are dead: he that eateth of this bread shall live forever, and that bread is the flesh of the Lord Jesus, which He would give for the life of the world. To the overcomers Christ would also give **a white stone,** and in the stone **a new name** written on it for the overcomer. At national games and wrestling matches of the past, the winners each received, from the judges, a white square marble plaque, (tessara), upon which their name was engraved, as well as the prize they had obtained; this stone gave the overcomer, on presentation, admission to the public festive banquet. Likewise, Christ also gives to the overcomers in the battle of faith a new name, (Rom. 8:17, 1 John 3:2) which no man knoweth saving he that receiveth it and therewith obtains admission to the communion of the marriage supper of the Lamb (Rev. 19:9).

This, as well as the rest of the closing promises of the seven Candlesticks, will be fulfilled in the Kingdom of Glory. At the fulfillment thereof we will look at these closing promises in greater detail.

Earlier on, (page 26), we said that with each new period, that is, with each following candlestick and seal etc., something new appears in the Congregation and the Church, which did not exist in the former period, but which would remain in the Church and Congregation up to the future of the Lord.

Were there not always believers, living where the throne of Satan is, surrounded by persecutions of superstition and unbelief, who nevertheless did not deny their faith, holding fast to the name of Christ and with Him remained overcomers? Here to belong the many witnesses of Jesus Christ in the Roman Catholic Church, the Protestant believers in the Roman countries, but also the upright believing Protestant teachers under the oppression of their modern anti-Christian contemporaries, Protestant fellow teachers, church ordinances, church meetings etc., the faithful witnesses who for peace sake did not want to renounce His Name, even though they stood as one against all (Antipas).[10]

But also the Nicolaitans, who misused the teaching of righteousness out of faith as a license for their sinful lusts, they were always in the Congregation and will remain in her, as much as the cunning Balaams, who wove their nets, to ensnare the poor souls and to seduce them to idolatry.

Against all these temptations of Satan, there is only one way to overcome and to partake in the promise of Christ, and this promise counts for all overcomers in the battle of faith, from Pergamos up to our time, and that way to overcome is: Not to renounce the faith and to hold fast to the name of Jesus Christ. Therefore: fight the good fight, that you may keep the faith, and obtain the crown of righteousness, which the Lord will give to all, who loved his appearance.

---

[10] One similar to Antipas was Luther on the Diet at Worms. "Here I stand, it cannot do otherwise, God help me."

THIRD SEAL

THE SPIRITUAL LIFE OF THE POWERS IN THE CHURCH AND STATE

> The days will come, when the bridegroom
> shall be taken from them, and then
> shall they fast.
> Matt. 9:15.

Rev 6:5-6.

The Third Seal is interpreted by some interpreters of Revelation as a prediction of *scarcity and difficult* times, by others *of abundance*, at least for the affluent and finally for the *upholding of Civil Rights* under Popedom and Islam by the believers (Gärtner) etc, etc. We shall see what God's Word will teach us about it.

The **third living creature** (Cherub), who, at the breaking of the third Seal of the historical scroll of the Church says: **"Come and see,"** what is depicted therein for this period and predicts, was the living creature with the **face as a man** (Rev. 4:7) or **the Evangelist Ministry**, which here is invited to see how the condition of the Spiritual life of the Gospel messengers or Priests and of the Christian state powers of that period will be. The preaching of the Gospel, correspondingly more or less pure and powerful, mirrors itself faithfully in the condition of the Congregation or the horse and leads it wherever it wills. The **horse** or **the Congregation** of that period was **black**, the colour of darkness, as it is referred to in (Prov. 7:9): "In the *black* and dark night," and (Prov. 20:20): "in obscure *darkness*"; also (Micah 3:6) "and the day shall be *dark* over them." (Ezek 32:7) "And make the stars thereof *dark*," and (verse 8) "all the bright lights of Heaven will I make *dark*", etc. The Congregation was thus covered in darkness, concerning her knowledge of salvation; she was deprived of the bright light of the Gospel and from the righteousness, which was valid only before God. We have seen, that the second vial, poured out over the Christian sea of nations (the red horse) caused the natural life, which then already had the upper hand in her, to completely kill the spiritual life, and estranged from the life which is of God. In this state, which was fully revealed at the end of the second period, we now

123

find again in the third period the congregation as the *black horse in spiritual darkness*.

He that sat on him, the rider of spiritual and worldly power, **had a pair of balances in his hand**. The hand, which should abundantly distribute the Bread of Life, as at the feeding in the desert, weighed it on the contrary scrupulously against the Spiritual scarcity. Thus, we find the meaning of *the scale* in (Ezek. 4:16), "Behold, I will break the staff of bread in Jerusalem: and they shall eat bread by weight," completely in contrast to what the Lord said (Isaiah 55:1),"And he that hath no money; come ye, buy, and eat; yea, come, buy wine and milk without money". - "He is a merchant, *the balances of deceit* are in his hand: he loveth to oppress." says (Hosea 12:7) and (Amos 8) with the description of the spiritual famine according to the Lord's Word (see verses 11 and 12), the Lord says (verses 4, 5): "Hear this, o ye that swallow up the needy, even to make the poor of the land to fall, saying, when will the new moon be gone, that we may sell corn? and *falsifying the balances by deceit*?"

"The merchants of the earth," says the prophecy in the 7th vial (the Spiritual leaders) shall weep and mourn over her (the modern Babylon); for no man buyeth their merchandise anymore." (Rev. 18:11)

The **balance** in the hand of the Spiritual leaders is, therefore, the image, both of her **deceitful trade**, by giving out the bread of life which was not the Word, the Living Word of God, (Isaiah 55:2, 3) as well as **the scarcity of Spiritual food** in these days.

This is totally confirmed by the following verse, verse 6. **And I heard a voice in the midst of the four living creatures.** This voice is like, as we shall see in Rev. 4:6 and Rev. 5:6, the *voice of the Lord himself*, which here speaks to John in *His Evangelist Ministry* and mentions to him the price of the Bread of Life for this period. The Lord says to him: **"A measure of wheat for a penny and three measures of barley for a penny."**

What the **wheat** means in the spiritual sense, God's Word teaches us very clearly. As the *wheat* **Jesus** shows himself firstly to (John 12: 23, 24)."The hour is come, that the *Son of man* should be glorified. Verily, verily, I say unto you, except a *corn of wheat* fall into the ground and die, it abideth alone: but if it die, it bringeth forth much fruit."

But secondly, **Jesus in the believers**, e.g. in the Parable in (Matt 13:24, etc.) where the enemy sowed *tares* among the wheat, and verse 30 the owner of the field says: "Let both (the wheat and the tares) grow together until the harvest: and in the time of harvest I will say to the reapers, gather ye together first the tares, and bind them in bundles to burn them: but gather the *wheat* into my barn."

That Jesus here with the *wheat* means the *believers*, this chapter teaches us further, verses 37-39, where the Lord explains the spoken parable to His disciples, the Sower is the Son of Men, the field the world, and the *wheat* (compare verse 25 with 38) are the children of the Kingdom or according to verse 24, the children of the Kingdom of Heaven, which are the *true believers, or the righteous*. (verse 43).

Barley is **the Sword of the Lord or His Word, spoken through His servants.** The proof we find in (Judge 7:13) is that you would not have guessed that the dream of a Midian man during the time of the Judges, still has to serve as God's council to teach you, believer of the 21st century, the meaning of barley and barley bread in the language of the Holy Spirit, and you will have to subject yourself to the interpretation of the dream by the man of Israel (verse 14), seen that God's Word approves and mentions it, and proved it with the victory of Gideon. That *barley bread* was, according to verse 20, the *Sword of the Lord or the Word of the Lord, spoken through his servants.* So were also the seven breads, *barley breads* (Matt. 15:36), wherewith the Lord fed the multitude (Mark 8:6), a foreshadowing and indication of the Gospel preaching by the 7 angels or Bishops of the 7 periods of the Church. If these 7 Congregations reflected to us the whole of Christendom throughout all the centuries, then also the 7 angels are all the servants of the Lord, and typically indicated by the 7 barley breads, wherewith the Lord fed the hungry multitude.

Barley is therefore the Word of the Lord or His Word spoken through His servants, being: **the preaching of the Gospel**. In a narrower sense, we would then have to understand the wheat to be *the four Gospels*, as containing the life, suffering and death, besides the words and works of the Saviour, and the b*arley* to be all *the rest of the writings of the New Testament*, except the Revelation and therefore the Word of the Lord, spoken by His servants as recorded in *Acts and Epistles of the Apostles.*

A *measure of wheat* was the amount, which in the moderate Eastern regions, was required to sustain one man per day and equals in nutritional value *three small measures of barley*. Both formed the usual ration of the more affluent in the region. One of both these quantities, or such a ration per day would cost 1 penny, actually a denarius, which is 30 cents in Holland, amounting to the salary of a labourer, at those times for a day of labour. See (Matt. 20:1–14), the remuneration of the labourer (verse 2) one penny (the same word denarius) of that time. But if a labourer could only earn enough daily to sustain himself, whereof must his wife and children be maintained, or housing, clothing and other life necessities?

We perceive a total picture of the scarcity of spiritual nutrition is accomplished thereby.

The Word of the Lord was scarce and expensive in those days (1 Samuel 3:1). Therefore, the Lord also says through his Evangelist Ministry **"and see thou hurt not the oil and the wine."**

Wine and oil consisted together with wheat and barley in the East, in older times as also nowadays, the most important victuals required by man.

What Spiritual victuals does man actually need for his salvation?

1st. Christ crucified, or the **wheat** (John 12:24);

2nd. God's Word and Gospel preaching to maintain his spiritual life or the **barley bread**;

3rd. The Holy Spirit. You find Him in the same verse, which we discuss, in the **Oil** and the **Wine**.

Was not the oil, which was used *to salve* the Priests and all that was *consecrated to the Lord*, (Exod. 30:25-32) under the Old Covenant the image of the Holy Spirit, verse 29, "whatsoever toucheth them shall be holy", verse 32 "It is *holy,* and it shall be *holy* unto you." In many places in the Old Testament, we encounter it, but also in the New Testament; or is not the oil of the wise virgins wherewith they kept their lamps burning, (Matt 25:4), the *sanctification* by and the testimony of *the Holy Spirit*? Also, Christ (Heb. 1:9) is salved by the Father with *Oil of the Holy Spirit*. (John 1:32, John 3:34, Col. 1:19).

If the *Oil* is the image of *sanctification by*, the **wine** is the image of **joy** in **the Holy Spirit**, the joy of the faith.

Christ names Himself (John 15:1) the true vine. The wine, which comes forth out of this vine, the Holy Spirit, gladdens the heart of the Christians. In the Holy Scriptures, we already find it in the prophecy of Jacob, (Gen. 49:11, 12) and indicated through Christ Himself in His parable of the Good Samaritan, (Luke 10:34).

Do you know the not-so-wholly coincidental deeper meaning of the images in this parable, of the general love for the neighbour? If not, read it again and think, that Christ presents Himself as the Good Samaritan in His Salvation work; the wounds of the injured man being his guilt and sin, his spiritual wounds, which were bound with the *Oil, the Sanctification,* and the *Wine, the joy of the Holy Spirit* for the redemption and the forgiveness extended unto him. The transportation on the beast of burden is the care of the Shepherd Ministry (see 2nd Seal), the inn is the Church, the inn-keeper is the teacher, the two pennies (denarius) are both the Sacraments: Baptism and Communion, the return of the Samaritan is the expected imminent return of our Lord Jesus Christ, which we will find in the 7th period of the Church.

As you see, the parable unwinds consequently; it is the way in which Christ meets the sinner on the way of repentance. The meaning of the images *Oil* and *Wine*, as the *Sanctification of, and joy in the Holy Spirit,* shall henceforth create no room for doubt anymore. Of these, so little would be present in the third period, that the warning of the Evangelist Ministry follows, "hurt them not, do not abuse them; there is only just enough left to go with the costly wheat and barley".

We have also found for all the images appearing in this third seal, clear explanations in God's Holy Word, which differ drastically from that which human intelligence earlier or later wanted to make of it. These meanings of the images were not chosen at random, but the only ones given in the Holy Scriptures. Taking up in short the full meaning of this third seal according to the given explanation, we then find, that in that period, the Gospel or the bread of life would be preached scarcely, seldom and impurely by the priesthood, but in its place, human reasoning, not suitable for nourishing the Spiritual life of the Congregation; who in turn would live in poverty regarding the Gospel of Salvation. The faith in Christ and the number of believers would diminish, for therewith the testimony of the Holy Spirit.

All this we clearly see confirmed in the church history of that period. The original Christianity, since the beginning of the previous period (since Constantine) thus during three centuries, amazingly weakened in purity and strength, through external prosperity, inner division and religious disputes, deteriorating in the West under Popedom, who tried to support it for spiritual mastery, trying to obtain it by connecting worldly power to the chair of Peter and to propagate the Gospel among the Heathen by the power of the sword.

In this period, many heresies came into existence in the Roman Church, such as idolatry, the Maria Cult and the Transubstantiation. In this period, the ground was also prepared for the division between Western and Eastern Churches. The last, the Eastern Church, earlier already deteriorating from the simplicity and purity of the Gospel into all sorts of sophisms (fantasies) and heresies, fell as a defenceless victim in the claws of Islam, which just as the Pope, binding Priesthood and worldly power into one person, ensconced its teaching on the blind Eastern Christianity, destroying numerous Christian Congregations and cities, and penetrated up to the gates of Constantinople. This was the state of affairs of the Priesthood and the powers of this period.

THIRD TRUMPET

or

THE CONDITION AND EFFECT OF THE GOSPEL PREACHING

> But Jesus called them unto him, and said, Ye know that the princes of the Gentiles exercise dominion over them, and they that are great exercise authority upon them. But it shall not be so among you: but whosoever will be great among you, let him be your minister.
>
> Matt. 20:25, 26.

Rev 8:10, 11.

The Priesthood and Congregation had, after the outpouring of the second vial, not repented to the Living God in this third period, but continued in their set ways and heresies. Therefore, the Gospel preaching and its effect in this period, became as we shall see in this third trumpet, verse 10. **And there fell a great star from heaven, burning as it were a lamp.**

"How art thou fallen from heaven, O Lucifer, son of the morning! How art thou cut down to the ground, which didst weaken the nations!" was clearly said (Isaiah 14:12) by the king of Babel at the fall of the Babylonian empire. If the **stars**, as we have already seen, and will still see further on, are the image of the *powers in the Church*, they are also, as we see in this case, of the *powers of the state*. Thus, the Christian kings together with the spiritual leaders, form the star or the angel of the Congregation.

In the same way (Dan. 8:10), the kings and the great in Israel, who would be vanquished and humiliated by Antiochus (1 Macc. 1:21-27) are spoken of, as the *stars* who would be thrown down *to earth*. *Heaven* is here not meant to be the church Heaven of God's Kingdom but as *an elevated place* (see Isaiah 14:13-15) *and great power*.

In this period, a great state power or a great church power, formerly shining as a burning torch (Isaiah 62:1) would be brought down from an elevated state, destroyed and extinguished. The fulfilment of this prophecy in this period is easy to find. No great spiritual power was destroyed during this period, but on the contrary, such a one, (Popedom) came into being. With difficulty, one would find a more appropriate image than the destruction of the Roman Empire, which formerly, shone brilliantly with power and greatness as a great star and burning torch, completely extinguished at the beginning of this period, by Swintila, king of the Visigoths, who between 621 and 630, destroyed the once so great Roman Empire.

Thereby the second mountain of (Rev. 17:9), which began with Constantine the Great, as the Christian-Roman Empire, came to nought. Concerning this second mountain we touched on it with its rising in the second trumpet and referred to it again. Here, the third mountain rises as a spiritual world power, Popedom, which the fallen world power of the Roman Empire appropriated for itself.

The fallen star from heaven we could easily mistake as Popedom or the fallen from the heaven of the Church and Priesthood that had become a worldly power. This can however not be; for then according to the language of Revelation, this star would have fallen *from heaven* upon *the earth*. This actually only occurred at the beginning of the Fifth Trumpet (Rev 9:1). Here, on the other hand, the star or *power* fell on the spiritual canals (rivers) of the priesthood, and the star already existed and *was* named: Wormwood, or the heathen unrighteousness, and Christendom of the second period could not be meant here, which was bitter yet sweet-smelling as myre and not horribly bitter as wormwood.

This star **"fell upon the third part of the rivers [11] and upon the fountains of waters."** Pure water is, as we also further shall see, and as is already known to us from the words of Jesus during His walk on earth, the image of pure Christian teaching, of pure Christian faith. See for example (John 7:38) "He that believeth on me," says the Lord: "rivers of living waters shall flow from him," and (John 4:14): "But whosoever drinketh of the water that I shall give him shall never thirst; but the *water* that *I shall give* him shall be in him a *well of water springing up* into everlasting life."

And this is therefore *the faith* in him, the Son of God, the Saviour of the world, and the *testimony of the Holy Spirit* in the preaching of the Gospel to the sinners; because "In that day there shall be a *fountain* opened to the house of David and to the inhabitants of Jerusalem for sin and for uncleanness." (Zech. 13:1). "The mouth of a righteous man is a *well* of life," says Solomon, (Proverbs 10:11). Peter says in (2 Peter 2:15, 17) "Which have forsaken the right way, and are gone astray, following the way of Balaam the son of Bosor, who loved the wages of unrighteousness; - These are wells without water." - The streams of drinkable water are thus

---

[11] Actually, SWEET water streams or streams of DRINKABLE water (Patamos), the Gospel teaching.

the spiritual canals through which the Gospel teaching flows and originate from the springs and the fountains of water.

These last are therefore again the image of the heads of the Church, as the springs, from which the wide water streams gushed forth, flow through the many branches of spiritual canals into the Christian Sea of nations.

The meaning of **the third part** we learned to know in the first and second trumpets, is **the part susceptible to the influence of the Holy Spirit**.

The star now fell, according to verse 10, not first on the sources (springs), to therewith poison the spiritual waters. It fell upon the third part of the rivers, (sweet water streams) and upon the fountains of waters simultaneously, a correct image of the degeneration of the Christian teaching in the Roman Church, not just emanating from the Pope and higher spirituals and flowing over into the lower spiritual canals, but originating in the higher and lower spirituality simultaneously. The fig tree of the Church decayed in roots and branches at the same time. - What was the reason for this decay? The prophecy says it to us in verse 11. **And the name of the star is called Wormwood: and the third part of the waters became wormwood,** or bitter as wormwood, for as the verse ends, **the waters, "where made bitter**." "*Bitter* as *wormwood*", says Solomon. (Prov. 5:4).

What do we have to understand about **wormwood** and bitterness? Those who *turn judgement* to *wormwood,* and leave off righteousness in the earth, answers (Amos 5:7), for ye have turned judgement into gall and the fruit of *righteousness into wormwood/hemlock.* (Amos 6:12). "Because they," says the Lord (Jer. 9:13, 15) "have forsaken my law which I set before them, and have not obeyed my voice, neither walked therein; - therefore thus saith the Lord of Hosts, the God of Israel, also: "Behold, I will feed them, even this people (river), with *wormwood*, and give them water of *gall* to drink." And (Jer. 23:15): "Behold, I will feed them with *wormwood*, and make them drink the water of *gall*; for from the prophets of Jerusalem is profaneness gone forth into all the land." Because, says Peter, (Acts 8:23) to Simon the sorcerer, "For I perceive that thou art in the gall of bitterness, and in the bond of iniquity." - This comprehensive warning and prophecy of the third trumpet, is clearly explained in the words of Moses to Israel (Deut 29:18), "Lest there should be among you man, or woman, or family, or tribe, whose heart turneth away this day from the Lord our God, to go and serve the gods of these nations; lest there should be among you a root that beareth *gall* and *wormwood*." That is thus the meaning of *wormwood* and *bitterness* in the language of the Holy Spirit. *Departure from the only true God, idolatry and unrighteousness* together had poisoned the fountains

131

of waters and the resulting streams (spiritual leaders), the freshwater of life, which the Christian Congregation had to drink, had become so bitter through idolatry and unrighteousness, that **many** died a **spiritual death** as a result.

All of this caused the fall of *the great star from heaven* on the streams of water and fountains or the fall and destruction of *the Roman Empire*, by which the patriarch of Rome, who, from then on was named *Pope* obtained the spiritual mastery over the whole Western church, also appropriating *worldly power*, two things which can never be united in human hands without dire consequences. Christ is and wants to be the King and the Head of the Church, which is His Kingdom, the Kingdom of Heaven. His Kingdom is not of this world.

Yet not only Popedom with its power and false doctrine was the cause of it all; it only applied to the Western church. Simultaneously, in Asia, a false prophet arose, **Mohamed**, who also united the worldly power and the spiritual power under one hand, and became the bitter **Star Wormwood** for the already straying Eastern Church. The eternal salvation, for which we all hope and pray, was malformed into an establishment of women or harem, with all its luxurious licentious lusts, the supposed prophet Mohamed brought the unholy fire of the altar, instigating the fiery imagination and uses of the Eastern Christians, and by gratifying flesh and blood, extinguished the little Christian faith and life which still was present in the Asiatic and European congregations of the Eastern church. Many people died a spiritual death because the fresh waters of the Gospel of our Lord Jesus Christ became bitter through blending with the godless teaching of Islam. "For if ye live after the flesh," says Paul (Rom 8:13), "ye shall die: but if ye through the Spirit do mortify the deeds of the body, ye shall live."

If the trumpet is the condition of the Gospel preaching and its effect for each period, here we at least again see it clearly sketched in the prophecy of the third trumpet, according to the indications in God's Holy Word. But its sound did not correspond with what the Lord had intended. It was not the trumpet of God's Word anymore, but a trumpet of human sound and teachings. Erring Christianity did not hear the call to life being preached anymore and did also not feel the need for the Gospel of Jesus Christ, so the third Angel was ordered by the Holy and Righteous God to pour out his vial, full of the judgments of God, upon the sinful earth.

THIRD VIAL

or

THE JUDGEMENT OF GOD

> And this is the condemnation, that light is come
> into the world, and men loved darkness rather
> than light, because their deeds were evil.
> John 3:19.

Rev. 16:4-7

And the third Angel poured out his vial upon the rivers and fountains of water, and they became blood.

In the third trumpet, we have seen that *the streams and fountains are the spiritual leaders* in the straying Eastern and Western church, that *the water of life*, given by her to the Congregation to quench the thirst of the souls longing for righteousness, had become *bitter* by *idolatry* and *unrighteousness,* and therefore not drinkable anymore. Upon these putrid water sources and streams, a new judgment of God is poured out, and the waters **become blood**.

The Angel, who blew the trumpet in the third period, is the Priesthood and State power of the Roman and Greek countries, and this same Angel is also again the Vial Angel, who pours out God's judgment upon the Christian nations. They themselves caused the water of life to be polluted with blood. In the second trumpet and the second vial, it became like blood in the Christian sea of nations. In this third vial, it became as blood in the spiritual leadership, the sources of waters of life, which ought to have flowed from her pure and refreshing as from gospel messengers of Christ. (John 7:38, 39).

Blood, we have learned to know in the second period, (see 2nd seal, 2nd trumpet and 2nd vial) as the image of decaying **spiritual** and natural **carnal life**. If in this period the spiritual leadership and with her the Congregation became estranged from the life that is from God, and again further partly sank into the natural and carnal living, - the teaching of Salvation, the Word of God, the Gospel of our Lord Jesus Christ, continued to exist, although for Christendom it was generally not seen as a power of God to Salvation anymore.

133

After the outpouring of the second vial, the waters became *bitter* through the third trumpet; now it became blood, which is *carnal, human*. If our way of explaining the images of Revelation is pursued, is the only correct explanation, then we must find in this period (622 – 914), that the pure teaching of God for salvation and the worshipping of God in spirit and truth, made way to all sorts of human reasoning, for sensual representations, carnal high-mindedness and superstitions.

The candlestick, the seal and the trumpet of this period have already shown, how Popedom, Roman spirituality and Mohammedanism, made the waters bitter; the short overview, presently given at the end of this period, will show, which effect this 3rd vial had on the powers in the church, as well as on the Christian state, on the preaching of the teaching of Christ and on the spiritual condition of the Congregation. In this period to be sure, the open and unashamed strife began to subject not only the Roman Empire but all the States to the Church, to subject civil and constitutional law to the church hierarchy and to the church laws. This was already the actual striving *for the Pope's infallibility*, which was reserved until our days, to be proclaimed as dogma, as an article of faith of the Roman church. We actually write this on the day (7 July 1870) when the first news of the decision of the Council of Rome concerning the declaration of the infallibility of the Pope reached us.

Not without impunity Popedom did try to obtain power for itself and for its successors over Church and State; therewith all Christian life also disappeared from the church and made way to high-mindedness, the most horrifying licentiousness and the satisfying of all the lusts of the flesh and blood. So, we also find at the end of this period, the beginning of the Regnum scortorum (the prostitute government) in Popedom, thus we find Pergamos, the high citadel or tower of Popedom erected, and in contrast with the 1st rider, who (1st Seal) on a white horse went out to preach the peace of God and righteousness in Christ Jesus, now Pope John X (in 914 AD) standing, arrayed in full armour, and at the head of an army. That was the sad end of Gospel preaching, which began at Pentecost (33 AD).

In this third vial, we also hear in verses 5 and 6 the righteousness of the Lord being praised by **the Angel of the waters**, which is *the streams of water and water fountains*, named in verse 4, which we naturally understand to be the Cherub, representing the *Evangelist Ministry* in this third seal. (See page 121).

Verse 5. **"Thou are righteous, O Lord, which art, and wast, and shall be, because Thou hast judged thus"**.

Verse 6. **"For they have shed the blood of saints and prophets, and Thou hast given them blood to drink; for they are worthy"**.

The praise of the righteousness of God is again confirmed in (verse 7) by **the Altar**. *The Altar* is the image of *the worshipping and the glorification of God by the still living and the already departed believers,* as the 5th seal will show. Worshipping, they also call out: **Even so, Lord God Almighty, true and righteous are thy judgments.**

That these represented witnesses of the Lord in the image of the Altar, in truth did praise His Judgments, cannot be denied. In this third period the Roman Church had *not yet* killed the witnesses of Jesus, she had not sunk so low yet. How then can God's judgement be righteous?

The Heathen-Roman Empire had killed the saints and prophets, the blood witnesses of Jesus in the first period. In this Third period, the Roman Empire fell, (the star that fell from heaven). The spiritual leaders of the Christian church claimed this fallen worldly power for themselves, but therewith also accumulated the eternal clinging blood debts upon themselves. With the unlawful heritage, they also inherited the thereunto cleaving curse. Where the church fell from God to take up worldly power, there they also had to undergo its accompanying judgement.

As the Heathen-Rome had shed the *natural blood* of the witnesses of Jesus, to Papal Rome it was given to drink blood, in a **spiritual** sense. God left them to their own lusts, when they left Him, *because that,* (Rom. 1:21) *when they knew God, they glorified Him not as God, neither were thankful; but became vain in their imaginations, and their foolish heart was darkened. (22) professing themselves to be wise, they became fools, (23) and changed to the glory of the incorruptible God into an image made like to corruptible man, (24) wherefore God also gave them up to uncleanness through the lusts of their own hearts, (25) who changed the truth of God into a lie, and worshipped and served the creature more than the Creator, who is blessed forever. Amen.*

This is, therefore, the opinion of God concerning the worldly power of the Pope, which was so dearly striven for. This curse, which Popedom acquired for itself herewith, it later appallingly increased in the fifth period. It's debt thereby reached up to Heaven, but also God's judgement came over it, and will yet become even more horrible.

OVERVIEW OF THE HISTORY OF THE CHURCH IN THE THIRD PERIOD

FROM 622 TO 914 AD.

TRANSLATION OF THE THIRD CANDLESTICK

<u>Rev 2:12–17.</u>

12. Write to the bishop of the Congregation and to all the congregations of the third period, wherein the Tower of Popedom, Babylon is built; so says He who teaches according to God's Word:

13. I know what you do, and that you live amidst the seductions and temptations of the worldly-minded Popedom and the carnal teaching of Mohamed. However, you have not denied my name and the faith, not even in the days of the heftiest temptations, wherein many of my faithful witnesses died a spiritual death.

14–15. But I have this against you, that you suffer amongst you, those who through idolatry and false teachings seduce you, and that you do not reject those who give themselves over to fleshly lusts as you did in the past but allow them to live among you.

16. Acknowledge this, but if not, I will execute My judgment over them.

17. Whosoever has ears, hear what the Spirit says to the congregation: who overcomes in this battle, him shall I give to eat of the bread, which gives life in Eternity, and I shall give him the name of Child of God and access to the Communion of the Lamb in the Kingdom of my Father.

FULFILMENT IN THE HISTORY OF THE CHURCH

VAN LOON says (Pag 90–22) about this period:

"Three centuries of external prosperity and inward schisms (in the 2nd period) had passed over Christianity and had weakened it. Not only was the unity of the church nearly everywhere broken up by the many conflicting opposing sects, but also the part which named itself Orthodox,

had not yet openly denied any of the great tenets of faith, but yet buried many of them under works of faith, self-righteousness and outward religion.

The church, sunken in worldly opinion and security, deserved a judgement of admonishment; yet she never once took a step backwards on the way to repentance of the pure Gospel from human reason and Salvation through works."

GUERS says of this period, (pages 38 and 39)

"The Eastern (Greek) church had already with swift strides erred from the simplicity of the Gospel. Each day saw new heresies sprouting forth in her midst. In the 8th century (787) she introduced image worshipping, a new type of idolatry to which she gave herself up with a sort of enthusiasm."

About the Western (Roman) Church in this period GUERS says pages 102 and 103:

"What a great difference there is between the Roman Church of the 1st and that of the 7th and 8th centuries; what a contradiction; what a decay! Like the heathen, of which the Apostle Paul speaks in the Epistle, which he directed to this Church, she held the truth and unrighteousness; knowing God, she did not glorify Him as God; she was filled with all unrighteousness, wickedness, avarice, strife, corruption and malice." And page 146; "The time, which elapsed between Gregorius I and Gregorius VII was for the world of the West a time of darkness and confusion." Page 147; "The Church was shaken. Before her was a time of tribulation and humiliation; the testimonies were weak, the word of God was scarce, heresies and superstition multiplied greatly, like thistles and thorns in an abandoned field."

"In the 9th century, the canonisation of Saints and the veneration of their remains formed the budding characteristic of national religion. Priests and monks populated the invisible world, as in battle, with imaginary protectors. One celebrated their feasts, counting on their intervention and attributed imaginary powers to heal sicknesses."

TRANSLATION OF THE THIRD SEAL

Rev. 6:5, 6.

Verse 5. *And when Christ opened the third period of the historical scroll of the Church before me, I heard it said in Heaven: "Come, and see how the preaching of the Gospel of salvation shall come to nought" And I saw the congregation shrouded in spiritual darkness, and the spiritual leaders giving her all sorts of human findings and teachings of Satan instead of the true bread of life. And spiritual famine came at this time.*

Verse 6. *And Christ, faith in Him, the preaching of His Gospel, the sanctification and comforting by the Holy Spirit, all this disappeared more and more from the Church, to make place for superstitions, idolatry and priestly supremacy.*

Van Loon says on Page 95:

"The Church extended her borders in Germany and North Netherlands by means of a new way of conversion: force of weapons. The vanquished rulers were forced to be baptized with their subjects. It was actually to allow access to the missionaries, that one understood it to be necessary to use the sword. It can only be seen as a fall, and the acknowledgement, that Christendom had lost much of its spiritual character, to rule over heathendom without worldly help."

With Guers, we find on page 99:

"In the town of Constantinople Emperor Constantin Copronymus held a council in 754 for 338 bishops, where it was firmly decided, that all statues would be ejected from the Church as abominations. But on page 100, the resolutions of the Council of Constantinople did not remain in force for long. Several years later another council was convened in Nice (787 AD), which was the seventh general council, attended by more than three hundred and fifty bishops, brought together by the influence of the Roman town Clark. The conclusions arrived there, come to this: that statues had to be erected of our God and of our Savior Jesus Christ, to our blessed lady, the mother of our Lord, to the glorious angels and to all the saints." It added as usual: *"All the heretics are condemned! Cursed is the council, which rejected the venerable statues!! - The Holy Trinity has caused them to be erected."*

Page 101. *"It was not only the statue cult, which Rome tried to implant in her through her lies in the seduced West. She openly taught that one should show reverence to the angels the Virgin Mary and the relics. In this way, she gave to the god-fearing souls the most ungodly direction.*

At the same time, she gave spiritual leadership over to the gravest ignorance. One single fact clearly illustrates this. When she ordained a bishop she generally demanded not, that he understood the Holy Scriptures; it was sufficient, if he could read and sing, know the Lord's prayer could recite the articles of faith from the book of Psalms, and could calculate the new moons, the Easter times and the orbit of sun and moon."

Thus was the spiritual leadership in this third period. With a few exceptions, leaving out Emperor Charles the Great, Leo De Isaurier, and his son and successor Constantine IV Copronymus, etc., the powers in the state were, as Christian princes, not better, than the Priests as Christian Priesthood

TRANSLATION OF THE THIRD TRUMPET

Rev 8:10, 11.

Verse 10. *During the third period of Gospel preaching on earth a brilliant worldly power has fallen, and its power came into the hands of the already fallen spiritual leadership.*

Verse 11. *And the name of this power was: the unrighteous kingship of this world, with its falling away from God and its idolatry; and what still remained Holy of the Gospel preaching was destroyed thereby, so that many souls through the mutilation of the teaching of salvation died the spiritual death.*

Guers says of the appearance of Papal power in this period on page 86:

"The end of the 6th and the beginning of the 7th century was characterized by scandalous scenes between the bishops of Constantinople and Rome; both ambitious and carnally minded, challenged each other for supremacy, because of the great privileges, which were bound thereto. John IV, Bishop of Constantinople, heftily ignited the dispute, when he in 58 [12]took up the title of universal Bishop. Pelagius II, Bishop of Rome, forcefully rejected such claims. Cynachus, successor of John, retained the title of universal

---

[12] Therefore at the end of the previous time period.

Bishop, to which Gregorius I, (who died in 604, therefore before the beginning of this period) replied: "I acknowledge freely, that all who take up the title of universal Bishop, possesses the high-mindedness and the character of the antichrist, and to a certain degree is his forerunner, through the arrogance, with which he tries to elevate himself above his peers."

"What amazing guidance and Godly Providence is found therein that already beforehand the prideful and godless title of universal head of the church was branded as blasphemous and a forerunner of the antichrist by a man who himself occupied the seat of Peter, and whose name is lauded up to our days in the Roman Church!"

"Gregorius I died in 604. Two years after his death Bonifacius III (patriarch of Rome) sought the title of universal Bishop from Emperor Phocas, with the privilege to carry it over to all his successors. Phocas (page 93) took away the title from the Bishop of Constantinople, gave it to Boniface and additionally declared that the church of Rome was head of all the other Catholic churches.

Page 93: "Behold the bishop of Rome is become lord and master over his brothers; yet a short time and he shall, elevated to the worthiness of worldly honour, possess states in Italy and presumes to be the ruler of the princes of this century." "One prince of the Lombards, (page 94) named Aistolph, thought to invade Rome and her territory and formulated the plan to bring the whole of Italy under the yoke of the Lombards. He already threatened the capital city of the old Roman Empire, when Pope Stefanus II made up his mind to ask Pepin the Short for his help. At the head of a mighty army (page 95) marching over the Alps in 754, Pepin vanquished Aistolph and forced him to cede the Exarchate of Ravenna (comprising 22 cities), Pentopolis, and all the castles and properties which he had incorporated in the Duchy of Rome, to the Papal chair. When the Bishop of Rome became a worldly prince, he placed himself in the ranks of the European princes. By combining the predatory expeditions with the uprisings, he added to the keys, the sceptre, to the priestly dignity, the Empire, and enriched himself with that which the Lombard kings and the Greek Emperors of Constantinople had left behind.

Page 96. "Risen to the highest power, one will see him furthermore endeavouring with all his might, to introduce the image cult everywhere, a *new sort of idolatry, under the guise of superficial Christendom, whereby the fall became complete."*

Not satisfied only with worldly power, the Pope, naming himself the steward of Christ, searched for military fame on the battlefields. The messengers of peace and of love, sent by Christ, the martyrs of faith from the Apostolic time, the rider on the white horse from the Ephesian period, had exchanged the bow of the Gospel with a warrior's spear, the sword of God's Word with the bloody battle-sword, and so we see at the end of this period, in 914, Pope John X as the first Pope, who stood at the head of an army.

(Van Loon page 101. 914 AD.)[13]

Pergamos, the high tower of the new Babylon, is nearly completed. But not only the false teaching and idolatry introduced by the Pope, also the sensual teaching of Mohamed poisoned the Gospel of Jesus Christ and made it bitter in the Eastern countries.

GUERS page 44.

"At the beginning of the 8th century, Mohamed's successors were known under the name of Caliphs, the most powerful rulers on the earth, the Arab realm occupied an extended area of two hundred days' journey, namely from the steppes of India to the shores of the Atlantic Ocean."

Concerning the preaching of the Gospel in the Roman church of this period, we find described in a few words by Guers on page 102.

"The famous Eligius, Bishop of Noyon in Picardy, canonized as a saint, taught the following; he is a good Christian, who often goes to church, who brings offerings to the altar, gives to God a tenth of his possessions, etc. Buy the freedom of your souls from punishment, which rests upon you through your sins, while you have the means thereto: - give offerings and tithes to the church; - maintain the waxen candles in the Holy places; - strive to obtain the protection of the saints with humble zeal; - if you do it, you will fearlessly stand before the eternal Judge on the Judgement Day and say to Him: Give Lord, because we have given."

---

[13] "For all they that take the sword shall perish with the sword." Said the Lord Jesus. 33 AD. (Matt 26:52). Nine centuries later Popedom took up the sword (914 AD) but also nine centuries later it perished by it (1870 AD) with the capture of Rome and the destruction of the worldly Popedom, which will never be restored, according to the Revelation of Jesus Christ."

That was then the teaching of salvation of those, who named themselves: substitutes of the Apostle Peter, who taught: We believe to be saved by the grace of the Lord Jesus Christ. And many souls died of the waters, says our prophecy, because they became bitter.

TRANSLATION OF THE THIRD VIAL

<u>Rev 16:4–7.</u>

Verse 4. *The powers in church and state poured out God's judgement upon the church in this third period, because they themselves replaced the pure waters of the Gospel, with a concoction of human findings, sensual notions, superstitions and idolatry. The sensual, unrepentant heart gave itself over completely to all lusts of the flesh, high-mindedness and falling away from God.*

We read from Guers, page 84:
"Until now, the Bishop of Rome covertly came out concerning his claim to supremacy. Henceforth he would speak out more freely of a spiritual supreme power. He will even want to rule over the princes of the East, and exploit the weakness of the Emperor, to elevate himself at their expense. At the third period of the striving Church, we will see him openly strive for general world supremacy; during the next seven centuries we will see him gathering riches and power."

And page 98: "Gregorius III had barely occupied the Roman chair in 731 when he wrote the following to the Emperor (Leo): "While you are ignorant and illiterate, we are forced to write hard, important words based upon God's Word (!) to you. We conjure you, to let go of your high-mindedness and to hear us in humility. You say, that we worship stones, walls and planks. Not so, Sir! These symbols only bring those persons to our remembrance, whose names they bear, in order to elevate our sluggish spirit. We do not see them as gods, but say when we have Jesus' image before us: "Lord, help us!" and by the statue of His mother: "Pray your son, to save us!" and by the statue of a martyr: "Holy Stephan; pray for us!" Since the power of Saint Peter is vested upon us, we could speak out punishment over you, but since you have brought the curse upon yourself, may it rest upon you. Stop destroying the statues, and all will be well!"

And page 101: The establishing of churches and chapels, to embellish them, to give to the monasteries, to build monuments, to dig up the remains of saints and martyrs to honour them, and to move the saints to intercede through rich offerings, was the religion, which the spiritual leaders sought to propagate everywhere, by exploiting the credulity of the people to their own advantage."

Verse 5. *And I heard the Cherub, representing the Evangelist Ministry say: Righteous are you, Lord! Who is and who was; Holy are you, that you have judged thus.*

Verse 6. *While they spilled the blood of saints and prophets, so did you also give them blood to drink; for they are worthy of it.*

Verse 7. *And I heard the martyrs, resting under the altar, say, Yes Lord, You Almighty God! True and righteous are your judgements.*

That was the voice of the blood witnesses of Jesus, who were killed by the Heathen-Roman power in the first period. Now that Popedom with its worshipers had appropriated the Roman worldly power for itself, it also inherited the curse of the spilled blood of the early Christians, according to Godly justice, which Christ also indicated, when he said to the Jews who rejected Him, (Matt 23:35) "That upon you may come all the righteous blood shed upon the earth, from the blood of righteous Abel unto the blood of Zachariah. " The souls of the killed, blood witnesses of the Lord praise His righteousness, while He, causes those of the Heathen-Roman Empire who bodily had harmed them, now, the "fallen away" Christians of the Papal-Roman Empire to experience the same spiritually.

END OF THE THIRD PERIOD

FOURTH PERIOD

HYATIRA

The Unbridled Run-Away

FROM 914 TO 1215 AD.

FOURTH PERIOD

THYATIRA: *The Unbridled Run-Away*

FROM

Pope John X heading an army, 914 A.D.

TO

Pope Innocent III and the 12th Council, 1215 A.D.

This period covers the tenth, eleventh and twelfth century of the Dark Ages, when the poor Christian nation, drained by the clergy, plundered by the predators, thinned out by the princes in wars, living in utter spiritual darkness, and apart from this also threatened by pests, famine and the terrible incursions by foreign plunderers from the South and the North, or to have to sacrifice their lives in Crusades. The period begins in the year 914 A.D, when whores and crusaders sat on the seat of Peter and ends in the year 1215 A.D. with the highest revelation of the worldly and spiritual power of Popedom.

In this period the fourth head of the beast reveals itself. (4th beast of Daniel; the Roman Empire.)

(Rev 17:9, 10.)

FOURTH PERIOD

THYATIRIAN TIME

THE MIDDLE AGES UNDER THE POPES

4th Candlestick. Chapter 2,	4th Seal. Chapter 6,	4th Trumpet. Chapter 8,	4th Vial, Chapter 16,
And unto the angel of the church in Thyatira write; These things saith the Son of God, who hath his eyes like unto a flame of fire, and his feet are like fine brass; 19. I know thy works, and charity, and service, and faith, and thy patience, and thy works, and the last to be more than the first. 20. Notwithstanding I have a few things against thee, because thou sufferest that woman Jezebel, which calleth herself a prophetess, to teach and to seduce my servants to commit fornication, and to eat things sacrificed unto idols. 21. And I gave her space to repent of her fornication; and she repented not. 22. Behold, I will cast her into a bed, and them that commit adultery with her into great tribulation, except they repent of their deeds. 23. And I will kill her children with death; and all the churches shall know that I am he which searcheth the reins and hearts: and I will give unto every one of you according to your works. 24. But unto you I say, and unto the rest in Thyatira, as many as have not this doctrine, and which have not known the depth of Satan, as they speak; I will put upon you none other burden. 25. But that which ye have already hold fast till I come. 26. And he that overcometh, and keepeth my works unto the end, to him will I give power over the nations: 27. And he shall rule them with a rod of iron; as the vessels of a potter shall they be broken to shivers: even as I received of my Father. 28. And I will give him the morning star. 29. He that hath an ear, let him hear what the Spirit saith unto the churches.	And when he had opened the fourth seal, I heard the voice of the fourth living creature say, Come and see. 8. And I looked and behold a pale horse: and his name that sat on him was Death, and Hell followed with him. And power was given unto them over the fourth part of the earth, to kill with sword, and with hunger, and with death, and with the beasts of the earth.	12. And the fourth angel sounded, and the third part of the sun was smitten, and the third part of the moon, and the third part of the stars; so as the third part of them was darkened, and the day shone not for a third part of it, and the night likewise. 13. And I beheld, and heard an angel flying through the midst of heaven, saying with a loud voice, Woe, woe, woe, to the inhabiters of the earth by reason of the other voices of the trumpet of the three angels, which are yet to sound!	And the fourth angel poured out his vial upon the sun, and power was given unto him to scorch men with fire. 9. And men were scorched with great heat, and blasphemed the name of God, which hath power over these plagues: and they repented not to give him glory.

FOURTH CANDLESTICK

or

THE LIGHT OR THE SPIRITUAL LIFE IN THE

CONGREGATION

> It is written: Thou shalt worship the Lord your God
> and Him only.
> Luke 4:8.

Rev 2:18–29.

Thyatira was a city in Asia Minor, which lay between Pergamus and Sardis. It still exists and still boasts a small Christian Congregation.

Thyatira means: **unbridled run-away,** (Thuein ateirys) and indeed the Christian Congregation of this period continued to run away unbridled on the road to perdition. To the spiritual leaders and the Congregation, as they would be in this fourth period, John had to write;

Verse 18. **This sayeth the Son of God, with his eyes as a flame of fire.** Moses says to Hobab: "Do not leave us, for you know where we should camp in the wilderness, and *you* serve as *eyes* for us." (Num 10:31.) Job says in (Job 29:15): "*I was eyes to the blind.*" In both instances, the word "*eyes*" does not refer to one's own personal eye, but *another person,* whose service is used to attain a goal. This image the Lord also uses here. The Apostle John saw, (Rev 4: 6), the four living creatures around the throne of the Almighty, who were: "Full of *eyes* before and behind". We have already previously shown, that these four creatures are the four ministries, the Apostle, Prophet, Evangelist and Shepherd ministry of our Lord Jesus, and the eyes of the four living creatures are thus all the *bearers of these ministries,* who watch over the whole Congregation, therefore the *servants of the Lord.*

In (Rev 5:6), however, the Lamb is described as having *seven eyes.* The Holy Spirit immediately adds the explanation: "Which are the *seven spirits of God,* sent out to all lands,", of which we already find the prediction in (Zach 3:9), "upon one stone (Christ) shall be s*even eyes*", and also (Zach 4:10) "*They are the eyes of the Lord,* which run to and from through the whole earth.*" The seven spirits of God are, according to (Rev 4:5) seven lamps of fire burning before the throne". In the 5th candlestick (Rev 3:1), we will find further explanations, that these seven spirits or seven lamps of fire are different powers, revelations or *gifts of the Holy Spirit*, wherewith Jesus equips His servants (*eyes*).

The **eyes** of the Son of God are thus **His servants**, standing in the full power of faith and of the Holy Spirit, in whatever ordination in church or state. This is totally confirmed by the following image: **"And his eyes where as a flame of fire"**, and also: Who maketh his angels spirits, his ministers a **flaming fire**." (Psalm 104:4), and "the voice of the Lord", or the word spoken according to his will," divideth the **flames of fire,"** (Psalm 29:7). The fire is already shown to be the fire of the Holy Spirit in the first trumpet. If the revelation then shows us that the eyes of the Lord Jesus and His servants, and the seven eyes of the Lord the seven powers of the Holy Spirit, wherewith He equips His twelve servants, then the image reoccurs as in itself. **The Lord's eyes as a flame of fire**, are therefore: **His servants, filled with the Holy Spirit, and His gifts**, as they were in the first period of the church, but not existing in the church in this period. The body of Christ or His congregation (1 Cor. 12:27) is not protected by the eyes anymore. It only moved forward through **His feet** (verse 18) which in this period were like **burnished bronze**. "How beautiful the mountains are the feet of Him that bringeth good things, that saith to Zion, thy God Reigneth," (Isaiah 52: 7). According to verse 6 it is the Lord Himself, who brings the good tidings and is, therefore, **His feet, His messengers**, or, according to verse 8, His watchmen, whose voice proclaim the tidings. "Behold upon the mountains the feet of Him that Bringeth good tidings, that published peace" (Nahum 1: 15), both also mentioned in Rom.10, and 1 Cor. 12:15: "If the foot shall say, because I am not the hand, I am not of the body, is it therefore not of the body?" All these texts refer to the **feet** of the Son of God, as **His servants, His messengers**, who propagate the Gospel to the world. The same image we meet again later in Rev. 10:2, where the Angel of the Covenant, Jesus Christ, sets His right foot upon the sea of nations and the other on the earth (the existing society), which is, the **evangelists and shepherd ministries**, during the Reformation period.

The feet of the Lord or His evangelist messengers in the fourth period were not like unto gold (image of truth, Rev. 3:18, Eph. 6:14, Rev. 1:13), but like bronze, which according to (Jer. 6:28), in the language of the Holy Spirit, is the image of grievous **revolters** and **corrupters;** a true reflection of the Evangelistic standard of the priesthood of the Roman and Greek church in this period. The thought contained in verse 18 is therefore, that the body of the Lord, the congregation in this period, would not possess

150

representatives of the Lord, filled with the Holy Spirit, but dissidents and corrupters under the name of priest of Jesus Christ. In this form, John saw the body in (Rev 1:15a see page 14). The Lord now presents Himself to render her accountability for where His servants or eyes in the congregation have gone.

What the Son of God says, the following verses will show.

Verse 19: **"I know your works, and service, and love, and faith, and your patience and your works: and** that **the last** are **more than the first."** From this verse, we see that in this period of the church, as well as previously in the congregation of Thyatira, the faithful remained patient under the removal of the Gospel of Jesus Christ in the Roman Church. In verse 20 the Lord now condemns the fact that the believers do not protest the false teaching of *this woman Jezebel*, who poses as a *prophetess*. Did not Jezebel (1 Kings 16: 31 -33) change the Religion of Israel into Baal worshipping. Do we not see in these few words, **"The woman Jezebel, which proclaims to be a prophetess,"** the Roman church of this time pictured in her arrogance as if, like previously through God's prophets, so also now the Holy Spirit spoke through her councils, Popes, etc.; the teaching that the voice of the Church was the voice of God; the infallibility of the Church, etc. The servants of the Lord, who allowed themselves to be *seduced* by this false prophetess, truly practised well, what is called **whoring** in many places in God's Holy Word which is: falling away from the only True God; eating of the **Idol offering** (Maria Worship, idolatry) of the false prophetess and seeking their salvation in good works according to her teaching which disdained Jesus' merit. In this period the edifying of Maria, the worshipping of saints and statues and the veneration of relics strongly penetrated the church, as well as the teaching of the transubstantiation of the total transformation of bread and wine, with the Holy Communion, into the natural body (flesh and blood) of Jesus Christ, a teaching which was confirmed at the end of this period (1215) by the Lateran Council and remained in the Roman Church since then.

According to tradition, the woman Jezebel was meant to be the wife of the bishop of the congregation of Thyatira, who by means of certain sorcery seduced the servants of the Lord to heathen licentiousness. The woman Jezebel did not actually live in Thyatira. However, we see in each case in her actions in this time, a clear proof of the typical meaning of many Old Testament events.

Verse 21. **"And I gave her time, to repent from her whoring, and she did not repent".** On the contrary, Popedom, as the name of the candlestick already implies, ran away unbridled on the way leading to covering up the Gospel. Therefore:

Verse 22. **"Beware, I will cast her into a bed"**. The Son of God throws the False prophetess with her lovers on a **bed** (kliny) or **to bed**. This is *not a sickbed* such as v.d. Palm freely interpreted, but a **bed of rest**. It is clear to us that here we have to do with an *image*, of which God's word will again give us the solution. We thus read: (Isaiah 28:18–20) "And your covenant with death shall be disannulled, and your agreement with hell shall not stand; for *the bed* is shorter than that a man can stretch himself on it", and (Ezk 13:2, 10, 18, 20) "The word of the Lord came to me" verse2, "Son of Man prophesy against the prophets of Israel that prophesy and say thou unto them that prophesy out of their own hearts" verse 10, "Because, even because they have seduced my people, saying peace and there was no peace; and one build up a wall and is low, others daubed it with untempered mortar." Verse 18. "Woe to the women who sew *pillows* to armholes and make kerchiefs upon the heads of every stature hunt. Behold, I am against your *pillows*, wherewith ye hunt the souls to make them fly."[14] A **bed**, a place of **rest**, what else can it mean in the given texts than the image of a *false*, an unfounded *soulish rest*, not leaning on the Word and the promise of the Lord, but on the false teachers and prophets; and therefore here a **false rest** of the soul, in penitence, absolutions, masses, merits of Saints, etc. of the Roman church. The bed, referred to in verse 22, was therefore the Church with her teaching, which she regarded to be the only true, the only way to salvation. This bed here was too short to stretch upon "to find rest for the souls." (Matt 11:29). The hope of salvation was built on sand.

"And whosoever committed adultery with her, I will throw in great tribulation, if they do not repent of their works." Indeed, as we will see in the fourth vial, Christianity unfaithful to God, and flirting with Popedom of this period, was subjected to great need, by the great wars, pests, famine, the invasion of the Sarracens, Normans, and later through the forced crusades to the Holy Land.

Verse 23. "**And her children** (of the prophetess Jezebel), the spiritual children, procreated by Popedom in this period, even as Paul procreated the Galatians, (Gal 4:19), **I will kill** by the spiritual **death; and all the congregations will know that it is I, who searches the kidneys and hearts. And I will give you each according to your works"**.

Verse 24, "**I say unto you, and those who remain in Thyatira, as much as they do not have this teaching** (of the prophetess Jezebel) **and did not**

---

[14] Although Ezekiel here does not refer to a bed, but of pillows, the image and the original thought of false rest remains the same.

know the depts of Satan (as they say) **I will not place any other burdens".**

"The Depths of Satan", as they name this teaching, against *the depths of God*. (I Cor 2:10). In this period there were thus still believers in the church, as there always had been, who remained in the truth and did not accept the darkening of God's truth and Word by Papal decrees and by the councils etc., and their strife and suffering in this period was truly heavy enough to cause the Loving Saviour to promise them: *I will not "Place any more burden upon you."*, but (verse 25) **that which thou hast, hold fast, until I come**. The hope on the return of Christ and the establishing of the Kingdom of His Glory, had remained alive in a few, from the Apostolic times throughout all the centuries, as Church history abundantly testifies. To the believing Christians of that period no greater burdens were imposed, but to those at the end of the following period as we shall see.

Verse 26. **And he that overcometh, and keepeth my works unto the end, to him will I give power over the nations** (verse 27) **and he shall rule there with a rod of iron**. This end promise to the spiritual overcomers of this period, finds its fulfillment with the end promise of the previous candlesticks at the return of the Lord, where all the overcommers of the previous period appear with Him again on the clouds of Heaven, to judge the anti-Christian earth. (Rev 14:14, 17-20; Rev 19:11-16) "What would you prefer?" says Paul, (1 Cor 4:21) "shall I come unto you with a **rod** or in love, and in the spirit of meekness?" and (1 Cor 5:3-5): "I have judged already in the name of our Lord Jesus Christ, with the power of our Lord Jesus Christ, to deliver such a one to Satan, and (1 Cor 6:3): "Know ye not that we shall judge angels?" In (Isaiah 11:4) it is predicted of the promised Messiah: "And He shall smite the earth with the *rod of His mouth*, and with the breath of His lips shall He *slay the wicked*." Whosoever heareth you heareth Me, says Christ", and did not the Apostle Peter *kill* the deceiver Ananias with the *rod of the mouth* of the Son of God? So will Christ, at His return personally, as well as through His glorified witnesses, execute judgement over the anti-Christians.

Verse 27 **"As the vessels of a potter shall they be broken to shivers"**. In the House of the Lord, says Paul (2 Tim 2:20), "There are not only *vessels* of gold and silver, but also of wood and of earth; and some to *honour*, and some to *dishonour*."

The whole verse 27 therefore sketches the *admonition through mutual strife*, and the punishment by the rod of His mouth, which the Son of God, according to the power, which He **received from His Father**, will exert

153

over the fallen-away nations and Kingdoms at the establishing of the Kingdom of Glory, as we shall learn to know in the seventh period.

Who overcomes and remains faithful to the end,

Verse 28 **"I will give Him the morning star",** that is, as we already said previously, the "**Royal Power**". "I am the morning star says Jesus (Rev 22:16). Jesus will give His royal power to the overcomers and make them Kings and Priests, (Rev 5:10; 20: 6) and they will reign with Him as Kings and Priests and sit with Him on His throne. (Rev 3:21)

Also, in this corrupt period of the church, the Lord acknowledges His own, who did not bow their knees to Baal, but obtained the victory against superstition with all its seduction, and on the day of the Lord will receive the promised Morning star. The greatest part of Christendom however *ran unbridled* on the road which leads to perdition. The fourth candlestick was also not dimmed at the end of this period but shines forth as in the previous and following candlesticks, in other words, the condition of the spiritual life of the congregation from the Thyatirian period continued to exist during all the times of the church in a part of the members of the Roman and Greek churches.

FOURTH SEAL

or

THE SPIRITUAL LIFE OF THE POWERS IN CHURCH AND STATE

> Ye cannot serve God and mammon
> for that which is highly esteemed
> among men is abomination
> in the sight of God.
> Luke 16:13, 15.

Rev 6:7-8.

Verse 7. "And when he had opened the fourth seal, I heard the voice of the fourth living creature call out, Come!"

The **fourth Cherub**, which speaks in verse 7, is the **prophet ministry**, or the living creature, **like unto an eagle** (aetoy), (Rev 4:7, Ezek 1:10). The *eagle* is in the language of the Holy Spirit, the *image of prophets* (Exod 19:4; Deut 18:15, 18; Deut 34:10; Hos 12:14; Hos 8:1).

The prophet ministry in the Old Testament had the duty to watch over the belief in and the worship of the only true God; to watch against falling away from God and idolatry. And exactly during this period the falling away from God and idolatry reached its peak. No prophet of the Lord watched against the falsification of the Christian teaching anymore. For this reason, the fourth cherub says, **come and see**, how in this period the prophet ministry comes to naught.

Verse 8. "And I saw, and behold, a pale horse, and he who sat on him, was death; and Hades followed him".

We know already that the colour of the horse is the condition of the congregation, which is described to us in this fourth candlestick as being *estranged from the only true God and His Son Jesus Christ*; here with one word, this condition is sketched as **pale**, e.g. without colour, **death pale**. Likewise, we find this word also in (Jer 30:6.), "Wherefore do I see every face turned in Paleness?" and in (Joel 2:6) "all faces grow pale (NRS**). Pale is the colour of death**, and the congregation of that period; the **life** in her **which was from God** was dead.

He who sat on the horse, or the powers in the church and in the Christian state, the priests and kings therefore – **his name was death**, which is the **spiritual death**, such as we find in many places in the Holy Scripture, death in sin and unrighteousness; e.g. (Luke 15:24), in the parable of the prodigal son, "For this my son was *dead* and is alive again." (1 Tim 5:6):

155

"But she that liveth in pleasure is *dead while she liveth*. (Eph 5:14): "Awake thou that sleepest, and arise from the *dead*!."." (James 2:20): "That faith without works is *dead*." (Rev 3:1) "I know thy works, that thou hast a name that thou livest, and art *dead*." (Prov 21:16): "The man that wandereth out of the way of understanding shall remain in the congregation of the *dead*."

The realm of the departed, which followed with the **spiritual death**, is here not to be understood to be the actual *land of shadows* only, but also the image of *worldly wretchedness*. (1 Sam 2:6): "He brings down to Sheol, and brings to life," (NRS), and David (2 Sam 22:6) "the sorrows of *hell*[15], (Sheol, Hades) compassed me about, and (Psalm 116:3): "The pangs of *sheol* laid hold on me,"[ψ](NRS). But also the non-overcomers of that period, and their number of all the periods is the greatest, shall have no part in the first resurrection, because they are the spiritually dead, partly fallen, but remaining in the realms of the departed until the day of judgement, when the books shall be opened. And *then*, (according to the best reading in the original text, and here seeming to be the correct reading) unto *them*, thus the rider, which are the kings and priests, **power was given to kill,** (1ˢᵗ), **with the sword**. This cannot be the sword of God's Word but is again the **natural and the spiritual sword of this world**; the same as that which the rider in the second seal carried; the bloody **sword of war**, but also as we found there (page 96) the sword of mutual strife and **bitterness**. To them power was given to kill, (2ⁿᵈ), **with famine**. In (1 Sam 3:1) we find, "that word of the Lord was rare in those days," (NRS) there was therefore also *spiritual famine* of which Amos speaks, (Amos 8:11) "Behold, the days come, says the Lord God, that I will send a *famine* in the land, not a famine of bread, nor a thirst for water, but of *hearing the Words of the LORD*." That was thus the famine, wherewith the spiritual leaders, themselves dead in sin and unrighteousness, caused the congregation which has such a great need of the fruits of the tree of life, to die of *spiritual hunger*. "Blessed are they which do hunger and thirsts after righteousness, for they shall be filled," said the Saviour (Matt 5:6), yet the priesthood of Thyatira killed the hungry congregation with spiritual starvation, and themselves satiated, through the eating of Jezebel's idol sacrifices, accumulated the judgement upon themselves spoken of by Jesus in (Luke 6:25): "Woe unto you that are full! For ye shall hunger."

---

[15] Totally incorrectly the state Bible as well as the Lutheran translation use the word Hell. Van der Palm better translated the word in its actual meaning as dead, or land of shadows. The fifth seal will further clarify this to the reader.

ψ The Hebrew meaning is Sheol; Greek is Hades.

The unfaithful priests and kings also killed the congregation (3rd), **with death,** not only **natural** but also **spiritual death**, of which Paul says, (Rom 7: 11) "For sin, seizing an opportunity in the commandment, *deceived me* and through it *killed* me." (4th), The priests and kings would also kill the congregation **through the wild beasts of the earth**. A literal tearing apart by wild beasts of the earth can naturally not be considered here; this only occurred in the Ephesian period, as ordered by the Roman emperors. Immediately we here remember that the **worldly powers**, who are **hostile to God**, are represented to us in (Dan 7:3-7, 17, 23; Rev 13:1-11) as **wild beasts**. Just open the books of history or that of your memories, and consider how the poor, lost in darkness Christianity of the Dark Ages, were killed by the wild beasts of the earth, in the unceasing Godly or rather ungodly disputes about and amongst the spiritual and worldly powers, the continuous wars, through the terrible invasions of Saracens and Normans, and the later murderous crusades to the Holy Land. We do not risk picturing the terrible scenes of strife and suffering, of this dominion of the realm of darkness on earth. "My sheep were scattered because there was no shepherd; and scattered, they became food for all the wild animals," (Ezk 34:5). This sorrowful power would be exerted by the rider over a **fourth part of the earth**. The earth we already know as the existing *Christian Society*. A much greater part than a fourth part of the people were actually killed by the sword in that period, by natural as well as spiritual famine, by wild beasts of the earth, but especially the spiritual death. It is therefore not again a particular numerical value, which we have to understand under a *fourth part*, just as little as in the case of a *third part* (page 59). If we actually found that the *third part* was explained as the *part sanctified by the Holy Spirit*, while *three is the number of God*, similarly four is the symbolic **number of the earth**. Four kingdoms would have power over the earth (Dan 7: 3-17; Mark 13:27). From the four winds of the earth, (Rev 7:1; Rev 20:8), therefore from the whole earth, Jesus shall gather his faithful. The **fourth part** is therefore the **earthly-minded part**, which does not want to belong to the children of God. And on them, the sad judgement of the natural and spiritual death would be executed by the idolatrous priests, the apostate kings or wild beasts of the earth, as they would be scorched by the fire from the bottomless pit at the outpouring of the fourth seal. The few believers from this Thyatirian period, who did not know the depths of Satan, belonged to the beloved of God upon whom Jesus would place no further burdens (Rev 2:24), but they made up a minority compared to the earthly-minded or the fourth part of the earth, which in its blindness ran unbridled on the way, which leads to perdition.

FOURTH TRUMPET

or

THE CONDITION AND EFFECT OF THE GOSPEL PREACHING

> If therefore the light that is in thee be darkness,
> how great is that darkness.
> Matt. 6:23

Rev 8:12–13.

Against the incomprehensive wonders of nature which most interpretations of revelation give concerning words, and the impossibilities, which must take on natural concepts, it will become clear how these verses *through their solution out of God's Word*, attain a striking simplicity and naturalness.

Verse 12. **"And the fourth angel sounded his trumpet"**, that is, therefore, during the fourth period of the church, and the condition in which the Gospel preaching of that period took place, becomes, as this prophet teaches us:

"The third part **of the sun was smitten, and the third part of the moon and the third** part **of the stars, so as the third part of them was darkness"**. Who is the *sun*, the *moon*, who are the *stars*? The **Sun** is **Christ**, *the sun of righteousness*, who rises for them, who fear his name, under whose wings there will be healing (Mal. 4:2). Also, in (Psalm 84:11), the *Lord is named a Sun*. In (Psalm 19:4, 5.), we read that God hath set a tabernacle in heaven for the sun. Comparing this with (Heb 9:11), it appears that this heaven is the church heaven; the tent tabernacle or hut, the New Covenant and the High Priest therefore Christ, the Sun. In (Rev. 12:1), the woman, the congregation, is presented as clothed with the sun, Christ. "But *put ye on* (that is*: put on as a robe*) *the Lord Jesus Christ,"* says Paul (Rom. 13:14). Christ is therefore the sun in the church, but also in this period, where the Church and State were one under the power of Popedom, also the Sun in the State. Reading more in (Gen. 37:9, 10), where Joseph dreams that the Sun and the Moon and eleven Stars bowed down before him, we see that the highly spiritual elevated Jacob immediately understood this image and understood himself as the father of the family to be the Sun then, as **Christ in Church and state and Family**, or as Christ in the Bishop of the congregation, in the leader of the state and in the family. For the congregation was subject to their head, Bishop or Angel, the state to its ruler and the woman to the man, these three again are subject to their head Christ, who now had not yet come to establish a Kingdom of this world, but to gather the faithful of God under His banner as a Christian Kingdom, living under His rule and institution, (Matt 28:19, 20). And this Kingdom or the **congregation** is presented under the image of the **Moon**, which receives its light from the ruler, the Sun; the soft, feminine *Moon*, as the *Congregation*, which is the *bride* of *Christ*, her *Sun* and *Bridegroom*, (see Eph. 5:22–32; John 3:29). When the Psalmist says: (Psalm 8:3) That heaven is the work of God's fingers, then heaven is not to be taken only as the blue vault above us, but as the Kingdom of Heaven, of which *Christ* is the *Sun*, and the *Moon* and *Stars*, "which Thou hast ordained," are the *Congregation* of Christ and her *Teachers*, and these are the *Sun*, the *Moon* and the light-giving *Stars*, who together with all angels and heavenly hosts praise God in heaven, (the congregation), (Psalm 148:2, 3). We read in (Psalm 89:2) *"Your faithfulness* is as firm as the heaven" and verse 5, "Let the heavens *praise your wonders*, O Lord, your faithfulness in the *assembly of the Holy Ones"*. For the **stars** are, this needs almost no reminder, the image of the **teachers**: e.g. (Dan. 12:3). The **teachers** shall shine as the *stars*. But not only in the Old Covenant, also in pages of the New Testament we find in (Jude 13), the *unrighteous teachers* named, *wandering stars*. So also, in (Rev 1: 20), Jesus Himself gives John the interpretation, that the *stars*, which he saw (verse 16) in His right hand, are the *Bishops* and Angels of the congregations. We also find these three images together in (Isaiah 13:10), at the announcement of the judgement over old Babel which is still prophetically valid for the modern Babylon of the seventh period: "For the *stars* of heaven and the constellations thereof shall not give their light; the *sun* shall be darkened in His going forth, and the *moon* shall not cause her light to shine." But just as the heads of the church, the heads of the state or the kings, are also called *stars*, as we have shown (page 127).

The meaning of the word *smitten* is clear enough to us from the plagues of Egypt and other judgments of God in Old Testament history. Concerning the third part, we must here remember what we said in the second trumpet about the meaning of the *third part*, as the sanctified part, or the part susceptible to the influence of the Holy Spirit, sanctified and purified by Him.

The *third part* of the *sun, moon* and *stars is smitten*, that is thus: Christ would not live through the Holy Spirit in the congregation anymore, neither in the teachers, and of the little, which in this period remained of Christian life in the church, state and family - of the little of Christ's original tenets still adhered to - of the small number of true believers and Christian teachers, which in this period were still present in the Roman and Greek church, (there would be, as in Elijah's time, still yet 7000 remaining, who did not bow their knees to Baal) – of the small remaining Christian element in the church, a *third*, or those susceptible to the influence of the Holy Spirit would be smitten and *darkened*. The church, the state, the family, the congregation and the teachers only had the name of Christian but had completely lost Godliness.

"And the day shone not for a third part of it, and the night likewise." What does the Holy Spirit understand with *day* and *night* here? Paul says: (Rom. 13:12), "The *night* is far spent, the *day* is at hand," and verse 13: "Let us walk decently, as in the day," because (1 Tess. 5:5), "Ye are all the children *of light*, and the children *of the day*; we are not of the *night*, nor of *darkness*, but (verse 8) let us, who are *of the day*, be sober, putting on the breastplate of faith and love, and for our helmet, the hope of salvation." This was therefore the characteristic of the *day*; faith, love and hope of salvation. We find the same in the words of our Saviour in (John 8:56), where Jesus speaks to the Jews: "Your father Abraham rejoiced to see my *day*: and he saw it and was glad." Abraham had not seen Christ in the flesh, only in *faith*, and rejoiced in the hope of salvation. This meaning of the word *day* becomes even clearer when we read in the first five verses of the next chapter (nine), what happened with the man who was blind from birth. (Verses 4 and 5), Jesus says: "I must work, the works of Him that sent me, while it is day: the night cometh, when no man can work." (Verse 5) "As long as I am in the world, **I** am the *light* of the world." Christ therefore names Himself the light of the world, that is, the Sun. Where **He** is and as long as *His light* shines, it is *day*. It is now clear to us, what the words of this prophecy mean. Where Christ, the Sun of righteousness, is darkened in church, state and family, where the Gospel preaching completely disappeared, there the light which shines forth from Him, also darkens. Life which is from and in Him the bright **daylight** of **faith**, **love** and **hope**, the **hope of salvation** darkened, but also the **moon** (the congregation) and the spiritual **stars** (the teachers) who both receive their light from the Sun, Christ, are similarly darkened, so that the little light of the Holy Spirit, which was still present in the Roman and Greek churches, would completely darken. This is how the third part of the day was darkened. The church would not shine in her anymore.

"And the night also." The *night*, the opposite of the day, the time wherein Christ does *not* shine, is the image of **darkness and ignorance**. See (Micah 3:6; Matt. 25:6; Rom. 13:12, 1 Tess. 5:5–7). The moon and the stars, which should have illuminated the night (congregation and teachers), were also darkened by the lack of light from the sun, from which they should have received their light. Also, no third part of the stars (Teachers,

Bishops 1: 20) or of the moon (congregation) is illuminated anymore. The light of the gospel was totally removed from the candlestick. They still meant to see, but they wandered about in the spiritual night. With all the splendour and power and feigned God-pleasing life of church and congregation, they were blind leaders leading the blind, in this night of spiritual darkness. That was the condition of the Gospel preaching of the fourth trumpet and its effect on the congregation.

After the picture of the sad condition of the church of Christ, such as John saw in the fourth trumpet, he receives a new vision which still belongs in the fourth period.

Verse 13. **"And I beheld and heard an eagle** (aetoy) **flying through the midst of heaven, saying with a loud voice, woe, woe, woe to the inhabiters of the earth by reason of the other voices of the trumpet of the three angels which are yet to sound!"**

The first question is: What do we have to understand under the word heaven? While it is still the same vision as in verse 12, wherein the sun (Christ) the moon (the congregation) and the stars (the teachers) were darkened, and John then sees an eagle flying in the midst of this darkened heaven, wherein previously the sun, the moon and the stars shone, this heaven must also be the church, and indeed the darkened church of Christ. The word church-heaven is freely used by the writers concerning the revelation, and not without reason. See what was already said on page 159. One must however not understand it in the sense of an earthly, external church institution, but as a Godly Kingdom on earth, the sum of all true believers, in which church denomination whatever, who together form the body of Christ, of which He himself is the head, (see page 26). So, when Paul says: "God hath raised us up together and made us sit together in heavenly places in Christ Jesus." (Eph. 2:6), he speaks of the past and the present and not of the future salvation, also not of the endless space, which apparently encircles our earth as a blue vault. Paul here speaks of the earthly church of Jesus Christ, as of the first of the three heavens of the Kingdom of God, which we will learn to know better in the fifth seal. Also, when the heaven, at the end of the sixth seal (the Reformation) such as it continues until the Day of the Lord, (Rev. 6:14), "And the heaven departed as a scroll when it is rolled together", it is not meant that the blue vault of heaven around us disappears, but the total abolition of the anti-Christian *church* by the anti-Christian state power. The **heaven** in our text is therefore the *darkened* Kingdom of God or the darkened *heaven of the* **Christian church**, as it was in the fourth period. Therein John saw an eagle or an angel flying. In the best handwritings, both versions are found, in some, we find probably included as an explanation, an angel as an eagle. We used the word eagle, because it appears so in the most reliable versions, and seems to us to be the true meaning, also while we found the *eagle* in that period as the image of the *prophets*, and in the seal of that period, as the image of the starving *prophet ministry* of Christ. At the end of this fourth trumpet, the eagle or cherub representative of the prophetic ministry of Christ, once more made his appearance, here, with the description of the condition and the effect of the Gospel preaching, to testify prophetically, that this condition, at least in its effect on the inhabitants of the Christian earth, would not improve. If the word eagle is the original one, it can here mean, a supernatural prediction, that in the three following periods of the church, the preaching of the Word of God (trumpet), would bring great catastrophes upon the believers. This vision is thus similar, to that at the end of the third vial and brought by heavenly witnesses. We would in that case seek in vain for an earthly fulfilment thereof in the history of the church.

That precisely the number of **three** angels who still had to sound their trumpets occurs in this prophecy, causes us to believe that the first version is the most correct one. That the eagle actually flies in the midst of the **heaven of the church**, again suggests another probable meaning.

In Deut. 28:49, a whole nation is compared to a flying eagle, and similarly the cherub represents the image of a flying eagle (Rev. 4:7) which appears in the seal of that period, as the servants of the Lord, who in His prophetic ministry, brought His testimony to His people and congregation. The flying eagle can therefore also in this trumpet mean a whole nation, which acts as a witness against the decay of the Roman Church and predicts to the believers the eminent consequent prosecutions.

Indeed, in this period the Waldense, the believing mountain dwellers, whose dark origin perhaps goes back to the fourth century of our timetable, courageously raised their heads and powerfully began to witness against the apostasy of the Roman Church and her false teachings. "The year 1120," says Martinet in His church history of the Waldense, "is renowned for their great boldness, as reflected in their public writings about the *Anti–Christ* and the particular heresies of the Roman church." This writing about the Anti–Christ, of which the libraries of Geneva and Cambridge each possess an old original document, of which J. MILNER (similarly to GUERS, page 430 etc.) while writing, in his history of the churches of Christ, gives an extract, (1838, part 6, pages 306–309) which shows, that the Anti – Christ, who will persecute the believers, is embodied in Popedom and that it soon will reveal its Anti-Christian character.[16] There must also still exist a short treatise, of which the date is not known to us, about the forthcoming persecutions or the *great tribulation*. Despite all the research, we could not acquire it.

If the word **angel** was the original version, while angel means "spiritual powers", then in this period in the body of the Christian church a similar prophetic testimony should have been brought by a part of the spiritual powers of the Eastern or Western churches. It is not written: *the* angel, that is: who sounded the fourth trumpet, but *an* angel. We, therefore, have to understand that this *angel who flew in the midst of the darkened heaven of the Roman church, are all the witnesses of Jesus*, who in this *fourth period*, raised their voices against the decay of the Roman church, such as Arnolphe, Bishop of Orleans, and Smaragdus, Giselbert, Radulphus, Adalbert, Bèranger, Anselmus, Fruentius from Florence, Bernard from Clairveaux, etc. of which some of them, probably at the inspiration of the Holy Spirit, predicted the forthcoming persecutions of the believers.

It is undeniable, that the Holy Spirit first gradually withdrew from the church, and amidst its growing decay, from time to time still spoke prophetically through individuals of holy disposition. Church history gives enough examples thereof. During this period, it appears to have completely died off in the Roman church, indeed it was also the prophetic ministry of Christ, which in the seal of that period, as the last of the four Cherubim said: Come and see, what will become of this ministry.

It is therefore not impossible, that similar prophetic testimony was uttered in the Roman church, eg: by the prophetess St Elisabeth, Abbess at Schonau, (died 1165 AD), or by the Abbess Hildegardis, famous prophetess and visionary, (died 1197 AD), zealous preacher against the moral decay of the spiritual leaders. While these prophecies are unknown to us, we deem it necessary, to mention them, in case one of our readers could gather more information.

To these angels also belongs Bernard the Abbot of Clairveaux (died 1153 AD) who, during the 12th century, in ignorance of their true principles and hostile to the Waldense, was the most renowned spiritual and greatest witness of Jesus in the Roman church itself. He said and taught amongst others, one century before the Inquisition began:

"It seems, that the time of persecution is past, but experience showed us clearly that neither the Christians nor the Lord Jesus Christ is free from

---

[16] Basnage: Histoire de L'Englise, etc. Book 26. Chapter 5 Par 8,9 (1699.)

persecution. And what is even worse, the persecution comes, for them, who bear the name of Christ". (Guers, page 215)

This is therefore a prophecy.

"Also, Joachim, abbot of Calabria, who died before the year 1215, taught that the Anti-Christ was born in the Roman States and that he would be elevated on the Roman seat." (Guers page 241)

If it is still uncertain whether the reading must be eagle or angel, and if this prophecy only in the vision to John, or also in this period was brought on earth, this is sure, that the Lord in His Revelation 19 centuries ago, already prophesied, that in the three last periods of His church, with the preaching of His word and truth, great tribulations and woes would come over those who accepted His witness. One has therefore named the three last trumpets, the three woes, yet unfairly, while the trumpets are not the woes, but at the sounding of each trumpet one of the woes lets itself be felt. The first of the woes was the horrible persecution of the Waldense in the 5th period (1215 – 1517): The second persecution of the protestants in the following period (1517 – 1815), emanates from Popedom and the Roman church, and just as certain as both these first woes came, the last and most horrible of all is to come. Then however the persecution will emanate from the totally revealed anti-Christendom and also hit both the Roman and the Protestant and all other Christian denominations. Then the seventh or the healed heathen head of the beast shall again appropriate the watchword of the first heathen head: *Pereat nomen Christianorum!* (the name "Christian" perish!).

FOURTH VIAL

THE JUDGEMENT OF GOD

> For from within, out of the heart of men, proceed evil thoughts,
> adulteries, fornication, murders. Thefts, covetousness,
> wickedness, deceit, lasciviousness, an evil eye,
> blasphemy, pride, foolishness: All these evil
> things come from within, and defile man.
> Mark 7:21 –23.

Rev. 16:8, 9.

The judgement of God, wherewith the apostate Christendom of that period are threatened, are poured out upon them, because they did not repent.

Verse 8. **"And the fourth angel poured out his vial upon the sun"**. The angels as we have already seen, are the powers in church and state, thus the kings and priests on earth, who, through their chasing after their own purpose and the satisfaction of their own lusts are used as tools in God's hand, wherewith He executes His judgements. None of them satisfied in seal neither trumpet what the Lord had actually called them for. Their own falling away from the Lord becomes a judgement to them. The trumpet angel becomes at the same time the vial angel!

The vial is poured out upon the sun of righteousness, Christ, as we said in the fourth trumpet. The church becomes a church without Christ. Robbed of the light from Him who is the light of the world, they wandered in spiritual darkness, a prey and plaything of earthly lusts, carnal passions, and influence of the prince of darkness.

"And unto him, the angel, thus to the kings and the priesthood, *power was given to scorch men with fire"*. In the state bible we read: To her power was given, that is *to the sun*. The words *angel* and *sun* are both masculine in Greek. The understanding of who is scorched is therefore arbitrary. The usual translation however fails, where the sun, Christ, is not scorched by the outpouring of the vial, but, just as in verse 10, darkened. In this, as well as in the other vials, the angel is, or are the powers in church and state of that period, even the persons, who by yielding to their sinful tendencies and passions, poured out God's judgements upon themselves and their nation. So it here also was the angel, who scorched the people by fire. Here we do not have to consider a holy fire or the image of the Holy Spirit, for they blasphemed the name of God, which does not come from the Holy Spirit. It was not the fire of the Holy Spirit (see first trumpet), but

167

the unholy fire of human passions and satanic anger, which reveals itself in discord, anger and strife. "What shall the false tongue give?" is asked in (Psalm 120:3) and the answer in verse 4, "sharp arrows of the mighty, with coals of juniper." "And the tongue is fire, a world of iniquity; and it is set on fire of Hell," (James 3:6), and it was not only its words but also its works, wherewith Christendom of that period blasphemed the good name by which ye are called. (James 2:7).

Verse 9. **"And men were scorched with great heat, and blasphemed the name of God, which hath power over these plagues".**

They were *scorched by the fire of anger* against God and their neighbours.

The fulfilment of this prophecy we see amongst other in the manifold quarrels and wars for supremacy, which took place between worldly powers and popedom during this period, and in the division, which after many quarrels and disputes, eventually occurred in this period between the Greek (Eastern) and the Latin (Western church, 1054 AD). To blaspheme God's name, the scripture describes as placing man above God, to desert Him and to rob Him of His honour (Isaiah 1:4; John 10:33; Mark 14:61–64) and to expect forgiveness not only from God but from man, (Matt. 9:3; Mark 2:7). In both meanings, the apostate Christendom scorched by the fire of Satan, committed this blasphemy. But the judgement of the Lord also hit the godless Christians of that period with falling-away, unrighteousness, blindness of those who did not walk in the truth, and thereby came to all sorts of foolishness. We here only mention the Easter laughter, or the creation of all sorts of laughing scenes performed by the spiritual leader at the Easter festivals in the church, to cheer up the congregation, the dancing and singing of songs in the church during festive services, instituted in 957 AD, Pope John X in full armour at the head of an army (914 AD), the indulgences (buying of sins) in 1002 AD, (probably the first in the church). The priests are forbidden to marry, with all its tragic consequences of immorality, etc. (1074 AD), the selling of spiritual ministries, named Simony, after Simon the sorcerer, the total corruption of the Roman court, which was ruled by all sorts of prostitutes, the well-known regnum scortorum (prostitute government), which began in the 10th century. The well-known crusades against the Saracens in Palestine, the so-called holy war, through which so many catastrophes were poured upon Europe, also belong to that period. The sorrowful consequence of this all is given in:

Verse 9. **"The people repented not to give God glory".** They ran unbridedly onward on the chosen way, which leads to perdition, and thereby came to the darkest time of God's word on earth, as we will find in the following period of the church.

OVERVIEW OF THE HISTORY OF THE CHURCH IN THE FOURTH PERIOD

FROM 914 – 1215

TRANSLATION OF THE FOURTH CANDLESTICK

Rev 2:18–29.

Verse 18. *Write to the bishop of the congregation, and to the whole congregation of the fourth period, which runs unbridled on the way to perdition: This says the Son of God, whose servants should be full of the Holy Spirit, yet through false shepherds and teachers, without the power of the Holy Spirit, corrupt His congregation of that period.*

Verse 19. *I know your works, and love, and faith, and service, and your patience, but your patience at the denial of My name, is greater than your courage in faith, to testify against it.*

Verse 20. *And I have against you, that you allow a godless spiritual power, calling herself a servant of God, to seduce My servants to apostasy and idolatry.*

Verse 21. *I gave her time to repent, but she repented not of her apostasies and false doctrine.*

Verse 22. *Therefore, I will cause her, and those who allow themselves to be seduced by her, to be delivered to their own heresies and find a false rest for their soul in their idolatry, but I will pour out great tribulation upon them, if they do not repent.*

Verse 23. *And those who follow in her teaching, will die the spiritual death, and My congregation of true believers will notice, that I am He, who searches the reigns and hearts, and I will give unto every one of you according to your works.*

Verse 24. *But those among you who do not accept the false doctrine of Satan, they have persecution and tribulation enough, I will put none other burden on them.*

Verse 25. *But that which you have, hold fast until I return.*

Verse 26. *He who endured unto the end, will in My day judge the unbelievers.*

Verse 27. *And he shall perform the judgement of My mouth upon them, and they will be avenged according to the power which I have received from My Father.*

Verse 28. *And I will give him Royal Power, and he will sit with Me on My throne, as I sit with My Father on His throne.*

Verse 29. *He that has an ear, let him hear, what the spirit says to the Congregation.*

FULFILLMENT IN THE HISTORY OF THE CHURCH

With VAN LOON we find, page 130:

"The most obvious condition of that period of the dark ages is the darkness to which Christianity generally had sunken," and page 136, *"The internal history of the church in that period reveals the most sorrowful scenes. All honest and upright believers whose accounts reach us in our time, unite their testimony to give us a picture of the greatest moral decay, which a church can produce.*

We found from GUERS about the previous period, page 147:

"The church sighed. For her it was a time of tribulations and humiliation; the testimonies were weak, the word of God was scarce, heresies and superstition greatly increased, like thistles and thorns, in a deserted field. In the 9th century, the invocation of saints and the veneration of their remains formed the emerging character of national religion."

Of this period GUERS says, on page 147:

The tenth century was truly worthy of its predecessor, it is the century which Cardinal Baronius, a zealous papist, names "an iron and barren century, a leaden century, fruitful in all evil: A century of darkness."

So dark was the light of the fourth candlestick, when it began to shine in the tenth century (914). But also, in this period of the church, some believing teachers and their followers still remained in her. For there would still be, as in verse 24, and according to our explanations, those who did not have this doctrine and had not known the depths of Satan. Church history names a Beranger, an Anselmus, an Adelbert[17], with their many followers and already existing Walsdense and Albigense and Manicheers of Orleans and Arras.

---

[17] Adelbert, the so-called apostle of Prussia said:
"Nothing is easier that to wear a mitre and a cross, but it is an earnest matter, to give account of a bishop ministry before the judge of the living and the dead." (Guers, page 177).

In that period there were also; as at all times, many simple believers, who had not bowed their knees to Baal. Luther says of them:

"There were souls, whom God called through the word of the Gospel and through Baptism. They walked in simplicity and humbleness of heart. Thinking that only the monks and the bishops were holy, while they considered themselves as laymen, worldly and impious persons. As they found nothing in themselves to be worthy of God's grace and to withstand His wrath, they cast themselves at the feet of the cross, they had taken refuge in the suffering and death of Jesus Christ and thereby in their simplicity were saved." (GUERS page192).

Remarkable is yet verse 24 the promise of Jesus to them, who had not known the depths of Satan. *"I will put upon you none other burden"* Indeed the tracking down of the so-called heretics in the church, and the severe persecution against them and against the heretics outside the church, only began in 1200 AD and thus belongs to the history of the following period, wherein the prince of darkness settled himself on the apostolic seat.

TRANSLATION OF THE FOURTH SEAL

<u>Rev 6:7, 8.</u>

Verse 7. *And when Christ opened the fourth period of the history of the church, I heard someone say, see, how the prophet ministry will come to nothing, and nobody shall guard against apostasy and estrangement from God and His anointed.*

Verse 8. *And I saw the congregation estranged from God and spiritually dead, and the name of the powers in church and state was: the spiritual death, and the spiritual and corporal realm of the departed both followed. And they killed the whole worldly-minded Christendom in terrible wars, and spiritually, through denying the Gospel of salvation, through death in sins and unrighteousness and through the power of all sorts of evil-doers.*

FULFILLMENT IN THE HISTORY OF THE CHURCH

VAN LOON says of this period, on page 130:

"The church (or priesthood) is the first to become unfaithful to her great calling, by hiding the living and illuminating word of God under a measuring bucket, and exchange and offer a series of human institutions to the truth. Seeking souls," page 136; *"from the pope to the lowest clergy*

are confronted with Simony, immorality, ambition, greed, unfaithfulness, contempt of the Holiest matters, unbelief and superstitions."

With GUERS concerning this, we find, on page 152, a statement by the Cardinal Baronius. *To fully understand the import thereof, we must remember, that he was a zealous defender of the Pope.*

In the year 1162 AD, Pope Alexander III riding his horse to his palace had Louis VII, king of France and Henry II, king of England walking beside him on each side, holding the horses' bridle like stable boys. Baronius described it: "A spectacle, *abominable to God, angels and humans*." (Milner 6:313).

"The 9th century," says the same Cardinal Baronius, "saw upon the seat of Peter, the throne of Jesus Christ, monsters with a scandalous life and totally corrupted morals. The popes of the 10th century even exceeded them in depravity. How despicable was then the Roman church under the tyranny of the scandalous prostitutes (Meretrices Sordidisimae), and what type of people do you think were the priests, deacons or cardinals, who were chosen by monsters?"

"In order to make the clergy independent from the civic powers, with the goal to form a separate body, which only Rome would acknowledge, Pope Gregorius VII forced the priests into celibacy, against the explicit prohibition of the Holy Spirit." "Out of this, the most horrible disorderliness was born."

"About the middle of the 11th century, three popes, men of pleasure, together sat on the throne of Rome, naïvely; Benedictus, Sylvester and John, they divided the income of the Holy Seat amongst each other, to lead a restful, sensuous and scandalous life, to the aggravation of the whole earth," says the Catholic Mainburg.

The bishop occupied their lives by enriching themselves and pursuing their passions, such as hunting, feasts, lusts and the war alternately as their pastime."

Compare this with what Paul through the Holy Spirit taught in the first Christian church about the Bishop, (1 Tim. 3:2, 3 and Titus 1:7, 9).

"The priests and monks scandalously wasted the income of the Roman Church with their mistresses. All flesh, say Baronius, had corrupted its way so badly, that a flood would have been insufficient, to wash away such impurities. The abominable sins of man required the fire of Gomorra."

"And I saw a pale horse, and His name that sat on Him was Death, and Hades followed with Him." This is according to the prophecy of the fourth seal, concerning this period of the church of Jesus Christ.

Here we saw the power, which the fourth rider possessed, to kill with spiritual hunger and death, his power to kill with the sword and the wild beasts of the earth, we will presently find its fulfilment in the fourth Vial.

TRANSLATION OF THE FOURTH TRUMPET

Rev. 8:12, 13.

Verse 12. *During the fourth period, the whole apostate church lost the little of what still remained in her of Christ, His light, His life and the comfort of the Holy Spirit, so that all Godly life completely disappeared from the church, from the state and from family life, and Christendom possessed neither any light of the Gospel, neither received it from its clergy.*

Verse 13. *And I heard in a prophetic testimony over the kingdom of God on earth, three times, Woe! called out over the believers, which still will come upon the earth, through the persecutions, which they will have to endure because of their faith and the testimony of the Gospel, in the three last periods of the church.*

FULFILLMENT IN CHURCH HISTORY

"Only inspired with the desire to spread her dominance to the conscience of mankind and even to the thrones of the princes, dominated by this one thought, Rome guided into the dark ways of heresies and revolt, those whom she had been commissioned to lead in the ways of the Lord. The prince of the powers in the air triumphed. Cardinal Baronius says of the 10th century; "Christ seemed to be in the throes of a deep sleep, the little ship was inundated by the waves and still worse, while the Lord slept, He had no disciples to wake Him up, whilst they themselves had fallen in a deep sleep." (Guers page 147, 148). The amount of ceremonies increased proportionally to their ever-growing name list. The feast of the dead is added to the existing or non-existing saints. The Maria cult is celebrated with more solemnity. Bells received the water baptism. At the same time, Purgatory daily received more power and recognition with the multitudes, who feared it just as much, or even more than the torment of Hell. One thought it possible to escape the punishment of the condemned, by dying under the prayers of monks and clergy, or by finding support in the merits and the protection of saints, one found many ways to escape the terror of Purgatory which the clergy increasingly propagated amongst the misled multitudes.

Page 150. The 11th century was also the period of the greatest austerity. Flagellation and voluntary torment originated. One believed that each sin had to be expiated in a corresponding way. And the penance, which one performed, existed in the reading of Psalms, in genuflection, especially under severe discipline, all things, says the Abbot Racine, which one can do, without repentance."

"Likewise, an unholy spirit took possession of the service, and the holiest memories of the church were disgraced by farces. The "Pentecost laughter" took a prominent place in the activities of the church. As the feast of Christ's resurrection had to be celebrated with joy, one sought in the preaching everything that could entice the laughter of the people. Many a preacher sang like a coo-coo, and many others mimicked the cry of a goose. The one told the unseemliest histories, the second recounted the journeys of Peter amongst others, how he cheated on the landlord by his 'laughter', and not having paid him (oecolan padius, de risu paschali). The lower clergy made use of the opportunity to deride their superiors. The temples were changed into theatres, and the priests in clowns. "If the service was like this, how must the morals have been?" (Merle d'Aubigne'. History of the reformation. I, Page 67. Medell, Translation 1837.)

About verse 13 enough has been said on pages 162 – 166.

TRANSLATION OF THE FOURTH VIAL

Rev. 16:5.

Verse 5. *The powers in church and state, poured out, in this fourth period, the judgements of God upon the Christian nations, by completely darkening Christ and His Gospel, they thereby have completely given their hearts and that of the people to all the sinful lusts and tendencies which are from the devil. And the people were scorched and angered by the fire of the bottomless pit, seeking forgiveness of sins by man and completely left the Lord God, who has the power to allow these plagues upon them, and they repented not, to give Glory to Him.*

FULFILLMENT IN CHURCH HISTORY

The Christian people from this fourth or Thyatirian period repented not from its broken vessels to return to the source or living waters and ran unbridled on the taken road of perdition and, thereby the end of this period, where it flows into the next, is totally revealed in the dark, most sinful time of Christ's church on earth. We read from Guers about this period, page 154, the following:

"The Saracenes, a rod of the Lord, constantly threatened Europe. These proud followers of Mohammed inundated France, Spain, Sardinia, and Sicily, who experienced the power of their weapons. They captivated several cities in Calabry and spread unrest up to the gates of Rome, Crete, Corsica and other Islands at last came under their power."

"They had only just completed their destructive work, when another, no lesser terrible rod, brought great fear to the idolatrous and depraved Europe. The Normans, a barbarous swarm, nations used to plunder and bloodletting, repeatedly invaded Germany, England, Friesland and France. They infiltrated Spain and in the heart of Italy. The old history of the French is filled with particulars concerning their bloody heroic deeds. In the 10th century their violence was so terrifying, that in France, England and Scotland, at public prayers, the following sorrowful word had to be added: A furore Nornanorum libera nos Domine! (Lord God, save us from the anger of the Normans!) Talking of plundering and destruction, wrought by these terrible children of the North, one writer wrote; "The courageous France desisted, as soon as it knew the power of their weapons, proud England is kidnapped, the rich Apuly saw his crown decay, the renowned Jerusalem and the illustrious Antioch bowed their heads under the yoke."

Page 148. "In order to increase their treasures, the priest spread a multitude of absurd opinions. There was not one, which instilled more fright than this, that judgement day was at hand. The imagination, which found its origin in Revelation 20, of John, filled the whole of Europe with fear and alarm. A great number of people daily broke off all civil and menial relations and gave all their possessions to the Roman church. Others gave themselves over to the priests with a solemn oath, literally becoming their slaves, meaning thereby softening the severity of their well-earned punishment. If a sun eclipse or a moon eclipse occurred, the unhappy citizens left their town, to hide in the deepest caves or rocks. The rich tried to appease heaven and the saints by giving beautiful presents to various spiritual orders. In various places, churches, palaces, and houses were razed to the ground, so strongly were people convinced that the end of the world had come. No language would be able to sketch the hopelessness of the people at this time, they did not lose their fear until they had seen the unhappy period come to an end, without having experienced the horrible happenings which they had feared so much come into fulfilment."

The scorching by the fire from the bottomless pit also resulted in 1054 AD, after appallingly many disputes, in the final schism between Eastern or Greek and Western or Roman churches, a schism, which is still prevalent in our days.

"Also, the crusades became the terrible rods, wherewith the Lord armed His arm. The famous crusades of the Dark Ages, which carried a religious and warring tendency, began at the request of the Popes, who sought to consolidate their territory in the East. The most famous and expensive monuments to human foolishness, which originated in any century, are the Crusades, which cost Europe millions of people. The Roman court was the true cause of it all, therefore heaven and earth will one day exact their accountability for all the blood, that it caused to flow. The promise of heaven, the threat of hell, curses, Anathema's, excommunication, nothing was to bring the West into complete revolt, and to fire a fanatical zeal against the East." (Gruers, page 221).

Open the book of worldly history even further, and you will find the tenth, eleventh and twelfth centuries described as centuries of disaster and need for the Christian nations. Pests, famine, terrible wars, servitude and oppression, this all harassed, as a rod of God in the three centuries, the sinful, apostate Christendom, who tried to forget its plagues in its intoxication with the greatest licentiousness and carnal lusts. "They blasphemed", says the prophecy in the fourth vial, "the name of God who has power over these plagues, and they did not repent to give Glory to Him."

That was the pouring out of the fourth vial of God upon the apostate Christendom. At the close of this period, we indicated to the reader, that Revelation further on is silent about the Greek church since she remained virtually unchanged from that time on up to now, as well as the Eastern sects which originated from her. From now on the Roman Church remains the stage on which the important happenings of the fifth and sixth periods take place.

The Greek church expanded more to the north, in the remote unpopulated Russia. The south and middle parts of Europe, infinitely more populated and the seat of civilization of that time, and of the greatest spiritual and worldly power, also remain the main stage of the performance of *"the Roman or Roman Empire," the fourth beast* of Daniel, which will continue until the return of the Lord (Dan. 7:7, 9, 11, 19–22, 23–27; Dan 2:34, 35, 40-45).

END OF FOURTH PERIOD

FIFTH PERIOD

SARDIS

The Remnant

FROM 1215 TO 1517 AD.

FIFTH PERIOD

SARDIS: *The Remnant*

FROM

Pope Innocent III and the 12th Council, 1215 AD.

TO

The Beginning of the Reformation, 1517 AD.

This period spans the thirteenth, fourteenth and fifteenth Centuries, when the highly elevated power of Popedom began to wane. Through the institution of the infamous Inquisitions, and the banning of the reading of the Bible, the church itself began to persecute and torture the believers and the witnesses of Jesus, but also through inner division and disputes, her worldly power and spiritual authority was gradually undermined, until with Luther in 1517 AD, the Reformation began.

In this period, **the fifth head of the beast**, (4th beast of Daniel: the Roman Empire), revealed itself.

This fifth head or Kingdom is **the fifth or the Anti-Christian Papal Mountain.** (Rev 17:9, 10).

FIFTH PERIOD

SARDISIAN TIME

or

THE FALL OF PAPAL POWER

5th Candlestick. Chapter 3,	5th Seal. Chapter 6,	5th Trumpet. Chapter 9,	5th Vial, Chapter 16,
And unto the angel of the church in Sardis write; These things saith he that hath the seven Spirits of God, and the seven stars; I know thy works, that thou hast a name that thou livest, and art dead.	And when he had opened the fifth seal, I saw under the altar the souls of them that were slain for the word of God, and for the testimony which they held:	And the fifth angel sounded, and I saw a star fall from heaven unto the earth: and to him was given the key of the bottomless pit. 2. And he opened the bottomless pit; and there arose a smoke out of the pit, as the smoke of a great furnace; and the sun and the air were darkened by reason of the smoke of the pit.	And the fifth angel poured out his vial upon the seat of the beast; and his kingdom was full of darkness; and they gnawed their tongues for pain, 11. And blasphemed the God of heaven because of their pains and their sores, and repented not of their deeds.
2. Be watchful, and strengthen the things which remain, that are ready to die: for I have not found thy works perfect before God.	10. And they cried with a loud voice, saying, How long, O Lord, holy and true, dost thou not judge and avenge our blood on them that dwell on the earth?	3. And there came out of the smoke locusts upon the earth: and unto them was given power, as the scorpions of the earth have power. 4. And it was commanded them that they should not hurt the grass of the earth, neither any green thing, neither any tree; but only those men which have not the seal of God in their foreheads.	_____ **Chapter 9, cont.** 8. And they had hair as the hair of woman, and their teeth were as the teeth of lions.
3.Remember therefore how thou hast received and heard, and hold fast, and repent.	11. And white robes were given unto every one of them; and it was said unto them, that they should rest yet for a little season, until their fellow servants also and their brethren, that should be killed as they were, should be fulfilled.	5. And to them it was given that they should not kill them, but that they should be tormented five months: and their torment was as the torment of a scorpion, when he striketh a man. 6. And in those days shall men seek death, and shall not find it; and shall desire to die, and death shall flee from them. 7. And the shapes of the locusts were like unto horses prepared unto battle; and on their heads were as it were crowns like gold, and their faces were as the faces of men.	9. And they had breastplates, as it were breastplates of iron; and the sound of their wings was as the sound of chariots of many horses running to battle. 10. And they had tails like unto scorpions, and there were stings in their tails: and their power was to hurt men five months. 11. And they had a king over them, which is the angel of the bottomless pit, whose name in the Hebrew tongue is Abaddon, but in the Greek tongue hath his name Apollyon. 12. One woe is past; and, behold, there come two woes more hereafter.
4. Thou hast a few names even in Sardis which have not defiled their garments; and they shall walk with me in white: for they are worthy.			
5.He that overcometh, the same shall be clothed in white raiment; and I will not blot out his name out of the book of life, but I will confess his name before my Father, and before his angels. 6. He that hath an ear, let him hear what the Spirit saith unto the churches.			

FIFTH CANDLESTICK

THE LIGHT OR THE SPIRITUAL LIFE OF THE CONGREGATION

> If thou hadst known, even thou, at least in this thy day
> the things which belong unto thy peace!
> but now they are hid from thine eyes.
> Luke 19:42

SARDIS, Rev 3:1–6

Sardis, in Asia Minor, was once the capital of Lydia and residence of the rich king Croesus, who the wise of that age, Solon, named unhappy. Presently, it is an extensive graveyard of ruins of heathen temples and Christian churches, destroyed by earthquakes and human hands, where there also exists no more Christian congregation. The poor little village of several huts, which one still finds there, is still named **Sart.**

The congregation of Sardis did not repent at the Son of God's admonishment and therefore, the threat predicted in verse 3 was fulfilled upon her, and not only in the first meaning of this letter to the original congregation of Sardis, but, as we shall see, also already fulfilled in its prophetic meaning, to the Christian church in her Sardisian condition and time.

Sardis, according to the Hebrew dictionary of the British Bible society and derived from the Hebrew *Sarad* means, **the Remnant.** So, the few names of verse 4 form the only remnant of the church of Christ, as we shall see, and it is from the small remnant of the church of that period, that the name "remnant" was taken.

Verse 1 **"Who has the seven spirits of God, and the seven stars?"** He is the Branch of the stem of Isaiah, upon whom 1st the Spirit of the Lord rests, 2nd the Spirit of wisdom and 3rd of understanding, 4th the Spirit of counsel, 5th of might, 6th the Spirit of knowledge and 7th the fear of the Lord. (Isaiah 11: 1, 2).

What are the **seven spirits of God**, already mentioned in (Rev. 1:4)? Rev. 4:5 says to us, that they were **seven lamps of fire**, burning before the throne of God. In this case, we have to think about seven different **powers** or **Revelations of the Holy Spirit.** For Paul teaches us this clearly, (1 Cor 12), when he would not have us ignorant concerning the spiritual gifts;

183

(verse 1) which (verses 4 and 6) there are diversities of gifts and operations, all given by the same God, the Holy Spirit, which works all in all.

Seven is the perfect number of God's revelation in man, and as such here is the symbolic number of the powers of the Holy Spirit in Christ Jesus, who is the fullness. If however, we rearrange the powers of the Holy Spirit, as Paul mentions them in (1 Corr 12:8–10), according to their individual and similar character then, we find the following seven individual gifts:

1. The gift of wisdom and knowledge of God.
2. The gift of faith.
3. The gift of healing.
4. The gift of might and miracles.
5. The gift of prophecy.
6. The gift of discerning the spirits.
7. The gift of tongues and interpretation of tongues.[18]

Yet, verse 11, "But all these worketh that one and the self-same Spirit, dividing to every man severally as he will."

These seven powers or gifts Christ exercised in his servants or bishops (**stars**) and His faithful, whom He equipped therewith, each according to what he required in his calling and personality. In the first or apostolic period these **gifts** of the Holy Spirit, as we have seen, were poured out upon the congregation. The Son of God, who had given these *seven powers of the Holy Spirit* to His congregation, now introduces Himself to the congregation of the Sardian period, to ask her which of these gifts, once entrusted to His church, still remained in her. The Sardisian congregation had however, like the useless and lazy servant in the prophetic parable of (Matt 25:15-30), buried the only remaining talent of wisdom and knowledge of God in the earth, under earthly power, glory and lusts of the flesh.

"I know thy works," says the Son of God. We cannot consider it as good works anymore, because immediately follows, **"that thou hast a name that thou livest and you art dead."**

These were therefore not works out of a living faith, not *works out of God* or pleasing to Him.

Jesus spoke of His own works, (John 5:36); "The works which My Father hath given me to finish, the same *works* that I do, bear witness of Me, that the Father hath sent me," and in (John 10:25): "The *works* that I do in My Father's name, they bear witness of Me." It follows that, He also spoke to

---

[18] A prophesy or prayer uttered in an incomprehensible language, which according to (1 Cor 13:1) seemed to be a heavenly or angelic language.

His Apostles, (Matt 5:16): "Let your light so shine before men, that they may see your *good works*, and glorify your Father which is in Heaven," and the Apostle Paul teaches us in (Eph 2:10): "For we are His workmanship, created in Christ Jesus unto *good works*, which God hath before ordained that we should walk in them," and of the unbelievers he says, (Titus 1:16): "They profess that they know God; but in *works* they deny Him, being abominable, and disobedient, and unto every good work reprobate." The **works of darkness** were therefore, those the Son of God saw in the congregation of Sardis, for *"thou hast a name that thou livest"* the name of Christians, and that thou livest in Christ, yet you have not the life, the characteristics of the Christian. I, Christ, have obtained no image in you, and without Me you can do nothing. *"You are dead"*, that is *dead in sin* and *unrighteousness*. Because, says (James 1:15), "and sin, when it is finished, bringeth forth *death*," and (James 5:20), "He that converteth the sinner from the error of his way shall save a soul from *death*."

Not to hope on the offered grace, not to believe in the Christ of God, as the Saviour of sinners, not to come to Him in humbleness and repentance, that is death, of which the Son of God speaks, therefore the Apostle John could, in the conviction of his faith say to the fellow believers, (1 John 3:14), *"We know,* that we have passed from *death unto life*, because we love the brethren," because that is the characteristic of our faith and is its fruit, "the love of the brethren," which love however in that period had nearly died off, to become alive again in the following period (Philadelphia, or brotherly love).

That is why the congregation of Sardis also receives the call of the Son of God,

Verse 2, **"Be watchful**, (from your death sleep in sin and unbelief), **and strengthen the things which remain, that are ready to die; for I have not found thy works perfect before God."**, and continues in with the call to repentance:

Verse 3 **"remember therefore how thou hast received and heard, and hold fast and repent",** but also the warning that the Lord would **come upon her as a thief** suddenly and unexpectedly.

This was the condition of the congregation of Sardis, as it is sketched to us in this candlestick, not less – as we will see in the seal and the trumpet and furthermore clearly in the overview at the end of this period – not less correctly is the condition of the so-called church of Christ in that period sketched in the prophetic meaning of these words. If the warning conveyed to the congregation of Sardis, in verse 3, that Christ would come as a thief, was literally fulfilled (see page 179) even so, in its prophetic meaning,

Christ in the Reformers came so unexpectedly as a thief, to disturb the temples of self-righteousness and the works of darkness of Popedom and the Roman church and to judge by the word of God. There were, however:

Verse 4, **"In Sardis**, as also in the Sardisian period of the church, **a few names** of people, e.g. yet a few believers, which have not **defiled** their **garments** with unrighteousness, but had washed the *spotted garment of the flesh* (Juda : 23) in the blood of Jesus Christ as pure and white as wool. (Rev 7:14, Isaiah 1:18). Church history teaches us to know the *witnesses of Jesus* in this dark period of the church: the Waldense, Thomas á Kempis, Wyklif, Wessel Gansfort, the Hussites, Savonarola, etc, all forerunners of the blessed heroes of the Reformation, and witnesses against the heresies of Popedom and the Roman church. Together they formed the small *remnant* of the once-established church of Jesus Christ.

Jesus Christ, who is the True and Faithful (Rev. 3:14, Rev 19:11), will also surely fulfil His promise upon those who overcome the terrible battle against Satan and His seduction with the word of God and,

Verse 5, **"clothe them in white raiment**; and (Matt 10:32) **not blot out their names out of the book of life, but confess their names before His Father, and before His Angels"**, (Luke 12:8, 9). The **white robes** mentioned here and in the previous verse, are well known as the image of **righteousness** and **holiness,** as the garments of salvation, and the robe of righteousness. (Isaiah 61:10). The Lord Himself uses this image in the parable of the lost, but found again, son (Luke 15:22), and of the man who was not wearing a wedding garment (Matt 22:11). In this context, Paul also says: (Rom 13:14), "But *Put ye on* (clothe yourselves with) the Lord *Jesus Christ*." i.e. Clothe yourselves with His righteousness. Over and above this the Revelation itself gives in (Rev 19:8) the meaning of the *fine linen,* as the *righteousness of the Saints,* and John also sees in (Rev 7:9 and 14) the great multitude, which came out of great (now imminent) tribulation, in *white raiment,* because (verse 14) "they had washed their robes, and made them *white* in the blood of the Lamb."

"The book of life, also mentioned in (Phil 4:3) and in (Rev 20:12), is not to be understood to be a physical book, (worldly things are not to be found in eternal life), but in the same sense as Paul (2 Cor 3:3), describes the congregation as an epistle of Christ, written not with ink, but with the Spirit of the living God, not in tables of stone, but in fleshly tables of the heart. Christ is eternal life, the **book of life** is: **all the merits of Christ,** for as many as by faith, were found therein, the name of the believers were also written **in that book** and were recorded therein with their new name as the overcomers in the dark ages of God's church on earth, whom their Lord and Head will confess as His **fellow overcomers** before **God and His angels**.

The actual congregation in Sardis no longer exists. In the prophetic meaning of members of the Christian congregation, having the name that they live, but are dead, she continues to exist and will exist until the return of the Lord. In the last years, alas! their number has alarmingly increased. In name only, Christendom, without the life of faith in Christ, expands itself more and more, together with the anti-Christian unbelief and the Laodicean self-sufficiency. If the prediction of Christ is fulfilled, His warning will also fulfill: "I will come upon you as a thief," "as a thief in the night" (Matt 24:43, 1 Thess 5:2–4). This time is not far away. The time is near. The time is here. In the sixth vial, which has already come and gone, the Lord warns once again and lastly, that He will come in the seventh period and again with these words, (Rev 16:15), "Behold I come as a thief. Blessed is he that watcheth." We already live in the seventh, the Laodicean period of the congregation for quite some time, and that will not last three hundred years. Godly patience is depleted concerning the denial of His name. The seventh vial is poured out, and the signs of the time announce it: He comes, who is to come, He comes unexpectedly, as a thief in the night. Therefore, **he that hath an ear, let him hear** (also a warning) **what the Spirit saith unto the churches.** "Watch therefore: for ye know not what hour your Lord doth come." (Matt 24:42).

And you, believers! Who love the appearance of Christ, and wait for His return, you who know the signs of the time, which the Lord has indicated, who know that "when these things being to come to pass, (Luke 21:28), then look up, and lift up your heads; for your redemption draweth nigh."

FIFTH SEAL

or

THE SPIRITUAL LIFE OF THE POWERS IN THE CHURCH AND STATE

> And fear not them which kill the body;
> But are not able to kill the soul.
> Matt. 10:28.

Rev 6:9-11.

In the first four seals we have seen that the colour of the horse which went out was the image of the condition of the congregation, concerning her spiritual life in each period. The white horse, the congregation, justified by the blood of Christ and living in all His institutions, was managed by her rider, who went out as a messenger of peace, with the Bow of Gospel Preaching, to overcome, and overcome.

The second, or red horse was the congregation in the following period, risen to outward honour, power and recognition, yet lower in Christian faith and divided by inward religious conflict, for the rider which sat there upon, was given a great sword and power to take away peace from the earth.

The black or third horse was the congregation sunk in spiritual darkness and governed by the rider or the clergy who with a fraudulent scale sold what was not the bread of life but exchanged the saving word of God's grace for human reasoning and superstitions. That was the first period of Popedom and the Roman church, which would be fully revealed in the following or fourth seal, as a pale or colourless horse, whose rider was named: death. We have seen in that fourth period how congregation, priesthood and powers in the state, all sunk in the deepest spiritual darkness, and were dead in sin and unrighteousness, even as if Christ never had come to earth to preach the way to Salvation, to seek what was lost, and as if He had never chosen and sent His representatives into the world with His commandments and promise recorded in (Matt 28:19, 20).

The fifth seal is now opened. The fifth period of Christ's church on earth and in heaven is predicted to John. Why did he not see a horse or rider in this period, but rather **the souls** of the Martyrs **under the altar**?

189

The answer is simple. In this fifth period, no visible church of Christ existed on the earth.[19]

Jesus says it already in the fifth candlestick, there are only a *small remnant* of believers in this Sardisian period of the church on earth, too few to be named a congregation. The church of Christ on earth is destroyed, killed and buried under the throne of Popedom.

With the church on earth, Christendom disappeared from the state. Instead of the powers in church and state on earth, who did not exist as Christians anymore, John **saw,**

Verse 9 **"When the Lamb had opened the fifth seal, under the altar the souls of those, who were killed for God's word and the testimony, which they had.**

As simple as these words may sound: **the souls under the altar**, we have here one of the most comprehensive images of Revelations. When the reader would with interested attention gather what we will find in God's word as an explanation of this comprehensive image, we can predict, that this explanation, although very easy to understand, will reveal to us deep mysteries from the Kingdom of God on earth and in heaven. Mysteries, not so well known, yet whose knowledge and understanding are necessary, so as to enable us to understand the happenings in the sixth and seventh periods.

The **altar** is an image, derived from the religious and worship of the Old Testament dispensation. That this dispensation was a foreshadow in earthly form, of the New Testament dispensation or the worshipping of God in spirit and truth; - that the Jewish temple with its priestly service was the fore-shadow of the Christian believers, whose High Priest is Jesus Christ, this all we must assume to be well known. If not, we can read it in: (Heb 8:1, 2, 5. Heb 9:8, 9, 11, 12, 23, 24. Heb 10:1, 19–22. Heb 13:10)

This foreshadowing of the Kingdom through the Israelitic temple is two-sided.

The *first* generally embraces all people: heathen, Jews and Christians, and depicts their relation to and their standing in the Kingdom of God. This is however not the case here.

---

[19] Our intention is definitely not to deny the Waldense and Hussites as witnesses of Jesus, as will later be seen, we only mean herewith, that the Popedom of the Roman church of that period was the immediate continuation of the church from the apostolic period and of the Church Fathers, now was not the church of Jesus Christ anymore, but of the father of all lies.

In order to fully clarify this, and to prevent confusion, we will refer to a note.[20]

The *second* or particular Christian meaning refers to the Christian nation only, and while Revelation is given to the Christians only, only this last one can be meant. For the congregation of Christians is the New Testament temple. (John 2:19–21. 1 Cor 3:16, 17. 1 Cor 6:19. 2 Cor 6:16. Eph 2:21, 22).

In her, we therefore must find the similarity with the temple of Israel, to which the Revelation here refers.

Altar (alta ara) means an **elevated place**. In the Tabernacle of Moses, (the hut, according to Luther) there were as in the later temple of Salomo, **two altars**. The first stood under the open sky in the forecourt of the tabernacle, *in front* of the Sanctuary or second part of the temple. This was the **burnt offering altar.** In the Sanctuary, behind it, was a second altar, the **incense altar**, to the worship and glory of God. *Only the priests* had access to it.

This altar of incense stood *in front* of the veil, behind which the Holy of Holies was hidden, where only the high priest could appear before the face of the Lord, who there spoke to the high priest from above the covering cherubim or the holy seat. This all we find clearly described in (Exod 25 and Heb 9:1–10) and was a foreshadow of the Christian service (Heb 8 and 9:11–28).

We will first examine the New Testament meaning of the Old Testament **burnt sacrifice altar**, upon which animals and offerings were sacrificed for the redemption of the sins of the people. This had to end when Christ, at the beginning of the new dispensation gave Himself as a ransom for sinners and died on the cross as a sacrifice, which was ever valid (Heb 7:27, Heb 9:23–28, Heb 13:10–15).

Christ is therefore the **ransom**, and the **cross** of Christ the **altar** of the New Testament dispensation. (Heb 13:10)

Whoever wants to have a part in Christ must also share His suffering, carry the cross as He did and as Christ died on the cross, to rise glorified,

---

[20] The general foreshadowing of the Kingdom of God through the Israelitic temple contains the following similarities:

OLD TESTAMENT TEMPLE	NEW TESTAMENT KINGDOM OF GOD
1. The forecourt of the Heathen	1. The Heathen
2. The forecourt of Israel	2. The Jews
3. The Sanctuary with the seven arms candlestick, etc. as material foreshadow of the spiritual goods in the New Covenant.	3. The Christians, with the New Testament spiritual holy goods as the church on earth.
4. The Holiest of the Holy	4. The Heaven of Salvation.

the old man in the Christian must be crucified, to rise renewed according to Christ's image in righteousness and holiness. (Rom 12:1).

Just as one would speak in an imaginary language, of "a cross to bear" or to bring sacrifices, e.g.: on one's country's altar, where only *sacrifice* for fatherland is considered, so also is the cross and altar upon which the Christian is sacrificed and upon which he is killed, of a spiritual nature. (Luke 17:33). This **altar** is the New Covenant or **Kingdom of God**. This New Covenant requires of us the sacrifice and death of the old man or threatens us with eternal death as sinners; for flesh and blood will not inherit the Kingdom of God.

On this altar, we must also offer our life in the name of Christ, if He requires it of us. This the witnesses of Jesus, the Martyrs, have done, the true Christians were always prepared for this "as men (Acts 15:26) who hazarded their lives for the name of our Lord Jesus Christ." Yet not only for the name of the Lord, and not to deny Him, who loved us, when we were still sinners, but Christians must try to bring their unbelieving fellow brethren to Christ and bring the gospel of mercy to them. For this, they must not love their own lives but be willing to sacrifice for Christ and be ready to sacrifice their life on the altar of the New Covenant. Paul was ever ready for this; (2 Cor 12:15, Luth, translated. Phil 2:16–18. 2 Tim 4:6). He also has, as most of the Apostles, except John, given His life in sacrifice to Christ and His brethren. Many missionaries and evangelists have done the same, even under Popedom, up to the previous fourth period. In this fifth period, however, this all died in the Papal church and only lived forth in the Waldense, etc. who were horribly persecuted as heretics. They found themselves unsafe on their high mountains and remote valleys and had to hide in the most unreachable caves and cliffs, and yet were killed in their thousands for the word of God and the gospel of Jesus Christ.

These living therefore, who did not love their soul unto death, but were corporally and morally killed, made ineffective and bound by Popedom, could therefore not openly bring the witness of God's word to the world, neither live according to their heart's desire and the requirements of God's word to serve and glorify Him before heaven and earth, **it is them, who lay under the altar**. They bore the revilement of the world for Christ's sake, and were crucified and killed on the altar of the New Covenant.

With these living were bound, however, as souls also belonging under the altar, **the souls of all the believers**, whom from Stephen, the first Christian Martyr, (Acts 7:59, 60) up to this period had been **killed for God's word** and the testimony they had to bring.

John was transposed in the spirit on the day of the Lord and looked back from there, from the beginning of the Christian church up to the fifth period; he thus sees all the martyrs up to that time gathered *under the altar*, or at the *foot of the altar*. The blood of the sacrificial animals was poured out at the foot of the altar (Lev 1:5). The life or the soul was however in the blood (Gen 9:4. Lev 17:11), and so, according to this image, the souls of the witnesses of Jesus, who are sacrificed upon the altar of the New Covenant, lay gathered at the foot of that altar. **They, with the yet-living and future believers, form the New Covenant people**.

Therefore, Paul also says, after he had spoken concerning the departed believers, (Heb 11:39, 40), that they **had not received the promise**, "God having provided some better thing for us, that **they without us should not be made perfect**."

The living believers cannot therefore be made perfect without the departed, nor these latter without the former. They belong together and are bound to each other, for as much as both altars were **one altar**, they together formed **one body**, of whom Christ is the head, and He is Lord of the living and the dead. That is the higher meaning of the "fellowship of the Saints", which the church adopts in her articles of faith, over which we later will still shed lighter.

Summarising once more all the aforesaid, we must understand the **souls under the altar** to be the **still living believers** in that period and all the **previously departed** people, "who sacrificed their souls (Acts 15: 26) for the name of our Lord Jesus Christ," and who morally and bodily were killed on the altar of the New Covenant, which was foreshadowed by the sacrificial altar to the old testament. But also all the witnesses of God of the Old Covenant, who suffered and died for the name of the Lord, or sealed their faith with their death, belong to these souls under the altar.

There was however, as we mentioned, a second altar in the tabernacle: the *altar of incense* where the words '**souls under the altar**' receive a second meaning. The smoke on the altar of incense was the second part of the service. They however form a **unity, one altar.** Even so the souls at the sacrificial altar, with those of the altar of incense. The incense of the New Covenant are the prayers of the believers (Heb 13:10, 15. Rev 5:8)

There is much in the Old and New Testament, which is normally regarded as poetic language and metaphorical expressions. However, when one compares the shadowing of the Old Covenant and the essence of the New Covenant, and therewith follows the indications of the Lord Jesus and His Apostles in the New Testament, then one comes to altogether different solutions, a deeper insight of the meaning, and glorious revelations, which otherwise remain mysteries.

We thus find here also, based on the undeceiving word of God, a clear representation of the whole **Kingdom of God on earth and in heaven** in their respective connection. The Saviour names it in its entirety: the Kingdom of Heaven, distinguishing it from the Heaven of Salvation.

Let us once more remember the layout of the temple or tabernacle of Israel. This consisted of three parts, encountered from the front, as follows:

1st. *The Forecourt with the burnt sacrifice altar.* This court was not divided into two parts, as long as Israel wandered, and the Tabernacle stood in the midst of Israel. In the stone temple of Solomon, this forecourt consisted of two parts, the outer: *the forecourt of the heathen*, and the inner: *the forecourt of Israel.* These both were not covered but in the open air.

2nd. *The Sanctuary with the golden altar of incense.* Only the *priests* had access to it. At the back, it was separated by a *veil* from:

3rd. *The Holiest of Saints, or the Holy of Holies,* wherein was the arc of the Covenant or the seat of mercy. Only the *high priest* could enter here.

The Sanctuary and the Holy of Holies therefore together formed *one building, the Holy Temple*, and were divided by a veil, through which the high priest only had access.

This picture of the temple, which we will still require in the sixth and seventh periods, represents an image of the *earth and heaven for believers*, or the *Kingdom of Heaven*, as Jesus names it. This is not our idea but is specifically taught in (Heb 8:5) where it literally says in the original text, "who serve unto the example and **shadow of heavenly things**," and in (Heb 9:23, 24), "It was therefore necessary that **the patterns of things in the heavens** should be purified with these (blood); but the heavenly things themselves with better sacrifices than these. For Christ did not enter into the Holy places made with hands, which are the **figures of the true**; but into heaven itself, now to appear in the presence of God for us."

That this *temple* was to be an *exact image of the Heavenly things*, we read in (Exod 24:15–18 and Exod 25:40) where Moses receives the command from God: "**And look that thou make them after their pattern, which was shewed thee in the Mount.**" Also referred to in (Heb 8:5).

If therefore the layout of the earthly temple is a true image of the Heavenly temple, which is: the New Testament congregation on earth and in heaven, we then obtain the following similarities:

- THE TABERNACLE OR TEMPLE of the
  - OLD TESTAMENT

- The forecourt of the Heathen

- 1. The forecourt of Israel with the burnt sacrifice altar of the Old Covenant

- 2. The Sanctuary with the altar of incense, where only priests had access.

- 3. The Holy of Holies, where Jehovah sits on the throne of mercy, and the high priest only was allowed.

- THE KINGDOM OF HEAVEN of the
  - NEW TESTAMENT

- The preaching of God's grace to the unbelievers on earth.

- 1. The already saved believers on earth or *first* heaven, the church heaven with the altar of the New Covenant, the cross of Christ and of the Christians.

- 2. The *second* heaven, or the residence of the believers, (*Priests*, Rev 5:10), **after** death, (Paradise)[21] where they wait for the day of the Lord.

- 3. The *third* heaven, or heaven of heavens, where God the Father sits on the throne of grace, and Christ at His right hand as our High Priest, here all the saved will be gathered to the joy of the Lord.

For the unbelievers, who refuted the preaching of God's grace, and therefore did not enter the Kingdom of Heaven here on earth, no place is prepared there, they first come in the dark realm of the departed and thereafter in hell (Gehenna) (Matt 5:29, 30).

If this should sound strange and unbelievable to you, we will refer you to several texts in the New Testament, which totally agree with it and not only clearly prove this image, but in return enlighten and clarify it.

Paul teaches us, (2 Cor 12:1–4), that a great revelation was given him in a vision. In the first two verses, he relates that he was transposed to the *third heaven*. Then there must also exist a *first* and *second* heaven. Whether he was there in the body or not, he claims not to know, as well as having heard nothing in this heaven. With the same testimony, that he does not know whether he was there in body, he begins anew in verse 3, and relates also, to have been transported to paradise, and there heard unspeakable words.

---

[21] The scriptures probably name this blissful part of the realm of the departed: Paradise, because the fallen man in Adam, is restored to paradise conditions through the Salvation work of Jesus Christ.

It is clear, that Paul here speaks of *two* different places, the first, as the highest, he names first and thereafter the lower or paradise, where he had to go through, to come in the third heaven, just as the high priest in the temple could only come into the holiest of Holy *by going through the sanctuary.* More so it seems, because Paul speaks of the *third heaven,* which cannot be understood in any other way, as the habitation of God himself. There must therefore be a second heaven; and this is paradise, through which he went when ascending and descending, to and from the third heaven. The first heaven, corresponding to the forecourt of Israel, is the church of Jesus Christ, the New Covenant nation, which is spiritual Israel (Gal 3:7, 16, 29) and therefore the Kingdom of God on earth or the church heaven.

In this sense Paul also says: "Blessed be the God and Father of our Lord Jesus Christ, who hath blessed us with all spiritual blessings in *heavenly places in Christ.*" (Eph 1:3), and: "Even when we were *dead* in sins, hath *quickened* us together with Christ, (by grace we are *saved*); and hath raised us up together and made us *sit together in heavenly places* in Christ Jesus." (Eph 2:5, 6). Blessed are the believers therefore already here on earth in the first heaven or the fellowship with Jesus Christ, and the incorporation in His body, the church, of which He is the head and the High Priest.

When holding fast to the concept of the three heavens in the Kingdom of God, all the texts mentioning heaven or different heavens in the Holy Scripture become clear to us, and the natural, visible, blue atmosphere is obviously not in question here.

When Jesus and the Apostles then say, that in the last days signs will appear in heaven, that the stars (teachers) will fall from heaven, etc. then we do not expect this to happen in the firmament, but with us and around us in the church of Christ, the heaven in which we live, and the signs are there, they are present in great numbers for those who have spiritual eyes to see and recognise them.

The second heaven is then the part of the spiritual realm, where the souls of the believers are preserved and live. This the Lord Jesus also indicated in His word to the murderer on the cross. "Today shalt thou be with Me in paradise." This paradise (where paradise means *place of bliss*) is therefore nothing else than the heaven of the blissful; for, Jesus did not go to heaven when He died, but to paradise, (Luke 23:43-46), risen on the third day and only later ascended to heaven. He, Himself also teaches that the judgement and the allocation of and the entrance into eternal salvation will only take place on the great judgement day, when (Rev 20:12, 13) the books will be opened, and each shall be judged according to their works and the sheep shall be separated from the goats, the believers shall enter eternal life, and the unbelievers into eternal perdition. On the great day of Judgement, the souls of the believers, who up till then were preserved in paradise, or the second heaven, reunited with their glorified resurrection bodies, go to the third heaven, where God sits on the throne of mercy in actual fact, just as He was foreshadowed by the seat of mercy.

This image is the teaching of the Holy Scripture. One should, however, be mindful of the fact that this teaching has not yet been brought to its perfect development. In (Acts 2:27), Peter says, that David prophesied of Christ: "Because thou wilt not leave my soul in *hell*[22] (Psalm 16:10). Here the word S*cheol,* in Hebrew, and *Hades* in Greek, both names for the realm of the departed, are used. Peter names the departed (1 Pet 3:18–20) "the spirits in prison." The same truth we also find again in (2 Pet 2:4), "For if God spared not the angels that sinned, but cast them down to hell, and delivered them into chains of darkness, *to be reserved unto judgement."* Similarly, in (Jude 6) exists also, under a pseudo (false) name, a so-called gospel of Nicodemus, in which the second part consists of a narration of the descending of Jesus into hell, as the title of that gospel suggests. The power of language, the glow and living representation which characterise this writing points to an earlier origin perhaps already in the first, at least in the second century. The high value, attached to this gospel during the first century, may not be accepted as proof of the *correctness* of this dogma, but is definite proof that it existed in the Christian church. So it was also, though somewhat later, maybe because this dogma was doubted, included in the apostolic creed as "descended into hell". Jewish theology also teaches a dark realm of the departed (*scheol)* and names it the beginning of our time base: paradise.

---

[22] The translation of the New Testament in the state translation made no distinction between the Greek words, Hades, Gehena and Tartarus, but translated all three with hell. V. d. Palm rendered the difference more clearly. As reproof he mentions that *hades* means the habitation of the souls after death, the realm of the departed or spiritual realm. This word we find and read as realm of the departed in (Luke 16:23, Acts 2:27-31, 1 Cor 15:55, Rev 1:18, Rev 20:13,14). The blissful place, where the believers reside in Hades, is the paradise.

Gehenna is actually hell or the place of punishment of the lost. (Matt 5:20, 30, Matt 10:28, Matt 23:15, Mark 9:43, Luke 12:5).

Tartarus is a deep pit, (2 Pet 2:4), and the residence of devils. In other texts, where hell is read, this word does not reflect its actual meaning, but as image for death, or powers of darkness.

The Western church fathers generally believed this until the fifth century and was continued into papal times, when it was malformed into "purgatory", from which the priest had the power to deliver the souls, and immediately make them go to heaven.

It could not be different, when also in the protestant church, after the Reformation, this belief from the first centuries had to appear, although in a slightly altered form. It was certain, that at death the soul separated from the body. The body goes to dust, to be raised immortal on judgement day. But where did the soul reside? It must surely be somewhere. One then believed that the souls of the believers were already blissful with God in heaven, and those of the unbelievers tormented in the place, where the worm does not die, nor the fire extinguished. Then, however the great judgement day, on which Jesus lay so much weight and emphasis, and of which He says: "and then He shall reward every man according to his works." (Matt 15:27), would become, forgive us the word, a travesty, a forgiveness centuries after the forgiveness, to a condemnation, centuries after the incarceration. Moreover, one understood, that on the day of judgement a much higher state of Salvation, and a heavier state of misery would follow. One found in this, that the souls of believing departed, in their longing for their resurrection body, did not yet enjoy full salvation, but on the day of judgement, clothed and reunited therewith received greater salvation, just as the lost, clothed with their resurrection body, will experience a deeper misery.

This whole explanation is not founded on any text in the Bible, and conflicts against all that is revealed in the Holy Scriptures concerning the future things; then for instance: Samuel with the witch of Endor, the son of the widow of Sarepta by Elias, Tabitha by Peter, the son of the widow of Naïn, the daughter of Jaïrus, and Lazarus by Jesus would all be **called back from heaven**. What then is the meaning of the preaching (1 Pet 3:19) to the spirits, which are in *prison* or *place of rest*, as it literally is stated.[23]

If we now take and understand the following part of Revelation, summarised in a few words, how that the Holy word of God teaches us concerning the life of the believers in and after this life, and as in the blue-print of the earthly temple, is shadowed as a visible image of the invisible heavenly temple.

1. *The forecourt of the temple is the earthly life.*

---

[23] The word *prison* here does not mean *punishment*, but *preservation*. The word in the original text does not only imply the place of the *preservation* but also the *condition* of the *waiting* souls. "They have not yet received the promise, that they without us should not be made perfect," (Heb. 11:40), but they are waiting for us. See also (Rev 6:11).

    a.   *In the forecourt of the heathen,* are the unrepentant, who are without Christ here on earth.

    b.   *In the forecourt of Israel,* are the believers or the spiritual Israel; they offer flesh and blood, the old man, on the burnt offering altar of the New Covenant (this is the cross of the Christian), of which Christ is the High Priest. This forecourt of the Kingdom of heaven is the *first* or *earthly heaven*: the heaven of the church of the New Testament.

  2. *The Sanctuary of the temple is probably the place or condition of the Christians after death* and before the resurrection of the flesh, therefore till the day of the Lord. This place and condition is named *paradise* and is the blissful part of, or the blessed condition in the realm of shadows, or Hades. The Lord Jesus is also there the High Priest, and offers the prayers of the believers on the *incense altar* of the New Covenant. (Rev 8:3, 4). This tabernacle is the *second heaven* or the condition of the believers after death in paradise, where Paul heard unutterable words. Here the souls wait under the altar of the fifth seal.

  3. *The Holy of Holies* is the heaven, *where God the Father* sits on the *throne of mercy,* where Christ went alone as our High Priest (Heb 6:20) and pleads for His own, who also on the day of the Lord will enter with Him in that Holy of Holies and will sit with Christ on His throne, as He sits on the throne with the Father, for God then is all in all. This *third heaven,* or the heaven of heavens, to which Paul was transported, and which Stephen, full of the Holy Spirit, saw opened and the glory of God therein, and Jesus standing on the right hand of God. (Act 7:55, 56).

This third heaven is the actual residence of the Son of God, from where He as High Priest goes out to the realm of the departed (the Sanctuary) and offers the prayers of the departed on the incense altar, but also comes to us in the forecourt of Israel, at the burnt offering altar and is *among, with* and *in* us. (Matt 28:20, 2 Cor 6:16, Eph 3:17).

"And would our beloved departed not be in heaven?", would perhaps ask a mournful heart, who mourns a beloved departed. "We thought they already had it so good." – Be satisfied, mournful soul! Your departed who died in Jesus have it well.

The scriptures here also have provided comfort for you. Their death was gain. Read (Luke 16:20–25), what the Lord tells you of the poor Lazarus: "He is comforted." If the disciple of Jesus here on earth, although under much suffering and persecution, is already blissful in the communion of faith with his Lord and Saviour, how much more there, where in paradise he experiences what he believes, where no temptations of flesh and blood grieve the faithful anymore, where he lives in bliss with his fellow disciples. If you entrust your *life* and that of your beloved to Jesus, how *eagerly* will He not preserve the souls for which He suffered and died. He loves them; also in the realm of the departed they are His, for He is Lord of the living and the dead. They are already blissful in the surety that they have gained the crown of life and wait for their glorious goal at the end of days.

Verse 10. **"And they cried with a loud voice, saying, how long, o Lord, holy and true, dost thou not judge and avenge our blood on them that dwell on the earth?"**

In this fifth period the Roman church was as the direct successor of the apostolic church, fallen away and degenerated so far from the gospel preaching of Jesus Christ, that there existed no priests in her anymore. On earth only the Waldense and the few forerunners of the Renaissance were the carriers of God's word. They however were killed for God's word and for the testimony, which they had to bring. This testimony was different in each period, according to the degree the church or the people deviated from keeping the word of God and truth. If the martyrs of the first period had to testify against heathen idolatry with its unrighteousness, those killed in the Arian disputes and persecutions of the second period against the denial of Jesus' Godhead, against the incorporating of human reasoning into Godly truth, in both the following periods the blood witnesses of Jesus had to raise their voices against the accelerating decay of the church to all sorts of unrighteousness, carnal-mindedness and superstitions. All these blood-witnesses of Jesus, as well as the departed overcomers (Rev 2:7, 11, 17, 26) from the four elapsed periods, John sees in this fifth seal, laying at the foot of the altar, i.e. of both altars, shouting with loud voices to Jesus, but not for revenge. They, who allowed themselves to be killed as sheep, call out not for revenge for their blood, for then they would have called out to Jesus the righteous; but they who had been unappreciated in their testimony, which they had brought, and were persecuted and killed for their testimony, they, who were called heretics by the Roman church: they call to Jesus as the Holy and True.

They ask, they plead with Him to reveal Himself as the Holy and True one, and to confirm that the testimony, which they brought and sealed with their blood, was His commission, by His judgement over His enemies and their followers, and thereby to justify them before heaven and earth as His messengers and witnesses.

Verse 11. **"And white robes were given unto every one of them; and it was said unto them, that they should rest yet for a little season, until**

their fellow servants also and their brethren, that should be killed as they were, should be fulfilled".

From the contents of verse 11 it also seems, that in their prayers and sighing of verse 10 there lay yet another meaning. From the answer in verse 11, that they would yet rest a little time, it seems for all that they looked forward, full of longing, to the coming of the Lord on earth, which would coincide, as they knew with the terrible judgement over His enemies, and the revenge of the Lord over the spilled blood of His witnesses. At His return they would be clothed with their resurrection body and would be allowed to enter the kingdom of glory (1 Thes 4:16), as the first born from mankind resurrected from the realm of the departed.

From this revelation of the fifth seal, we again clearly see proof, of what we have shown concerning the conditions of the souls in the realm of the departed. For they still had *to rest a little time and abide there*, until Jesus would resurrect them to eternal salvation before the throne of God, to their experience, what no eye has seen, what no ear has heard, and has no come up in any human heart, but which God prepared for those who love Him. (Compare the ref. Catechism, Question 58). In this last sentence, their pleading was not yet answered. They were given white robes or robes of honour, as V. D. PALM says.

For the Martyrs of Jesus, killed in this period, white robes of Salvation were promised to them in the candlestick (Rev 3:5), or the righteousness of the saints (Rev 19:8), to enter into paradise. For the already killed Martyrs from the previous periods, it was however not the robes of righteousness of their Saviour Jesus Christ. For, as believers they were already clothed in garments of salvation and the robe of righteousness (Isaiah 61:10), yet these were garments of honour, which they received, that is: the answer to their prayers for righteousness before heaven and earth, that the testimony they had brought was not their own but that of Jesus Christ Himself.

In the scriptures, we often find the ancient custom described, that one upon whom honour was to be bestowed or to be restored, would be clothed with a pure white robe.

This image is used here in the heavenly vision of John to show, that Jesus would justify the testimony of all His martyrs in this time in heaven and earth. And indeed, in this period, man from many quarters stood up as witnesses against the teaching of the Roman church, as messengers of the same truth, which the martyrs had confessed and who thereby justified their testimony. These are the many forerunners of the Reformation, which church history mentions in this period, which continually increased; finally at the end of this period culminated in the great figure of Luther, the pioneer for the restoration of the word of God and faith to salvation.

In the day of the Lord John saw (Rev 7:9–17) among the great multitude, which no man could number, all these Martyrs of the Lord clothed with white robes, yet now not under the altar anymore, but standing before the throne of God and the Lamb.

The souls under the altar had to wait a little while until their fellow servants and brethren would join them, who would still be killed, as they had been. They arrived there already in this period, the Martyrs for the word of God; the Pattarenians, the Cathars, the Albigense and Waldense in their thousands and thousands under the persecutions of the inquisitions, yet in greater numbers in the next period, that of the reformers; and still the souls rest under the altar, united with their brethren, who joined them. They still rest, for their number is *not yet fully there*; more brethren must still join them, who will also be killed for their faith as the Martyrs from the anti-Christian time. And this time is not far off. We do not have to wait for a personal anti-Christ, just as little for a personal great whore (Rev 17), neither will ever come. They are, as we shall see later (in the seventh period) the representatives or images of the anti-Christian state power, and the fallen away church of God. That the whore already exists in the modern, ungodly destructive teaching and preaching in the Protestant, Roman, Greek and other Christian churches, no one who compares her with God's word will deny. But also the anti-Christian state power reveals itself in neighbouring countries. Her aim is: one European republic, her motto: humanity, her programme: "Abolition of Christian religion, away with the clergy! Hang the last king to the intestines of the priests! (historical).

And her power will come over the earth, as surely as God's words predict it, and her humanity will degenerate into anger against everyone, who will not recognise, respect as holy or worship the beast (Rev 13,14), the anti-Christian state and the ungodly humanity as the only true government and single human obligation:

> "See here your gods: Art and Power and Industry!
> And hence! No religion anymore except that of a genie!"

That will be for those of the truth, the time of great persecutions, such as was never yet on earth, as Jesus teaches us (Matt 24). Then, the last brethren will come, who still have to be killed for their faith, the Martyrs, still before the eminent glorification, as workers hired at the eleventh hour; but the hour is also there, that to the faithful witnesses of Jesus, the voice from heaven will come: "Enter thou into the Joy of the Lord." (Matt 25:21). But then also the word will be fulfilled, which was written for their fellow servants, their brethren, who still have to be killed as they were; "**BLESSED** ARE THE DEAD WHICH DIE IN THE LORD, **FROM HENCEFORTH.**" (Rev 14:13). These will not see Hades, but go *directly* in – in the joy of their Lord.

FIFTH TRUMPET

THE FIRST WOE,
OR
THE CONDITION AND EFFECT OF THE GOSPEL PREACHING

> The time cometh, that whosoever killeth you
> will think that he doeth God service.
> John 16:2.

Rev 9:1-12.

We have seen that in this period the church of Jesus did not exist anymore. Of gospel preaching no specific mention can be made, nor of explanation of the gospel among the heathen, which had completely stopped in this period. The Crusades, which took place in this period, under the semblance of religious fervour (crusades), did not deserve the name of gospel preaching to the Gentiles. The actual subject, which the trumpet sketches to us in imagery is therefore the condition of the Roman church in the three centuries before the Reformation and her actions against those who still believed in the gospel of Jesus Christ.

At the **sounding of the fifth Angel**, or at the beginning of this period, the Lord allowed John to see, verse 1, **a star, fallen from heaven on the earth**. If this image is a true reflection, as the reader of the previous explanations immediately will understand, of Popedom in this period, that of a **preacher of the gospel (star)** which had become an **unbelieving world ruler**, and, **fallen from heaven**, now stood at the head of worldly powers and rule (**the earth**); a perfect impersonation of this image we find in Pope Innocent III, who, at the beginning of this period, had attained the peak and highest revelation of papal power. He deposed emperors and kings, appointed others in their place, released the nations of their faithfulness and obedience to their rulers, banned their kings and emperors[24], took away their lands, to appropriate them for the worldly crown of the church; in one word, nearly

---

[24] The papal ban in those days meant something totally different than presently. King Victor Emanuel laughed at it, and the clergy themselves disregarded it. Previously it stood equal to a declaration of freedom.

the whole earth lay under the despotism of Popedom, which with the greatest arbitrariness and cruelty yielded its iron sceptre.

From the humble Apostle Peter[25] an emperor Nero had emerged. "How art thou fallen from heaven, o morning star." (Isaiah 14:12) King of the new Babylon!

What this fallen star achieved and the consequences thereof, we find described in the following 11 verses. This image has been explained in many different ways. V.d. PALM regarded it as a description of roaring zealots and plunderers, who at the siege of Jerusalem by the Romans, infested and destroyed the land. (70 A.D.). Gärtner considered it as the Arian Gothic Nations (400 – 600 A.D.); LE ROIJX as the future armies of the anti-Christ. These happenings occurred during the time of 1800, as we said in our introduction. The explanations of the fifth trumpet must therefore not be clear when they are interpreted so differently and at such diverging times.

That with this trumpet a highly remarkable and special event in the church history is predicted, we can expect, 1^{stly} because of the great detail, wherewith this trumpet is described in the otherwise short but powerful images of revelation, and 2^{ndly} from the totally strange and personal images. If our maxim and explanation is the true one, we again must find all these images explained unconstrained and clearly in God's Holy Word, and recognize the explanation of the prophecy immediately in the history of this period. We will recognize them as the most remarkable and the most devilish phenomenons in the Christian church: the Dominicans, Franciscans and Inquisitors in the persecution of the Waldense, Albigense, Hussites, etc.

To the star, which had fallen on earth or the unbelieving Popedom in this period**, is given the key of the bottomless pit. And he opened the bottomless pit.**

The Lord Jesus gave to His disciples (Matt 16:19) the *keys* of the *kingdom of heaven*; which were 1st according to the last part of that verse *the power* and 2nd according to (Luke 11:52) the *knowledge*.

To the apostate disciples here is given the key (power) to open the bottomless pit.

In (Rev. 20:1–3) the angel comes with the **key of the bottomless pit**, to bind the old serpent, the devil; that this *bottomless pit is the habitation of the fallen angels or devils,* is revealed by (Rev 9:11) and (2 Peter 2 4). Popedom in its superstition and unbelief had the key to the realm of

---

[25] "Silver and gold have I none." (Acts 3:6).

darkness, and through awakening the religious desires it granted to the evil spirits from the bottomless pit access to the hearts of men. (Matt 15:19).

Not without particular meaning does it speak here of the *bottomless pit*. We find herein the shadow image of the *pit of living waters*, which springs forth to life everlasting, of which Jesus speaks. (John 4).

The gospel was not yet mutilated enough by human findings of Popedom and the Roman clergy; the darkness was not yet deep enough. The word of God had to completely disappear from the earth. The Council of Toulouse in 1229 forbade the reading of the Bible.

The pit, wherein the living water of the pure gospel welled forth, and wherewith the priesthood of the first centuries had quenched Christendom believers' thirst, was not dried up and became a bottomless pit, wherein only evil spirits resided. The apostate priesthood opened this bottomless pit and released the evil spirits to destroy the remaining believers on earth of this period.

In verses 2 and 3, a total image of a swarm of locusts is represented, which came out of the pit, destroying all greenery in the unlucky fields, over which they migrated. Do you know the description, which travellers gave thereof, how they rise as a cloud on the horizon? Coming nearer, the cloud becomes smoke, gliding thickly over the earth, still nearer locusts are seen in the apparent smoke, as if they came out of it. In a blink of an eye, they have devoured all green and grass and trees, and leave behind only famine, destruction and death in the unlucky affected regions.

What a destructive swarm they are, we find described in the Bible in (Amos 7: 1, 2. Nahum 3 : 15 – 17. Joel 1, 2.).

A more appropriate comparison for the rise and deeds of the Dominicans, Franciscans and Inquisitors, than the plague of locusts, would be hard to find, and that these evil persecutors of Christendom for all that are depicted thereby, becomes clear when we analyse each separate image of this whole parable by the word of God.

Verse 2. **"And there arose a smoke out of the pit, as the smoke of a great furnace."**

As a **smoke**, which rises, is described in (Isaiah 14:31), as the *destructive hordes*, which would come over Palestine, from Babylon.

A *smoke* in His nose is God's description of the unrepentant sinners. (Isaiah 65:3–5).

The *lifting of smoke* is the result of *wickedness and bitterness against his brother*. (Isaiah 9:18, 19).

A fiery oven is what David calls (Psalm 21:8, 9) the **enemies and haters of God.**

For a *destructive judgement*, the image of a furnace or *fiery oven* is also used in (Mal 4:1, and Zech 12:6); for *persecution* in (Deut 4:20). The meaning is thus, the godless, blinded by self-righteousness clergy of the Roman church, would come out of the bottomless pit as evil spirits.

"**And the sun and the air were darkened by reason of the smoke of the pit.**"

The sun is **Christ,** the Sun of righteousness, (Mal 4:2), as we clearly saw in the fourth trumpet.

The **air** (actually atmosphere, *ayr*) is the spiritual atmosphere, of which Paul also speaks (Eph 2:2, and Eph 6:12).

Later we will see that the seventh or the Laodicean period, wherein the people rule (*aou dikaia*) the seventh vial is also poured in the air. When we observe the revolutionary-democratic tendencies in political circles, and the anti-Christian hatred against Christendom, as it already spread amongst the nations and rapidly grows, we involuntarily compare the public opinions with a contagious sickness of epidemic proportions, which reproduces itself amongst the people through the atmosphere, and we now understand what not only Paul, but also what we mean with a spiritual atmosphere.

The spiritual atmosphere in our trumpet was actually a Christian believing one, for she was corrupted and darkened by the destructive smoke out of the pit. Christ and the Christian believing atmosphere was at the time only found with the Waldense and Hussites; in the Roman church they did not exist anymore; on the contrary, the persecutors came out of her, who wished to rid the earth from all the believers in Christ, and to darken the atmosphere there where the Sun of righteousness still shone, by their inhuman anger and horrible cruelty and their spiritual evil.

Verse 3. "**And there came out of the smoke locusts upon the earth**". We have to understand this eastern image of a destructive swarm of locusts, not a natural locust plague, but men, is clear from (Num 13:33), where the spies of Canaan compared themselves as locust and from (Judges 6:5) where the Midianites and the Analekites "came over Israel as grasshoppers for multitude" and further from the eleventh verse of this trumpet, where it states that they had a king over them, yet Salomon already says (Prov 30:27) "the locusts have no king."

The earth we already know as the image of the order in church and state of the period, which is spoken of.

When we test this trumpet with her explanation so far, with history, we then find Innocent III at the peak of papal worldly power, and in the deepest spiritual darkness, as the star or bishop, which was fallen from heaven down to earth.

We also find him in (1215 A.D.), at the beginning of this period, as the president of the fourth Lateran council, the most general of all councils. Resolutions were passed there over church discipline, heresies, teachings, etc., and the Inquisitions or the religious investigations by the papal legates were arranged and enforced. The Albigense, Waldense, etc. were strongly condemned and banned. In the following council of Toulouse (1229 A.D.) all the ordinances concerning the heretics and the inquisition were strongly reinforced and the reading of the Holy Scripture in vernacular language, as the source of many heresies at first forbidden. That was thus the smoke, which as a threatening thunderstorm, pregnant with destruction, would rise out of the oven of persecution under Popedom and totally darken the Sun of righteousness (Christ and His word) and the spiritual atmosphere.

From this smoke, locusts came on the earth. We also then see in the year after the above-mentioned council, (1216 A.D.) the Dominican monks begin to take action, and, approximately simultaneously with the following council, the order of the Franciscans. Both were burdened with the inquisition or the commission to bring the heretics to repentance or to persecute them. How they fulfilled their commission is abundantly recorded in history. The Dominicans especially excelled in particular cruelty, so that soon their name through a word spelling was changed to Domini Canes, hunting dogs of the Lord. So-called "heretic" believers had also previously been persecuted in the previous period, shortly before the beginning of this period, but always by worldly powers, (Frederic II, emperor of Germany, the king Louis VII of France, Henry II of England.), albeit at the incitement of the clergy. With this period, however, the spectacle pleasing to hell and devils unfolded itself, where the clergy themselves became the persecutors of the witnesses of Jesus and took over the task of torturers.

"And unto them was given power, as the scorpions of the earth." In the whole Bible, excluding the Revelation, we only find one place where *men* are represented by *scorpions*. This one place, however, is sufficient; it is (Ezek 2:4, 6) where the rebellious children of Israel were named, *impudent and stiff-hearted, rebellious thorns and* **scorpions**. A better character description than this of the spiritual order, to which the inquisition was entrusted, is difficult to expect.

Also, *the power, which was given to them,* was *like the power of scorpions.* The sting of a scorpion is, in many cases, not deadly, but always causes great pain; when it does not lead to death, it results in an important anaesthetic, followed by a very painful infection, which ends in abscesses. Also herein lies a deep meaning.

The intentions and commission of the inquisitors were not to kill all the heretics, but to bring them back to repentance by all sorts of torment, torture, pain, etc., and so possibly to return in the lap of the Roman church, wherein, after recanting their former beliefs and proper penitence they were adopted again. Only those who remained steadfast in their belief and seemed unyielding were referred to the stake. Those therefore who through force and fear returned to the Roman church, would not find the food to eternal life there but experienced a state of spiritual numbness, painful remorse, and what the Holy Scriptures names in (Isaiah 1:4, 6) "wounds and putrefying sores", forsaking and going backwards from the Lord.

Verse 4. "**And it was commanded them, that they should not hurt the grass of the earth, neither any green thing, neither any tree** and yet this is exactly the feared occupation of locusts. From this, it appears that the locusts here are only an image and a very accurate one. They could only hurt **those men which have not the seal of God in their foreheads"**. In this *"not"* lies a seeming contradiction. When they had to hurt *only* **those** *men*, then there lies herein the admission, that under *grass*, the *green* and the *trees also men* must be understood, and as we shall find, those men who had remained faithful to the Roman church. If however, we consider correctly the Waldense as the believing witnesses of Jesus and if those here meant are the true men, who would be persecuted and hurt by the inquisition, then we will superficially see that it should read, those who *have* the seal of God on their foreheads. Yet it read that they did *not* have it, but then *faith in Jesus* cannot be the seal of God.

Is our maxim true, that the Holy Scripture is the only and true source to explain the Revelation, then we must also find this contradiction irrevocably solved in the explanation of this parable.

Just as in the first trumpet (page 60) the earth here is the whole Roman empire, but now, it was subjected to papal worldly power. The *grass*, the *green*, and the *trees* are the image of the people and the lower or higher placed persons in the Roman church and in the state of this period, who must not be hurt by the inquisitors (locusts), because they believed and were faithful (green, first trumpet) to her godless teaching. Only the fallen away heretics, so-called by the Roman church (we name them, according to God's word, witnesses of Jesus) had to be traced and hurt. In contrast with the grass, green and the trees, which soon had to be cut off and thrown in the fire, the witnesses of Jesus, the Albigense, Waldense, Hussites, etc. of this period, are called *men* – men, recreated according to the image of

God, disciples of Jesus through their faith in Jesus Christ. But why does the Lord here name them *men*, who have not the seal of God on their foreheads?

What is the seal of God? – According to Paul the first Christians in the first century possessed a *seal* of God in the Holy Spirit; e.g.(2 Cor 1:21, 22): "Now he which stablished us with you in Christ and hath anointed us, is God; who hath also *sealed* us, and given the earnest of the spirit in our hearts," and in (Eph 1:13) "In whom also after that ye believed, were sealed with the Holy Spirit of promise." Therefore, he also said (Eph 4:30): "And grieve not the Holy Spirit of God, whereby ye are *sealed* unto the day of redemption."

When we now compare the Waldense and other believers of this period with the Christians of the first century, we find both a similarity and a difference between them.

The Waldense and other believers, like the first Christian, according to Jesus' promise (Luke 11:13), were led by the Holy Spirit, which had brought them to repentance and faith even to such a powerful faith, that they steadfastly and faithfully brought the testimony which Jesus had given them for that century, and sealed it with their death. By further comparison with the first Christians, however, we miss in the Waldense etc. the power and *gifts* of the Holy Spirit, which occurred so mightily in the first congregation, and it appears, in Revelation to the above-mentioned texts from Paul, that a certain fullness of the Holy Spirit exists, whereby His powers and gifts are revealed in men. This measure of the fullness of the Holy Spirit is thus the *seal of God*, and lack thereof: *"not having the seal of God."*

One example of such believers we find in (Acts 19:1–6) in the twelve disciples, who already (verse 2) believed in Jesus, and yet had not received the Holy Spirit and thus did *not* have the seal of God on their foreheads.

Verse 5. **"And to them** (the inquisitors) **it was given that they should not kill them** (the Waldense, etc.) **but they should be tormented five months".**

In verse 4, it was already said, when the commission *was* given, only to hurt those who believed in Christ, thus only the heretics, not the faithful of the Roman church.

This commission and power was given to them during 5 months, or 5 times 30 prophetic days, that is 150 years[26]. The calculation of year-months we consider well known from scripture.

---

[26] The prophecy calculates with year-weeks and year-months as round numbers. The exact number of years cannot be determined off-hand. It cannot however be 164 or 165 years,

Most remarkable is the fulfilment of this prophecy in the history of the Inquisition and the persecutions of heretics. The prophecy says (verse 4) that they had the *commission*, not to hurt the faithful Romans, but only those, who diverged from her teaching, and (verse 5) that they received power not to *kill*, but to *torture*, during 150 years, approximately. Indeed as GUERS says, on page 281:

"At the onset, the inquisition was very simple and not as cruel. The first inquisitors restricted themselves to investigate the heretics, whom they then referred to as the bishops, who in these times were only allowed to express their judgement, consequently, the clergy gave the unlucky ones over to the secular powers."

LLORENTE[27] historic writer of the Spanish Inquisition, says, on page 121 in the Dutch translation:

"That the inquisitors of the thirteenth century (1200 to 1300) considered themselves to have the right, excluding the punishment of death, to all sorts of tortures. Although in their own authority, they had no power over life and death, they had invented the rack and the relaxation[28], and they knew very well, that the worldly judge could not avoid bringing the relaxed to death, because, according to the highest power, only the reading of the verdict of the inquisition-council was required, which declared the perpetrator to be a heretic. From this any reasonable person will find it strange, that the inquisitors, at the end of their verdict, added the words, pleading that the worldly judge *should not kill* the heretic, while it was certain that the worldly judge, if he complied with the plea of the inquisition, would himself be suspected of heresy, and would himself appear before the inquisitors.

In the resolution to persecute the Waldense hiding in Arragon, the following words appear, which PEGNA conserved for us in his: *Remarks about the formulary of the inquisitor;*

"*Each one, who will find one of these wretches, know ye, that if he* **torments, ill-treats** *and* **persecutes** *them,* **without however killing them,** *we will be thankful to him.*" GUERS, page 279.

One more literal fulfilment of the prophecy, than both these examples is unthinkable. In this still mild form, the inquisition continued from (1216

---

then according to corresponding prophecies we would here speak of $5^1/_2$ months, and neither 135 years, which would be $4^1/_2$ months.

[27] D. Juan Antonio LLorente, old secretary of the Inquisition. History of the Spanish Inquisitions. 1821.

[28] The *Relaxation* was: that those found guilty of heresies were handed over to the worldly judges, who according to law, had to kill them.

A.D. Dominicans) and (1223 A.D. Franciscans) until (1378 A.D.) therefore, therefore approximately 150 years or 5 years of our prophecy. We also find with GUERS, page 308:

"During one and a *half century* the strictest measures were taken to eradicate the name of the Waldenses."

Although the worldly powers during this time referred thousand upon thousand Waldense heretics to the stake, and more than two million Albigense and Waldense died in the persecutions, at the instigation of the clergy; this does not change the fulfilment of the prophecy, that the inquisitors and their agents, who in multitudes, as the locusts of Revelations, overran all the Roman states, were only given the *commission* to seek them, to force them to renounce God, to *torture*, to *mistreat*, as with the pain of the sting of a scorpion, yet the *power* to *kill* was not given them. In the second half of this period, however, things will change as we soon will see.

Verse 6. **"And in those days, shall men seek death, and shall not find it; and shall desire to die, and death shall flee from them".** Already in a natural sense, this was true. GUERS says (page 279) concerning the coming formulary of the inquisitor, *"but this persecution charity, which spared life, was more unbearable than death itself; because for the believer life is a punishment and death a release."* In these words, we also see a spiritual meaning. How many thousands, under terrible tortures and persecution by the inquisition, coupled with onslaughts by Satan and impulses of the flesh, would not have felt the urge to renounce Christ like Peter and thus return to the former state of **spiritual death** wherein we naturally sink. How many, under the bitter horrible tortures of the inquisition, experienced the flesh's desire against the Spirit, in spite of the apostolic warning: If you live according to the flesh, you will **die** (spiritually). But if the flesh longed for spiritual death, shaken and weak in faith as it had become under this frightful woe, it was in vain! **Death would flee from them**; they could not convince their own conscience that they would find salvation without Jesus; the Spirit would testify against the flesh, that exactly under these tortures they had to glorify the name of the Lord and they, in spite of this suffering, were disciples of Jesus, and that openly falling away from Him, would lead to their eternal damnation.

Who among the Christian readers, in moments of weakness, did not sometimes envy the foolish while undergoing long, deep and heavy temptations on the way of Christian suffering, when seeing the godless peace; he who spoke with Israel of the olden days, when a cup full of water was wrung out of them: Verily I have cleansed my heart in vain and washed my hands in innocence. For all day long have I been plagued and chastened every morning. (Psalm 73:13, 14). Whosoever had such thoughts, felt this way, will also understand the condition of the Waldense.

When we consider the next part of the fifth trumpet of verses 7 to 10, it will immediately be apparent, even at a superficial reading, that here we have a new image of the same type, which has already been explained, the locusts or inquisitors; but that they now receive other characteristics, under which they once again will exist for a further 150 years. It now appears that they are **not** forbidden to kill yet receive full power to damage. The new commission of five months in verse 10, is not an aimless repetition of this time restriction in verse 5; - this would completely disagree with the shortness of the Revelation, - but points to a new period of 150 years in the Inquisition. Indeed we shall see that in 1378 the Inquisition underwent a change as it is depicted here in verses 7 to 10 and that instead of being a spiritual tribunal, it now becomes an avenger against the believers, as it is already depicted with the great similarity in (Joel 2:2–5), where the destruction of Jerusalem by the Babylonians is predicted.

The inquisitors now become, according to

Verse 7, **"like unto horses, prepared unto battle"**. If this depicts a more cruel desire for destruction, we find this image clearly explained in (Jer 8:5, 6) "Why then is this people of Jerusalem slidden back by a perpetual backsliding? They hold fast to deceit; they refuse to return. I hearkened and heard, but they spake not aright: no man repented him of his wickedness, saying, what have I done? Everyone turned to his course, as the horse rusheth into the battle." Snorting with battle-lust, they went out to exterminate the disciples of Jesus from the earth.

After, in (1378 A.D.), many believers died at the stake, in (1380 A.D.) the inquisition began in even more horrible ways to persecute the Waldensians and all who also in the Roman church were suspected of heresies. If the inquisitors in the first 150 years were hunters of heretics (Domini Canes) and commissioned with tracking heretics, to bring them to the tribunal of the bishops, now they begin by by-passing the bishops, to condemn the heretics themselves, established prisons to keep the heretics at hand, to torture them there and often killing them, without calling upon the worldly powers. GUERS says, on page 444:

"While the horrible persecutions (in 1378 A.D.) had not eradicated heresy, Francois Borelli, a monk-inquisitor, began, armed with a bull from Pope Clemens VII, two years later, a new persecution. He summoned them before his tribunal and questioned them concerning their faith, and on refusing to appear he condemned them, without other form of process, to death and gave them over to the arm of the law, to be burned as heretics. The inquisitors appropriated half the riches of the condemned; the rest was for the worldly power. What great efforts can we expect from both parties in each case, as this was supported by greed, evil and superstition?

VAN LOON says on page 149:

"The inquisitor Borelli (in 1400 A.D.) committed horrible cruelties in the valley of Pragela against the Waldense in Piëmont."

This monster had already persecuted the believers. These persecutions in the valley of Pragela, is described by GUERS on page 443.

"It was also approximately the time", as LLORENTE said, "that Nicolas Eymerik compiled this: Guide for inquisitors, for use by his fellow servants. The title of this infamous work is Directorium Inquisiterum. Later, after the invention of the art of printing, it was published (1578 A.D.); it contained everything ever decreed by papal bull, instructions, etc. about the heretics and the hunt for heretics. VAN LOON mentions that this person was the chief inquisitor for 44 years.

"And on their heads were as it were crowns like gold." The heads of these locusts are their ancient honourable heads (Isaiah 9:15) or leaders.

The *crown* is well known, also as Biblical symbol of *honour* (page 52) and the *golden crown* as that of *royal power* (2 Kings 11:12, Est 1:11, Est 2:17, Est 6:8 and Est 8:15); and indeed the inquisitors in the second half of this period were, not only in great regard by the different popes, whose already shaking throne they tried to support, by suppressing the strong rising unbelief of that time, and by forcefully extinguishing the rapidly growing light of the gospel; but they also possessed a nearly royal power, as the rulers and powers had to subject themselves to their command, and had to assist them by all means. LLORENTE says, on page 106:

"When an inquisitor was appointed by, or because of the pope, he then announced this to the prince or ruler of the country and he in turn to all the tribunals in all cities, which he would visit, and strongly commanded to assist this person in all he desired. According to the same prescription of the government, full accommodation and care had to be provided for the inquisitor and his entourage, and care should be taken, that not the least obstacle should hinder him.

At his arrival, he summoned the authorities of the region, in order to instruct them of his intentions."

These prescriptions LLORENTE gathered from the work of EYMERIK. He adds to it these words:

"One sees here, that royal or even the highest authorities are not respected, that the authorities, who represented these powers themselves, had to react immediately at the inquisitor's command."

Their crowns were therefore not of gold, but like gold; that is: their power was not really royal, but as great and like unto it, they had:

"the freedom to negate any city privileges and laws, for as much as these would appear to oppose the interests of the inquisition, and to fire all those who considered themselves responsible for these laws." LLORENTE, page 69.

"And their faces were as the faces of men." In these words, we do not only find an indication, that the locusts are an image, in which we understand that we here have to do with men but we are reminded of the third living creature from the third seal, who according (Rev 4:7) *had a face like that of a man*, which represented the *Evangelist ministry*. The almost unlimited power of the inquisitors was given them by the popes, so that they would uphold the gospel, i.e. the teaching of the Roman church, and their teaching was:

"that their gospel was the eternal gospel, the gospel of the Holy Spirit, destined to replace the gospel of Jesus Christ, which was not of the kingdom, and that only the beggar monks (Franciscans) were able to teach and practice a perfect life." GUERS, page 219.

Verse 8. **"And they had hair as the hair of a woman.** This is probably a contradiction of the outward appearance against the following words describing the inner disposition of the inquisitors, "and their teeth **were as the teeth of lions."**

Paul teaches us (1 Cor 11:14, 15) that the *long hair of a woman* is her *glory*, for her hair is given her for a *covering*. Long hair is, therefore, an *ornament of woman*, and the external sign of her spiritual ornament, *meekness* and *humbleness*. As zealous fighters for the gospel, the inquisitors were an *ornament* of the church (the woman, Rev 2:20, Rev 12:1, Rev 17:3, Rev 21:9) to her **glory**.

The *teeth* are in comparison not only in the normal way of speaking but also in Biblical language, the image of the *inward disposition*. (Dan 7:5, 7, Psalm 57:4). Here the disposition is *like* the teeth of *lions*. "My soul is among *lions*", says David, "and I lie even among them that are set on fire, even the sons of men, whose *teeth* are spears and arrows, and their tongue a sharp sword." (Psalm 57:4). In this period the Roman church was also the fifth head (Rev 17:9), of the fourth beast, (the Roman Empire), which Daniel (Dan 7:7) saw, and which: "was dreadful and terrible, and strong, and it had *great iron teeth*, it devoured and brake in pieces." This fifth head was also named, as we shall see, *Abaddon* of *Apollyon*, meaning *"corrupter"*.

Indeed, the image of the *hair of a woman* and the *teeth of lions* is the correct image of the *external appearance of meekness and humbleness*, wherewith the inquisitors hid their *cruelty and arrogance* under a *cover*, just as a woman can hide herself under her *long hair* as a veil.

These characteristics of the inquisitors are well known from history. We already gave (page 216), an example of this hypocrisy; how they, knowing that their conviction of *guilty of heresy*, was an inexorable command to the worldly arm, to burn the heretic, yet wrote at the end of their deposition, that the worldly power must not kill the heretic. This **feigned meekness**, at the actual **thirst for blood**, the prophecy names: **hair of women** and **teeth of lions**. How could human feelings ever live in hearts, surrounded with breastplates as if were **breastplates of iron** (verse 9). From (1 Tess 5:8 and Eph 6:14) we know the breastplate or armour as an image of **righteousness of faith**. Even Christ put on *righteousness* as a *breastplate* (Isaiah 59:17).

The *righteousness* of the inquisitors was therefore not of *gold* (image of Godly truth), neither of *silver* (image of love), but of *iron* (Dan 2:40, 42), *so hard, so loveless*, an anti-Christian Phariseeism. LLORENTE gives on page 123 an example of hardness, wherewith the inquisitors handled those who after repentance returned to the church and were *adopted in her once more*.

"And the sound of their wings." (see Isaiah 8:7, 8 and Hab 1:8). The image of their invasion of the whole expansion of the Roman empire, was as great *as the sound of chariots*, of *many horses running to battle*. We remember in this image, that the warriors and armies in the old Biblical times as well as in the Greek and Roman periods went to war standing in chariots, led by two horses. The many *chariots and horses* are thus the image of *great power* as in (Psalm 68:17) "The chariots of God are twenty thousand," the short meaning of these words is this, just as *great in number as in power, they would invade the Roman countries*. One single example of the terrible persecutions, which the Waldense of that period had to endure, also from the crusades, which were preached against them, we take in short from GUERS page 446–448.

"Pope Innocent VIII proclaimed in (1487 A.D.) a bull, to exterminate the heretics, to destroy them as poisonous snakes to preach a crusade against them and to awaken the believers, to go against these pests with force of weapons. He actually prescribed to all the clergy to absolve all those, who would help in this lawful extermination, from all church punishment; he offered these new crusaders absolution for all apostasy and, to offer all those who would participate in this *holy war*, a still better bait, Innocent gave them license to confiscate all moving and fixed property. LÉGER, who left us this bull, assures us, that it cost the lives of over 800,000 people all over Europe.

This high commission was allocated to the arch-deacon Albert. He moved with his army into the valley of Loyser; the frightened inhabitants fled to their caves in the mountains. He hunted and found their hiding places eventually. He had then had great loads of wood brought to the entrance of the caves and ordered it to be set alight. Four hundred children suffocated in their cribs or their mother's arms. A multitude, fearing to be burnt alive, threw themselves from the high rocks and were crushed, the remainder were murdered by the angry army. "It is sure," says PERRIN, "that in this valley not more than three thousand people lived, we can say, that all the inhabitants, whether old or young, simultaneously died.

After their works of destruction in the valley of Loyser was completed, the murderous hordes, moved to Fraissinere in the name of the pope. The persecution which followed was one of the most terrible ever known, all the Waldense, judged without appeal, were doomed for the fire."

About the *locusts*, named in verse 10, we have already spoken. That the scorpions do not bite, but sting with their tails, is known. The locusts however of this fifth trumpet **had tails, like unto scorpions, and there were stings in their tails,** wherewith they stung like them. (Isaiah 9:15) teaches us the meaning of this image of the Holy Spirit, "*the prophet that teaches lies, he is the tail.*" Just as the prophets of the Old Covenant not only had to bring God's word and commandments that the people of Israel would not fall into idolatry, so indeed the commission was given to the swarm of locusts of the inquisition with her agents, to the inquisitor-general, to strictly watch; that the people did not fall from the teaching and belief of the Roman church. Therefore, the Inquisition was named **the holy service** by the church. As *maintainers of this false teaching*, they were the *false prophets* or the tails of the *scorpions*, who with their *sting* poured out soul-killing poison in the hearts of those, who found not enough peace for their conscience in the teaching of the Roman church.

That we have to understand under the *sting*, the seducing, partly flattering, partly threatening *tongues* of the inquisitors, is apparent not only from the consequences of the parable but also from (James 3:8) "But the *tongue* can no man tame, it is an unruly evil, *full of deadly poison.*" And (Prov 12:18) "There is that *speaketh* like the *piercings* of a sword, but the tongue of the wise is health." David also says in (Psalm 52:3) that against the violent, "thy *tongue* deviseth *mischiefs*; *like a sharp razor*, working continually." The effect of the venom we have already seen on page 213, is how it causes spiritual death or painful abscesses (falling away from the only God).

"And in their tails, power was given to hurt men five months." These false prophets (tails) who brought another gospel, than that of Jesus Christ, had the power to hurt the believers, that is: full power to do with them as they wished.

The restriction, that they would not kill them (verse 5), Revelation does not repeat in this second half of the inquisition, and history again completely agrees. If the inquisition in the first half of this period, as we have seen, was still bound by commission and restriction of power, in the second 150 years of this period she was not bound anymore. Not only did she form her own tribunals, and was thus the prosecutor and judge, but often also the executioner in the infliction of pain and death penalty, or the warder of prisoners to life sentences in her own dungeons. No one, who knows anything about the history of the inquisitions, will claim that she did not make use of her evil power in horrible ways, and her victims have to be counted in their millions. On page 223 we have given one of the many examples thereof.

According to the registers of the inquisition, LLORENTE said (page 272), that for example, the inquisitor Torquemada singly, in Sevilla, in the course of eighteen years burned 10,220, tortured and punished, condemned to death, etc., 104,181, a total of 114,401 people.

The 5 months or 150 years of this second period of the inquisition form together with the first have three hundred years. We see, therefore, that this fifth trumpet and the whole fifth period of Revelation lasted three hundred years, and that our estimation of the duration of time for this period was not arbitrary. Here, we have an indication of the length of this period in Revelation itself, with the previous period's church history clearly showing, that every three hundred years a total change took place. This period of 300 years also ended with the Reformation in (1517 A.D.).

Verse 11. **"And they had a king over them, which is the angel of the bottomless pit"**. Locusts have no king, as Solomon already stated. Their spiritual ministers, the inquisitors, had a *king* in the *pope*. They were responsible or obedient only to the pope; they only received commands from him.

Many times, the (so-called) holy office, made bold to openly humiliate the authorities, and force them to satisfy the pretended accusations and to receive the imposed sentence on their knees, under the reading of high mass, with a candle in hand and a robe of repentance. LLORENTE, page 260.

The **pope**, who originally was no king, but a spiritual overseer had also appropriated the royal worldly power, was the **angel or star**, which had fallen from the church heaven and had the key to the bottomless pit; from which, as we saw in verse 1, the evil spirits were released to destroy the believers; this is why his name is **Abaddon** or **Appollyon**, both meaning corrupter.

Popedom, as we already said, is one of the heads or great kingdoms of the fourth beast of Daniel, (Dan 7:7, 19, 23) which was characteristically a destroyer and corrupter among all its heads. As the first head of the heathen Roman empire, it killed the believers. As a second or Christian head, it corrupted the brotherly love. As third or papal head, it unthroned Christ. As fourth, also the papal head, it destroyed the whole Christian teaching. As fifth, Christian in name only, but actually anti-Christian papal head, it reverted to the role of the first heathen head and again killed the believers. Both the last heads will also meet in the sixth and seventh periods.

Verse 12. **"The one** or first **woe** for all that, the inquisition before the Reformation, or the Waldense and Hussite persecutions **is past;** and behold **there come two woes more hereafter".** The *second* is the *inquisition after the Reformation* and the *third,* is the *coming Christian persecution under the anti-Christendom,* when the beast, which as the heathen Roman power *was,* as Christian Roman kingdom seemed *not to be,* although *it was* (Rev 17:8), lastly again as the heathen anti-Christan kingdom had come up out of the bottomless pit.

FIFTH VIAL

or

THE JUDGEMENT OF GOD

> Every kingdom divided against itself is brought to desolation; and
> every city or house divided against itself shall not stand.
> And if Satan cast out Satan, he is divided against
> himself; how shall then his kingdom stand?
> Matt 12:25, 26.

Rev. 16:10, 11

If the Lord God is patient over sinners, and delays his punishment over those who withstand Him, He would not be a Holy and Righteous God if He in His own time had not poured out the vial of His wrath over the abominations of unrighteousness of the angel out of the bottomless pit, the "*beast*" which seemed "*not*" to be, although *it was*. Just as God the Lord acted in the previous periods, He now also punished the godless through their own vices. The tower of the new Babylon of Innocent III was erected to "reach unto heaven" (Gen 11:4), the fullness of unrighteousness was fulfilled, and the Lord came down to confound their language. The clergy themselves poured out this judgement. The angel with the trumpet of blasphemy was also again the angel with the vial.

Verse 10. **"And the fifth angel poured out his vial upon the seat of the beast, and his kingdom was full of darkness".**

That the *throne* here is not literally meant to be the royal seat of the "beast" of that time, but as *his kingdom* and *rule*, is apparent, except from ordinary use of language, also from (Psalm 45:6, Psalm 89:4, Isaiah 16:5).

It was the **empirical worldly power**, which Popedom had appropriated for itself, wherewith it glittered in its highest glory from 1215 A.D. till 1300 A.D, although at the time the foundation for the coming decay was laid. That **the beast** was not a single person, but the **power of Popedom**, carried by many consecutive persons, is evident from the peculiar language of the prophecy, which speaks of the throne of **the beast** and **his** *kingdom* in the singular form, but immediately adds the plural **they**.

The beast, we repeat it here once more, was the fourth, God-hating worldly power, or the fourth beast of Daniel (Dan 2 and 7) the Roman empire, which apparently was or *existed* as the heathen worldly power and persecutor of the Christians in the first period (Rev 17:8), as we already learned to know in the first vial. With Emperor Constantine, when the state power became Christian, and under the Popedom which followed, it *appeared* to cease to exist. And was *not*, although in the fifth period with the persecutions of Christians by Popedom and its inquisition, it seemed, that it still was and still existed. And so, it CONTINUED TO EXIST through the period of Reformation and up to our time: although apparently IT IS NOT (that is: not heathen), the beast still rages forth, although hidden, to destroy the kingdom of God on earth.

In the *seventh* period, however, in which we now live, it will again rise as "the beast" under the seventh trumpet (Rev 13), and already comes out of the sea of nations, with its new unbiblical and unchristian religion, first to be as the anti-Christian worldly power, **the seventh head**, and thereafter under the seventh vial (Rev 17) as Christian persecutor again to come out of the bottomless pit, as the eighth head, which was also the first of the seven.

This beast, rising again, in the *sea* of nations, out of the *bottomless pit* of spiritual darkness, is the *anti-Christ*, or the Christ-hating power of the people. That we do not have to expect one person, or a personal anti-Christ, is clear from the plural **they**, wherein the fifth vial of *the beast* is mentioned.

His kingdom is darkened. Not only the **worldly** but also the **spiritual authority** of Popedom began to darken, especially from 1300 A.D. As quickly as this power had risen to its peak, it also descended again. But also the church, as the spiritual kingdom of Popedom, had sunken in the deepest spiritual darkness; literally nothing Christian had remained in her. The greatest superstitions and unbelief went hand in hand with a complete ignorance of the main truths of Christendom. All the efforts of the popes to elevate their power again and the efforts of the councils and clergy, to purify and reform the church, only served to publicly proclaim the impotence of the former or the total corruption of the latter.

This also brought about that popes and councils often disagreed and clashed with one another, which resulted, as the prophecy teaches us: **And they gnawed their tongues for pain.** That we do not have to take it literally, not even as a Greek narration of our sayings "they gritted their teeth," or "they bit their lips", needs no explanation. This would be too unimportant for the exalted Revelation. Whether there lies a deeper meaning to these words, the word of God will again teach us.

We read in (Exod 4:10), that Moses said to the Lord: "Oh my Lord, I am not eloquent, but I am slow of speech, and of a slow *tongue*." The Lord answers to this: (verses 14, 15, 16): "Is not Aaron the Levite thy brother? I know that he can speak well. And thou shalt speak unto him, and put words in his mouth, and *he shall be thy spokesman* unto the people." So also (Exod 7:2) the Lord says to Moses: "Thou *shalt speak* all that I command thee; and *Aaron* thy brother *shall speak* unto pharaoh." **Aaron** was therefore the **tongue** of Moses.

David also says (2 Sam 23:2): "The Spirit of the Lord *spake by me ,and* His word was in my *tongue."* David was then the *tongue of the Lord.* Similarly, the *herald* (Dan. 3:4), was the *tongue of the king,* and in our church prophecy the **councils, the Cardinals** and other clergy were the **tongues of the beast** (Popedom) *who had to speak for them,* and sustain its power and honour, as they had done in the previous periods. But also reciprocally, *the popes were the tongues of the councils*, and had to confirm and maintain their resolutions, because the councils and church authorities together formed the anti-Christian Roman power or the beast. When we then read in the church history, that the council of Constance (1414 A.D.) and Bazel in (1431 A.D) granted themselves the right, even to dethrone a legal pope, made use of that right and revealed all the scandalous deeds of the popes to the whole of Europe, we then find the prophecy fulfilled, that the kingdom of the beast darkened, and the image becomes clear, that they, who together formed "the beast", bit their tongues, which had to speak for them because of the adversity. This **"biting"** we find in (Hab 2), where against him, (verse 5) "who cannot be satisfied," it is said, (verse 7): "shall they not rise up suddenly that shall *bite* thee?" Also Paul uses this image, (Gal 5:14, 15): "Thou shalt love thy neighbour as thyself. But if ye *bite and devour* one another, take heed that ye be not consumed of one another." This was perfectly fulfilled in the acts of popes and councils against each other, and we can rightly speak of **biting**, consuming and devouring of each other, when the popes **resisted** the efforts of the councils (Martinus V, Eugenius IV); when the councils dethroned the popes, (Eugenius IV, 1437 A.D.) and he in turn **excommunicated** the whole council (1438 A.D.). When in (1379 to 1429 A.D.) two popes reigned simultaneously, one in Rome and one in Avignon, who *banned* each other and all their followers, so that effectively the whole Christendom was *excommunicated.* (v. LOON, page 164). But not only the mutual disputes and accusations between popes and councils darkened the power and glory of the beast, but also between the worldly power of emperors and kings and the spiritual power of Popedom and amongst the latter again against the former, disputes and conflicts arose.

Over and above all that, many noble and god-fearing men, contributed to the darkening of the power of "the beast", comparing the lives of the clergy with the gospel which at the time became more and more known, and thereby became the forerunners of the Reformation. We have only to remember Wycklif, Huss, Savonarola, Erasmus, etc.

Verse 11: **"They,** the beast, **blasphemed the God of heaven** (the Lord of the church), **because of their pains and their sores.** This blaspheming of God we already know as total falling-away from Him, and granting themselves the power, which only God has a right to, to forgive sins (page 164), all the sad results of superstition and unbelief, (*abscesses,* first vial). Isaiah said (Isaiah 1:4, 6): "Ah sinful nation, a people laden with iniquity, they have *forsaken the Lord,* they have *provoked the Holy One of Israel unto anger,* they are gone backwards. From the sole of the foot even unto the head there is *no soundness* in it; but wounds, and bruises, and *putrefying sores.*" The godless in Israel were thus the abscesses of God's people. Similarly in this period, the godless priests were the abscesses of the church in their falling away from and revolt against God; and the persecution of His people the *sores* of the beast or of the anti-Christian, papal power, **and repented not of their deeds"** at this judgement of God, on the contrary, they continued in their falling-away from Him and in the persecution of His people, running unbridled on the way of destruction, from blasphemy to blasphemy. Pope Jules II threw his prayer book in the fire after the defeat at Ravena (1512 A.D.), swore by the devil and cursed God. His successor Leo X, two years later, sent a tariff throughout the whole Roman empire, listing the prices at which sins could be bought off (GUERS 554):

20 pennies for the murder of a father, mother, brother.
20 pennies for incest with mother, sister or daughter.
24 pennies for prostitution or perjury.
28 pennies for false witness, sacrilege, and revealing a confession.
68 pennies for falsifying apostolic letters!!!

"How long, O Lord, Holy and True, dost thou not judge and avenge our blood on them that dwell on the earth? cried the souls under the altar with loud voices, which were slain for the word of God. (Fifth seal, Rev 6:9, 10).

OVERVIEW OF THE HISTORY OF THE CHURCH IN THE FIFTH PERIOD

FROM 1215 – 1517 A.D.

TRANSLATION OF THE FIFTH CANDLESTICK

Rev 3:1–6.

Verse 1. *Write to the Bishops of the congregation and to the whole congregation of the fifth period of the church, wherein only a few believers have remained, who can only in fear and trembling remain faithful to Me.*

This says the Lord of the church, who once gave the powers and gifts of the Holy Spirit as an inheritance to His church, and who had wanted to continue working with these powers and gifts in the congregation.

I know your works of superstition and unbelief, and that you are Christian in name only, but are living dead.

Verse 2. *Awake from your spiritual sleep and strengthen the little Christian life that still remains in you, and which would also die, for I have not found your works perfect before My God.*

Verse 3. *Remember, therefore, how you received and heard My gospel in the beginning, return on the old ways and preserve it.*

But, if you do not awake, I will come as a thief, and you will not know at what hour I will come.

Verse 4. *But you still have a few as a small remnant of My church among you, who have not soiled themselves with your unrighteousness and carnal disposition. They will have a part in the kingdom of My Glory as overcomers.*

Verse 5. *Because who overcomes; will participate in the glorification of the saints, and I will not erase his name from the Book of Life, but I will confess his name before My Father and before His angels.*

Verse 6. *Who has ears, let him hear; what the Spirit says to the congregation.*

FULFILLMENT IN THE HISTORY OF THE CHURCH

A few extracts from the work of Guers will clearly reveal the fulfilment of this prediction by the Son of God for this period. We find on page 207:

"One thinks to find Salvation in building or restoration of churches, or at least, by carrying bricks and to pull the wagons as beasts of burden. The saints – and what saints! – have more worshippers than Jesus Christ. The cult of Maria has replaced that of the Saviour".

Page 208. *"The bread of the communion has become the subject of religious worship, - the bread which had become God, as Rome called it. According to legend, still professed by the Roman church in our days as proof of transubstantiation, or the changing of communion bread into the fleshly body of Christ, the following occurred in the street of Pamphlets in Paris in 1290 A.D., a Jew pierced the host, blood flowed from it, the host ascended to heaven and disappeared, while Jesus on the cross revealed himself. The Jew is taken into custody, delivered to the provost of Paris and burned alive.* (GUERS, page 211.)

Page 209. Matthew Paris (13th century), after *relating the scandalous deeds* of Jan Zonder Land, adds the following:

"We may hope and can be certain of it, that some good works, which he performed in this life, will plead for him before the throne of Jesus Christ; because he had commissioned an Abby to be built, and at his death left a sum of money to someone."

Page 210. *"Johannes Marijns, abbot of St. Albans (end of 13th century), spoke these sad words on his death bed: "O Holy Albanus! Whom I loved as my best help and often invoked, while I experienced your help and lived by it, guarantee me, illustrious Saint! against the punishment of hell." – Stephen, dying, entrusted his soul to Jesus Christ. Johannes Marijns entrusts his soul to St. Albanus."*

That was the piety which reigned in those days. The righteousness of the Saviour is trodden under foot. One preferred to buy heaven, rather than to accept it out of grace."

Page 211. *"The writers of legends assure us, that in the year 1221 A.D., the angels took over the house, which the blessed virgin (Maria) had lived in, in Nazareth, and transported it on a mountain in Dalmatia."*

"Three years later – probably rested from their great effort, as one writer reports, they brought it to Italy in the forest of the country of Anconia, which belonged to a widow Loretta. (Our beloved ladies of Loreta)

Page 553. *"The services only consist in the exercise of manifold ceremonies, which were from heathen or Jewish origin. Human values were worshipped; the Saints called upon, and God's perfection, through sanctification, divided amongst the creatures by the pope."*

This was the condition of Christendom in the Sardisian period of the church. We remember that the Son of God revealed Himself to the

Sardisian congregation or Christianity of the Sardisian period as He who had the seven spirits of God, (the gifts of the Holy Spirit, as we said), and asks her to account for what is still left in her of those gifts, wherewith He equipped His church at its foundation. These gifts of the Holy Spirit had disappeared from her.

The congregation of the Lord in this period was covered in spiritual darkness and full of the natural life of this world, the lusts of the flesh and the pride of life, which did not come from the Father, but is from the world. (1 John 2: 16). The poor Waldense and Albigense, even in the loneliness of their mountains, persecuted by the Roman church, and fleeing in caves and holes were, with the forerunners of the Reformation, the only *Remnant* (Sardis) of the church of Jesus Christ on earth, but *a remnant*, which lived in *fear and trembling* for the power of the anti-Christian Popedom.

TRANSLATION OF THE FIFTH SEAL

<u>Rev 6:9-11.</u>

Verse 9. *And when Christ Jesus unrolled the scroll of the history of the church in the fifth period, I saw no Christian congregation, nor spirituality in her anymore. However, I still saw a few witnesses of Jesus living on mountains and caves, suffering for His name's sake and persecuted, tortured and killed by the anti-Christian power, which called itself His church and His body. And I saw the souls of the Martyrs from this and former periods which were killed for His names' sake, resting in bliss in the paradise of God.*

Verse 10. *And they with the still living blood witnesses cried with loud voices: "How long, O Holy and True Ruler! Until You come to judge, to avenge our blood from those who rejected You and killed Your witnesses, and to fulfill Your promise to Your servants?"*

Verse 11. *And to the believers on earth, persecuted for the testimony of Jesus Christ, white robes were given, the righteousness of the Saints, and to them and the formerly killed blood witnesses of Jesus it was said, that the Lord would confirm their testimony before heaven and earth as His own word, spoken by them as His servants, but they had to rest a while longer in their initial bliss in the realm of the departed, until their brethren also, the blood witnesses of the Lord, from both the last periods of His church would have joined them; to then partake of the first resurrection as the overcomers of all the periods and to the kingdom of Glory of Jesus Christ.*

Earlier we have shown (page 84), that from the second period of the church, when the state became Christian, the kings together with the priesthood formed the seal. In the second, third and fourth periods the kings remained Christian, at least faithful to the teaching of the church. In this period, however, kings as well as priests were completely unbelieving.

We read from GUERS, page 220:

"Ignorance and corruption lead straight to ungodliness. In these unhappy times hypocrisy and superstition brought about a multitude of unbelieving and free spirits. Writers from the thirteenth century attacked the gospel, without identifying themselves. Some went so far as to deny the existence of God and His perfection. Due to lack of teaching, one confused the religion of the pope with that of the Bible and rejected Christendom as a deception. The book about the three deceivers, ascribed to emperor Frederick II, is from that period. Pope Gregorius IX at least banned it, and issued a bull against him, wherein he accused him to have said, that three deceivers had deceived the world: Moses, Jesus Christ and Mohammed, but he made out Jesus to be very inferior to both the others, because, he said: "Moses and Mohammed remained famous until the end of their lives, while Jesus Christ was scandalously crucified. (GUERS, page 203).

About the clergy, VAN LOON says, page 163:

"When we consider the condition of the clergy in the church in the two centuries before the Reformation, we need no other Protestant sources to confirm the conviction that corruption surpassed all thought, all description. The writings of Roman contemporaries exhibit a picture thereof, so dark, that one does not stand amazed, that the people, led by such leaders, also sank in deep immorality".

About this period, GUERS says, page 206:

"The clergy saw in Jesus a worldly ruler, who had to allow them to rule over a universe, which was totally subjected to their laws, and over His church as they desired, as a power of this century, to which all the other powers had to subject themselves." And page 212:

"The priests knew how to take advantage of the ignorance and superstition of the nations. The indulgences opened an inexhaustible source of riches. They preached, that there existed an immeasurable treasure of merit, composed of good works, which were done by the Saints above that which was required for their salvation, and they confirmed, that the pope had use of this immeasurable treasure, and had the right to let anyone whom they thought fit, to experience the benefits thereof, stipulating that

this or no penance, which he prescribed, with this or no sum of money, according to the set tariff, had to be bought."

"All religious feeling was extinguished. The clergy even lost the semblance of shame, page 328. The bishop of Lodi commented at the council of Constance, that the Latin clergy had given themselves over to scandalous lusts and immorality, that Diogenes, if he had sought a human being amongst them, would have found only wild beasts and swine. Page 331.

"The only care of the clergy from this time consisted in maintaining their privileges and to extend their power. Their head, the pope, was the centre point around which everything revolved, and the kings had to humble themselves, to serve as stirrups for him to climb on his horse." Page 551.

"The duties of the preachers were generally neglected, and great ignorance prevailed. The church ministries were sold to children and lay people, who, in turn, hired them out to sub-tenants, of whom not one fulfilled the duties for which he was paid."

"The pope allowed himself to be given blasphemous titles and developed an attitude as if he wanted to expand his territory to heaven and hell, even as an intermediate place, called purgatory. He had, he said, the keys of all these places." Page 552.

"Behold, what was called the holy, catholic, apostolic church, which was considered to be headed by Jesus Christ." Page 553.

What John further saw happening in the realm of the departed in the fifth seal, naturally will not be found fulfilled in *earthly* history books.

TRANSLATION OF THE FIFTH TRUMPET

Rev. 9:1-12.

Verse 1. *And in the fifth period of the church I saw no more gospel preaching anymore, but the clergy, instead of being the angels and servants of the Lord, had become worldly rulers and important persons of the earth. They thereby had power to allow the evil spirits to come out of the bottomless pit and infest the hearts of men.*

Verse 2. *And they allowed them to seduce the people to all sorts of evil, and thereby bitter hatred and great persecutions against the believers came into existence in the hearts of and by the unbelievers, who deluded and called themselves members of the universal apostolic church of Christ.*

Verse 3. And out of the desire to persecute the witnesses of Jesus, spiritual ministries were appointed in the Roman countries, the inquisitors, to bring back or to persecute all those, who diverged from the teaching of the Roman church. And by force or the instilling of fear they held the people to be faithful to the church and poisoned the souls of the unbelievers with godless teaching.

Verse 4. And they were commanded not to hurt all those, who were faithful to the teaching of the Roman church, rich or poor, high or low; but only those, which did not adhere to her teaching, and who sought their salvation preferably in the word of God.

Verse 5. And to the inquisitors power was given, during 150 years, not to kill them, but only to torture and plague them, and their torture and pain was cruel and destructive for soul and body.

Verse 6. And in those days the persecuted believers will desire to die in soul and body; but they will not be able to extinguish the faith in their hearts, neither find rest for their soul in the teaching of the Roman church.

Verse 7. After the persecution of the believers had lasted in this form for 150 years, without getting rid of them, the inquisitors, raging with combativeness, went out to eradicate them from the earth by fire and the sword, and as a royal power, wherewith they went out over the earth, to expand the blasphemous teaching of the Roman church, as the only true gospel.

Verse 8. And they were considered the glory of the church, and under the semblance of humility and humbleness they hid their blood thirstiness and high mindedness.

Verse 9. And instead of Christian faith and love only high mindedness and cruelty filled their hearts, and their power was spread over all Roman countries.

Verse 10. And false prophets which they were, they enforced their soul killing teaching on the people by force and fear and poisoned the souls of the straying Christendom. And in this crueller form the inquisitors had power again for 150 years, to persecute all those, who disagreed with the teachings of the Roman church, and they received, now without any restrictions, power over life and death.

Verse 11. And their only ruler and commander was the anti-Christian popedom, which had subjected themselves to serve Satan, and carried the name of the corrupter of God's kingdom on earth.

Verse 12. After this persecution is past, two more will follow.

With the explanation of the trumpet in this period, we indicated, because of the volume of each image, apart from its explanation, also its fulfilment in church history, to strengthen and consolidate them. The Inquisition was extensively dealt with. Not to write the same twice, we have, in this translation given the relevant pages, where its fulfilment is to be found. We therefore here only have to show the condition of the gospel preaching in the Roman church of this period.

In the year 1215 A.D., at the onset of this period, the twelfth general council confirmed the already discussed teaching of transubstantiation or the changing of the communion bread in the fleshly body of Jesus Christ, the confessional was advocated, the inquisition was regulated, etc.

In the year 1229 A.D., the council of Toulouse forbade the reading of the Bible in vulgar language. Before this time, it was still allowed. The conclusion of the council read as follows:

"It will not be permitted that lay people possess the books of the Old and New Testament, only those who in piety so desire, can possess a Psalter or breviary. *But we forbid them strongly to possess the above-mentioned books in vulgar language.*" GUERS, page 272.

In 1260, the flagellants and the self-chastisers arose, who meant to find salvation by chastising themselves. Also, the teaching of the immaculate conception of Maria dates from this period; accompanied with the use of the Ave Maria prayer.

"The Bible," says GUERS, page 549 "made way for papal traditions, for the books of Peter Lombard, of John Scot and of other writers of the sort, a new collection of trivialities or unconfirmed reasoning. The people robbed of sound instruction in the word of life were given ridiculous legends as food. Aristotle was mentioned more often than Paul. Usually, the books of this old philosopher, or the works of Scot or of Thomas d' Aquina were the source, from which the preachers took their texts. It was said to the people, that the Holy Scripture, far from being necessary, was rather detrimental, and that it was sufficient to adhere to the teaching of the church." "One could just as well have lived in peace and oneness, even though there was no gospel in the world." Said the Vicar of Constance at the time of the Reformation. – "The affairs of the church (Roman) would be in a much better condition," said Cardinal Hosius, "if the gospel had never appeared on this earth." GUERS, page 550.

"It is the power of God unto salvation to everyone that believeth," said Paul (Rom 1:16) and: "If any man preaches any other gospel unto you than that ye have received, let him be accursed." (Gal. 1:9).

TRANSLATION OF THE FIFTH VIAL

<u>Rev. 16:10, 11.</u>

Verse 10. *And the Roman popes and priests, through their apostasies and total estrangement from the gospel, themselves executed the judgement of God over Popedom, and the glitter of his spiritual and worldly power was darkened, and the popes began disputing with their defenders and maintainers, the councils and clergy, over and over they accused each other bitterly, and cursed each other in their spiritual misery.*

Verse 11. *And the whole Popedom became a pool of blasphemy, abominations and hellish disputes through sin, superstition and unbelief, and they repented not from their works of darkness.*

FULFILLMENT IN CHURCH HISTORY

At the outpouring of the fifth vial, the kingdom of the beast was darkened.

"The scandalous disputes between Emperors and the Popes, the increasing of false or true heretics and other circumstances" says GUERS, page 322, "had some influence on the Roman power since the previous century (1200 A.D. – 1300 A.D.); it was reserved for the 14th century, to observe the first clear signs of her decay."

"All the disputes (between popes and kings) caused Rome an incalculable harm. Until now the heads of the false church were considered as saints, untouchable beings, against whom one could not raise a hand, without incurring the immediate wrath of God. Europe now heard that one could without punishment, restrict their unashamed impudence.

About the division in the papal church, both through the transfer of the papal seat to Avignon, in subjection to the king of France, and the resulting great schism, when two popes existed simultaneously, one in Avignon and one in Rome, who excommunicated each other with all their followers.

"Due to all these schisms, (v LOON says, page 165) which had wrought irreparable damage to the moral authority of the pope, the governments of individual popes, who through immorality and mischief of all sorts, amply worthy of general contempt, so that both emperor Maximilian and Louis XII from France were filled with disgust and anger against the papal seat.

Louis XII had a medal minted, with the title: Perdam Babylonis nomen, (I will extirpate the name of Babylon (Rome)), v LOON, page 159.

The time of God's judgements against Rome is nearing, (says GUERS, page 340); everything she attempted to establish her supremacy, turned out against her. The council of Constance already proved this; that of Bazel also, (1431 A.D.). Pope Eugene IV wanted to dismantle this council and convoked another in Ferrara, but with the help of the Emperor of Germany and the king of France, it was declared unruly and prejudiced by default. (page 341). Nevertheless, pope Eugene in person opened his Italian council the following year and flung his anathema (banning curses) against the clergy, who were still gathered at Bazel. His anger did not disturb them, and they in turn issued the sentence of his dethroning. About this, rising in anger, the pope for the second time condemned the clergy of Bazel to eternal damnation. (*see they bit their tongues*). All these disputes continually affected papal power negatively.

In this way, the kingdom of the beast of that time, and its worldly and spiritual power, darkened. The Lord came down on Babylon, to confuse their tongues and speech.

END OF THE FIFTH PERIOD

SIXTH PERIOD

PHILADELPHIA

Brotherly Love

OR

The Scented Bush.

SIXTH PERIOD

Philadelphia: *Brotherly Love*

FROM

The Beginning of the Reformation, 1517 A.D.

TO

The Fall of Napoleon, 1815 AD.

This period spans the three centuries after the Reformation, during which time the Reformation, in spite of the persecutions by Popedom, the inquisitions and many dissensions within their own ranks, spread over an important part of Europe, and the Protestant church, whether in Lutheran or in Calvinistic direction, was accepted as a state church in most European countries.

It ended in 1815, when Europe, after all the upheaval and consequences of the French Revolution of 1789, finally came to rest again.

In this period, **the sixth head of the beast**, (4th beast of Daniel: the Roman Empire), revealed itself.

This sixth head or Kingdom is **the sixth mountain** or the mountain of the Protestant state powers.

(Rev 17:9, 10)

SIXTH PERIOD

PHILADELPHIAN TIME
or
THE PERIOD OF THE REFORMATION

6th Candlestick. Chapter 3,	6th Seal. Chapter 6,	6th Trumpet. Chapter 9,	6th Vial, Chapter 16,
And to the angel of the church in Philadelphia write; These things saith he that is holy, he that is true, he that hath the key of David, he that openeth, and no man shutteth; and shutteth, and no man openeth; 8. I know thy works: behold, I have set before thee an open door, and no man can shut it: for thou hast a little strength, and hast kept my word, and hast not denied my name. 9. Behold, I will make them of the synagogue of Satan, which say they are Jews, and are not, but do lie; behold, I will make them to come and worship before thy feet, and to know that I have loved thee. 10. Because thou hast kept the word of my patience, I also will keep thee from the hour of temptation, which shall come upon all the world, to try them that dwell upon the earth. 11. Behold, I come quickly: hold that fast which thou hast, that no man take thy crown. 12. Him that overcometh will I make a pillar in the temple of my God, and he shall go no more out: and I will write upon him the name of my God, and the name of the city of my God, which is new Jerusalem, which cometh down out of heaven from my God: and I will write upon him my new name. 13. He that hath an ear, let him hear what the Spirit saith unto the churches.	And I beheld when he had opened the sixth seal, and, lo, there was a great earthquake; and the sun became black as sackcloth of hair, and the moon became as blood; 13. And the stars of heaven fell unto the earth, even as a fig tree casteth her untimely figs, when she is shaken of a mighty wind. 14. And the heaven departed as a scroll when it is rolled together; and every mountain and island were moved out of their places. 15. And the kings of the earth, and the great men, and the rich men, and the chief captains, and the mighty men, and every bondman, and every free man, hid themselves in the dens and in the rocks of the mountains; 16. And said to the mountains and rocks, Fall on us, and hide us from the face of him that sitteth on the throne, and from the wrath of the Lamb: 17. For the great day of his wrath is come; and who shall be able to stand?	And the sixth angel sounded, and I heard a voice from the four horns of the golden altar which is before God, 14. Saying to the sixth angel which had the trumpet, Loose the four angels which are bound in the great river Euphrates. 15. And the four angels were loosed, which were prepared for an hour, and a day, and a month, and a year, for to slay the third part of men. 16. And the number of the army of the horsemen were two hundred thousand thousand: and I heard the number of them. 17. And thus I saw horses in the vision, and them that sat on them, having breastplates of fire, and of jacinth, and brimstone: and the heads of the horses were as the heads of lions; and out of their mouths issues fire and smoke and brimstone. 18. By these three was the third part of men killed, by the fire, and by the smoke, and by the brimstone, which issued out of their mouths. 19 For their power is in their mouth, and in their tails: for their tails were like unto serpents, and had heads, and with them they do hurt. 20. And the rest of the men which were not killed by these plagues yet repented not of the works of their hands, that they should not worship devils, and idols of gold, and silver, and brass, and stone, ad of wood: which neither can see, nor hear, nor walk: 21. Neither repented they of their murders, nor of their sorceries, nor of their fornication, nor of their thefts.	And the sixth angel poured out his vial upon the great river Euphrates; and the water thereof was dried up, that the way of the kings of the east might be prepared. 13. And I saw three unclean spirits like frogs come out of the mouth of the dragon, and out of the mouth of the beast, and out of the mouth of the false prophet. 14. For they are the spirits of devils, working miracles, which go forth unto the kings of the earth and of the whole world, to gather them to the battle of that great day of God Almighty. 15. Behold, I come as a thief. Blessed is he that watcheth, and keepeth his garments, lest he walk naked, and they see his shame. 16. And he gathered them together into a place called in the Hebrew tongue Armageddon.

238

SIXTH CANDLESTICK

THE LIGHT OR THE SPIRITUAL LIFE OF THE CONGREGATION

> The gates of Hell shall not prevail against my church.
>
> Matt 16:18

PHILADELPHIA, Rev 3:7–13

Philadelphia, a former larger town in Asia Minor, still exists today under the Turkish name of Allah-Sherr (the town of God) and still boasts a considerable Christian congregation, in the midst of its Mohammedan population.

The name Philadelphia suggests a resemblance with a **blooming and scented bush**[29], a very apt image, as we shall see, of the church of Jesus Christ in this period.

The Lord Jesus reveals himself to the congregation, which had risen from the dead through the Reformation, as **Holy and True**, who Himself also rose from the dead and lives, and is presently the true treasurer and steward of God's mysteries, (1 Cor. 4:1) who has the key to the kingdom of heaven[30]. He stands before His congregation, to call her to account. of her newly entrusted treasure of God's Word, the Gospel of Grace.

The *keys of the kingdom of heaven,* given by Jesus unto his disciples, are 1st according to (Matt 16:52) the *power* and 2nd according to (Luke 11:52) also the *knowledge.* In the fifth period, we saw, that the clergy of the Roman church took away the *key of knowledge,* by forbidding the reading of the Bible, and used the *key of her power,* to hinder the congregation from entering the door of the kingdom of heaven. What Jesus said to the Jewish lawyers in (Luke 11:52) and in (Matt 23:13) "Woe unto you, lawyers! For ye have taken away the *key of knowledge*" applied very fittingly to the Roman priesthood. "For ye shut up the kingdom of heaven against men, for

---

[29] Philadelphos. A bush with scented flowers (Athenaei p. 682)

[30] We remember what we said in the fifth seal, (page 185) about the kingdom of heaven, as the kingdom of God in this life and in the hereafter.

239

ye neither go in yourselves, neither suffer ye them that are entering to go in."

Through the blessed church reform in 1517, this would all change. The door to eternal life, Jesus Christ, and faith in Him, (John 10:7, 9), would again be opened. The once risen Saviour again gives unto His resurrected congregation the keys of heaven, and the door, which, when He opens it, no one can shut, but when He closes the door, no one can open it again. *And no one will from now on* until My return *close that door* is the promise, contained in the following words:

Verse.7. **"He that hath the key of David, he that openeth and no man shutteth, and shutteth, and no man openeth."**

They find their further explanation in (Isaiah 22:15–22), from which the Lord himself not only makes use but which He actually herewith indicates as a prophetic type of foreshadowing of the Reformation. An attentive reading of the words of Isaiah will, for all that, give us the deeper meaning of this prophecy, given *for the Reformation*. It is surely not acceptable that the Prophet Isaiah would have been given such an elaborate prophecy by the Holy Spirit, if it was of a purely domestic nature, concerning only the firing of the unfaithful servant of king Hizkiah (2 King 18:18), and the appointment of another in his place. The pettiness of this happening already makes us suspect, that this prophetic burden of Isaiah has a deeper typical meaning. The reference to these words for the sixth period by the Lord Jesus proves it, and it becomes quite clear to us when we examine the meaning of the names occurring in this prophecy. We already said that names in the Holy Scripture generally have an important meaning. So it is here.

Shebna means *mind*, also *youth*, and here it is the type for the *Priesthood in the Roman church*, who left God's truth and from their own mind formulated a teaching of Salvation.

Eliakim means, *appointed by God*, and is a foreshadowing of the *reformers appointed by Jesus Christ*, who had to replace the unrighteous Roman preachers for His faithful of that period.

Hilkia, the father of Eliakim, means *heritage of the Lord*. With this name Peter also described (1 Pet 5:3) the *congregation* or the flock of *the Lord*. The reformers where also the spiritual sons of the congregation from apostolic times.

The *house of David* is the image of the *kingdom of God* of which Jesus Christ is the spiritual *king David*. (Jer 30:9. Ezek 34:23, 24.Ezek 37:24, 25 Hos 3:5).

The *key to the house of David* is also the same as the *key of heaven, the knowledge and the power in the kingdom of God.*

The whole typical meaning of this in Isaiah is therefore: Jesus Christ, as the head of the church will take away the keys of the kingdom of heaven from the unfaithful servant Shebna, the apostate priesthood of the Roman church, and reject them as unfaithful servants (verse 19) and as He once rose from the dead, so He once again rises from the dead church, as its Head, through the reformers, Eliakim (verses 20, 21), who are the spiritual descendants of the first Christian church, (the son of Hilkiah, verse 20). These would replace Shebna, and He would give over to them the keys of the kingdom of heaven, therewith to open the door to His Father's Kingdom (verse 22).

Verse 8 "**I know thy works**", says the Lord. This is not followed by any reproach. The works were thus good and works of faith.

"**Behold I have set before thee an open door, and no man can shut it.**" The **door** is **Jesus Christ**, as He named himself (John 10:1–9) "I am the door, by me if any man enter in, he shall be saved." But also by **faith in Him** (Acts 14:27), and **the preaching of His Word** (Col 4:3). By Him and His knowledge (key) the sinner comes to self-understanding, repentance, faith and renewing of the heart, as already the Father predicted about Him (Isaiah 53:11) "By His knowledge shall my righteous servant justify many for He shall bear their iniquities." If Jesus was the door in the reformers, by which access to the kingdom of God was opened again, the princes, who were involved with the Reformation, were the door, through which the Gospel was again accessible to the nations, the teachers the door to the congregation, the father to the family. (Psalm 24:7; 1 Cor 16:9; Col 4:3). We have already seen (fourth trumpet), that in a Christian kingdom, Christ must be the king or sun in the teacher, in the prince and in the head of the family.

Christ therefore, with the Reformation, stood up anew in the teacher, in the king and in the family father, as the spiritually risen one, to give the congregation the opened door with the key of knowledge.

"**Thou hast a little strength, and hast kept my word,**" says the Son of God to the believers in the time of the Reformation. This strength, however weak in itself (2 Cor 12:10), relied on the Word of God, which had again become alive in them. With the sword, the reformers overcame the power and the anger of Popedom. These were the works of faith, which Jesus saw in them, the rejection of papal fables and the attention given to the word of the Lord, wherewith they repelled the violence of devils. Who does not here think of the well-known words of faith of Luther, at the warning not to go to the Diet at Worms: "Although there be as many devils at Worms as there are tiles on the roofs, I would still go there."

"And hast not denied my name," that is: the name of the **Redeemer** and **Saviour**, upon whom the believers could again hope for eternity, instead of upon the Saints of the Roman church.

Christ our righteousness. Through faith in Him, the sinner is justified before God. This was the motto, the basis of the Reformation and on that belief, Christ again founded His church, on that belief alone, it still exists as such today.

That belief would, however, not generally remain in the resurrected church of Christ. For He said further on: **"Behold, I will make them of the synagogue of Satan** (the school) **which say they are Jews and are not, but do lie."** Already in the second period, that of the church fathers, we learned to know these Jews, deniers of God, as those who deny the divinity of Jesus Christ, and refute the trinity of the Almighty: - the Arians of the second period. Also, in the time of the Reformation, this teaching denying Christ would rise again. It is perhaps known to the Christian reader, how belief in the divinity of Jesus Christ, whereupon the whole Christian religion is based, was already contested in the previous century, first in France, later in England and especially in this century, in Germany, with such good results, that this doctrine has become an object of derision by the greater majority of the members of the Protestant Church. How few believers in the Protestant-Christian church are there presently; who worship Jesus as their God and Saviour, as the true Divine man and the mediator between God and man? How few teachers in this church could underwrite a testimonial in faithfulness and righteousness? How many in comparison, who say, they are worshippers of God, or Jews, and are not?

Indeed, it is easier for flesh and blood, for the world and its adherents, to believe in one God, who once created heaven and earth, and in Jesus Christ, as the greatest moral teacher and the most exalted human being who ever lived here on earth, than to admit before this loving, but also Holy God, to be a damnable sinner, and to place all hope for Salvation only on the offered grace of God the Father, and the merit of His Son Jesus Christ, as God revealed in the flesh.

We therefore also clearly see in the present state of religious conviction of the greatest part of Christendom, the fulfilment of this particular prophecy of Jesus Christ, in that which He has foretold in His Revelation, concerning the belief in His Divinity in the present time. Already John said it (John 1:11) explicitly "He came unto His own, and His own receiveth him not." And Jesus himself said (John 5:43) "I am come in my Father's name, and ye received me not."

This will not remain so forever.

If anything could convince the unbeliever of the truth of Christ's divinity, then it must be this, His own Revelation, not only because of the divine wisdom of that which has already accurately been fulfilled in the past periods of the Christian church but also, especially in the striking happenings, which He has predicted to His servants for these present times, which we will presently learn to understand.

"Behold," says the *Holy and True*, as He called Himself in verse 7, "Behold, I will make them who deny Jesus' divinity, to come and worship before thy feet, and to know that I have loved thee." This acknowledgement by the modern clergy, that the old believers for all that, had the only true understanding of the biblical truth and teaching, has not been realised up to now. If this promise is not yet fulfilled, it apparently still lies in the future. But then it does not belong to the sixth period. Actually, the sixth period of the congregation ends with the words of Jesus in verse 9, **"Behold, I will make,"** etc. The remainder flows into the seventh period and is thus still to come. It is already clear, that Jesus, just as in verses 7 and 8, also in the 9th verse, begins to speak in the present tense "I know" and ends with, just as in the following verses, to speak in the future tense: "I will make" etc. Those who deny the divinity of Christ, have come to tempt those who live on earth with their acknowledgement that they did not stand in the truth, they shall come in "the hour of temptation", of which Christ speaks in the 10th verse, which will come upon all the world to try them that dwell upon the earth. This however belongs to the end of the seventh period. We must therefore leave the rest of the sixth candlestick, to find it again at the right time and place in the seventh period and to explain it.

The reader must not speculate about this, but remember that we have already said in the beginning of this work that each candlestick, seal, trumpet and vial does not stop at the end of that period, but remains evident until the return of the Lord, and that with each new period something new occurs in the church and in the congregation, which had not yet occurred before, that all the former remains in existence, the one in *more* the other in *lesser* degree, with and next to each other until the return of the Lord. So does the Roman church, which began in the third period, still exist, up to now, in all her diverging ideologies and greater or lesser apostasy from God's Word, in her Pergamosian, Thyatirian or Sardisian form. Also, the other candlesticks, seals, trumpets, etc.

The first trumpet still sounds in the missionary work in the present time among the gentiles, as it becomes quite clear to the reader after all that has been said.

Similarly, the Philadelphian congregation, or the present Protestant church, survives through the seventh period, until the return of the Lord, and the promise given her in verse 9 up to the end of this candlestick, will eventually be realised as surely as those already fulfilled. We will go over this promise in the seventh period, where the time of its fulfilment in the church history is expected. With the explanation of this sixth candlestick, we have now come nearer to the present time.

The name of this period: Philadelphia, indicates a similarity (Filadelfeia) with a bush with scented flowers. Although we named this period of the Reformation a revival of the Smyrnian period, it lacked the bitterness, the mutual bloody strife with the battle sword, which characterized the period of the church fathers. If it was to the Lord; mire, which is scented but bitter, the period of the Reformation notwithstanding all her sects and religious conflict, did not show bitterness before the Lord, but the revelation of the *savour of His knowledge* (2 Cor 2:14), a *sweet savour of Christ* (2 Cor 2:15) in them that are saved, a *good savour unto life* (2 Cor 2 :16) and an additional *brotherly love*[31], to God as a *sweet-smelling savour*. (Eph 5:2. Phil 4:18)

The old fig tree of the church (Luke 13:6–9), already rotting in branches and roots for over 1000 years, apparently already withered and dead, began to bloom anew (Mark 13:28), and caused a new shoot with scented blooms to sprout forth. That it bore *blooms* in this period, *sweet smelling to the Lord*, but *without ripe fruits*, His Revelation will presently reveal unto us.

---

[31] Philadelphia means also brotherly love, and this also revealed itself to a higher degree, although especially in love to the brethren of the same religious confession, and greater separation from those of a different opinion.

SIXTH SEAL

or

THE SPIRITUAL LIFE OF THE POWERS IN CHURCH AND STATE

> Suppose ye that I am come to give peace
> on earth? I tell you, nay; but rather
> division. The father shall be divided
> against the son, and the son against
> the father.
> Luke 12:51, 53.

Rev 6:12–17 and Rev 7:1–47

Verse 12.**"And I beheld when He** (the Lamb) **had opened the sixth seal, and, lo, there was a great earthquake."**

Thus, with this period of the Reformation, a great **earthquake** would develop. The earth we learned to know as the image of the social conditions of the ordinances in church and state in Christian Europe (the Roman Empire), during the period under discussion. Earthquakes must therefore indicate great **changes in the condition of Christian Europe**. In this sense, the word in (Heb 12:16) is thus also used "Whose voice *shook the earth*", namely by the appearance of Jesus Christ on earth during the existence of the heathen Roman Empire. In (Isaiah 29:3–6, Isaiah 13:5-13, Psalm 18:7, 8, 16, 18; Hagg 2:6, 7), *earthquakes* are clearly sketched as *unrest among nations*. Through the testimony of Luther and his co-workers against the Roman church, unrest took hold of the heart of Christians and all states in Christendom. We need not write about the appalling changes in the existing order of things, brought about by the Reformation, as this is well known by our readers. Our prophecy names this, a *great earthquake*.

"And the sun became black as sackcloth of hair, and the moon became blood."- From the fourth trumpet we already know *the sun as Christ* and the *moon as the congregation*, and also *black* as the colour of *darkness* we found in the third seal. **A sackcloth of hair** is the image of **repentance** and **sorrow**. The preacher of repentance John the Baptist was clothed in *camel's hair* (Matt 3:4, Mark 1:6). According to Jewish religious customs the wearing of *sackcloth* is well known as an act of repentance and a *sign of sorrow*. (see Joel 1:8).

The *two witnesses* from (Rev 11:3) are also represented as *"clothed in sackcloth"* during the coming anti-Christian tribulation.

The attentive reader will probably find it strange that Christ, the sun; the congregation, the moon; and the teachers, the stars, who were already embattled and darkened in the fourth period (fourth trumpet and fourth vial), so that in the fifth period they did not shine, are yet again represented, the sun to become as black, the moon as blood, while in verse 13 we will presently find the stars as in heaven again, which restoration Revelation has not mentioned yet.

As correct as the reader's comment may be, just as correct is the proof that this peculiarity again confirms the truth and consequence of our explanation. Simultaneously with this seal, the sixth trumpet began sounding in 1517, which in chapter 10:1 describes the condition of the gospel preaching, and verse 1 shows that, with the onset of this period, Christ as the sun, had appeared again in the heaven of the church, while in verse 2, the forming of a new congregation (moon) and new teachers (stars) is described. The seal now shows us the actions of these teachers or stars, who are simultaneously pictured as resurrected. The latter announcement of the trumpet does not pertain to a later date in the history of the church, but only the sequence in which the different happenings in history were shown to John in different images.

In order to understand the whole picture of (verse 12), we must not present the Protestant church as the only congregation of Philadelphia, as THE church of Jesus Christ.

In the Roman church, we also find, especially during the awakening of the Reformation, many believers, who, shaken out of their Sardisian sleep, through belief in Christ the Saviour, belonging to His body, the church, relating with the believers from the Protestants, together forming the church of Christ in that period. Christ, the sun, who wanted to remain with His church until the end of the world, and live in the hearts of His own, was darkened in His church by the testimony of the Reformation. The reformers accused the clergy of the Roman church of that time, albeit correctly, as false teachers, but these reciprocally accused the reformers of preaching a doctrine "whereby one would go straight to damnation." This caused doubt in the hearts of the simple, and the impartial, the unsure, the seeking had to ask: "Where is Christ, the Saviour, with which of both churches is He, that I can find Him?" The Reformers further renounced all authority of the councils and elevated the Bible above the councils.

The Roman church on the other hand, placed their traditional teachings and the pronouncement of the councils concerning the Gospel above the Bible, and thousands upon thousands in the Roman church, who were earnest about the salvation of their soul, but had been fed since birth with all the heresies of their church, and had never known the authority of the Bible as the Word of God, naturally had to ask: "where is the truth?". Thus,

God's believers in both churches experienced sorrow and repentance, that each other had to be fought against, and Christ, the sun, in His love and fullness, was darkened in His church and servants.

When one, however, decided firmly for the Protestant faith, the heart once again was filled with lack of love for the undecided and such as think otherwise, and in the heart, Christ, the sun of righteousness, was darkened in His love; when the time of persecution of the Roman church started, then one grasped the worldly sword, to win and defend the freedom of religion to salvation, by taking ones neighbours' life, and seal the belief: "*the blood of Jesus Christ cleanses me of all sin,*" with the spilt blood of fellow sinners. These were not the works of the son of man[32], here *the sun of heavenly love became as raiment of repentance and sorrow.* This was not the life that is from God, this was the earthly, the *natural* life, which we often already represented with the image of *blood.* The unholy longing for the holy Word of God, the bitterness against the neighbour and the grasping of the worldly sword to defend the faith made the congregation, (the moon), as blood.

Alas! Instead both, in love with each other, would seek Jesus the Head of the church and serve Him, both fed and maintained the mutual hatred since that time up to now. If both are guilty herein before the Lord, the greatest guilt falls upon the Roman priesthood, who set their human statements above God's Word, and appropriated an apostolic authority, of which she had become unworthy through her actions, and, as the sixth head of the fourth beast of Daniel (the Roman empire) remained faithful in its sorrowful role as persecutor of the believers. The Protestant church, instead of using the Word of God and the meekness of Jesus Christ against them, as did the church of the first three centuries, grasped the worldly sword, and was thereby filled with un-Christian hatred and bitterness against her persecutors, just as the church of the second period. Thus was the image of Christ, the sun, darkened in His church. Thus was Christ, the heavenly love, covered in *black* sackcloth of repentance in His congregation, His body. Thus the *moon*, the congregation, became as *blood.*

If the reader perhaps finds this judgement over the blessed and its effect in the sometimes too highly praised church reform too harsh, it is not our view only. We will presently find a similar finding from our writer Van Loon. Above our own and all other writers stands the judgement of Jesus Christ, the Lord of the church and we have seen in the twelfth verse, how the Lord showed John the *condition* of the *congregation* of Philadelphia (as

---

[32] Here Christ is darkened in His church.

blood) such as she appeared before His own holy eyes, but also the manner in which she reflected *His image* (the sun) on the world (*black as sackcloth*), and against the judgement of the Son, to whom the Father gave all judgement (John 5:22), no mortal will dare oppose himself. That through the Reformation the congregation was not brought back to the original condition of a bridal congregation of the Lord, as she was in the first apostolic period, but only to the Smyrnian condition of the second period, is not only clear from the resemblance of both religious conditions and religious strife but is also evident in the words of Christ in the prophecies of both periods. Also in the second seal, the second trumpet and vial, we find the congregation predicted, not as a white horse anymore, but *red as blood*, and the clergy, not armed with the bow of the Gospel, but with a great sword, and with "the power, to take away peace from the earth." (Rev 6:4)

This judgement is also confirmed by what the Lord says in the following verse, concerning the teachers and kings in the period of the Reformation. We do know that these together form the seal.

Verse 13. **"And the stars of heaven fell unto the earth, even as a fig tree casteth her untimely figs, when she is shaken of a mighty wind."**

The *stars* are already known to us as the *teachers and Christian kings*, the *heaven* is the church heaven or the recently restored *kingdom of God* on earth in that period. The *earth, the earthly ordinances* in the Christian states. The second part of this verse, as much in comparison to explain the first part, depicts the same happening, yet under another image more flamboyantly.

The fig tree is in (Joel 1:7, Hos 9:10 and Song of Songs 2:13), the image of the believers of **the church of the Lord** in the vineyard of Israel. The same image is also used by the Saviour himself in (Luke 13:6–8). It is God the Father, who planted the *fig tree of the church* in His vineyard, Israel. His only begotten Son, Jesus Christ is the vinedresser. For three years He walked upon the earth, yet the fig tree bore no fruit.

Only in the fourth year (verse 8) did the fig tree begin to blossom and to bear fruit[33]. The *figs* of the fig tree are therefore, because the one image flows into another, just as much as the *stars of heaven*, the *teachers* of the church, and they were thrown down, and *fell* unto the earth, when *the fig tree was shaken by a strong wind*.

Wind is the image of **the teaching**, that of the **pure teaching** of the gospel as well as that of **false teaching**. See for example as *false doctrine*

---

[33] Jesus walked and preached for three and a half years on the earth.

(Job 8:2, Psalm 1:4, Isaiah 41:29, Isaiah 57:13, Jer 4:10 – 12, Jer 5:13) "The *prophets* are nothing but *wind*, for the word is not in them." As *lies* and *deceit*, (Hos 12:1–2, Mica 2:11, Eph 4:14), "tossed to and fro and blown about by every *wind of doctrine*." (Matt 7:25–27, Jude 12)

As the *pure doctrine* and *works of the Holy Spirit,* we find the *wind* used as an image and parable in (John 3:8), as also in (Acts 2:2, Ezek 37:9).

The appropriate explanation of this image is simply this: When the fig tree of the church was shaken to and fro by the gospel preaching of the Reformation, and by the powerful opposition of the Roman false doctrines, she threw her not yet deeply rooted and planted in Christ teachers and kings, away from the just restored kingdom of God unto the earth as unripe figs. Until the Reformation, the clergy stood *above* the state ordinances. With the Reformation, they not only resorted *under* the state, but instead of being purely heavenly, became worldly in their feelings, and religion melted to a great extent with politics, totally to the disadvantage of the first. The prophecy expresses this more accurately by naming the *figs* as *unripe*. The judgement of Christ, the Lord of the church, also over the Reformation, is therefore, that her fruits were *unripe*. The Reformation had not gone far enough. Instead of going back to the total separation from the state and not using the worldly sword anymore, and therefore to become the Christian church of the first period again, instead of, as Luther so urgently and repeatedly admonished, to let the Word of God be the only guide, without the assistance of the worldly arm, the Protestant church became a state church, just as in the second period under Constantine. Thereby she remained *unripe*, as Jesus calls her. If this judgement should appear much too harsh to the Protestant Christian in his unlimited respect for the Reformation and the Protestant church, he will have to accept the judgement of the Lord of the church, although with sorrow, in faith and resignation, and when he further follows this explanation of the Revelation from God's Word attentively, the judgement of the Lord will become clear to him.

The Reformation did not come to the perfection, which she could have achieved, through her own fault, and thus remained *unripe*. What still lies hidden in the future for her, the Word of the Lord in His Revelation will further teach us. That the judgement of the Lord of the church is not only reflected in our view, but many Christian writers of church history say the same, the reader will soon realize from a statement by Mr. Van Loon.

Just as it was in the case of the sixth candlestick, we have hereby come up to our time in the sixth seal. That in our time great winds of false doctrines are blowing in the so generally expanded modern doctrine,

249

wherewith the fig tree of the church of Christ throws off her unbelieving modern teachers as unripe figs, - will not be strange to the Christian reader.

The further predictions of the sixth seal, which carries through to the seventh period, are not yet fulfilled but belong to the time of the end. The church heaven (verse 14) is not yet dissolved, it still exists although her days are numbered, and the time of the third woe approaches under the seventh trumpet, when the death penalty will be coupled to the testimony of the name of Christ, and the beast, which is not, although it is, again rises out of the bottomless pit, to the destruction of believers. To him, who knows the prophecy and compares it with the signs of the time, it is not dark anymore[34].

To this sixth seal still belongs the whole seventh chapter of Revelation, for only with the eighth chapter, is the seventh seal opened. Forthwith we find described in Revelation *more events*, which *occur simultaneously*, but which could not be seen or described simultaneously by John. In chapter 7 another action, which belongs to the earthquake of the sixth seal, but could not, without causing confusion, have been revealed in the story of that image, and was therefore shown to John (Rev 7:1) by the Lord. The word *"After this"* thus indicates the order of things, wherein John saw these images, but not the time frame, wherein they will be fulfilled. This is evident from the meaning of the imagery and its comparison with church history.

---

[34] To his amazement the reader will perceive in the seventh period, how much of the great events of our time are the fulfilment of what Revelation predicts in imagery as the beginning of the last days.

SIXTH SEAL

or

THE SPIRITUAL LIFE OF THE POWERS IN THE CHURCH AND STATE.

> Blessed are you when people revile you and persecute
> you and utter all kinds of evil against you falsely
> on my account.Rejoice and be glad, for your
> reward is great in heaven.
> Matt. 5:11, 12.

REV 7:1

Verse 1.**"After this I saw four angels standing at the four corners of the earth, holding back the four winds of the earth so that no wind could blow on earth or sea or against any tree."**

The *four corners of the earth* are well known as the *four points of the compass,* (Jer 49:36) meaning: *roundabout.*

The *corners* are also mentioned in the Holy Scripture in the sense of *strength* or *pillar of strength,* (Jer 48:45, Jer 51:26, Zeph 1:16, Zeph 3:6) (high towers). The earth is the social and religious condition of Europe in this period. **The four corners of the earth** are therefore also four pillars of the existing order of things, or **four great Roman princes**.

The further images in this vision are already well known to us. The four angels or teachers are the four main reformers: Luther, Melachton, Zwingli and Calvin. As the Christian teachers and Christian rulers together form the seal, we must also find four protestant princes in the time of the Reformation, who defend the Reformation. We find them in the four well-known persons, the Elector of Saxony, the Earl of Hessen, the Earl of Brandenburg and the Prince of Anhalt[35]. These formed together with the four reformers the four angels, who had to withhold the four winds, and therefore stood at the *four corners* or *pillars of strength of the Roman churches*. Wind we know to mean doctrine, pure as well as false. That the four winds were opposed to the angels, is indicated by the fact that the latter

---

[35] From the *protest* delivered by these four princes on the second day of the Reichstag in Spiers (1529) against the Roman church, the *Protest*ants and the *Protest*ant church still derive their name today.

had to hold them back. We therefore here have to cope with false doctrine, and as there existed *four* false doctrines, with four personal powers, who, in opposition with the four reforming protective powers, maintained the false doctrine, and wanted to destroy the evangelical doctrine. In the same spirit, we find the image of the wind used in (Jer 4:11–13). The four winds must be *great* princes, the four angels *smaller*.

For these latter had to hold back the persecution of the *greater* princes. If however, the roles had been reversed, and the great princes had become the defenders of the gospel, the smaller princes would not even have thought of persecution. Leaning on God's Word and power they could easily have acted as protectors of the Reformation against the four great princes, the enemies of the Reformation. We find these four winds, who were at the same time the four corners of the earth, or the four pillars of the existing Roman church and states, clearly depicted in the history of church reform. 1st *the pope* as *ruler of Italy*, 2nd *Charles V, Emperor of Germany*, (at the same time king of Spain and Earl of Netherlands), 3rd *Frans I, king of France* and 4th *Ferdinand, archduke of Austria, king of Bohemia and Hungary*. When we bear in mind, that the epicentre of the Reformation, totally included and encompassed by the *four* just-named protestant states and their defending princes, lay exactly in the middle of these four hostile states and powers, we also find therein the fulfilment of the first meaning of the four corners of the earth. The four reformers would therefore oppose the four proponents and instigators of the Roman doctrine on a spiritual level.

The four previously named Protestant princes, the great Roman world powers in worldly spheres, hindered the smothering of the Reformation. This actually literally occurred. The Lord of the church, in His adorable providence, gave His resurrecting church not only wise and steadfast princes as defending angels, to firstly tame her enemies in a peaceful way, so that they would not disturb the social condition (earth) of the Protestants, nor the Protestant nations (sea), nor exterminate any Protestant prince or particular person or reformer (trees), but He further caused the hostile princes to mutually disagree amongst each other, and to war against one another, until the Reformation had gained enough ground, and was well enough established, never again to be destroyed, but gloriously resist the impeding persecutions.

Also in the following times of the Reformation, up to our century, four lesser kingdoms and countries have always by excellence been the Protectors and seats of the Reformation in Europe, namely England, Netherlands, Prussia, and the Scandinavian kingdom, against the four great

Roman countries: Italy, Spain, France and Austria. Up until our days, the first verse of the seventh chapter has remained in force; from (verse 2) it flows further until the end of the seventh period. We will discuss this again at the appropriate time and place.

SIXTH TRUMPET

or

THE CONDITION AND EFFECT OF THE GOSPEL PREACHING

Rev 9:13–21. Rev 10:1, 2.

If the manner in which the gospel preaching in its increasing degeneration was so far the only subject and content of the description, now with the Reformation, a second church appears openly in the Roman countries of Europe. If the trumpet truly sketches the condition and effect of the gospel preaching, we must beforehand expect that in the sixth trumpet, next to the Roman church, the Reformation and the origin of the Protestant church are predicted. In this expectation, we did not err. We find the first described in (Rev 9:13 21), and the last in (Rev 10:1, 2.) The Lord allowed John to see firstly the mutual strife in, and the actions of, the Roman and Protestant churches in this sixth period in (Rev 9), as the second woe, which followed immediately after the first woe of the fifth trumpet. In (Rev 10:1, 2) the origin and being of the Reformation is sketched, although this happened simultaneously with (Rev 9:13–21). Yes, in the history of the church, it was even somewhat preceded by it. While we now see not the way in which these things were shown to John, but their reaction and fulfilment in history as a directive to the order of explanation, we will deal first in (Rev 10) with the predicted Reformation, and thereafter in (Rev 9) with the predicted actions of the Roman church. We only do this to allow the reader to follow the order of history, not to try and improve the work of the Lord, whom, we later shall see, had the most valid reason for His order of action. History of the Protestant church for all that flows from (Rev 10:1) through to (Rev 11:14). There the sixth trumpet ends in the last portion of the seventh period, wherein it continues, as it will later become clear to the reader.

THE REFORMATION

> And this gospel of the kingdom shall be preached
> in all the world for a witness unto all
> nations; and then shall the end come.
> Matt 24:14.

Rev 10:1, 2.

Verse 1. **"And I saw another mighty angel coming down from heaven, wrapped in a cloud."** *Angel* means clergy. *Another angel* is therefore *another clergy*, than the formerly described clergy of (Rev 9) the Roman church, therefore *the Protestant teachers*: **the reformers.**

The **mighty angel** was however also **Christ, the messenger of the covenant**. (Mal 3:1). For shortly He will say (Rev 11:3) *"I will give power* unto **my two witnesses**, etc."

He came **down from heaven**. The Lord himself names His first coming down to earth, His coming in the flesh (John 6:41, 50, 58), as He walked visibly on earth, and came to preach the gospel of Salvation and the kingdom and *to make known* to His own *the only true God*. (John 17:3, 6, 25, 26). Now, however, he came anew to reveal the knowledge of the true God and His Son, Jesus Christ, which Popedom had destroyed, and came anew to earth, from heaven, but now not in the flesh, not personally visible. For He was **"wrapped in a cloud, the cloud of His witnesses,"** (Heb 12:1) the **reformers.** Although personally invisible, it was however the Lord himself, who came back through the reformers to renew the covenant of the lost gospel of grace on earth for all who wanted to seek him; because **the rainbow**, *the sign of the covenant*, (Gen 9:12, 13), **was over His head**. If the angel, the clergy, was the body of the Lord, the figure or bodily form into which He *was wrapped*; - He Himself was the head of the body and upon that head shone the image and sign of the renewed covenant of grace. However the Roman church may have slandered, the Lord Himself here testified irrefutably in His Revelation, that the Reformation was not the work of man, did not originate from human self-interest or insight, but that *He Himself* had, *in* and *through* the reformers, descended from heaven, to reveal the knowledge of the Father and the way to Salvation anew, which had been darkened and lost through the Roman church.

Thus did the Lord appear again on earth, **"and His face was like the sun."** Since the congregation must reflect the image of the Lord, in this period of the Reformation she displayed anew the righteousness valid before God, now Christ, the sun of righteousness, who in the fourth period had been darkened, again became alive in His church, and the reformers once again preached the righteousness through belief in Christ, which the Roman church had for so many centuries replaced with the supposed merits of the saints. Just as the Lord revealed *His face* at the end of the Old and the beginning of the New Covenants, *shining like the sun* (Matt 17:2), so also does He again appear anew in the full splendour of righteousness at the reawakening of His church at the end of the New Covenant, because "this Gospel of the kingdom shall be preached in all the world for a witness unto all nations, and then shall the end come." (Matt 24:14). In this way John also saw the face of the Lord. (Rev 1:16)

"And His feet like pillars of fire."

The feet or the messengers of the Lord, already like unto *copper* in the fourth period, meaning *apostate and corruptors,* were again full of the fire of the Holy Spirit in the reformers and their supporters, yes, mighty pillars full of the fire of the Holy Spirit, for the congregation; just as the apostles (Gal 2:9) were considered pillars of the congregation. *Both feet* were for one part the *Lutheran testimony* (Luther and Melancton), and for the other part, the *reformed testimony* (Calvin and Zwingli), where through the body of the Lord, the congregation, again moved upon the earth. The feet of the Lord have yet a second meaning, which will appear in (verse 2).

Verse 2. **"And He** (the mighty angel, Christ in the reformer) **had in His hand a little book open."** This hand must have been the LEFT one, as Christ, the angel, in verse 5, raises the *right hand* in a solemn oath to *heaven.* The meaning of this *left hand* will be clarified later.

The small rolled down or opened book, cannot be the still remaining, or unfulfilled part of the book with seven seals, while in the fulfilment of Revelation, at the time of the sixth period, the seventh seal was not opened yet and the little book is said to be open. It may be understood to be the New Testament, the reading of which was forbidden by the pope in the previous period (1214 A.D.), yet now is again opened by the reformers and made known to the nations, so that they would see therein, not only what serves to their Salvation, but also the whole counsel of God. (Acts 20:27).

The whole counsel of God, contained in the New Testament, is completely revealed in His last book, "The Revelation". For therein the last testimony for Christendom, of what will happen with and at the return of the Lord, is revealed to the servants of the Lord, although it remained a mystery at the beginning of the Reformation[36]. The understanding and hope of the imminent return of the Lord became evident and alive again with several writers in the sixth period and in the seventh period, in which we are living now, as well as in a great portion of the congregation, just as with Christendom in the first century, - efforts were made to decipher as much as possible what the Revelation predicted about it, but what will happen before and at the return of the Lord, remained a mystery, just as it is still today in the seventh period. This is also very natural. The angel had the opened book in His hand, so that the mystery, if one would have sought it in the correct way, would already have been understood in the seventh period, but it being open, had no particular reference on the seventh period, or to be read and understood then. On the contrary! The contents of this book consisted (verse 8-11) of what John again had to prophesy in the seventh period (see verse 7) before many nations, people, tongues and kings. In that period, we will also find the contents of this book in its correct place again.

"And he set his right foot upon the sea, and his left foot on the earth." It is clear, that in the short and to-the-point Revelation, it would not be stated with emphasis that precisely the *right foot* of the Lord would stand upon the *sea*, and the *left* on the *earth* if there would not be a particular meaning to it. The fulfilment of this action of Christ must be found in the history of the Reformation. When Paul (1 Cor 12:14–31) speaks so much about the different members of the body of the Lord, (the congregation), among others about the *feet*, then it is, or an outdrawn inconsequential parable, and who would claim in faith it to be by the inspiration of the Holy Spirit[37], or there must be a spiritual meaning to it.

The feet of the Lord we already know as His messengers of peace (Angels) and servants to the congregation.

Here it appears that each must have a different sphere of activity, while the right foot is placed on the sea, the Roman sea of nations, and the left foot on the earth, the Christian society. When Christ, the Reformation angel, first places His right foot upon the existing Roman sea of nations, the *right foot* cannot mean anything else than the *Evangelist ministry* of

---

[36] We are reminded of the highly unfavourable judgement (later somewhat elaborate) of Luther about the Revelation of John, and yet he would, if he had applied our key, been able to understand.

[37] Not a mechanical, literal, where the writers are only instruments, but only for as much as it concerns the truth of God, the pure teaching of the Gospel, and the meaning of the imagery of the Holy Spirit, therefore organic, where the human mind connects to the Godly Word.

Christ, which He exerted in and through the reformers and their contemporary teachers, to preach the Gospel of Salvation, to tear away poor lost souls from the clutches of Rome and to win them for Christ. When the Lord placed His right foot, or the Evangelist ministry *upon the sea of nations*, the waters parted just as in (Gen 1:9, 10) and dry land, mountains and the *earth* appeared as the *Protestant congregation* and *state ordinances*.

Upon these the Lord now places His left foot, to care for them as His flock, to conserve and keep them in His name. But then the *left foot* cannot be anything else than the *shepherd and teacher ministry* of the Lord, who tried to keep the souls won for Him in the truth, and lead and feed His flock. Both these ministries belong with each other in the Protestant church, the Evangelist ministry to win souls for Christ, and the Shepherd ministry to keep the souls won for Christ. Both are the feet of the Lord, wherewith His body, the congregation, moves over the earth, whereby she is supported, the pillars, whereupon she stands and leans against, in order to grow to a holy temple of the Lord (Eph 4:15, 16. Eph 2:21).

In this manner, the Protestant church was founded by the Lord, formed and preserved during the period of the Reformation. How the Roman church reacted to her in this time, is mentioned in the Revelation already in the previous, but simultaneously in the current chapter.

SIXTH TRUMPET

OR

THE CONDITION OF THE GOSPEL PREACHING

> The servant is not greater than his Lord. If they have persecuted me, they will also persecute you; but all these things will they do unto you for my name's sake, because they know not him that sent me.
>
> John 15:20, 21.

Rev 9:13–21.

The wonderful vision with which this sixth trumpet begins is repeated and explained in many more wonderful places. To mention it all would take us too far away and is definitely of no value and therefore unnecessary. GARTNER correctly stated in his "Morgen Licht van den Werelsabbath" concerning this vision: "The prediction is wonderfully profound," yet declares them as the conquering expeditions of the followers of Mohammed, which started approximately in 630 A.D., and whose consequences would continue in the possession of the Holy land by the Turkish Empire. To which ridiculous human wisdom one can arrive, is illustrated by Baxter in his "Louis Napoleon, the predicted ruler of the world," a view, not taken from God's Word, but from his own power and ingenuity, in trying to explain the Revelation, when he explains the vision of (verses 16, 17, 18), as a battle of the cavalry of Napoleon III in the war of Armageddon and verse 19 as *mounted cavalry*.

After having read the explanation of the fifth trumpet (the locusts), this sixth trumpet, through its resemblance therewith, as well as through its effect in this period of the Reformation, will immediately be realised and understood by our somewhat developed reader, as the Roman clergy in her persecution of the Protestants and of the Protestant church. This supposition is well founded, as the Word of God will make it clear to us.

Verse 13. **"And the sixth angel sounded."** This is already known to the reader as the gospel preaching during the sixth period of the church of Jesus Christ on earth, the Philadelphian period of the Reformation. The *sixth trumpet* is thus the *trumpet of Reformation*. The fifth still sounds next to it.

261

Verse 14 **"And I heard a voice from the four horns of the golden altar which is before God, saying to the sixth angel which had the trumpet: Loose the four angels which are bound in the great river Euphrates."**

The **voice** out of the horns of the golden altar is that of **Jesus Christ** himself, the Lord of the church. The **golden altar**, (Rev 8:3) is the image of the **high priestly ministry of Jesus**, wherewith he brings the prayers and praises, of both the living, and the waiting believers in the realm of the departed, up to God the Father, and therefore the heavenly realization of that which is represented by the smoke or incense altar from the sanctuary of the earthly temple or the tabernacle, as we described it in the fifth seal (page 188). **Horns** are the image of **power**, spiritual as well as earthly. (1 Sam 2:10. Jer 48:25. Dan 7:11, 21. Dan 8:21. Rev 5:6. Rev 17:12, 16). The four horns of the altar are therefore the four spiritual powers or the quadruple office of Christ, as we have shown in the first seal (pages 51).

As the Lord of the church on earth and her Apostle, Prophet, Evangelist and Shepherd, He makes His servants on earth preach His gospel, and also by virtue of the four ministries or offices, gives His commandments concerning the lot, the suffering and battles to His church. Therefore the voice of Jesus Christ came out of the four horns (ministries) of the altar, to command the believing teachers and kings, that is: the sixth angel, who had the trumpet of gospel preaching: *sound loudly the trumpet of My gospel and awake the enemies to the battle; loose thereby the hostile princes and priests, whom so far I bound through you, so that they may come over you as a trial of your faith.* In other words: the Lord of the church, as we just saw in the sixth seal, who in His wise guidance first had held back the persecution of the Protestants, so that the reform would not be smothered at birth, now releases the hostile powers of Satan and the Roman church over her, to test their faith or glorify him through their martyr's death. The powerful gospel preaching itself had to awake and loose the hostile worldly and spiritual powers (the four evil angels) through her trumpet sound. That here on earth the angels of God and the angels of Satan interact, and influence the earthly angels, we learn from (Dan 10:13–21). The fulfilment of this prophecy is clearly seen in history. After the Reformation started in 1517, one could already consider it to be well-established, yet only in 1546 did the actual persecutions begin against the Protestants. The merciful Lord had called His servant Luther out of this life before this time (18 February 1546), to spare him the sorrowful prospects.

The Protestant church and state or the angel with the sixth trumpet received the command of Jesus in (verse 14): lose the four angels or the hostile princes and clergy, who are bound by the river *Euphrates*.

It is remarkable, that the Euphrates River, the outer boundary of the Turkish empire in Asia, is almost unanimously, yet without proof, described to be the image of the whole Turkish empire and its power. From this also, one then expects, based on the sixth vial, the eminent fall of the Turkish Empire, an expectation which, due to the condition of that Empire, apparently is confirmed. In order to clearly illustrate the difference between such an explanation and our own, we here want to immediately state, that *based upon God's Word*, the *river Euphrates* in the Revelation is to us not the image of the Turkish Empire, but of the *shepherds and teachers* of the Protestant church in this period of Reformation. To illustrate this, we must here use the typical or the teaching of foreshadowing of the New Testament spiritual things by the Old Testament histories and things. The fulfilment of history will eventually not only prove the truth of our explanation, but also the greater worthiness, of the prophecy, and of our view.

Over and above what we previously said, the Revelation does not contain the history of the world, least of all that of Napoleon, nor of the Turkish Empire, but the history of the church of Jesus Christ.

The Euphrates we find mentioned firstly in (Gen 2: 10 – 14), still named Frath today. Paradise, or the Garden of Eden and its state of bliss, were lost through the fall of the first Adam, but restored through the second Adam (Christ, 1 Cor 15:45), through the reconciliation of sinners and their justification before God. Paradise, before the fall of men, or the earthly heaven on earth, was, therefore, the foreshadowing *of the re-establishment of the spiritual heaven*, the kingdom of heaven, as Christ calls it, here on earth the struggling and later in heaven victorious Christian church. Adam was, in this paradise, just as Paul says to us, (Rom 5:14), a type or example of Christ, who was to come in His church, but then his wife, Eve is the image of the congregation, the bride of Christ, the wife of the Lamb. With this, a mutual, more external relationship between Christ and His congregation is described. There is however an even more inward side to it.

The spiritual life of the church of Christ (paradise) also had to be fed and made fruitful to good works through the outpouring of the Holy Spirit, through Godly comfort and admonitions, through the preaching of the gospel and through shepherdly care of the souls won for Christ.

"And" we read in (Gen 2:10), *"a river flows out of Eden to water the garden, and from there it divided and became four branches."* Living water we already know as *Christ and the belief in him*, by the Holy Spirit, and the main river in paradise was therefore the image of the type of Christ, (Rev 22:1, 2), and the four proceeding branches, the type of His fourfold

ministry, which we learned to know in the first seal, through which Christ spread His grace in the congregation. The meanings of the names totally confirm this.

The 1ˢᵗ PISON means *the pouring stream,* that is: THE APOSTLE MINISTRY, through which the Holy Spirit with its gifts, is poured out through the laying on of hands in the name of Jesus Christ. (Acts 8:17. Acts 19:6. Eph 1:13. 2 Tim 1:6, 14).

The 2ⁿᵈ GIHON, *the pathfinder stream,* is the PROPHET MINISTRY, through which the Holy Spirit speak to the congregation. (Acts 11:27, 28. Acts 13:1, 2. Acts 15:32. Acts 21:10, 11. 1 Tim 4:14.)

The 3ʳᵈ HIDDEKEL (TIGRIS), *arrow-like or cheerful hopping stream,* or the EVANGELIST MINISTRY in its fast spreading upon the earth. (Acts 21:8. 2 Tim 4:5)

The 4ᵗʰ EUPHRATES, *sweet waters,* that is the SHEPHERD MINISTRY and teacher ministry. (Eph 4:11. 1 Pet 5:2. Acts 20:28).

Of these four ministries of Christ, which He exercised in the first century in and through His servants (Eph 4:11), just as He later, in the kingdom of glory and peace, will again exercise through human beings, as the Revelation later will teach us, the four living creatures or Cherubim (Rev 4:6–8), as we said on (pages 51), and the four horns of the altar, (Rev 9:13) on (page 253), as also the four rivers of (Gen 2:10) are all *images* of the four ministries.

Involuntarily the question arises, why does the Holy Spirit use three different images for these four ministries of the Lord, namely: the four horns of the altar, the four cherubim and the four rivers of the Garden of Eden? From the use of each of these images in the conditions wherein they occur, we believe to be able to draw the following conclusion:

1ˢᵗ. The four horns from the altar indicate the *origin* of these four ministries *of Jesus Christ.* Just as the altar is the actual body, and the main thing, while the horns only shoot thereof, Jesus Christ is the actual ministry in His human representatives. He was the Apostle in the apostles, the Prophet in the prophets. He is still in this sixth period of the church the Evangelist in the evangelist, and the Shepherd in the shepherds.

2nd. The four cherubim indicate the sphere of activity and the *activities in the congregation* in these ministries of Jesus, whose servants they are in their ministries.

3rd. The four rivers, or sweet streams, (page 255) indicate *their effect in the congregation* in the heart of men, how they poured out and spread the waters of life from the mainstream Christ in different ways.

Just as the shepherd ministry in the second period is depicted *in its activities*, by the cherub with the likeness of an ox, here *its effect* is represented by the river Euphrates. Both were however lost during these periods, in the mutual strife, which characterised these periods.

We have repeatedly indicated in the first four seals, how in the first period the first cherub or the apostle ministry disappeared from the church, (page 53) in the second period the second cherub or the shepherd ministry, (page 95) in the third period the evangelist ministry, (page 121) and in the fourth period the prophet ministry of Christ (page 151). In the fifth period, nothing of Christ nor of His fourfold ministry remained anymore (page 184).

In the sixth period, two of Christ's ministries were restored by the Reformation in the clergy of the Protestant church, the evangelist and shepherd or teacher ministry. Of the last named, the great river Euphrates is the image and type in the ministry of Revelation, and THAT THIS IS SO, the reader will shortly discover, when in the sixth vial (Rev 16:12), we see the great river Euphrates dry up, whereby Revelation does not predict the fall of the Turkish empire, but the loss of the shepherd or teacher ministry of Jesus Christ in preachers in the Protestant church of our time. And that this great river Euphrates, which, with the heart of Christ, irrigated and fructified [38]with the waters of life in all good works and spiritual life, - that this shepherd and teacher ministry according to the heart and requirements of Christ totally dried up in the modern teaching and the modern teachers, each thinking believer will immediately concede.

Now we can return to the sixth trumpet, and both the first verses (13, 14) become very clear. The words, where we left off: "Loose the four angels which are bound in the great river Euphrates," therefore mean that the four hostile Roman state and church powers, whose anger and desire for persecution against the Protestants had remained *powerless* and *bound* till now through all sorts of mutual state questions, enemies and wars, under the wise guidance of the Lord of the church against the newly re-established Christian shepherd and teacher ministry (the river Euphrates) –

---

[38] The newly won hearts in Christ, with the waters.

are now allowed to cool off their incensed satanic anger against the believers.

This could not have taken place earlier according to the wise insight of God:

Verse 15. **"And the four angels were loosed, which were prepared to persecute for an hour, and a day, and a month, and a year."** That is, just as in (Zech 1:2. and Hagg 2:1), on the *hour of this day, and of this month, and of this year*, decided upon by God's unfathomable decree. Christ also says (Matt 25:13): "For you know neither the day nor the hour," and (John 2:4): "My hour has not yet come." The Lord therefore also had His hour and knows how to hold back the trial, till His time came, that it may come upon His servants. But they know that Christ is also with them in the oven of tribulations until the end of the world and that without His will not one hair on their head goes lost. (Luke 21:18. Acts 27:34). In the year 1543, the 1st of April, was the designated year, the month, the day and the hour, where, in the pronouncement of the bull of Pope Paul III, the persecution was declared. At the epicentre of the Reformation, (Saxony), it started on the 27th of October 1546, after the death of Luther (18 February). On that day the Protestant prince of Saxony was deposed by the emperor, and the hostile Maurits of Saxony was named as his successor.

The four great, hostile state and church princes (angels) had therefore received the power: **"for to** (verse 15) **slay the third part of men."** Here, **men** are again just as in the fifth trumpet, the believers, the *Protestants*, in contrast with the horses and their riders of (verse 17), or the faithful of the Roman church of the different nations in Roman countries, who here form the enemy party. We here again find confirmed, what we have often (page 102) found from the *third part* of men. *The part sanctified by the Holy Spirit*, the believers, of the faithful Protestants and the believers in the Roman church.

Verse 16. **"And the number of the army of the horsemen were two hundred thousand thousand, and I heard the number of them."**

In other words, 200 million. John does *not say that he counted them himself*, but that *their number was told to him*, probably by the angel, which is mentioned in (Rev 1:1. Rev 22:6, 9), who had to explain the visions to him. We consider this number given just as in (Psalm 3:6), to point out an exceedingly great number. Whether we here have to think more of the number of the hostile angels, than whether here men are implied, we will not decide on.

If one knows the history of the persecutions, which the Protestants and believing Romans had to endure from the Roman church, Jesuits and

Inquisitions, from 1546 till the beginning of the 19th century, for two and a half centuries, then it is not yet one million per year who participated in the persecutions, and the literal meaning and fulfilment of this number is definitely not impossible, even more so as the persecutions did not cease in 1815, but continued with the sixth trumpet in the seventh period.

Now follows a clearer description of this vision.

Verse 17. **"And this was how I saw the horses in my vision and the riders who sat on them."** We already know them as the congregations and the clergy, bishops, etc., of the different Roman realms. As a religious congregation is a spiritual society, the various orders of monks with their heads, the inquisitors and especially the Jesuits with their generals are collectively described by the spiritual riders.

"They wore breastplates the colour of fire, and of jacinth and brimstone (sulphur)." The breastplate is, as the fifth trumpet already indicated, the image of righteousness. *Fire and sulphur* are in the words of the Lord still the image of *hell*, (Rev 14:10. Rev 19:20. Rev 20:10. Rev 21:8. Similar to Gen 19:24. Psalm 11 6. Luke 17:29). Fire and fiery we already know, from the first trumpet, as unholy fire or wrath and anger.

Black is the colour of the *smoke* to be mentioned in the image of *spiritual darkness* (third seal).

Their *breastplates*, or what they considered to be their *righteousness*, was therefore not righteousness valid before God, but a *delusion of Satan*. They were righteous in their own eyes, but before God, sunk in *spiritual darkness* (*black*). Inflamed by this *hellish fire of anger*, they stood with their self-righteousness in the *service of Satan (Sulphur)*. They persecuted the witnesses of Jesus with a zeal, which did not emanate from God, but *from the evil one. (fiery)*.

"And the heads of the horses were as the heads of lions." The heads we know from (Isaiah 9:15) (see the fifth trumpet) as the **elders and dignitaries, and** the lion is the symbol of royal power, as the image of the apostles, (first seal). In an evil sense, as it is here, the lion also is the image of the devil. (1 Pet 5:8, and of evil persecutors, Psalm 22:21, Psalm 57:4, Proverbs 28:15, 2 Tim 4:17). They are therefore the Popes, as supposed occupiers of the apostolic seat and stewards of Christ, who are sketched here as the satanic origin of the persecution of the Protestants, for: **"And out of their mouths issued fire and smoke and brimstone (sulphur).**

The **mouths** of the horses are the same persons, which we already found in the fifth vial as the **tongues**, the **defenders** and dignitaries of the Roman church, who just as *Aaron* was the *mouth* of Moses, **spoke for her** in the councils and meetings, according to the words of the Lord Himself. (Exod 4:10, 16. Exod 6:29. Exod 7:1, 2).

The *archbishops, bishops, Jesuits,* etc., all who declared the teaching of the Roman church as the truth and defended her were thus the *mouth* (Council of Trent).

Over and above, we remember the well-known historical figures from the Reformation, Dr. Eck, etc. against Luther. The inquisition benches consisted of the bishops, as the watchmen over the teaching.

Smoke (see the fifth trumpet) is the image of **destruction and devastation.** From the hellish satanic angry popes and their defenders, the order went out to destroy the Protestants.

Verse 18. **"By these three plagues, a third of humankind was killed, by the fire** (anger)**, and the smoke** (persecution)**, and the sulphur coming out of their mouths."**

Once again, we have proof that everywhere in Revelation *the third part* means *the sanctified believers through the Holy Spirit,* the powerful witnesses of Jesus. However violent the persecutions against the Protestants may have been, no third part of humankind was killed. *Humankind or men,* just as in the fifth trumpet, we have to see as the *Protestants,* in contrast with the *troops* and the *horses,* or the *Romans* of (verses 16 and 17). But those, who mightily rose up as witnesses of Jesus, and who did not deny Him in the hour of persecution, but possessed power from the Holy Spirit, to glorify Him, by the martyr's death, only these were considered that sanctified third part, because also amongst the Protestants, although honourably distinguished through God's Word as men, there was still much dross amongst the cold, weak, apostate, or unfaithful, whose faith could not withstand an open confession or persecution.

Verse 19. **"For the power of the horses is in their mouths and in their tails."** The power of the horses or Roman elite is their worldly or armed power. The *mouth* we learned to know as the *defenders* of Popedom, the *tails* in the fifth trumpet as the *false prophets,* or *false teachers,* the Dominicans and Franciscans from the fifth period, and the Jesuits from the sixth period, where they originate (1540) precisely with the goal to protect the Papal seat and the Roman religion, to support and restore her from the devastation of the Protestants.

The armies of the various Roman realms stood in the service of their archbishops and the Jesuits, Papal legates, etc., to the persecution of the Protestants.

"Their tails are like serpents, having heads; and with them they inflict harm." Their *false teachers,* the *Jesuits* and others, are therefore likened to *snakes*. The serpent was craftier than any other wild animal (Gen 3:1), and wise, as the Saviour gave as an example (Matt 10:16) but yet poisonous, as Jesus names the hypocritical and false teachers in Israel: "You snakes, you brood of vipers!" (Matt 28:27–34). It would be difficult to find a more appropriate image than the serpent for the hated and dangerous order of the Jesuits or followers of Jesus, with their soul poisoning, cursed teaching, "the goal justifies the means" in other words: the most honourable crime ceases to be a sin, when it is done to the wellbeing of the Roman church and (which to them is the same) to the expansion of the power of the Jesuits. Murder, etc., thus became God-pleasing works.

"These Jesuits and other snakes **have heads and harm therewith**." These *heads* or chiefs are the generals of the Jesuits, the Inquisitors, etc. To anyone familiar with the military discipline amongst the Jesuits, whereby the subordinates in their unconditional obedience are no more than the blind tools of the thinking and cunning plotting generals, it is most strikingly expressed in the prophecy, that the *heads* of the serpents are those who harm. How much harm they have brought upon the Protestant world, will only be revealed from the secret and deeply hidden roots of this so-called *society of Jesus* on the day "when the books will be opened." It is enough, that because of their dangerousness and dreadfulness they often were expelled and banned by Roman states and countries, even by some Popes. No wonder then, that the Protestant leadership of the German Empire in (1872), tried to remove this feared Jesuit order (named the black Internationals) from its state.

Hereby the persecutors and the persecutions of the Protestants during the sixth period of the church are depicted prophetically in the sixth trumpet. The fulfilment in history, in particular in Holland through Phillip II, king of Spain and the Duke of Alva, even the eighty-year war, commemorated in our time, the celebration of memorial feasts, may be so well known by our readers, that we should not have to elaborate on them. In the overview at the end of this period, we will be forced to give them in general form.

Although the prophecy of the persecution of the Protestants in the sixth period by the Roman church is ended herewith, there follow in (verses 20 and 21) two more verses, which also belong to this period and this prophecy, concerning *the rest of the men who did not die by these plagues*. Who are these men?

The reader will probably raise his eyebrows in wonder at the explanation of these verses, as we did when we received insight into the meaning. We trust, however, that he will examine himself at the judgement of the Lord of the church upon the congregation and see whether he himself perhaps also falls under the judgement of the Lord!

Verse 20. **"The rest of humankind, who were not killed by these plagues,"** do not belong to the Roman church, for these are depicted by the *persecuting armies* in (verses 16–19). They possibly comprise a small part from members of the Roman church, who, although having come to better insight, remained faithful to her, but *all the rest of the men, who were not killed,* belong to the opposing party, just as the believers in the fifth trumpet were also called *men* in contrast with the *locusts* of the Roman church. The *men* named in (verses 15 and 18), or those who were persecuted and killed by the Roman church, therefore also belong to the Protestant church. The *rest of* MEN, *who were* NOT KILLED, must therefore be from the Protestant, and so the whole Protestant church must be considered here, right up to our days, for **"they did not repent of the works of their hand,** (thus remaining caught up in their apostasy) **or give up worshipping demons and idols of gold and silver and bronze and stone and wood, which cannot see or hear or walk."** Is the Protestant church guilty of the horrible sins in (verses 20, and 21), the worshipping of demons and idols, killing, etc? The reader will remember that Revelation speaks in images, that we thus do not have to take these sins literally but have to inquire as to how God's Word classifies these wrongs. If we then find these clearly in the Protestant church, we must also bow our heads before the judgement of the Lord of the church.

To *worship the devil* is evident from the temptation of Jesus in the wilderness, (Luke 4:1–8), *not to worship and serve God the Lord only,* because "no one can serve two masters," one cannot serve God and Mammon" (Matt 6:24), "You cannot drink the cup of the Lord and the cup of devils" (1 Cor 10:21). Therefore John says: "Love not the world, neither the things that are in the world. If any man loves the world, the love of the Father is not in him, for all that is in the world, the lust of the flesh, and the lust of the eyes, and the pride of life, is not of the Father, but is of the world." (1 John 2:15, 16). And now, dear reader! Examine your heart. Is the Protestant church, her Protestant Christians, so Godly and heavenly-minded since the Reformation that they do not flirt with the world and worship devils in the lusts of the flesh, the eyes and the pride of life?

Did the Protestant church completely break off from the world, as did the original church of the first period?

But the gold, silver, copper, stones and wooden idols? The Protestant church does not worship saints or idols. God's Word will actually teach us, that she had many more idols than there ever were in the Roman church. In the Holy Scripture, we find that:

Gold is the image of the *truth of God.* (Revelation 1:13. Isaiah 11:5. Eph 6:14. Rev 3:18).

Silver "of *Christian purity and love*". (Mal 3:3. Prov 10:20. Zech 13:9).

Copper "of *apostasy and corrupters*". Fourth candlestick (page 146) (Jer 6:28).

Stone "of *immovability*" (Job 6:12. Job 41:15), and of "*Unfeeling*" (Eze 11:19. Matt 3: 9. Luke 19:40).

Wood "is that which commeth of a tree" (Isaiah 44:19), thus what is made from a dead tree. Trees we have learned to know as persons rising above others. *Wood* is therefore *honouring deceased persons.*

Idols are all the *objects, which we worship and venerate beside God.* "Thou shalt have no other gods before Me." (Exod 20:3), is the first Commandment. In the scripture, gods are often described as *high-ranking and honoured people,* who exert rule over others as their subjects. The Lord Himself says to *Moses* (Exod 4:16), "And thou shalt be to him (Aaron) instead of God," and in (Exod 7:1), "I have made thee *a god* to Pharaoh." Moses sings in his song (Exod 15:11) "Who is like you, o Lord, among the *gods*?" and David (Psalm 82:1) "God holds judgement in the midst of the *gods*", and in (verse 6), "Ye are gods, and all of you are *children of the Most High.*" Jesus Himself refers to these words in (John 10:34, 35). And who are now the gods and idols in the Protestant church? Paul answers this in (1 Cor 1:12), "that every one of you saith, I am of Paul and I am of Apollos X, and I am of Cephas, and I of Christ," and (verse 13) "is Christ divided? Was Paul crucified for you? Or were you baptized in the name of Paul?, and (verse 10) "Now I beseech you, brethren, by the name of our Lord Jesus Christ, **that ye all speak the same thing, and that there be no divisions among you**; but that ye be perfectly joined together in the same mind and in the same judgement."

There is but one Christ, and one Christian church. Did the Protestants restore the church in the unity of faith? On the contrary! We find that during this period, the Reformation in Protestantism not only in Pauline, Appoline, Cephism Christians, there are Lutheran Christians, Reformed Christians, Remonstration Christians, Mennonite Christians, Episcopal Christians, Presbyterian Christians, Methodist Christians, etc. So many in fact, that hundreds of different sects can be found among the un-Roman Christians. But is there a Lutheran, a Reformed, a Mennonite, a Remonstration, or an Episcopal Christ? Were there more than hundreds of Christ's Great God! Your beloved Son Jesus Christ, whom you have sent, may have been *in* the

Protestant church, as we hope and believe, - but the Protestant church *cannot* be THE church of your beloved Son Jesus Christ!

You see and understand Christian readers! Who *the idols* of the Protestant church were and still are: a Luther, a Calvin, a Menno Simonsz, the Dordtshe Fathers, etc. and not only them, but all praised and beloved and admired single teacher in the congregation, a Socinus, Afminius, Gomarus, Voet, Coccelijus, Brakel, Smytegeld, etc., who were if they had stood *in the truth of God*, **gold**, if they had been *loving teachers*, **silver**, if they had *corrupted and maimed God's Word*, **copper**, if they were *cold and orthodox*, **stone idols**, and if men continued to honour them as *half gods after their decease*, **wooden idols**, as the Revelation of Jesus Christ describes them. How much more, how much deeper than all these was Christ in their hearts? Or who was Lutheran, only because his own religious conviction corresponded with that of Luther? Who was Reformed, because he totally agreed with the formulary of unity? Did not the authority teaching and formulary power in the Protestant church often stand above the personal belief, founded upon Biblical religious conviction? Did men in the Protestant church not rely more often on defending opinions with the feelings and statements of the church fathers from the old and new dispensation, than on the clear Word of God? This is how it was however in both previous centuries, after the Roman church ceased to persecute in the countries where the Protestant church had become a state church. In our time, this all gave way to Anti-Christian views and indifference to religious, and Biblical convictions.

But although the strict believers in our time do not deny their God and Saviour before the spirit of our time, are not *often still* the statements of father Luther, who passed away hundreds of years ago, for many Lutherans – or those of the Dordtshe Synod, several hundred years ago, *still* the directive for the strict reformer of how the Word of God *should and must* be understood? Do these statements not stand *next to*, or even *above* God's Word, and their authors, Luther and the Dortsche fathers, almost next to God? Is this any different from the presumption in religious matters of the Roman Jezebel that the Holy Spirit speaks in the decisions of the popes and councils, which we see in the extreme consequences of the declaration of the infallibility of the Pope? When we consider that there are hundreds of un-Roman church denominations, all protesting against Rome, and each of them still has highly honoured first founders, and latter still living maintainers, - are then those religious societies, crumbling and mutually opposed to each other, the congregation of the body of Christ? Reader! Cross your heart! Has the Protestant church also sometimes her golden, silver, copper, stones and wooden idols, as the Lord of the church says? And were not **all these idols**, which the Protestants honoured, all these churches, **the work** of their own **hands**, while the *church of Christ*, or the kingdom of heaven, *must be the work of God's hands*? (Psalm 8:3.). Were all those highly honoured sect founders and champions, in opposition to the Lord, who wanted himself to be the living and speaking head of His church, (Matt 28:20. John 14:16–18, 25, 26. John 15:26. John 16:12–15.), anything else, than idols, **which cannot see** in the hearts of the believers, **nor hear**, what the Spirit says unto the congregation, **nor walk** according to the instructions of the Lord on the old ways, upon which the church of the first period walked, when the Holy Spirit with its gifts lived in her?

The Lord not only spoke to the Apostles, but also to the seventy, therefore to all His workers, (Luke 10:16): "He that heareth you heareth Me, and He that rejects you, rejects Me." It is therefore impossible, that the Lord can speak through all the mutually dissenting Protestant sects. And where they in their teaching fight and reject one another, the Lord can only at best speak out of one of them, for Christ is not divided (1 Cor 1:13). And while they all *claim to be the one*, the Lord here judges *them all* in His Word.

Verse 21. **"And they did not repent of their murders, nor of their sorceries, nor of their fornication, nor of their thefts."** *"Whosoever hateth his brother* is a *murderer."* Says (1 John 3:15). How many sorrowful scenes of religious hatred between the confessors of her different denominations, as well as against the Romans, has the Protestant church not been guilty of, during the last three centuries?[39] And where we see this dividing and religious hatred diminish in our days, is it there due to an awakening Christian brotherly love, or perhaps partly to the growing indifference towards religion? But also the giving of *unbiblical soulish poison*, which is fatal for belief in Christ, such as the rationalists and modernists, which the Lord Jesus named, serpents, a generation of Vipers, (Matt 23:27–33), in their unchristian teachings, (James 3:8) – but also her *fornication* with Rome, with the world, with the state church, with philosophy, etc. but also the *theft of heresies* from others, from the church fathers of the second century, this was all in the Protestant church and remains from the beginning of the Reformation, up to now, there is not a single page of her history, on which we cannot find all this in clear words.

---

[39] Whilst the Lord Himself accuses the Protestants of *hating their brothers* (verse 21), He could never have meant to use *brotherly love* as the meaning of Philadelphia. The Holy Spirit never speaks against itself.

SIXTH VIAL

or

THE JUDGEMENT OF GOD

> For whosoever hath, to him shall be given;
> and whosoever hath not, from him
> shall be taken even that which he
> seemeth to have.
> Luke 8:18.

Rev. 16:12–16.

Verse 12. **"And the sixth angel poured out his vial upon the great river Euphrates, and the waters thereof were dried up."**

We already know that the sixth angel is the clergy of the sixth period, who through their deeds and teachings poured out the vial, when the sound of her gospel trumpet did not have a God-pleasing sound, neither had any influence on men. Thus, Christ came for the preservation of Israel when it *would not* accept Him, and the promised blessing became to them a curse, which continues into our days. This is why they accept the Love of truth that they might be saved; this is why God sent them strong delusion, that they should believe a lie. (2 Thess 2:10, 11).

The Euphrates is the shepherd and teacher ministry, re-erected by the Lord in the Reformation to the blessing and preservation of lost sinners. If, however, one despises the blessing of the Lord, God again takes it back from men, for whosoever hath, to him shall be given, but whosoever hath not, from him shall be taken even that he hath. (Matt 13:12).

After the persecutions by the Roman church had diminished, the church began, just as in the second period, to lose the purity of the teaching. All sorts of old heresies came up and caused great divisions in the different Protestant church societies, resulting in bitter disputes. The worldly power, which had in the interim placed itself above the clergy, acted as judge, even in religious affairs. All the fatal influences, united with dead orthodoxy, strict sect spirit, and sharp division of the different parties, caused the *fresh waters of life*, which *the Euphrates, or the shepherd and teacher ministry* as it was called in the congregation, to *dry up*, **"that the way of the kings of the East might be prepared,"** who must come in the seventh period. They are mentioned here in the sixth vial in this manner in contrast with the kings of the earth and of the whole world of (verse 14).

That at the end of this sixth period, during the last half of the previous century, up to the beginning of this century (1815), a time of great unbelief and godlessness, the waters nearly totally dried up, is well known.

Other reasons also contributed to this.

Verse 13. John saw in this period **"three unclean spirits like frogs, came out of the mouth of the dragon, and out of the mouth of the beast, and out of the mouth of the false prophet."** Which according to (verse 14) **"are the spirits of devils."** *Devil* (diabolos) means *blasphemer. A spirit,* personally depicted here, is the image of *teaching, which is preached* (2 Thess 2:2; 1 John 4:1, 6). *What is not from God and His truth,* the Lord calls *impure.* (Luke 4:33–36. Matt 23:25–27).

The *mouth* we already know (sixth trumpet, pages 259) as *the preachers and defenders of teaching.* We therefore here have *three blasphemous teachings,* which would be preached, three "seducing spirits and doctrines of devils," as Paul says (1 Tim 4:1), which had to have come up in this period having a great influence on the church and congregation. History indeed teaches us to know them as **Deism, Atheism** and **Pantheism.**

The Dragon is according to (Rev 20:2) *the old serpent* (Gen 3), *the Devil* and *Satan.*

The first **unclean spirit from the mouth of the Devil** is **Deism,** *or the single belief that there is one God.* This, however, the Devils also believe. (James 2:19). The devil is not so stupid, that he would proclaim to men "there is no God"; he would harm himself that way, and his teaching would become suspicious to men. And this single belief does not harm him in his power over their hearts. The devil however also knows very well, who Jesus is (Acts 19:15) namely the Holy one of God (Luke 4:34), the Son of God, who was revealed to destroy the works of the devil (1 John 3:8). This is why the devil is interested in keeping the knowledge of the Saviour of men from the world, and he caused the *doctrine of Deism* to be preached in that period. In this doctrine God is recognized as the only God and Creator, at the most the caring providence. Sin and Salvation fall away. Moses, Christ, etc. become gifted persons and reformers of society. Religion becomes a moral doctrine and, - the devil also knows that well, - a powerless and fruitless doctrine, because in the heart of the unconverted man, who does not consider himself a sinner and has not learned to know Christ Jesus as His Saviour, neither could bring forth fruits, and the branch, which is cut off the tree (John 15:4–6).

In the beginning of 1600, as VAN LOON says on page 253: "Cherburg already opens the row of English Deists, who in this and the following centuries nearly drove the church in an abyss of unbelief." Later teachers in this were: Thomas Hobbes, Baylz, Locke, Lord Bolingbroke, etc.

Deism is thus *the unclean spirit out of the mouth of the dragon,* and the source of Rationalism in the Christian church and the denial of the divinity of Jesus Christ. It's followers we already saw predicted in the congregation in the sixth period, (sixth candlestick), as the Jews which would come. (Page 236).

The second **unclean spirit went out of the mouth of the beast,** and this is **Atheism** or *the denial of the existence of God.*

The beast we already know as the fourth worldly empire[40] or the power hostile to God (Dan 7), which had already made itself known, as heathen Roman empire, as Atheist; *denier of God,* of which John already says, (1 John 2:22): "He is antichrist, that denieth the Father and Son": and (1 John 4:3): "And this is that spirit of antichrist, whereof ye have heard that it should come; and even now *already is it* in the world."- The four great worldly powers *hostile to God,* which would succeed each other on earth, are depicted by the Holy Spirit as **"beasts".** (Dan 7:3–7). Throughout the whole history of the world we then also see the beasts deny the true, revealed God. The Babylonian empire for example in Nebuchadnezzar (Dan 3), the Persian empire in Darius (Dan 6), the Greek empire in Antiochus (Dan 8), and the Roman empire in its Emperors (first period of Revelation, pages 66 – 68). – the devil denied therefore only the Son, the beast also denied the Father. Since 324 A.D., when Rome became Christian, the beast or the antichrist *apparently was not,* although *it is* (Rev 17:8), at least here it again shows itself as Atheism in the Christian empire.

One of the first mouths of the beast was VOLTAIRE, a free-thinker and unscrupulous mocker of all religion, whose many writings had an extremely corruptive influence on his time and that which followed. He died in 1778. Simultaneously, JEAN JACQUES ROUSSEAU lived and wrote writings which contributed very much to making all religions suspect. Further, the so-called Encyclopedists, d'Alembert, Diderot and Helvetius, Montesquieu, la Mettrie, Holbach, Frederick II, King of Prussia, etc. with all their admirers and followers.

All *these servants of the beast* formed *his mouth,* from which the doctrine of Atheism came forth; and were the forerunners and the cause of the terrible upheaval in France, whereby in the year 1793, by decree of the administration, Christian religion was banned, and the worship of reason was introduced.

---

[40] The reader will remember that this fourth empire, under its seven different forms or heads, still continues to exist until the return of the Lord. (Dan 7:13, 14, 27).

One hundred years ago, the Convention of France, under the famous Robespierre, introduced a new timetable and a new calendar.

Forthwith there would not be any Sundays in France any longer. First, the day of rest was completely abandoned, but when this did not go well, the so-called "Decade" was introduced. On each tenth day, the people came together to rejoice in their freedom. Each day received a new name, to eventually put aside anything that could remind one of Christendom.

On 21 January 1793, king Louis XVI was led to the guillotine. The queen, the king's sister and her son followed nine months later in an unjust death. The rightful heir to the throne died a miserable death in the house of a drunk; who slowly poisoned the royal child with brandy.

GOBEL, archbishop of Paris, appeared with all his clergy before the Convention on 7th November, to deny the whole Christendom. Gobel threw down his mitre, staff and ring on the floor and donning the red Jacobin hat, declared: "There is no religion other than of freedom and equality."

Three days later, the religion of Reason was introduced by the Convention, and it was openly declared: "There is no God! Therefore, none must be worshipped! Reason only is our guiding lady, our goddess!"

On 21 November, the populace of Paris, adorned with spiritual robes, and paraphernalia of the churches in their hands, marched through the hall of the Convention, mocking and blaspheming. The president spoke to the multitudes: "In one wink of an eye you undo the senselessness of eighteen centuries." A wretched, debauched woman was elevated as the goddess of Reason, carried through the streets and placed on an altar of roses in the church of Notre Dame.

All crucifixes were destroyed, and the church was recreated into temples of reason. Those who still wanted to celebrate Sunday in a Christian way were (at the hand of freedom?) put to prison. Marriage was abolished. Funerals could take place in a formal way but not according to Christian rites. Graveyards were daubed with the name of "Eternal sleep!"

The people were let loose. In order to restore some order Robespierre gave the senseless command: "From now on there will be a God again, and in all churches, He must be preached about again!" Sunday was also reintroduced.

After a vain attempt at suicide, Robespierre's head fell under the guillotine. Very poor and insane, the "goddess of reason" died in a stable in Italy.

Of these two un-Christian doctrines, Deism and Atheism, Deism was for many people too much, and Atheism too little. The faith, which the devils themselves still had, was yet too religious for them; but on the other hand, the healthy and unprejudiced mind of man could not for all that condescend to the utter materialism of the Atheists, as it clashed everywhere with the origin of all life symptoms. Here human science had to intervene, as the **false prophet**, and mediate both factions and at least recognize one God, but not a personal God, in opposition and separation of the earthly, visible world. To this end, they found, as **a third unclean spirit**, a new idea of God, which had to answer all riddles and questions, namely: *the cosmos, or the sun of all life-giving principles and powers in the universe, is God.* This is **Pantheism** or "God is all and all is God."

The false prophet, of which John speaks, is the same as the beast from the earth of (Rev 13:11–17), we only compare this last reference with (Rev 19:20. Rev 20:10), where everywhere he is mentioned simultaneously with the beast from the sea and gives him all his power. In (Rev 13:11–13) John describes the false prophet, how he, as "the beast from the earth" in the last days (seventh trumpet), will *openly* perform before the world as a great spiritual power, hostile to God. When John however sees in the sixth period (sixth vial) an unclean spirit come from the mouth of the false prophet, this false prophet must already have originated and been active in propagating his doctrine over the earth. Indeed, this was so, and in the seventh period, we will see, how in our time this false prophet as the beast from the earth performs, and already has many confessors under the teachers of the Christian churches.

The prophets of the Old Covenant were commissioned to preserve and preach the knowledge of the true God. Abraham was such a prophet (Gen 20:7), Moses (Deut 34:10), and Jesus Christ, (Deut 18:15, 19. Acts 3:22). A false prophet is, therefore, one who spreads a false doctrine or understanding of God, such as the false prophets in the Old Covenant, and this is the role which Pantheism fulfilled in its world wise endeavours, to reconcile Atheism, but brutal unbelief of the beast, with Deism, or the even more acceptable doctrines of devils.

Although the principles of Pantheism could already be found in the first century after Christ, Toland was the first to openly use the word and its doctrine, in 1705.

Currently, in the understanding and belief of the people, it has mostly repelled belief in the biblically revealed religion.

While we definitely do not have to deal with the finer definitions and understandings of philosophy about these doctrines, but only about their practical results as they in raw, sometimes banal form, reveal themselves in the reasoning and the belief of the people, influencing their religious convictions, we must now, after the description of Deism and Atheism, also give an intelligent description of Pantheism, as it is revealed in the reasoning of the illiterate masses. Pantheism is the doctrine that God is the world and the world is God. All life-giving principles or inspiring powers together are a oneness, and this oneness is the cosmos or God. Just as one wave elevates itself momentarily above the sea, as a partially self-relying entity, but yet not separated from the sea, and after its momentary elevation sinks back in the general great sea, and again forms part of it, to partly rise up again in other waves, - thus also is the cosmos or God revealed, through humans, plants and animals in their life cycle. At death, however, the life-giving spirit flows back in the general cosmos, to be absorbed into it, and to rise again in other forms or persons. A personal existence of God is thus denied, as well as a personal existence after death. The worst consequence of this doctrine, however, is that man, as the highest revelation of the cosmos, is also the highest godly being or God himself, whereby then the practical religion, or God-worshipping, becomes a worshipping of man, humanitarian.

The seventh period will teach us to which end this doctrine of Pantheism takes man, only then will it play its leading part, as the father of deifying man, just as Deism has been the father of rationalism since 1600, and Atheism the origin of Materialism, Saint Simonnism, Jacobism and the French Revolution with her terrible bloody scenes and the worshipping of the goddess of reason.

How the three unclean spirits of unchristian doctrines, Deism or the belief of the devils, Atheism or the unbelief of the beast-like man, and Pantheism or the false doctrine that man is God, - how these three teachings during the period of Reformation up to our time, have undermined and deformed the Christian churches, especially in the Protestant countries, - how much influence they had on belief and morals, - how they infiltrated and wove into the whole Christian church, - how thereby the clear waters of the gospel of the great river Euphrates are already greatly dried up, - this all would be unnecessary to describe for the more intellectual reader, and too bulky for the less learned Christian.

It is enough to know that through them rationalism, liberalism and modern ideologies came into existence and that nearly no heresy is found in the church or congregation, which does not sprout forth from these three main branches: Deism, Atheism and Pantheism. Thereby the whole Christian church: Roman, Greek and Protestant, of which the angel in (Rev 18:2) testifies, *the great Babylon*, became a dwelling of *devils*, and a haunt for all *unclean spirits* **in the eye of the Lord**.

"Like frogs" were the Spirits. The word *like* used in the text can mean *alike in number*, just as the frogs of Egypt, and then the prediction is fulfilled, or *alike in quality*. The characteristic of the frog is that, as an amphibious animal, it lives alternately on the earth (world ordinances) and in water (gospel).

While the frog is not used in the figurative language of the Holy Spirit in the Scriptures, it must mean, that the teachers, inspired by these spirits, wanted to serve God and the world at the same time and consider it easy to be a Christian. Indeed, where the Lord so explicitly says, that the way is narrow and the gate is straight, there the devil preaches, the high-mindedness of the flesh and worldly wisdom, that the way is broad and the gate wide, there they even preach it in the churches through Deist, Atheist and Pantheist preachers. Whether the meaningless croaking and the bloated appearance of the frogs may be applied to the nonsense in these three doctrines, and the arrogant preachers placing themselves above God's Word, we leave it to the reader to decide for himself. Luther took it up in this sense, "they (the false teachers) often came against the gospel, and themselves achieved nothing."

So far the sixth vial in the history of the church is fulfilled, as a preparation for the pouring out of the seventh vial, as is mentioned in (verses 14, 16). The content of both these verses for all is a short explanation of what will happen at the end of the seventh period, when the *three unclean spirits rising* in the sixth period continue through the seventh *to perform signs and go abroad to the kings of the whole world, to assemble them for the battle on the great day of God Almighty*. These signs we will find mentioned further in the seventh period in (Rev 13:11-17), as well as the war of the great day of God Almighty in (Rev 19:11–21).

That this all goes on till the last time is apparent from (verse 15), where the Lord himself again appears speaking (speaking through the Angel Rev 1:1) and at the end of the sixth vial gives the warning to His congregation for the last time, just as at the end of the sixth candlestick (Rev 3:11) that *His coming is near*. "Behold, I come quickly," He said there, **"Behold I come as a thief,"** He says here. (Rev 16:15)

The former holy city or the spiritual Jerusalem, (Heb 12:22), we will find again in the seventh period, as "the great city," which is described in the seventh trumpet (Rev 11:8, 13) as the spiritual Sodom and Egypt, in comparison with the believing Christians of the holy city of (Rev 11:2), who will be trampled upon by the anti-Christ.

Similarly, we find in the seventh vial (Rev 16:19 and Rev 18:20, 21) the great city mentioned, the great Babylon, to which in (Rev 18:10, 16, 19), the word Alas! Alas! is applied three times. This great city or the great Babylon (Rev 18:2), is the whole apostate Christian church, as she will reveal itself in the last period. On these pages the Christian churches are named *Babylon* by the Lord. *Babylon* means *confusion*. All the Christian churches, with their contradictory doctrines, are therefore **in the Lord's eye** a Babel of confusion. In the middle of the old city Babylon flowed the river Euphrates. But also through the spiritual Babylon flows the spiritual river Euphrates, or the shepherd and teacher ministry (page 254), and, just as the Euphrates in the old Babel dried up, the shepherd and teacher ministry of the spiritual Euphrates in the new Babylon also dried up (page 266). With these similarities, no more doubt is left as to the meaning of *Babylon* and the *Euphrates*.

That the sixth trumpet and vial Angel, that is the Protestant clergy, has been increasingly active since the previous century, to gather the three unclean spirits or doctrines against God's Word, Deism, Atheism and Pantheism into the Christian churches, forming thereby the great Babylon, is clear to everyone.

OVERVIEW OF THE HISTORY OF THE CHURCH IN THE SIXTH PERIOD

FROM 1517 - 1815 A.D.

TRANSLATION OF THE SIXTH CANDLESTICK

Rev 3:7–9.

Verse 7. *Write to the bishop of the congregation, and to all My congregation of the sixth period, which as a new shoot, on the old shrivelled fig tree of the church, through her faith and love is a pleasant smell to Me:*

This says the Holy and True, who has the keys of knowledge and of power to the kingdom of heaven, and who has taken them away from the unfaithful Roman priesthood, to give them to other faithful servants, this says He, who can open the kingdom of heaven, so that no one can shut it, but who can also shut it, so that no one can open it.

Verse 8. *I know your works of faith and love. I have given Myself and therewith faith in Me and in My Word back again, as an opened door to the kingdom of God, and this door shall never again be shut.*

You are weak in yourselves, but you are powerful, because you lean upon My Word and promise, and have not denied My Name, as that of your Lord and Saviour.

Verse 9. *But there will come among you from the school of Satan, who say, that they know God and Me, as the True God and reject eternal life. See I will cause that the…*

FULFILLMENT IN THE HISTORY OF THE CHURCH

The fulfilment of the predictions of the Son of God about this sixth period will perhaps not be indicated too strikingly by both our historians VAN LOON and GUERS, as in the previous periods, because they consider the period of Reformation still ongoing, which is an error, and their overview about that period is incomplete.

We will however find enough facts from them, which will confirm our translation of Revelation. The actual history of the Reformation does not belong to our subject. We believe the Christian readers are already well informed. Whoever wants to research it, will find it briefly with VAN LOON pages 179 – 211, with GUERS, (pages 557 – 622), and in addition to many other works, extensively but highly entertainingly with MERLE D'AUBIGNE.

With GUERS, we read on pages 536 and 558:

"Throughout the whole West resounded a single note of sorrowful music of complaints (about the condition of the church). Anyone who had an upright conscience prayed for a new total, conclusive reformation. Jesus heard the sigh of His own. He speedily came to their rescue. After several centuries of struggles between darkness and light (in the previous periods), the sun of grace rose again (Page 557). Martin Luther, the most important vessel in God's hand, to reform Germany, studied at the University of Erfurt. One day, while looking through the university library in search of information, he laid his hands on a dusty Latin Bible, the first he had seen in his life. From that moment on, he did not cease to ponder about the Godly book. In this way, God prepared him for the great battle, in which the Holy Scripture would be his only support (page 242), and which he would use victoriously against human authority.

An expression in the letter to the Romans especially attracted his attention, recorded in (Rom 1:17): *"The just shall live by faith."* During all his daily activities he kept on pondering over this. Eventually, when God opened his heart, he could understand what *righteousness* meant, which was given anew to the sinner through faith in Jesus Christ, and this knowledge became to him the key to the whole scripture. "I felt suddenly", he said, "that my whole being was renewed, that I had found AN OPEN DOOR (page 241) to enter paradise."

Page 562. "The evening before All Saints Day, 31 October 1517, Luther posted his memorable 95 theses against indulgences at Wittenberg. Five months prior to this, on 1 June 1517, Rome witnessed a miracle, a great catastrophe predicted against its seat. While the Pope was busy choosing 31 cardinals, a great storm arose. One lightning bolt struck off the Angel that was placed on the castle St. Angelo, another struck the image of the child Jesus from his mother's arms, and a third caused the keys in the hand of Peter's statue to fall to the ground."

It is generally well known that, next to Luther and his friend Melanchton, as well as Zwingli and Calvin, other men stood as the reformers, and again preached the full council of God for Salvation. VAN LOON says:

"The Reformation originated in various countries and through various vessels. While Luther was referred by Staupitz to accept Christ as the only Saviour and called to preach, that the just will live by faith, Zwingli, his contemporary and later opponent, without knowing of each other, also introduced the idea of the sufficiency of Christ, and almost simultaneously Lefévre with his disciple Farel in Paris, were likewise brought to the knowledge of truth through reading the Bible; and so many allies stood up

for Luther on all sides in the struggle against Rome. Apart from those in England, we also find disciples of Wycliffe working and preparing the country for accepting the doctrines of the reformers. The scattered Hussites in Bohemia preserved their heritage from their believing Fathers. The Waldense in Piermont were ready to accept the new doctrine with Joy."

"The Reformation was not the work of a single person; it originated out of the need common to all Christians, and if Luther or Zwingli would have kept quiet, then Farel and Viret would have spoken; in this was her power, her unity, which regardless of all differences of doctrine between Swiss and German reformers, powerfully protested against Rome's unanimity.

Since the time of the Reformation, the students of Socinus appeared: the unhappy ones, who degraded Him, whom heaven and earth worshipped, and at whose feet the redeemed will throw their crowns, to the rank of one of the first sons. Next to that, Arianism dared to raise its godless head. This old heresy (see page 87, especially the footnote), which wanted to rob the Lord of glory, of His sovereign divinity, again rose in England shortly after the Reformation and gradually corrupted the whole continent of Europe" (GUERS, page 628).

TRANSLATION OF THE SIXTH SEAL

<u>Rev 6:12, 13. Rev 7:1.</u>

Verse 12. *And when Christ had opened the sixth period of the scroll, I saw a great disturbance come into existence amongst the Christian nations of Europe, and Christ, the sun of righteousness was darkened in His newly resurrected church and believers, through their mutual religious quarrels, and the congregation again reverted to the carnal life, which is not from God.*

Verse 13. *And the Christian kings and teachers fell as unripe figs from the fig tree of the church, because of the hefty religious quarrels between Roman and Protestant churches, out of God's kingdom upon the earth and became carnally minded. Religion amalgamated with state politics and the church was subjected to the state.*

Rev 7:1

Verse 1. *And I saw four head teachers and four Protestant princes, who stood at the head of the Reformation, preserving the mutual peace, defending the Reformation against the divided Roman states and church powers, until they had won enough support and had received enough strength, never again to be destroyed through persecutions.*

FULFILLMENT IN THE HISTORY OF THE CHURCH

"What was now the condition of the church at the moment that the Reformation had taken up its official place, and what chances did she have of survival and success?" asks Mr. Van LOON, page 205, and answered as follows:

"When one superficially traces the way in which she travelled in the thirteen years from 1 October 1517 till 25 June 1530, (the Augsburg confession through the Protestant princes to Emperor Charles V), and the victories achieved during this short period of time, one tends to imagine that before the end of this century, Popedom would be deprived of all power, and be without any ecclesiastical or political meaning. Although we know differently from history, we ask ourselves with some wonder why the Word of God, given back to the people, was less successful in the following years, than in the first half of the sixteenth century, especially since the newly converted could find support in the already established churches, and could enjoy the protection of the reformer princes against the persecution on the side of the Roman governments. One must remember, that precisely these conditions, apparently so advantageous for the Reformation, formed a difficult hurdle for her to overcome. The two parties had sharply defined their spiritual and political aspirations, neutrality was mostly impossible; nations and princes were forced to don the weapons for or against Rome; and the peaceful propaganda of preaching was curtailed, to make place for religious wars, treaties, the signing of peace accords, and the granting or suppression of particular religious trends. The whole Roman church was awake, which she was not in 1517, and aware of the danger, which threatened her from the increasing influence of the Reformation ideas, she used all her expediency, which cunning and violence indicated, to repel the danger. In the countries where she was still in power, she reverted to inquisitions and the most systematic and well-organized persecution. In the countries where this was not possible, treaties were concluded, political negotiations achieved, and all civil tricks were used to take advantage of peace and war, division and zeal of the nations and the princes, and to suppress Protestantism, at least to stem its growth." And page 207:

"Yet not only the condition of the Roman church, also those, in which the Reformation made an impact, stood in the way of her progress. Rome reverted to persecution, and those recently converted Protestants had to choose between subjection or factual opposition. They chose the last and took up arms. Whatever the judgement may be, which one takes concerning this opposition, the case of the Reformation was stemmed. It was not by killing, but by being killed; that the Christians of the first three centuries overcame this heathen Rome, and it is apparent, that one can be won by the preaching of the defenseless, whom one persecutes, rather than by the enemies, that one sees standing against you with a sword. But also the preaching is totally different there where religion has taken a political character, and it seems not to be the Salvation of the sinner which is important, but rather the supremacy of one civil faction.

In light of the fulfilment of (Rev 5:1), the following comments of VAN LOON, pages 208 and 209 are given here:

"But what were now the chances of success for the Reformation? In the first place: it was prepared over a long period and the timing was so chosen, the condition of Europe, of Germany especially, so planned by God's providence, that the young plant could thrive and develop solid roots, before she was subjected to too great storms. The Reformation had infiltrated various countries, that stood hostile to each other, the persecutions could not therefore develop the unity, which it needed to restore Rome's authority in the whole West, and both Roman and Protestant princes were not unhappy, that the Reformation diminished the arrogance of the Pope somewhat, and used the Reformation and its political meaning, to become more or less independent from the seat of Rome."

TRANSLATION OF THE SIXTH TRUMPET

PART ONE: THE REFORMATION

Rev. 10:1, 2.

Verse 1. *And I saw Christ Jesus, the Angel of the New Covenant, not in the flesh, but in His witnesses, come down again to earth to, through them, the fallen away teachers from the Roman church, bring back the lost knowledge of the Gospel, and to preach again here on earth the covenant of grace and righteousness which is valid before God. His servants were mighty witnesses, through the power of the Holy Spirit, and they brought* the Word of the Lord which had been darkened by Popedom, back to the congregation. Thereby they were also empowered, if they had sought it, to find therein, what would happen at the return of the Lord, and that, now that the Gospel of the kingdom would be preached to all nations, the end of this dispensation would be near.

Verse 2. *And in the power of His Evangelist ministry, Christ through His messengers again formed believing (Protestant) congregations in the Roman sea of nations and through His shepherds and teachers He kept, as the head Shepherd and teacher, His believers in the truth, and fruitful in good works.*

About the exact fulfilment of this prophecy, the performance of the Reformation, we have said enough already on (pages 240 – 242). With the next part of this sixth trumpet we will, just as with the fifth trumpet, again and again, give page numbers concerning this explanation, where its fulfilment can be found.

PART TWO: THE PERSECUTION OF THE PROTESTANTS

Rev. 9:13–19.

Verse 13. *In the sixth period of the church, when the gospel was brought back on earth by the Lord, I heard Him, as the living head of the congregation,*

Verse 14. *Say to His servants on earth, the Protestant teachers: "Sound the trumpet of My Gospel (pages 28, 52, 53), loose by it the four hostile Roman state and church princes (Angels) who thus far were powerless to disturb the peace and to take up arms against My witnesses (pages 253, 254).*

Verse 15. *And the four Roman civic powers were unbound and loosed, on the hour appointed by the Lord, so that they could kill the mighty witnesses of the Lord, sanctified by the Holy Spirit. (page 256).*

Verse 16. *And the army of the Roman church was so great, that they were uncountable to me; and their number was told to me to be twice ten thousand times ten thousand. (Page 257).*

Verse 17. *And I saw also the hostile Roman armies (horses) with their spiritual and worldly generals (riders) and they presumed to be the Christians and zealots of the Lord; and they were instruments of Satan, sunk in the deepest spiritual darkness, and ablaze with a hellish fire of anger against the believers. And the popes, as the leaders of these persecutions, acted as if they were apostles of our Lord Jesus Christ and yet were roaring lions of Satan. And the defenders of Popedom, the bishops,*

Jesuits, and Inquisitors, given to evil anger, everywhere gave orders to exterminate the Protestants. (pages 257, 278).

Verse 18. *Through Satanic hatred, angry persecutions and hellish murderous desires, the mighty witnesses of Jesus, who openly stood up for their faith, were killed at the instigation of the defenders of the Roman church (page 259).*

Verse 19. *For the armies of the Roman princes, unreservedly stood at the service of Papal legates, bishops, Jesuits and these last, who named themselves followers of the meek Jesus, are like unto poisonous snakes and have leaders full of murder, lust and evil. (pages 258, 259).*

About these persecutions, we read in a short overview of GUERS, page 623, the following:

Satan, jealous of the progress of the Reformation, developed a terrible opposition against her. Firstly he gathered against her the infamous Council of Trent (1545 – 1563), which activated everything needed to re-establish Popedom on the ruins of the crushed Protestantism. But God's goodness confounded the conspiracy of the enemy, and in spite of the great Council, Protestantism still stands and truth is victorious. While far from having brought the least damage to the Gospel, Trent and Rome had committed an irreparable blunder. By confirming all the heresies, which originated in the Middle Ages, by sanctifying all the foolishness of the previous centuries as unchangeable laws, by confirming the doctrines and tenets, against which the reformers were mostly opposed, with so much terrible Anathemas, Trent caused the rift between light and darkness to be complete.

Satan similarly used amalgamations and conspiracies against the Reformation but with as little success as the Council. The same God, who under the empire of Rome, had confused the best-formed plans of the prince of the powers of darkness, again showed, that His might is only weakness, His wisdom is but foolishness. The life of the Reformers threatened more than once by the godless, is repeatedly wonderfully spared by Him, whom they serve in faithfulness. He held them hidden in the hollow of His fatherly Hand.

The wars and invasions, which the devil resorted to, to erect his throne among the Christians, did not succeed.

The *Emperor of Germany* threatened the Arch Duke of Saxon and all the princes, who defend the doctrine of the gospel, to destroy them with the full force of his weapons, but all his plans floundered, and Protestantism victoriously came out of the struggle.

The persecutions against the Reformation did not stop. Those, prepared by the murderous Popedom, exceeded in horror all those, which the Romans formerly had devised. The heathen Rome had been terrible in their persecutions, Papal Rome excelled in its persecutions, its Inquisition studied and nursed them as a science; it used torture implements which the former centuries had not known, and spread horrible skills in the art of torturing people. The blood of Christians flooded the whole of Europe. Bohemia, Moravia, Hungary (the current Austria) became during a series of years, the stage of horrible barbarism. Also France will speak of the sorrow with which Rome burdened the Reformers. In the short interim of 30 years, 39 princes, 148 counts, 234 barons, 147,518 noblemen and 760,000 citizens were murdered for the sake of the gospel. On the 21st August 1572, 70,000 Protestants fell under the axe of the executioner[41].

PART THREE: THE FURTHER CONDITION OF THE GOSPEL

PREACHING IN THE PROTESTANT CHURCH

Rev. 9:20, 21.

Verse 20. *And the rest of the believers, who were not killed by these persecutions, continued in their errors, and with their individual different confessions of faith and church sects, with their state churches and with their fornication with the world. They are also faithful to their, partly believing and loving, partly corrupting God's truth, or cold-hearted, and also continued venerating their long since deceased teachers, sect founders and maintainers, next to, if not above the Lord of the church, and have accepted as tenets of faith, the conflicting proclamations of these men above the Word of God, as if they were the proclamations of the Lord Himself. They continued steadfastly in all this, although all these teachers were just as fallible people as they were, and not as the Christian teachers from the Apostolic time, who had the Holy Spirit, who led them in all truth, living in them with His gifts. Through missing this, they could also not see the full counsel of God, could not hear, what the Spirit formerly spoke to the congregation, nor walk in the old ways and institutions of the Lord.*

---

[41] The above-mentionedd four kingdoms with their princes were the four winds of the earth of (chapter 7 : 1), or the four great Roman civic and church powers, who formed the four corners of the earth, or the defenders of the Roman civic and church ordinances. (Page 245).

Verse 21. *They remained faithful in their hatred for their brothers who disagreed with them, in their fornication with the world, with the state, with the wisdom of this world, and with the taking over and preaching of old heresies.*

This prophetic judgement of the Lord of the church concerning the different Protestant sects is in its fulfilment clearly described on (pages 260 – 265). To give an oversight of all these sects which during the Reformation have sprung up, would be far above our scope. We can find them all with VAN LOON from pages 213 – 299. They describe nearly exclusively the whole history of Protestantism in the period of reform.

TRANSLATION OF THE SIXTH VIAL

<u>Rev 16:12–15.</u>

Verse 12. *Protestant state and church powers poured out the judgment of God upon the shepherd and teacher ministry of the Protestant churches of the sixth period; and the formerly preached gospel dried up in the Protestant churches, so that the way may be prepared for the royal witnesses, who will come in the last days.*

Verse 13. *And in this period three false doctrines came up in the Protestant churches, which were not from God, but blasphemy from the father of lies, which are preached by his instruments as the true religion. His own servants in the church denied the divinity of Jesus the Christ, who is one with the Father. The servants of this world totally denied the existence of God, and the servants of human wisdom taught that all living principles in nature, the living spirit in men, animal or plant together forms God.*

Verse 14. *These three are blasphemous doctrines of devils, whereby he seduces man to the rejection of the gospel of Jesus Christ and of the belief in God.*

Verse 15. *And the Protestant clergy spread these false doctrines of Deism, Atheism and Pantheism among Christianity and in the Christian churches.*

FULFILLMENT IN THE HISTORY OF THE CHURCH.

GUERS says, on page 627:
"While the devil externally attacked the church with violence, he inwardly attacked her with heresies, lies and vexation. Since the time of the

291

Reformation, the Anabaptists rose again, weapon in hand, spread the most dangerous doctrines. These children of unruliness, these Jacobites of the former times, began with all sorts of revolts, therewith willfully blaming the Reformation. The Enthusiasts, the other children of the prince of darkness, cast suspicion on the Reformation. After them appeared the disciples of Socinus, the unhappy ones, who degrade Him, whom heaven and earth worship, and at whose feet the redeemed will throw down their crowns, to the sons of the highest rank. Next to that, Arianism dared to raise its godless head. This old heresy, which wanted to rob the Lord of the glory of His sovereign divinity, rose up again in England sometime after the Reformation, gradually poisoning the whole of Europe."

"Your lot on earth will soon change, a small flock of Jesus Christ. Eventually, you will take possession of the kingdom. After being trodden upon for a long time by your enemies, the time approaches, where you will rule over them. As deep as your humiliation was, as high will your glory be. Rejoice in the Sabbath, for which you long, tired as you may be from so many sorrows and of so much strife, it will be yours. Yet one battle and the tribulation will end."

"But by which happenings must the church go from strife to victory? Which circumstances will lead her from her low state to glory? – If we respect the darkness, with which the prophecy covers itself, we rejoice at the same time at her light. Did God not give her to strengthen our faith, and to kindle our hope?" and page 639: "What the prophecy predicts is a total new establishment of the fourth empire (of Daniel). It assumes in advance the complete undoing of the present state of affairs, to make way for a totally new dispensation. Before one builds, one must break off. And for this, the political upheavals which we experience in our days prepared the way."

That GUERS spoke truthfully in his suspicion, will irrefutably be shown, when we, in the seventh period, compare the history of the day with the prophesies of the Revelation.

Mr. VAN LOON says in the closing words of his work in 1862:

"Although it would be desirable to add an overview about the time, which evolved up to the end of the eighteenth century (since the Reformation), a totally impractical view of the last sixty years and especially of the happenings, which we experience in our days, would preferably be left over for a later judgement. Over and above that, this period is definitely not over; many important questions at issue about hierarchy as well as of faith, are in a state of crisis and await a factual, or at least a reasonable conclusion. An overview would presently be like a report in the middle of an undecided battle. However much the Christian assured of the promise of the Lord, knows that the end of all turbulence of the nations, all revolutions against Christ, from the kings of the earth, as well as of the princes of science and of "the many findings, which men seek," will occur, - that the kingdoms of this world will belong to the Lord, and to His anointed, that He will reign as king for all eternity (Rev 11:15), and that the earth will be full of the knowledge of the Lord, like the bottom of the sea with water (Isaiah 11:9). It is therefore not yet possible, to determine the times and happenings which God reserves in His hand to any extent, until their end fulfilment, and how all apparent contradictory and controversial happenings are working together to the fulfilment of God's plan and to the advantage of His chosen as well as to the glorification of His Name."

So wrote VAN LOON in 1862. During the following years, so many important happenings took place in church and state, - we remind ourselves only of the declaration of the infallibility of the Pope, with the consequent complete loss of his worldly power, to the blows inflicted upon both the eldest and most faithful sons of the Roman church, Austria in 1866 and France in 1870, - so much has taken place since 1862 in the church and in the states, such as increasing signs of demolition and decay of the existing order (Anarchy), that now, as the Lord has given to His servants the only and true way to the correct understanding of His Revelation, it could now perhaps be possible, to see the future happenings based upon that understanding or at least from His Revelation learn to known the individual characteristic, whereby the future fulfilment of events will be recognized.

The present time is of the greatest importance. The atmosphere is pregnant with dark clouds, on the point of bursting. And so much stands firm and sure based on God's prophecies, that the moment approaches with all speed, (God knows how near) of the return of the Lord; the moment of God's final hearing of the moving high priestly prayer of His beloved Son Jesus Christ: **"Father! The hour has come; glorify Thy Son, that Thy Son also may glorify Thee: O righteous Father! The world hath not known Thee: but I have known Thee, and these have known that Thou hast sent Me, Holy Father! Keep through Thine own name those whom Thou has given Me; that they may be one, as we are. Father! I will that they also when Thou hast given Me, be with Me where I am, that they may behold My glory."** (John 17:1, 25, 11, 24.)

END OF THE SIXTH PERIOD

End Of Volume One

Final notes from the translator

I firmly believe that the reader has now gained an exciting and deep insight into the Revelation of John and can truly acknowledge the accuracy with which the wonderful wisdom of God, through His Son Jesus Christ and the Holy Spirit, predicted the development of His Church in the past centuries.

I look forward to meeting you again in **Volume Two**, which will deal with the **recent past, the present and the future.** I, for one, cannot wait to start translating the remaining pages and share them with you. Due to the time elapsed since the original book was written, it can be expected that events which occurred in the last 130 years will have to be taken into account and will require some research.

God bless you and may the Return of our Lord Jesus Christ be the goal to which we strive. **LORD COME SOON!**

The Translator

VOLUME TWO

SEVENTH PERIOD

Laodicea

Democracy
Or
The Will Of The People

Introduction To The Seventh Period

With the fulfilment of the prophecies of Revelation and the history of the Church of Jesus Christ, we have now approached our own century and therefore we can understand the current events better.

Before going on, the reader may ask whether our explanation of Revelation so far seems to be true, and if throughout the six periods, the meaning of the prophetic images taken from God's Word fulfilled themselves accurately and clearly in the history of the church. The answer to this question is important as Revelation was given for our time.

The happenings in church and state which occur in the seventh period, are sketched infinitely more amply and in detail than those of the first six periods. It appears to us the Lord therewith had a twofold goal in mind, namely:

1.) That we would readily recognize these happenings as they occur, and would thereby be warned against evil, which the Lord wants to spare us, and at the same time accept as good, which He we want us to inherit.

2.) The Lord in His revelation appears to want the predictions of the first six periods to serve as a letter of credit for His extensive prophecy of the seventh period, so His congregation, as a result of the accurate fulfilment of that which was predicted for the expired eighteen centuries, would also accept in faith and confidence, that which the Lord predicts for the present and future days.

The reader may with the greatest earnestness, as if in the presence of God's holy countenance, asks whether his heart and mind are completely satisfied with what we have thus far explained about the Revelation. Strange things are further predicted for the seventh period of such a portent as to exert the greatest influence on accepting or rejecting the lot and participation of the Christian in both the here and hereafter.

We must warn the reader seriously, not to rely on the universal thinking: "This will not happen in my lifetime!" To trust in this will be a false rest. Revelations, for all that, teaches the contrary, and God gave it to us as a clock on which we can see how late it is on the world time. When the reader learned to read it, he will see the end of this dispensation and the return of the Lord is near.

At the transition of the sixth into the seventh period (Rev. 10:5-7), Christ Himself swore with a solemn oath: *"There will be no more delay, but in the days when the seventh angel is to blow his trumpet, the mystery of God will be fulfilled."*

This seventh angel already sounds his trumpet, the happenings under this seventh trumpet already occur around us, escalate daily more and more, and as soon as they are completed, the mystery of God shall be fulfilled. Therefore: who has ears, let him hear what the Spirit says to the congregation.

We will not, as we have done up to know, give a historical overview of this period taken from Van Loon and Guers as it is not completed yet, and we will discontinue the way which we worked until now, by immediately showing the fulfilment of the prophecy as it is explained. Since we live in the second century of the seventh period, it is wise to divide this period into three parts:

A. **The recent past**: This will encompass the fulfilled part since 1815.
B. **The present**: Everything concerning our time.
C. **The future**: All Revelation predicts for the coming times.

Of the yet unfulfilled part, we must especially give the *characteristics, whereby we immediately can recognize and judge the predicted happenings as they occur*. In this manner, we will follow the fulfilment of Revelation from day to day, in order that we may awake and prepared on the day of the Lord. For this purpose, the Lord revealed to His servants: *"What must soon take place."* (Rev, 1:19).

SEVENTH PERIOD

LAODICEA:

A. The Recent Past

FROM
The Restoration of Peace in Europe, 1815 AD,
TO
The Return of the Lord

This period pertains to our 19th century with all its religious, state, and civil questions and upheavals, with all the expression of unbelieve and superstition, with its grievous wars, the striving of the nation for State Power, and the decay of Christian religion.

In this period, the **seventh head of the beast** is revealed (4th beast of Daniël: the Roman Empire).

This seventh head or Kingdom is **the seventh or universal anti-Christian Mountain.** This seventh head at the same time becomes the eighth as the persecutor of the Christians.

LAODICEAN TIME

Or

THE ANTI-CHRISTIAN PERIOD

A.   THE RECENT PAST

<u>Revelation 3: 14-21</u>

14. Write this letter to the leader of the church in Laodicea. This message is from the one who stands firm, the faithful and true Witness (of all that is or was or evermore shall be), the primaeval source of God's creation:

15. I know you well – you are neither hot nor cold; I wish you were the one or the other!

16. But since you are merely lukewarm, I will spit you out of my mouth!

18. My advice to you is to buy pure gold from Me, gold purified by fire – only then will you truly be rich. And to purchase from me white garments, clean and pure, so you won't be naked and ashamed; and to get medicine from me to heal your eyes and give you back your sight.

19. I continually discipline and punish everyone I love; so I must punish you unless you turn from your indifference and become enthusiastic about the things of God.

20. Look! I have been standing at the door and I am constantly knocking. If anyone hears me calling him and opens the door, I will come in and have fellowship with him and he with me.

21. I will let everyone who conquers sit beside me on my throne, just as I took my place with my Father on his throne when I had conquered.

END OF THE SIXTH CANDLESTICK

10. Because you have patiently obeyed me despite the persecution, I will protect you from the time of Great Tribulation and temptation, which will come upon the world to test everyone alive.

11. Look, I am coming soon! Hold tightly to the little strength you have – so that no one will take away your crown.

12. As for the one who conquers, I will make him a pillar in the temple of my God; he will be secure, and will go out no more; and I will write my God's Name on him, and he will be a citizen in the city of my God – the New Jerusalem, coming down from heaven from my God; and he will have my new Name inscribed upon him.

13. Let all who can hear, listen to what the Spirit is saying to the churches.

SEVENTH CANDLESTICK

Or

THE LIGHT OR THE SPIRITUAL LIFE OF THE CONGREGATION

> But woe unto you that are rich! For ye
> have received your consolation.
> Woe unto you that are full! For
> ye shall mourn and weep.
> Luke 6: 24,25

Rev 3:14-22

Laodicea, previously named Diospolis (City of God), where this seventh congregation in Asia Minor was established, is described as a great, rich, and renowned city. The congregation is also mentioned in (Col. 2:1 and Col 4:13, 16). The name Laodicea means **Government of the people** and the city itself was destroyed by an earthquake in 1402 A.D. In this time and in the fate of the city of Laodicea, lies hidden the typical condition and the end of the congregation of the seventh or last period. Government by people for all that is the individual characteristic, the strange striving of the Christian nations of Europe in this century. As such, the condition of the congregation is the result of the sixth vial. Through the severe shocks and earthquakes of the French Revolution in 1789, with its consequences of unbelief, the people awoke, tried to shake off the yoke of kingship and priesthood and recognize their so-called rights. Since this could not always happen by force, and the kings would not in the long run be able to resist the awakened people's will, the politics of the nineteenth century found a settlement in the constitutional kingship replacing the absolute kingship or sovereignty. [42]

This constitutional kingship, presently accepted in nearly all the kingdoms of Europe, is nothing but a transition between kingship and people's rule, and just like all transitions between irreconcilable principles, it is an absurdity and of a passing nature. Just like the condition of the

---

[42] Government by the people, actually the judgment of the people, which makes out the law, both in the meaning of executing a judgment by the people, as well as a judgment on the people, will take place.

Laodicean congregation, neither cold nor hot, it has no lasting viability in itself, and had all the important happenings, since 1848 up to the present not occurred, we could still foresee, grounded on Revelation, that the days of kingship are numbered and that the general people government is at hand. The democratic spirit wins appalling ground over the whole of Europe, the old Roman Empire.

Besides, the fate of the earthquake destroying Laodicea is a shadow of the future, as predicted to the congregation of Laodicea of the seventh period, in the anti-Christian earthquake and turmoil amongst the nations, when the Christian religions will be totally abolished, and the churches will be used for the purpose of human worship.

In the Roman and Protestant states the sovereign kingship and priesthood were previously coupled to the Shepherd and Teacher ministry (Euphrates) as a state church. (324 A.D.), the Christian kings and clergy together formed the seal. (Page 84). This bond between church and kingship allowed no freedom of religion. With the disappearance of absolute royal power in the seventh period, the bond between Christian kings and clergy, in the sense of Revelation completely stopped. The logical result must thus be a separation between state and church, irreligion; all things, which we have already seen happening in Europe, and daily further develop even to Papal Rome, in the loss of worldly power of the pope. In this way, both the Euphrates or Shepherd and Teacher ministry, as well as the absolute kingship, dried up in the seventh period.

Two great cancers, gnawing at the life of church and congregation, came into existence:

> *1. The commencing separation between state and church resulted in the state taking responsibility for education upon itself, and, in order not to offend anyone, in their religious convictions, to erect religious-less or neutral schools. Biblically, however, a religious-less school is a godless or anti-Christian school, (1 John 2:22,23) where one logically must deteriorate to materialism (matter worship) and Pantheism (all is God), just as they then also, alas! Became hotbeds for unclean spirits of the beast and their false prophecy. (Page 285).*
> *2. Freedom of religion resulted in the Protestant church dividing itself into countless sects, churches, and congregations, and will continue to divide herself until she becomes easy prey to anti-Christendom. The Christian idea, in so far as it was still present in the Roman church, received the death blow through the proclamation of the infallibility of the Pope (1870). The anti-Christian ideas (socialism, anarchism) flourished profusely in the Roman countries.*

This, in short is the social condition of the congregation in the seventh period, as it is understood in the prophetic word Laodicea, and is presently experienced. This opinion about the condition in Europe is not exclusively ours. Multapatior in his *Algemeen Handelsblad* of 21 July 1872, totally agreed as follows:

"In the last forty years, such enormous, radical and far-reaching changes occurred in political and in general social spheres; totally new world perceptions and principals are presented, all the old, formerly so Holy, or at least highly respectable matters of state and economy, are forcefully and ruthlessly removed from their pedestal; education and political life advanced at such giant leaps, that we in this respect, just as many others, find ourselves as it were in a new world."

We will now, in the seventh period find the judgement of the Son of God over the spiritual condition of the congregation for our time.

Verse 14. "And unto the angel (the whole clergy) **of the church of the Laodiceans** (or the Christians of the seventh period) **write These things saith the Amen, the faithful and true witness, the beginning of the creation of God".** None of the former candlesticks begins with a solemn assurance of the veracity and credibility of the promise of the Lord, as in this last, whereby He takes action against the Christians of the last period. Christ here names Himself:

> 1. *The Amen.* Amen means: *so shall it be.* In (Isaiah 65:16), the Lord names himself in the original: the God Amen, or the God, who keeps His Word. He therefore starts this last candlestick with the assurance that He will keep His Word in these last days, in all, that He promised His servants and threatened His enemies and that in the days of the voice of the seventh angel, the mysteries of God will be fulfilled, just as His servants the prophets declared. (Rev 10:7).
> 2. The Lord also names Himself: *the faithful and true witness.* He could say of Himself, that His testimony was true (John 8:14), and His testimony concerning the history of His church, received so far from His Revelation, appears to be faithful and true.

His testimony concerning these last days will appear true, just as His testimony directed against Jerusalem and the people of Israel. (Matt 24:1-8, Mark 13:1-8, Luke 21:5-9), truly was fulfilled.

Furthermore, He names Himself *the beginning of the creation of God.* The meaning of the original word is not a passive beginning, as if Christ names Himself the firstborn of the creation, but a *causative beginning,* as the *author of the creation of God.* This testimony of Christ concerning Himself finds its total solution in the words of (John 1: 1-3). *"In the*

307

beginning was the Word, and the Word was with God, and the Word was God. The same was in the beginning with God. All things were made by Him; and without Him was not anything made that was made." Similarly, we find in (Col. 1:15, 16), Christ naming Himself the beginning of the creation of God, because He will show the end of the present dispensation but also thereafter the beginning of His New Creation in the Kingdom of Glory. This omniscient God, creator of all things, Jesus Christ, who as the faithful and true one, keeps His Word and promises in all eternity, speaks out His judgment over the Christian congregation of our time as follows:

Verse 15. **"I know thy works, that thou art neither cold nor hot: I would thou wert cold or hot."** Above these and the following words numerous explanations were given, yet nowhere perhaps in the whole Revelation, will greater differences exist than here, between the general understanding of these words that which God's Word and the meaning Revelation gave us. The general understanding is that these words of Christ are directed to the *indifferent* Christians, who do not value and have not yet come to a definite faith, but serve Mammon and God, the world and Christ simultaneously, and therefore waver between hell and heaven, Christ could not have meant faithful and true believers. Our conviction is a totally different one, according to God's Word.

The judgment in (verses 15-17), spoken by the Lord, does not concern the indifferent, liberals and modern, but believers in the Christian church of the seventh period. The Lord for all that, directs this letter to the so-called Christians of our time and does nowhere differentiate between indifferent and believers, while He, who knows the hearts, and usually is so especially painstaking in His Words, that He in all the former letters praise the good and condemn the bad*, and even in the most corrupt Sardinian period of the church[43], knew how to single out and praise the few names of the Waldense, etc. (Rev 3:4). Of this no trace can be found in this last candlestick; on the contrary, the subject of the whole judgment of the Lord is, that the believing Christians of our time are not really against Christ (cold), but yet also not with their whole heart for Him (hot), and therefore live in an intermediate state (lukewarm), in which they consider themselves to be rich, happy and seeing (verses 15-17), and yet they all miss what Christ offers them in this last time (verses 18-20).

This undertaking agrees more with the whole content of the letter, than the general understanding of admonition to weak, indifferent Christians, whose condition and character unjustly, according to our views, we have

---

[43] See Rev.2:2, 4, 6, 9, 13 – 15, 20, 24, and Rev. 3:4, 8, 9.

named Laodiceans according to this letter. This understanding of ours should not be strange to our reader; for, indifferent Christians do not consider themselves spiritually rich, happy, and seeing. They do not concern themselves with their spiritual condition and do not even think about such matters. Moreover, we expect something strange in the judgment of the Lord over His church.

Previously, we said and seen it confirmed throughout all periods that, after approximately three hundred years, something new occurs in the church, which was not present in the previous period, by which it differs from the previous period. In such a way, the Christian religion was freed from persecution (324) and even became the State religion of the Roman Empire, with the third period (622) Popedom came into existence in Rome, with the fourth period (914) whores and knights took the place of the angel (the spiritual messengers or teachers) of Christ, with the fifth (1212), the reading of the Bible was forbidden and the servants of Christ were persecuted and killed for the Word of God by the clergy of the Christian church and not by the heathen, with the sixth period (1517) the light of the Gospel was restored through the blessed Reformation; and with the seventh period (1815)…?

The above-mentioned great happenings were great signs of those periods in the church. If Revelation, as the history of the church of Christ, in its construction, develops consequently, we have to expect something new, a special sign in the church, since another three centuries have expired after the Reformation[44].

Whether this expectation is valid, and what events in the church will answer the expectation, Revelation will show us in good time.

Verse 16, **"Because you are lukewarm and neither cold nor hot, I will spew you out of My mouth",** at My coming, and when you then say: "Lord! Lord! Open the door," My answer will be: "Verily, I say unto you, I know you not." These words of Christ clearly show that the congregation was in a terrible condition, and all efforts to restore her would be in vain. The keynote for all that of the Lord's complaint in verse 15: *"I would thou wert cold or hot,"* is thus, that the church henceforth is irreparably lost, and no believer, who is familiar with the conditions of the church of Jesus Christ, will dare to claim or expect, that the pure Gospel of Jesus Christ in the church, will triumph over the infiltrated modern and liberal feelings, and to drive them out again, to give way for the unity of faith in the Son of God. This is just as impossible as it was impossible for Luther and the other

---

[44] We put the prophetic words in Luther's mouth, that the results of the Reformation would only last three hundred years.

Reformers, to bring back the original purity and Evangelistic truth into the corrupt and apostate Roman church.

The admonition of the Lord: *"I will spew thee out of my mouth"*, may seem somewhat strange, however, we know the mouth (pages 229 – 230), as *the defender of someone's doctrine.* The *mouth* of the Lord is therefore *His witness.* The spewing out of the mouth we see fulfilled in (Rev. 18: 20), where the angel says to the Lord's witnesses: "For God hath avenged you on her". (The apostate church). The Lord gives the reason for His sentence in Verse 17: **Because thou sayest, I am rich, and increased with goods, and have need of nothing; and knowest not that thou art wretched, and miserable, and poor, and blind, and naked."** This must therefore be the spiritual condition of the churches of our time. Indeed, one fact is clear to us, each church considers itself rich, the Roman as well as the Greek and the Protestant, and each considers itself to be the right one, standing in the full dispensation of Christ. However, since there exists so much diversity among churches, so much separation, contradictions, and division between the Roman, Greek, and Protestant churches, and in the last-named again so much discord amongst her different denominations, this is impossible. The question, where are the riches, is at the same time totally irrelevant, where Christ Jesus, the faithful and true witness, says to them all, to the total Laodicean church, in the seventh period: *"You think you are rich, but you are poor. You say you are increased in goods, but I say unto you, you are wretched and miserable. You feel you have need of nothing, and you don't see, what I see in you, you are blind and naked."*

The unbeliever does not fall under this judgement of the Lord, it is therefore not written for him, but to the believers; and he can now only choose concerning His judgement, or to inquire as to his poverty, his *nakedness* and *blindness*.

To this last the Lord invites him. For in the following (Verse 18), He says: **"I counsel thee to buy of me gold tried in the fire, that thou mayest be rich; and white raiment, that thou mayest be clothed, and that the shame of thy nakedness do not appear; and anoint thine eyes with eye salve, that thou mayest see".** If then the Christians of the nineteenth, twentieth, and twenty-first centuries, would hear the voice and advice of the Lord, they will have to investigate, wherein their poverty, their nakedness, and blindness lies. This investigation will best be done, when we compare the present conditions of the church with her original condition in the first period of the first three centuries of the church, when she was still the *white horse* (first seal). When we see that the church was then organized differently than now, and possessed gifts of the Lord, which now are missing, then we suspect that the Lord wants to give back these gifts to the church of our time, so that our poorness changes to riches, and raiment to cover our nakedness. And even if everything does not immediately become clear to us during our investigation, we may expect the loving Lord, who wants to save us, that He will show us this further on in His Revelation; for He Himself advises us, to buy of Him the eye salve, that those who are blind, might see. We immediately notice one big difference between the former and the present church in that the latter completely lacks the gifts of the Holy Spirit, which none possessed in its entirety, as we have seen in the church of the first period, as testified to by the writers of the church history. This gift of healing the sick through the laying on of hands or salving with oil and prayer in the name of Jesus, which James described as something very common, these gifts of talking in tongues and interpreting them, these gifts of prophecies, to raise the dead (miracles), etc., we name them still the extraordinary gifts of the Holy Spirit. However, when we read (1 Cor. 12:1-3, 27-30, and 1 Cor. 14), it becomes clear to us, that the gifts of the Holy Spirit were definitely not considered extraordinary in this former congregation, but very customary, like something which ought to be inseparably part of being Christian. Nowhere in the New Testament scripture do we find that these gifts were given exclusively for the church of the first period and not to ever be restored at any later period.

Similarly, the same must be said about the fourfold ministry, through whom Christ worked in His congregation, the Apostles, Prophets, Evangelists, and Shepherds, as they were active in the Christian church of the first century, as they were also described and fore-shadowed in (Ezek. 1) in the four Cherubim, in (Gen 1) in the four main streams, and in the four horns of the altar, and as Paul mentions in (Eph 4:11-13), they were present and active in the congregation. We have seen, that in and after the first period of the church these ministries disappeared and up to the seventh period did not return in her, then we must admit that the Christians of the first three centuries possessed therein a great treasure of Grace, which we now miss, and the missing of them we do not even feel or regret; we must then come to a decision, that our water Baptism is not the Baptism instituted by Christ, since John the Baptist so clearly predicted of Christ, (Matt. 3:11, Luke 3:16), "I indeed *Baptize* you with water, but He that cometh after me is mightier than I, He shall Baptize you with the Holy Ghost, and with fire. *"But also then the Word of the Lord (verse 17), becomes the full truth; "For you say, I am rich and have need of nothing, and knows not thou art wretched and, that the church had these gifts, and we can do without them?* But Paul writes to the congregation of Thessalonica (1 Thess. 5:19, 20),

"Quench not the Spirit. Despise not prophesying." Or is this not also written for us, just as all the other apostolic admonitions? If not, then we do not have to concern ourselves with all the other apostolic writings. Or may we accept and be satisfied, that the church had these gifts, and we can do without them? But then we are completely like the Laodiceans. Actually, the Lord put us on a par with them, for they also spoke likewise. The question is, however, whether the Lord wants to miss them in us. In the congregation of Laodicea, the Lord did not want to miss them but offered to give them back. But we also belong to the Laodicean congregation and in the judgment over Laodicea, we find at the same time His judgment over us. But how was the condition of the congregation of Laodicea, when the Lord caused this to be written to her? During His life, approximately twenty-five years previously, Paul already complained (2 Tim. 1:15), to His disciple Timothy, "This thou knowest, that *all* they which are in Asia be turned away from me". To them also belonged the congregation of Laodicea. The consequence of this apostasy was an amazing decay during the fourth century. They also had possessed apostles, ministries, and gifts of the Holy Spirit, but they did not have them anymore, did not value them anymore, did not feel that they missed them, but build on the fact, that they possessed them all, and imagined, in their unconscious decay, to be rich and in need of nothing.

The Lord not only describes Her in verse 17, but therewith at the same time, the whole Christendom of our seventh or Laodicean period, who live in the same condition. Therefore, who hath ears, hear what the Spirit sayeth unto the congregation.

Verse 19: **"As many as I love, I rebuke and chasten";** says the Lord: **"Be zealous, therefore, and repent."** And He loves us as He loved the Laodiceans because they wandered in good faith, and because He loves you, He teaches you and says:

Verse 18: **"I counsel thee to buy of me gold,** *that is the truth of God,* **gold, tried in the fire,** that is the pure truth of the Gospel, preached by the faithful and well-tried servants of the Lord (1 Cor 3:9–25), **that thou mayest be rich,** and repossess all that which you lost. He counsels you to buy of Him **white garment,** *the hidden man of the heart* (1 Pet 3:3, 4*), the white garment of light* (Psalm 104:2), to walk as the children of the light (Eph 5:8), the *garment of the Holy Spirit* (2 Cor 5:4, 5) to come to the great tribulation, (Rev 7:13, 14.) which they who remain Laodiceans will experience; the white wedding garment of the Kingdom of Heaven (Matt 22:2, 11, 12), necessary to be called to the marriage supper of the Lamb (Rev 19:7–9); **that the shame of thy nakedness do not appear",** at the moment when they, who possess these white garments, will be clothed upon with our house which is from heaven (2 Cor 5:2), and be caught up together with them in the clouds, to meet the Lord in the air. (1 Thess 4:15–17).

We do not doubt for a single moment that here and there some things in the last pages will not be readily acceptable to the reader or credible in our understanding of the words of the Lord to the congregation. The reason for this is not difficult to find. The Lord told you (in verse 17) that you are spiritually blind, we, therefore, will not try to bring you to have the right insight of your condition, thereby not perhaps to be blind leaders of the blind. The Lord Himself promises you in (verses 18 and 19), as many as I love, I rebuke and chasten, and counsel thee to anoint your eyes (Spiritual eyes) with eye-salve, the unction and the light of the Holy Spirit (1 John 2:20, 27) that thou mayest see what your condition is, what is expected from you. Where the Lord Himself counsels you, you can also freely trust that He will give you the eye-salve in His Revelation; that He will further on show you, what will serve to your peace.

Just believe Him, even though everything is not clear to you, just accept in good faith this judgement concerning your condition, and open your heart to Him, because the Lord says to you:

Verse 20. **"Behold I stand at the door, and knock: if any man hears My voice, and opens the door, I will come into him and will sup with him and he with Me."** And He stands at your heart's door and knocks, also with this writing. But He also knocks at your door, teachers (the angel's verse 14), of all denominations, and if you will hear His voice and open to Him, He shall come into you and sup with you and you with Him.

The Lord comes into you and sups with you? And He Himself named you (verse 17) miserable and poor? What would you have to present to Him at a supper? Rest assured! He does not need, that anyone should prepare something for Him. When He comes into you, poor one, to sup with you, He brings with Him and offers you what is needed for the supper, and what He used with His apostles in the night that He was betrayed, He brings along:

1. *The slaughtered lamb*, that is: *His own body, given into death for you,* to redeem you from eternal death (Isaiah 53:7);

2. Over it the *bitter sauce of His suffering*, for your iniquities (Isaiah 53:4–6, 11);

3. *The unleavened bread*, that is: the bread of life, or His Word, which itself is the *wheat* (page 123, 124), and the bread, purged and pure (1 Cor 5:7, 8), not mixed with the *leaven of false doctrines* (Matt 16:12);

313

4. *The wine,* that is: *His blood,* the blood of the New Testament, *shed for your sins* (Matt 26:28, 1 Cor 11:25).

Therefore, if you hear His voice, and open your heart's door, He will come into you in this seventh period, to celebrate the communion with you, that is, to bring you to a higher intimate relationship with Him, for in the communion of the Lord, celebrated up to now, was there not the cup of thanksgiving, a *communion of the blood* of Christ? Was the bread, which we brake, not a *communion of the body* of Christ? (1 Cor 10:16)? And as often as we ate this bread, and drank of this cup, did we not celebrate the Lord's death, till He comes. (1 Cor 11:26)? And now His coming is near, but before He takes you unto Himself, to be where He is (John 17:24), He wants to celebrate communion with you in a higher form, here on earth in these last times, before you are called to the supper of the marriage of the Lamb. What this supper with Christ means, is not revealed by the Lord in this seventh candlestick, and we thus find no license to anticipate Him in His Revelation.

Enough that the Lord in this earnest admonition to you in the seventh candlestick, wants to warn you to realize that you as Christians, do not possess all He once gave to His church, and wants to find in Her at His imminent return and require of you. Your excuse, that the talent was buried in the earth, will not profit you, no more than the fact that the church had not possessed the means of salvation for so many centuries. For *those times* they were so necessary, as will later be apparent. In *this time* they are indispensable for you if you want to partake of the glorious promise which the Lord makes to you and to the last times, and for which He needs you.

The Lord in this letter not only directs an admonition and counsel to us but also an invitation to us in (verse 19). *"As many as I love, I rebuke and chasten."* Endeavour to see this. Do not persevere in your thinking that your faith, that your church denomination is the only true one, is totally sufficient. If all the members of the Roman church had done that in the days of the reformers, the blessed Reformation, of which we still harvest the fruits today, would never have been established. Therefore, intelligent reader of this century who has so much more than the poor Romans of that time, act at least as intelligently as they did, and do not build on the incorruptible of your faith, on the steadfastness of your hope, but accept as they did, the Word of God as a guide. Mirror yourself in it, research what Christ warns you about! See what you lack, and what He promises to give back to you in this time, that you may follow His counsel. Because in the Reformation He wants to give in this last period a new, a last Reformation. With the first Reformation not everything was restored as it was in the first

Christian church. And yet the Lord, at His return, wants to find His church as He established her. Do you want to know how the church, how the congregation should be, then read attentively, as we already counseled you to do in the first candlestick (page 35, 36.Vol.1), the letter to the congregation of the Ephesians, as an example of the congregation of the first three centuries. Do you fully understand this? Do you posses everything, of which is spoken therein? Are you the persons to whom Paul writes? You should be – this letter is also directed at you, since it is a universal epistle to all Christians.

And this self-examination is worth it, because great is the reward, which the Lord of the church promises in the last verse, the most glorious of all end promises of the seven candlesticks.

Verse 21. **"To him that overcometh,** - overcomes his own opinion, his prejudice against that which I want to give back to My church, - who overcomes the seduction of the last days, but hears My voice, opens the door of his heart and as teacher (angel) the door of his congregation to Me, - **Will I grant to sit with Me in My throne, even as I also overcame, and am set down with My Father in His throne."** You do not realize or understand what a great measure of Glory it is, to be seated with Christ on His throne, to live with Him and to reign in the Kingdom of His Glory.

Revelation will later give you some indication as to this splendour. This Glory is especially promised to the overcomers of the last period and also to you, if you overcome. Therefore, if you hear His voice today, harden not your heart and who hath ears, let Him hear, what the Spirit in its prediction still further says to the congregation, because, should you belong to the overcomers behold, I will make them, who deny Me as their God and Saviour (the Jews from the sixth candlestick, Rev 3:9) to come and bow down before your feet, and they will learn that I have loved you.

With this promise, we had to take up the sixth candlestick again (Rev 3:9), where we left it, as unfulfilled and pouring over into the seventh period because this is where it joins the chronology of the church history in the seventh period and progresses next to it. May we remind you, as we have often stated before, that the seven congregations reflect the seven conditions of faith of Christians, as they occurred in succession in church history, that all these conditions of the spiritual life of the congregation remain in existence with and next to each other until the return of Christ, at His return He will thus find Christians of all these different views and faiths on earth, but also only then will the seven different promises to the overcomers, given at the end of each candlestick be fulfilled on the day of the Lord. We must also not imagine the congregation of Philadelphia as having come up from nothing in the sixth period. On the contrary! It was the same testimony of Jesus, which prevailed throughout all the periods of the church, as we learned to know them as the Cathars, the poor of Lyon, the Waldense, Hussites, etc... during the periods of papal power, who openly appeared in the sixth period as the Protestant church, but which as the sixth candlestick in the period of Reformation (up to 1815) was fulfilled only up to (verse 9), while the rest only occurred after 1815, and continues into the seventh period up to the end.

Behold, promises the Lord to His faithful, *I will make them come*, and, just as Nebuchadnezzar offered Daniel the highest honour (*worshipped*, Dan 2:46, 47), and recognized him as the servant and messenger of the true God, so will they also *recognize* that you are My disciples, that you have in truth believed in Me, as the true God and eternal life, and *that I love you*. In the already unfolded portion of the seventh period, this promise is not yet fulfilled and could not yet come to fulfilment. We will see this happen in a spectacular manner in the hours of the Great Tribulation.

Before this fulfilment, however, what the Lord promised must first occur (verse 10): **"Because thou hast kept the word of My patience, when you were persecuted by the people, for My name's sake, and, like Me, have suffered patience and endured, I also will keep thee from the hour of temptation, which shall come upon all the world, to try them that dwell upon the earth."**

This disdain of those, who believe in Christ as their God and Saviour, did not occur in the sixth period. The Arian teachers (Jews) who denied the divinity of Christ had appeared, but their teaching was not yet so deeply rooted in the church during the sixth period until (1815);

The Christian worshippers were scorned and disdained. On the contrary, the Arians comprised, in accordance with the meaning of (Rev 3:9) the minority. Only after (1815) did everything change, and presently the minority has become the great majority, and he, who openly dares to come out for His belief in the divinity of Jesus Christ, is scorned by the greater majority as a heretic, disdained as pious, as one who has not enough intelligence, to discuss religion.

Christ, the King of the universe, names them Blessed (Matt 5:11, 12), and wants to preserve them, as He here promises, from the hour of temptation, which will come over the whole world; - a time of trouble, such as never was since there was a nation even to that same time. (Dan 12:1), - for then shall the Great Tribulation, such as was not since the beginning of the world to this time, no, nor ever shall be. (Matt 24:21) – the anti-Christian time, as described in (Rev 12:13–17; Rev 13:14–17 and Rev 15:9–13), when they are beheaded for the testimony of Jesus and for the Word of God, which do not want to worship the beast and its image and receive the mark on their foreheads and hand (Rev 20:4).

The Philadelphian congregation, therefore, the scented sprout of the old fig tree of the church, such as she still existed in the seventh period in the believers who see God's truth, Christ wants to preserve them from the coming persecution. Those who, by patient continuance (Rom 2:7), kept His Word, who endured unto the end in the promise of His return, hoped and waited for it (Matt 24:13, Mark 13:13); - to them the Lord will offer a way of salvation, now that His return is imminent. The Lord says from this seventh period:

Verse 11. **"Behold I come quickly: hold that fast which thou hast,** the faith in My return as your God, as your Lord and Saviour, who wants to save you from the hour of Great Tribulation. Keep that faith, **that no man take thy crown",** the incorruptible *crown of Glory* (1 Peter 5:4), the crown of righteousness, which the Lord, the faithful judge, (who presently stands at the door, (James 5: 9), will give to all in that day, who loved His appearance (2 Tim 4:8). Be ye steadfast and unmovable, because,

Verse 12. **"Who overcomes** the battle against unbelief and superstition, in the battle against authority and personal prejudice, in the battle against the anti-Christian seduction of the seventh period, **I will make a pillar** of My congregation, as James, Peter and John were pillars (Gal 2:9) in **the temple of My God",** the church, the striving church here on earth, as well as the victorious one in My Kingdom of Glory. Or do you not know that you are My congregation, My Body, (1 Cor 1:27), God's temple, and that the Spirit of God lives in you (1 Cor 3:16. 1 Cor 4:19)?

Who overcomes, I will make him a pillar of My church in the last period, and **he shall go no more out** and fall prey to the Laodiceans and the Anti-Christians again, because, through Me, he belongs to the Father (John 17:22, 23), and is revealed as a letter from Me, written not with ink, but through the Spirit of the living God in the tables of the flesh of His heart (2 Cor 3:3). "I will write on **him the name of the city of My God**, mount Zion, the city of the living God, the heavenly Jerusalem, of which he possesses citizenship, as belonging to the congregation of the firstborn, who are written in heaven (Heb 12:22, 23), the name of **New Jerusalem**, to be living stones thereof (1 Pet 2:5), and to belong to My Bridal congregation, the New Jerusalem (Rev 2:2, 9, 10) which **cometh down out of heaven from My God"** (Rev 21, 22:1–15).

"I will write upon him **My new name,** not the name of Jesus (Saviour) for there were amongst men those who bore that name, (Jesus, Saviour,

Acts 7:45, Hab 4:8, Col 4:11), not the name of Christ (anointed), because there were also false Christs (Matt 24:24. Mark 13:22); - not the name of Son of God because you are already children of God, but My new name of **King of Kings**, (Rev 19:16), which I, as overcomer will exercise in My Kingdom of Glory, where you also, as overcomers will sit on My throne with Me (Rev 3:21), and reign with Me as kings on the earth (Rev 1:6. Rev 5:10. Rev 20:4, 6. Rev 22:5).

All these glorious promises of the Son of God are therefore given to the upright Philadelphian Christians, who in the seventh period, not as scented blooms, but now as ripe fruits on the old fig tree of the church (see Vol. 1) are not fallen to the Laodicean self-sufficient condition, or those who have overcome by listening to His voice, and thereby became unshakable, as pillars in the great battle of the anti-Christian seduction, during the time of the great apostasy.

They, and they alone, will not partake of, but be saved from the coming Great Tribulation. When they open their heart's door to Jesus, when He, also through His writing knocks on it, they will not have to strive in this terrible battle until the end, but will soon (Rev 4-5) find an open door in heaven, to go therein, and to sit with Jesus on His throne, because they overcame as He did, and sit with His Father on His throne (Rev 3:21).

The writing of the glorious name on the forehead of the overcomers by their Lord, as an outcome against the anti-Christian persecution, will soon be explained to us. Therefore:

Verse 13: **"He that hath an ear, let him hear what the Spirit,** also here, **saith unto the churches."**

With all that which we have disclosed in this last candlestick, here completely there halfway, and with all the things which come to mind concerning the future happenings of the seventh trumpet and vial, the thought may arise in the reader that such wonderful happenings, such as for example we find in chapters 11, 12 and 13, could not happen here on earth. The readers of Revelation in the eighteen centuries gone by, must have had the same feeling, and yet, how naturally and simply has everything come into fulfilment so far. Similarly, the strangest images, once we have learned to understand their meaning, will not only appear to be possible, that they will be fulfilled in a natural and simple way, but we will even see, that presently, we already live amidst these happenings. Revelation henceforth becomes very important to us, because it teaches us the judgement of God over the present world and church history, but also what still lies ahead for both in the very near future.

SEVENTH SEAL

Rev 8:1-5

1. When the Lamb had broken the seventh seal, there was silence throughout all heaven for what seemed like half an hour.

2. And I saw the seven angels that stand before God, and they were given seven trumpets.

3. Then another angel with a golden censer came and stood at the altar; and a great quantity of incense was given to him to mix with the prayers of God's people, to offer upon the golden altar before the throne.

4. And the perfume of the incense mixed with prayers ascended up to God from the altar where the angel had poured them out.

5. Then the angel filled the censer with fire from the altar and threw it down upon the earth; and thunder crashed and rumbled, lightening flashed, and there was a terrible earthquake.

1. And I saw another angel coming from the east, carrying the Great Seal of the Living God. And he shouted out to those four angels who had been given power to injure earth and sea,

2. "Wait! Don't do anything yet – hurt neither earth nor sea nor trees – until we have placed the Seal of God upon the foreheads of his servants."

3. How many were given this mark? I heard the number – it was 144,000; out of all twelve tribes of Israel, as listed here:

Judah	12,000
Reuben	12,000
Gad	12,000
Asher	12,000
Naphtali	12,000
Manasseh	12,000
Simeon	12,000
Levi	12,000
Issachar	12,000
Zebulum	12,000
Joseph	12,000
Benjamin	12,000

SEVENTH SEAL

OR

THE SPIRITUAL LIFE OF THE POWERS IN CHURCH AND STATE

Can ye not discern the signs of the times?
Matt 16:3c

Rev 8:1-5; Rev 7:2-8; Rev 6:14-17

Rev 8:1. **"And when He had opened the seventh seal, there was silence in heaven about the space of half an hour".** When we consider that just before this, John in (Rev. 7:10-17) described the calling with a loud voice of an uncountable multitude, and the explanation of the angel, he now wants to say, that in heaven approximately one-half an hour of silence occurred after the opening of the seventh seal, during which silence the acts took place as described in (verse 2 to 6). The first happening was:

Verse 2. **"And I saw the seven angels which stood before God, and to them were given seven trumpets".** With this verse, many writers were thrown off track. It was generally accepted, that, after the fulfilment of the seven seals, the seven trumpets followed, yes even, that the seventh seal had no portent of its own but consisted of the seven trumpets. Once off track, it became impossible to find the way again. And yet, the matter is very simple, when one remembers what was already said in (Rev. 1:10) that John after being *transported in the spirit to the day of the Lord* (not Sunday, but of the future of the Lord), received this Revelation. That was indeed the point in time in History, where John was transported in the spirit, when the Lord in prophetic visions allowed him to see all that still had to happen in the church before this day would come. The visions of John were thus retrospective, a look back at the things, which on the day of the Lord would have *happened*, but at that earthly point in time, where John saw them and indeed was still on the Isle of Pathos, in effect still would happen in the *future*. In the previous chapter, he actually saw how the congregation of the sixth period, together with the clergy of the sixth seal, had come out of the great anti-Christian tribulation (verse 14) into the Kingdom of Glory where *"God shall wipe away all tears from their eyes"* (Rev. 7:17). The sixth seal is therefore completed on the day of the Lord. The seventh is now open. During the half-hour silence, which followed, the seven angels representing the Christian kings and priests of the seven periods appeared before God, and received, while the happenings of the seventh seal (verses 3 to 5) take place, their respective trumpets. After the happenings of the seventh seal are completed, only then do they prepare (verse 6) to sound their trumpets. Now, at the conclusion of the seven seals or the description of the condition of the clergy in the seven periods of the church, the Lord wants to make John see, what the condition and effect of the gospel preaching during the seven periods would be, through these same seven angels of the seven periods.

This is the simple explanation of it all. We can thus consider (verse 2 of Rev. 8), as an interjection, which does not pertain to the actual content of the 7th seal, but, after (verse 5) follows:

Verse 1. **"And when He had opened the seventh seal** and wanted to show John, what would happen in the seventh period of the church, beginning in 1815, as exceptional and new in the Christian church and with the Christian teachers and state powers, and add it to that which remained and still existed from the previous periods, - **there was in heaven**, thus in God's Kingdom on earth as well as in heaven, **a silence about the space of half an hour"**. This silence we must find in the earthly history from 1815 if our classification and time frame of Revelation is correct.

"With 1815", so do we read in the "*Handelsblad*" of 25 April 1871, in the report on the readings about the Newer History, held by Dr. Doorenbos in Amsterdam.

"With 1815", - so said Dr Doorenbos, "a new era begins. I deem this period important, because, - the rest which it brought, - developed (thus in silence) that which took a few years to realize. Our time (1871) is a time of the greatest confusion in the political condition, - of *the heaviest religious revolutions and the most violent upheavals in social life*." Who does not agree with him? He also recognizes, that after 1815, a rest and silence prevailed in state, church and social life. How long did it last? Revelation says: *Half an hour in heaven*, or in God's Kingdom. In the Bible it often speaks of "one hour" as a point in time and thus in an indefinite sense. Here however it is a decided time frame or duration. But how long is half an hour in our earthly calculations? In order to know the time and determine its duration in a realm, we must also follow the time and the time frame of that realm, and thus also in the realm of God, the time frame of God. - Without taking recourse to the known Israelite representation of six days, each of 1000 years, and the seventh 1000 years as Sabbath or day of the Lord, - a representation, which incidentally totally concurs for the first part with history and the second part with (Rev. 20), - we thus have a place in the Old and one in the New Testament, which provides us with the same divine time reckoning.

Psalm 90:4 says: *"For a thousand years in thy sight are but as yesterday when it is past, and as a watch in the night."* Thus 24 hours, and Peter says (2 Pet. 3:8), with emphasis: "Be not ignorant of this one thing, that one day is with the Lord a thousand years (in our time reckoning), and a thousand years (for us) as one day" (for the Lord). It is remarkable that while we, true to our principle, to resolve the unknown in Revelations with the Bible, find that this time frame of 1000 earthly years, which equals 24 hours for God and in His Kingdom for us, - accurately fits in with the time frame of history.

Taking therefore 1000 earthly years as being one day in the Kingdom of God[45], then half an hour, is approximately 21 years. Adding these to 1815 will give us a silence up to 1836. It however states "about", and could therefore be 1830 or 1832. Indeed, our historical writer Van Loon, finds *no important happenings* in the *Kingdom of God on Earth*, nor major wars between the *Christian nations* in Europe. This was therefore the silence, that John saw in heaven, a silence however before the storm. In 1830, an important phenomenon began to develop in the church, but at the same time a series of upheavals on earth, continued in rising measure up to our time. But it is pure coincidence that the time frame falls in place with this or that will the reader say! Please read on, we pray, and then you will see that the seventh seal coincidently is fulfilled according to this time reckoning as was the whole Revelation so far throughout all periods. The year 1830 for all that is the origin of all the great happenings, which we experience today. During this silence, John however saw what is described in (verses 3-4). If our time reckoning is correct, then we must find it on earth in the Kingdom of God. Because

Verse 3. **"And another angel came and stood at the altar, having a golden censer; and there was given unto him much incense, that he should offer it with the prayers of all the saints upon the golden altar which was before the throne".**

This other *Angel* is *Jesus Christ, the Angel of the Covenant*, who, as the High Priest of the New Testament, lays the prayers of the living and deceased believers as a costly odour (Rev. 5:8, Psalm 141:2) on the golden altar of incense, which is in the sanctuary of the temple, or in paradise,

---

[45] Then many New Testament prophetic sayings concerning the last days, (two days) as divine time reckoning become simple and clear. The apostles probably did not understand that, just as prophesying persons also often did not understand the actual meaning of their prophecies.

before the throne of the Father, (see fifth seal. Vol.1). For only through and in Christ Jesus can the prayers, even of the holiest and most pious souls be pleasing and heard by God the Father. The *golden altar of incense* is already known to us (page 193), as the image of the *High Priestly ministry of Jesus.*

There must, therefore, have been many prayers in and for the Kingdom of God, during the 20 years of silence, whether on earth or in paradise by the deceased and still resting believers, because:

Verse 4. **"And the smoke of the incense, which came with the prayers of the saints, ascended up before God out of the Angel's hand."**

Did this occur on Earth at that time? We need not refer to historical books to confirm this. The aged, as living witnesses still live amongst us, who remember how, after 1815, in churches as well as by particular persons, in separate societies, long and earnest prayer meetings were held, for the restoration of the church. How was the condition of Europe, the condition of the church *before*? And, how it remained *after* 1815?

Terrible was the shock, also on a spiritual level, felt by all at the outbreak of the French Revolution. The persecuted and angered French nation broke all rules, and all the evil lusts were freed. Godlessness, cruelty, bloodthirstiness, and satanic hate against God and His service, raged all over civilized Europe. Murder was the politics, cursing the Christian religion, the moral law, exalting man to godhood the religion of the French nation. As an infernal spirit, it spread out over Europe with the banner of unchristian Freedom, Equality and Fraternity, to cause the nations to partake of this supposed national prosperity. Its poisonous breath plagued the hearts everywhere. Unbelief and the revilement of Christianity had reached its top. Many thought that the end of the world was near, especially when, out of the sea of nations, as predicted in (Rev. 13:1), Napoleon I, rose to power, who knew how to bridle the freed lusts, and to apply them to attain his own ambitious goals, so that many thought him to be the predicted anti-Christ. Through his invasions, Europe went up in flames and was drenched with blood.

The earnest believers compared the signs of the times with the prophecies of God's Word. Many thought that the return of the Lord had to be imminent and that the great falling away, which had to precede the advent of the Kingdom of Glory, would soon rise to its peak.

Then from the Lord's mouth sounds: *"Till so far and not further."* With broken wings, the French eagle lay down. Napoleon, the conqueror, is dethroned, banned and imprisoned. Europe comes to rest (1815); but what a rest. The state coffers are empty, the fields destroyed, fortunes dissipated, prosperity is undermined, trade and industry not functioning, the flower of men killed, but above all, the Christian faith poisoned, the hearts of the youth plagued by horrible unbelief, and the hope of the believers on the advent of the great day of rest is disappointed. Thus did Europe, with its destroyed faith, broken hope and devastated prosperity, tired to death, sink in despair.

Now, from the silent believers, prayers began to be raised to the almighty to restore religion and faith. Supplications ascended up to His throne for the restoration of the church of Jesus Christ. And not only a few prayed. Over the whole of Europe, writings were sent out, especially from England, to awaken the believers, to unite at specified times, to plead the Lord of the church, and to have mercy on the devastated vineyard. Separate prayer meetings were held. Thousands of prayers rose up for the promised latter rain of the Holy Spirit, (Zach. 10:1), for the return of the gifts of the Holy Spirit given by Christ to His church; prayers for the disbanded missionary and Bible Societies; prayer for everything and for all, which Christians deem holy and costly, but above all this one, the holy prayer: **"Let Thy Kingdom come!"**

Did all these prayers remain unanswered?

Verse 5. **"And the Angel took the censer, and filled it with fire of the altar, and cast it into the earth".** This fire we know as the fire of the Holy Spirit (first trumpet, pages 60-61. Vol. 1), Jesus himself had once come to earth, to send fire on earth (Luke 12:49), and which He once more pours out into the heart of His servants.

"And there were voices, and thunderings, and lightnings, and an earthquake." Will we find these on earth again at the end of the silence in the year 1830 or 1832? Which were then *these voices, these thunderings, these lightnings*? They were *the voice of the Lord spoken through His servants* (Ex. 5:1, 2), *the voice of the preaching of the gospel of the seventh trumpet* (Isaiah 58:1), which again began to resound in Europe through a renewed awakening to repentance and faith, to announce the pure gospel of Jesus Christ; voices which found a wide response, as evidenced in the foundation of the Société Evangélique in France in 1830, the Sociéte Evangélique in Zwitserland in 1831, the establishing of a Seminar for orthodox preachers in Geneva in 1832; the origin of the Separation in the Nederlandsche Hervormde Church in 1833 and 1834; the second separation of Old-Lutherans in Germany in 1835, from the state reunited Evangelistic church in 1829. They were the *thunderings of the glorification of the Lord's name*, through His angels or messengers once again preached on earth (John 12:29), for *the Spirit of the Father spoke through them* (Matt.

325

10:20). They were the religious awakenings which arose everywhere in Europe and which, not restricting themselves to their own circle, but also to the establishing and expansion of bible and missionary societies, to spread the word of God and the gospel of salvation to heathens and Jews across the whole world, so that all should see the salvation of God. For this gospel of the kingdom must first be preached in the whole world as *a witness to all nations*; and then the end will come (Matt. 24:14). And *that the end of this dispensation was near in the future of the Son of man*, the voices also went out as the voices calling in the desert: "Prepare the way of the Lord, for His coming is nigh." And these voices speedily resounded over the whole earth as lightning, which shineth from the east to the west (Matt. 24:27).

The **Maranatha, Maranatha, the Lord comes**, went out from the Apostolic church and worldly authorities in all countries; like **lightning** (Matt. 18:3) her teachers, as the angels of the Lord, caused all over the world to hear the cry: Awake! Awake! For ye know not what hour your Lord doth come (Matt. 24:42).

But not only *these voices, these lightnings, these thundering*s were the results of the outpoured fire of the Holy Ghost on earth. Already the first trumpet showed us, that this fire of the Holy Spirit was unacceptable to the enemies of the Lord Jesus, and that it awoke in them the opposite, the devilish fire of enmity against God and His anointed. And also since 1830 this fire was again revealed in the *voices* of Buonarotti (1830), disciple of Babeuf, who preached communism, the abolition of family and property, and the exaltation of materialism to a religion; of Robert Owen, the socialist (1836), who wants to abolish religion and marriage; in the *lightning*, in which satan (Luke 10:18) revealed himself in David Strauss (1835), who's Life of Jesus (or the Gospel as a collection of fables) sounded as a *thundering* of hell over the Christian earth; in his still outshining spiritual colleagues, Bruno Baver and Feverbach, who declared the gospel as deception and suggested self-worship instead (van Loon, page 315), in his French-superficial follower Renan and further rational prophets, through which mouths the lying spirit spoke (1 Kings 22:22). But also, the hostile *voices* against Christ and the Father rose out of the friends of the light in Germany, the free thinkers in Belgium and France, the Day-Break new in Holland, out of the spiritists with their diabolic (Lev. 20:6, 27) whoring with spirits (1 Tim. 4:1) in England, America and the whole of Europe etc., etc. – all came out of the unholy fire of our anti-Christian time, the fire from the bottomless pit, which also would cause the earth to be shaken.

But did this *earthquake* after 1830 come as the storm after the silence? *Earthquake* (see Haggai 2:7, Isaiah 13:13, Heb. 12:26), we know as the *changes in the condition of Europe* (page 248, Vol. 1), as *revolutions and wars amongst the nations,* and see, just as God the Lord spoke before the first coming of the Son of men: *"I will shake not only the earth but also the heavens,"* now also began before His second coming *earthquakes and revolutions amongst the nations, wars and rumours of war*, beginning in the year 1830;

> 1830. The second French Revolution, the Belgian separation from Holland, the shocks in Germany, and the upheavals in Poland.

> 1831.The revolution in Palermo, the war between Russian and Poland, and between Russia and the Caucasus, the wars of the French in Algiers.

> 1832.The revolution in Paris, the revolutionary movement in Germany, the civil war in Portugal.

> 1833.Civil war in Spain, shocks in Germany.

> 1834.Upheavals and murder in Ireland in its rebellion against England. Unrest and insurrection in France. War between Sardinia and Barbary.

> 1835.Unrest in France. Civil war in Greece and Spain.

> 1836.Unrest in Portugal. Military rising in Spain. War between Turkey and Kurdistan. Persecution of the Separatists in Holland.

> 1837.Unrest in Hanover. French war in Algiers, continuous wars in Spain and between Russia and the Caucasus (Shamyl), and not to include further little skirmishes, we just remind ourselves of the war in Turkey 1839;

> 1840. War between England and China;

> 1842.War with Afghanistan.

> 1843.The revolution in Greece.

> 1844.Financial crisis in Holland. War between France and Morocco.

1845.The great potato infestation.

1846.Revolution in Switzerland.

1847.Civil war in Switzerland.

1848.The terrible year, started with the revolution and the declaration of the Republic of France; a revolution, which caused all the thrones in Europe to be shaken, and democratic revolutions, civil war resulting in terrible upheavals in England, Italy, Austria and almost the whole of Germany; but also brought with it total freedom of religion and religious expression. Also the English war in Punjab.

1849.War between Austria and Hungary, between Sardinia and Austria.

1850.Revolutions in Germany.

1852.Revolutions in France and Portugal. The second French Empire with its: "l'Empire c'est la paix".

1853.Turkish – Russian war (Crimean war).

1854.England, France and Austria.

1855.Sardinia, joined the Turks.

1857.The terrible war of England in British-India.

1859.The war between Austria and Sardinia with France, and the resulting forming of the Kingdom of Italy.

1860.War of the particular and adventurer Garibaldi against Frans II, King of Naples; the murders in Syria; the English French war in China.

1862.The Greek revolution and the French-Mexican War;

1864.The Sleewyk-Holstein; and

1866.The Austrian – North Germany war.

1870.The declaration of the infallibility of the Pope, with its consequences, and the French-German war in 1870-1871, a war of such colossal proportions and unheard-of results that one fails to find its equal in Christian History.

1871.The civil war and communes in France, with its plundering and closing of churches, its civil and priests murders, arson and destruction in Paris; a condition, which Revelation in her imagery would describe as: "*Blood came out even unto the horses bridles.*" (Rev. 14:20)

1877.The Russian-Turkish War.

What revolutions, what changes, what thrones fell and others were established (Belgium Italy, the German Empire), what a different form of Europe and how many strong men were killed and maimed in three short decades? But also, what revolutions in spiritual spheres, in the kingdom (heaven) of the church, and in the faith of the congregation; what splitting, divisions, dissolutions and decay of church and religions in the same period. And with this all, the social question, the upheavals of the social democrats, anarchists and nihilists, the famines in India, Ireland, Syria and Russia, the shocks in the financial world (state bankruptcies, Panama and Bank scandals), the general malaise in all spheres; since 1830 repeatedly swarming over the whole world, and in spite of the general vaccination, for all that is, 1870 and 1871 the best angel of smallpox, raging over Europe, from North to South, from West to East while lately influenza infects many.

What Revelation understands with earthquakes is therefore something totally different than what John Cumming tells us about it in his "Seventh Vial", with a useless and detailed summary of factual earthquakes. We must warn against this work. It is based on the false premises of human wisdom and will be proved wrong in the end.

Believer! You, who instinctively assume and feel according to half-understood prophesies about the signs of the times, that the end of this dispensation is near, freely let the worldlings ridicule your superstition and apostasy; you have the word of God and this Revelation of Jesus on your side. Because all this is only the beginning of the tribulations. For, if all these revolutions, upheavals and wars, were only the fulfilment of that which Revelation expressed with that one-word *earthquake*, what can we then not expect from that which Revelation so amply describes in the sixth trumpet, (Rev 11:15-19), about the great earthquake in the seventh vial, (Rev 16:18-21), "*such as was not since men were upon the earth, so mighty an earthquake, and so great.*" A description, which totally corresponds with that which Daniel in (Dan 12:1) and Jesus himself (Matt. 24:21) predicted about it, as a time of great tribulation, such as was not since the beginning of the world to this time, no, nor even shall be, and *which will shortly come to the living generation on earth.* Then not only the *earth* will be shaken, but also the *heavens* (God's Kingdom, the Christian church) *which will be rolled up as a scroll.*

With these words, we could again take up the sixth seal where it is still unfulfilled in the above-mentioned troubled days. We would however then anticipate the time of its fulfilment. Consequently, we would rather here ask the Christian reader this question: "Is the silence, which John saw in heaven, of approximately one-half hour, clearly fulfilled in the rest of 1815 to 1830? Is also the breaking of this silence and rest in 1830, by the voices, thunderings, lightning and earthquake, remarkably fulfilled, through the movements in religious circles, social and statesmanship, which occurred since 1830? The reader may well earnestly answer this question, to become certain, that the pinning down of the year 1830 is the point of departure, for what is to follow in the last and seventh period of Revelation.

The reader may here make the observation that we really are jumbling Revelation, grasping here, then there, describing a part, applying it, while it actually does not clearly appear to him from Revelation itself, that it must be understood and be fulfilled in this way.

If the reader has not yet observed this up to now, it would shortly appear so to him by further reading. We, therefore, want to answer in anticipation and refer him to what was already said on (Vol. 1). When a novel writer describes the adventures of four families or persons in different houses or places, he would, while he is busy relating to one happening in one family, he would have anticipated the other three considerably, and mostly, at the end of that chapter, have to go back in time, to describe one by one the happenings of the others, and eventually come to an end at one point of time. Similarly, our explanation, because the order in which the Lord *showed* John the *happenings*, totally differs from that in which they occur. While the historical succession of happenings in the church nevertheless are the most appropriate, to understand Revelation and the particular order of their fulfilment in history, we, in contrast with other writers, followed the above way, giving rise to the above-mentioned question from the reader. With our order of successions, we are *completely safeguarded* against arbitrariness in the conception and apostasy of the fulfilment. Whenever we resolved the prophetic images from God's word, we up to now never had to seek their fulfilment in history, but they, of their own volition, became apparent to us, and while they so accurately, as up to now, corresponded with the predictions, any deviation from our side in the understanding and order of succession would immediately reveal itself in the deviation in fulfilment. It needed to be said, as we now here, just as with the candlesticks, again pick up the sixth seal in its unfulfilled part. At first glance, for all that, in its content (Rev. 6:14-17), lets us see that we herewith are transported to the end of this dispensation at the return of the Lord. This event is furthermore amply mentioned twice more in the seventh trumpet (Rev. 14) and in the seventh vial (Rev. 16:17-21, Rev. 17, 18 and 19). In order not to write the same three times, we will, as we come to those days, deal with the end of the sixth seal, in the seventh period, with the simultaneous happenings in the seventh trumpet and vial, because they are one and the same event, seen from different points of view. Before we come to this time however many other events occur on the earth, as well as the particulars of the seventh period, as they still belong to the sixth seal and the sixth trumpet, and flow through in this seventh time through their fulfilment.

For the sake of completeness and because we already presently *spiritually see, the beginning of its fulfilment* we want to go through the further part of the seventh seal explicitly to show, how in the last days of the earthly heaven, *the Christian Church* (Protestant, Roman and Greek), although not fully according to God's will, yet just as Babel for Israel still being the only refuge of the believers, *has strayed*, and is *rolled up as scroll*, which is read, the scroll of the church (Rev. 5:1,7) of which all seven seals are open, and the whole content is read and fulfilled. That the Roman and Protestant church in our days already has begun to roll up, through the declaration of infallibility of the Pope and the resulting consequences in the first, and through the similar dividing modern direction and denial of the most important basic truths of Christendom in the latter, is all clear, to everyone, who is not an irreconcilable optimist. The Christian Baptism is the incorporation into God's Kingdom, the church. Where the Baptism of Christ (another does not exist) is not obligatory to the clergy anymore, as presently in the Reformed church, one begins to roll up the heaven of the church, the Kingdom of God on earth, to set it aside as redundant. Does not every thinking believer already say: What is to become of the church, what will come out of all this? And all these things are only the beginning of the tribulations, and it is only the introduction to these last terrible times, when already the mountains or state churches (Rev. 17:9), are removed out of their places, that the mountain of the House of the Lord (Isaiah 2:2) may be established in the top of the mountains. Similarly, the Islands or missionary congregations, where the Christians could still find refuge, as on the solid ground in the up-roaring sea of nations, they also are moved and slung around by the storms of all sorts of winds of teachings, and the raging waves of the sea (Eph. 4:14, Jude 13). Also, the *rocks and mountains* (1

Cor. 10:4, Matt. 16:18) or the *Christian denominations* and *State churches* split up, and fell in ruins, and the kings of the earth, the nobles and rich (the Pope, Roman and Protestant bishops) the overseer over thousand, (the preachers) and the servants or faithful members of the church, tried to take refuge in the caves, caverns and grottoes, the sad remains of former greatness. Do we not clearly see the splitting and divisions of church denominations and state churches or rocks and mountains since 1830 resulting in all sorts of churches and denominations to almost infinite numbers and often without any reasonable cause? Although this presently occurs especially in the Protestant churches, in the Roman churches we have external unity also inner conflict. This is all a sifting, yet, before the sifting takes place, the threshing of the wheat has to occur (Isaiah 41:15, Matt. 3:12). Sand and dust will fall through the sieve, and the chaff will be blown away, but good wheat will lie on the winnow.

What a sadness, what pain does this cause to the believing Christian, who is still attached to his earthly church denomination, because in her he has found his faith, found Christ in her/his heart, and consequently honours her in particular as the church of Christ. *Your mountains, you cracking rocks! Fall on us; hide us, from the wrath of the Lamb!* That I may perish with my beloved church and be buried under her ruins, rather than see God's judgement over her, and the wrath of the Lord of the church, who once promised, that the gates of hell will not prevail against His congregation, those who are built upon their faith in Him. Is this not the complaint of the hearts of thousands of pious believers in the Roman and Protestant churches?

That the great day of wrath is near, and the judgement of the Lord over church and state has begun, that is felt and perceived by every believer from the appalling accumulation of terrible events and judgements, which burst loose over Europe, in an unbroken pattern since 1830. in the midst of which we live. If the spiritual meaning of this imagery already indicates such a terrible time, what will it not be, when this will also be fulfilled in its natural meaning, and the cry will resound: The great day of wrath has come and who can exist?

Who can exist? Where can we flee to?

Who can, with such a future, cry out with a whole heart!! "Come, Lord Jesus, come!"

And yet He himself promised, that a rescue would take place, just as in the days of Noah, for the remnant of His people, an ark for the protection of those, who believe His word and grasp His saving hand; for those, who do not despise (scorn) the words of the prophecies of this book, as the contemporaries of Noah did with his prophecy, and, just as they realized too late that their own wisdom, which is foolishness by God, was unbelief, when the Lord had shut the door after Noah (Gen. 7:16, Matt. 24:38, Matt. 25:10).

He promised this to those of the congregation of Philadelphia, *who kept His word* (Rev. 3:10), *"I will keep thee from the hour of temptation."* And would He, who called himself the Amen at the beginning of the seventh period, the faithful and true witness, would He not keep His word and His promise? Would He not already put in place the rescue, the perception thereof and the means thereto, and made them known, that His servants having accepted His saving hand, and being assured of their protection, cry out the heartfelt *"Yes! Come, Lord Jesus!"*?

To this question, Revelation also has an answer. The sixth chapter ends with the description of the great day of the Lord and with the question: *"Who shall be able to stand?"* The seventh chapter immediately gives the answer.

The seventh seal only starts with chapter eight. The preceding seventh chapter therefore still belong to the sixth seal, and describe how the servants of the Lord from the Philadelphia congregation, land in the kingdom of glory through the seventh period. The whole seventh chapter has as a subject and could lead to the title: *The saving hand of the Lord over His church, from the beginning of the Reformation (1517).*

The first verse immediately begins the description of how the servants of the Lord, at the start of the Reformation, were protected against persecution by the Roman church and state powers. With verse 2, another one starts another protection, against the anti-Christian persecution of the last days. It is clear, that the four angels named in (verse 1), are not the same as those of (verse 2), but that these last are *angels of wrath*, to whom it is given to destroy, while those in (verse 1) are *protecting angels*, who have to keep back the four destructive winds. The fulfilment of (verse 1) has clearly enough been proven on (Vol. 1).

This is where the persecutions of Protestants by the Roman church began, which, slowly diminishing, ended only at the beginning of this century, with the end of the period of Reformation. Whether the sealing described in (verses 2 to 8), occurred during the period of Reformation, as a protection against the persecution of the Roman church, or, only occurred after that period ended, as a protection against the anti-Christian persecution of the last days, must become apparent, when we have solved this sealing from God's word, and found its fulfilment in history. All the wonderful explanations, given concerning this sealing, we can positively discard.

This simple natural fulfilment of this prophesy, as it up to now appears to us, leaves us to suspect, that under the sealing, something is to be understood, that it is not a strange occurrence in God's kingdom.

THE SEALING

And there shall be signs in the sun, and in the
moon, and in the stars (page 155) for the
powers of heaven shall be shaken.
Luke 21:25, 26

Rev 7:2-8

Verse 2. **"And I saw another angel ascending from the East, having the seal of the living God."** This angel is again a clergy, but different from the four angels of the Reformation (Vol.1). Its commission is a preserving, protective one. If this had occurred during the three preceding centuries of the presently past period of the Reformation, these acts should then immediately be known to us, as they would already be fulfilled and completed. We do, however, find nothing in the history of the church, where it is made understandable to us, even less the fulfilment thereof, and yet, after all the experienced clear fulfilment of Revelation, we could certainly expect an explanation. Moreover, the angels of the Reformation stood, (verse 1), *at the four corners of the earth*; while this clergy **comes from the east**. We thus have to consider a clergy which ascends after the sixth period (after 1815) and therefore in the seventh period, it is also clear, that its function continues throughout the seventh period and only ends in verse 9 with the Kingdom of glory.

This angel *is not one person*, for he names himself in (verse 3), **we** and speaks in the plural of his fellow angels. It is thus one spiritual body, but consisting of more persons, who are sent in the service of the Lord, to fulfil a commission.

They come from the East. *Who is he, who comes from where the sun rises, that he may preach the name of the Lord?* (Isaiah 41:25). It is Jesus Christ. **Jesus** is thus **the other angel**, who, as the dayspring rising from on high (Luke 1:78), appears again in His servants on earth to those who sit in darkness and the shadow of death, to guide their feet on the way of peace (verse 79). Just as the wise from the east knew of the coming on earth of Jesus, the King of the Jews and, probably from (Mica 5:1 and Dan 9:25), knew the exact time and place, where He would be born, so also are these, as we later will see, the wise from the east, *the kings, who would come* (sixth vial Rev 16:12) from the east, who knew that the return of the Lord is near, and would preach this over the whole earth. We have seen in the

335

sixth vial, that the shepherd and teacher ministries would dry out, that the three unclean spirits of denial of Christ (*Deism*) of denial of God (*Atheism*), and man being God (*Pantheism*) would infiltrate the Christian church, and amongst the people, in order to *prepare the way for the kings,* who later, in the seventh period, would *come from the east.* And they have already arrived, for they are the **thunderings** and the **lightning**, which John saw emerging in the seventh seal, after the half hour of silence, as a result of the pouring out of the fire of the Holy Spirit on earth by Jesus, the angel of the covenant.

They are *the thunderings of the glorification of the Lord's name, and the lightnings or angels of the Lord,* who had to announce His imminent return, and which we have seen taking action in 1830-1836, especially in the Catholic Apostolic church in England. But not only through her, but also in different Protestant denominations the conviction began to assert itself and was revealed in writing and preaching, that the return of Christ is near. Do these together form *the angel,* who rose from the east? Or is there amongst them one, who is that spiritual body, *the other angel* of Christ in the seventh period? The revelation gives us the signs, whereby we will recognise Him, since it is Him *"who has the seal of the living God, to seal therewith* (verses 3 and 4) **on their foreheads the servants of God from all generations of the children of Israel."**

The first question is: "What is to be understood with the seal?" The second: "What is to be understood with all the tribes of children of Israel?" The third: "When does this sealing take place?"

The answer to the first question will become easier when both the other questions are answered because then the terrain *where* and the time *when* this will occur will have been determined.

Therefore first the question: are those sealed from **all** the tribes of Israel, as many think to be sought amongst the **Jews**? No! Certainly not!

> 1. Revelation is given not to the Jews, also not to the Heathen, but (Rev 1:1) to the servants of Jesus Christ, the sealed are thus Christians, more so because the sealing angels are a Christian clergy.
> 2. They must be from every (verse 4) tribe of the children of Israel, and, wonderfully! John, who hears the number of the sealed and the names of the tribes from the angel who explains everything to him, (Rev 1:1), this John, who certainly knew the names of the tribes of the children of Israel, he does **not** name **every** tribe, but leaves out the tribe of **Dan** and replace it with

Manasseh. Up and above that, Judah, the fourth son of Jacob, he named first and Ruben, the firstborn second, and except for the four last, the order of the remaining tribes is totally changed.

James writes (James 1:1) his general epistle, to the *twelve* tribes, who are scattered around. There were however only two tribes who returned from captivity in Babylon, Judah and Benjamin and a portion of the tribe of Levi. The rest are still scattered amongst the nations. James did not write to the Jews but to the Christians. The Jews have rejected the Gospel, and so it came to the heathen, and since the coming of Christ, the word stands. Circumcision is nothing and uncircumcision is nothing with God (1 Cor. 7:19, Gal 5:6, Gal. 6:15), but a new creature in Christ Jesus. For not all are Israel which are of Israel (Rom 9:6); They which are the children of the flesh, these are not the children of God: but the children of the promise (Rom 9:8).

James, therefore, meant with the twelve tribes, "that those, who are of the faith, are the children of Abraham (Gal 3:7), because "that the blessing of Abraham might come to the gentiles through Jesus Christ." (Gal 3:14) "And if ye be Christ's then are ye Abraham's seed, and heirs according to the promise." (Gal 3:29) James thus meant the New Testament Israel of God (Gal 6:16), and names *all the Christians, the twelve tribes scattered abroad*, because they, just as formerly the twelve tribes under Babel, were also scattered and persecuted under the gentiles. Revelation will later on give us more light about these twelve tribes of Christians.

The sealed are therefore Christians. Israel means *fighters for the Lord*, and the twelve tribes of the New Testament Israel form the whole striving church of our Lord Jesus Christ on earth, or the whole New Testament Congregation. The sealed from these tribes of the church of Christ are those, which we later will find again as the believers saved from the great tribulation or the bride of Christ, in the Kingdom of Glory (Rev 14:4) "as the redeemed from among men, the first fruits unto God and to the Lamb".

But then there must be a hidden meaning in the naming of the tribes, in the changed order, in the omission of Dan and the addition of Manasseh, since so far we never found anything meaningless in Revelation. Indeed it is so, and we find this meaning in the names of the tribes, (Gen.49:32-35) and in the parting words of Jacob to each of his sons. The earthly promises and predictions for their offspring, are also spiritually fulfilled in the twelve tribes or sorts of sealed Christians, whose lot, character, level of faith and persuasion are typically revealed in their names. To wholly research, this

337

would lead to extensive work, but later we will again refer to this. We restrict ourselves to answering the question: Why is not Ruben but Judah named first? Jacob said it in his blessing, (Gen.49:3,4) "Ruben, thou art my firstborn, thou shalt not excel, and in (verse 8), "Judah, thou art He." Judah, as we already said in the second and sixth candlestick, means: "He who praises God." And the real Judah, who in the sealing praises the Lord the most, will be the firstlings amongst the sealed. Also, Jesus, who taught us to know and to praise His Father, was from the Old Testament tribe of Judah.

But why is Dan not included, and Manasseh added? Dan means: "Judge", and "Manasseh" means forgotten. The New Testament tribe Dan cannot, therefore, belong to the sealed because this tribe consists of all the pious, and the blind Pharisees, who think they exclusively possess the Kingdom of God, and who will disdain the sealing, the work of God in the last days, while in their piety they imagine not to need it, and who as judges will condemn it, because God the Lord does not call them as the pious, great and honored men as sealers, but without taking into account their piety, righteousness and popularity in the congregation, follows his own Godly way. They will, as the rulers in Jesus' days on earth, say: If Christ had come out of us, we would have accepted Him, but since He came from without, He cannot be the true Christ, away with Him!

Replacing these judging and condemning great, wise Christians, are the small and forgotten, the sinners in their own eyes, who recognize that grace is extended to them and thankfully accept what the Lord offers them in these last days. The placing of the tribe of Manasseh instead of Dan is totally included in the prophetic judgement of Christ over the Pharisean high priests of the people: "Verily I say unto you, that the Publicans and the Harlots go into the Kingdom of God before you". (Matt21:31)

Dan can also not belong to the sealed, because that tribe will also fulfil the prediction of Jacob concerning him:" Dan shall be a serpent by the way, an adder in the path, that biteth the horse's heels so that his rider shall fall backwards." (Gen.49:17) When the Lord will send His promised angels, to seal, to prepare in their hearts the way for Him (Mark1:2,3) and to even the path, so that He may come, then the mockers and unbelievers will not be those who stand by the way, but the honoured and pious, the pillars of the congregation, the orthodox, the church believers, the serpents on the path and the nest of adders (Matt 23:13, 28, 33, 34), here also as the seed of the serpent (Gen.3:15), bite the horse (the congregation of the sealed) in the heels, so that this rider (the clergy or sealers)[46] falls and does not reach his goal. As if Jacob experiences a dark premonition, of the later sad spiritual meaning and fulfilment of this prediction, he bursts out in a soul-wrenching cry "I have waited for thy salvation o Lord!" A cry which did not occur anywhere else in his words, seemingly testifying, that he himself had an undefined premonition, that a higher meaning was attached to his words for the inheritance in the glory, for which he hoped, from which the tribe Dan would be excluded.

The New Testament tribe Dan must therefore consist of the important leaders of the congregation of Laodicea, and all in her, who consider themselves rich and increased in goods, and yet are poor and miserable (Rev.3:17), who consider themselves seeing and yet are blind, -at least that part of her must form the tribe Dan, who will not accept Christ's counsel to buy the gold of truth, the white raiment for the communion of the Lamb and the eye salve of the Holy Spirit from the sealing Angels sent in the last days.

We believe that we have so far sufficiently proved that the sealed consists of Christians, of believers from all tribes, denominations and creeds of the New Testament people of God, the repentant whores and publicans of the tribe Manasseh, as the ever faithful confessor of God from the tribe Judah, excluding only the pious of the tribe Dan. Now that the terrain of or research of where the sealing will take place has been established, we can proceed to the research of the time, when this sealing will take place. Revelation indicates it to us, with the cry of the Angel who rose from the east with a loud voice to the four Angels, to whom it was given to hurt the earth and the sea." Saying (Verse3), *"hurt not the earth, neither the sea nor the trees, till we have sealed the servants of our God in their foreheads."*

The beginning of God's judgment in this seventh period (the hurting) is not only here, but also further on, the predicted overthrow of existing civic

---

[46] That is farfetched! the reader may exclaim, again take up the horse and the rider, of which Jacob spoke 2000 years before Revelation was given, as having the same imagery and the same meaning, as the horses and riders of the first four seals. Considering that many of these predictions of Jacob extent up the last days, e.g..: That of John up to (Rev.5:5) (The Kingdom of Glory), that of Benjamin to Saul, and that it is one and the same God, the Holy Spirit, the unchangeable, for whom no time exists, who spoke prophetically through Jacob and John, then there must lie deep meaning in these predictions, and once again we find proof of the consequential meaning of the imagery of the language of the Holy Spirit, as we already mentioned in our prologue on (page 8 Vol.1). Besides, the cry of Jacob which follows it, is very strange and unexplainable as it appears from the following words, that his strength had not left him, from which many want to explain this cry.

and religious conditions (the earth); the beginning of revolutions and upheavals of the nations (the sea) and of the fall of kings and clergy (trees). The beginning of the great earthquake of the seventh vial (Rev.16:18-24) is, therefore, the point in time, within which the sealing of the 144000 must be completed. The present happenings in state, church and society clearly indicate that the great earthquakes are approaching and perhaps already lie before us in the near future.

On the other hand, this sealing as an important event in the Kingdom of God, could not have begun earlier than after the completion of the half-hour of silence, which John saw in Heaven, thus after 1830 to 1836. From that time on up to our days, that sealing must have started and must now be in full swing.

The question is, however: Have the four Angels already begun to hurt? Who are these Angels? In the order in which John saw and described the images, nothing but the four Angels is mentioned in the immediately preceding (verse 1), of the four Angels, which we learned to know as the four Reformers and the protective Protestant princes. Their task was, however, to withhold the destruction of the four winds, the Roman church and civic powers at the onset of the Reformation. The four angels of (verse 2) in contrast are four destructive angels. They can therefore not be the same as those in (verse 1). Over and above the beginning of (verse 2) describes another event in (Rev 1). The four angels of (Rev 2) must therefore be four Christian states and church powers in the seventh period, who represent four church denominations. They are thus the Calvinistic, the Lutheran, the Roman and the Greek nations of Europe with their state churches, and with the princes of their confession, who themselves not only speak out the judgement over their state and their church denomination but even execute them.

This should not be strange to the reader. He will remind himself, that the angels or powers in the church or state of each period themselves poured out the vials of God. Nowhere did we find for the vials something else, than that God in His wrath did not subject men to strange and arbitrary punishment, but that He allowed the consequences of their own sinful actions to overtake them and thereby allowed them to experience the effect of their own bad deeds and their apostasy. Even so, where the church formerly supported the kings, and the kings the church, in the seventh period, Liberalism, in religion must lead to Republicanism, and liberalism in the state to anti-Christian views, resulting therefrom, first a mutual persecution of the believers in their midst, thereafter division and schism, and eventually enmity with each other (Rev.17:17) In this way, the four angels of the presently formed state and church will themselves destroy the church, as we will see in the seventh vial, and although the four mentioned great church denominations still stand according to the Lord's command (Rev.7:3), we already see, that God released them, and gave them over to their own evil lusts, which will end in destruction.

When, therefore, the powers in state and in the four Christian denominations in this Laodicean time do not recognize Christ in His total being, His power and His commission, they have become anti-Christian, (1 John 4:2, 3), and instead of protecting, these same angels destructively influence the Christian order (earth) and the Christian nations (sea.). Are not Pope Pious 1X, with his Jesuits, with their lustfully enforced decree of the infallibility of the Pope, the greatest enemies of the church, which they had to defend and confirm. Do we not already see in the great upheavals and schisms between the Pope and the Roman state powers, among the Roman nations and in the whole Roman church, who allow this human edification, that this dishonouring abomination will lead to the fall and dissolving of papal and spiritual power, just as immediately after the promulgation of his infallibility his worldly power fell.

And where so many teachers of the Protestant churches deny the fundamental truths of the Christian religion and, instead of preaching the power of God to salvation (Rom.1:16) preach a cold heathen moral teaching, under the watchword of following Jesus, did they not become angels of destruction to the Christians and the Christian nations? Do they not bring total unbelief in the Protestant churches, next to the superstition in the Roman and Greek churches?

And when, for example, the church rulers, the Synod of the Nederlandsche Hervormde church, not only allow all modern teachers freely to preach their anti-Christian views, and in some cases abolish the obligation, to use the instituted tenets of Christ, are they there led by anti-Christian principles or not? Do they not work destruction on the Christian earth and the Christian nations? And where the Protestant civic powers ban Christian teaching in schools, and under the guise of natural science, introduce Deism, Atheism and Pantheism freely to the young hearts, have they not become destroying angels instead of protecting angels of the Church of Jesus Christ? We thus see that of the four angels some already begin to destroy. But then the sealing must also come to its end, and we have to search for it in the last year of 1830 up to today.

This is therefore the time of the sealing; the place was the Christian church with her different denomination; What is the seal and the sealing?

341

One thing we know for sure from the fifth trumpet (Vol.1) is that the belief in Jesus is not the seal of God. We therefore have to seek something else.

The word sealing is not unknown in the New Testament writings. We find it, firstly in (John 3:33), where John the Baptist says, "He that hath received Jesus' testimony, hath set to His seal that God is true." Similarly, Jesus Himself said (John 6:27) *"That God the Father had sealed Him."* Paul gives light on this when he wrote to the Ephesians (Eph.1:13,14)". In whom (Christ) after ye believed, ye were sealed with that Holy Spirit of promise, which is the earnest of our inheritance," (Eph.4:30)". And grieve not the Holy Spirit of God, whereby ye are sealed unto the day of redemption." According to these words, the seal of God is also the Holy Spirit, which the believers receive from the Father, as a seal and mark that they belong to Him. Receiving the Holy Spirit is therefore the sealing. It now becomes clear, that the sealing of Jesus Christ by God the Father (John 6:27) means, that Jesus, the Son of man, received the Holy Spirit, in the form of a dove descending over Him and lighting upon Him, after His baptism by John the Baptist, as the seal of God the Father, (Matt.3;16,17. Mark1: 9-11. Luke 3:21,22. John 1:32), and testified after His baptism of what God the Father had revealed". The same is He which baptized with the Holy Spirit,"(John 1:33) except the baptism with water, as the bath of rebirth as children of God, the Father would through Christ also perform a baptism with Fire or of the Holy Spirit on His servants, as a seal or sealing, that they belong to Him; just as Paul wrote to the Corinthians (2 Cor. 1:21,22) "Now He which stabilized us with you in Christ, and hath anointed us, is God. Who hath also sealed us, and given the earnest of the Spirit in our hearts." Both these baptisms, water and fire, we also found in (Heb.6:2), where the writer expressively says, that he does not want to speak of principles of the doctrine, and laying on of hands, and of the resurrection of the dead, and of eternal judgement. Both baptisms and laying of hands (Acts 8:17,18. Acts 9:12, 17.and Acts 19:6), were therefore principal and important teachings of the church of Christ. It is also clear, that Paul himself (Acts 9:17) also received the Holy Spirit through the laying on of hands by Ananias, and (afterwards) was baptized (verse 8) we here see that two totally different actions took place; the one, the water baptism, the other the sealing or the receiving of the Holy Spirit as a pledge of our eternal inheritance (Eph.1:13,14). One or the other reader may perhaps say: But this we received at our confirmation as members in our church.

Allow us to investigate how the sealing took place at the beginning of the New Testament, and which were the signs, whereby the indwelling of the

Holy Spirit, as the scripture names it (Rom.8:9.11. 1Cor.3:16. James 4:5 2 Tim.1:14), became apparent. In Acts, we find this action clearly described in two places.

Firstly in (Acts 8:5-12), where many Samaritans were baptized by the evangelist Philip, (not an apostle, see verse 1) After they were baptized in the name of the Lord Jesus Christ (verse 16), wherewith they naturally as adults had confessed their faith in Jesus, and were adopted as members (See Acts 19:1, 2), only afterwards, the apostles in Jerusalem (verse 14) sent Peter and John to them, who (verse 15), prayed for them that they might receive the Holy Spirit, because (verse 16) He had fallen upon none of them, but they were only baptized, and (verse 17), then laid they (the apostles Peter and John) their hands on them and they received the Holy Spirit, as a gift of God (verse 20). It is here apparent that not Phillip the evangelist, but only apostles had the authority to lay their hands on the baptized believers, to thereby impart the Holy Spirit to them as a gift from God.

The second event we find in (Acts 19) is the moment Paul, in (verse 1:1-4), found some disciples in Ephesus, about twelve, (verse 7), who not only had not received the Holy Spirit, but did not even know that there was a Holy Spirit. Paul even found out that they were baptized with the baptism of John the Baptist and first baptized them in the name of the Lord Jesus (verse 5) and afterwards, just as in (Acts 8:17), when Paul laid his hands on them, the Holy Spirit came upon them and they spoke in tongues and prophesied.

In the first case, nothing is mentioned about speaking in tongues or prophecies, although something similar must have taken place, because in (Acts 8:18,19) Simon the sorcerer saw, that through the laying on of hands of the apostles, the Holy Spirit was given. Simon must have seen some unmentioned visible signs, otherwise, such a stingy sorcerer would not have offered the apostles money (verse 18) to also possess this power (verse 19). In any case, we see from (Acts19;6) that speaking in tongues and prophecies were gifts of the Holy Spirit, which here were immediately revealed as a result of receiving the Holy Spirit, just as with the apostles themselves in (Acts 2:4), when they received the Holy Spirit, and just as they were present in the congregation during the Apostolic era. The Holy Spirit was always active on earth to work repentance and faith in the hearts of the people, for all, who believed and were baptized, experienced His activity. This was however not the receiving of the Holy Spirit with His gifts, which only occurred at the laying on of apostles' hands. But when we now compare the condition of the Christian congregation of the last centuries, with those of the earliest centuries, we immediately miss the characteristic of receiving the Holy Spirit with His gifts, and now come to the conclusion of the following dilemma, a twofold result:

Either we do not stand in the original tenets of Jesus anymore. But then we miss the baptism with Fire of the Holy Spirit, which for all that was not superfluous or, we do not need this baptism with the Holy Spirit in our time anymore. But then we have the right, to also demand the scriptural proof from those who profess this, to this we would invite them in vain; the contrary would be apparent.

Therefore… Revelation will later give its conclusion.

One accomplished proof, that the sealing or the baptism with the Holy Spirit existed in the church in the first centuries we find, that in her three most important immediate off-springs, the form thereof has been conserved, although without its former power.

In the Roman church, we find the confirmation as *a ratification and supplement to the baptism,* and the formula of that confirmation reads as follows:" I confirm hereby in the name of the Father, the Son and the Holy Spirit, *that you may be filled with this same Holy Spirit* and have eternal life".

In the Greek church as inseparable from baptism, after the baptism with water, the salving with Holy Oil. They name this salving:" *The seal of the gifts of the Holy Spirit".* These words also appear in the formula spoken by the priest during this act.

Also, the Albigense (approximately in the 10th century) were *baptized with the Holy Spirit through the laying on of hands.*

The preservation of the same image and the same form in these three divergent direct off-springs of the original church, indicates most clearly, that this act did not only exist in the Apostolic church but also, that formerly it was deemed highly important for the church.

Based on the New Testament and church history, it is certain that in the first church of Christ, besides the water baptism, there was also *another baptism with fire and the Holy Spirit named the sealing.* Just as Jesus dispensed the Holy baptism with water through human hands, so did He also dispense, through the human laying on of hands, the Holy Spirit with His gifts to His believers, and this is presently totally missing in the Christian church today. Would the reader receive this conclusion of our research with suspicion or unbelief, we remind him, of what the Lord Himself said to the congregation in the seventh candlestick (Rev.3:17, Page 320.) in our time.

This baptism with fire or sealing must have been reinstituted in the Christian church from 1830 up to our days. The place where it must take place is already known as the presently existing church of Jesus Christ (see page 338), the time been known to us since 1830 and is in full swing in our time. The meaning of sealing itself is also known to us, and yet we search in vain for it in the writings of our so-accurate writer Van Loon in this time.

We must therefore ask the question in another way; Who are the sealing Angels, that is: through which persons is the sealing done? When reading (Acts 8:1-17) again, we see that Philip the evangelist could not seal, but exclusively (verses 14-17) the apostles Peter and John were sent to Samaria. Similarly, we see in (Acts 19) that apostle Paul dispensed the sealing in Ephesus and that he reminds Timothy (2 Tim.1:6) *to stir up the gift of the Holy Spirit, which is in thee by the putting on of my hands.* Similarly, Paul reminds the Corinthians (1 Cor.9:1,2) and (2 Cor.12:11-13) of the gifts of the Holy Spirit, whereby the Corinthian congregation was the seal of Paul's apostleship, And here we do not have to think of receiving the gifts of the Holy Spirit through preaching, but through the laying on of hands of Paul. The sealing was therefore an Apostolic commission, unless it pleased the Lord in special cases through immediate commission to call another person for this single case, such as Ananias in Damascus who was called to seal Saul. The reason why the Lord changed His own order here, must be, that Saul, for the sake of his later destination and calling to the Apostle ministry (Acts 13:2, Acts 14:14), would not receive anything from the first apostles, in order not to be considered less than them (Acts 9:15, Gal.1:1). Yet even here the laying on of hands was necessary

In comparison the Lord immediately gave the Holy Spirit to Cornelius and his own, without the laying on of hands (Acts 10:14), only to show, that the Gospel had come to the Gentiles (Acts 11:17,18). Peter, raised as a Jew, had difficulty in laying hands on a gentile, and, although he was prepared by God in the triple vision in his dream on the roof, he still had to be convinced that the gentiles could also be included in the salvation plan. The result of this immediate sealing by the Lord Himself is revealed in (Acts 10:46) in speaking of tongues, and when Peter in (Acts10:48) commands, that they must be baptized with water (verse 47), it is clear, that this water baptism belongs to the evangelist ministry, while the baptism with fire and the Holy Spirit or the sealing was the exclusive power of the Apostle ministry. Paul therefore also says, that in the congregation in which he established himself in Corinth, he baptized no one but Crispus, Gaius and the household of Stephens (1 Cor.1:14,16), but he glories therein (2 Cor.12:11) that in nothing he was less than the chief apostle, and in (2

Cor.12:12) that the sign of an apostle, the spending of the sealing with the Holy Spirit by laying on of hands, was apparent in her, because, he asks in (verse 13): "For what is it whereby ye were inferior to other churches?", and that these gifts were abundant in her we learn from (1 Cor.12 and 14). But if the sealing is the exclusive power of the Apostle ministry, then necessarily apostles must be active in the seventh period, called and commissioned by the Lord Himself. It will presently become clear to us why in the fifth trumpet the Waldense are described as those who had not the seal of God on their foreheads (Vol.1). They had no apostles, nor the gifts of the Holy Spirit anymore.

The Sealing must be done (verse 3) to the foreheads We have already seen, that the external handling except for prayer, consisted of laying one of the hands of an apostle on the forehead of those to be sealed, whereby they become a Holy Temple of God, wherein His Spirit lives (1 Cor. 3:16, 17) a temple of the Holy Spirit, which was in them, which they received from God (1 Cor 6:19, 2 Cor.6 16) an habitation of God (Eph.2:22).

The number 144,000 of the sealed in this place is of little importance to us; we will therefore rather handle this when in (Rev. 14:1) under the seventh trumpet we again come to the sealed.

If we now take our findings together we come to the following translation of what is predicted in (Rev.7:2-8) which as an overflow of the Reformation into the seventh period, would happen after the half-hour silence, thus in 1830, a translation which at first might seem strange.

TRANSLATION OF REVELATION 7:2-8

Verse 2. "And I saw Christ the Lord appear on earth again in other servants, sent by Him as apostles with the seal of the Holy Spirit, and He commanded the clergy of the apostate Christian churches, who live in decaying condition, and to the Christian princes".

Verse 3 "Saying; remain standing a while longer and do not further destroy your faith nor that of your members; do not complete the decay, which, through your own actions and your unbelief will come over your denominations, until, through My apostles, which I will send again in the last days, the servants of God will have been sealed with the Baptism of Fire of the Holy Spirit, and the renewed outpouring of His gifts, and have written the name of My God (sixth candlestick) on them".

Verse 4 -8 "And I heard the number of those who were sealed 144,000 From all Christian countries and denominations, believers from all persuasions; only the pious, who profess to possess the Holly Spirit, and *do not desire His gifts (the tribe of Dan), of them none were sealed, because they did not want to accept the seal of Christ, to be saved from the great tribulation ".*

However strange this translation might sound to the reader, it fits in perfectly with what God's word has taught us as an explanation of this prophecy, and up to now we have never been misled or disappointed in what the word has revealed unto us but have so far seen everything fulfilled in church history. Calmly we want to investigate with the reader, if this sealing has already appeared in the church, or if we still have to wait for it. That we have to find something new and strange in it, a totally individual characteristic occurrence in church life is clear. One thing we must hold fast to, namely: that Christ Himself is the Sealer through His servants, the sent sealing angels, as Paul says; "For I will not dare to speak of any of those things which Christ hath not wrought in me"(Rom 15:18), and just as Christ Himself said to the seventy disciples; "Who heareth you heareth Me, and he that despiseth you despiseth Me; and he that despiseth Me despiseth Him that sent Me" (Luke10:16) But also therefore we must not only be careful in our judging, but even more cautious in the judgement and discarding of that which history still has to teach us about the fulfilment of this prophecy.

Van Loon writes, on page 307, the history of the church in 1830, how Joseph Smith with his "Saint of Latter Days" or Mormons, named according to his new bible, the Book of Mormons. In 1827 we see him perform as a prophet. In 1838 we find him fleeing as a bankrupt salesman, and in 1839 as general at the head of an army of four thousand. This cannot be the sealing angel, because the apostles of the Lord do not use the worldly sword. The new bible of Smith and polygamy in 1843 makes things even more suspicious so that we can clearly discount the Mormons although they were somewhat misjudged.

In 1844, the Seventh Day Adventists, through the writings of the self-appointed prophetess Ellen Harmon White, separated from the Adventists (believers waiting for the return of Christ) and explained the seal based on (Ex 31:16): "Wherefore the children of Israel shall keep the Sabbath, to observe the Sabbath throughout their generation, or a perpetual covenant" (verse17) "It is a sign between Me and the children of Israel". This sign is not a seal and is not applied to the forehead but according to them is "in your forehead, in your mind". Let us just add that this Old Covenant was between God and the children of Israel. Jesus Christ brought a New Covenant between God and the spiritual Israel.

We therefore once again do not find sealing done by laying on of hands by apostles of Jesus.

The non-Christian appearance of communism in 1830, the new Templars in 1831, the socialists in England in 1836, etc…, of which some found their own early death, we find with Van Loon in 1833, with Pusey's in the English church, in the Romanesque persuasion, *"everything external in the church is counted as of the highest value"*. This also, because it was totally restricted to England, was doomed to fail. Instead of being a carrier of the seal of the Living God, Pusey's actions and the appalling progress of his Roman-minded teaching in the English State church, was nothing else than a dissolution and demolition of the once mighty stronghold of Protestantism. Transeat cum caeteris! (He goes through with the others).

In 1834, the splitting in the Nederland's Gereformeerde church took place. This phenomenon, which we and many others, have followed with great interest, spread out and gained ground in our Fatherland, in America, South Africa, Belgium, the separation in Scotland under Chalmers, etc, but did not give Christendom back that which she had in the beginning. From an apostolic sealing activity to a preserving from the hour of temptation which will come over the whole earth (Rev 3:10), nothing can be found. For this reason, this can also not be the one. Which of the Christian church denominations can in thankfulness to the Lord, point to the spiritual gifts in her, as we find them in scripture?

In 1836, we find with Van Loon: the open action of "The Catholic Apostolic church" of the Irvingians with a letter to all clergy and world princes in all countries". Already in 1831, Van Loon reports: "The speaking in tongues in the church of Edward Irving in London takes form". This speaking in tongues was not preaching in strange tongues when we see that in 1832 Edward Irving, because of it, was banned from the Presbyterian church. We thus have to think of a strange occurrence on a spiritual level, just as in (Acts 2:4 Acts 10:46. Acts 19:6), on the gifts of the Holy Spirit, and if it were true, we should not have to wonder about this. We have already seen in the seventh seal how, during the silence from 1815 to 1830, especially in England many continuous prayers were uttered for the restoration of the church in her original condition, for the renewed outpouring of gifts of the Holy Spirit; we have seen since 1830 Christ, the angel of the Covenant, throw the fire of the Holy Spirit on earth, how from this Apostolic church in England followed the cry *Maranatha, Maranatha, the Lord comes!* all over Europe. Our interest increases when we read about this Catholic Apostolic church in Van Loon's writings about the year 1836; "This church is led by twelve apostles, called through prophesying persons, having evangelists and teachers or angels, who each in turn have six elders and six deacons to help them". Except for strange liturgy, dress form and ceremonies their Eschatology (the teaching of the last things) is the most remarkable, as well as the preparation of the church for the imminent return of Christ. Their typical symbolism of the Old Testament is strange and unusual. They have been established especially in Germany as well as in most countries of Europe, various congregations. Rothe, Köppen and especially H.W.J.Thiersh are their main theologians,

In these revelations of Van Loon, we find nothing which disagrees with the characteristics we are looking for as a result of the prophecy. On the contrary, the tone of reverence with which Van Loon speaks of them immediately strikes us, even the speaking in tongues 1831, and not on a tone of suspicion, as with the Mormons revelation in 1830, but almost as of a fact, which is above all doubt. Over and above, it strikes us, that we find three things in her, which we seek. 1. The gift of the Holy Spirit: speaking in tongue, 2. apostles and 3. the naming (or rather calling) of those apostles through prophets, which reminds us to the calling to Apostleship of Paul and Barnabas, also through prophets as we see in (Acts13:12). Lastly in the general actions of this movement in religious circles, the Catholic Apostolic church, with her prophetic testimony of Christ's imminent return, with her written testimonial to all church and world leaders, with her fast expansion over the earth, we find something dignified, something impressive, such as we can expect with the appearance of the sealing angels of our Lord Jesus Christ. Of the sealing, we do not find a word with Van Loon. We have therefore too little information to successfully research, whether the apostles of this church as predicted in our prophecy of the sealing (Rev7:2,3) if the last is correct, we will, in accord with the previous periods (if Revelation is consequent) since we hear work with the seal necessarily find it in the trumpet of the seventh period. We will probably find more facts and lighter there, to continue our research. So much is sure, that in the specified time since 1830, the Catholic Apostolic church is the only one, which showed the characteristics that she **could be** the predicted angel of our Lord Jesus Christ.

Of the other religious movements no further mention need be made. The further separation of the old Lutherans in Prussia from the united Evangelical church in 1841 was only a rectification of earlier matters and remained a local matter. The same can be said of the Free Scottish church in 1843. We there miss the waiting for the imminent return of Christ, and by their renouncing of all spiritual ministries, the apostolic character of the sealing angel.

And herewith the rising of the sealing angel, as a continuation and perfecting of the Reformation of the sixth period into the seventh period, provisionally comes to an end. We later will find it in Revelation again as the golden thread, which runs through her. But for now, the continuation of the sixth seal in the seventh period has ended, because John, in (verse 9), after seeing a great multitude with long white raiment and palm branches in their hands standing before the Throne and the Lamb, it is clear that he was again transported in the day of the Lord when the end happenings of the sixths seal (Rev 6:14-17) are concluded.

SEVENTH TRUMPET
Or
THE CONDITION AND EFFECT OF THE GOSPEL PREACHING

> And He sends His angels with a great
> sound of a Trumpet, and they shall gather
> together, His Elect.
>
> Matt 24:31

Rev 10:3-11 and Rev 11,12, 13, 14.

So far, we have clearly seen in the history of the Kingdom of God on earth the proof that the trumpet describes the strife between the realm of light and darkness, between the servants of Christ and the world (Vol.1). This same battle, in the seventh period of the church is elaborately described in the last portion of the sixth trumpet, as it flows into the seventh period (from Rev11:14),[47]

We will thus firstly take up the sixth trumpet, where we left it at its fulfilment up to 1815, (Rev10:3).

First, we must remember, that with the end of the fourth period, the Greek church was never mentioned again and the Roman church remained the stage of the happenings predicted in Revelation, (Vol.1) whereupon the Reformation took place. Similarly, after the mutual battle between the Protestant and Roman churches during the sixth period, the last is not mentioned any further during the seventh period, but the Protestant church, especially in Europe, became the stage upon which the coming happenings will develop.

Verse 3: **"And He"**, Christ the Angel of the covenant in His servants, the Reformers**, "cried with a loud voice, as when a Lion roared".** The Lion (Vol 1) and in (Hosea 11:10 and Amos 3:8) is the image of Christ Himself and of His representatives on earth, the apostles. The Lord spoke again on earth through apostles, because He spoke *like a roaring Lion.* This however did not occur in the sixth period. We have to expect it in the seventh period, and it is clear, that chapter 10 was fulfilled up to and with verse 2 in the

---

[47] The uninitiated reader may find it strange, that the periods do not always end at a chapter and a new period starts with a new chapter, but the sixth trumpet for example, ends in the middle of a chapter (Rev10:2 and 11:14) and the seventh trumpet starts at (Rev11:15).To clarify this, we must note that the dividing into chapters and verses happened at a later date and is totally arbitrary. In the original writing this does not occur, but all the texts uninterruptedly follow one another.

sixth period, and with verse 3, a new happening, in the seventh period, is predicted.

We said on (Vol.1) that the Lord had wise reasons to describe the persecutions of the Roman church (Rev 9) against the Protestants, and only in (Rev 10:1, 2) to reveal the Reformation itself. The reason is, that chapter 10 predicts the *whole Reformation*, not only in verses 1 and 2, as it happened in the sixth period.

But also in the following verses up to (Rev 11:6) as it continues in the seventh period, and becomes perfect, to bring back the congregation fully to the first apostolic form, as the Bridal congregation of the Lord, who finally receive the fulfilment of the promise, upon which the church of the first century hoped for, "To be taken home and be with the Lord forever" (John 14:3, 1 Thess 4:17,18.)

This action of the new apostles of our Lord Jesus Christ in the seventh period is confirmed by the immediate following: **"and when He had cried, seven thunders uttered their voices."** *The thundering, is the voice of the Lord or His word, spoken through His servants* (Vol. 1) It sounded only in the first period, through the apostles, as it was not them who spoke, but the Spirit of the Father who spoke in them (Matt 10:20). If the thundering is the Word of the Lord spoken through His apostles what do we then understand by the seven thunderings? About this, much has been thought and written. Revelation gives no light here, as John immediately continues with:

Verse 4**. "And when the seven thunders had uttered their voices I was about to write: and I heard a voice from Heaven saying unto me, seal up those things which the seven thunders uttered, and write them not".**

A similar command was given to Daniel in (Dan 12:4) *"O Daniel, shut up the words, and seal the book even to the time of the end."* Because in (verse 9) these words are closed up and sealed till the time of the end. "For then (verse 10) the wise will understand."

Through this command to Daniel, it is shown, that the prophecy will only be understood in the last days, when Christ's return is near, probably through the explanations added to it by the Revelation of John, however, he was not allowed to write the thunderings down but had to seal them up. At the end of Revelation, he received the specific command, not to seal the predictions (Rev 22:10). If John could not reveal the contents of the thunderings, the command not to write them would suffice. Since he was not allowed to write them but to seal them, it can only mean that the meaning expressed by Daniel with the sealing of the words, did not mean anything else, than that the seven thunderings are mentioned at another place and are hidden in a way, that they will only be understood in the last days.

In the course of the centuries, different writers and interpreters of Revelation have tried to research these thunderings and their meanings. We will not tire our readers with their different explanations, but as an example convey the explanation of the Holy Brigita. According to legend, she dearly wanted to know what these thunderings revealed to John meant. She prayed to God for a special Revelation and received it, whereby it was told her, that these thunderings predicted terrible judgement over the persecutors of the church. Her totally wrong conception as seen from her Roman point of view, is the nearest to the truth of all.

We for ourselves did not seek an explanation of these thunderings, in the confidence, that the Lord of the church, when He deems it necessary in His time would give that light. During our research to explain Revelation, we however found mention of the thunderings sealed in another place, and it became clear to us, why John could not write them down for everyone. These thunderings or voices of the Lord relate to the contents of everything the Lord will allow His servants on earth to preach as an admonition, and warning before His imminent judgement which only could be revealed in the seventh period and be made known, and that we will find everything in its rightful place.

John speaks of THE, it literally and specifically speaks of THE seven thunderings, from which would follow, that we already met them in Revelation and John presents them thus as known to us. Indeed it is so. According the thread of the whole record of John they already appear in (Rev 4:5): *"And out of the Throne proceeded lightnings and thunderings and voices;* and in the seventh seal (Rev 8:5) *"and there were voices, and thunderings, and lightings"*. We will find them further on in the seventh trumpet (Rev 11:19) *"and there were lightnings, and voices, and thunderings"* and in the seventh vial (Rev 16:18*) "and there were voices, and thunderings and lightings."* All four of these concerns however, the same happenings which according to the first mentioned (Rev 4:5) will sound out of the Throne of God and as His Words spoken through His servants, in the seventh seal, the seventh trumpet, and the seventh vial.

That this is the meaning, that already appears from the text itself. For the seven thunderings did not sound but *spoke*, and *they spoke their voices*, and just as the original text implies, and as we later shall see *each his particular voice.* And these voices are for all that the Glorification of the Lord Jesus and the preaching of the pure Gospel.

But what are the *seven thunderings*, may the reader ask, even though we do not want to run before the Revelation, the reader has the right to. wonder. This can however only be derived from the formally resolved images, and if our principles of explaining Revelation is correct, and the Holy Spirit is consequent in its imagery, the answer must later be revealed by Revelation.

The thundering we only found described in the first period of the church, as the apostolic testimony (Vol. 1). The seven thunders, which were consecutive, because their seven voices would not have been understood all at once, must be seven different Apostolic testimonies, which occur in the seventh period, prior to the return of Christ, and seven different, perhaps not all glad tidings, they have to convey to His congregations. But then in the seventh period, the Lord must again give apostles to His congregation, and so the part of verse 3 corresponds with the first part, where we saw that the Lord would again in the seventh period speak through apostles (the Lion). Here we are for the second time, just as with the sealing, told of the appearance of apostles in our time, who must act after 1830, after the half hour of silence, but also reminded for the second time of the risen Apostolic church in England in 1832.

There is still one peculiarity in our text, which draws our attention to this last new appearance in the church. It is this: When the Lord himself, after the half-hour silence in the kingdom of God, opens the seventh period, with the cry, "like a lion roars", that is, begins to speak himself through His sent apostles after 1830, and the seven thunders extend over the whole duration of the seventh period, then the first thundering must or at least can have started as the first apostolic testimony in 1830-1832. Highly remarkable is, therefore, this resemblance in time, between that which Revelation predicts, and the actions of the Apostolic church in England. Even more remarkable will it become, when we compare the oral and written testimony which this (whether true or false Apostolic church) spread over Europe, compared with what Revelation will still teach us about the future.

Most interpreters of Revelation believe to find the seven thunders in Psalm 29 in the seven voices of God, (verses 3,4,5,6,7,8,9., we can also unite ourselves with this, yet only in so far as that they are prophetic pointers, of the actual seven thunders, which occur in the seventh period, we will compare one of them with each of the seven thunders. After the Lord according to (verse 3), sent apostles as His representatives on earth at the beginning of the seventh period, He gives to His church in (verse 5,6) a solemn promise, (verse 5) *"And the Angel which I saw stand upon the sea and upon the earth,"* Christ the Angel of the covenant, who through the Reformers had again formed a Christian society in the sea of nations (earth), lifted up His right hand to Heaven at the beginning of the seventh period for a solemn warning. We must here remember what we said previously that the Reformation, begun in (Rev 10) did not end with (verse 2), but is a continuous reform in the church stretching over the whole seventh period.

Christ did not personally appear on earth at the beginning of the sixteenth century but appeared in the Reformers (Vol.1) but then, since He worked similarly in apostles in the seventh period, His solemn promise by the Almighty God must already have been brought by apostles in this period, or must still be brought. It also agrees with the fact that the right hand of the body of Christ (the congregation) which He uses here for His solemn Oath, is the image of the Apostle's ministry just as the left hand is that of the Prophet's ministry.

Verse 6 **"And swore"**, that is: He solemnly promises through His apostles as a warning for us, His servants, living on earth after 1815, **"by Him who lives forever and ever, who created Heaven and what is in it, the earth and what is in it, and the sea and what is in it"**, thus by the eternal, Almighty God, the Creator of heaven and earth, but also the Creator of his church (heaven), as of the condition of society (earth) and the Christian nations (sea) of the seventh period, -**"There will be no more time"**.

The meaning of the original word is 1ˢᵗ an *indefinite time*, but also 2ⁿᵈ *a delay*. The word does not lend itself to any speculation. This would be contrary to the intention of Christ which is: He swears by His Father, the Almighty God that it will not be long, that there will be no more extension of Godly long-suffering for the sinful earth and the corrupted church, but (Verse 7) in the days of the voice of the seventh angel, when He shall sound the trumpet, the end of this dispensation begins, and then:

"The mystery of God will be fulfilled as He announced to His servants the Prophets." Whether this solemn promise "That the end of this dispensation is near and the mysteries of God will soon be completed," whether this warning and solemn assurance by the Almighty God, is already brought through apostles and prophets, as stated in our text in (verse 7) in our time, or still has to be brought, will be made clear in the vial (Rev 18:1-7). Apostles are the dispensers of the mysteries of God, Paul teaches us (1 Cor 4:1.). These mysteries will therefore also be revealed in this seventh period, for assuredly the Lord will not do anything unless He reveals it first to His servants, the prophets. (Amos 3:7). Indeed, the seventh trumpet (Rev 11:15) ending at (Rev 15:20) contains the following mysteries of which Paul speaks:1ˢᵗ The mystery of unrighteousness (2 Tess 2:1-12), 2ⁿᵈ The taking up to heaven of living believers (1 Cor 15:51, 52).

These mysteries will not only be fulfilled in the seventh period, but as Amos already said, will be revealed beforehand to the servants of the Lord, the prophets. This last is the meaning of the verses which are to follow in (Rev 10).

Verse 8 **"Then the voice that I had heard from Heaven spoke to me saying, " Go, take the scroll"**, the testimony of Christ concerning the last days, (page250,Vol 1), "which is open," of which the content is known, and which is "in the hand of the Angel, who is standing on the sea and on the earth" while Christ works through apostles in the seventh period (the Lion and the first thunder of verse 3) the Angel of the seventh period must consist of apostles, (Rev 7:2,3), and the testimony concerning the last days and the imminent return of Christ must also go out from apostles, and once again Van Loon writes in 1836 that such a testimony went out from the Catholic Apostolic church in England.

Verse 9.**"So I went to the Angel and told Him to give me the little scroll."** John is not on this earth for over 18 centuries, yet he says in the nineteenth century: "Give me this testimony of the last days." But then John could not have referred to himself in person, but in his ministry, his apostleship; but then we also have to expect apostles sent by the Lord, as his substitute, because John received this testimony in order to announce it, not by writing it in Revelation, but by word of mouth through his substitutes in the last period. Prophesying (Rev 10:11) according to Biblical meaning, is not a received vision to be written down, but to be spoken, driven by the Holy Spirit, and announce future happenings. Therefore Christ says to him:**"Take it and eat, it will be bitter to your stomach, but sweet as honey in your mouth."**

Verse 10. **"So I took the little scroll from the hand of the Angel, and ate it; it was sweet as honey in my mouth, but when I had eaten it, my stomach was made bitter".**

To receive this Revelation, to write it down, and send it to the congregation in Asia, may have been sweet to John, but it could however not be possible to become bitter in his stomach. This can only be said of them, who in the seventh period, as substitutes of John, received this testimony of the last days, and orally conveyed it to the world. The whole image, which we also find in (Ezek 3:1) is derived from fruit, sweet to the taste, yet unpleasant in after taste. Its effect is described in:

Verse 11. **"And He said unto me: You must prophesy again before many peoples, and nations, and tongues, and kings."** Receiving the commission, to announce this testimony of the last days (the contents of the scroll) in the name of Christ and as His personally chosen ambassadors to all nations and peoples and tongues and kings is probably sweet, it is a glorious privilege to be chosen by God's grace to such a commission in his service, but the consequences thereof is bitter. When in our days of unbelief, after that for so many centuries the prophecy, as a gift of the Holy Spirit, ceased to exist in the church, when now these gifts are given again to some persons through Christ, and these, convinced of their truth and of their calling from the Lord, in His name announce to the nations: the Lord Jesus sent me to say unto you that His return is at hand,- how would such a prophet, even if his calling was just as true as those of the old Testament, how would he be received? The unbelievers would mock him as a crazy fanatic; the weak in faith doubtfully raise their shoulders and the pious Christians? - They must answer this themselves. Lucky for them, if they do not belong to the testament tribe of Dan but follow the advice of the Jew Gamaliel (Acts 5:38,39.), but luckier still, if they take the words of the *gentile* Cornelius (Acts 10:33) to heart: "Thou hast well done that thou art come, now therefore are we all here present before God to hear all things that are commanded thee of God."

Nothing else could have been meant, that as the chosen prophet and driven by the Holy Spirit, to announce this testimony of the last days, John would again have to prophecy before many peoples, nations and kings. John received this prophecy on the island of Patmos a few years before his death in (100 AD). After his banishment, he returned to Ephesus, almost one hundred years old, and so weak, that in the gathering of the congregation, he could not speak more than to say: "Children, love one another!" John did therefore not prophecy again before many people, nations tongues, and kings, and after him in the first Christian centuries no prophets with a similar testimony rose anymore. This *"again"* can therefore only take place in our days, at the end of this dispensation. We also remember that John, at. the beginning of Revelation was transposed in the spirit on the day of the Lord, and spiritually lived through the time, which up to that Great day, would still have to develop. He was therefore in the seventh period, when he received this commission, to prophecy again. But then, in our days, there must be prophets of our Lord Jesus Christ active again, with His testimony of the last days. It is remarkable, that Van Loon (1836) mentions not only apostles in the Apostolic church but also prophets. Moreover, the testimony, orally and in writing, of the Laodicean condition of the church, the imminent return of the Lord and the preceding restoration of the church in its original apostolic form according to His will, went out to all church leaders and worldly leaders of all countries (before many people and nations and tongues, and kings). In no other church denomination did such a happening take place. This is the third time that we can find the fulfilment of Revelation prophecies only with this Catholic Apostolic church, the third time that we, with such emphasis, are shown this.

How will the reader receive this pointer to the Apostolic church? What will he think about the writer of this work? Probable that the writer wants to make propaganda for her; but the reader will never be more wrong.

We do not wish more than, now that the Lord has given us light on Revelation, to find great wisdom therein, and unprejudiced, together with the reader to seek, where to find the fulfilment of the prophecies. The search of whether the revealed fulfilled prediction of an event is truly from God remains, for the writer as well as for the reader, their responsibility according to each one's personal conviction and individual tendency and belief, as well as the accepting or rejecting thereof.

The feeling that we would appear in a strange light to the reader is also reflected in Revelation. The receiving of the testimony was sweet to John, but when he had eaten it and had to bring it out, it became bitter in his stomach. From the body, the congregation, of which Christ is the Head (Col 1:18, 24) we have learned to know both feet in the Reformation period (Vol. 1). The hands, as part of the body, must come to the fore again in the seventh period as the Apostle and Prophet ministries as we find them again in the seventh vial (Rev 18:20) in their judgement over Babylon.

But this body or Apostolic congregation of the last period, especially her prophesying persons, will experience that this testimony, which is the Spirit of prophecy (Rev 19:10), after having absorbed it, becomes bitter. Mockery by unbelievers, suspicion of separatism and hypocrisy, and disdain and rejection by believing Christians from the Laodicean churches will be her lot. What her Lord and Head had to suffer with His first appearance on earth from the pious Jews and Pharisees, she must also suffer; but her comfort will also be that which the Lord spoke to the first Apostolic congregation! *"Blessed are ye, when men shall revile you, and persecute you, and shall say all manner of evil against you falsely, for my sake. Rejoice, and be exceedingly glad: for great is your reward in Heaven: for so persecuted they the prophets which were before you"* (Matt 5:11, 12).

We remind the reader here of what we remarked on (page 334) about the simultaneous histories of several happenings, which cannot be described at the same time. Henceforth because of the detailed and multi-faceted description of events in Revelation, it becomes very difficult, to explain them in a set order. For instance (Rev 11:1, 2), happens as a result of (Rev 10); but (Rev 11:15-19, Rev 12:1-5 Rev 16:17 and Rev 18:1-7) all occur approximately simultaneously and the best rule for our explanation will be to handle the events as much as possible in the order, in which they flow from one another, and the chronology in which they occur, as it appeared to us from our resolving of each image. Therefore, (Rev 11:1,2) must come first.

MEASURING THE TEMPLE

He that is not with Me is against Me; and he that
gathered not with Me scattered abroad.

Matt 12:30

Rev 11:1

Verse 1. **"And there was given me a reed like unto a rod, and the Angel (Jesus) stood saying: Rise, and measure the Temple of God, and the Altar, and them that worship therein".**

This verse connects itself immediately with the last verse of the previous chapter. We do not here find as elsewhere in Revelation the word *after this* or *then*, but the connecting word *and*, by which this commission to measure also belongs to the prophesying. Therefore, the persons, who shall prophecy as substitutes of John, are the same as those who will measure the Temple.

The temple in Jerusalem was already destroyed for 23 years before John received the Revelation. Besides, this was not given to the Jews but to the servants of Christ. The measuring of a building is ruled out here since those, who worship therein, must also be measured. The measuring is therefore an investigation or an examination.

This commission is also given to John in the seventh period; therefore, it cannot be the temple in Jerusalem, but the New Testament temple, the congregation of the Lord, and the church of Jesus Christ. The Old Testament temple, with all its regulations and goods, was the foreshadowing (type) in the earthly form of the spiritual New Testament congregation or church. (See: the fifth seal, page 183-197 Vol. 1). "Know ye not asks Paul in (Cor 3:16,17.) that ye are the temple of God?" and "Ye are the temple of the living God" (2 Cor 6:16).

When therefore this spiritual temple, the whole Christian church, must be measured, it is the image of examination according to the measure of her increase in Christ (Eph 4:13, 16. Col 2:19.). The measuring or examination must be extended to all, who worship in the temple or in the Christian church. The rod for this cannot be anything but the Word of God. This rod Luther and his fellow Reformers also used to measure the Roman church. According to the utterances of this word, it must be investigated in how far the Christian churches of the seventh period of Laodicea, still belonged to THE church of Jesus Christ, how much of the original church still remained in her, in how far the church was still the Kingdom of Jesus Christ, and not of this world, and in how far those, who worshipped the Lord in this church, where still Christians.

The institution of the church from the first Apostolic period was a totally different one than at present.

She was, according to the promise of Jesus (Matt 28:20), a true Christian Government, a living church, which He ruled himself, as her living Head, and exerted His power, not through dead, but living apostles and prophets. If we compare the congregation or the spiritual temple of God (1 Tim 3:15) with a building or earthly temple, (Eph 2:21, 22), then living apostles and prophets were the foundation of that building and Christ Himself the Chief Cornerstone, in whom the whole building was fitted together (Eph 2:20-22, 1 Peter 2:4, 7. Matt 21:42. Acts 4:11) the congregation forming the living stones of the building (1 Peter 2:5)

If we however take another image and name the congregation the body of Christ (Eph 4:12, 16. 1 Cor 12:27), then He was the ruling Head (Col 11:18), speaking to her through the Holy Spirit (Acts 13:2. Acts 16:6, 7), through prophesying persons as mentioned in (Acts 20:23. Acts 21:4, 9, 11), and guiding and caring for her through His four ministries, or the members of His body, Apostles, Prophets, Evangelists and Shepherds (Acts 13:2, Acts 20:28).

When the substitutes of John compare the Christian church according to these standards with what they find after 1830 up to our time, they find in the Greek church a mighty worldly prince, the emperor of Russia, who by proclaiming himself high priest (1721), united the spiritual power with the worldly power, thereby making the church a slave of the state. In the Roman church, on the other hand, they find a high priest, the Pope, who first made himself the vicar of Christ and then the Emperor, and along this reversed way, binds the worldly power with the spiritual, and wants to make the state the slave of the church; besides which they there find the councils of church princes, who assume, that the Spirit speaks through them, so that their utterings and decisions, are spoken by God Himself and must be binding for Roman and non-Roman, who even in our days declare the Pope infallible.

In the Protestant church which once, as the spiritual Israel, came out of the Roman Babel, they here find the worldly head of the country at the same time the head of the state church, (England, Prussia) where the church was under the rule of a Synod, which in her Protestant council, reveals the same

Roman arrogance in matters of faith, and by consolidating all the rules of faith declare themselves a Protestant infallible pope.

In this, they would find nothing else than anti-Christian dissolution, which reveals itself in continuous quarrels, divisions, charges of heresy against one another, schisms and splitting into numerous denominations. In one word they would find all possible matters in Greek, Roman, Lutheran, Reformed and other Christian churches, but nowhere would they find the Christian church, as she was instituted in her original form by the Lord; nowhere find what they came to look for; one body, one spirit, one hope, one Lord one faith, one baptism (Eph 4:4, 5). Nowhere would they find one temple, but all sorts of small chapels and prayer cells in the clefts and caves of the exploded temple of God.

That was the external condition and the construction of the Temple of God. But also the internal condition of the Kingdom of God, the altar and those, who worship in the temple, they had to measure, and at the same time receive the command:

Verse 2 **"But the court which is without the temple leave out, and measure it not, for it is given to the gentiles!**

From the fifth seal we remember that the temple consisted of the outer forecourt, open to the Gentiles, corresponding with the condition of the unbelievers around the spiritual temple of the church of Christ on earth. The inner court or the forecourt of Israel is the image of the believers. In this last stood the burnt offering or the atonement altar. In the next part of the temple stood the golden incense altar, for the Glorification and worshipping of God. These two actually formed a unit and were the image: firstly, of repentance and forgiveness of sins, and secondly of the worshipping of the Lord in the Christian church.

*Here we must touch on very sensitive matters, about which many a reader will perhaps take offence when he sees his church denomination being judged. Everyone considers his own to be the only true and best and thereby judges the other denominations. If this were not the case, he would belong to another denomination. The free choice which the reader has, the writer also asks for himself. He may do this boldly, while not his own feelings and judgement, but God's infallible word is the touchstone, and the Lord Himself has spoken out His judgement and opinion about the Christian churches in His Revelation.

In the Christian churches of the seventh period the spiritual condition of the believers, their reconciliation and worshipping of God must be measured. The outer court of the temple, or the unbelievers among the

Christian nations, who are outside the kingdom of God, did not have to measure.

When they measured the Christian churches, in how far in their internal condition they still belonged to the kingdom of God, they would have to take as a measuring rod the words of the apostle Peter, (Acts 4:12) "Neither is there Salvation in any: for there is no other name under heaven given among men, whereby we must be saved", a measuring rod, given by Christ himself in His words: "But he that believeth not is condemned already, because he hath not believed in the name of the only begotten Son of God" (John 3:18).

In the Roman and Greek churches, John's substitutes would now find next, with, and above Jesus Christ, all sorts of names of so-called saints, who during their lives were no more than poor sinners, just as we are. Above all, however, the name of Maria, the mother of God. They would see them seeking their salvation by invoking the saints, by fasting, etc.....

The worshipping of God they would see, consisted of waving with incensers, prayers and songs in unintelligible Latin, which the congregations could not understand. Sorrowfully, having seen the Roman and Greek churches returned to heathen idolatry, they would with joyful expectation turn to the Protestant church, which for already three centuries had left the Roman church, to restore and preach the gospel to salvation in its full purity. But where to begin, for her number of sects is legion! Evangelists, Free Evangelicals, Lutherans, Reformed, Remonstrant, Mennonites, Baptists, Separatists etc.

Yes, amongst them all, they would find believers, who set their hope of salvation on the offered grace of God in Jesus Christ; more than seven thousand, who had not bowed their knees to Baal;- but they would find the majority of the members of the Protestant Christian churches, with their hearts open to and filled with the evil spirits out of the mouth of the dragon, that is, denying Christ, out of the mouth of the beast, denial of God, and out of the mouth of the false prophet, the pantheistic Nature religion and deification of men. And upon all these, Roman, Greek and Protestant churches, they would write the name, of the place where these three evil spirits would be gathered, the name, which in Hebrew is called Armageddon (Rev 16:13, 16) that is the (once) holy city (Eph 2:19, Heb 12:22) now the great Babylon, an habitation of devils and a place of preservation for all evil spirits. (Rev 18:2)[48]

---

[48] Babylon means confusion, actually confusion of speech and everywhere in Christendom, there is confusion and differences in the form of church leadership, as well as in belief and the preaching of the Gospel, in the sense of Revelation is Babylon.

But then they would also at the same time think, that for our time, in the seventh vial, the command is given: ***"Come out of her my people so that you do not partake in her sin"*** (Rev 18:4) and in the seventh period there must be a Babel; for how can the people of the Lord come out of Babylon if they do not find themselves in Babylon. And the people of the Lord (or the believers) do not find themselves in the Roman church, except for a smaller part, the greatest part will be found in the Protestant church since they came out of the Roman church, and therefore Babylon does not refer to the Roman church only, but them, as also the Greek and Protestant churches, in one word, the whole presently existing apostate Christian church.

With the command: **"Come out of Babylon, My people,"** a series of remarkable memories come to mind out of the occurrence of the former temple at Jerusalem, which developed to the following parallel between the earthly temple of the Old Covenant and the spiritual temple of the New Covenant or the Christian church. From this, it appears at the same time that the similarity between them does not only concern the institution, as we learned to know it in the fifth seal, but as their history, and the first to be a foreshadow or type of the last.

These points of similarity between the history of the Jewish and the Christian temples are too manifold and too remarkable to be coincidence or to be of no meaning for the future. We will just look at a few of these similarities.

Solomon, the son of David built the first temple at Jerusalem, Jesus, the Son of God, yet more than Solomon, built the Spiritual temple.

Gold, Silver, precious stones in the temple.

Truth, Love, and Gifts of the Holy Spirit in the church.

The temple is robbed of its gold, silver and precious stones.

The church is robbed of its Truth, Love and the Gifts of the Holy Spirit

The first exodus of Israel out of Babel.

The first exodus of Christians out of Babel (Reformation 1517) Gold, and silver were brought back to the temple. No precious stones.

Truth and love were brought back to Babel. No gifts of the Holy Spirit.

Second exodus under Ezra, at God's command.

Second exodus out of Babylon, at God's command (come out of Babylon my children Rev18:4).

Before the Reformation, the Roman church had become a Babel of confusion. Then Luther and his followers encouraged the believers, to leave Babel and named those who had returned from Babel, the Protestants. Through him and his fellow reformers the devastated Christian temple was firstly measured, and thereafter rebuilt; also the altar service, that is the confession of sins with the absolution of sins, and the worshipping of God according to the Gospel were restored. They build up believing congregations as the houses of the spiritual Jerusalem. This development continued for as long as Roman believers went over to the Protestants. This was the first exodus. It is remarkable, that Luther himself predicted that the Reformation processes would last for three hundred years.

Indeed, at the end of that time (1825) the Temple building was stopped, and since then up to our days, the Protestant church itself has become a Babel of confusion and unbelief, as we already found on (Vol 1) and no believing Christian will deny this. In our seventh period, the substitutes of John received the commission to measure and investigate the whole Christian church (Greek, Roman and Protestant) or to investigate the condition of faith of the Christian congregation, and after they had found them a Babel of confusion, the Lord gives His servants in the seventh vial (Rev 18:4) the command to a second exodus out of the whole Babel of Christian churches, to the completion of the incomplete temple, to the restoring of the ruined walls of the Spiritual Jerusalem, and to the rebuilding of the city itself.

In the seventh period, there would not only be a measuring of the whole Christian temple, but also under the Spiritual Ezra (Helper) a new exodus would take place in order that complete temple service could begin. But then the Spiritual Ezra must be the same, as the substitutes of John, because through Ezra the serving priests and the people of God, or the believers, were measured or investigated, purified and sanctified and the heathen cast out, just as it was commanded in (Rev 11:1, 2). However, since we came across only one religious body risen since 1830, wherein apostles and prophets where found, who could be the substitutes of John, then, if these apostles and prophets are the true and predicted ones, then they must be the same body, the Catholic Apostolic church, who received and execute the commission to measure the temple. It would also be the fourth time, that we are emphatically referred to the same remarkable and important appearance in the Christian church, which had to act in the seventh period after 1830, 1st as the sealing Angel 2nd as the restored apostle ministry, through which Christ would again give the Holy Spirit with His gifts to the believers, 3rd as the prophet ministry, with the testimony of Jesus concerning His return, to be brought to many peoples and nations and tongues and kings, and 4th here, as the body to investigate the outer –and inner condition of the whole Christendom.

The first three characteristics we could find with our writer Van Loon only in the Catholic Apostolic church. Of the fourth characteristic, we found nothing, not with her or any other religious denomination. And yet, this event must have taken place, while at its completion the second exodus out of Babel begins, and has already begun, as we shall see.

We had to find other sources to see if the measuring of the temple through the same Catholic Apostolic church did occur. We laid our hands on a little book titled: *"Erzaling von Thatsachen in verbindung mit jetzigen lage und zukunft der ganzen Christlichen kirche,"* Frankfurt, Heinrich Zimmer, 1884. (Report of matters in connection with the present condition and the future of the whole Christian church. Frankfurt by Heinrich Zimmer1884). Herein we find specifically mentioned, that at the Lord's command, through prophecies, that of the 12 apostles of the Catholic Apostolic Church, 11 were sent out of England with the already mentioned oral and written testimony to all the religious and worldly leaders concerning the condition and the decay of the Christian church, the re-establishing of the Apostolic church and the imminent return of the Lord. They also had the commission to investigate the religious condition of the countries they visited; to observe their various morals and customs, and to investigate, in how far and how it would be possible to bring to them the truths which they themselves had received. They further had to learn to know the form of divine services in the different countries and their spiritual condition, and finally, gather the Gold (the truth) from all parts of Christendom, the reason for this last task was that in every denomination of the church, a certain amount of truth is to be found, often hidden and buried under the mud of human teachings and traditions, as, the pure Gold in the bowels of the earth. The results of their investigation, on their return to the meeting of all the apostles, would be weighed, reweighed and sifted, so that all the good in the whole of Christendom would find its place in the worshipping of God and in the service of His House. They are also given the commission to consider themselves more as observers and learners, than teachers.

However inadequately prepared the apostles were for their commission, they nevertheless went out trusting in the help of Him who had called them thereto. Thus Russia, Sweden, Norway, Germany, Greece, Spain, Portugal, Netherlands, Dennemark, France and Switzerland were each visited by one of the apostles. According to the word of the Lord to them, that they would return after 1260 days, they left on 7th July 1835, and having fulfilled their commissions, all came back and gathered on Christmas day the 25th Dec.1838 after (1260 days).

It definitely did never appear that the Catholic Apostolic church boasted, that by this investigation at the command of the Lord, she fulfilled the prophecy of the measuring of the temple.

Perhaps, she unknowingly fulfilled the commission as John's substitute. It becomes clear to us from this commission why John did not have to measure the forecourt (the unbelievers), because amongst them not a single grain of Gold of Godly Truth was found, and they, therefore, were outside the temple.

The facts named from the little book, appeared on our investigation to be correct. No other denomination ever undertook such an investigation. There is absolutely no valid reason, why those events would not be the measuring of the Christian temple. It is therefore the fourth big characteristic, which we found in this denomination. Even though we do not consider everything good in the Apostolic church, e.g. ceremonies and dress, we must be impartial enough to recognize, that this religious body is the only one, wherein we find the predicted characteristics given in Revelation that could be explained through the Word of God. Whoever does not agree, of him we have the right to expect, that he will show us when and how this measuring of the temple occurred in our time; for it did occur. Later already fulfilled events prove this.

The following in (verse 2) "*And they* (the gentiles or unbelievers) *will trample over the Holy City for forty-two months*" which is an event still in the future and the same, which is described in detail in the rest of the chapter (Rev 11:7-10) It is the three and a half years of tribulation of *Christendom* (*Holy City*, page 274 Vol 1) by the anti-Christian power, such as we will presently find in the chronology of time, wherein those events occur. We here must remark, that this *Holy City*, which will be trodden upon, is not Jerusalem and its invasion by the Mohammedans, since this prediction refers to our time. This Holy City is described (Rev 21:2, 9, 10) as the Heavenly Jerusalem, the Bride of the Lord, or the city of the Living God, the congregation of the firstborn (Heb 12:22, 23 compare Vol 1).

THE SEVENTH TRUMPET ANGEL

or

THE NEW WAY OF GOSPEL PREACHING IN THE SEVENTH PERIOD

> The Kingdom of God cometh not with observation,
> behold the Kingdom of God is within you.
>
> Luke17:20,21.

Rev11:15-19

Up to now, we followed the sixth trumpet, as it flowed into the seventh period and for as much as it has been fulfilled since 1830 up to our time. The rest of the sixth trumpet in (Rev 11:3-4) belongs to the coming days and occurs in the third part of this seventh period: **The future.** With or shortly after the end of the half-hour silence, thus after 1830, together with the seventh seal, and as a result thereof, the seventh trumpet also begins to sound.

Verse 15. **"And the seventh Angel sounded"**. The sixth trumpet angel was the clergy of the Reformation. The seventh must therefore be a reforming in the Protestant movement corresponding with previous periods, at least bringing a change in it.

At the sounding of the seventh trumpet, that is: The new way of gospel preaching after 1830, there were (verse 15), great voices in Heaven, saying, *"The Kingdom of this world has become the Kingdom of our Lord, and He shall reign forever and ever"*. The first impression of the reader will be, that the Kingdom of Glory, the so-called Thousand-year Kingdom as predicted in 1830 has already begun, and God knows, the condition of the world is all but so that we should think ourselves to be in the Thousand-year Kingdom. And yet, we will see that the first impression of the reader was not wholly untrue, but that indeed with 1830 the first Light of the Great Day of peace over the whole earth has dawned. With the dawning of the first light in nature, there are moments, when day and night are equal, when night has not yet gone, and the full day has not yet come; when over the depth and ravines of the earth nightly darkness still hovers, while the golden seams around the clouds in heaven already call to us; *the night is past, the day has broken, soon comes the sun, which will ban all darkness from the depths and precipices.* Just like such a moment in time in nature, it also is in the Kingdom of Grace, the time in which we live. The last day of the world is past, midnight darkness, long ago already covered the Christian earth,

369

nightly vapour and darkness cover the depths and ravines of the earth, where Satan with his fallen angels and human servants dwell, as the prince of darkness, yet the golden seams (truth) shine around the clouds of witnesses (the church of Christ); the morning stars (teachers) have already risen, who announce the Day of the Lord, who announce the coming of the Sun of Righteousness.

Verse 15. **"And there were great voices in Heaven,"** this could be a great rejoicing among the Angels around God's throne, **"saying: The Kingdom of this world are become our Lord's"** The sound of the seventh trumpet teaches them, that it will happen, the intention of God is to them the deed itself, the beginning already the completed event.

But at the same time in the Kingdom of God here on earth, the heaven of the church, great voices sounded, as we saw in the seventh seal; Great voices, who announced over the earth: *"Maranatha, Maranatha, the Lord comes, the kingdom of Glory is near; the Lord comes, to reign as King in eternity!"* From the Catholic Apostolic Church in England, we saw this testimony proceed with great power.

Verse 16. **"Then the twenty-four elders who sit on their thrones before God fell on their faces and worshipped God".** In most translations, we read THE twenty-four Elders, indicating the already described elders in (Rev 4 and 5). The best writings of Revelation do not contain the article THE, and the translators have arbitrarily added it because otherwise, this verse became unexplainable to them. But it would be just as unexplainable to us with the added article. It is remarkable; as we already often mentioned (page 257 Vol. 1) that *true readings*, although rejected because of their being unintelligible, always seem to be to us, the true, the simplest, the clearest explanation; also in this instance. According to the best scripts we therefore read: AND twenty-four Elders etc. With A. Lachm the second article WHO is also missing. Twenty-four is nowhere to be found as a symbolic number in scripture, we therefore have to take it literary. Who are these twenty-four Elders, sitting on their thrones before God? Some say, the representatives of the Christian congregations, without specifying anything concrete. Others say, the twelve Patriarch of the Old and the twelve apostles of the New Testament, are all arbitrary and without biblical proof. Only to the apostles it was promised (Matt 19:28 and Luke 22:30), that when the Son of man shall sit on the Throne of His Glory, they also shall sit upon twelve thrones, judging the twelve tribes. The patriarchs themselves belong to the twelve tribes of Israel. *When they are judged by the twelve apostles, they cannot at the same time sit as judges on the throne.* We would however err if we would presume the apostles to be in the Glory of God and around His Throne; the time is not yet there. They still rest with the souls under the altar; see the fifth seal, (Vol.1). These twenty-four Elders have not received their crowns yet in this seventh period (verse 16), the crown of Glory (1 Pet 5:4) wherewith they are adorned after the completion of the seventh period in the day of the Lord (Rev 4;4,10,11). *There* they cast their crowns before the Throne of God. *Here* (Rev 11:16) they do not do this, because they do not yet possess a crown. And not only these crowns, but the four living creatures, who in (Rev 4 and 5) always appear with THESE elders, are not present here.

The twenty-four elders of (Rev 11:16) cannot be understood to be the first apostles of the Lord, while the Kingdom of Glory has not yet fully commenced, and they moreover still rest in paradise, until also their fellow servants and their brothers will join them, who will be killed as they were (Rev 6:11). "For that they, without us should not be made perfect" (Heb 11:40). And these last brothers must still be added in the coming anti-Christian persecution. Only after that will they come to life together (Rev 20:4-6). If this vision of John cannot be sought under the departed servants of Christ, we have to seek them among the living, and the thrones must be an image of a Royal Power, such as we saw in the fifth vial, (page 215, Vol 1) and here therefore a Royal Power in the Kingdom of God (Luke 22:29, Rev 1:6, Rev 5:10, Matt 16:19) and from the power of Kings of old, the right to speak out judgement (Luke 22:30, Rev 18:20).

What clergy or spiritual office was known during the life of John as Elder?

In the Jewish state, at the time of Jesus' coming on the earth, they were honoured and distinguished men, who ruled the people together with the chief priests. (Matt 28:11, 12. Luke 7:3 Luke 2:66, Act 4:5,8. Acts 22:5, Acts 24:1)

In the young Christian congregation, we find (1 Tim 5:17, Titus 11:30) similarly the heads or rulers of the individual congregation named Elders. From (Acts 11:23. Acts 15:2, 4, 6, 22, 23. Acts 16:4. Acts 20:17. Acts 21:18. 1 Peter 5:1) it appears, that they were subject to the apostles. The apostles Peter and John however also named THEMSELVES ELDERS (1 Peter 5:1, 2 John 1.) **The apostles** were therefore also **elders**. However, they did not stand at the head of the local congregation, but at the head of the whole Christian church, they were **the elders of the whole Christian church**. Since this Revelation of Jesus Christ is not directed to local congregations or sects, but speaks of His whole Church, we have no right, according to the New Testament scriptures to assume, under the **twenty-four elders** of (Rev 11:16) anything else than the **twenty-four apostles.**

The reader will probably testify that we strictly and consequently adhered to our principle; only to solve the entire unknown in Revelation from the Holy Scripture. And if through our consequence would bind our own hands, we cannot, will not and may not diverge from our pattern, and must come to the following conclusion:

There must and will again be twenty-four living apostles of our Lord Jesus Christ, sent and given to His church in the seventh period (since 1830).

It is remarkable, that we already found twelve apostles in the Catholic Apostolic church in England after 1830 and are herewith **for the fifth time** specifically shown this strange appearance in the church,- involuntary the question arises, where are the other twelve apostles? The reader must remember that (Rev 11:15-18) stretches over the whole seventh period of the church, from 1830 up to the return of the Lord. In case the twelve apostles of the English Apostolic church are the true apostles of our Lord Jesus Christ, we then have to expect another twelve. With (Rev 11:4) it will later become clear. The reader must not wonder about such a great number of apostles, and will not remain under the old understanding, that only the first twelve chosen by the Lord eighteen centuries ago, were true apostles and no more than these twelve would come. For then already, after the death of apostle James, two others were called to replace him, Paul and Barnabas (Acts 13:2, Acts 14:14.) Then already there were more than twelve apostles.

After this clear indication in prophecy, that in the seventh-period apostles will again be active, we must come to a decision,- whether the Catholic Apostolic church rose in England since 1832 is the fulfilment of this prophecy, and whether her apostles are truly the predicted apostles of Christ, chosen and sent, and the first half of the twenty-four elders of the seventh trumpet; or the Revelation, which in our time so accurately is fulfilled in the history of the Christian church, henceforth becomes an unfulfilled prophecy of our Lord Jesus Christ, which do not show in truth to His servants; "Those things which must soon take place" (Rev 1:1, 19). Another choice is impossible.

Agreed! Says the reader, there will again be apostles in our time, as we earlier said, also prophets will come, but then they must still come, it cannot be the present ones. But then the Christian reader would be guilty of the same judgement as the Jewish scribes with Jesus' first appearance on earth.

They expected the Messiah, they knew or could know from the prophecies of (Dan 9 and Mica 5) when and where the Messiah would be born. But when Jesus, the Christ, was born at the specified time and place, they did not accept Him (John 1:11). This was not the Messiah. Just like the Jews, the reader could also perhaps disdain an offered blessing.

But how can I discern, whether these are true apostles and prophets of the Lord or false?

In case they were false, the Loving Lord and Savior would have warned you in the seventh candlestick. Did He not warn of false apostles who would come in the first period of the church, the Ephesian Christendom? (Rev 2:2). In the seventh candlestick, the letter to the congregation of Laodicea, the letter, which is directed at you, He does not do this; on the contrary, He warns you against yourselves, about the self-deception of thinking yourself rich while you are poor, and He councils you lovingly to buy Gold of Truth from Him, purified in the fire; that is the Truth of GOD, preached by tested servants whom He will sent in this period. He even indicates in His Revelation, that He will send His sealing angel, His servants, the apostles, who imprint the seal of the Holy Spirit, the name of our God upon the foreheads of His believers, who recognize Him in this sealing work, and accept it as preservation from the coming great tribulation, to belong to the 144,000, redeemed from mankind as Firstlings of God and the Lamb (Rev 14:1-4) He also shows you, that He will send His prophets in this time, to testify from His word of all the things, which will happen in the last time of oppression, and with all this can you still doubt?. Do you not have a sign, that the false prophets deny the Lord who bought them? (2 Pet 2:1) Are you not commanded to test the spirits, whether they are of God (1 John 4:1) *"Because many false Prophets are gone out in the world.,* and (verse 2) *"By this you know the Spirit of God; every spirit that confesses that Jesus Christ has come in the flesh is from God,".* and in (verse 3) *"And every spirit that does not confess Jesus is not from God."*

When now these apostles and prophets of the Apostolic church, do not deny Him who has bought them, but confess, that Christ is come in the flesh, -and this is easy to investigate, -then they must be the true apostles and prophets, or Peter and John although inspired by the Holy Spirit would have been wrong or a third possibility, the reader, who rejects these apostles and prophets as false is perhaps also wrong? In this case, there exists still another characteristic. Are not the characteristics of an apostle signs, wonders, mighty works, dispending the Holy Spirit and His gifts (2 Cor 12:12,13) and must not an Apostolic congregation be the seal of His apostleship (1 Cor 9:2), as a letter of Christ, written on our hearts, to be known and read by all (2 Cor 3:2, 3).

373

For those who want to investigate this, it must be very easy to determine, whether the apostles and prophets whose appearance in the seventh period is predicted by Christ Himself in His Revelation, are true or false apostles and prophets when they act as such. If it is not possible for everyone, because this apostolic congregation can be found, in small numbers and at too great a distance away, it becomes easier for all by the testimony of their belief and their hope, which they will utter according to the prophecy in the following verses: They worshipped God, saying:

Verse 17. **"We give you thanks, Lord God Almighty, who are and who were, for you have taken your great power and begun to reign."** This is the same as what the great voices in heaven (verse 15) uttered. The kingdom of the world has become the Lord's and of His Christ, and He will reign forever and ever. But how, will the reader say, has the Kingdom of God already come in 1830 or 1836, and through the Apostolic church? It does truly not appear so in the world.

What is the Kingdom of God? Jesus says in (Matt 12:28) *when* and *where* the devils are driven out by the Spirit of God, *then* and *there* the Kingdom of God has come, and from (Matt 16:28. Mark 9:1 and Luke 9:27) it appears clearly, that with the Kingdom of God the Lord did not mean an external kingdom (Luke 17:21) but the Christian church such as she existed in her complete organization about 30 years after the death of the Lord, and is described for us in the epistle to the Ephesians. In this completed form and structure the Lord was her living Head, reigning through His apostles, speaking through His prophets, and the members of the congregation, who are His body, who had the Holy Spirit living in them with all His gifts and through this Spirit the power to drive out the devils, heal the sick, etc—in one word; the Kingdom of God is the total government of Christ, now in His striving church, but soon also in His victorious church. There the state goes into the church, the state laws in the commandment of God and the state office in the Royal Priesthood. But did the government of Christ in the church commence again after 1830? It is exactly the testimony of the Catholic Apostolic Church, that in her, Christ, as Head of the congregation, again reveals Himself as living governing King through His apostles and speaks through His prophets; that the Holy Spirit with His gifts again inhabits her. For this reason, the words (verse 17) *"Who shall come"* are missing in the best readings, because He already has come, although not visible to the world.

Verse 18. **"The nations raged, but your wrath has come."** This was also the testimony brought by the Apostolic church and, although between 1830 and 1836, it was not yet clearly perceptible in the religious and political areas, the latter years have brought to light the Godly truth thereof. With astounding speed and power, the social-democratic principles spread under the people, the liberalist principles under the middle classes and the anti-Christian principles under all classes of Europe. Old state institutions fell as a result of their onslaught, church denominations disbanded, and thrones abdicated, others were undermined. Lordship is a figment of the imagination, an empty word. No prince can or dares to oppose the will of the people anymore. The voice of the people rules, as if they were the voice of God, and where the people now still rule through their elected representatives, the day is near when they will grasp the reins themselves and the name of the seventh period, Laodicea, people rule, people justice, will become the full truth. For not only have the people become angry, the nations furious, but also *the wrath of the Lord has come*; His wrath against the rulers, those who had become Christian kings through God's Grace, kings through the choice of the people, and ceased to defend the church. The wrath of the Lord comes over them, when the people in their anger will exert their judgement over the kings who fell away from God, but similarly the wrath of the Lord will thereafter come as a judgement over the people who fell away from Him. All this, as we will see, as the judgements announced by the Catholic Apostolic church become more and more visible.

The revolution in France in 1870 and the communists in 1871 are but a prelude on a small scale, of all the drama which Europe soon will experience, which the seventh seal in Revelation, will describe to us as future events.

"And the time for judging the dead has come, and the time for rewarding your servants, the Prophets and saints and all who fear Your name, both small and great, and for destroying those who destroy the earth."

Also, the contents of this verse refer not to the general judgement of the world, but to the first Resurrection (Rev 20:5) and the judgement over the anti-Christian people, both of which will occur at the beginning of the Kingdom of Glory, belong to the future and are better described in further parts of Revelation. Then will the souls of the martyrs of Jesus, who still rest under the altar (fifth seal, Rev 6:9-11) resurrect to their lot in the end days, (Dan 12:2, 13. Rev 20:4) and their blood will be avenged from those, who destroyed the earth or the Christian ordinances.

After the twenty-four elders glorified God on earth, wherein they praised Him and thanked Him for what He had started on earth and what He would still bring about, John saw in Verse 19 **"Then God's Temple in Heaven**

375

was opened, and the ark of His covenant was seen within His Temple."
Would there still be any doubt in our reader whether our explanation, that
the beginning of the seventh trumpet (Rev 11:15-19) fulfils itself wholly
on this earth, is the truth, this last verse will convince him. *The temple of
God in Heaven*, is not to be found in high spheres, for there is no temple
there, *"For the Lord, the Almighty God Himself is the temple and the
Lamb."* (Rev 21:22). It is therefore on earth in the first Heaven, the church
of Christ, that we have to seek it and we already found the Christian
congregation, and the particular persons of the congregation from the
apostolic period, who had received through the fire baptism or the sealing,
the Holy Spirit, with His gifts inhabiting them, described to us by Paul as
the temple of the Living God (2 Cor.6:16. 1 Cor.6:19. 1 Cor.3:16.
Rom.8:9). When then, at the sounding of the seventh trumpet in 1835, this
New Testament temple is opened in the church, there must also have been
Christians, who received the baptism of fire of the Holy Spirit, but also
apostles, through who's laying on of hands Jesus Christ, the sealing angel,
gave them the Holy Spirit with all His gifts; for the ark of His covenant
became visible in His temple. The New Testament temple we already know
as believers is inhabited by the Holy Spirit. In these baptized with the Holy
Spirit, people were therefore the Ark of the covenant, the Ark of the
testimony was to be seen. But what was to be seen of the Ark of the
Covenant in its typical meaning:

1) It was covered with Gold, the image of truth;
2) It contained The Manna, the bread which came down from: Heaven
   (John 6:31-58), or the pure word of the Lord
3) The Tablets of Testimony, written by the Finger of God (Ex.
   32:16. Ex 34:1) or living stones (1 Pet 2:5), written not with ink, but
   by the Spirit of the Living God,(2 Cor 3:2, 3) and also the apostolic
   Christians served with the Holy Spirit, the living witnesses of the truth
   of the Apostolic church.
4) The Budding Staff of Aaron, the image of the Rich Priesthood, as
   planted in Christ (Heb 9:4. Num 17, 18. John 15:4-8)
5) That God Himself spoke through and from the Ark to the people.

When we summarize all that which must have been present in the sealed
people since the seventh trumpet, then they must:

1) Stand in the pure truth of Christianity (Gold);
2) Possess the pure Word of God as the bread of Life, which came down
   from Heaven, through the coming of Christ;

3) Stand in the right covenant with God and be as a letter of Christ, written by the Finger of God, prepared through the service of apostles, written by the Spirit of the Living God, not on   stone tables, but in the fleshly tables of the hearts   (2 Cor. 3:2, 3)
4) Have the right priesthood, not appointed by man, but by Christ Himself and planted in Him;
5) God must speak from and through them to His people, that is the Holy Spirit must speak through prophets.

Such Christians, such a Christian church, as she was in the first century, must therefore again be active as a new appearance in the church after 1830, next to the existing Christian churches.

In order to see, if and where these predictions can be fulfilled, the reader is urged to read on (pages 365-369), which church denomination or religious appearance claims; what her characteristics were, and which characteristics correspond to the above-described ones. None of the others can say this of themselves or dares testify of it. Only the Catholic Apostolic church testifies of herself. The investigation, however, whether this testimony is true, is not within our scope or plan, we only seek, where Revelation is fulfilled. The personal investigation, in how far the fulfilment is of value to the reader, is left entirely to himself and is his responsibility.

We however have enough ground to accept with probable cause, that the actions of the Catholic Apostolic Church in 1835, are the reestablished church in its original form, predicted 18 centuries ago, and that further:

1) The apostles of the risen Catholic Apostolic church form the angel, having the seal of the Living God (Rev 7:2), who would come in the seventh period.

2) That the sealed servants of God (verse 3), are the congregation of the 144000, who later (Rev 14:1-5) stand on Mount Zion with the Lamb, are the believers who received the Seal, the Holy Spirit, from Jesus Christ through the laying on of hands of these apostles.

3) That the apostles with the prophets of this church of Jesus Christ are the substitutes of John, who again prophesied, and will still prophecy before many peoples, and nations and tongues and kings. (Rev 9:11), just as they still do today in many countries and among many peoples, where they have their congregations, with all ministries and gifts of the Holy Spirit.

4) That they have measured the temple of God and those who worshipped therein since 1835. (Rev 11:1)

5) That they are elders, predicted in (Rev 11:16-18) of the seventh trumpet, and that they form the Ark of testimony together with the sealed in the temple of God: That they have received the Holy Spirit with His gifts and that the Lord Himself speaks through the Holy Spirit by means of their mouths (prophecy);

6) That the eating of the scroll (Rev 10:8-10) which is the testimony of the last days, is revealed to them, to be announced to the whole world.

The likelihood of this all becomes even greater when we compare the similarity between the Old Testament and that of the Christian church:

The second exodus from Babylon under Ezra.

The second exodus from Babylonian Protestantism.

The second temple is completed, in a time of anxiety.

The second Christian temple is completed, in a time of earthquakes.

The stone with 7 facets on the temple. (Zech 3:9).

The cornerstone Jesus Christ with the 7 gifts of the Holy Spirit.

The Glory of the latter house will be greater than the former.

The Glory of this last church will be greater than the original.

The prophecies concerning the coming of Christ.

The prophecies concerning Christ's imminent return.

In case then, that the history of the church since 1830 is the true fulfilment of that which Revelation predicts, then it cannot be doubted, that the Realm of Glory herewith begins to develop on earth. Revelation describes it clearly later on, that in this Realm of Glory, with the happy life and spiritual condition of the people, the establishment of the church will be, similar to what we found in the Apostolic church, and that Christ will again personally rule in the church on earth, through His four reestablished ministries, Apostles, Prophets Evangelists and Shepherds, and in the state through His Royal Priests. Then it will be a true Realm of Christ and a true Christ government; Peace on earth and goodwill to man!

But since on earth these happy outward and inward conditions have not yet developed, it must be clear to everyone, that, in case everything the Apostolic believers claim to possess in prophecy and other gifts, is true, - in case they are truly the Temple of God and the Ark of Testimony seen in them, then also for them the day of the Lord has begun to rise, and the kingdom of the world already in them has become the Lord's and His anointed. But then the angels (the stars) and teachers of this church already begin to shine in the Heaven of the church as the morning stars of the Great Day of Peace, who announce the coming of the sun of righteousness, while deep darkness still covers the rest of Christendom, and Satan with his fallen angels out of the abyss already rise in conflict against the realm of light.

The last escape, that this part of the seventh trumpet is not fulfilled yet, but could well come to fulfilment, this last escape or excuse is denied us through the last words of (verse 19): **"And there were flashes of lightning, rumblings, peals of thunder, an earthquake, and heavy hail."** Simultaneously therefore with or just after the actions of the predicted church in Apostolic form, these flashes of lightning rumblings (voices), Peals of thunder, earthquakes, and hail, must occur, and we have already heard the rumbling in the seventh seal, since 1830, as the voices, of the Lord, but also as the voices of seducing spirits. We heard the thunderings of the glorification of the Lord's name, but also of His being denied. We saw the lightning flashes of the return of the Lord, but also the lightning of Satan in the denial of the eternal Gospel. And also in 1830 we saw the earthquake begin, increasing continuously up to our time.

But with all this, we also saw, how the Catholic Apostolic church began to develop in 1831, to openly confess before the whole world in 1835-1838, and bring her Apostolic testimony concerning the condition of the Christian church, and her prophetic witnessing of the imminent return of Christ to all religious and worldly leaders. It would be a wilful distortion or denial of the truth, to expect in the future, that which already lies behind us or still occurs around us, because the great hail started in 1830 and we live in its fiercest destructions. Did the Christian reader not already understand, that just as the gospel preaching in the first trumpet was a destructive judgement? (hail) for the Roman heathen religion and state politics, that similarly also the modern heathendom, the rising beast of anti-Christiandom, exerted a destructive judgement (great hail) since 1830 over Christian, social and political institutions, over church denominations and belief? Did not the anointed kings disappear, and is not therewith in 1830 the kingship by God's grace abolished[49] to give way to transition, to the rule of the people, the constitutional kings, who can only act according to a constitution or fundamental law? Are there not even under the ruling royal families, those who rose from the revolution? Did not liberalism ban all religious classes from schools? Is not everywhere the motto: Religious-less schools? Did not since 1830 rationalism, thereafter liberalism, then modernism, bring the protestant church in such a condition, that they (except for a few believing teachers) preached a so-called Christendom, without Jesus Christ, God's Christ?

Did not Popedom itself dig its own grave by its proclamation of infallibility, and thereby gave the Roman Church prey to dissolution?

In one word; wherever we look, do we not see in church and state and society, popular belief and way of thinking, everywhere, a growing demolition, dissolution and destruction of the existing order, as a destructive hail-storm over Europe, to prepare for the day of the wrath of the Almighty God? Not in vain does Revelation here speak of a great hail, against the hail of the first trumpet, because in the course of less than half a century, it caused almost a total reversal in church and state, while the first hail required three centuries. The Christian church is already nearly destroyed by the anti-Christian power.

He, who hopes for her restoration and victory flatters himself with an expectation, which is in total contradiction with the word of God and this prophecy of Jesus Christ. In His Revelation He names the degenerated Christian churches, collectively, the great Babylon (Rev 16:19), the great whore, which sits on many waters (Rev 17:1) or peoples, and multitudes, and nations, and tongues (Rev 18:15). They have become a habitation of devils and a preserving place for all impure spirits, therefore the voice sounds also in the seventh vial in our time from the Heaven of the church; **"Come out of her, My people !"** –believers in each church denomination.- **"So that you do not TAKE PART in her sins and so that you do not share in her plagues (Rev 18:2, 4)".** Because on her, God executed the judgement of the apostles and prophets (Rev 18:20) and the execution of this judgement has already commenced. Whosoever denies this, is free to do so. But then the apostles and prophets, who have spoken this judgement over them, must already have come. The history of the church did not

---

[49] Charles X, kings of France, was the last anointed king. Through the revolution in 1830 he abdicated and was succeeded by Louis Philip, first king by the choice of the people. Thus began all remarkable events from 1830, after the half hour silence.

anywhere allow us to find apostles and prophets, other than in the Catholic Apostolic Church, which since 1830 arose in England.

Herewith the introduction to the seventh trumpet is completed. What still occurs under this seventh trumpet, we will learn from the three following chapters of Revelation (Rev 12, 13,14). We have however often spoken about the Catholic Apostolic Church, about her performance since 1830 and about her testimony before kings and nations; we have in this seventh trumpet already often seen, that only she can form the one whose preaching and her testimony are the sound of the seventh trumpet or the gospel preaching of the seventh angel, that we would like in a few sentences, and to inform our reader about the origin, the form and the teaching of this church. We can only derive from her own open communication, from the facts, which cannot be denied, and the reader will be able to judge, if this whole work is the result of imagination and fanaticism or that it is indeed the work of God; as Revelation teaches us.

In the seventh seal we have seen, how during the silence of approximately half an hour (from 1815 to 1830), many prayers went up from the believers in Europe, for the reestablishment of the church in her original form and power, for the outpouring of the Holy Spirit and His gifts in the church. We saw also that Christ brought these before the Throne of the Father, and that He consequently threw down the fire of the Holy Spirit on earth, as in the first apostolic time on Pentecost.

What occurred thereafter in the kingdom of God on earth?

In the summer of 1829, a pious man died in Scotland, who on his death bed, as if in a trance, shouted, that it was revealed unto him the awesome mystery, the imminent reestablishment of the gift of prophecy in the congregation.

In the year 1830 in different places in Scotland, the gifts of Healing and the gifts of Prophecy, revealed themselves simultaneously, Christians hearing these rumours travelled from London and were convinced. In London, prayer meetings were conducted for further revelations of these powers and gifts of the Holy Spirit, whereupon in April 1831 the voice of prophecy through the Holy Spirit was heard. The first words, after a silence of 15 centuries, spoken by God through a human mouth were: **"Behold! The Bridegroom comes, go out to meet Him."**

Up until now the voice of the Holy Spirit had only been heard in particular prayer meetings. In October 1831 it happened for the first time in a Sunday morning service in a church building of the Scotch preacher Irving in London. On the same day in the evening service, while Irving, in consequence of what took place in the morning service, spoke of (1

Cor.12), the power of the Holy Spirit revealed itself, in that one of the worshippers began to speak in tongues.

The great, but also the only gain, that Irving contributed towards the Apostolic church, is that he recognized the voice of the Holy Spirit in the prophecies, and in spite of all the efforts of his church, he did not want to quench this voice fearing to go against the prophecies and the Holy Spirit. (1 Thess.5:19, 20). Because such scenes did not agree with the church regulations, Irving was disrobed from his ministry by the National Scottish church in London. Although he died in 1834, the Apostolics were nicknamed Irvingites. This was the origin of the Apostolic church.

Those who believed the truth of these revelations of the Holy Spirit, gathered in prayer and in bible studies, whereby streams of light upon the word of God were poured out through prophecies, and yet unknown depths and meanings were revealed, especially on the Old Testament.

As the believers grew in knowledge, wisdom and strength to bear everything that naturally goes with human weakness and misconception, the Lord showed more and more through prophecies the outward form which His congregation should take on, until in October 1832 a lawyer from London, member of the Episcopal church, was called as apostle through prophecy. Soon thereafter the number of called apostles grew to 12, and, at the same time prophets, evangelists, and shepherds were called to the four-fold ministry of Christ, while angels or bishops were appointed as heads of forming congregations. All the persons, who carried those ministries, were called through prophecies and ordained through the laying on of hands. Together they formed the Elders of the congregations. The deacons serving the poor were chosen by the congregation and ordained by the apostles.

The above was drawn from an interesting work by Mr. Is. Capadose: *A Page from the History of the church of Christ.*

We may think what we will, concerning this origin, but it is remarkable, that we find the reestablishing therein of the four ministries of Christ, such as can be seen in the vision of Ezekiel and Revelation, where John describes the first seal, seen as the four Cherubim just as they existed in the first century of the church (Eph 4:11-16).

Concerning the authenticity of the gift of prophecy, solemnly assured by apostolic and other respectable and credible men, is so strongly doubted by their enemies, denounced and mocked, it becomes difficult to believe, that so many congregations of the church of England, that over fifty congregations in North- Germany, except the remaining in South- Germany, Switzerland, France etc, such an involuntary self-deception or intentional deceit could have taken place during nearly 40 years without the deception being discovered or the eyes of the congregations themselves would be opened, and the whole matter would end in nothing. The history of the church clearly shows, how such human heresies and supposed prophecies could never ever last that long, even less, establish itself in such a steadfast form and spread over so many divergent countries.

One example of prophecy and the gift of tongues we would like to share with the reader. The first is a prophecy uttered by a simple servant girl. We can vouch for its genuineness.

"Zion thou beautiful City of peace! What salvation is allotted to you, Zion, thou Bride of the Lamb! Keep your hearts pure, serve no false Gods,

but give your heart wholly to your Jesus, Behold, as I sent My Son into this world to suffer and to die, so that He could free you from the power and the punishment of sin, behold so will I send Him again soon, to lead you, His Bride, into His Father's House, before the terrible tribulation will come. Then you will know no more strife or pain, but then you will experience perfect peace. But Woe! Woe you, who heard the voice calling and yet did not come. Woe! Woe you, because terrible will be the tribulation. It will be difficult for you, to remain steadfast in the Faith. Flee therefore to Zion, flee to your Jesus, that He may lead you to the Father's House before the terrible tribulation shall come. Come therefore to your Jesus, for He comes soon.

Come! Yes, come! For terrible will be the tribulation."

Concerning the gift of tongues, we find in the "Bible dictionary for the Christian people," of H. Zeller, translated into the Netherlands by J.A.G. Westhoff, on the article Tongues, page 569 the following comments about the speaking in tongues, experienced by an eye witness in the Irvingian congregation (in England)."

"The whole body of the speaker is shaken as if by an electric shock; he experiences cramp-like convulsions. Then follows a stream of strange words, mostly in Hebrew sounding words, issuing from the mouth of the speaker. They are mostly repeated three times and uttered with exceptional vehemence and sharpness. Thereupon follows a shorter or longer address in English, in a reduced vehement tone, and consisting of earnest and severe admonitions, of terrible warnings, but also of short balming words of comfort. Lastly a deep silence and slow relaxation."

To better understand this phenomenon it serves well to read the foregoing said page 568 of the dictionary and page 569, "about the speaking in tongues."

What is individualistic in the teaching of this Apostolic church, what differentiates her from the believing church denominations, we will allow her enemies to enlighten us. The reader will see therefore how far this, positively not-so-favourable judgement and information corresponds with that which Revelation has taught us and will still teach us concerning God's actions with His judgement over the church. From the Lehrbuch der Kirchengeschichte von Dr. Joh. Heinr. Kurtz (6 aufl .Mittau 1808), who is freely hostile against this church, and ranks her amongst the sects and heretics, we find about "The Catholic Apostolic church or Irvingites" page 755 the following: "Most come out of their new Revelation, the promise of the very near return of the Lord. It can occur any day, any hour. This will commence with the first Resurrection (Rev.20:5) and the simultaneous change of the living saints (The wise virgins, that is: the Irvingites) who are taken up to the Lord in the clouds, and are united with Him through the wedding of the Lamb. They are protected while the antichrist persecutes the remaining Christians (the foolish virgins) who only can be saved by torture, and executes the judgement over the Babel of Revelation (the remaining Christian churches). After the total yet short-lived victory of the antichrist, the Lord appears visibly amidst some of the resurrected saints. The kingdom of the antichrist with Christ 1000 years on the curse-free earth. Thereafter Satan will be loosened, for a short period, and he causes a great falling away. Finally follows the fall of Satan, the second Resurrection and the judgement day. The Apostolic church rejects the Roman teaching of the bloodless repetition (in communion) of the bloody sacrifice (of Christ) as well as the teaching of transubstantiation. (She accepts the communion with Luther and believers on the sacramental communion with the body and blood of Christ) by principle she goes out through her missionaries to the already believing, and does not involve herself with mission work amongst the heathen, since she claims, not to have been sent to the heathen or to unbelievers, but only to assemble and save the believers".

This last would again relate to what we found in (Rev 7:2-8, page 352) concerning the commission of the serving Angel to the servants of God.

About the sealing the very hostile and mocking George Kreitmar mentions in his "Apostles and Prophets of the old and new times," Amsterdam H.De Hoogh 1867, as the teaching of the Apostolic church, page 30: "The Apostles are the highest authority of the Catholic Apostolic Church, the source and keepers or stewards of the teaching, those who impart the Holy Spirit through the laying-on of hands,- sealing- whereby the believers received many gifts and power from the Spirit" so that they;

(page 37) imbued with the sealing and the salving of the Holy Spirit, can be saved from the snares of the antichrist and of the outpouring of God's wrath over the world of the ungodly.

Concerning the walk of life and the personal characteristics of the apostolic clergy, Kurtz in his above-mentioned work gives on pages 756 and 757, the following testimony. "Morally religious earnestness, coupled with dignity, goodness, humbleness and personal amiability distinguish their working representatives in Germany in an advantageous manner. Likewise, it cannot be denied that irrespective of their Apostleship without foundation and that which goes with it, from their views, their judgement and their striving, mostly in unexpected ways, they seem to have healthy, clear, sober and real church sense".

This last testimony of Kurtz, of healthy, clear, sober and real church sense strongly contradicts the judgement of heresy, which he himself wrote against them. For that matter with each writer, we find a totally different judgement, and seldom have so many diverging judgements been expressed over a single church denomination. It is therefore inconceivable for us Protestants, with our enlightened, clear and understandable Evangelistic teaching, that in our days, apostles must come again, and that they with their believers would stand in a higher communion with the Lord of the church, and not only would have higher promises and advantages than the remaining Evangelical churches but also could boast of clear insight and clear perception of also that which will occur in the future with the church and the believers, while these matters, for Protestants, we concur, are very obscure. When, however, we consider, that in 1835, when no one could foresee the present condition, through their extended testimony concerning, the condition of the Christian churches, her total speedy decay etc., has since then appallingly and at an unbelievably fast pace become truth,- when we also consider, what Revelation has already predicted for our time, and what history caused us to find only in the Apostolic church (the sealing, the gifts of the Holy Spirit, apostles, prophets, the measuring of the Temple, the seventh trumpet, etc....) then we become careful, not to condemn her without further earnest investigation. The praising testimony of Kurtz about the walk and acts of the Apostolic reminds us of the word of the Lord: *"For the tree is known by its fruit."* And our conclusion, whether this is truly from God, and if her teaching concerning the last things and the imminent times are truly teaching from God, can only be ascertained when we know, what Revelation still predicts for the times ahead, and when we compare this with that which the Apostolic church taught and preached since 1835. This is certain, she did not do it because she understood

Revelation and its fulfilment, and to arbitrarily accommodate and thereby commit a terrible blasphemy. If she had only understood Revelation, then this interpretation would have gone out of her; that it would have been her duty, her glory, her own righteousness, to preach to the nations, what the Spirit hath to say to the congregation about it, and what the Lord wanted to show unto His servants. She however did not do this, and from that, we may assume, that she only understood parts of Revelation. It was possibly exactly the intention and the way of the Lord, that the whole meaning of Revelation, which so prominently indicates the veracity of the Apostolic Church as truly God's works in our days, did not originate from her, but from outside her. God Himself stands above His own rules and can give light, where He deems it profitable and necessary. And if she is the church of the Lord in the last days, then He is the true and faithful, who will show this to the world. And herewith enough said about the Apostolic church, whose origin, form and teaching, we for our purpose have learned to know sufficiently.

THE SUN WOMAN AND HER CHILD

> So also, when you see these things taking place,
> you know that the kingdom of God is near.
> Luke 21:31

Rev 12:1-5a, Rev 12:7-9

Verse 1. "A great portent appeared in Heaven: A woman clothed with the sun, with the moon under her feet, and on her head a crown of twelve stars!"

This great sign, which John sees, is not the woman only, but her fate and history, to which the greatest part of chapter seven is dedicated. While this event takes place in the seventh period, the heaven, wherein John sees this happen, is the first earthly heaven: the church.

Similar to all the events in the seventh period, the fate of the woman must also have begun after 1830, at the end of the half-hour silence.

Who is this woman?

The covenant of Jehovah with His people is compared by the Lord Himself and by His prophets to a marriage covenant: and the desertion from Him by His people as a breach of faith or adultery; (Deut 31:16, Isaiah 54:5, Isaiah 1:25, Isaiah 50:1, Jer.2:2, Ezec16 and 23) Also, in the New Testament, John the Baptist uses this image, where he says of Jesus: *"He who has the Bride, is the Bridegroom."* (John 3:29) The Lord Himself (Matt 9:15, Matt 25:1, 5, 6, and 10) is *"The Bridegroom"*. This is still taken further by Paul in (2 Cor. 11:2) and especially in (Eph 5:23-32), as the great mystery of the relationship between Christ and His congregation.

The woman of (Rev 12:1) is therefore the congregation of the Lord, as she is seen after 1830 in comparison to the congregation from the sixth period, which we left in the sixth vial (Rev 16:13), where the three unclean spirits entered into her, who further misled her to fall away from God, whereby in the seventh period (Rev 17) she appears as the great whore.

Indeed, we already met the sun woman in the seventh seal, as the multitude of believers sorrowful about the apostasy of the church, earnestly praying for the reestablishment of the church of Christ, for the outpouring of the Holy Spirit, for the promised latter rain, seeking Jesus and Him alone.

387

They stood there, silently developed as reborn children of God, the Bride of Christ the woman clothed with the sun. The sun is the Light of the world (Jesus Christ). They came out of Babylon in obedience to the cry *"Come out of her My people."* Imbued with the Holy Spirit and all His gifts she stood elevated above the rest of Christianity (the moon). The moon is a heavenly body, a planet, which in comparison with the sun, has no light of its own, but only reflects the light of the sun. This is a perfect image of the so-called Christians who only reflect the light of Christ, seeming to be Christians but in effect walking in darkness. Her feet, the Evangelist and Shepherd ministries, travel over the moon to save those believers who still have to come out of Babylon and be sealed.

"Upon her head a crown of twelve stars".

The head of the woman or the congregation of Jesus is the Lord Himself. (Eph 5:23, Cor 1:18)

A crown, we learned to know (Vol.1) as the image of the redeemed souls won for Christ! Here, we have a living crown of twelve stars, reflecting the twelve-fold Apostle ministry of Christ. Remembering the sealing (Rev 7) with the exclusion of the tribe of Dan, the twelve tribes of the New Testament Israel together form the Sun woman from which her son will be born or the Catholic Apostolic church. The twelve stars are the sealing Angels, the living apostles given back to the church or the sun woman.

The sun woman, with the moon under her feet and the crown of twelve stars on her head, is thus the congregation of believers, such as John saw her in 1832, when the Lord had given back to His church the Apostle ministry.

Verse 2 **"She was pregnant and was crying out in birth pangs, in the agony of giving birth".**

The commission of the woman, the church, was to find and gather the bride of Christ and prepare her for the great day of His return; She had to fight against unbelief, superstition and all the human reasoning of the existing church, also to overcome the three unclean spirits and the increasing moral decay. She had to lead the fallen believers out of Babylon and incorporate them into the newly formed Apostolic church through the rebirth by the Holy Spirit.

This task was in opposition to Satan and his servants as well as under much prayer, pains of persecution and mockery. From this, the pangs of giving birth to something totally new.

Moreover, the reestablished gifts of the Holy Spirit, the prophetic calling of Apostles and Prophets, coupled with much effort, prejudice and human misunderstanding, must have been a highly strange phenomenon in the church.

Verse 3. **"Then another portent appeared in Heaven; a great red dragon, with seven heads and ten horns and seven diadems on his head"**.

The dragon is the old serpent, the devil, Satan (Rev 20:2) red from evil hatred and wrath, (Eph 6:16), because he is aware that here something will be born, which will disturb his kingdom. He appears in the Heaven of the church after 1830 to hinder the birth of the woman's child, not in the form of a serpent, but as an angel of light in and through the deceitful servants (2 Cor 11:14,15), who repudiate the testimony of the woman concerning the decay of the church. While the dragon represents himself in the church as a spiritual principle, his seven heads and ten horns are also to be taken spiritually. The heads with royal crowns are the image of princes, elders and important men in the church.

Seven, as the number of the full revelation of God on earth, has, just as all images of the Holy Spirit, a similar meaning in the opposite sense; thus the full revelation of Satan on earth (Luke 11:28).

It was not the Holy Spirit, but the dragon who spoke through the princes and officials in the state churches, when they opposed the effect of the fire of the Holy Spirit.

The horns of the dragon are the image of royal power (Dan 7:7, 8, 21, 24. Rev 17:12). Ten is the perfect number, the number of the Kingdom of God. The ten horns or powers of Satan represent his total power in the realm of darkness, such as it began to reveal itself in the beginning of the Christian period (1830) later to come to total fullness (Rev 17:12).

In the established state churches, the father of lies spoke through the kings as head of the state church, and through its clergy, synods etc - as the horns, with the claim; that *we are the old, unadulterated, church. We have the Kingdom of God in our church; we have the power in God's realm.* It was the old voice of the dragon (Luke 4:6,7): "All this power will I give thee, and the glory of them. If thou therefore wilt worship me, all shall be thine". Anything developing apart from us is heresy and fanaticism. We, Roman and Protestant infallible popes are the only ones who can decide what is religion, what God's will is and what He wants.

Verse 4. **"His tail swept down a third of the stars of Heaven and threw them to the earth":** This tail or false teachers of the dragon swept away the third part of the stars of Heaven, or the believing and susceptible to the influence of the Holy Spirit sanctified teachers, and threw them out of

God's realm (the Heaven) down to earth. They decided to stay loyal to their various denominations.

"Then the dragon, now endowed with all earthly power in the church, stood before the woman, who was about to bear a child so that he might devour her child as soon as it was born". Since the reestablishment of the Apostolic Church after 1830, the dragon's greatest interest is to undo the works of the Sun woman and attack the reborn children of God in any way he can, trying to undermine their faith and confidence in God and in Jesus Christ, pointing out the weaknesses of the bearers of blessing, who after all are also sinners. Jesus warned against such tactics in (Matt 24:23) *"Then if any man shall say to you, lo, here is Christ, or there; believe it not!!"*

We now leave the Sun woman as she develops throughout the next three centuries up to the great Day of the return of Christ.

THE RISE OF THE ANTICHRIST

> So likewise ye, when ye shall see all these things,
> know that it is near, even at the door.
> Matt24:33

<u>Rev 13:1- 3</u>

Verse 1. **"And I stood upon the sand of the sea, and I saw a beast rise up out of the sea, having seven heads and ten horns."** This beast, even though it has ten horns and seven heads, just like the dragon in (Rev 12), is not the dragon himself, but another apparition, while, in (verse 2), this beast received its royal power from the dragon, the devil. It is, therefore, just as we said with the Sun woman, the worldly state power, wherein and through which Satan reveals himself, just as in Rev 12, he revealed himself in the clergy of the churches. The beast in its visible form has ten horns and seven heads; seven and ten we know in their meaning with regard to the Kingdom of God. The beast must therefore, when it rises, still appear to be Christian, at least carry the outward form and name of Christian, but be anti-Christian inwardly, just as we saw this in the church under the influence of the dragon.

Where do we have to seek the beast? What is it?

Verse 2. **"And the beast which I saw was like unto a leopard, and his feet were as the feet of a bear, and his mouth as the mouth of a lion."** Daniel saw four consecutive kingdoms in the form of four beasts, who would form four consecutive powers on the earth. The first was the Chaldean-Babylonian, the second was Persian and Medes, the third the Greek kingdom and the fourth the Roman Empire. This last one would continue to exist in various forms until dominion and glory and Kingship were given to Jesus Christ (Dan 7:7-14). Revelation predicts the history of the New Testament people of God under the fourth beast or the Roman Empire until Jesus Christ is crowned King.

The territory of the beast or the Roman Empire principally extended over the whole of Europe. It is therefore foolish to limit the scene of Revelation to the borders of the old Roman heathen Empire as some writers do. Revelation is not given to the heathen, but to the Christians, and for as far as they spread over Europe, this is the scene of Revelation. Thereto also belong to Russia as the Greek-Christian Empire, and Turkey as the former Greek-Christian Empire, although currently under Islam's power.

Of the remaining parts of the world, Asia and Africa, except the profitable regions along the coasts of the Mediterranean Sea, are excluded just as the Americas and Australia, which were discovered in the last centuries and were never part of the Roman Empire.

Europe, is almost a totally Christian part of the world, and the main power of the whole world is, therefore, the scene of Revelation, but we have to seek for the beast in Europe.

We know *the beast* as the fourth world power; it here consists of all the kings or state powers of Europe, as they rose from the fourth or Roman Empire and reigned after 1830. We have already seen *the beast* rising as the Roman Emperors in the first vial, in the fifth vial, as the anti-Christian Roman popes, in the seventh period we again find it as the anti-Christian world powers in Europe.

It is totally impossible to understand the full meaning of *the beast* in our time, as meant by Revelation, and of *its rising from the sea*, without comparing it with the Christian kingship, according to God's order. While here we refer to what was said in the second candlestick (Vol.1), we will in a few words describe the characteristics of the kingship through God's grace.

There is no power than from God. It was already said from the heathen Roman Emperors :(Rom 13:1-6), the authority is the servant of God, thus: "Fear God, honour the king." Kings therefore received their power from God and must rule according to God's laws. For this reason, since they became Christians they received their crowns, in the House of the Lord, from the hands of the clergy as also the salving and swore to reign faithfully over the people and the fulfilling of all their royal duties. Through this, they also became the representatives of Christ on their thrones, until He accepts His own Kingdom.

By receiving the salving from the hands of the priest of God, they subjected themselves also in spiritual matters as simple lay people to the spiritual power, just as those who were subject to the kings in earthly issues. They did not rule over each other but next to each other and formed a unity in Christ.

The kings are given by God for the people, and not the other way. They must be Christian rulers, not oppressors, but fathers to the people, not for one but for all.

To be anointed and crowned, and reign in this way, is true Christian kingship through God's grace. All the rest is kingship through violence or the choice of the people. Christianity however produced few true Christian kings. They have mostly misused the God-given power, forgotten His commandments and become oppressors of their people. Eventually, the angered people drove away the successors of these kings and replaced them with kings of their own choice.

King Charles X of France was, as far as we know, the last anointed king (Rheims 1824). From 1830, beginning with Louis Philip, kings started to be chosen by the people rose to power and the constitutional laws replaced God's commandments. These anti-Christian powers form the beast.

This beast came out of the sea. It would be difficult to give a better image concerning the state powers since 1830 than used by John here. He stood on the sand of the sea, here the sea of nations.

Just as the sea, throws everything which floats and foams on it upon the shores, John also saw what drifted upon the tossing sea of nations, the people voting for their rulers and representatives who drifted from the sea of nations. Let us remember that we live in the Laodicean period, the period of Democracy.

To name a few, Charles X 1830, the last heir of the Bourbons, was dethroned and Louis Philip chosen by the people replaced him. Similarly, King Bernadotte of Sweden and Norway.

In 1830, Belgium also became an independent kingdom as well as Greece, and their kings were chosen by vote. Also in 1848, Napoleon III ruled first as president, and later as Emperor. Also, Victor Emanuel, king of Italy and his son Amadeus were placed on the throne of Isabelle of Spain.

In one word, it is remarkable to note how, since 1830, the anti-Christian driving and striving revealed itself, and an appalling change in the political conditions of Europe and the power of European princes took place. This did not all occur at once, but developed until having reached a certain level, the total change appeared as a fact in history.

"And upon his horns ten crowns." The European state powers must therefore consist of seven heads and ten horns, and on the last ten royal crowns. The seven heads according to (Rev 17:9) are seven mountains or realms. We know that the heads or mountains (Vol.1) as greater and the horns or hills as smaller powers, and as the latter wear royal crowns, they are personal kings. Since 1872, Europe consisted of seven greater powers and ten smaller kingdoms.

The heads are not said to wear royal crowns as is the case with the ten horns, because in 1870 France became a republic. Switzerland, as a republic, has no crowned king and thus falls away from the horns.

The king of Hungary is already accounted for in the Empire of Austria. The king of Sweden is also king of Norway and notwithstanding the forming of the German Empire in 1871, the kings of Beiere, Saxony and Württemberg remained independent kings in their own states and must therefore be recognized as crowned horns. Rumania, and its prince Charles, are subjected to Turkey and therefore do not belong to the horns.

GREATER POWER	SMALLER KINGS
The Emperor Of Russia	The King Of Sweden And Norway
The Emperor Of Germany	The King Of Denmark
The Emperor Of Austria	The King Of Netherlands
The Republic Of France	The King Of Belgium
The Queen Of England	The King Of Wuttemberg
The King Of Italy	The King Of Beiren
The Sultan Of Turkey	The King Of Saxony
	The King Of Greece
	The King Of Spain
	The King Of Portugal

If this condition in Europe is remarkable, it becomes even more remarkable, when we consider that under the seventh vial, shortly under the great earthquake (Rev 16:18. Rev 17:3, 12.), the kings will fall, and that at that moment the seven heads and ten horns without crowns are already present in Europe.

On the surface, it appears very simple and natural, that when the ten kings fall, ten republics come into existence. This is however not so, because some kings had two different countries under their jurisdiction, besides Switzerland must also be counted as a republic.

We only have to imagine the ten kings falling away, and Europe automatically resorts to seven greater and ten smaller republics, the latter consisting partly of other countries.

Austria divided into two republics, Austria and Hungary since both are totally different kingdoms with individual legislation and only have in common that the Emperor of Austria is king of Hungary. Similarly, Sweden and Norway also split into two republics, and Switzerland must also be counted among the republics.

Beiren, Württemberg and Saxony completely disappeared as independent kingdoms, and are included in the united Germany.

Europe will now, in 1872, consist of the following seven greater and ten smaller republics:

GREATER POWERS	SMALLER KINGS
France	Spain
England	Portugal
Germany	Belgium
Russia	Netherlands
Austria	Sweden
Italy	Norway
Turkey	Denmark
	Hungary
	Switzerland
	Greece

These greater powers and smaller kingdoms together form the beast that rises out of the sea of nations and encompasses the territory, occupied by the Roman Empire in the days of Jesus Christ. As long as there are Emperors and kings who are repentant believing Christians, the anti-Christian beast is forming itself and is still rising out of the sea of nations. As soon as they all become unbelievers and anti-Christian, then also as in Mene, Tekel (Dan 5:26,27), the moment when God's wrath will affect the rulers and the judgement of the people (Laodicea) will be fulfilled in a declaration of a people government. But in a people government, the antichrist is totally revealed. In answer to the question of whether in Europe the powers are already anti-Christian, Revelation gives us the answer in (verse 1).

"And on its heads were blasphemous names". Blasphemy, we know, is the falling away from God and placing human authority above God. (Vol.1)

From the list of names and principals of the seven greater powers in Europe, the reader can decide for himself, who carries a name of blasphemy.

1 The Emperor of Russia is head of the Russian-Greek church.

2 The Emperor of Germany, Archbishop of the Evangelistic- state church in Prussia

3 The Emperor of Austria, Apostolic king of Hungary.

4 The republic of France is the country of revolution.

5 The Queen of England head of the English church

6 The king of Italy is born out of the revolution.

7 The Sultan of Turkey, head of Islam.

It is also remarkable that during 1835-1838, the Apostolic church published and distributed their testimony to all clergy and rulers of states, stating that they all had left the ways of God, and had misused the power God had given them, and if they would not repent and return to God's instituted ordinances, His judgement by means of the people would be executed. The fulfilment which we since then already could experience is our guarantee, that the commission of the Apostolic church, was truly a God-given commission and a guarantee of the further fulfilment of her testimony.

Verse 3. **"One of its heads seemed to have received a death blow, but its mortal wound had been healed."** The heads we know to be the present seven greater powers of Europe. Rev 17:9-11 will presently show us, that the seven heads must be considered in twofold meaning: 1. As the current seven great powers of Europe. (Rev13:1) and, 2. As the seven consecutive mountains or state churches, of which five are already gone, one still is and the seventh has not come yet.

If our explanation is true, then we must find, in both cases, a wounded head back in history, whose deadly wounds are healed in our time, firstly one of the current greater powers in Europe, which seemed destroyed and revived, and secondly, one of the past five mountains or state religions, which is re-established.

At the first question, we have to remark, that with the beginning of this event of the seventh period, thus before 1830, this great power was already wounded, which wound must have been inflicted in the previous or even earlier period, and which was healed in the seventh period.

Indeed, the German Empire, established by Charles the Great in 803 B.C., had gradually lost its power and was destroyed in 1806 by Napoleon 1. In that year, the Emperor of Austria abdicated as Emperor of Germany and the German Empire came to an end. In 1815 the Vienna Congress declared *the German Empire to be dead forever* and divided the German country and states. Since then, Germany was divided into many small states by French politics and kept divided by internal differences as if bleeding to death, until, through the French declaration of war in 1870-1871 Germany suddenly united and by the glorious victories of Germany, the German Empire was restored in full power.

This German Empire is currently the most powerful state of Europe in material and intellectual power, and the fulcrum of Europe shifted from

France to Germany in 1871. The great role of France in the balance of power has ended.

The German Empire is the only power in Europe which fulfils the prediction completely and it is clear that Germany currently leads Europe, and as we will see will continue to do so. *"The whole earth follows the beast"*. The one healed head of which the verse begins to speak, becomes *"The Beast"* in the same verse, and shows thereby, that the healed head, stands as the most important and the leader of the remaining anti-Christian states, and according to (Verse 7): "It was given authority over every tribe and people and language and nation, the personification of the whole beast, and that in him the anti-Christian principle and the whole anti-Christian power will be brought together and will emanate from him". For all that, Germany appears to be ripe for this, under a future anti-Christian ruler. However, much godliness and Christian faith there may still be in Germany; nevertheless, no matter how much the narrow connection between the state and Evangelistic church is still supported and maintained, the overall thinking of the people, just as in other countries, has become anti-Christian.

Germany has become the breeding ground of knowledge, of Philosophy, the fruitful breeding ground of scientific onslaughts against the Gospel, the mighty source of Pantheism, the breeding ground of all sorts of Pantheistic societies and of Freemasonry, whose lodges can be found in the smallest cities and even in villages, who, under their brotherhood count a number of protestant clergy, then no other country is more suited than Germany, to become the focal point of the coming legalized anti-Christian religion. What this will be, Revelation will presently teach us.

We do not stand alone in those feelings. Dittmar already says in his World History in connection with the newest materialism: "In this way, one of the scientific fights has been prepared, which normally precedes a social upheaval, and accompanies it. Just as the first struggle of this type, by the English Atheists in the 17th century, resulted in a revolution, the second struggle, that of the French Encyclopaedists in the 18th century, resulted in the French revolution, so it appears that the third and severest will come out of Germany, in order to shake the nations of Europe in their deepest principles and turn these upside-down, if this danger is not prevented by God".

The great God will not prevent this danger but allow the disastrous consequences of the falling away from God and the apostasy to befall the sinful Europe. The English Atheists of which Dittmar speaks, were actually Deists (see page 268 Vol. 1); the French Encyclopaedists, were Atheists

(Vol.1). Behold the unclean spirits out of the mouth of the dragon and the beast. The third will go out of Germany, the spirit of the false prophet, Pantheism. (Vol.1).

In this first meaning, the wounded head of the beast is therefore healed. In this second meaning as one of the five already fallen mountains (Rev 17:10) which will be re-established, it meant, *the beast, that was, is not, and will rise again out of the bottomless pit.* (Rev 17:8,11) On investigating which one it can or must be, we have to remember, that it formerly existed, but did not exist at the beginning of the seventh period but had already fallen *before the seventh period in one of the first five periods*, while the sixth, or the mountain of the Protestant state power still exists (Verse 10). The three papal mountains are thereby excluded, while they had so far not been inflicted with a deadly wound, and if one would take the invasion of Rome in 1870, as the wound by the sword, this was only inflicted well in the seventh period. John however saw, that at the beginning of the seventh period, this head <u>was</u> already wounded.

Also, the second or Christian-Roman Mountain cannot be considered, since this one did not receive a wound by the sword, not naturally, nor spiritually, and moreover, had already been revived in the Protestant-Christian state church and all the sectarian disputes.

There only remains one mountain, the first mountain, the mountain of *Heathen*-Roman power, which in its end-form of the Roman Empire can rise again. And this one had received a deadly wound by Constantine, both by the war sword and by the sword of the Word of God.

This heathen religion and state were mortally wounded by the Gospel of Christ. (Vol.1).

"In amazement, the whole earth followed the beast". Just as the whole world was amazed at the great victory of Germany in 1871, and at the resulting resurrection of the German Empire, so also, and even infinitely more so, will the whole world stand amazed, when the beast, in its end-form, as the revealed anti-Christian, stands there at the peak of its power and the whole of Europe will accept its anti-Christian state rule and follow in amazement.

Thus the two meanings of "The head" flow together into one entity. As the seventh or anti-Christian mountain, it is at the same time the highest of the seven heads of Europe, and thereby this previously so-dark prophecy is fulfilled.

THE SEVENTH VIAL
or
GOD'S JUDGEMENT

> Watch ye therefore; for ye know not when
> the Master of the house cometh,
> at even or at midnight
> lest coming suddenly
> He find you asleep
> Mark 13:35, 36.

Rev 16:17

Verse 17 "And the seventh Angel poured out his vial into the air." Natural air, indispensable to the maintenance of natural life is, as we previously said in the fifth trumpet (Vol.1), the image of spiritual atmosphere where in our spiritual life breathes. Just as the first must be pure, and not be poisoned, with toxic fumes, so also must the spiritual Christian life not be endangered.

Which believing Christian, who attentively regards the political, religious and social conditions in Europe, does not think of the evil in the air, of which Paul spoke? In the states of Europe, unrest from without and from within. From without, because of mutual mistrust, envy and fear of the violence and the power of a stronger neighbouring state. The political condition of Europe is highly strained, resulting in long-term, pretended peace, although armed to the teeth, which engulfs millions from the treasury every year, to the sweat and blood of the nations. From within, unrest in the states through the continually increasing upheavals of the social democrats and anarchists. The kings of Europe feel their thrones are threatened.

In the church, conditions are not better, evil spirits triumph in the air, and the church is mostly brought down to its most humanistic form, a recommendation of the *moral* teaching of Christ, whom they reject in His actual personality and sending.

This results in increasing indifference to religion actually dissolves into hatred against the Christian *faith*.

In Industry the rising battle between workers and capitalism begins to take on such disproportional effect, due to large scale workers strikes, that the media openly announces "The question *must* be resolved, is not Europe doomed to ruin?"

According to what the Lord says in (Luke 21:25) and Revelation, it is probable that the question will not be resolved. The people, having come to understand, that unity is power, unite themselves in the battle against capitalists. The incited sea of nations becomes restless, rises higher, her waves roar, and once the storm breaks loose, the weak dams of egoism and insufficient concessions will not prevent the flood from being contained and swiping everything into the abyss. All bonds between state, church and society, which for so long kept Europe together, are severed. The seventh Angel poured out his vial over her. The judgement begins. It is not yet the Lord, who lifts His hand in *wrath*. Just as in the previous vials, the Lord here also allows the consequences of their own actions to come over them.

Or did the kings, through their pursuit of glory, greatness and the lusts of life, through forgetting their duty and calling to live as Christian kings and to watch over the welfare and the true interest of their subjects, bring about these inescapable results upon themselves? Did not the clergy through her liberal rational views and teachings destroy the worship of God in the heart of the people, the Christian belief and the Christian satisfaction in the earthly things? Is not their preaching of striving for a moral perfection, which is however unreachable for those who are not reborn, the cause of indifference towards religion, and of the loss of God's fear? The fear of the Lord is the beginning, of wisdom! (Psalm 111:10). The "Fear God, honour the king" (1 Pet 2:17) is in a Christian state, where a Christian nation is ruled by a Christian king, not only a prescription but also a guarantee of happiness, and, where the fear of the Lord disappears, human wisdom, through its reasoning begins to race into perdition.

In this way, both clergy and kings of the seventh period, have brought the judgement upon themselves. This seventh vial clearly predicts that they will both fall and be destroyed by the people's government (Laodicea). But they have at the same time also drawn the people under this judgement, the people who misled and seduced, became angered and stretched out their hand in revenge.

When the seventh vial was poured out, **"And there came a great voice out of the Temple of Heaven, saying: it is done,"** what still had to be done; with this seventh vial the wrath of God is completed (Rev 15;1).

The great voice is that of the Lord Himself, who in the 1st verse of this chapter (16) commanded the vials to be poured out; this voice comes from the Throne of God.

After the last vial is poured out, He Himself speaks: *"It is done"*. The battle between light and darkness is thus concluded. The voice of the Lord however comes out of the temple, and this we know quite well as the congregation of the believers (Rev 11:19). It must therefore be the Lord who speaks through prophecy from the Holy Spirit. We however found no gifts of prophecy in any church denomination except in the Apostolic church. After the outpouring of the seventh vial in 1830, the voice of the Lord must have predicted through prophecy in the Apostolic church, that the end of this dispensation is near, and the judgements of the Lord are poured out over the earth; that what had to be done was done, before the wrath of God over the sinful people is completed. Indeed we will still see, that this is the main contents of the written and oral testimony of the Apostolic church to all heads of states and churches in all countries in Europe in their Manifest. It was not them who spoke, but the Spirit of the Father who spoke through them (Matt 10:20). But then again the Apostolic clergy, together with all the believing teachers, forming the Angel of the seventh trumpet, again form the Angel with the seventh vial, and just as the clergy of the first Apostolic period, by their testimony against the anti-Christian, poured out the judgement of God and the vial of His wrath over them.

When the Lord says *through His servants* at the beginning of the seventh period: **"It is done,"** it totally corresponds with what we found in (Rev 10:6), where Christ swears with a solemn oath to the Almighty God, that in the seventh period, no more delays will occur, but that when the seventh trumpet shall sound, all the mysteries of God will be fulfilled.

This testimony that the time is short (no more delay), is strengthened not only by the appalling changes which occurred in church, state and industry since 1830, but also by the present condition of Europe, where, in the leading states everything is prepared, all fuels are acquired, so that just one spark is required to ignite the whole of Europe.

Remembering that the Lord warns us at the end of the sixth candlestick (Rev 3:11): "Behold, I come quickly", in the seventh, vial (Rev 16:15): "Behold I come as a thief," and in the seventh candlestick (Rev 3:20) "Behold I stand at the door," in ever-increasing nearness, then there is good reason for everyone who loves his soul, to watch, and to be clothed with the robes of righteousness, that he may not be found naked on the Lord's day. For now, follows (Rev 16:18): **"And there were voices, and thunderings, and lightnings".** We learned to know the *voices, thunderings and lightning* in the seventh seal and trumpet. Considering however that these voices, etc. occur in the vial, describing the consequences of the anti-Christian state powers and clergy falling away from God.

They can therefore not be the voices, thunderings and lightnings of the Holy Spirit, but those of Satan and his angels active through the anti-Christian leaders in church and state, voices who preach revolutions, abolition of marriages and of Christian religion, redistribution of property. The thunderings of denial of God and worshipping of human genius. The lightning with which Satan and his angels preach government by the people or democracy, the contempt of royalty and clergy and all that his unholy fire will still dish out in the future to the souls of the unbelievers.

"And there was a great earthquake", *such as was not since men were upon the earth, so mighty an earthquake, and so great.* In the seventh seal, we already considered the earthquake as disturbing the order of the day, upheavals, wars and revolutions of nations continuing in increasing measure and increasingly more severe since 1830 up to our days (1872), and we cannot expect better days ahead. On the contrary, the conditions in Europe are highly unstable and fit in with what the prophecy teaches us. We stand almost immediately before a new, still unknown world order.

From what we learn in this Revelation of Jesus Christ, we may also with certainty predict, that from now on, wars, upheavals and revolutions on earth will not cease until the Son of Man returns.

This seventh vial is only fulfilled up to and with the beginning of the great earthquake; its further fulfilment, effect, and the fulfilment of the remaining part of this chapter lies in the near future. The reader living in the 21st century will readily agree that the above-described predictions have so far been fulfilled. We experienced two catastrophic world wars started by Germany, devastating Europe, the atomic bombs killing and maiming thousands, daily labour unrest, technological inventions placing a man on the moon and rockets to the planets, etc…

This seventh vial is described in short terms in (Rev 16:17-21). Revelation again takes up its three parts and describes them in greater detail in the following chapters. (Rev.17, 18, and 19)

The first part thereof (Chap.17) predicts the total separation between church and state in Europe.

The second part (Chap.18) predicts the abolition of the Christian religion by the anti-Christian state powers.

The third part (Chap.19) predicts the judgement of God over anti-Christian states and nations.

Of the first two parts, we will find (Rev 18:1-7) already fulfilled. This therefore still belongs to this part in the seventh period. "The past". In

(Chap.17), we see the initial fulfilment of (verses 1, 2, 4 and 5). In total, however, this all belongs to our days, and therefore to the 2nd part of the seventh period, "The present". In order not to break up the sequence of events, it will be better to cover it all there. Chapter19 still belongs to "The future".

THE TESTIMONY AGAINST BABYLON

> And then shall they see the Son of man coming in
> a cloud with power and great Glory.
> Luke 21:27

<u>Rev 18:1-7</u>

Verse 1. "And after these things I saw another Angel come down from Heaven, having great power, and the earth was lightened with His Glory".

The *"After"* with which John starts this chapter, again concerns the sequence in which these visions were shown to him and not the sequence, wherein the events will be fulfilled. As we will yet see, this chapter is already partly fulfilled, simultaneously with the remaining events, which have already occurred in the seventh period since 1830.

The Angel comes down from Heaven. He, therefore, comes from the Throne of God. He has great power and enlightens the earth with His Glory (actually: with his teaching). All these characteristics indicate to us, that here no created angel, but the uncreated Angel of the Covenant, Jesus Christ is described. It is again as with the Reformation (Rev 10:1), Jesus Christ, who comes down from Heaven to the earth through His servants with great power, so that the Christian society (the earth) may be enlightened by His teaching, through His judgement and through His expectation of the things which will occur. The original text contains all these meanings. So, we must find something corresponding with the fulfilment of (Rev 10:1). The *coming down from Heaven there seemed to be, the bringing back of the Gospel to the Apostolic church*, through the Reformers. Something similar must also occur through His witnesses of the seventh period, (the cloud: Luke 21:27), wherein the Lord comes before the Redemption (verse 28).

It cannot however be a total Reformation, since the gospel truths, once again brought to the light, had not totally disappeared from the church. It must be, a perfecting of this Reformation, a greater light and glory, which Jesus Christ gives anew through His servants concerning His whole Word to the believers, a new and clear insight into God's counsel, such as it is revealed in the Holy Scriptures, but not totally understood during the three centuries of the Reformation. We find ourselves in the seventh vial, which has nothing to do with the gospel preaching, but with God's judgement. When Christ then takes action through this angel in the vial, it can only take

405

the form of an admonishment or awarding and we must already have met this angel in the seventh period in his Priestly character and in the seventh trumpet in his character of an Evangelistic messenger.

If we ask: where in the history of the church since 1830 has Christ taken action with great power in His servants, with a yet unknown clear look and deeper insight in His Word, a disapproving judgement concerning the condition of the church and knowledge of things, which in the near future will occur, before, with and at the return of Christ? Then, the reader will no more than we ourselves, give another answer than this: in the *Catholic Apostolic church.* When we, without prejudice, consider upon which important matters this Apostolic church sheds a bright light, that against all odds, gradually seeps through all the believing denominations of the Protestant church, we count the following:

1. The doctrine of the typical or fore-shadowing meaning of the Old Testament, for the New Testament.[50]

2. The total falling away of the church and the lack of uniformity in what Christ instituted.

3. The doctrine of both Baptisms, water Baptism and the Baptism with fire or the sealing with the Holy Spirit as the Rebirth to children of God.

4. The resulting gifts of the Holy Spirit, healing of the sick, tongues, prophecies etc.

5. The knowledge of the correct church ordinances in her fourfold ministry, with Christ as the living Head of the congregation, speaking in her through prophecies.

6. The doctrine of the last days, and the preparation of the church for the return of Christ.

The teaching from the Holy Scriptures, which the Apostolic church through Godly enlightenment and direction by prophecies presented to the

---

[50] Prof.H.W.J.Thiersh, formally in Marburg, a highly respected theologian, in his introduction to "The Genesis", Basel 1870, found that the doctrine of the typical, which recently was brought to a unified concept by Menken. Herstenberg, Bähr, Olshauzen, Hoffman, Deutsch and other Protestant theologians, in a much richer form in the Apostolic church through prophetic enlightenment, and simultaneously the correct church tenets. The later conversion of this theologian to the Apostolic church, is enough proof of his creditability.

world, are not unintelligible matters, but exactly that which the church in our days needed, to escape the persecutions and destruction from the anti-Christ.

It was, therefore, Jesus Christ, the Head of the church, who came down from Heaven, in answer to the prayers of the believers (seventh seal), in 1830, in His servants, appointed by Him, apostles, prophets, evangelists and shepherds, with great power (the Holy Spirit and His gifts) and with the Glory of His now wholly known word and gospel, to restore the church in her original purity, power and ordinances, in preparation for His return.

Verse 2 **"And He cried mightily with a strong voice, saying, Babylon the great is fallen, is fallen, and is become the habitation of devils, and the hold of every foul spirit, and a cage of every unclean and hateful bird".**

Verse 3. **"For all nations have drunk of the wine of the wrath of her fornication, and the kings of the earth have committed fornication with her, and the merchants of the earth are waxed rich through the abundance of her delicacies."**

Who Babylon, the great whore is, Chapter17 will clearly and amply teach us. From the sixth vial, we already know it sufficiently as the great city Babylon, through which the river Euphrates flowed (Vol.1), that is: As the whole apostate Christendom with all her differences, quarrels and confusion on religious matters. Babylon or confusion is therefore a collective name for all the different denominations of Christendom who deviated from God's truth. That it is **"fallen"** cannot mean that it is materially destroyed and judgment was already executed. In (verse 4), the Lord Himself says *"Come out of her, My people!"* It follows that it is still in existence in its outward form, but inwardly it has fallen out of God's Kingdom, out of the Covenant of God's Grace. The bride has become a whore (Rev 17:1). She has fallen; and **has become a habitation of devils and the hold of every foul spirit,** such as we already saw in the sixth vial, that the three unclean spirits out of the mouth of the dragon, and out of the beast, and out of the mouth of the false prophet, or deism, atheism and pantheism, who went out as spirits of the devils to nestle in the church. **"And a cage of every unclean and hateful bird."** What is the meaning of the image **"birds"** in the kingdom of God? Jesus teaches us (Matt 13:4,19. Mark 4:4,15. Luke 8:5,12) that it is Satan, and his servants, the evil spirits, who come and devour the Word of God sowed in the heart of the people so that they would not believe and be saved. It is the prince of the power in the air, the spirit that now worketh in the children of disobedience! (Eph 2:2). "For we wrestle not against flesh and blood, but against *spiritual* *wickedness in high places.*" (Eph 6:12). Just as Christ works through His servants, so also does Satan, and even as the Roman and the Greek denominations of the Christian church are full of servants of Satan, who devour the sowed word of God from the hearts to replace it by the superstitions of their church, so also are the Protestant churches full of evil spirits, unbelievers and mocking "lukewarm" Christians; full of modern, *so-called protestant teachers*, who only protest against superstition in order to preach unbelief, and try to devour the good seed in the believers, that they should not believe and be saved (Luke 8:12). These are the birds, the unclean and hateful birds, who are not from God's truth. (Titus 3:3 and page 271 Vol.1), of which Babylon, the fallen Christian church, has become the hold.

How **all nations have drunk of the wine of the wrath of her fornication** (verse 3) that is: how they are corrupted through all the different false teachings of the apostate Christian churches, how the kings of the earth fornicated with Babylon, will be described in the 17th Chapter.

"And the merchants of the earth are waxed rich through the abundance of her delicacies". Since we are dealing with the apostate Christian church, the *merchants of the earth* cannot be merchants of earthly goods, as is usually presumed, but must also have a metaphoric meaning in the church. The Lord Himself is compared to a Merchant, who bought the believers with His blood and sacrifice. (1 Cor 6:20.1 Cor.7:23. 2 Peter 2:1 Rev 5:9. Rev 14:3, 4). But even so, Peter says in the same text that "False teachers," who secretly shall bring damnable heresies, who with made-up words, "Make Christians into merchants" and thus make the House of the Father into a marketplace. These false teachers waxed rich from the great treasures of Babylon. These *riches* of the whore Babylon we will also find described in (Rev 17:4), where she is *arrayed in purple,* and *decked with gold and precious stones and pearls, having a golden cup in her hand* full of abominations before God. This Babylonian treasure of the false teachers in the whole of Christendom (earth) the Lord already pointed out in the seventh candlestick, the congregation of the Laodicean period (Rev 3:17,18), "Because thou sayest, I am rich, and increased with goods, and have need of nothing; and knowest not that thou art wretched, and miserable; and poor and blind and naked: I counsel thee to *buy* **of Me** *gold tried in the fire,* that thou mayest be rich: and white raiment, that thou mayest be clothed, and that the shame of thy nakedness do not appear; and anoint thine eyes with eye salve; that thou mayest see". This judgement of the Lord is not only directed to the false teachers, who deny their Lord as saviour but also to the remaining teachers, who live in Babylon, because they deny the Lord in His work in these last days, the Holy Sealing with the Holy Spirit and the restoration of the church as Bride of Christ.

If we want to summarize what the Lord says here in judgement over the combined Christendom and the Christian churches as they appeared to Him since 1830, (Vol. I), then the interpretation of the text is as follows: *She has fallen, she has fallen; the Christian church, out of God's covenant of grace, she is full of confusion, and teachings of the devils. The good seed of God's word is trodden down in her, and the souls of men are fed with all sorts of lies and human reasoning. She does not lean on Me anymore but on her own worldly power. Her false teachers consider themselves rich in knowledge of Me and in faith, and they are poor and blind and naked. They consider themselves to be gospel preachers and trade in the souls of men.* (Rev 18:13)

However bitter this judgement may be for all Christian churches, it is the true judgement of Him before whom nothing is hidden, and the truth of this judgement will still become clearer to the reader.

We still have to take note of one important matter. This testimony and judgement of the Lord concerning Babylon is not described only here in Revelation, neither is it only revealed by the Lord to His reinstated apostles and prophets in the Apostolic church, but according to (verse 2), the Lord *cried out with a loud voice*; and if it is a testimony against Babylon, then this warning must also have been brought and preached to Babylon, through apostles and prophets, through whom the Lord as Head of His congregation wanted to work. Indeed also here the prophecy was fulfilled and this testimony given by Christ to His apostles was brought to Babylon by them.

Our investigation concerning who the sealing angel could be, led to Van Loon. "Open action of the Catholic Apostolic church with a letter to all church and worldly authorities of all countries". We have later seen that this letter, or rather this manifest was handed over and verbally explained to all above mentioned authorities. Now is the time and place for us to reveal the contents of this manifest, because the content is the original fulfilment of (verse 2) and describes the testimony of Jesus Christ, concerning the fall of Babylon, such as it was brought to the heads and teachers of the whole Christendom of Europe. The manifest itself covers 89 pages in A5 size and is thus too extensive to wholly copy it here. We have therefore by means of extracts, with reservation, where possible, tried to give the content in our own words and in the same train of thought, and printed the important sentences especially the predictions concerning the future of the church and of Europe in Italics. We cannot emphasize enough the importance of reading this work, since it sheds light on many matters and lets us see things from another perspective;

Four points we have to emphasize for extra attention:

1. The statements concerning the corruption of the whole of Christendom, the apostasy of the kings from the living God, and the Babylonian condition of the church, all this is revealed through the Holy Spirit by the prophets of the Apostolic Church.

2 The Lord also announced His will through prophecy, that this testimony against Babylon, and the writing of Mene, Mene, Tekel above all Christian denominations, should be brought to all authorities in church and states in all European countries.

3 In 1836, when this testimony was revealed, the fearful conditions of the future of Europe were not even anticipated yet, and that the present condition of Europe has not only already fulfilled many of these predictions, but also makes known the nearby fulfilment of the remaining predictions.

4 The reader must make his own decision, whether the statements and predictions contained in the manifest must be taken as human reasoning or as a proof for the Godly origin of the Catholic Apostolic Church.

EXTRACTS FROM THE TESTIMONY

or

The Manifest of the Catholic Apostolic Church,

Written in 1835

To the patriarchs, Archbishops and Bishops and other heads of the church of Christ in all countries; and To the Emperors, kings, princes and other rulers of the baptized nations.

In the name of the Father and the Son and of the Holy Spirit. Amen! The church of Christ is the community of all who are baptized in the name of the Father, the Son and of the Holy Spirit.

To this church, we apply through her clergy, to whom the souls of the baptized are entrusted by our Lord Jesus Christ, the great Shepherd.

To Christendom, the nations united in God, we apply through their anointed heads, the kings and all her rulers, whose duty it is to rule according to the laws of God.

We pray you, for Christ's sake, not to let our word be either unheard or hastily rejected, as though we spoke it arrogantly of ourselves, for we solemnly declare to have received the commission from Him, who is your and our Head, whom we may not disobey, and who shall judge us, if we high-mindedly assumed to bring you this testimony, but also judge you if you reject those whom He sent to speak to you.

Even in the darkest hour of the church, in the greatest need from without and the deepest decay from within, God always preserved and saved His people. Also in these last days, in the last hours of the history of the church and of the world, God appears again to seek His people, and bring His voice to all, who still remained faithful amidst the floods of ungodliness.

The sea and the waves begin to roar (Luke 21:25), and people think in their hearts, that the time is come, to overthrow all thrones, to destroy the altars and to revolt against all belief and honour. But God, who never forsakes His church, now also rises to judge the foolishness of the nations, to comfort the heart of His children, who call upon Him to visit the sins and to separate the pure from the impure.

The Holiest truths of God are rejected, the Priestly ministry despised, and unbelief and revolt threaten to reject everything in church and state and to establish a new order of Godly denial and confusion on the ruins of Christian belief. Hatred against the Christian faith wants to destroy the

411

bond between church and state, not only there, where it is misused and where the church becomes the servant of the state, or vice versa, but also there, where in its most adequate form, religion still affects human relations. And they, who do not belong to the enemies of Christianity, do not understand what the authority of the Christian Priests or the dignity of the Christian king means any more. Kingship through God's grace, the old title of Christian kings, is only retained as a formality in most European states (1835). Forgetting both of these concepts caused Christianity to split up into numerous sects, differing in the worship of God, teaching and inner spirit, biting each other, and consuming each other. They have forgotten that the body of Christ, the congregation, must be united and that differences are sin; that one brotherly bond must embrace all those baptized in the name of Jesus.

This forgetfulness results in the slogan, that power is derived from the people, whereby each wants to choose his own form of government and the kings become the servants of the people and are responsible to them instead of God.

When the kings forget that they are anointed by God for the people, and, instead of becoming like fathers, become persecutors of the people, then they are not kings according to God's grace anymore, but kings through the will of the people or through raw violence, and they themselves give the people proof, that the government is better off in the hands of the majority than in one person.

But when the anointed king and the ordained Priest of God give in to the dissolution between society and religion, when they disregard the people's opinion, renounce their place as a divine institution, and acknowledge the people as the origin of their power,- when the Priests of God are no more the servants of the one church of Christ, but of numerous sects, and both do not repent of their heresy, the judgement of God is poured over them.

The powers in church and state are confronted by terrible crises. Many flatter themselves vainly with the hope to be able to subdue it or to direct it. But the power of those who stand up against God increases by the day. The opinion of the people, such as it was revealed in the previous century in France, spread out over the whole of Europe and destroyed all feelings of loyalty of the subjects, all piety and God's fear amongst the people. Separation of church and state will result in the plunder of the first. (Church)

Many see and agree, that such a terrible storm will come over Europe, but trust, that it will be of a transient nature and that it will drag all her poisonous matters along with it. But they do not know that the time of the end has come and therewith the judgement of God over all, who have forgotten Him and His ways. Do not deceive yourself, the church of the Living God, and baptized nations! It will not be a passing cloud, or transient evil, from which you shall emerge unscathed. All the tribulations from former periods will not be taken into consideration here.

But there will be a rescue, a refuge, for those who return to the old paths. We therefore urge you all to hear our message and to recognize that God once more visits His people. Consequently, we must reveal to you the evil wherein Christendom lies and the even more terrible evil which strengthens her.

Then follows an explanation of what the sacraments must mean to the congregation, as the sure pledge of the Lord's love and faithfulness, and the means, whereby He blesses her and give her spiritual life. After this, how the institutions in the church of Christ, which He instituted, were in the beginning; He the Living Head, who carries and rules His congregation through His four ministries, as described in (Eph.4 and 1 Cor.12), as apostles, prophets, evangelists and shepherd, to the perfection of the body of Christ, who were supposed to remain active in the church. Through the lack of these ministries, the body of Christ is not perfect yet, the whole congregation has not come to a perfect man, and the church is not prepared as a pure virgin for the wedding of the Lamb (Rev.19:7). Therefore, these ministries have to be reinstated in the church, to prepare the congregation as the Bride of the Lord, so that He can come.

Now follows a description of the characteristics of each of the four ministries.

Apostles as the Ambassadors of Christ for the whole church, the dispensers of the Holy Spirit with His gifts, and the stewards of the mysteries of God (Acts 8:14-17.Acts 19:2, 6 Acts 2:42.1 Cor.4:1).

Prophets, as the organ through whom God speaks to the congregation, and reveals His will. Together with the apostles to form the foundation of the visible church on earth (Eph.2:20).

Evangelists; who as preachers of the gospel, of the message of the coming Kingdom, of the imminent judgement, and of the prepared refuge, work externally and present the converted souls to the apostles for sealing.

Shepherds tend to these gathered believers and sealed souls, as the flock of the Lord. Their work sphere is thus inward, in the congregation herself.

Through these four ministries, through whom Jesus, the Lord Himself worked in the congregation, she was, equipped with the gifts of the Holy Spirit, a unit as the body of Christ, one in faith, one baptism, etc. (Eph.4:3-6). The manifest goes on as follows:

413

This is how the church, in its original condition and form, was built upon a rock, against which the gates of hell would not prevail. That is the one, Holy, Catholic Apostolic church, the bride, the firstlings of God and the Lamb, who wait upon the return of our Lord Jesus.

Looking around us, to seek this church amidst the baptized, we find that the apostle ministry was lost, and the goal for which they were given (Eph.4:11-16), was not reached.

The voice of the Lord through prophecies has also been silent for a long time, and the congregation has sunk in the silence of death. The comforter does not speak to her anymore, and also the healing of the sick, the driving out of devils has disappeared. And which part of the baptized reveals in its form or its spirit the character of *One, Holy, Apostolic church*? The baptized have all fallen out of the glorious institution, which God in the beginning had given to His church.

The church, feeling they missed this unity, tried to restore it by means of the worldly arm or through the presumption of power of one Bishop over his fellow Bishops. **Babylon the great has fallen.** (Rev.18:2) [51] This resulted in splitting, separation and deviation in faith and discipline, the domination of worldly power and the forceful presumption of one universal bishop. And it will not stop at this. The decay and the degeneration will continue to increase until all power and each ministry is lost and the whole of Christendom has become a confused mass, from which the antichrist can select the building blocks to establish his realm of lies. **And is become the habitation of every foul spirit.** (Rev 18:2)

The church is not a human institution for human goals, but a divine one, for a Godly goal.

The claim that she is one in her invisible head in heaven, Jesus Christ, without visible unity on earth, is an error, the fruit of which is, continuous and endless splitting in the body of Christ here on earth.

The Roman and Greek Church stand on the one side, and the history of their opposing Protestantism, is not that of one church, but of many sects, not of one faith, one baptism, but of numerous beliefs, hopes, and baptisms. They did not live together as brethren, and eat and drink at one table, but separated themselves, biting and consuming.

---

[51] These and the following words printed in bold are references from Revelation, they do not appear in the testimony of the Apostolic church but are interpolated as being the prophecies of Revelation which through this statement by the Apostolic church are fulfilled. The angel of Rev.18:1! the Apostolic clergy cried with a loud voice, that which is written in verses 2 and 3.

Originally the church was united through the indwelling of the Holy Spirit, later she was held together through ambition and violence, but since the Reformation there definitely exists no unity anymore but a multitude of contradicting sects, whose only claim to unity is, that they acknowledge the Holy Scriptures as the only basis of true faith, but at the same time the untenableness of this claim as proof of oneness, that they base all their individual characteristics, their often contradicting points of view, on the Holy scripture. **A cage for every unclean and hateful bird**. (Rev 18:2)

This division in Protestantism, this right of everyone, to judge for himself, where he strove against darkness and heresies, without being led by the voice and utterances of the Holy Spirit, revealed unto us the depth of the origin of the anti-Christian spirit, who in such a short time revealed itself and spread out over the whole society.

Because, according to those principles, each one becomes his own judge, whereby he holds in contempt all authority in king and priest, authorities and parents, and rejects everything that stands next to and above him, most of all God's Word. In this way, the concept that the lawful power originates from the people, is born. Thereby the favour of the people is sought after, and the truth is silenced. Even the regent lost all knowledge, that his power is derived from God; and one consequence of this terrible decline is the claim: that the state must consider all forms of religion as equal, and thereby deny the church of God, which is Atheism. But thereby the kings also lost the only means to fulfil their duty according to God's will and to erect a dam against the evils, which will flood the people of Europe. By forgetting God, from whom they received their power, they became persecutors and bad rulers; through despising the anointing, the measure of their sins was filled, and they became anti-Christian kings. But because of this, their kingdoms were also visited by the judgement of God and upheavals. The people, tired of governments, who did not assure them of rest and happiness, and together with their kings forgot God, as the source of all rescue and salvation, rose in angry violence to help themselves, and in the hand of a few leaders become willing tools to a total revolution of all existing institutions in church and state. **For all nations have drunk of the wine of the wrath of her fornication, and the kings of the earth have committed fornication with her**, and the merchants of the earth are waxed rich through the abundance of her delicacies. (Rev 18:3) The condition in France in 1793, was only a local occurrence of the general destruction, which now spread over Europe, a first rumbling of the great earthquake, which would destroy every society and religious institution.

This revolution occurred, while there generally were better insights and principles, which they tackled with unheard of anger, but to which they eventually yielded. But now, the whole of Christendom, contaminated by this poison is threatened with a revolution, of which none was ever an example and prelude, and before whose anger all undermined institutions will succumb. Then the last flood of anti-Christian blasphemy will rise and carry away church and state, as well as the few remaining institutions of God, to replace it with that of hell. Godlessness then becomes law and God and His anointed will be blasphemed in every conceivable way, not by the foolish rumblings of angry people, but by the regulations of constitutions of a subdued government, who however came out of the all-powerful nations. *The bonds of society, formerly* (1789) *torn by the anger of human lusts, will now be quenched through the godlessness of human wisdom. Lawlessness will permeate everything* until all its power is combined *in the man of sin*, the lawless, who exalted himself above all that is called God and religion. (2 Thes.3, 4, 9.)

And he will soon be revealed because, with the increasing upheavals among the nations of Europe, the appointed time announced by God is rapidly approaching. (Luke 21:25-27), *that the Son of man will return in the clouds in the heavens, to judge the nations and to establish His kingdom, which will be Everlasting.* (Dan.7:13, 14.)

And this is the terrible crisis in the history of humankind, which confronts the world; this is the hour of temptation, which shall come upon the world (Rev.3:10). And it will come as a snare upon all who live on the earth. (Luke 21:35)

The falling away and the coming judgement, the total disunity of the so-called churches, singly and together, whether in external form. or in inner purity and holiness, *with that body of Christ, which is described in the Holy Scripture as* **"The Church"**, *and her total unpreparedness for the return of Christ, we have presented to you,* and in confirmation thereof, we refer to everyone's conscience, to whom this testimony is given. And our witness of the truth of all these things is not only the agreement of conscience but the involuntary fear and uneasiness for that which is to come in the future. The general unrest of the world, the general cry for change and improvement, testify to this truth. Since you priests and kings still are God's anointed, God has revealed unto you the signs of the times, and uncovered the hidden causes of evil, the threatening, terrible judgement, and the imminent return of Him, who with His mighty angels will be revealed from the Heavens. (2 Thess 1:7, 8)

416

But who may abide on the day of His return? For He is like a refiner's fire, and like the fuller's soap. He shall melt and purify the silver. (Mal 3:2-4) Only a holy people can abide before His countenance, who walk as children of light and as children of the day. (1 Thess 5:5); only a people filled with the Holy Spirit, the servants of God, whom He seals on their foreheads, before the destruction is loosened. (Rev.7:2,3) And this announcement of the Holy Spirit cannot take place, the sealing cannot occur, the church cannot be brought to perfection, except through the ordinances, which God gave in the beginning for this purpose, and they will be restored. All the promises given in God's Word shall be fulfilled and His intentions shall be executed by His means and not by human inventions. Apostles (not of men, neither by man, Gal.1:1), prophets, evangelists, shepherds and teachers, will execute God's work in His church and will perform the work of the ministry, whereby the body of Christ is erected, as firstlings of God and the Lamb. (Rev 14:1-5). And Jesus Christ, the Head of the church, is ever ready to reinstate these ordinances so that His servants are able to fulfil their commission. Therefore, venerable Bishops and Fathers of the church! Let God tell you, to bring your flock to Him as a Holy people, who can withstand His judgement, and be found worthy to stand before the Son. And you, princes and regents! be faithful to God, and save your nations from the flood of godlessness, when you acknowledge your responsibility to Him, and seek Him in His church. *But this salvation will not be the restoration of your earthly power and glory. Already the noise of the death knell resounds in this world. The only hope left is* which was always the hope of the church, *to be taken up in the clouds, meeting the Lord in the air, and thus be with the Lord for eternity, saved from the great destruction and from the great tribulation, which shall come upon the earth. But will you listen to us? God only knows!*

Without a doubt, many will hear and be preserved through the sealing from destruction and be hidden in His tent in the evil times. *Whosoever does not hear and accept God's seal, how shall he flee from the judgement, of which is written* (2 Thess 2:11, 12), "And for this cause, God shall send them strong delusion, that they should believe a lie: That they all might be damned who believe not the truth but had pleasure in unrighteousness".

But you, who grieve over the miserable condition of the church of Christ, who wishes, that all the baptized would developed to the image of Christ, the Son of God, and walk in Holiness and love,- that God's image might be restored, and the congregation of believers might be filled with one heart and one mind and with the Holy Spirit, who – having no individual high-minded plans, but only wish, that these things might be attained through

God's ordinances, *you in particular we adjure that you do not resist His grace, which we proclaim unto you, and do not consider the truth of His counsel, which we have presented to you, as something inconceivable.* Do not believe that God's gifts and callings are forever taken away from us. Lift up your heads, for in the midst of darkness He lets the light come, the time of approaching judgment was always the time, that He raised His voice, and prepared a refuge.

Once again, He decided to reestablish His sanctuary, and from there His testimony goes out to all the baptized. It is brought to you by the hands of men, called to the Apostle's ministry by the voice of the Holy Spirit, and set apart for Christ's sake to serve in all countries. Their ministry is to share God's blessings with the baptized in all lands, which Jesus, the true apostle, longs to pour out upon His church through apostles.

For God heard the cry, of those who grieved about the miserable condition of the church and called upon Him to take them under His wings.

During this century many came together in different places, especially in Great Britain, to plead for a rich outpouring of the Holy Spirit. In the year 1830 these prayers were heard, and in the west of Scotland, answered by the Holy Spirit. The members of the Scottish church where the long silent and forgotten voice of the Spirit of the Lord made itself heard, were simple unlearned members (Isaiah 28:11) who, just as the remaining churches, did not understand (1 Cor.14). Also some persons in London, members of the English church, received a similar answer to their prayer

God there performed a wonderful and mighty work, when He again made His voice heard amidst His assembled people. And this voice will not be silent anymore but go out to the ends of the world.

Relatively few could recognize this voice as God's voice, but they experienced the power of the Almighty, when through His grace and from Him, they received the power to build His church, according to the original ordinances of Jesus Christ. This work is not a new sect. It is God's own work to offer His salvation to all Christians. *It is the testimony of God.* Everywhere in Christendom, lawlessness, separation and the sectarian spirit reign supreme. Here is one body, one faith, in which all teachers preach the same. There outside are schools of the anti-Christ, with teachers appointed by the people themselves; here one body, guided by ordinances, given by God Himself and not by man. Outside, there is an unbelieving world, rejected kings, church leaders and all institutions in church and state. *Here* we see God's church, the king and all authority in church and state being glorified. Not only are these the signs of the reestablished Apostle ministry, but also the sensually *perceptible signs of manifold healings of the sick and driving out devils.*

We, therefore pray, venerable Fathers and Brethren in Christ Jesus our Lord! Hear our words. *We do not come as your judges, but as messengers of the Lord of Hosts,* to restore that life, which was always the prayer, the hope and the great comfort of the church of God, *to proclaim unto you the acceptable year of the Lord* (Issaiah1:2), *but also that the day of vengeance is fast approaching.* We may not recognize all the different names, whereby the members of the *One, Holy, Universal, Apostolic church* divided itself into numerous sects, but to all, Roman, Greek and Protestants *we proclaim, that the time of judgement is near, and the Judge stands at the door.*

And should one ask, why God revealed these things to us; it is not because of our righteousness or that we are without sin, but for His Name's sake and to fulfil His intentions with His church. He has separated us from all churches, to send us to everyone. If He had poured out His Holy Spirit upon one of the sects, He would thereby have justified them above the others while, for all that, they all erred. If on the other hand, He had poured out His Holy Spirit upon all of them, He would have confirmed their self-sufficiency and separateness. But God's intention was, to appoint apostles and prophets, to once again lay the old foundation, to build thereon His Spiritual temple, and from there to send out His messengers, and to invite all the true believers, in order to bless them. *Because all believers must be visibly separated from the unbelievers into one body and be prepared for the return of the Lord.* And when the Lord again sends apostles and prophets to His church, and the baptized reject them, they then thereby declare themselves to be fallen away. And in this way, separation must come between light and darkness.

And now, you servants of God! Bishops and Shepherds of His church! The first to believe the blessing, but also the first in responsibility, we adjure you, Fathers of the church and Shepherds of the Lord! do not reject our testimony. We offer you faith, power and help from God in the difficulties, wherein the evil, which the church suffers, has involved you. Do not take any step in your own power, and do not seek to shirk your responsibility for any reason. But this God desires of you, that you, remain standing where you are, and recognize His hand in this His present work; that you confess the sins, which cover the face of the heavens like a thick cloud, and in steady prayer you rejoice in the hope in the approaching salvation and rescue, through the power of God in the Holy Spirit.

And you, Princes and Authorities of Christendom! Be assured that your true power and any security in these times of confusion lies in the God-given glory of His church. We assure you in the name of our God that you stand fast as good soldiers for His truth and for His church. Be faithful in the fulfilling of all your duties; purify your courts from sin and malice. Appoint honest, faithful and god-fearing men in your service. But above all, consider that you are called to protect the church of Christ. Do not allow that she, even under the pretext of reformation, is torn apart and destroyed. But in spiritual matters be subject unto them, who are appointed over you, as well as over all those baptized in the Lord.

And now that He brings back His original ordinances in the church, fear not to admit it. As far as your lawful power is concerned, promote the completion of this work of God, because only through this can you and your nations be saved. *Against the storm, which is ready to break loose over you, no human power has control. The only way to escape it, is, that you would be taken away in the future of the Lord before the coming evil, and to this end, this work of God is the only preparation.*

We have tried to bring you all this in good faith and truth. Concerning ourselves, it does not matter if we are judged by man. God will execute His counsel, whether through us or through someone else. But for your own sakes, you anointed priests and kings! for the sake of the church, and the children of God, who find themselves amongst the nations over which you have been placed in spiritual and worldly things, *we once more adjure you, to accept the true message of God which we bring. But whether you believe or not, and accept us as messengers of God or not, we know, that we received this commission from Him.*

But, may God, the almighty Father, who holds in His hands the hearts of the people and leads and guides them: grant you knowledge and perfect in you the good pleasure of his will.

May the grace of our Lord Jesus Christ, your Savior, fill you with all the blessings of his goodness. May the Holy Ghost, the comforter, the spirit of the Father and the Son, guide you now and forever in His perfect way until the end, to the honour of God and to the salvation of your souls and of souls of all His people. Amen.

Glory be to the Father and to the Son and to the Holy Ghost; as it was in the beginning, so now and forever and from eternity to eternity. Amen.

This in short is the contents of the manifest of the Apostolic church. Much of what is predicted therein has since then shown itself much clearer and been fulfilled. The Protestant church has since 1836 continued to divide itself into increasing numbers of sects and accepted teachers, who do not suffer a sound doctrine anymore, but according to the itching of their ears (2 Tim.4:3). Where the individual disputes and sharp separation between the different sects is reduced, it is in most cases caused more by unconscious anti-Christian indifference, than in true Christian longsuffering and brotherly love.

The Roman church also begins to dissolve, partly because of unbelief, and partly because of extreme superstition. Jesuism drove her to her grave with her declaration of the infallibility of the pope.

In all the countries, where this testimony was brought to all heads of church and of state, those who, by keeping it amongst themselves, and not making it known to the Christian people, that these should not be acquainted with the revealed will of God's counsel, and would not be able to choose between the way of the Lord and that of man, have accumulated a heavy burden upon themselves. In this way, the decay of Babylon continues and in all countries the cry! "*Separation between church and state,*" does not only resound, but the thrones of kings stagger, the people have become angry and grasp the reins of rule for themselves. With the increasing power of the social-democratic and atheistic workers societies, the cloud of evil has already spread over Europe, from which the lightning can strike with destruction in church and society.

The contents of the manifest are also, in short, a warning about the threatening judgements and the preparation for the return of Christ, as they occur in the preaching and the prophecies in the Apostolic church. But she also proves herself to be the seventh vial angel, as we mentioned before, or the clergy, which arose in the seventh period and in fact proclaims the judgement of the Lord over the church to the world.

Upon this testimony brought to Babylon by the mouths of His servants (Rev 18:1-3) follows:

Verse 4: **"And I heard another voice from heaven, saying, <u>Come out of her, My people</u>, that ye be not partakers of her sins, and that ye receive not of her plagues".**

It is remarkable, that this other voice is the voice of the Lord Himself since it comes from Heaven just as the previous one (verse 2), and says, "*My people*" and yet: it does speak with great voice or power, as normally the case with the voice of the Lord in other places in Revelation. It is even called "*Another voice* "from heaven being the same voice of the Lord, because in (verses 1-3) the Lord, caused His apostles and prophets to proclaim His judgement over the church, as His witnesses, while here the Lord in His newly reestablished church, *speaks to His people Himself.* Therefore, this voice is called **another** *voice from Heaven.* Even more remarkable is that John or an angel is commissioned to proclaim to His people what His voice says, but that, in the seventh period, the Lord speaks directly to His people. It is however the first time that, in Revelation, the Lord Himself *speaks* to His people. What we have to understand by this other voice from Heaven, Paul teaches us in (1 Cor.14:21), "In the law it is written, with men of other tongues and other lips will I speak unto this people;" and in (Isaiah 28:11), the Lord says: "For with stammering lips and another tongue will He speak to this people" and we can also read in (1 Cor.14:22), "Wherefore prophesying serveth not for them that believe not but to them that believe." This other voice from Heaven, the voice of the Lord Himself, which since 1830 speaks to His people, is not the personal voice of the Lord, but the voice of the Holy Spirit speaking in prophecies through human mouths, as amongst the people of the Old Covenant, and as it occurred in the first century of the Christian church, and again speaks since 1830 in the Apostolic church. This voice of the Holy Spirit is therefore a sign only for her believers. The other believers and unbelievers in Babylon despise this voice as vain imagination, nervous excitement, hysterical ecstasy, fanatical high-mindedness, etc. It is unbelievable to them, that God Himself should speak through human lips. For the believers, this testimony of Jesus from the seventh period is the Spirit of prophecy. (Rev 12:17, Rev.19:10). This voice of the Holy Spirit says to those who want to believe her: "*Come out of her,* (the fallen great Babylon, the apostate Christian churches of verse 2), *my people! That ye be not partakers of her sins, and that ye receive not of her plagues*", (through your connection with her guilt) which, as the following verses will teach us, will come over her, for:

Verse 5: **"Her sins have reached unto heaven, and God hath remembered her iniquities.".** These sins of the Christian churches are her doctrines and institutions contrary to the teachings of the bible, her denial of the only Saviour, and her failure to recognize and her contempt by believers as well as unbelievers, of the great work of God, which HE, in the seventh and last period, wrought as salvation for His people and the restoration of His church. For this reason, God remembers her iniquities, and He will reward her accordingly.

Verse 6. **"Reward her even as she rewarded you, and double unto her double according to her works: In the cup which she hath filled to her double".** A natural reward or wrath for God's people cannot be considered, because this would conflict with all the prescriptions of Jesus.

To know which rewards are contemplated, we have to ask:

1.How in general did the Christian churches act against the Apostolic Church; what cup (Mark 14:36) did they fill?

2.What line of conduct did the Lord here prescribe for His people?

Christendom, especially, accused the church:

1: That fanaticism, spiritual high-mindedness and imaginations, were the foundation of her pretended gifts of the Holy Spirit, prophecies, etc.-

2: That therefore the calling of persons into the ministry of Christ was false, and was only human arrogance, especially the calling of the new apostles, who therefore were not apostles of Jesus Christ, but spiritual seducers;

3: That, therefore, the Apostolic church was not the church of Jesus Christ, but an assembly of high-minded fanatics, who imagine that through the laying on of hands of their self-made apostles, they receive (the sealing) the Holy Spirit and the 144000 sealed form the Bride of the Lamb, who will rise alive to Heaven, before the anti-Christian persecution, and will not come under the tribulation.

4: That She imagines herself to be the body of Jesus Christ, or the only, Holy Catholic Apostolic church.

5: That nowhere in the Holy Scripture it appears, that after the first twelve, in the last days, new apostles must again come.

These are in short the not-so-mild accusations, with which Babylon attacked the Apostolic church, the cup, which she filled for her, the Babylonian power, wherewith she threw out her believers, cursed, reviled, and still rejects, blasphemes and reviles.

This, - so says the commandment of God to the Apostolic church through prophecies: "Reward Babylon with that which she has done by testifying with double strength":

1: That she is Babylon or the fallen Christendom. (verses 2-7).

2: That God's judgement awaits her (verses 8-20) by the destruction of all Christian churches;

3: By warning her of the anti-Christian woes, which she will suffer, and wherefrom she herself, the Apostolic congregation, will be spared.

The Apostolic church did this in the above-mentioned manifest and still testifies continually through preaching and writings against all these accusations and revilement.

1: That whatever the Holy Spirit may inspire in the hearts of the believers in the various denominations of Christendom, the Holy Spirit with His gifts do however not live in them as in the older days and has generally left the Christian churches.

For herself, she urgently invites all to diligently investigate without prejudice whether, the gifts of the Holy Spirit, the healing of the sick, prophecies, etc. are active in her.

2: She testifies against Babylon's clergy, that they are not called, appointed and competent shepherds of the flock, but called and appointed teachers by man, or spiritual usurpers, who force themselves upon the congregation. She refers to the condition of the congregation, apart from God's Word, mentioning her deep apostasy in her spiritual life, her moral decay, and denial of the Son of God. her incompetent and anti-Christian attitude of her teachers as proof.

3: That Christendom therefore does not form the universal Christian church, even less can she belong to the Bride of the Lord, which must be prepared as a pure virgin, sealed with the Holy Spirit, and that in this unprepared state, and without the wedding garment (Matt.22:11-14, Rev.19:7, 8), she cannot go in to the super of the wedding of the Lamb, but becomes prey to the anti-Christian persecution and seduction;

4: That the many sects of Christendom, cannot in any way form the only body of Christ, the church (Eph. 4) while, disregarding that the outer unity must be present, their mutual biting, eating and consuming each other proves, that she also misses any inward unity, which must be present in the church of Christ (Eph 4:3-6, John 13:35, John 17:11); That they on the contrary form a Babylon of confusion, in which everyone says: "Here is Christ!" (Matt. 24:23)

5: That the sealing, such as it must occur again in the last days, can only be performed by apostles, and that the judgement over Babylon, as it is proclaimed in our last days by apostles and prophets at God's command and insight (Rev 18:20), could, and cannot be proclaimed by the dead apostles of eighteen centuries ago; and that therefore God's word and this Revelation of Jesus Christ must lie, or that in time true apostles and prophets of our Lord Jesus Christ must come again.

This is in short the testimony in preaching and in writing of the Apostolic church against Babylon, as it is proclaimed in greater detail in the manifest, and this is the double reward to her according to her works, and the double pouring in the cup, which Babylon must drink; because biblically it is impossible for Babylon to contradict this testimony and to refute this judgement over her on any ground. This double outpouring still continues and will in future still come to greater powerful might and effect.

Verse 7. **"How much she hath glorified herself, and liveth deliciously, so much torment and sorrow give her: for she said in her heart, I sit a queen, and am no widow, and shall see no sorrow".**

This testimony, which the Lord commanded His Apostolic church to proclaim over Babylon, also causes her pain and mourning, because it forms such a major contrast with the glorification of which she deems herself worthy, with earthly riches which she enjoys, and with the spiritual riches which she imagines to enjoy. Each of the Christian denominations Roman, Greek, Protestant as well as other smaller sects however, each consider themselves to be the true people of God and by excellence to represent the Kingdom of God here on earth. Each one boasts: I am the queen, the true church, the bride of Christ, and am not a widow, and not one of them knows or realizes, that because of her unfaithfulness she is a rejected woman, whose husband went on a journey in a far away country, to there receive a kingdom for himself, and then to return (Luke 19:12) to take unto himself a pure virgin as His bride. (2 Cor. 11:2. Rev .21:2, 9. Rev .22:17)

None of them believed, that they would mourn as foolish virgins; to be admonished at the return of the Bridegroom by Him; "Verily I say unto you, I know you not". (Matt. 25:10-12)

And yet to all of them the word of God predicts not only this mourning, but even poverty, destruction and annihilation of all her glory and riches.

This then is the lot which is predicted for them all in the following verses, and although we already perceive the beginning of the fulfilment, this prediction actually belongs in its entirety to the coming future days and will find its place in connection with the remaining future events.

The predictions of Revelation, for as far as they are already fulfilled in our days are hereby concluded. Any future events originating in the past will be mentioned in its right context.

SEVENTH PERIOD

LAODICEA:

B. The Present

The Present Condition Of Europe 1874 To 2006 According To
The Opinion Of Our Lord Jesus Christ

This period "THE PRESENT" lies entirely in the seventh period. It commences with the restoration of the German Empire and the inauguration of King Wilhelm of Prussia as German Emperor. This period of political unrest in Europe seems to be, according the indications of Revelation itself, the time wherein it will be declared to the congregation.

Dear reader considering that this is a literal translation of the author's writings at that time and that in retrospect, after another century of events has been added since then, much more can be said of this period "The Present" covers the period from 1874 to 2006. As the translator, having personally experienced ¾ of that period, I intend to include here and there some important events which occurred since 1874.

Since we will show the reader which part of the predictions of the Lord are fulfilled in our days, we must first look back, upon that part of the seventh period already explained still occurring today.

We saw how, in the seventh candlestick, that the Lord Jesus still advises the believer (Rev 3:18), while it is still the present, to buy of Him the gold of His truth, the true gospel, as it is still being proclaimed through apostles, the servants whom He sent for this purpose in the seventh period, - that He still counsels to buy of Him the white robes, necessary to take part in the supper of the wedding of the lamb and the eye salve of the Holy Spirit. Yes, yet today, as the Lord himself says (verse 20), He stands at the door and knocks for you to open. Therefore, who has ears, let him hear what the Spirit says to the congregation.

Fully in accord with that, we also saw in the seal (Rev 7:3), that the great tribulation of society is held back, until the apostles of the Lord will have sealed the servants of God on their foreheads.

In the interim we saw how through their (Rev 8:5) voices of pure Gospel preaching, the thunderings of glorification of the Lord's name, and the lightnings of the return of the Lord continuously occur. But also the satanic thunderings of denial of God; the voices of abuse against His only begotten

Son, Jesus Christ, the lightnings of scorn concerning His eminent return, the belief in a self-creative nature and powers of nature on the one side and the peak driven superstition, the infallibility of the Pope, on the other side – we also see these voices, thunderings and lightnings in full power over Europe, together with the self-inflicted upheavals of nations and changes in the conditions of society (earthquakes).

In the seventh trumpet we saw that the anti-Christian power in her seven headed and ten horn form already exists. And, although nine of her 10 horns still bear royal crowns, the time is near, such as the seventh vial shall teach us (Rev 17: 12), that also these will fall. Europe in the meantime goes on in developing herself into an anti-Christian direction. Total separation of church and state is, in almost all countries of Europe, the watchword, the question of the day.

But also amidst all these signs of the present last times, another great phenomenon developed unexpectedly and unobserved, of which the origin is in the past, but which in the last years, in the present, has revealed itself in its true meaning. This phenomenon, whose knowledge is highly necessary for each believer, who wants to be prepared against the seduction of the last days, is the performance of the false prophet, such as is dissembled in the seventh trumpet.

THE FALSE PROPHET

Or

The Beast Out Of The Earth

> For false Christs and false prophets shall rise, and shall show signs
> and wonders, to seduce, if itwere possible, even the elect.
>
> Mark 13:22

Rev. 13:11, 13

Verse. 11. **"And I beheld another beast coming up out of the earth, and he had two horns like a lamb, and spake as a dragon."** This beast from the earth is according to (Rev 19:20) the false prophet, the same, as the one who, in the sixth period (sixth vial) spread his doctrine of Pantheism in the Christian congregation. The beast out of the earth is again a power, consisting of a number of persons, although, just as the antichrist, figuratively is represented as a unit, as a beast.[52] Here already the Lord predicted (Matt 24:24. Mark 13:22) for the end time, when there will be great tribulation, these false prophets, will show great signs and wonders (Rev 13:13) to, if it were possible, also deceive the very elect. Apostle Peter also (2 Pet 2:1) says, that in his time there were already false prophets, and shall still come. Likewise, John says: (1 John 4:1–3) "Many false prophets are gone out into the world." Both however give us the characteristics whereby one can distinguish between these false prophets from the prophets of God, whether they deny the Lord, who redeemed them, and do not confess that Jesus Christ came in the flesh. This totally agrees with what we know about the Gnostics during the first three centuries, who primarily deny the appearance of Christ in the flesh and deny His redeeming suffering

---

[52] The False prophet in (Dan 7) is not mentioned separately. We find however in (Dan 7:8, 20) that in the small horn of the anti-Christian power there where "eyes like the eyes of a man, and a mouth speaking great things." The eyes of Christ we know as His servants (page 146, Vol. 1), a mouth as preachers of a doctrine (page 268, Vol. 1). We will learn to know these "eyes of man" and "mouth" as the servants of the antichrist, the false prophets, the preachers of the anti-Christian doctrine.

429

and death. In (Acts 13:6) such a false prophet is mentioned, a Jew, Bar-Jesus, that is: Son of Jesus.

The Holy Scripture, therefore, clearly indicates what we have to understand under "false prophets". We have already seen how the Spirit (doctrine) out of the mouth of the false prophet in the sixth period as Pantheism, penetrated the church, although not openly accepted as the truth in the church. With the seventh period this has changed, and in pantheistic modernism we clearly see, how the false prophet, *as an earthly power* or *beast,* openly performs and passes itself off as **The** truth in Christianity (without the true Christ), how they repel the Christian Gospel truth from the church, and only maintain the Christian moral doctrine.

The modern, pantheistic teachers, with their followers, are therefore *the false prophet,* or the ecclesiastic power, which as beast (power) performs out of the Christian ordinances (earth) just as the anti-Christian state power performs as a beast out of the sea of nations. This will never increase. The false prophets of the first centuries shall again perform in anti-Christian Pantheism, but then as the only recognized truth by the state. Gnosticism in the first three centuries was nothing else than a still-developing emblem of Pantheism mixed with heathen idolatry and philosophical dreams.

Of all this inconceivableness, purified through the philosophy of the eighteenth and nineteenth centuries, Pantheism, as we described it in the sixth vial, will not only perform again in our time, but will be accepted and believed everywhere as the only possibility, as the only understandable and irrefutable truth for everyone, - as the true religion concerning the whole origin and life in nature, and of man in particular – as the only and simple doctrine, which solves all riddles.

Just like the "Beast out of the sea" in politics, the *other beast* or the *false prophet* also imperceptibly came up in spiritual spheres after 1830, as a result of the effect of the *spirits* or *doctrines* of devils, which had infiltrated Christendom and filled her pantheistic ideals.[53]

"And he had two horns like a lamb." This is the only external sign, which is mentioned about the false prophet, his whole personal description. *His total nature must therefore lie* **in these two horns**. *Horns* are the image of *power* and *might,* spiritual as well as earthly.

They were like the horns of a lamb. While this false prophet, as the servant of Satan is the opposite of the Lamb of God, and *speaking as the*

---

[53] In order to prevent any misunderstanding, we will henceforth name the beast out of the earth, just as Revelation does, the false prophet, to distinguish it from the beast out of the sea which remains the beast or the antichrist.

dragon, is the enemy of Christ Jesus, *the horns of a lamb* also mean *the horns of the Lamb of God.*

These are seven in number, according to (Rev 5:6). As we will see, these seven horns are powers and might wherewith Christ reigns and rules in the Kingdom of God, that is, the seven gifts of the Holy Spirit, and as such the same as the seven Spirits of God.

The false prophet only had two horns *like unto* the horns of the Lamb, (therefore not *alike*) and thus two satanic powers or might, of which his whole being was composed. We must therefore analyse the seven gifts of the Holy Spirit, as we found them mentioned by Paul (Vol. 1) and see which of those can be imitated by Satan. We follow a reverse order:

7. The gift of unknown tongues. He that speaks it, does not speak unto men, but unto God (1 Cor 14:2), edifies himself (verse 4) and prays in the Spirit (verse 14). This, Satan will not do, fearing to disturb his own kingdom, as also interpreting tongues, because he who interprets the unknown tongues, edifies the congregation. (Verses 5, 12, 13)

6. The gift of discerning the Spirits, especially serves to recognize evil spirits. (1 John 4:1–3). Satan knows this, for him, it is therefore of no value. He does not want to be recognized as a false prophet.

5. The gift of prophecy. Those who prophecy edifies the congregation (1 Cor 14:4), and the prophecy is only for the believer. (Verse 22)

4. The gift of miracles (Acts 13:11). Since his kingdom is disturbed by Jesus Christ, the devil cannot perform miracles, as he did in the time of Moses in Egypt, and only has power over the children of darkness. To plague them is not his intention.

3. The gift of healing. This is to him an abhorrence. Sickness and death came into the world by him, and he would not want to destroy his own kingdom. (Matt 12:25, 26)

There are now only two more gifts (horns) of Jesus left: _faith_, and _wisdom and knowledge of God_, and these Satan cannot only imitate in the form of a lie, but we will see, that actually *false wisdom and knowledge of God* and *an untrue faith*, are the two horns or powers, like those of the Lamb, of which the whole being and works of the pantheistic, false prophet consist. For the beast **spake as the dragon**. *How he speaks* we find in (Gen 3:1, 4, 5): *"Yea, hath God said?* what you deem to be God's Word; but believe what I say unto you, your eyes will be opened and ye shall be as gods, knowing good and evil." If in this denial by the modern theologians, that the Bible is the revealed Word of God to man, the already perfect first limb of this speaking of the old serpent is hereby repeated, just as much as these many believers are also guilty of this dragon language, where it concerns the restoration of the gift of prophecy. Also with them sounds the doubting or denial: "Did God really say so?" Pantheism adds the second limb through this denial: "Believe my doctrine, this is the true knowledge of the universe, your eyes shall be opened, and you, man, as the highest revelation of the world spirit, will feel yourselves to be equal to the God of the Christians, and be gods." However strange it may appear to the unenlightened reader, just as sure as the first is since long ago, the doctrine of the liberalists and of modern theology, even so, the later pantheistic doctrine is already deeply ingrained among lay people and clergy, and will reveal itself in her extreme consequence in the near future. As a remarkable sign of the times we may here mention, that already in 1871 in Vienna a new religious sect formed itself in this spirit.[54]

Verse 13. **"And he** (*the beast, the false prophet*) **performs great signs and wonders so that he maketh fire** (*seemingly*) **come down from heaven on the earth in the sight of men."** When Revelation was still a closed book to us, the usual translations, that the false prophet caused fire to come down from heaven before men, were already strange to us. Such a miracle would identify the false prophet immediately after the above prediction, and the temptation, to accept him as a true prophet would thereby be destroyed. Exactly because the character of seduction by false prophetdom must not be of a material, but of a spiritual nature, and be highly cunning and enticing, so that one finds oneself in his power without knowing it. Moreover, miracles do not only stand in irreconcilable contraction with the pantheistic doctrine but would also be a specific impossibility, if Pantheism were true. Such a miracle would therefore not only reveal the untruth of the pantheistic doctrine to her supporters and the lies of her preachers, but also the *believers*, after this warning, could not be

---

[54] She has already announced her existence to the government and revealed her programmes. She worships the creative power of nature as the universal spirit, and man as one of uncountable forms, in which the universal Spirit reveals itself in its continual development. She considers death as a steppingstone to a new form of temporal existence. Under the word: God, she understands an ideal of the highest step of perfection, to which the reasonable man must strive. Her norms are purely Humanitarian, firstly with regard to oneself; moderation, cleanliness, honesty, zeal, etc.... secondly, with regard to the neighbour; universal and particular humanity. The form of service is not yet finalized or has not yet been revealed. The doctrine of this new church is therefore purely pantheistic, and a true model of the future religion. (See Hollandsche Illustrasie, 1870-1871. No.48).

seduced by such a miracle, and this is actually the goal of the false prophet. (Mark 13:22) The usual reading and translation of the text can therefore impossibly be true. Therewith our translation not only gives the true text but also the whole character of seduction, whereby the false prophet will reveal himself, much more accurately and simply.

What the signs are is not unknown anymore. That they will be strange and highly seductive is sure, because the Lord Jesus says so Himself, (Matt 24:24).

Paul also said, (2 Tess 2:9-11), that they are the working of Satan, who uses all power, signs, lying wonders and every kind of wicked deception for those who are perishing by believing his lies.

What concerns the character of these signs, it does not only appear from Paul's prediction to be the work of Satan, but Revelation also teaches us in the sixth vial (Rev 16:14), where it flows into the seventh period, that the three unclean spirits out of the mouth of the dragon, the beast and the false prophet, are spirits of the devils, who perform signs. Under these signs therefore the signs of the false prophet are also included.

Whatever form these signs will take, we can definitely not imagine that they will be supernatural, or so-called miracles. In our days of unbelief, where all miracles, including those recorded from Jesus Christ, are rejected, the performance of miracle workers would be sufficient for condemnation by public opinion.

We see this in the attitude of the majority of people concerning the Apostolic church, and her obstinate resolve not to deny prophecies and the gift of healing in her, or, to attribute the last to natural causes. And, let us be honest, it is not only the miracles of Christ, of Moses, of Elijah, of the apostles, which are denied, but one just the same denies them from Satan.

One denies all miracles these days and therewith also Christ and the devil himself. By the false prophet performing miracles, one would again have to believe in supernatural causes, and thus ascribe them to God or the Devil. And none of these are the intention of Satan, because just as the service of God exists, in recognizing Him, the service of devils exists in denying it. In one word, a miracle would, according to our view, ruin the whole case of the false prophet. But why consider miracles here? Are we not too much under the influence of the traditional translation and understanding of the "miracles" of the false prophet? Does the text give us a reason for a better, more comprehensive and natural translation? Indeed! The word, translated by "signs" (revised King James), is used in a totally different sense. In (Matt 16:3), the Lord uses it for the sign of the times. Similarly, the disciples use it in the same sense (Matt 34:3). In verse 30, it can also not

433

mean miracles as in (Matt 26:48); and when in (Mark 16:17, 20) it is used; it is not in the sense of miracles themselves, but of the signs of Christ's discipleship.

In Revelation (Rev 12:1, 3. Rev 15:1) it refers to a *portent*. Likewise, the words used by Paul (2 Tess 2:9) and by Jesus (Matt 24:24), translated as miracles, actually are *unusual signs of the future* (portents), and this meaning is exactly what is the case here. A miracle cannot be a lie, except in the sense of a miraculous lie, which is represented as a truth. Here the meaning is at most *strange signs* and *wonderful matters*.

In Revelation, the word used by Paul (Teras) does not appear. The *great signs* of the false prophet in (Rev 13:13) and the *wonders* in (2 Tess 2:9), can therefore, in their actual meaning as well as in the Biblical use of these words, simply only mean: *Great Portents*, **by which he will reveal himself by his performance, to proclaim wonderful things as truth, which are nothing but lies and deceit**. We understand very well that our authority is not sufficient, in order to make our interpretation of the usual traditional text acceptable as the correct one. We can, however, add the words of our Lord as confirmation. When John describes it he says, that the false prophet does or *makes* great signs. He uses his own human imperfect language to describe this vision.

The Lord is infinitely more accurate in His words, and when He speaks in (Matt 24:24 and Mark 13:22) of this false prophet, he uses in the original, according to the testimony of both writers, these words: they will produce great signs. The Lord uses the same words, written in (Matt 26:48) about the sign which Judas gave, whereby Jesus had to be recognized. Hereby all foundation for the traditional interpretation of signs disappears as well as the same references to miracles in (Matt 18 and Mark 13). On the authority of the Lord's own words, we may therefore present our translation as the true one. **(In 1971 the new revised King James version was published and confirms the above Statements).**

For that matter, the interpretation and fulfilment will wholly confirm it. The sole intention of the false prophet will be: to prove, that the true God of the Bible does not exist, and to replace the Christian Biblical doctrine with the pantheistic one. Just as the beast came up in 1830 out of the Christian Sea of Nations and became physically recognizable in 1871, the false prophet also came up in 1830, and in the last years has become increasingly recognizable in his blasphemous striving. **The great signs** which he will perform, and the wonderful lies, which he will proclaim as true, and by which he will deceive men, are already clearly defined in our days in all subjects of science and education. They are such remarkable signs of the times that we would like to point them out.

In our century, the seventh period of Revelation, which began in 1815, the more general study of science has replaced the former more cultivated, speculative philosophy. Unheard-of inventions are also the practical results thereof. Consider the steam engine, with its resulting manufacturing of manifold machines, factories, railways, electricity, photography, spectral analysis, etc., all things which one could not even dream of before 1815 - that fifty years later they would have developed to such an extent. A very pious and understanding man already said to us in the years 1835-1840 several times: "With all these fast-developing inventions and general applications of the steam engine, railways and the magnetic telegraph, which abolish all time and distance, it is clear that we come to the end of our present dispensation and that the time will be shortened." (What would he say in 2006?)

Indeed, the coincidence of all these inventions with the beginning of the seventh period is too remarkable, not to mention it. The parallel or shadow of the spiritual must reflect in the natural. At the beginning of the seventh period in 1830, God again spoke through His prophets and apostles bringing light into the darkness and new spiritual life could be experienced. Today, we say that we live in an enlightened time. This also applies to the natural life and we thus live in a time where both spiritual and natural life are enlightened.

The restless study of science has however, come to conclusions from other discoveries about world philosophy and the history of creation, which are much too unripe fruits of science, and however unripe and founded on too little evidence they, however, were accepted with remarkable eagerness, spread around and swallowed, only because they contradicted the hated doctrine of the Bible concerning one God and Creator, and to make out the creation story of the Bible for once and for all to be a lie. Geology, or the knowledge of the forming of the earth, claims to have discovered, that the earth must already exist for billions of years, and not only was habitable for millions of years, but was also populated. One irrefutable proof of this for her was when, several years ago, during excavations, a human jawbone was found in the so-called tertiary layer, considered one of the oldest, and before then declared uninhabitable.

Now it becomes an undisputed fact, that this old tertiary layer was inhabited by man for billions or trillions of years. A healthy unprejudiced mind could here ask the geologists whether the so well-known landslides could be involved; or, on denial thereof, doubtfully make the remark, that the people who lived on the tertiary layer, only consisted of one jawbone, for otherwise more human fossils should have been found.

Such a remark is in vain, it only testifies to stupidity, not placing enough value upon science and not relying on her declarations, and even as Samson conquered the Philistine with the jawbone of a donkey, the geologists mean, that should the former discoveries not be enough, now with this donkey-like jawbone the Christians, with their Biblical doctrine of the age of man, yes even the Bible's birth registers are conquered for good.

Zoology, the knowledge of living beings, likewise came to the same results, by the evolution theory of Darwin.

This presupposes that all living beings including man originated from single original forms through self-development, and through self-changes, according to circumstances under which they had to live, evolving into manifold intermediate forms, after millions of years and so came to be in their present form, while all the intermediate forms which were not viable disappeared. With astounding approval, this theory was received and immediately accepted as an indisputable truth. A Christian scientist may remark that Geology should have found fossils of appalling masses of intermediate forms, and since it is not so, unchristian Zoology totally contradicts unchristian Geology, and both sciences are too undeveloped to make any statements. One could utter the well-founded remark, that experience teaches, that with animals, divergence in species always reverts to its original primitive form in succeeding generations, and that formerly totally different laws must have ruled the animal world than today, and that once more a pantheistic world order is an impossibility, - all for nought! The Darwin fantasy is accepted as truth, and the Biblical doctrine of the original creation of man and animals in their present condition by God is declared foolishness.

"But what is it then?" asks an admirer of this theory "that suddenly caused suggestions to be accepted, which during half a century, had to waver repeatedly under the criticism of the most advanced Systematics?" Revelation answers: the anti-Christian principle, the false prophet. The longing to deny the God of the Bible causes moreover intelligent and scientific men to overrate the poor results of their striving to such an extent, that they take the boldest leap in their conclusions, and accord infallibility to the decisions, so bold and so lacking in support, that they themselves would contradict them with all might if they occurred in any other science.

Likewise, the same pantheistic principle reveals itself in plants and chemistry, for in as much as they are open to it. It should be clear to everyone, that, out of some observations, it resulted that under favourable conditions, raw material can take on life and form, and that thereby the sharp borderline between the soulless and living nature has been bridged, and the universal soul or world spirit can penetrate all substance and change dead particles into living organisms. If these particles produce only **one** form, then the theory of Darwin, the **one** cell takes over, allows itself to split or bring forward bacteria, which infinitely multiply, group into all sorts of forms, and there you have the self-created origin of all living creatures on earth, who further multiply in all sorts of directions and variety.

The results of Astronomy are similar. Her greatest discoveries date from 1822, since the giant Herschel telescope.

In the last 50 years, this took on an appalling flight of the imagination, and although her textbooks, even in our days, still teach us that God is the creator of the universe, the ideologised pantheistic doctrine already has infiltrated this science. Some observations, even though insufficiently proved, caused the minds of the students of this normally exact science to reel. The steady contraction of core formation, which one seems to observe in some nebulae, in conjunction with some nebulous stars, already suggests the continued forming of new universes. This does however not prove, that this does not occur through God's creative hand, and that the earth and our whole universe could not have been brought about in the same way, but self-creation, self-forming and perfection, also now becomes the watch-word in this science which previously glorified God, and the world can expect the performance of a Darwin, as an apostle of unbelief, with a completely pantheistic doctrine concerning the origin of the universe (Cosmology). Alexander of Humbolt was already a forerunner, although this type of universe was proposed by Alexander Friedman and Abbe Georges Lemaitre in the 1920s, the modern version was developed by George Gemow and colleagues in 1940. (Encyclopedia Britannica). The building blocks for this theory were sought after everywhere. Her reason is again: no personal God! Away with the Biblical teaching!

And what will we say of scientifical theology, the theology herself? She, who should be at the peak of the defenders of the Bible, stands in the front row to break down her own Bastion and fortress. Of the Old Testament, nearly not one book, according to her infallible critique, was ever written by the person named as the author.

According to her recent bulletins, only the letters to the Romans, Galatians and the Corinthians of the New Testament are authentic. The Revelation of John only contains Jewish dreams and riddles, - fortune-telling in the style of that time, from which anyone can make what he wants, and which was written by an impostor who named himself John.

The Gospels are declared as non-authentic, and written from 150 to 300 years after Christ, by people, claiming to be eyewitnesses of Jesus life and suffering, but are exposed as deceivers by modern theological critique. The Gospel teaching therefore has just as much worth and authority as that of Mohammed and is only an expression of the mindset of that time, which in our days must make way for more accurate conceptions. In return for what the newer theology breaks down, she does not give anything back except her vague pantheistic teachings, and of all the sciences, in her present pantheistic direction, modern theology itself is most advanced in anti-Christian spirit and instead of divine, theology has become a philosophy. One should not suspect us of wanting to end free scientific research. We here only come up against the fact, that scientific research in whichever field, is not free, does not go out with an honest and unprejudiced view, but is already caught up in the anti-Christian mindset, and endeavours to gather everything, which can lead to the denial of Biblical revelation.

All these anti-Christian revelations would be less damaging if the present conclusions and declarations of the scientists were limited to the scientific arena, but the servants of the false prophet see to it, that they make known as much as possible, as irrefutable truth, amongst the people, and while in the state schools, for good appearances, and for those who want to attend, one hour is set aside for the teaching of cold Deism and morals, the young students are immediately bombarded with the Bible denying declaration of Geology and the teaching of Darwin, whereby all faith in the Bible is destroyed in their young hearts. Although we would like to believe, that with this good faith and conviction of the teachers is still prevalent, it is exactly this conviction in good faith which is the proof, that the false prophet has already come and all their Bible contradictions, and her whole authority with so many contrary destroying declarations of the new sciences, are the signs, which the false prophet performs, and the false truth which he proclaims, while they are indeed nothing but lies and deceit of Satan, whereby he seduces the souls. In the present climate it will all continue in rising measure and sketch itself ever sharper until it resolves itself in the establishment of the public religion of the false prophet, such as Revelation will shortly reveal unto us.

We have intentionally described this anti-Christian tendency in science, church and school quite extensively because in this we see the signs and wonders of lies of the false prophet, and that every reader may understand these signs, which the prophet already performs in our days, and to draw the attention of those, who expect miracles, that they perhaps unwittingly are already seduced by the false prophet, while they, because of the lack of miracles, still consider him not to have come. And if we should be wrong in our interpretation, the reader is still warned by our writings against the finer seduction of the presently available, popular proposed results of science, and her fatal influence on the Christian faith.

We for one cannot expect any seeming wonders or supernatural signs from the false prophet. Should they ever occur, then they would warn against themselves.

In both cases however, the warning must be written with blazing letters in the soul of our reader, which for more than 3400 years was also recorded for us in (Deut 13:1–3): *"If there arise among you a prophet, or a dreamer of dreams, and giveth thee a sign or a wonder, and the sign or the wonder, whereof he spake unto thee, saying, let us go after other gods, which thou hast not known, and let us serve them. Thou shalt not hearken unto the words of that prophet or that dreamer of dreams; for the Lord your God proveth you, to know whether ye love the Lord your God with all your heart and with all your soul."*

As another sign of the times, we see that in our 21st century, the words of (Isaiah 4:1) are increasingly being fulfilled. **"And in that day seven women shall take hold of one man, saying, we will eat our own bread, and wear our own apparel; only let us be called by thy name, to take away our reproach".** This is exactly what takes place in our days and to understand this prophecy we again make use of the imagery language of the Holy Spirit. A "woman": is a group of believers, and "seven" here refers to a number of denominations with different views, they want to eat their own bread: "They formulate and live by their own doctrine", all having the same recipe, namely the Bible, but each adding or subtracting some of the ingredients according to their reasoning. They also want to wear their own robe of self-righteousness instead of the robe of righteousness which Jesus offers, believing that their sins are already forgiven through the sacrifice of Jesus Christ and they do not need anyone to forgive their sins in the name of Jesus Christ. They firmly believe like the scribes of old (Mark 2:7) that only God can forgive sins. The **one man** they approach is our Lord Jesus Christ because they are very interested in being called by His name, they want to be known as *Christians*. Does the cry: *"Take Jesus as your personal Saviour and you will be saved",* sound familiar?

This prediction of Isaiah truly reflects the condition in the Protestant church which is divided and is continually dividing in our time. Each denomination formulating its own view of the gospel, (*baking its own bread.*), usually inspired by human reasoning, and categorically rejecting the truth. Whilst translating this work I encountered several adverts in various daily papers concerning newly formed churches inviting believers to their services with the slogan: *"All about love."* Nothing about Christ or His teaching, but purely moral doctrines, in a truly pantheistic spirit.

"And (maketh) **fire"**. – Fire is well described in the first trumpet as holy or unholy fire. With the false prophet it can only be the last. This whole sentence is a contradiction of (Exod 19:18–20. John 3:13, 31. John 6:3-58. and Acts 2:2–4). Because just as Jesus equipped His disciples with the fire or the gifts of the Holy Spirit, whereby they (Acts 2:11) spoke the words of God in all sorts of languages, so also the dragon equips the servant of the false prophet with the fire of unholy spiritual gifts, whereby they blasphemed God in all His works in all sorts of languages, and with great talent, acumen and persuasiveness, ascribed the creation of heaven and earth and of all that exists under heaven as the work of God, to the fusion of all matter by the universal spirit.

This fire of zeal for their unholy cause and of brilliant spiritual gifts reveals in them also the satanic fire of enmity against everything, that is of God, and therefore the anti-Christian trend of our century.

"Come down from heaven on the earth in the sight of men." This is the ultimate goal of the false prophet. The coming down of Christ, the great Prophet, from heaven, was to bring the true knowledge of God, the only true faith and the only true religion. And just as Christ equipped His servants with spiritual gifts, the false prophet also inspires his servants with this false zeal and unholy brilliant spiritual gifts, as these false theories of science, so that through them, he may be seen by all men as having brought a pantheistic doctrine which seems to totally agree with nature as the true understanding of God and the only true faith. For this reason, his two horns are described as those of a Lamb, because before men he will appear to be a new Christ, who finally is the right messenger of truth. Thus shall the false prophet, or the pantheistic doctrine be considered to have banished the mist of the old Christendom, and to be seen as a new Jesus coming down from heaven to earth, and just as He, to reform the ordinances in church and state (earth) or the Christian society to his new religious interpretation.

In this role, we will see him performing in the third part **"The Future"**, when he will openly perform in his true form as the false prophet. Revelation therefore names him in his coming up: the beast out of the earth (Rev 13:11) because his true nature is then not yet revealed. Only when he openly performs in his true role is he named: the false prophet (Rev 13:14, Rev 19:2).

And now, reader! Together we earnestly wish to seek the truth. Therefore the question: Can the reading of (Rev 13:13) be the correct one? Could the apostles and prophets of the Apostolic church be the false prophets against whom the Lord warns? Can the sealing with the Holy Spirit (fire), be the supposed fire of the Holy Spirit, which they let come down from heaven before men? It would be a terrible error from them, who would believe these apostles and prophets.

Revelation and history luckily give us such irrevocable signs, that we should not for a moment ever be uncertain. The true prophets must warn against the anti-Christian worldly powers of the seventh period, as we shall soon see; in contrast, the false prophet seduces the people to worship these with great honour (Rev 13:12, 17). The Apostolic church has in her manifest concerning all this, made sufficiently clear and announced her disapproving judgement and her warning against the coming anti-Christ. Up and above that we found nothing in that which her enemies communicated concerning her, which could be construed as such an accusation.

The false prophet already existed in the sixth period (sixth vial); the Apostolic church only arose in the seventh period. She can therefore not be the playing ground of the false prophet.

The future part of Revelation will also clearly show that the Apostolic church will be the first to be persecuted by the anti-Christian state powers because she shall be the first, to warn the world, that the anti-Christ or the predicted *"Beast"* of Revelation has come, and exists in its completed form.

For the false prophets are according (Rev. 13) the obedient servants and warmest worshippers of "the Beast".

We have already said that Germany is the true breeding ground of the pantheistic nature mindset. One of its greatest scholars and nature scientists, Prof. Rudolph Virshow, in his thesis *Concerning the calling of natural sciences in the new national life of Germany* boasts that the trend, which presently rules the natural sciences, the thought, that everything is in a constant condition of development, actually is a German thought; - that the German nation can boast, to have brought this pantheistic trend to its present height and expansion, and deems it to be the calling of the state and science to reject the Biblical traditions and to unite this persuasion with the existing unity of the states of the German nation.

This is already the true language of the false prophet, such as he will speak in the coming years.

We now know the signs, that the false prophet performs. But also *the unclean spirits out of the mouth of the dragon, and out of the mouth of the beast*, (sixth vial, Rev 16:13) or the doctrines of *Deism* and *Atheism*, perform signs (Rev 16:14) or give portents, whereby one will recognize them in the seventh period. That of those who deny God (Atheism) we saw rising in the French Revolution in the sixth period, with her "bestial" consequences and again reappeared in the seventh period after 1830 in materialism, communism, republicanism, revolution, etc. Later in workers strikes, the Internationals, the people's motto: away with religion, away with the rich, distribution of assets, etc. All these are signs in the spirit or teaching out of the mouth (defenders) of the beast. They reveal themselves mostly in political and social spheres and are presently the order of the day.

The teaching of Deism, or denial of Christ, which arose in the sixth period, has appallingly expanded in our seventh period. The signs, that it performs, are indifference to religion, disdain and hate against all that is Christian. They reveal themselves mostly in church matters. Pantheism, however, now only performing in church and scientific circles, will in the future be working together with church, state and industry.

Deism, this doctrine or spirit of devils, brought about another strange sign and wonderful deceit, which cannot be overlooked, such as spiritualism, table motion, rapping spirits, or the calling up of spirits of the departed.

However much it may be denied by those who did not research too well, it is factually true, above all doubt. The concept and explanations however are untrue. The Holy Scripture teaches us, that already 34 centuries ago this existed. (Deut 18:11. 1 Sam 28:11-15). God's prohibition proves the possibility of calling up spirits. Spiritualism will however very seldom call up the spirit of believing departed such as Samuel. They rest in paradise (Hades. fifth seal. Page 190, Vol. 1). It cannot but be unchristian, whilst it is forbidden by God. (Deut 18:10-12. Lev 20:6, 7), and the supposed revelations of these spirits do not agree with the teachings of Christ. What is forbidden by God, remains a sin, as much for the dead believers as for the living. Therefore, no spirit of believers will reveal themselves, unless the Lord, as with Samuel, for a specific reason decides on this. The spirits who do reveal themselves are therefore not of the truth, but evil spirits of unbelievers, or – according to our experience – spirits of devils (1 Tim 4:1), who give themselves out to be that of departed, to thereby infiltrate the Christian congregation (Rev 16:14, 16), in order to contradict the teaching of Salvation and damnation after death, as taught by Christ, and consequently to deny the whole calling, merits and personality of Christ. The general results of this supposed spiritual revelation concerning life after death, and the existence of God are that in the hereafter no damnation exists, but that everything moves on in perpetuity and perfection; that a higher power than God exists, and that Jesus was a totally normal human being, highly developed and many centuries before his time. All this is pure Deism (1 John 4:1-3).

It is known to us, that upon this testimony of the person of Jesus, some exceptions occur, and the so-called spirits sometimes uttered words in a more Biblical, Christian sense concerning Him.

A great, well-known spiritist explained, that the personal conviction of the medium or the person through which or to whom the spirits reveal, influenced this, and changed the revelations according to their own mindset. This man did not realize, that he actually contradicted his own theory. If these spirits for all that, really proclaimed the truth, they would have to speak uniformly. Many spiritists therefore name spiritualism a yet unknown and indescribable **power.** To us, it is not indescribable anymore. We regard it, according to this Revelation, to be the works of Satan, totally in opposition to, yet mimicking those of the Holy Spirit. Both revealed themselves after 1830. The revelations of spirits occur under spiritual trance, much like those moved by the Holy Spirit. (2 Peter 1:21). We regard this therefore as driven by Satan, and the speaking of spirits or of a medium, as prophetic lies from Satan, and, just as with prophecies from the Holy Spirit, human feelings can influence them, (Rom 12:7. 1 Cor 8:9), personal feelings can also influence the supposed revelations in spiritualist circles. Likewise, we consider rapping, the violent movement of tables and other furniture, the wonders and signs, openly proved by Gebr. Davenport and Hume, as Satanic mimicry and in contrast with the wonders and powers of the Holy Spirit such as they are, except those of the Lord Himself, mentioned in (Acts 2:43. Acts 3:2, 7, 8. Acts 4:16, 31. Acts 5:19. Acts 8:39, 40. Acts 12:7, 10. Acts 13:11, 12. Acts 16:26, 27, etc.)

And – oh! wonderful anti-Christian consequences of the nineteenth and twentieth centuries! The last-named wonders are considered never to have happened, and the first are happening before their very eyes. Through these satanic wonders and calling up of spirits of the nineteenth and twentieth centuries, the satanic wonders of the Egyptian sorcerers against Moses, the calling up of Samuel by the witch of Endor, the sorcery of Simon, (Acts 8:9,11) and the other magicians of olden days, do not only become explainable, but also historically possible and believable. (Eph 2:2)

In this way these spirits of devils penetrated Christendom (Armageddon, Vol. 1) who must be the congregation, the body of Christ, and undermine in her the true faith. All this unbelief and superstition are the spirits of devils, the unclean and hated birds, who pick the good seed out of the Christian's heart, so that they should not believe and be saved.

So do they perform strange signs and portents, which do not belong in the church of Christ, and are gathered in the Christian church, Armageddon, the Holy City. There already exists spiritist religious denominations, complete with liturgy, prayers, etc…to which even some believers partake.

Poor Christian churches! You are filled with devils, and yet, your Lord promised, that the gates of hell would not prevail against his congregation? But then, you are not His congregation anymore, and must be found somewhere else.

Poor believers! Who will support and defend your belief against seducing wonders and lies, now that the Lord himself does not allow His voice to be heard through the Comforter?

But yet His promises, also those to His church, must eternally remain true. Therefore, also in our time, the congregation of the Lord must still exist, where the spirits of devils did not penetrate, but where He reveals himself through prophecies and the gifts and wonders of the Holy Spirit as the living head of the church.

THE GREAT WHORE AND THE BEAST

OR

The Anti-Christian Church And The Anti-Christian State

> Then I will declare to them I never knew you;
> Go away From me you evil doers.
> Matt 7:23

Rev 17

Verse 1. "And there came one of the seven angels which had the seven vials, and talked with me, saying unto me, Come hither; I will show unto thee the judgement of the Great Whore that sitteth upon many waters."

The question, which of the seven angels spoke to John, was often raised. Only with our explanation can an answer be given here, and the certainty, of who this angel is, is not only highly necessary, but the answer came as if by itself through our explanations. We know that the angel is the clergy, which arises with every new period. If now Revelation is consequent in her imagery, and if we also are consequent in our explanation, then the clergy which arose in the seventh period, must again be the angel, who in fact reveals the judgement of the great whore unto the whole world, just like the angel in the vision shows John this judgement and vice versa, the clergy, which predicts this judgement of the great whore to the world, must also be the angel of the Lord Jesus for the seventh period. When we later see in (Rev 18), that the first indeed is so, the second must also be true, and thereby it is ascertained that it must be the seventh angel, who showed John the vision and explained it to him.

This angel says to John, who in Spirit experienced the whole history of the church: *"Come hither to me in the seventh period; I will show you, what will happen to the great whore in the seventh period"*.

Verse 2. "With whom the kings of the earth have committed fornication, and the inhabitants of the earth have been made drunk with the wine of her fornication." With this short description of the whore, the angel describes in a few words the whole history of the Christian church, from beginning to end. Likewise, the actual angel of the seventh

445

period will also have to reveal to the world the history of the church from God's viewpoint, as we shall see that it already happened.

That *whoring means: falling away from God,* and *a whore is a fallen away church,* is clear from (Eze 16. Jer 3:1,2. Isaiah 1:21, etc.) See also the fourth candlestick (Vol. 1).

In (verse 18) of this chapter (Rev 17), it is eventually disclosed who *the woman, the great whore is,* which sits upon many waters, or (verse 15) upon many peoples, and multitudes and nations, and tongues. It is the Great City, who rules over the kings of the earth. The *great city* we already have identified in the sixth vial is *Armageddon, the Christian church.* Why does the seventh vial angel name her the great whore, with whom the kings of the earth have fornicated? The interpretations of the history of the previous periods already gave us the answer. We saw, in the first period, that the church remained pure for as long as she was led by the apostles, as visible representatives of the ascended Lord, the head of the church, and as long as she, with no connection to the state, even though horribly persecuted by it, recognized Jesus as the only King. We also saw that after the death of the apostles, with the second century, earthly minded feelings assailed her, that gradually the longing arose, to make the Christian church a state church, and unfaithful to the only heavenly King, began to fornicate with earthly Kings, until with Popedom a total break occurred, when the worldly and spiritual powers were united in one hand.

From the first period, however, when in the third century, this striving began in her, she was already unfaithful in heart and mind to her heavenly bridegroom and lost her first love (Rev 2:4, Vol. 1). From the moment that the church and state united, the congregation became and remained in God's eyes, the great whore, which sits upon many waters of Christian nations, with whom the kings of the earth have fornicated. If she longed for them, they also longed for her. If it was later pleasing for the kings and state rulers of the Protestant countries, that the church recognized them as head of the church and subjected themselves to her rule, likewise was it and is still a pleasurable feeling for citizen to be able to say: "I am a member of the state church, I confess the religion, which the state recognizes as the only true one, as the authentic one." This reciprocal inclination between church and state becomes even greater in the Roman and Greek churches where the worldly and spiritual power is personified in one person, and led to a marriage between church and state, whereby these two "became one". So did the former bride of the Lord, instead of remaining pure and faithful, waiting for the return of her Heavenly Bridegroom, not only fornicated with the kings of the earth but committed bigamy, yes even polygamy. She simultaneously married several men, and committed adultery with others, and so became to God a whore, who will be punished.

"And the inhabitants of the earth have been made drunk with the wine of her fornication." *The wine* we already know as the image of the *joy of faith*, which flows out of the true vine Jesus Christ (John 15:1-5), of which each Christian must be a branch (verses 4–6). Already in the prophetic blessing of Jacob for Judah (Gen 49:10–12), she appears as this image. The woman could not have become the great whore, if she did not fall off the true vine. Her wine is therefore not that of the true vine anymore; not the true, the authentic joy of the faith, anymore, not the comforting of the Holy Spirit.

By their fruit shall you know them. Do men gather grapes of thorns? (Matt 7:16). "For their rock is not our rock, for their vine is of the vine of Sodom, and of the fields of Gomorrah: their grapes of gall, their wine is the poison of dragons, and the cruel venom of asps. (Deut 32:31–33) The deviations therefore, in all possible forms and degrees, from the only truth, such as that given through Christ and His apostles to the Christian church, all the deviations from the original church, all those so-called consolations, all the joy of her untrue faith, are thus the wine of her fornication, whereby she not only intoxicated the inhabitants of the earth, but also poisoned them.

The wine of her antiquated fornication with the state, is the doctrine, that one must believe everything the state servants declare. Who does not here think of the intoxicating wine of superstition and the false hope in Salvation, of the self-appointed only saving Roman church; of the self-appointed Orthodox Greek church, or the wine of the doctrine of predestination, or the recognition of the Reformed church as the only true, by the Synod of Dordrecht, appointed by the State in 1618, or the Evangelistic state church in Germany, etc. Upon all was applicable, that which is written in (Isaiah 29:8–14). This is thus the judgement of God upon not only the Roman or Greek churches, but upon the combined Christian churches, as she began to develop into a whore after the first century, and remained the great whore and still will be, until the judgement is fulfilled upon her.

Verse 3. **"So, he carried me away in the Spirit into the wilderness: and I saw a woman sit upon a scarlet coloured beast, full of names of Blasphemy; having seven heads and ten horns."** The wilderness or devastated place, where nothing grows, is the image of an apostate church, where no green of living faith is found anymore. So were the spiritually dead Jews a wilderness, wherein John the Baptist before the advent of the Lord, made his voice heard: prepare the way of the Lord" (Isaiah 40:3. Matt

3:1, etc.) The *wilderness* is described in (verse 15) as *the waters or peoples*, upon which the whore sits. She herself is described in (verse 18), as the great city or the apostate church. It is therefore the whole of Christendom of the various peoples and nations of Europe, which John sees as the unfaithful woman in our seventh period, the unfaithful congregation, in a spiritual wilderness, without the green of living faith, where she was removed from the fellowship with Christ, and *sat upon*, or according to (verse 7), was *carried by the seven great and ten smaller states of Europe*, or as Revelation describes them, *the* anti-Christian *beast*, as we learned to know from (Rev 13:1). "The beast" is formed by all the European peoples, whose heads are the great and the horns the smaller powers. This woman being carried by the beast, corresponds exactly with the condition of the church, such as she existed since 1830 up to our days. Even now some churches are still carried by a very few states, in the other states only just endured. In (verse 16), however, the angel says to John, that they will hate the whore, and shall make her desolate, and naked, and shall eat her flesh and burn her with fire. Do we not already clearly see the beginning of the fulfilment of this prediction in all the States of Europe? Or is not the popular slogan amongst the representative of the people: "Separation between church and state," both in Roman and Protestant countries, a proof that the patience to carry the church is ending, and hatred begins? This therefore is the proof that we live in the time of the fulfilment of (Rev 17). We only have to refer to the clashes in Prussia, Italy, in Hungary, etc... as we have seen them in recent years.

The beast or the anti-Christian state power was in God's eyes scarlet in colour, better said, *crimson*, that is: *at the peak of a sinful condition* (Isaiah 1:18), the greatest opposite of white, the colour of righteousness; *full of names of blasphemy*; that is: describing herself to be a Christian state power, even king by the Grace of God, yet fallen away from God, separated from God's ordinances and are anti-Christian minded, hating religion. The original meaning of the word blasphemy was; speaking revilingly or scornfully about someone or something.

"And it had seven heads and ten horns." It is thus *Europe with its seven great and ten smaller states*, again as described in (Rev 13:1), that forms the beast, which still carries the whore, and is therefore the same beast or state power, whose influence on the Gospel preaching in the seventh trumpet, and whose enmity against the church as a judgement upon her, is described here in the seventh vial. A definite difference is seen in both descriptions. In the trumpet the horns are described with royal crowns; here in the vial we miss them. The reason for this is later given to John in (verse

12); "The ten horns which you see, **are** *ten kings which have received no kingdom as yet; but receive power as kings one hour with the beast.*"

It is clear, that here we have to do with rulers, who possess the power, but not the worthiness of our constitutional kings, and must therefore be the presidents of the ten smaller republics. The role and position of Thiers and his successors in the French Republic are shining example thereof.

It is remarkable that John is shown the beast, with seven heads and ten horns as existing, and yet it later says that these horns had not yet received power. The only satisfactory explanation was given when we interpreted (Rev 13), that in 1871 this form of the seven headed and ten horned (presently still crowned) state powers in Europe came into being, but in her combined political condition at the same time the coming republican seven and ten are actually prepared.

With this also corresponds, that in (Rev 13) only the seven heads had names of blasphemy written on them, while here according to (verse 3) the whole anti-Christian beast, in its completed form, will be full of names of blasphemy.

These events, although still in the future had to be touched upon, because the history of the woman and of the beast appear interspersed in this chapter, and this chapter up to (verse 10) has been fulfilled in our time.

Verse. 4. **"And the woman was arrayed in purple and scarlet colour, and decked with gold and precious stones, and pearls, having a golden cup in her hand full of abominations and filthiness of her fornication."**

The believers who come out of the different denominations from that period together form the woman clothed with the sun, that is: with Christ and His righteousness (Rev 12:1). *The denominations of the unbelieving Christians are* **the woman** *or church* **arrayed with purple**, the image of the *high worthiness and royal power*, (Dan 5:7. Luke 16:19) and therefore of power and high worthiness in the external church life, a presumption, as if she truly had the kingdom of God and the true way to eternal life, or was the only true universal Christian church. With all of them, especially with the three big ones, the Roman, Greek and Protestant denominations, we find not only the outward high power and worthiness, but also inward self-emulation. Although they arrayed themselves with purple, they are in God's eyes covered with the scarlet of her great unrighteousness. The woman **is decked with gold**; outwardly only, the church is decked with a thin layer, **a glimmer of truth** (gold), inwardly she is whoring and an apostasy. She is decked with **precious stones and pearls. Precious** stones are not only jewels, but also **hewed stones to lay the foundation of the**

449

house, or **marble, porphyry**, etc.. (1 Kings 5:17; 1 Kings 7:9-11, 1 Kings 10:2, 10, 11. 1 Chr 29:2. 2 Chr 3:6. Est 1:6 and 1 Pet 2:5).

The woman is therefore not herself *a pearl, a treasure in the kingdom of Heaven* (Matt 13:45, 46): she is not even a *costly jewel*, nor a *carrier of the light of the Holy Spirit* (Rev 21:11, 19-21), she is only decked with this all; *with men in faith, Christian knowledge and shining examples*, such as can still be found in most of the denominations and who are her supporting *pillars, cornerstones or her adornment.*

"Having in her hand a golden cup full of abominations and filthiness of her fornication."

She therefore did not have the pure Word of God in her hand, to quench the people's thirst with fresh water, which flows unto eternity, neither with the wine from the true vine Jesus Christ, yet a golden cup full of abomination and filthiness of her fornication. Likewise was also the *godless* Babylonian *world power*, a *golden cup which made the nations drunk of her wine* (Jer 51:7): *this cup was the power to the destruction of the people, who had to drink from it.* (Isaiah 51:22, 23). Likewise Jesus also describes his rejection by the Jews, which he had to suffer, his suffering and death, a *cup*, which he had to drink (Matt 20:22. Matt 26:39, 42).

The woman also has the present Babylonian golden cup in hand, that is: the doctrine of state churches, and the power to the destruction of nations, through human conceptions and confessions of faith, Christian morality and subjection to the authorities, to preach her statements concerning religious matters. For this she calls herself the church, the true, pure, Christian church, not polluted with the fanaticism or apostasy of other sects, but the true descendants of the Apostolic church, and thereby drugs the nations with the abominations and filthiness of her fornication or falling away from God, which are found in the Christian states and in the conditions in the society of the earth.

Verse 5. **"And upon her forehead was a name written, MYSTERY, BABYLON THE GREAT, THE MOTHER OF HARLOTS AND ABOMINATIONS OF THE EARTH."**

John saw the name: "Babylon the Great", written upon her forehead. This name was a mystery. To him however, it would not remain a mystery, since the angel immediately gave him the explanations. To herself however, and to all, who drink the wine of her fornication, or of the doctrine of her unevangelical Christendom, it was and still is a mystery.

That she is the great Babylon, the fallen church, that she is the mother of all false doctrines and of all the *dissenting sects and church denominations*, of whom Jesus is not the living, speaking and ruling head, and who just as their mother, are called whores;- that she is the mother of earthly high-mindedness in the church, which is an abomination before God. (Luke 16: 13–15) is and remains a mystery to her, *that she is the great whore of Revelation, while she imagines herself to be the Christian church*.

Verse 6. **"And I saw the woman drunken with the blood of the Saints, and with the blood of the martyrs of Jesus."**

The state church always persecuted the believers, from the second period, when the state church denied the divinity of Christ, throughout all times of Papal rule. And alas! also the Protestant state church made herself guilty of the same thing in various countries, if not always physically, then with social death, through rejection, dismission, imprisonment, etc.

She (the State church) will also still in the last days, as soon as she is totally anti-Christian, and the anti-Christian human deification has become the state religion, horribly persecute and kill the believers, who do not want to deny the name of Jesus, as Revelation further on teaches us.

The State churches in all countries have claimed to have persecuted the heretics, as they described them, who differed with them in faith. The great whore was still drunk with the blood of the Saints or believers and stupefied (Isaiah 29:9) by her fanatic victory over the heretics.

In the last day she will also once more be drunken with the blood of the martyrs of Jesus.

"And when I saw her, I wondered with great admiration," says John, and this will surely not be strange to us. It was impossible for him to recognize in the great whore, the Christian church of the first century, as he had left her, and to understand, how gradually she would so degenerate, and remain in existence throughout so many centuries, and *perform as the great whore*, she, who was then still *the Bride of Christ*."

Verse 7. **"And the Angel said unto me, wherefore didst thou marvel? I will tell thee the mystery of the woman, and of the Beast that carrieth her, which hath the seven heads and ten horns."**

The angel promises the explanation of that, which to John was an incomprehensible appearance: Firstly, who the woman is (verse 18), secondly, who the beast is. (Verses 8–14)

Verse 8. **"The beast that thou sawest was, and is not; and yet it is"**[55], In order to better understand church history in Revelation we have, in the

---

[55] The New translations here contain instead of the words: <u>yet it is</u>, according to another text: <u>and shall ascend</u> or <u>and shall be</u>, though this last reading is based on the best writings, we regard the first to be the original and therefore to be taken as the truth, firstly, because the difference in the Greek text is so minute, we consider the words: <u>and shall be</u>, as an improvement, made by translators: because they could not understand the reading:

fifth vial, amply described the beast (Vol. 1), how it <u>was</u> as the Roman-heathen Christian persecutor during the first five periods of the church, how, since the State became Christian, it apparently <u>was not</u>, although by its persecutions of the believers it revealed that it <u>was,</u> and how at the end of this dispensation, in the second meaning of the wounded head, the heathen, anti-Christian beast again shall ascend from the bottomless pit and thereafter go to perdition.

"And they that dwell on the earth shall wonder, whose names were not written in the book of life from the foundation of the world when they behold the Beast that was, and is not, and yet is."

Who are the inhabitants of the earth, whose names are not written in the Book of Life? The Lord himself says it to Moses (Exod 32:33): "Whoever hath sinned against me, him will I blot out of my book." They therefore are the unbelievers, who are not of the truth, who are not written in the true book of life, while only the believer's *"names are written in the book of life,"* (Phil 4:3). For the believing reader of our time, this statement of the angel is not strange anymore. We already clearly see how the increasing unbelief marvels at the rising anti-Christian state power, which wants to have nothing to do with the church, considering it as the right institution. Both for the liberal in his constitutional state, and for the republican in his republic, the popular slogan is: total separation of church and state. In principle they are right.

This monstrous marriage between heaven and earth should never have taken place, but when the bond is torn with violence, the whole family is unavoidably affected; the Christian society is jerked apart and disbanded.

We clearly see the principles of this disbanding increasing due to the growing separation between church and state. And when the beast will have reached its full potential as an anti-Christian state, only then will the marvelling of the unbelievers occur. Then religion, already considered as foolishness by intelligent human beings, will be totally abolished by the state, and *men,* as the highest creation, will be restored to their rightful place in nature and receive their well-earned glory.

"<u>although it is</u>." Secondly, we consider it as true, because it exactly describes the peculiar and historical being of the beast, that it was, and then was not, although it was. For the beast, or the Heathen world power, ceased to be with Emperor Constantine, and in the fifth vial (Rev 16:10), it seemed, in name only Christian Popedom, yet to be as "the beast" and up to our days to be, although apparently "it was not". In case the newer translation and the old reading "and it shall be" is correct, the sentence becomes weaker, yet remains the same in so far as, that the Roman Empire (beast), which was anti-Christian in the first period, in its final form, in the seventh period, again will become an anti-Christian or modern-heathen beast.

452

Those who then still believe in God and Christ and will not honour man as the highest being, must be removed from society as mad fanatics, or be taken as traitors. Then the beast out of the sea of the seventh trumpet has become the beast from the bottomless pit of the seventh vial, which ascends as modern heathen state power and Christian persecutor. That is the direction in which Europe is moving, the goal that it will reach to its own destruction.

We now come to the complicated part, which led to so many divergent explanations. The angel testifies to himself, that a deep meaning lies hidden in the explanation, which he now gives to John.

Verse 9. **"And here is the mind which hath wisdom: the seven heads are seven mountains, on which the woman sitteth. And they are seven kings."**

We must honestly admit, we do not understand, how this text gave the interpreters so much trouble. The sentence is so simple when one literally holds fast to the text. The greatest trouble is also derived, from the fact that one wanted to hold fast to a previous conception. This was according to our understanding, that these seven mountains, on which the woman sitteth, must mean the city of Rome (others: Jerusalem.), because already before John up to our days, Rome popularly is known as the city built upon seven hills, Urbs Septipolis.

We do not understand how interpreters, with so much zest, can uphold this above all doubt. To say that Rome is a city built on seven hills is just as great news as to say Paris lies in France, and that to understand such schoolboy science, the Holy Spirit would through the angel have to call upon the attention and acumen of learned and intelligent Christians? One feels that this conception is too weak, to answer to the earnestness of the text, because it has a remarkable deeper meaning as will soon appear.

The angel himself indicates that in his words lies a special meaning, which one has to investigate. The seven heads of the beast therefore have a double meaning: Firstly, that of mountains; Secondly, that of kings or kingdoms, which Biblically is the same (Dan 7:17, 23).

To understand this one must consider that the angel here describes to John, the relationship between the Christian church or the woman and the beast, from the first century up to our days in the seventh period. The beast is here considered in another sense than in (Rev 13:1 and Rev 17:3) and considered in its total being during all its consecutive periods.

But which are now the mountains?

Revelation already gave us the answer. Let us first remember, that the beast still is the fourth beast of Daniel, or the Roman Empire, which would endure until the return of Christ (Dan 7:9–18), and that mountains are the state churches of powerful kingdoms (Vol. 1).

In the second trumpet, we saw, that a mountain burning with fire was thrown into the sea. This mountain was identified as the heathen-Roman state church (Vol. 1), or the first mountain of the Roman Empire, which as the heathen mountain under Constantine was destroyed. Then came the Christian-Roman Mountain, giving way to the Christian papal mountain. These were already three mountains or different state churches in the history of the Christian church.

With the fourth began the worldly papal mountain, thereafter, came the anti-Christian papal mountain, and as the sixth mountain the Protestant state churches, while the seventh or popular anti-Christian Mountain began to rise. These are now the seven mountains or consecutive state churches of the Roman Empire.

The seven kings or kingdoms are on the other hand the seven corresponding state powers, of which we learned to know the six previous ones, as allied to the state churches. Therefore, the heads of the beast are mountains or state churches as well as kingdoms or state powers. The beast is in its total form, seven-headed, and has thus the mentioned consecutive heads in the 18th centuries but is also in its final form seven-headed, and will in our time also again consecutively have seven great state powers and seven state churches in the seven great nations of Europe[56].

It appears also that "the seven-headed beast," which we saw ascending in (Rev 3:1) under the seventh trumpet, actually had only one head and was the seventh of the seven consecutive heads or state powers of the Roman Empire.

"On which the woman sitteth." This **sitting** of the woman is explained in (verse 7) as **being carried** by the beast. Indeed! In the first period the congregation or the woman was carried and suffered by some of the heathen emperors (sitting on the first mountain), almost in the same way as she is carried in the seventh period by the anti-Christian state powers in our days. How the woman was carried by the other mountains in the rest of the periods is known to the reader.

The whole riddle is solved in this simple meaning. The beast or the fourth beast of Daniel, the Roman empire, will, during the twenty centuries of Christendom, show seven consecutive heads, mountains or kingdoms, but the last head or the anti-Christian Mountain, will also again possess seven great kingdoms, both we learned to know.

---

[56] These seven kingdoms are mentioned together in (Rev 17:16): as "the beast". In the best translation it says "the ten horns AND the beast will," etc. (compare verses 3, 9, 12, 13).

Verse 10. **"Five are fallen, and one is, and another is not yet come"**. According to the Greek text, it refers to the seven state powers, but while they were inseparably bound to the church powers, it also refers to the state churches, more so, because the angel combines the state powers and state churches in the image of heads of the beast. (Verse 9) We here have a picture of the past, present and future. It cannot therefore be the seven simultaneous heads of the beast, which is spoken of here, but of the seven consecutive heads. To understand this, one must realize that the seven heads are not the seven periods, but that in each of the seven periods, one of the seven mountains and kingdoms reveals itself. In this way, from the above-mentioned seven mountains and kingdoms, five are fallen, and the one, the sixth or Protestant state churches is, and the other, the seventh, the general anti-Christian Mountain, is not yet come. Indeed, although we are already in the seventh period, the sixth mountain or the old condition of the Protestant state churches still partly continues in our time, and the seventh mountain or the completed anti-Christendom, as the wounded head, which will heal, has not yet come to its peak in its second meaning. When this mountain has come, he must continue for a short space.

The coming up of the beast in his final form we saw in (Rev 13:1). His seven heads and ten horns could be seen to develop in 1871. His full revelation as anti-Christian state power lies before us in the near future, and with the forming of this seventh mountain, the sixth mountain will fall, while Christendom will disappear.

We, in the 21st century, have experienced the growth of this seventh mountain and notice that its completion is near, Europe has come together and formed the *European Community* and Euro-market, presently consisting of 15 nations or kingdoms, while 3 have applied for membership, of which 2 will be accepted, forming the 17 nations, (7 great powers and 10 kingdoms) predicted in Revelation 13.

We must here still add a word to a better understanding of what the image of a mountain in the language of the Holy Spirit means. The believer knows, that in (Isaiah 2:2, 3. and Micah 4:1–4), the mountain of the Lord describes the New Testament religion, and in (Isaiah 44:23), the singing mountains, are believing congregations.

Just as in the olden days the sacrifice was brought upon the highest mountain as a divine service to God, the seven New Testament mountains on which the whore sits for over 2000 years, also shows us, the divine service, as they would be implemented consecutively in seven different ways by the worldly and spiritual powers. As soon as another mountain or a new period of worshipping and belief arose, the previous mountain with its power in church and state fell and was disdained. The newly risen feelings in religious matters fought against the previously ruling feelings until victory was achieved, and the new mountain was higher than the former, as the previous periods have taught us. The falling of the five mountains, therefore, does not mean their total disappearance, it only means, that the religious persuasion, which previously ruled in church and state, had to give way to another persuasion, not forming the only ruling power anymore, but co-existing as a crippled power. The previous religious persuasions still exist with and next to the sixth mountain yet weaker in power. Since the Reformation the main seat of power in Europe is in the Protestant churches; otherwise, Catholicism would have overcome Protestantism. Also, the sixth mountain or Protestant state powers must fall; that is, it will also, like the five previous mountains, see its temporary religious persuasion diminish and make way for a new, seventh mountain, a new persuasion. This seventh mountain or religion is anti-Christian, which will obtain power in church and state above the other still-existing Roman, Greek and Protestant religious persuasions.

If we consider seven mountains in a row, of which the next one is always higher than the previous one and the seventh is the highest, then this last rules the other six.

Likewise, will the anti-Christian persuasion of the Seventh Mountain rule over all the feelings from the previous six periods. Just like with the six previous mountains, the woman, the whore, will also sit on the seventh mountain, now in a new figure.

Therefore the Roman church with her declaration of the Pope's infallibility will never again gain power over Europe anymore, unless she totally denies her superstitions and beliefs, and converts to a fully fledged anti-Christian pantheistic belief. But then she would however completely lose her Roman character, cease to be the Roman church, and together with the other Christian churches go over to the pantheistic anti-Christian, or the seventh mountain.

Verse 12. **"And the ten horns which thou sawest are ten kings, which have received no kingdom yet; but receive power as kings one hour with the beast."**

These words precisely describe the time in history in which we live. John was shown the anti-Christian state power of Europe, with her seven greater and ten smaller kingdoms, as she will execute the judgement of God upon the fallen church. The ten horns have not yet received their power, but will (verse 12), together with the fully developed anti-Christian power (the beast) receive their power. This still belongs to the future, when the seventh general anti-Christian Mountain, which is still rising, has fully developed (verse 10), and the ten horns will have lost their crowns.

We have previously indicated that these ten horns without crowns will be presidents of Republics after the kings are deposed or rejected. It yet appears that some countries, eg: Russia, England, and Germany are not ripe enough for a Republican system. Since this book was written, we know that Russia has no Emperor and has become a Republic, Germany likewise, while England still holds fast to a monarchy with increasing pressure from the people for its abolishment. Truly, things are moving. The prophecy must be fulfilled!

According to our interpretation, the point in time when the angel says to John: five are fallen, one is, etc. is not in 93AD, as many interpreters wrongly assumed, but while he speaks in the seventh vial, the seventh period, beginning in 1815, and not only in the present time but even more so after 1871.

We saw the fulfilment of Revelation in history up to the middle of verse 10 and of verse 12, while the sixth mountain or the Protestant state churches still exist. It is remarkable that the explanation of the angel up to now was wholly in the past tense (verses 2, 9ᵃ, 10ᵃ) and present tense (verses 8ᵃ, 10ᵃ, 12), while from there on everything is in the future tense as still to come. (Verse 10ᵇ, 12ᵇ, up to and with verse 16). From this, it appears however, clearly and convincingly, that Revelation is given especially for our time, and only would be understood in our time.

We therefore named Revelation, and our interpretation thereof:

The Book For Our Time

Concerning this we owe the reader a further justification. The base for this we luckily do not have to find in our own wisdom, Revelation itself gives it to us. Therein we found a remarkable and an eye-opening particularity which we did not find with any other interpreters. They are these: Revelation speaks in the past (had, etc.), in the present (has, etc.), and in the future tense (will have, etc.). Herein lies something particular.

Understand us well! Everything shown in visions to John or said to him, he naturally describes in narrative tone, in the past tense, I saw; I heard; the angel said, etc.…. However, where the angel of (Rev 1:1) performs as the interpreter, to explain these visions to John, he speaks in the *past*, in the *present* and in the *future* tense. This is now remarkable, that everything, which this or another angel, or the Lord himself speaks in the past tense has already happened, what they speak in the present tense presently happens and is present, and that everything, which they speak in the future tense, is not fulfilled yet. Why and wherefore? Only one answer is possible. John experiences in the Spirit the whole history of the church (page 25, Vol. 1). The point in time, wherein the angel speaks here, is thus the time, where the things, of which he speaks in the past tense have already happened, those, of which he speaks in the present tense, are already present, and also, that the things, of which he speaks in the future tense, still have to happen. From this, it follows, that at the point in time in the history of the church or the world, when all the things which are present, whereof the angels speak in the present tense, Revelation must also have become understandable and readable to the congregation. This point in time is thus the point in time in which the angels speak. From this, we derive two consequences:

Firstly, that everything spoken in the present tense, must also occur simultaneously, and if our interpretation is the true and the first true one, all this must currently be present. But also on the other hand, if all this is currently present, our interpretation must be true, the only, the first true one. The unprejudiced and attentive reader may decide before God and his conscience, in how far all this is present and our deductions are well founded.

Secondly, in case all this is currently present, the heavenly angels, who explained to John in the year 93, (Rev 1:1), cannot be the persons, who actually explained all this to the congregation and the servants of the seventh period. (Rev 22:6, 16), but must be the foreshadows of other earthly persons, earthly angels or messengers of Christ (Vol 1), who represent them (the heavenly) for the congregation, and declare unto her what has happened in the predictions of Revelation, what currently happens, and what still lies in the future. That it is indeed an angel of the Lord, who in our time declares all this, will be found by the reader when we come to (Rev 22:6–16).

Now in short, we will show the truth of Revelation, concerning what we said above, how from the words of the Lord himself and of his angels it appears, that everything, spoken of in the past tense is already fulfilled and gone by; that, which is spoken of in the future tense, is still to come, but also, what is spoken of in the present tense, is currently present and happens around us. A conclusive proof and right to the title we gave Revelation and this interpretation: **The Book of our Time.**

THE PAST TENSE IN REVELATION

The Lord himself speaks in the seven candlesticks in the present tense, to the then-existing congregations, and in this sense, the present tense in the verbs corresponded with the then-existing conditions. Also in this meaning of the letters to the seven congregations in Asia, our maxim concerning the time frame in Revelation applies. So was the candlestick or the light of the gospel in Ephesus in 93AD, not yet taken away, and the Lord speaks of it (Rev 2:5) as a future matter (I will) if they do not return to the first love. Likewise, to the congregation of Smyrna (Rev 2:10), to Pergamus (Rev 2:16), to Thyatira (Rev 2:23, 24), to Sardis (Rev 3:3), to Philadelphia (Rev 3:9, 10) and to Laodicea in (Rev 3:16, 19). Moreover, all the end promises in the seven candlesticks (Rev 2:7, 11, 26-28. Rev 3:5, 12, 21.) are spoken of in the future tense, because all the overcomers of the first centuries have not yet received the promise, but still rest under the altar (in paradise) of the fifth seal until they, on the day of the Lord, will resurrect to their part in the kingdom of Glory.

But also in their second meaning, as the prediction of the conditions of churches in the seven consecutive periods of the congregation, the same maxims apply. So was (Rev 2:5b) still to happen, when this Revelation was given by the Lord in 93, and the threat only fulfilled in the third century (Vol. 1), similarly the predictions mentioned in the preceding pages, spoken off in the future tense, fulfilled not at the beginning of each period, but further on in each period, that of the sixth and seventh periods still to come. (Rev 3:9b, 10, 16b, 20), as also the promises to the overcomers of each period.

Considering the seventh period in particular, we find that all the described happenings are already fulfilled, for as far as the words of the Lord or His angels are not uttered in the present or future tenses.

The point in time in church and world history, which is represented by the angel in his explanation to John, corresponds totally to our present time. We find this point in time clearly described in (Rev 18:8, 10, 12).

We will again clearly see the present tense in (Rev 22:6, 11, 17) where in verse 6 the angel says: *"The Lord sent his angel to show unto His servants the things which must shortly be done.* The angel is therefore already **sent,** that which he announces, which is shortly to be done, is still in the future. Also, verse 11 gives the <u>present tense</u> in the words: "He that **is** unjust, that **is** filthy, that **is** righteous, that **is** holy." And the <u>future tense</u> in the words: "Be unjust still, be filthy still, be righteous still, be Holy still.

THE FUTURE TENSE IN REVELATION

The unfulfilled and future prediction in Revelation are also spoken of in the future tense: (Rev 3:9[b], 10, 16, 20 and Rev 4:1[b]) when John in verses 2–11 will be shown how, after the end of the seventh candlestick, the condition of the congregation will be in the Kingdom of Glory (still to happen).

In (Rev 7:3) the words *"until we have sealed"*, indicate that this process is not ended yet. Also (verses 15–17) speaks of the future Kingdom of Glory.

More future events are predicted by the Lord in the future tense in (Rev 11:2[b], 3, 7-10, by the angel in Rev 17:8, 10, 12, 13, 14, 16.)

In (Rev 18:8–23. Rev 20:6-8. Rev 21:3, 4, 5-8, 24-27. Rev 22:3-5, 15, 18, 19.) the future tense is also used.

And in this way, the tenses used with the verbs, wherein the Lord or His angel speak in Revelation concerning events, totally correspond with the performance of the latter in history and is in this time not only the point in time, where the Lord and his angel stand when they predict or interpret the future events, but now also the time has come that Revelation should be unveiled, and therefore the Revelation of John and our interpretation may aptly be named: *The Book for Our Time.*

SEVENTH PERIOD

LAODICEA:
C.THE FUTURE

The Future Of Europe According To The Predictions Of

Our Lord Jesus Christ

This time period "The Future" forms the end of the seventh period. It ends when the kingdoms of this world have become the kingdoms of our Lord and of His Christ. (Rev 11:15).

In the time preceding this, the completed anti-Christian beast presents itself as the seventh head, the beast out of the sea, which, as the beast out of the bottomless pit – becomes the eight but is of the seven. (Rev 17:11).

So far we have handled events which have already occurred and are therefore already known. Now we have come nearer the unknown, and stand ready to lift the veil which covers the future. That we do this in holy apprehension, each believing Christian will certainly understand. Yet we may not hesitate. Christ gave His Revelation to His servants, to "show the things, which must take place, and the things which shall be hereafter. (Rev 1:1, 19). And he did not reveal this to satisfy our curiosity (Acts 1:6, 7) but, as we said in the introduction (Vol. 1), so that we may learn to know the thoughts of the Lord, his judgement over the earthly and spiritual matters and thereby avoid evil and remain on a good way. For this reason, the Lord did not say to us in simple, popular understandable language, what would still happen on earth, but in the prophetic language of the Holy Spirit, in metaphors, given us the signs of the times, whereby the believer immediately and unfailingly would recognize them, what is of Him, and what is of the father of lies. The prophecy is not for the unbelievers, but for those who believe. (1 Cor. 14:22).

This goal of the Lord must therefore be the guide in the still following predictions, to us as well as to the reader.

We will have to adopt a different way to interpret future events than that used up to now. With the already fulfilled (past) predictions, we only had to look up the meaning of the images, to find them in the events of the past periods and to point them out. This was an analytic (analysing) way.

However, we must now adopt the synthesis (combining) way, and, out of the given images of the future, make up the history of the still following and coming days.

The interpretation of images alone would for many readers be inadequate. Therefore, we will, according to our understanding, combine them in a presumable way of fulfilment, according to the amount of light that Revelation will give us.

The incomprehensive things which will still occur in the coming days, we will not try to unravel with our own ingenuity, but always through the Bible. The total corresponding conditions described in the Old and especially in the New Testament, will in the latter history of the Christian church, be the only source, from which we can derive the manner of fulfilment of the prophecies.

This is the only way to come as near as possible to the truth, and if this should fail, we will in all cases explicitly indicate the characteristics, which the Lord gives us in Revelation, to be able to recognize the events when they occur. The warning of the Lord in (Rev 22:16, 18, 19) does not only apply to our reader, but above all, to us and everyone who intends to interpret this prophecy of the Lord.

In the method of Synthesis, which our interpretation of future events will adopt, we must still permit ourselves one more deviation from that which we used up to now.

Previously, with each period of the past, we interpreted first the whole candlestick, then the whole seal, followed by the whole trumpet, and finally the vial, and translated them into paraphrases, followed by their fulfilment in history by given writers. For a retrospective overview, this was very suitable. The whole therefore remained close to one another. Here this all changed. The predictions of future times are elaborately described, and we would have, as in the past, to use four times the same time frame of the present to the return of Christ and therefore describe each event four times.

We, therefore, suggest unrolling the scroll of Revelation in its future fulfilment, and interpreting it, according to the chronology of the future, as events will unfold in the future.

We therefore divide the further happenings of the struggling church on earth up to the return of the Lord in three parts.

Firstly, we can expect the complete revelation of the beast or the anti-Christian state powers according to (Rev 13:2, 3). Therewith begins the seventh head, or the anti-Christian Mountain.

Secondly, the first resurrection and the flight of the sun woman, followed by the war in heaven and the 3.5-year tribulation.

<u>Thirdly</u>, the judgement over the anti-Christ at the return of the Lord with His Saints.

We will now handle each of these three divisions separately and take the text verses pertaining to the future history of Europe, from the candlesticks, seals, trumpets, etc., interpret them and combine them in the chronology, so that the reader may find the presumed combined version, which encompasses all the predictions, to a whole.

Has the part of Revelation interpreted so far not proved to be the key to understanding it, the only true one, it will now still become clearer. Of the images, which will appear in the future parts of Revelation, most are already known. In order to avoid repetition, and for the convenience of the reader, we now give an alphabetical list of all the images already interpreted.

Angel -	Clergy	Vol.1
Babylon -	The Apostate Christian church	Vol.1
Beast -	The anti-Christian state of Europe	Vol.2
Blood -	Natural life	Vol.1
Body -	Congregation	Vol.1
Book of life	The merits of Christ	Vol.1
Bottomless pit	The habitation of devils	Vol.1
Brimstone & fire	Hellish	Vol.1
Destroy	destroy	Vol.1
Calf -	The Shepherd Ministry	Vol.1
Cloud	The witnesses of the Lord.	Vol.1
Crown	A newly acquired congregation.	Vol.1
Death	(Second) eternal damnation	Vol.1
Door	The entrance to the Kingdom.	Vol.1
Eagle	The Prophet Ministry	Vol.1
Earth	The existing social condition of Europe	Vol.1
Earthquake	Changes in the Conditions in Europe.	Vol.1
Elders	Apostles	Vol.2
Eyes	Servants of the Lord.	Vol.1
Feet	The Evangelist and Shepherd Ministries.	Vol.1
Fire	Fire of the Holy Spirit	Vol.1
Fire	Satanic fury and anger	Vol.1
Fountains	Preachers	Vol.1
Fornications	Unfaithfulness	Vol.2
Gold	The Truth	Vol.1
Great City	The Apostate Christian church	Vol.1
Hail	Destructive Judgement of God	Vol.1
Heaven	The Kingdom, the church.	Vol.1.
Horns	Spiritual or natural powers.	Vol.1
Horses	Congregations	Vol.1

Hunger	Need of Spiritual Food	Vol.1
Idolater	Who places man next to or equal to God	Vol.1
Image	State religion	Vol.1
Islands	Missions, denominations	Vol.2
Key	Power	Vol.1
Lightnings	Announcing the Return of Christ	Vol.1
Lightnings	Satanic strife against the Gospel	Vol.2
Lion	Satanic persecutors.	Vol.1
Mark	Proof of citizenship	Vol.1
Measure	Investigate	Vol.2
Moon	Congregation.	Vol.1
Mouth	Defenders of a Doctrine	Vol.1
Murder	Who hates his brother.	Vol.1
Pearl	Exemplary men of Christian faith	Vol.2
Poisoning	Giving unbiblical soul poison	Vol.1
Raiment (White)-	The righteousness of the Saints.	Vol.1
Rain	Outpouring of the Holy Spirit.	Vol.1
Rainbow	A New Covenant with God	Vol.1
River	Preachers of a Doctrine	Vol.1
Rod	The Word of God	Vol.2
Sea	The sea of nations	Vol.1
Serpent	The devil	Vol.2
Ships	Mission work among the heathen.	Vol.1
Smoke	Destructive Judgement	Vol.1
Spirit	A teaching, which is proclaimed	Vol.1
Sun	Christ in church, state and family	Vol.1
Sword	God's Word	Vol.1
Sword	Worldly	Vol.1
Temple	The Christian church.	Vol.2
Ten	Number of the Kingdom of God	-
Throne	Royal Power	Vol.1
Thundering	Voice of God through Apostles	Vol.1 Vol.2
Voices	Gospel preaching through servants of God	Vol.2
Water	The Gospel	Vol.1
Waters	Peoples	(Rev 17:15).
White	Colour of Righteousness	Vol.1
Whore	The unfaithful Christian church.	Vol.2
Wilderness	The apostate Christendom of Europe	Vol.2
Woman	Congregation of Believers	Vol.2

THE FUTURE ANTI-CHRISTIAN STATE POWER

Or

The Beast

> But these things have I told you, that
> when the time shall come, ye may
> remember that I told you of them.
> John 16:4.

Revelation 13:2-6, 11, 12. Rev 17:10^b, 12.

One thing is certain, that according to Revelation, the appearance of the anti-Christ lies before us, in the near future.

It is impossible to form a correct image of the future, nor to see the true meaning of the present days when one has not first received clarity as to what the Holy Scripture understands under "anti-Christ". Only then can one be safe against all the errors, perpetrated by so many interpreters of Revelation. Anti-Christ, not only means: *against Christ*, but also the anti-Christ, the counterpart of Christ, that is, His copy, but in a total opposite way.

What therefore was, what is, and what shall the anti-Christ be? What he was and is, John will teach us, and what he shall be, Paul will, in total agreement with Revelation.

John writes (1 John 2:18, 19), "As ye have heard that anti-Christ is coming, even now are there many anti-Christ. They went out from us, but they were not of us". And in (1 John 2:22, 23) "Who is a liar, but he that denied that Jesus is the Christ? He is the anti-Christ, that denieth the Father and the Son. Whosoever denieth the Son, the same hath not the Father". And in (1 John 4:3), "And every spirit (doctrine), that confesseth not that Jesus Christ is come in the flesh is not of God; and this is the Spirit of anti-Christ, whereof ye have heard that it should come, and even now already is it in the world."

The beast was therefore already in John's time. "For many deceivers are entered into the world, who confess not that Jesus Christ is come in the flesh. This is a deceiver and an anti-Christ". (2 John 7). This last explanation makes it all clear. The many people, who do not recognize Christ as having come from God in the flesh, form THE seducer and THE anti-Christ.

467

Therefore, John could say, that the anti-Christ already was present in the world in his time, in the Gnostics, the Docetists, etc., who denied Christ as the revelation of God in the flesh. The anti-Christ is named in Revelation "the beast", or the world power hostile to God. We have already learned to know him in the Christian persecutions by the Roman Emperors (first trumpet and vial) as "the beast". Revelation further described this plurality of the beast in the (fifth vial), where it was poured out "upon the throne of the beast, and <u>they</u> gnawed their tongues for pain, and <u>they</u> blasphemed God, and <u>they</u> did not repent. The beast consisted in that period of the whole Roman anti-Christian and persecuting power. All the Popes, Cardinals, Bishops, councils, etc., collectively formed the beast (see page 217, Vol.1).

According to John, the anti-Christ consists of:

1st All the people, who deny the divinity of Christ and declare Him only to be a natural human being.

2nd All those who persecute true believers and faithful Christians and suppress the truth. Christ commands us, even to love our enemies, how much more should each one, named after the name of Christ, love his brother and fellow Christian, even though he may differ from him in belief. But "whosoever hateth his brother is a murderer." (1 John 3:13–15).

While John describes the anti-Christ, as he appeared in his time, and as he is in his inner being, Paul likewise describes how he shall appear in the last days, in (2 Tess 2:1-12), where we read: "Now we beseech you, brethren, by the coming of our Lord Jesus Christ, and by our gathering together unto him, that ye be not soon shaken in mind, or be troubled, neither by spirit, nor by word, nor by letter as from us, as that the day of Christ is at hand. Let no man deceive you by any means: for that day shall come, except there come a falling away first, and the man of sin be revealed, the son of perdition, who opposeth himself above all that is called God, or that is worshipped; so that he as a god, sitteth in the temple of God, showing himself that he is God. Remember ye not, that, when I was yet with you, I told you these things? And now ye know what withholdeth that he might be revealed in his time. For the mystery of iniquity doth already work: only he who now letteth will let until he be taken out of the way. And then shall that wicked be revealed whom the Lord shall consume with the Spirit of His mouth, and shall destroy with the brightness of His coming. Even Him, whose coming is after the working of Satan with all power and signs and lying wonders. And with all deceivableness of unrighteousness in them that perish; because they received not the love of the truth, that they might be saved. And for this cause, God shall send them strong delusion, that they should believe a lie. That they all might be damned who believe not the truth but had pleasure in unrighteousness."

When Paul describes the anti-Christ of the last days in this way, he could not have gathered all this from the Scriptures, even less from his own understanding, but we here have a true prophecy from the Holy Spirit, the like of which Paul often could testify of. We therefore can interpret the language of the Holy Spirit in our usual way. When Paul names the anti-Christ the man of sin, we may, as is the case in many places in the Old and New Testament, where it speaks of the man instead of many men, also take up the plural, and when Paul names him the Son of perdition, the Holy Spirit (Exod 4:22) names the whole of the people of Israel as well as (verse 23) all the firstborn of Egypt; a son. In (Jer 3:1: 9, 20) the whole Israel and the whole tribe of Ephraim and (Num 3:12, 13) all Levites: my firstborn son. John and Paul both speak of the anti-Christ in the singular, yet it is also meant in the plural.

Revelation will solve this, where, with the anti-Christ as the beast, it indicates all the anti-Christian unbelieving people as his personal head and ruler, who, together as beast form one body, just like Christ with the congregation. The son of perdition in his personal being, will, according to Paul therefore come, as soon as the universal falling away has come, and reveals itself in its full power, when the bridal congregation of the Lord has been taken away in the air, to meet the Lord. (2 Thess 2:8, 9, 1, 7). It is clear to everyone who knows the condition of Christendom in our time that the falling away is taking place as we speak. This consists of the denial of the Son of God, and he that denies that Jesus is the Christ (1 John 2:22, 23) he is the anti-Christ and has not the Father, (1 John 14:6), for no man cometh unto the Father, but by the Son.

This is the apostolic biblical teaching concerning the anti-Christ. In total agreement, Jesus himself describes him in (Rev 13:1) in his external form and in (verse 2) in his internal being, such as it must now be revealed. We have to keep in mind, that the seventh trumpet, where under this is described, sketches the condition and effect of the Gospel preaching in the Seventh period.

(Rev 13:2) **"And the Beast which I saw, was like unto a leopard, and his feet were as the feet of a bear, and his mouth as the mouth of a lion, and the dragon gave him his power, and his seat, and great authority."** The beast is here described as consisting of the most characteristic parts of the body of the three former beasts or kingdoms of Daniel, and must therefore incorporate the three most important characters of those three kingdoms, which will reveal themselves in the anti-Christian kingdoms.

When the mouth is the mouth of a lion, the feet are bare feet, the leopard can then only reveal itself in the remaining part of the body. We will not interpret the animal characteristics of these body parts with human intelligence, but investigate their meaning in the Holy Scripture.

If the believers collectively form the body of Christ, the unbelievers form the body of the beast. This body is like that of the swift leopard, who, with four wings of a bird on his back, is described in (Dan 7:6), as the image of the Greek kingdom, which under Alexander with his four generals (wings), conquered the Persian kingdom and a great portion of Asia in a swift invasion lasting nine years (334 – 323BC). The Roman Empire which came after that, the fourth beast of Daniel, which in its final form is the beast in Revelation, would possess the same leopard swiftness and thereby, according to (Dan 7:7, 19 and 23), would tear apart or conquer the whole earth (Europe). Also in (Hab 1:8) the leopard is used as the image of swiftness. That the body of the beast is like a leopard, indicated therefore that the unbelief or the anti-Christian falling away, will astoundingly swiftly spread over Europe in the seventh period. To every believer, who considers how swiftly the falling away from Christ increases in our time, it becomes clear, that we live during the invasion of the beast, on a Christian spiritual level.

His feet would be like those of a bear. The enraged eastern bear of (2 Sam 17:8, Prov 17:12 and Prov 28:15) is the image of an unavoidable persecution rage. His power is not in his mouth, but in his feet. The characteristics described for the fourth beast of Daniel, we find in (Dan 7:7, 19 and 23) in the devouring of the vanquished, just as the Roman Empire also carried this character. The nails of the bear's feet were according to (Dan 7:19) of brass, that is "corrupter". The Roman power is also described in the fifth trumpet (Rev 9:11, page 213, Vol.1) as the fifth head of the beast, Abaddon or Apollyon which is *corrupter*.

The feet of the anti-Christian beast are, as opposed to the feet of Jesus (page 250, Vol.1) also the preachers (teachers and shepherds) of the anti-Christian religion, who thread upon all truth from God, and with the nails of their godless teaching and humanness take hold of the poor weak souls and drag them to perdition. (Eph 6:12).

"And his mouth as the mouth of a lion." This mouth possessed teeth of iron (Dan 7:19, 23), which is cruelty and bloodthirstiness, whereby he broke the whole earth to pieces.

The lion in the first beast of (Dan 7:4) was the image of the great power of the Babylonian kingdom, which destroyed the temple of the Lord vanquished the people of God and imprisoned them. The mouth we know as the defender and preacher of a doctrine.

If we already know the lion in a good sense as the image of the apostolic ministry and of royal power, in an evil sense such as here, it is also used (Psalm 10:9, 10. Prov 19:12. Zeph 3:3) for the wrath of the godless, and in the Messianic Psalms (Psalm 22:13, 21), the ruling high priest, Pilatus and Herodus are described as lions. Even the devil is likened unto a lion (1 Pet 5:8). The character of a lion of the anti-Christian beast expresses his great power over the subjected Christian earth and nations, and, in opposition with the apostle ministry of Christ, his satanic apostleship to proclaim the new anti-Christian doctrine, which he preaches everywhere through his teachers (mouth). Lastly, it depicts the cruel godless persecution against the believing Christians.

Taking into consideration the characteristics, wherein the anti-Christian principles reveal themselves, as we said in (verse 2), then it must be recognized:

1st, By its swift propagation over the whole of Europe and conquest of the heart of the Christians (leopard-body).

2nd, By the trampling of Christ and the Godly truth of the Gospel by his teachers, who take hold of and drag the souls of the people in their anti-Christian faith, (brass bear feet with nails, as opposed to the feet of Christ.).

3rd, His performance as the head of a new state institution and religious teaching, which is not of God, but from the father of lies, preached with great certainty and conviction by his teachers, as the only finally discovered truth. This teaching is not from God, but from Satan, he will prove by persecuting all those who do not want to accept the anti-Christian religion (lion mouth).

Since 1830 these characteristics have increasingly and proportionally developed with the outward form, so that it is already possible, with enough certainty to predict in accord with Revelation what the final form of the anti-Christian religion and state power will take.

"And the dragon gave him power, and his seat, and great authority." The dragon or the ruler of this world gives his kingdoms and power to whom he wants to. (Matt 4:8, 9. Luke 4:5–7). The present seven great and ten smaller kingdoms of Europe already form the seat of the dragon. The power of the people, the democracy and the state powers, chosen by the will of the people, are already the might and great power of the dragon, and the history of Europe since 1830, already convincingly shows, which of the state powers of Europe want to receive their crown from him, or have subjected themselves to him.

The separation between church and state, which is the order of the day, here forms the touchstone. However praiseworthy of themselves, when they go out with a true Christian principle, even more satanic are they, when they, like currently in Europe, go out with an anti-Christian principle. When the state powers do not rule according to God's commandments, do not protect the service to God, but make the will of the people their constitutional law, they exchange their God-given ministry for the service to Satan, and they, although not according to human consideration, but according to the opinion of the Lord, are not rulers by God's grace anymore, instead of Christian governments, became anti-Christian governments, and thrones, and powers, and great powers of the dragon, instead of predecessors of the people, such as king Hilkian was described by the Lord himself. (2 King 2:18).

The state powers of Europe will increasingly continue in this trend, until they have fully received the power and rule (thrones) and the great power of the dragon, as the completely revealed anti-Christian state powers of Europe or "the beast" of Revelation, of which the previously wounded heathen head was healed. The result of the healing of this head is: "all the world wondered after the beast," that is, the whole of Europe wondered over the new state regulations and followed them. This becomes understandable, when one remembers, what we said before, that the principal state of Europe probably will be the forerunner in this trend and all the anti-Christian states will adjust themselves to it, "whose look was more stout than his fellows. (Dan 7:20).

To these changes in politics and society, as predicted by Revelation for the future, there must naturally have to be a reason. We know this already as the rapidly growing unbelief, and the influence of anti-Christian pantheistic doctrines and teachers, the false prophet or the beast out of the earth.

Verse 12 **"And he excerciseth all the power of the first beast** (the anti-Christian state-power) **before him, and causeth the earth and them which dwell therein to give the first beast whose deadly wound was healed the highest honour**[57].

Liberalism in religion leads to liberalism in politics and the pantheistic religious teachers or false prophets are the origin and the cause of the anti-Christian sentiment of the people and state powers.

Through the influence of this modern doctrine, the Christian institutions are rejected and the anti-Christian state power and state laws are considered

---

[57] The ordinary translation "worship" is here totally unfounded and stood in relation with the traditional understanding of the personality of the anti-Christ.

as the finally achieved ideal of good state institution and law. The result of all this is indicated in the parallel verse:

Verse 4. **"And they** (the whole earth of verse 3, or the people who inhabit the earth or society as it exists), **worshipped the dragon which gave power unto the beast."** Here the translation "worshipped" is in its right place, because they, who do not give the highest place in their heart to God, but to the earth and to earthly things, are described as worshippers of Satan. The anti-Christian power originates from the ruler of this earth (verse 26). Those who honour it, worship the dragon unwittingly.

"And they gave (his servant**), the beast, the highest honour, saying; who is like unto the beast? Who is able to make war with him?"**

From the honour given to the anti-Christian power it appears that to make war has to be understood in a spiritual sense, as the non-acceptance of his state religion and the promotion of other Christian conviction. It is indeed obvious, that the great multitude, rich and poor, as they currently possess no worthy Christian conviction, will say in all sincerity of heart that this universal pantheistic state and church institution, whose goal is humanitarian love and glorification of man; "must really be the true way, who proclaim such noble principles; that it is a better religion, than that of the old narrow-minded Christians, who all professed to believe in the same Christ as their Saviour, but charged each other with heresy and killed one another. As long as the old Christian religion existed, no rest or peace reigned on earth, but the Christians, whose teaching also preached love, for more than fifteen centuries, continually killed each other in the most horrible wars and divided into numerous sects, remained bitter and without love against each other. They thereby trod on their own doctrine. How differently are the nations now, made one, under one law! All differences between them are now resolved peacefully by the international court of justice.

This unhappy blindness resulted from the intolerance of the Christians of former periods for which they will probably have to account for in the day of judgement.

The fulfilment of this prophecy has already begun, but will daily grow into its full development as John saw it. We currently live in this time of completion, and it is interesting to lay the daily papers next to the prophecies and to see the prophetic attributes daily fulfil in history.

About the anti-Christian kingdom or the seventh mountain, Revelation says in the seventh vial, simultaneously with the seventh trumpet, in (Rev 17:10[b]):

"And when he cometh, he must continue a short time." The duration of this Empire, once it has reached its full potential, will therefore be short, as we will still learn.

Verse 12. **"And the ten horns which thou sawest are ten kings, which have received no kingdom as yet, but receive power as kings one hour with the Beast."** – The reader will remember, that the point in time when we wrote this, is the point in time, from which the angel explains, what is already gone by, what is currently present, and what still has to come. Full power has not yet been attained by the Ten Horns or smaller kingdoms in Europe. The seven great powers forming the power in Europe, are represented as "the beast" (Rev 13:1 and Rev 17:16). When these yield to the will of the people and the people's power, the small kingdoms cannot exist as such anymore, but must follow the general trend either of their own free will or by force, together forming the United States of Europe. It is remarkable to notice that although this book was written in 1872, the above predictions are swiftly coming into fulfilment in our time in 2006, and the E.U. (European Union) is nearly complete. As a translator, I have in my possession several articles about the E.U. with the heading "WE ARE FIFTEEN", stating that 3 more countries have applied for membership, of which two are predicted to succeed, then there will be "SEVENTEEN".

Previously, we have followed the usual yet incorrect state translation of (Rev 17:12): "For one hour", as no further indication is given about these words. Here we again interpreted it as for **one** hour, because these words must here find their explanation, and in the original text do not signify a point in time, but a period of time. The Greek word for an hour also means a while. In the seventh seal, the word, because one half was added to it, probably meant a duration of time. Here it is uncertain. It can therefore mean a certain short time (as in Mark 16:35. Luke 22:53. Rom 13:11) and thus here the time, during which the beast has full power (Rev 17:10) – or a given period of time of approximately 42 years. From the parallel texts (Rev 11:2. Rev 13:5 42 months), (Rev 12:6 1260 days) and (Rev 17:10 a little while]), all relating to the same time frame, it appears, that the word 'hour' here is not meant as one hour in the kingdom of God, but as a short while, during which the ten horns without crowns will receive their power.

Verse 13. **"The ten horns or future regents have one mind, and shall give their power and strength unto the beast."** This is the uniting of the seven great and ten smaller kingdoms of Europe (E.U.), under one universal anti-Christian law, whereby "the beast" is fully formed.

Verse 14. **"These shall make war with the Lamb."** This battle is the battle of the beast against Christ in His servants. As the anti-Christian government and law in Europe attains its peak, Revelation describes the future performances of this Empire in the seventh trumpet: (Rev 13:5); **"And there was given unto him a mouth, speaking great things and blasphemies:"**

Verse 6. **"And he openeth his mouth in blasphemy against God, to blaspheme his name, and his tabernacle, and them that dwell in heaven."**

The mouth of the beast, or his defenders are the anti-Christian pantheistic teachers. Just as the disciples of the Lord on Pentecost, driven by the Holy Spirit, spoke great things of God (Acts 2:11), proclaiming His glory for sending His Son, Jesus Christ, they will also speak great things, that is: the praises of pantheistic world views and religion. They will not only deny and mock God's laws and institutions, but this being the greatest blasphemy, deny His personal existence.

The tabernacle according to (Heb 8:2 and Heb 9:11) is the image of true Christian religion, such as it existed in the apostolic time, and thereby also in this seventh period in the Apostolic church, where God himself dwells and speaks just as in the Tabernacle, wherein also the Arc was, the image of the correct religion. The heaven is the Christian church heaven, and those, who inhabit it, are the believers in all other Christian denominations who still have to come out of Babylon.

Again we clearly see the language of imagery in Revelation. If one denies the meaning of the word "heaven", one must come to the ridiculous conclusion, that the beast or his angels will blaspheme the departed believers, who live in the second heaven (Vol. 1). And what is then the meaning of the word tabernacle?

The Apostolics, as well as the believers, who daily come out of Babylon and form the Sun woman, will be blasphemed as stupid fanatics, who still believe, that there is a personal God, who guides the fate of the people, hears their prayers, and speaks to them through prophecies.

Verse 5^b **"And power was given unto him** (the beast) **to continue forty and two months."** This is not a calculation of time in heaven or in God's kingdom, as in the seventh seal, but purely an earthly time for earthly conditions. This first period of anti-Christian power will thus apparently last forty two literal months, that is 3,5 years.

It is now imperative to show the relation and the similarities between Revelation and the prophecies of Daniel concerning the anti-Christian Empire. Revelation has primarily the goal: to predict the fate of the Christian church, during the existence of the fourth beast of Daniel, or the

Roman Empire. This Empire would, according to (Dan 7:3, 13, 14, 22, 27 and Dan 2:34, 35, 44, 45) last until the Kingdom of Glory would begin.

The angel, who explains to Daniel, the meaning of the four beasts, describes in (Dan 7:23), the heathen-Roman Empire, in (verse 24), the Christian-Roman Empire, and in (24^b and 25), the anti-Christian empire, as the final form of the anti-Christian empire (the little horn, verses 8, 11, 20, 24^b – 26). The Christian-Roman empire would therefore consist of (verse 24), the ten horns or ten kings, who would rise from the heathen-Roman Empire. According to our understanding of this prophecy, all interpreters made the mistake to take these ten kings as the same as the ten kings of (Rev 17:12). They have nothing in common but the description "ten kings", and the ten kings of John only appear, when those of Daniel cease to exist. Their meaning in the Kingdom of God is totally in opposition. The ten horns of Daniel are Christian kings, those of John anti-Christian rulers, who receive power together with the beast (Rev 17:12), or the little horn of Daniel, which only rises AFTER the ten horns (Dan 7:24). The ten horns of John cannot possibly be the same as the ten horns of Daniel, but only come up after the latter.

Ten is the number of the kingdom of God. The ten horns or kings of Daniel are therefore the Christian kings, who would rise out of the Roman Empire (Dan 7:24^a) and rule 15 centuries over Europe from 323 to 1815AD

After them another would rise, which would be diverse from the first (verse 24^b). This is the anti-Christian beast or the little horn (verses 8, 20, 25), which according to John (Rev 13:1) would also have seven heads and ten horns, as anti-Christian powers of the kingdom of darkness.

Since this beast already exists, the ten horns of Daniel must already be gone (Dan 7: 24, <u>after them</u>). We know, however, that the ten anti-Christian kings of John have not yet received their rule. (Rev 17:12). They are therefore not the same

As soon as the beast reaches its full power, it will only rule for 3.5 years here on earth, we will therefore proceed to this period of forty-two months, or 1260 days.

THE 3 ½ YEARS

The events taking place during the 3 ½ years will now be described and interpreted as events occurring chronologically, sometimes overlapping each other.

1st The First Resurrection

2nd The 144000

3rd The Great Multitude

4th The Marriage Of The Lamb

5th The Flight Of The Sun Woman

6th The War In Heaven

7th The Two Witnesses

8th The Ascension Of The Two Witnesses

9th The Fall Of Babylon

10th The Harvest Of The Earth

THE FIRST RESURRECTION

The Bridegroom came; and they that were
ready went in with him to the marriage;
and the door was shut
Matt 25:10

Rev 12:5

Verse 5. **"And she brought forth a man child, who was to rule all nations with a rod of iron: and her child was caught up unto God, and to His throne."** The Sun woman, the Apostolic church, gives birth to a "man child". This expression mislead many interpreters. Some understand the woman to be "Mary" giving birth to Jesus Christ. Others realize that a woman, in the prophetic sense, means a church, which gives birth to Jesus Christ. This is absolutely impossible, as Jesus Christ established His church here on earth and this church could not give birth to her creator. Who then is the "*man child*"? This son is the future ruler of the nations with Christ, the future king of the Kingdom of Glory. He however did not personally appear in the flesh. It is Christ, who after 1830 again performs live through His servants. When the people of the Lord, are indicated in connection with Him, the Lord uses the image of a woman as the whole congregation. There, where the people appear as the executor of His Will against the Heathen, they are described in the masculine genre "*Son*". The Lord also named the whole people of Israel: My Son, my firstborn (Exod 4:22), to the pharaoh.

Likewise to Ephraim: (Jer 31:9), his firstborn. Similarly, after 1830, the sealed believers, reborn out of the Holy Spirit, together formed the manly child, revealing the overcoming characteristics of Jesus Christ. These are the 144,000 sealed, who have the name of His Father written on their foreheads, who followed the Lamb, wherever He goeth (Rev 14:1, 4), and as a manly strong child, fight the unbelievers (heathen) with the Sword of His Mouth, (Rev 19:14, 15) and rule with a rod of iron of mutual strife, just as the king of Assyria (Isaiah 10:5, 6), and King Ahaz (Isaiah 14:28, 29), were rods in the hand of the Lord to the apostate people.

"And her child was caught up unto God and His throne". This is the living ascension to heaven, the preservation from the temptation of the anti-Christian power, which the Lord promised to the believers of the Protestant congregation (Rev 3:10), who become pillars in the Temple of God, the congregation, who possess the Holy Spirit and His gifts, - who received the name of God (Rev 7:2,3), whom we find also in (Rev 14), safe on Mount Zion with the lamb, redeemed from the people as firstlings of God and the Lamb. This is the first Resurrection of (Rev 20:6), *"Blessed and holy are those who have a part in the first Resurrection: on such the second death hath no power, but they shall be priests of God and of Christ and shall reign with Him a thousand years."*

THE 144,000

Rev 14:1–5

Verse 1. "And I looked, and lo, a Lamb stood on Mount Zion, and with him a hundred forty and four thousand, having his Father's name written on their foreheads." The Lamb is Jesus Christ, the lamb sacrificed for us. Mount Zion is the New Testament people of God of the First apostolic period (Heb 12:22, 23), just as they stood in the original ordinances of Jesus, but likewise that of the present apostolic period, which, united with the first together form Mount Zion.

The city of Jerusalem was built on several hills and mountains; the highest one was Mount Zion, upon which the old city of David lay, (the upper city) which, although lying within the walls of Jerusalem, was surrounded by its own wall. Jerusalem lay lower down, as if at the feet of Mount Zion. On the Northeast side of Mount Zion, there was a mountain ridge, named Moria, upon which stood the temple.

This temple in Zion, was the place where the Lord abided (Psalm 9:11. Psalm 48:1-3. Psalm 99:2. Psalm 132:13,14), from whence the law or the Word of the Lord went out. There also lived the king and the high priest.

All these Old Testament earthly shadows we find in the New Testament spiritual Jerusalem or the church of Christ. (Heb 10:1). In His prophetic language, the Holy Spirit names the whole of Christendom: the Great City of Jerusalem, but the Apostolic church: Mount Zion, the city of the living God, wherein the living Lord of the church abides and speaks to its inhabitants, the 144,000 sealed from all the tribes of the New Testament Israel, (Psalm 2:6, Isaiah 2:3. Isaiah 28:16. Micha 4:2. Zach 9:9. Matt 21:5. Heb 12:22. Rev 11:2, 8, 13. Rev 14:8,20. Rev 16:16,19. Rev 17:18. Rev 18:2, 10, 16, 18, 19, 21). In the kingdom of Glory, the spiritual Mount Zion is shown to us in (Rev 14:1) and the heavenly Jerusalem in (Rev 21:10).

If therefore under the Old Covenant Zion was a natural mountain, upon which the Government over church and state was established, in the New Covenant Zion is a Spiritual Mountain, or a power in church and state, the mountain of the Lord, or the kingdom of Glory, predicted by Isaiah and Micha as stated above. Upon this mountain, Christ is revealed as the Lamb, because through His death, the royal priesthood, lost by Adam's fall, is given back to all, who stand on Mount Zion, namely according (Heb 12:22), the apostolic Christians. Christ, who is the King of Kings, and Priest of priests, here appears, surrounded by the 144,000 sealed, as His fellow kings and priests in His future kingdom. To that end, they had to

481

receive the seal of the Holy Spirit, whereby they were redeemed as firstlings from men by God and the Lamb, and carried the name of God the Father and His Son, Jesus Christ, on their foreheads.

That this sealing only started in the seventh period (after 1830) has already been explained.

This vision on Mount Zion is therefore not on earth, but in heaven, where they, as the Bride of Christ partake of the marriage of the Lamb, later to return on earth with him to establish His Kingdom for a thousand years and to live and reign with Him as kings and priests.

The 144,000, who stand with the Lamb on Mount Zion, are the same 144,000 of (Rev 7:2–8), who were sealed in the Seventh period. We postponed the explanation of the number 144,000 up to this point because it is of greater importance to handle it here. The question is: is the number to be taken literally or symbolically? The Bible does not give any indication as to this. But one thing is clear from (Rev 14:1–5) is that the 144,000 are overcomers who attained the highest degree of perfection as stated in the following verses of (Rev 14).

Verse 2. **"And I heard a voice from heaven, as the voice of many waters, and as the voice of a great thunder: and I heard the voice of harpers, harping with their harps."** The waters are the nations; here the glorified believers from many nations, with the formerly resurrected departed believers, who participate in this glorification.

Verse 3. **"And they sang as it were a new song before the throne, and before the four living creatures, and the elders; and no man could learn that song, but the hundred and forty and four thousand, which were redeemed from the earth."** The 144,000 are therefore these last-named singers. The other resurrected forming a chorus.

This is a sensual representation of unheard-off Bliss.

While no man can learn to sing this song, except the 144,000, the subject of their praise and glorification, will be the privilege and higher state of happiness, which they enjoy above the other resurrected believers.

Verse 4. **"These** (the 144,000) **are they which were not defiled with women; for they are virgins. These are they which follow the Lamb whithersoever He goeth. These were redeemed from among men, being firstfruits unto God and the Lamb."** Women are the image of Christian denominations or confessions, who do not live up to God's ordinances, as they were instituted originally in the one, holy, universal Christian church. (Jer 3:1, 6, 7, 10. Rev 12:1. Rev 17:1, 4–6, 18). Women have husbands, whose name they bear. Virgins are still free of the man. The 144,000 are described (Rev 7:3) as servants of God, in (Rev 12:5), as a man child, and here as virgins. As servants of God, indicating their manly characteristics as kings and priests, they are not polluted with women, that is: not bound to the different diverging human religious confessions. As virgins, these sealed believers were not guilty of any deviations from Christ's ordinances and institutions and belonged whole-heartedly to the Lord, and each of their congregations formed a faithful and chaste virgin in Christ, as Paul wanted to present the congregation of Corinth to Him. (2 Cor 11:1, 2).

"They followed the Lamb whithersoever he goeth", these virgins name Jesus their bridegroom, because He named himself so. (Matt 9:15. Matt 25:1, 5, 6, 10), and want to be found as wise virgins (Matt 25:4) at His coming, faithful in all His institutions, because He commanded it so (Matt 28:19, 20).

It is also important to note, that in order to be capable of following the Lamb, the Lamb must be visible and present here on earth. This is made possible when we remember that in the seventh period, the apostles of Jesus are active again and according to the words of Jesus in (John 13:20) **"Verily, verily, I say unto you, he that receiveth whomsoever I sent receiveth me; and he that receiveth me receiveth Him that sent me."**

The wise virgins receiveth the sent apostle ministry and followed them withersoever they led them, thereby following the Lamb. In Jesus' prayer for His disciples, He says (John 17:18) *"As you have sent me into the world, so I have sent them into the world."* And in (John 17:20), *"I ask not only on behalf of these but also on behalf of those who will believe in me, through their word."*

Accepting the words of the apostles in faith also implies subjection to their word, and to live according to it. This is the following. Dear reader, how this can be achieved is made clear by Paul in (Rom 10:17): *"So then faith cometh by hearing, and hearing by the Word of God,"* and in (Rom 10:15) *"And how shall they preach, except they be sent?"* We see that it is imperative that one must HEAR the word preached by those who are SENT, and then be obedient to that word.

"These were redeemed from among men, being first fruits unto God and to the Lamb." (see James 1:18). They are, just as the Apostolics of the beginning, the firstlings, who went out of the Old dispensation and entered the New Kingdom. They are the firstlings before the Great Harvest on Judgement day (Rev 20:5), to serve God with the firstling Christ (1 Cor 15: 23), in his kingdom of Glory, as kings and priests. They, together with the seal of the first apostolic period, form the Bride as the firstlings of Christ, who is the Bridegroom.

Verse 5. **"And in their mouth was found no guile: for they are without fault before the throne of God."** Their testimony and teaching is the pure apostolic doctrine, and, inspired by the Holy Spirit, they speak the truth, unlike the other Christians who allow human reasoning to mar their teachings. When they testify of themselves, their testimony is true, because they are Apostolic and do not want to know anything about other institutions and doctrines, than that which Christ originally gave to His church, and as He instituted her in Baptism, Sealing, Communion, and ministries of apostles, prophets, evangelists and shepherds. They therefore are without fault and are thus capable of being Kings and Priests with Christ on earth in His Kingdom of Glory. As sinners, they require the redeeming blood of the Lamb and the Grace of God in order to be sanctified and glorified. By accepting the sent ministry of reconciliation (2 Cor 5:18–20) and their authority in Christ (John 20:21-23), they washed their robe in the blood of the Lamb and all their sins where forgiven, making them without fault before the throne of God.

This is the First Resurrection of (Rev 20:6) **"Blessed and Holy are those who have part in the First Resurrection: on such the Second death hath no power, but they shall be priests of God and of Christ and shall reign with him a thousand years."**

THE GREAT MULTITUDE

Rev 7:9-17.

In (Rev 20:4) we find that besides the 144,000 sealed believers, another group of souls partake of the First Resurrection. **"And I saw thrones, and they sat upon them, and judgement was given unto them: And I saw souls of them that were beheaded for the witness of Jesus, and for the Word of God, and which had not worshipped the Beast, neither his image, neither had received his mark upon their foreheads, or in their hands, and they lived and reigned with Christ a Thousand years."**

These are the true believers who lost their lives as Martyrs in the past six periods, who waited under the alter in the fifth period and who were given white robes of righteousness and honour, as also those who died in Christ, and had received the Sacraments and the Holy Sealing and had refused to accept the mark of the beast in the seventh period. We find them beautifully described in (Rev 7:9–17). After describing the sealing of the twelve spiritual tribes of Israel, John saw a further multitude;

Verse 9. **"After this I beheld, and, lo, a great multitude, which no man could number, of all nations, and kindreds, and people and tongues, stood before the throne, and before the Lamb, clothed with white robes, and palms in their hands."** This uncountable multitude is seen apart from the 144,000 of the previous verses. They are also clothed in righteousness of the Saints (white robes).

Verse 10. **"And cried with a loud voice, saying: Salvation to our God, which sitteth upon the Throne, and unto the Lamb."** They talk of Salvation because they are saved by the Grace of God and by the blood of the Lamb.

Verse 11. **"And all the angels stood round about the Throne, and about the elders and the four living creatures, and fell before the Throne on their faces, and worshipped God."**

Verse 12. **"Saying, Amen, Blessing and Glory, and Wisdom, and Thanksgiving, and Honour, and Power, and Might, be unto our God for ever and ever. Amen."**

Verse 13. **"And one of the elders answered, saying unto me, what are these which are arrayed in white robes? And whence came they?"**

Verse 14. **"And I said unto him, sir, thou knowest. And he said to me, these are they which came out of Great Tribulation, and have washed their robes, and made them white in the blood of the Lamb."** This clearly indicates that these souls accepted the Sacraments offered by Jesus Christ in the seventh period, and these souls arrayed in white robes are the righteous believers who accepted the forgiveness and grace of our Lord Jesus Christ, offered by His servants the apostles.

The fact that they washed their robes in the blood of the Lamb must be clarified. The blood of the Lamb was shed for the forgiveness of sin, but dear reader, take note, they *"made them white"* in the blood of the Lamb clearly indicates that they subjected themselves to a washing process. This raises the question: "How are our sins forgiven?" and "Who can forgive sins?" The Protestant believers claim that Jesus died for all our sins and, just to believe this, is sufficient. They also claim that only God can forgive sins. They base this statement on the Bible (Mark 2:7), where the scribes reasoning in their hearts, "Why doth this man thus speak blasphemies? **Who can forgive sins but God only?"** Dear reader, consider carefully: Who said here that only God can forgive sins? The scribes! They still do today. Ask any Pastor, Evangelist, or Professor of Theology and Protestant denomination and they will all agree to this. Only God can forgive sins!

But what was Jesus Christ's response to this?

We read in (Mark 2:8–10): *"And immediately when Jesus perceived in His Spirit that they so reasoned within themselves, He said unto them, Why reason ye these things in your hearts? Whether is it easier to say to the sick or the palsy, Thy sins be forgiving thee; or to say, Arise, and take up thy bed and walk?* **But that ye may know that the Son of Man hath the power of the earth to forgive sins;** (He saith to the sick of the palsy, etc…).

Jesus contradicted the scribes in order to teach them that the Son of Man has power here on earth to forgive sins.

Jesus did not refer to himself alone, as the scribes would have us believe, but he referred to His apostles and servants who would later be empowered and commissioned to forgive sins in His name. After His Resurrection, Jesus appeared to His Disciples (John 20:19–23): *"When it was evening, being the first day of the week when the doors were shut where the disciples were assembled for fear of the Jews, came Jesus and stood in their midst, and saith unto them;* **Peace be unto you**. *And when He had so said, He showed unto them his hands and side. Then were the disciples glad, when they saw the Lord. Then said Jesus to them again, Peace be unto you: as my Father hath sent Me, even so send I you. And when he hath said this, he breathed on them, and saith unto them,* **"Receive ye the Holy Ghost":** (This is wrongly translated, as the disciples received the Holy Spirit on Pentecost, some weeks later, and they could not receive the Holy Spirit twice. It should have been translated: <u>Receive of my Spirit</u>: This was their <u>ordination</u>, confirmed by the commission: **as my Father hath sent Me, so do I send you.** This is further reinforced by what follows:

Verse 23. **<u>"Whosoever sins ye remit, they are remitted unto them; and whosoever sins ye retain, they are retained."</u>** These words authorized the apostles to forgive sins in the name of their sender, (*the Son of Man has the power here on earth to forgive sins*).

Since the apostle ministry is active again in the seventh period, the period of Great Tribulation, it becomes possible for believers in our time to wash their robes in the blood of the Lamb if they accept the authority of Jesus apostles.

THE MARRIAGE OF THE LAMB

Rev 19:1-9

The marriage starts immediately after the First Resurrection as described in the following verses, just prior to the end of the seventh vial.

Verse 1. **"And after these things I heard a Great voice of much people in Heaven, saying, Alleluia, Salvation, and Glory, and Honour, and power, unto the Lord our God."**

Verse 2. **"For true and righteous are His judgements: for He hath judged the Great Whore, which did corrupt the earth with her fornication, and hath avenged the blood of His servants at her hand."**

Verse 3. **"And again they said, Alleluia. And her (Babylon) smoke rose up forever and ever."** That is: the numerous Christian churches, which did not live up to the precepts of the Lord, will now be destroyed.

The Great Multitude who rejoices here must be distinguished from the elders and living creatures (verse 4).

Verse 4. **"And the four and twenty elders and the four living creatures fell down and worshipped God that sat on the throne, saying, Amen, Alleluia!"** This is answered as a chorus to the song of the multitude.

Verse 5. **"And a voice** (of one of the Cherubim) **came out of the throne saying, Praise** (all together) **our God, <u>all</u> ye His servants,** (not only the first choir of verses 1–3, but also the chorus of verse 4), and ye that fear Him, both small and Great." Thereupon both choirs combined in verse 6.

Verse 6. **And I heard as it were the voice of a great multitude, and as the voice of many waters, and as the voice of mighty thunderings** (apostles**), saying, Alleluia: for the Lord God omnipotent reigneth."**

Verse 7. **"Let us be glad and rejoice, and give honour to Him: for the marriage of the Lamb is come, and His wife hath made herself ready!"** (also Matt 25:10).

Verse 8. **"And to her was granted that she should be arrayed in fine linen, clean and white, for the fine linen is the righteousness of saints."**

The bride of the Lamb is here not introduced as speaking but only spoken off by the great multitude.

Verse 9. **"And He saith unto me, write, blessed are they which are called unto the marriage supper of the Lamb."**

These are not his words for John adds: "These are true sayings of God." The great multitude is thus the invited guests in contrast to the bride; they are the virgins, who accompanied Rebecca when she had donned the jewels and raiment given to her by Abraham's servant (Gen 24:53); the sixty queens and eighty concubines and maiden without a number of (Sons of Songs 6:8, 9) who accompany the bride, the dove, the perfect one, the only one, and praise her. Who are the believers who form this multitude? How do they come to be at the marriage of the Lamb?

The guests consisted of all the believers of the Old and New Covenants, who believed and looked forward to the Kingdom of Glory and the coming of Christ on earth and in the Resurrection of the firstlings. They, together with the martyrs under the altar (fifth period), form this multitude of guests, this voice of many nations (waters. verse 6). Just as Rebecca was fetched by Abraham's servants, so also the Bride of the Lamb now meets the resurrected servants of the Lord (1 Thess 4:15–17) forming the cloud of witnesses (Heb 12:1) in the air. Those still alive, are changed and ascend, to form the wise virgins of the seventh period, the Apostolic or sealed, who accepted and gathered the oil of the Holy Spirit and had trimmed their lamps. (Matt 25:7, 10). Amongst them is the bride of the Lamb and the many faithful believers who did not overcome but were found worthy to attend the marriage of the Lamb as guests.

The apostolic believers, who failed to gather enough oil for their lamps, will remain behind here on earth as the Sun woman.

Not all who resurrected and changed will sit on the thrones, neither are all of them the bride. Revelation clearly differentiates between the called, chosen, and faithful (Rev 17:14). There are small and great, who sing Alleluia (Rev 19:5). Except for the bride, the wife of the Lamb (Rev 21:9, etc.), we see at the wedding also the guests, the saved, called to the supper at the wedding of the Lamb. (Rev 17:14. Matt 22:1–14. Matt 25:10. Luke 14:15–24). For many are called, but few are chosen.

This supper will be a Heavenly supper, of greater holiness and glory, than the Holy Communion we celebrated here on earth, and instead of a constantly repeated supper for sinful and weak mortals, to unite them with Christ, so will the great supper at the union of the Bride with the Lamb, be the only, and last, for the resurrected firstlings, forever to be spiritually united with their Bridegroom, Jesus Christ. This supper will also be that of which Christ predicted, which Abraham, Isaac and Jacob will attend (Matt 8:11. Luke 13:28, 29), while the children of Israel, both of the Old and the New Covenant, who did not accept His Testimony, will be left out, but will remain in the darkness of Hades (Matt 8:12).

The called, the elect and faithful (Rev 17:14) will take part in this supper. Revelation described three different types of sanctified believers, and this solves a profound question which occupied the Christian church of the second period and the Protestant church in the sixth period to such an extent that it often led to great disputes. Indeed, it appears here that there is an election, yet only an election of Grace and not of rejection. The Augustine and Reformed doctrine of predestination is, according to this Revelation of Jesus Christ, a misunderstanding of His eternal love, which wants to have mercy on all who want to accept His revealed Grace, but also rejects all who reject it. *"Jerusalem* (Matt 23:37)! *I wanted to, but you did not want to."* In that word of Jesus, the whole doctrine of predestination and rejection is condemned. God's offer of eternal grace is universal. He only hardens the heart of those who despise His offer, and who argue against the testimony of the Holy Spirit. They could be saved yet did not want to.

"But to all who received Him, who believed in His name; He gave the power to become children of God." (John 1:12). And amongst all those who accepted God's grace, He elected some as firstlings, as the Bride of the Lord. This is the election, a special election of Grace, which does not clash with God's universal mercy. The Reformed church correctly understood, that there was an election, but because she did not understand, that this election only pertained to the Bride and that the Lord only choose from amongst the believers and because she also applied the election to the whole Salvation plan, it consequently also led to the false doctrine of rejection, although no such thing is recorded in the Bible.

While the marriage supper of the Lamb takes place in heaven, we now continue with the momentous events on earth.

WAR IN HEAVEN

Rev 12:7-12

After the First resurrection, there is war in heaven.

Verse 7. **"And there was war in Heaven: Michael and his angels fought against the dragon: and the dragon fought and his angels."**

Who is Michael? Most theologians named Michael described in (Dan 10: 13, 21 and Dan 12:1) the unborn angel of the Covenant, Jesus Christ. The name itself means: Who is like God? According to the strange name formation in Hebrew, the answer is: *Who else but I, is like God?* Only the Son is like unto the Father. This war takes place in the heaven of the church where Satan is overcome by Christ and His servants (Angels).

Verse 8. **"And prevaileth not; neither was their place found no more in heaven."** With the First Resurrection, the church of Christ is removed from this earth to a realm of bliss.

Verse 9. **"And the Great dragon was cast out, that old serpent, called the Devil and Satan, which deceiveth the whole world: He was cast out into the earth, and his angels were cast out with him."** The devil who deceived the majority of humankind is now confined to earthly things since the Spiritual Israel has been taken up.

Verse 10. **"And I heard a loud voice saying in heaven, Now is come Salvation and strength, and the Kingdom of our God, and the power of His Christ: for the accuser of our brethren is cast down, which accused them before our God day and night."** In the wedding chamber, this loud voice confirms that Satan's power is confined to the earth and that all power is given to Christ.

Verse 11. **"And they overcame him by the blood of the Lamb, and by the word of their testimony, and they loved not their lives unto the death."** This testifies to the overcomers and the martyrs who are now with Christ.

Verse 12. **"Therefore rejoice, ye heavens, and ye that dwell in them. Woe to the inhabitants of the earth and of the sea! For the devil is come down unto you, having great wrath, because he knoweth that he hath but a short time."** There is joy in heaven at the wedding feast, but on earth Satan rages and knows he only has 3 ½ years to achieve his goal.

THE FLIGHT OF THE SUN WOMAN

<u>Rev 12:6, 13–16.</u>

Immediately after the First Resurrection and the ascension of her man-child, the Sun woman flees to the wilderness.

Verse 6. **"And the woman fled into the wilderness, where she hath a place prepared of God, that they should feed her there a thousand two hundred and three-score days."**

Verse 13. **"And when the dragon saw that he was cast unto the earth, he persecuted the woman which brought forth the man child."** Satan could not infiltrate the heaven of the church anymore, to falsify the teachings of Christ, and to mislead souls, for the true believers have been taken away from the earth, and those who remained on earth because they were not worthy to partake of the First Resurrection, form the Sun woman against whom Satan wages war. But God protects his disappointed children and gathers them in the wilderness.

Verse 14. **"And to the woman were given two wings of a Great Eagle, that she might fly into the wilderness, into her place, where she is nourished for a time, and times, and half a time from the face of the serpent."**

The journey of Israel in flight from Egypt, through the desert, in order to take possession of their heritage, is the Old Testament type, which the Holy Spirit uses here for the flight of the New Testament congregation.

The wings of an Eagle are in (Deut 32:10–12) the image of Godly guidance and preservation for Israel in particular. Jesus Christ once said to Jerusalem: (Matt 23:37), "Jerusalem, Jerusalem, how often would I have gathered thy children; even as a hen gathered her chickens under her *wings,* etc." But two such wings are given to the woman to gather the believers into a state of wilderness.

Wilderness is a place where nothing grows, no fountains of water (ministries), and no food (the Word). We are talking of a spiritual wilderness since the church is taken up, no one will dare take leadership, no one will want to preach, no services will be held, and yet, this woman will be fed for a time, and times and half a time.

This refers to the 42 months of (Rev 11:3) where the gentiles will tread underfoot the court of the Temple, the Apostolic church, and to a thousand two hundred and three score days of (Rev 12:6) during which the woman will be fed. The fugitives will come together and be led and protected by

God in the same way Israel was cared for in the natural desert, (Manna from heaven, quails, water, etc.). All they need to sustain their spiritual life will be available. The time spent in the spiritual desert will last 3 ½ years. This is also confirmed in (Rev 12:12), "The devil is come down unto you, having great wrath, because he knoweth that he hath but a short time." The anti-Christian nations, due to their democratic governments and their humanitarian inclinations will be the tool in God's hand to achieve all this, for in (verse 6) it says: "that they should feed her there a thousand two hundred and three-score days."

Verse 15. **"And the serpent cast out of his mouth water as a flood after the woman, that he might cause her to be carried away of the flood."**

Satan also works through the powers on earth, the anti-Christ, and influences the false prophet and anti-Christian teachers against the Woman. Therefore the persecution of the woman does not end with her flight, but the serpent cast out of his mouth (the defenders of his blasphemous doctrines), water (doctrine) after the woman, as a river (preachers of a doctrine), to force on her the anti-Christian doctrine by the power of the sword, just as Saul did in (Acts 9:1, 2) and the Dominicans and Franciscans, as Inquisitors in the fifth period, sought and persecuted the Waldense in their caves and mountains. The goal is to totally destroy the woman in all the places where she has fled.

Verse 16. **"And the earth helped the woman, and the earth opened her mouth, and swallowed up the flood which the dragon cast out of his mouth."**

The earth (the existing anti-Christian democratic society in church and state) to which the woman fled, became her defender (mouth) and protects her against violence. The history of the kingdom of God gives us many examples, of how God knew how to move the hearts of some to help and protect His people in need. In the New Testament, we remember King Agrippa, who, after Emperor Nero in 70 started persecuting the Christians, willingly received the fleeing Christians, and showed them a refuge in the city of Pella (Van Loon, page 9).

Later the protection of the Roman Emperors Anthony Pious, Alexander Severus, Constantius, etc. even the Waldense persecuted by the popes found defenders and protection from landlords and princes in Roman countries, where they were free to practice their religion unhindered, although strictly forbidden by the Popes. This was the first woe. Similarly, the second woe during the Reformation, will again be repeated in the third and last woe, the anti-Christian persecution.

Verse 17. **"And the dragon was wroth with the Woman and went to make war with the remnant of her seed, which keep the commandments of God, and have the testimony of Jesus Christ."** Satan, realizing the futility of his efforts to destroy the woman, looks at the next best target, <u>the remnant of her seed.</u>

Who are the remnants of her seed? It is clear that they must also be apostolic believers, *who keep the commandments of God, and have the testimony of Jesus Christ,* which they could only have received in the Apostolic church. These are the many apostolic believers who for various reasons had left the church, some did not attend services anymore, and some went back to Babylon, to their previous denominations, but when they realized that the promised return of Jesus Christ had occurred, they realized with great sorrow that they were part of the foolish virgins who had remained behind. That they are the fallen apostolic believers is confirmed in their being the remnant of the seed of the woman, she had given birth to them through the rebirth.

THE TWO WITNESSES

<u>Rev 11:3-11.</u>

Verse 3. **"And I will give power unto My two witnesses, and they shall prophesy a thousand two hundred and threescore days, clothed in sackcloth."**

The vision and prophecy concerning the two witnesses is of great importance, since here it is predicted by the mighty angel Christ Himself. (Rev 10:1, 5, 9. Rev 11:1).

What and who are the two witnesses?

Wilhelmus Brakel wrote about this: "Witnesses are people, who know and confess the truth (Acts 1:8, 22). Here two witnesses are named; not because they are only two persons, but because of the testimony they have to give. These promised witnesses are not two persons, but a double testimony by many people, who proclaim the same truth." It is remarkable that Brakel already understood the character of the two witnesses so well.

We cannot consider that only two persons are involved, we learn from (Rev 11:7, 10). Two persons cannot torment all the inhabitants of the whole of Europe in the 3 ½ years, and it is even less likely that the anti-Christian state powers would wage war on two persons, overcome and kill them (verse 7).

That none other than apostolic believers from the seventh period form these two witnesses, and that we do not have to search for any other, is clear from the particularity of (verse 3), that these witnesses already exist and are considered to be known, before their prophesying during the last thousand two hundred and three score days begins, but also from the further description.

Verse 4. **"These are the two olive trees, and the two candlesticks standing before the God of the earth."**

When Paul (Rom 11:17–24), describes the congregation of the heathen (gentiles) as a "wild olive tree", and that of the circumcision a "good olive tree", he uses this image in another sense, and here describes the whole church, as carriers of the Holy Spirit (Rom 8:9, 11. 1 Cor 3:16). an "olive tree", standing before the unconverted heathen and Jews, in order to pour in them the Holy Spirit.

This completely agrees with (Eph 2:19–22), where Paul names the congregation a Temple of God, built on the foundation of apostles and prophets, to whom (Eph 3:4, 5) the mystery of Christ was revealed.

The two witnesses in the 3½ years are therefore just as in the first century, again two congregations (candlesticks), standing in the ordinances of Christ.

Zechariah saw the New Testament church of Christ described as a candlestick with two olive trees beside it. (Zech 4). It is remarkable that the Holy Spirit, here again, repeats his own image in Revelation, here again speaks of two olive trees, but also of two candlesticks. Therefore, there must be two Apostolic congregations in the 3 ½ years period, because nowhere in the Holy Scriptures does the candlestick represent anything else than a congregation. Our Lord Jesus himself irrevocably proclaimed (Rev 1:20) *"The candlesticks are the congregation,"* Dear reader, you may well ask: "But who are the two Apostolic congregations in the 3 ½ years?

We find the answer in (Rev 12:13, 17).

Verse 13. **"And when the dragon saw that he was cast out unto the earth, he persecuted the Woman which brought forth the man child."** We clearly see that Satan attacked the Sun woman, the apostolic believers who did not partake of the First Resurrection and who remained on earth. They still have the Testimony of Jesus Christ and know the truth. This is the first witness, the first apostolic congregation (Candlestick).

Verse 17. **"And the dragon was wroth with the Woman, and went to make war with the remnant of her seed, which keep the commandments of God, and have the testimony of Jesus Christ."** Who are the remnants of her seed? We are firstly reminded of what Paul said: (2 Thess 2:3), *"Let no man deceived you by any means; for that day (the return of Jesus) shall not come, except there come a falling away first."* This falling away takes place as we speak, and many apostolic believers either take offence, become tired of waiting for the Lord's return, or are seduced to return to Babylon from where they came.

We also remember the parable of the seed (Matt 13:19–28). Some seeds fell on hard ground and the birds of the air ate them, some amongst the thorns, the cares and burdens of this world and were suffocated, etc. But they all received the Word of God, the teaching of Christ, and although they had rejected it, they now realize that they had made a grave mistake, and will rally as the second witness, for they also know the truth.

We therefore have found our two witnesses, the two olive trees and the two candlesticks in the 3½ years.

THE TESTIMONY OF THE TWO WITNESSES

<u>Rev 11:3, 5, 11. Rev 14:6, 7. Rev 13:14</u>

Verse 3. "And I will give power unto My two witnesses, and they shall prophesy a thousand two hundred and threescore days, clothed in sackcloth." Here is further proof that the two witnesses are correctly identified as the Sun woman and the remnant of her seed. They will "prophesy". It is remarkable that Revelation clearly identifies them if we consider the following:

1st. To the Sun woman (Rev 12:13) were given two wings of a great <u>EAGLE.</u> (the prophet ministry, the Eagle faced living creature) proving that she was given the prophet ministry which ceased to function in the final stages of the Apostolic church.

2nd. The remnant of her seed (Rev 12:17) has the testimony of Jesus Christ which according to (Rev 19:10), *"for the testimony of Jesus is the spirit of prophecy."*

3rd. Both witnesses shall prophecy clothed in sackcloth. Sackcloth is associated with mourning (Gen 37:34) and especially with the public expression of humility and penitence, a token of grief. It should be evident that both congregations had much to grieve for and were mourning the fact that they did not partake of the First Resurrection. Being penitent they also brought warning to all other believers of the short time left to repent.

They will testify to Babylon concerning the Great Deception to which they have fallen They will predict the fall of Babylon and of the Second return of Christ at the end of the 3½ years. They will also specifically proclaim that the beast, predicted in Revelation, has come and that the state institutions and governments in Europe are the revelation of the beast or the anti-Christ of the Bible. This will also lead to the hatred and the war against them. (verse 7).

To prophecy is, according to the meaning of the Holy Scripture, not only preaching but a conversation, driven by the Holy Spirit, whereby the future events and the will of the Lord are proclaimed.

This, testifying, preaching and prophesying will last 3 ½ years, just as the testimony of the Lord Himself, His preaching and prophesying about the coming judgement over Israel lasted 3 ½ years. It began with His baptism by John the Baptist and ended with His Ascension.

It is interesting to note that the time given for the testimony of the two witnesses is expressed in days, while the same time of the performance of the anti-Christ is given in months. (Rev 13:5). We have already too much respect for Revelation, that we should here think of capriciousness. In former times, months were divided into ascending and descending parts, just as we still speak of a waxing or a declining moon. The symbolic meaning of the reference to months and days express, that the anti-Christian persecution, just as the former heathen Roman, will not always be as hefty, but alternatively wax and diminish, while the testimony of the repentant witnesses and their warnings against the beast will ever be faithful and undiminished, until at the end of the 3 ½ years they will be killed.

Verse 5. **"And if any man will hurt them, fire proceedeth out of their mouth and devoureth their enemies: and if any man will hurt them, he must in this manner be killed."** Since we here have to do with a battle on a spiritual level, this fire and killing is also of a spiritual nature, and those who see fire spitting miracles from the witnesses are totally wrong. The fire, which comes out of their mouth, we already know as the fire of the Holy Spirit. The "hurting" is also meant in a spiritual sense, just as the word also means "wrong". Whosoever mocks these witnesses and their preaching and prophecies, does not do it to them, who are only weak and sinful people, but he mocks and insults God the Lord who sent them (Luke 10:16), and the Holy Spirit, who speaks in and through them.

Just as out of the mouth of Elias no fire came out, but the fire of the Lord came down, the voice of the Lord also becomes a flame of fire in their mouth (Psalm 29:7), and the Lord will make His word in their mouth a fire (Jer 5:14), that devours their enemies as wood. "For I will give you a mouth and wisdom, which all your adversaries shall not be able to gainsay nor resist." (Luke 21:15). – "Is not my Word like as a fire?" (Jer 23:29); "as the fire of the refiner" (Mal 3:2, 3).

It is the fire that Christ came down to kindle here on earth (Luke 12:49), the fire of the Holy Spirit. Those who allow themselves to be purified unto the knowledge of Christ, experience that this testimony of the Holy Spirit is a sweet savour of life in them that are saved, but a savour unto death to them that perish. (2 Cor 2:14–16). Those who reject the Lord's testimony in these last days, are totally subjected to the power of the Anti-Christ and also experienced the Lord's judgement. Those who want to convince them to deny their faith, and to convert them to the anti-Christian religion, and thus tries to kill them, must in this manner be killed through their testimony and because of their own hard-headedness.

Verse 6. **"These have power to shut heaven, that it rain not in the days of their prophecy: and have power over waters to turn them to blood, and to smite the earth with all plagues, as often as they will."** This is an

Elias work, just as the following will be a Moses work. Both were in the natural state a fore-shadow of the Spiritual which will be performed in these thousand two hundred and threescore days. The rain is the outpouring of the Holy Spirit, the Spirit of truth which the world did not accept (John 14:17, 26), and which will lead to the truth of the Gospel. (John 16:13)

The believers who disdained to accept the Sealing from the apostles will know from all the signs of the times, that they have erred and will go to the (merchants), in order to be sealed. (Matt 25:1–10), but it will be too late, as the door will be shut, and the Sealing angels, the apostles are not active on earth during this 3 ½ year period. The two witnesses being the foolish virgins who remained behind will refuse "the rain (Sealing) during the days of their prophecy."

The second part of "verse 6" refers to a Moses-work, performed by the two witnesses. Just as he did in a natural sense, they also have power in a spiritual sense, to awaken the nations (waters) to sinful lusts (blood), (page 60. Vol. 1).

The earth is an anti-Christian society and its ordinances are plagued by their Christian testimony, just as the apostles and witnesses at the beginning of the church were a plague to the Jews and the heathen. (Acts 5:28. Acts 23:1–3), even as the sect of the Nazarene was called a pest (Acts 24:5). Likewise each new testimony, verbal or written, becomes a new plague, wherewith they smite the anti-Christian earth.

This leads to hatred and strife between the anti-Christian society and the two witnesses; which can truly be expected.

THE EVERLASTING GOSPEL

<u>Rev 14:6, 7. Rev 11:13, 14.</u>

Verse 6 **"And I saw another angel fly in the midst of heaven, having the everlasting gospel to preach unto them that dwell on the earth, and to every nation, and kindred, and tongue, and people."**

Another angel! Who was the previous one? The last named angel was (Rev 10:1, 3, 5 and Rev 11:13) Christ in His apostles and prophets, the seventh trumpet angel. The other angel can therefore be none else than a new spiritual clergy, the Sun woman and the Remnant of her seed. They receive an extra power from the Holy Spirit as their work is done during the great tribulation of the 3 ½ years.

Verse 7. **"Fear God, and give glory to Him, for the hour of His judgement is come: and worship Him that made heaven,** the true church of Christ in its complete institutions and ministries, **and earth,** with her true Christian society **and the sea** of nations, as it should be as a Christian society**, and the fountains of waters**, the preachers, in the power of the Holy Spirit." This testimony to Babylon and all believers does not only resound in all churches (the angel flying in the midst of heaven), but they also have to preach an eternal gospel to those who live on earth. This *"eternal"*, better said, **long lasting gospel**, is the glad tidings that the resurrected and ascended bride and guests are already in the Kingdom of Glory and that, at the end of the 1260 days, this Kingdom will also come on the earth with the Second return of Jesus Christ; then the Gospel of Jesus Christ cannot be corrupted by Satan anymore, but will soon everlastingly be preached in its purity for 1000 years. This testimony is brought by the Sun woman and the remnant of her seed, the two witnesses.

WAR BETWEEN THE BEAST AND THE TWO WITNESSES

THE BEAST AGAINST THE TWO WITNESSES

> Then shall they deliver you up to be
> afflicted, and shall kill you: and ye
> shall be hated of all nations for
> My Name's sake.
> Matt 24:9.

Rev 13:7. Rev 11:7.

Rev 13:7. **"And it was given unto him to make war with the saints, and to overcome them."** This verse, describing the performance of the anti-Christian state power, occurs in parallel with what is said of the witnesses in:

Rev 11:7. **"And when they shall have finished their testimony, the beast that ascendeth out of the bottomless pit shall make war against them, and shall overcome them, and kill them."** Both verses describe the same happening; except that in the first instance, it describes the persecution while in the last name it describes the persecuted.

The beast of (Rev 13:7) is therefore again the same fourth beast of Daniel, in its final form, as the small horn, or the anti-Christian state power of the seventh period, who also overcame the Saints. (Dan 7:21).

The democratic-anti-Christian state power hates these two witnesses, who in warning the nations, brand them as anti-Christian powers from the abyss, and persecute them most bitterly. The two apostolic witnesses are spread out over the nations of Europe, and are all subject to the same anti-Christian laws and governments. These two witnesses cannot escape, their churches will be closed, meetings forbidden, and they, as moral bodies, will be morally killed, because they will be considered a danger to the anti-Christian state rule.

It can be understood that the other believers in Babylon will remain quiet in order to escape persecution. However, the two witnesses, driven by the Holy Spirit of God, cannot be silenced and they prophesy the Second Return of Christ at the end of the 3 ½ years.

507

The outward persecution by the anti-Christ is not the worst, but the inward seduction by the false prophet, to accept the mark of the beast in order to live comfortably. But the two witnesses, deeply inspired by the Holy Spirit remain faithful.

To the faithful witnesses a promise in (Rev 14:13), is a great comfort.

Verse 13. **"And I heard a voice from heaven saying unto me: write, blessed are the dead which die in the Lord from henceforth. Yea, saith the Spirit, that they may rest from their labours, and their works do follow them."** This is a glorious promise to all those who **die "in the Lord"** during the 3 ½ years. They will immediately proceed to the wedding celebrations and be received as guests of honour by the resurrected saints and by the Lord and His Bride. In (verse 12) it mentions the patience of the Saints, of those who keep the commandments of God, and the faith of Jesus, and (verse 13) says: *"Henceforth,"* from now on, from the onset of the two witnesses prophesying; *all those who die "in the Lord" from a natural death or by martyrdom*, are blessed and will join the marriage feast as guests of honour.

The mark of the beast is described by the Lord in (Rev 13:18).

Verse 18. **"Here is wisdom. Let him that hath understanding count the number of the Beast: for it is the number of man; and his number is six hundred threescore and six."** The Christian is urged to use his acumen in solving this mystery. But then the puzzle must be easy to solve, even for simple Christians. All interpreters of Revelation, misguided by the words: "is the number of a man," have come up with a multitude of names of different men, dictators and Emperors, describing them as the Anti-Christ, eg. Bileam, Nero, Napoleon III, and lately, Adolf Hitler, Stalin and the last we heard off, Sadam Hussein. This is also wrongly based on the belief that the anti-Christ is ONE person. The translations of this text comply to this wrong belief but could also be correctly translated: from "it is the number of a man" to "it is a human number," a number according to the usual human way of counting, without any figurative meaning. This translation is the correct one, because it agrees with the rest of the verse, and John, to indicate one person, at least would have added the word: one (Henos or Tinos) like in (Rev 8:13): ONE Eagle.

How it was possible to speak of the anti-Christ as one person is incomprehensible. Already in the fifth vial (Rev 16:10) the word "the beast" is described in the plural: *they* gnawed, *they* blasphemed, *they* did not repent, etc." In (Rev 13:1) the beast is described as consisting of seven heads and ten horns, therefore at the time consisting of at least seventeen persons. The seventeen European republics forming the European

Community will have to be represented by proportionally elected representatives of each nation in parliament, who each will reflect the interest of their people. When the representatives number 666, this prophecy could be fulfilled.

We see in Europe a movement to end wars, to solve differences by peace-making institutions such as the Geneva Convention, International Court of De Hagen, the U.N. and the E.C.

Finally the E.U. could possibly have a particular name, wherein the number 666 is hidden, the number of his name (verse 17).

When the time is ripe, one will see that this prophecy, just like all the previous ones, is fulfilled in a very simple way.

THE TWO WITNESSES AGAINST THE BEAST

> The world shall rejoice; and ye shall
> be sorrowful, but your sorrow
> shall be turned into joy.
> John 16:10.

Rev 11:7–11

Verse 7. **"And when they** (the two witnesses) **shall have finished their testimony, the Beast that ascended out of the bottomless pit shall make war against them, and shall overcome them, and kill them."**

This is the beast, which the angel describes to John (Rev 17:8, 11) that it shall come "out from the bottomless pit", and that, although one of the seven heads, it is the eighth. The seventh head is the anti-Christian head, which becomes the eighth. From this verse, it is clear, that only after the two witnesses have finished their testimony during the 1260 days, the beast comes up in the anti-Christian state. In his first period, it was therefore only the anti-Christian beast and persecuted the Christians in his second period as a Christian persecutor, he becomes the beast out of the bottomless pit, the habitation of devils; it is therefore a world power serving Satan, just as the Pope; as the persecutor of the believers, in the fifth trumpet (Rev 9) was described as "the angel of the bottomless pit" (verse 11), who opened the bottomless pit. (verse 2). The Roman Empire as a Christian persecutor was the beast (first vial). Under Popedom it apparently was not, although it was (Rev 17:8. Rev 16:10). At the end of the testimony of the two prophets it again comes out of the bottomless pit (Rev 11:7, Rev 13:15, Rev 17:8).

"And shall overcome them, and kill them." The weapons used by the two witnesses are not earthly, but spiritual. The victory which the beast attains, and their death are therefore also of a spiritual nature and consist of forbidding their meetings, preaching and prophecies, whereby they are morally killed, hindering their prophetic testimony against the anti-Christian religion.

Verse 8. **"And their bodies shall lie in the street of the great city, which is spiritually called Sodom and Egypt, where also our Lord was crucified."** The congregation of Christ is His body. The **dead bodies** are therefore **banned** and **outlawed by two witnesses. The street** is the wide paved market street in the narrow Eastern cities (Neh 8:1, 2), where the merchandize was displayed, but which was at the same time the court where the judges or kings heard the complaints and spoke out their verdicts. (Job 29:7–21. Isaiah 59:14. Jer 5:1). The street is therefore the opportunity to present their spiritual wares, just like in Babylon (Rev 18:11–13), thus the image of **the Gospel preaching**, but also the image of the **law of the State**.

In the kingdom of Glory, the street or the Gospel preaching and the state laws will be of pure gold, of Godly truth (Rev 21:21).

The Great city is the great Babylon, already known as the anti-Christian states of Europe, which in a spiritual sense can be called Sodom (mystery, Rev 17:5), full of spiritual immorality, and Egypt (flesh) of bitter persecution of the people of the Lord. Europe, through the denial of Jesus Christ and falling away from God, crucified the Son of God (their Lord) again and openly put Him to an open shame. (Heb 6:4-6). These anti-Christian states will crucify the Lord Jesus again, when they forbid the two witnesses to worship, to gather, to preach or to prophecy, thereby overcoming them and leaving them defeated, as dead congregations (bodies), and refuse to listen to complaints and protests against them.

Verse 9. **"And they of the people and kindreds and tongues and nations shall see their dead bodies three days and a half, and shall not suffer their dead bodies to be put in graves."**

The people, tongues and nations, are the people of Europe, who see the apostolic congregations closed. Again a proof that we cannot think of two persons as the two witnesses, who lie dead in all the countries of Europe, but of two different church societies, spread out over the whole of Europe. It also proves that all the nations stand subject to one and the same anti-Christian law, and the ban on apostolic congregations is imposed in all the states.

Concerning the three and a half days, we will broach this subject when we come to (verse 11).

Consequently, it follows that with social and moral death, also the **graves** must be understood in a moral sense, and not in a natural one.

As an image we find the grave in the Holy Scriptures used for a place of refuge, (Job 14:13), "O that Thou wouldest hide me in the grave, wouldest keep me secret, until Thy wrath be past," and as a resting place in (Isaiah 57:1, 2), as a moral death in (Ezek 37:12,13). The words "they shall not suffer their dead bodies to be put in graves" means that the witnesses will find no rest or refuge against the anti-Christian persecution.

Verse 10. **"And they that dwell upon the** anti-Christian **earth shall rejoice over them and make merry, and shall send gifts to one another; because these two prophets tormented them that dwelt on the earth."**

The anti-Christian nations and people rejoice for at last the two witnesses who plagued them continuously for 3½ years have been silenced. Sending gifts to one another is a Biblical expression for "good wishes", which often was accompanied by presents.

Verse 11. **"And after three days and a half, the Spirit of Life from God entered into them, and they stood upon their feet, and great fear fell upon them which saw them."**

In (verse 3), the two witnesses are said to prophesy for 1260 days. Lying dead lasted 3½ days. Consequently, we must use the same measure for this time in days. Since this ban occurs at the end of the 1260 days or 3½ years, we can safely assume that here we can expect a literal 3½ days. The two witnesses predicted this in their prophecies concerning the Second return of Jesus Christ to establish His Kingdom of peace here on earth.

At the end of the 3½ days, as predicted, the two witnesses are now filled with an extra measure of the Holy Spirit which makes them resurrect from this spiritual death,

"And they stood upon their feet." The feet are the evangelist and shepherd ministries. The mighty final prophecy will resound everywhere "Maranatha! Maranatha! The Lord is coming!" No law, no fear, nor earthly power, will in this last hour, prevent the two witnesses from prophesying the last glad tidings, that the end is imminent.

"And great fear fell upon them which saw them." We must realize that these events will be televised to the whole world by the newsmakers and reporters who stand by to record all these happenings. On hearing and "seeing" the great prophecy of the two witnesses, great fear will come upon all who rejoiced at their "death" and now, shortly afterwards (3½ days), hear and see them alive and well, and fearlessly predicting the imminent return of Christ to establish a new heaven (church) and a new earth (society).

ASCENSION OF THE TWO WITNESSES

<u>Rev 11:12.</u>

Verse 12. **"And they heard a great voice from heaven saying unto them, <u>Come up hither</u>. And they ascended up to heaven in a cloud, and their enemies beheld them."**

The First Resurrection and ascension of the bride and her retinue took place just prior to the 3 ½ year and the wedding feast has been in full swing since then.

The resurrection and ascension of the two witnesses take place at the end of the 3 ½ years, and these faithful witnesses will join the marriage feast in heaven, as guests of honour, because of their testimony and courage during the great tribulation.

"And their enemies beheld them." The anti-Christian nations will all see these hated witnesses ascend up to heaven from this earth. With today's technology, this has become possible and we can be sure that the news-makers will not miss such a scoop. This is therefore a Second Resurrection and ascension. The believers in the anti-Christian churches will then realize with horror that the Apostolic church was the true church of Jesus Christ and will be angry with their preachers who misled them. This will cause the fall of Babylon.

THE FALL OF BABYLON

> Immediately after the tribulation of those
> days, shall the sun be darkened, and the
> moon shall not give her light, and the
> stars shall fall from heaven.
> Matt 24:19.

Rev 13:7[b]. Rev 17:13, 16, 17. Rev 16:18–20.

Rev 18:8–24. Rev 14:8.

After the ascension of the two witnesses, the anti-Christian states gained full control. In (Rev 13:7), **the beast is given power over all kindred, and tongues, and nation**s. The beast actually consists of the seven great kingdoms of Europe, its seven heads (Rev 13:1). The ten rulers however (Rev 17:12) are named there _with_ the beast. (Rev 17:16) also speaks of the ten horns _and_ the beast. Similarly, this giving power to the beast over all kindred, tongues and nations, we also find in (Rev 17:13). "For God hath put in their hearts to fulfil His will, and to agree, and give their kingdom _unto_ the beast." This is the uniting of all the kingdoms of Europe under one anti-Christian state rule. The consequences we find described in Rev 17 in the seventh vial;

Verse 16. **"And the ten horns that you saw, they AND the beast, will hate the whore; they will make her desolate and naked; they will devour her flesh and burn her up with fire.**

This is the destruction of the apostate Christian churches by the anti-Christian power, elaborately described in (Rev 18). Her existence is henceforth not only redundant but even dangerous to the anti-Christian states of Europe.

After having recently been freed from the hated two witnesses, the Christian churches are in turmoil, and growing unrest amongst the Christians flared up and threatened the whole anti-Christian state and legislation. The churches stand empty. The upright believers have left their churches; the good citizens have no longing for her. The managers of her funds enrich themselves. It becomes the duty of the state, in its state wisdom, to ban the Christian religion, to forbid it by death, and to declare all the church buildings, assets and capital, as un-owned, to the advantage of the state treasury. This is therefore the eating of her flesh (James 5:3), to eat someone's flesh; rob, destroy (Psalm 27:2), that is: to expropriate

Babylon's assets; this also is the meaning of to burn her with fire (Psalm 21:9), here the fire out of the bottomless pit (Prov. 26:27), which we already know as the working of Satan in human hearts.

That the daily press will urge the powerful states to act according to the will of the people is self-evident.

This will be the fate of the whore Babylon, because:

Verse 17. **"For God hath put in their hearts to fulfil His will, and to agree; and to give their kingdom unto the beast, until the words of God shall be fulfilled."** Without wanting to, and unknowingly the anti-Christian states will, in their sinful lusts, become a tool in God's intentions to punish a similar sinful church and to pour out His vial over her. This anti-Christian unity of the European powers will last until the Godly predictions are fulfilled, and the Lamb, (Rev 6:16, Rev 19:11–21), through His return, will overcome the beast.

In (verse 18) it says: **"And the woman which thou sawest is that great city, which reigneth over the kings of the earth."**

The woman therefore does not represent the waters or the nations (compare verse 1 with verse 15), yet she sits on the nation and reigns over their kings. From (verse 3) it appears that the waters are either in a wilderness, or the wilderness itself, and thus unbelieving Christians nations. The woman, which sits on these nations and reigns over their kings, can, since she is the whore (verse 1), be no other, than the apostate doctrine and institutions in the church and state, as they more or less in an anti-Christian spirit, all deviate from the ministries introduced by Jesus in His church, and from the Christian Royalty by God's grace, such as it should be in Christian kingdoms.

The constitutional kings, subjected to the constitutional law and to the representatives of the people, the kings chosen by the people, and presidents of republics in the state,- and the Pope, Cardinals, Archbishops, and the Bishops in the Roman and Greek churches, the Oberkirchenrath, superintendents, Synods, etc. in the Protestant churches, all together form the woman, the whore, the mother of whores (verse 5), which sits upon many waters and reigns over the kings of the earth. They all together form the Great City of Babylon. Each of their church denominations forms a district, each of their different denominations forms a street out of Babel, called Sodom and Egypt, where their Lord is again crucified in His truth and witnesses in this twenty-first century.

They, however, do not know that the angel of (Rev 14:6 and 7), must proclaim over the whole of Christendom: the hour of judgement has come, first for the apostate church, then for the anti-Christian states. The seventh vial is totally poured out first over Babylon, then over the anti-Christ. Its outpouring in the judgement over Babel follows in (Rev 16:18);

Verse 18. **"And there was a great earthquake, such as was not since man were upon the earth, so mighty an earthquake, and so great."**

This earthquake is the same as the one described in the seventh seal (Rev 8:5) and in the seventh trumpet (Rev11:9). We said (Rev 11:13) that the sixth trumpet ended in the seventh period with "a great earthquake". In the seventh trumpet, we also found: "a great hail" (verse 19). In the seventh vial, each hailstone will be equivalent to one talent in weight (43 kilos). It is clear that a progressive climb in power is described here. In the trumpet, the occurrences are heftier than in the seal, and in the vial again heftier than in the trumpet.

The following comparison of these events shows this:

SEAL	TRUMPET	VIAL
Earthquakeke (Rev 8:5)	Great Earthquake (Rev 11:13)	Great Earthquake, such as was not since men were on earth, so might and so great. (Rev. 16:18)
	Great Hail (Rev 11:19)	Great Hail one talent in weight. (Rev. 16:21)

This earthquake of (Rev 16:18) is, therefore, the same as the one we considered in (Rev 11:13), as the great uproar amongst the nations, because of the ascension of the two witnesses, and the total ban on Christianity by the anti-Christian states of Europe. This all peaks to its top in the last events of the seventh vial, as predicted by Christ Himself (Matt 24:21) and by Daniel (Dan 12:1), as a time of great tribulation, such as was not since the beginning of the world to this time.

All the previous earthquakes in the church, even the great earthquake of the Reformation (Rev 6:12) are not to be compared with this one. Each tremor since 1830 shook off a piece of the Great Mountain Babel, forming smaller mountains and rocks, new religious denominations; also Islands, or dry places in the great sea of nations; on which earth the Lord could place His feet (Evangelists and Shepherds), thus new believing religious denominations were formed by that great earthquake, but by this great earthquake everything is destroyed, and (Verse 20): **"And every island fled away, and the mountains were not found."** The Roman, Greek and Protestant mountains or state churches totally disappeared, and Babylon is destroyed. Also, the islands, all the other believing sects and churches, are discontinued and Babylon, as the Great Millstone, is cast into the depths of the anti-Christian sea of nations (Rev 18:21).

This is what is predicted in (Rev 6:14): **"And the heaven departed as a scroll, when it is rolled together, and every mountain and island were moved out of their places."**

Verse 19. **"And the Great city was divided into three parts, and the cities of the nations fell: and great Babylon came in remembrance before God, to give unto her the cup of the wine of the fierceness of His wrath."** This last is the judgement of God over the apostate Christian churches, which (Rev 18) will describe in full detail.

The dividing of the Great city contains a special meaning and is the consequence of the sixth vial (Rev 16:13), where we discussed Deism, Atheism and Pantheism rising in the clergy and the church as well as in the states. These three spirits come to their full power in this time of great tribulation. It can be understood that the anti-Christian religion, although ONE over the whole of Europe, still will have different shades of belief, since the mind of all the people in Europe, from North to South, and East and West, will not easily unite in harmony.

Since Christendom spread over Europe, the Slavonic or Eastern nations adopted the Greek religion, the Latin or Southern nations, the Roman religion; while Protestantism was primarily adopted by the Germanic nations of Central Europe. At the same time, the unbelief revealed itself in the Greek nations mostly in the form of Deism, with the Romans in Atheism and with the Protestants in Pantheism, in clergy as well as in layman. Each of the three races appears to have a particular ground, to the development of one of these three forms of belief or unbelief.

If now under anti-Christian law the Christian religion is abolished as dangerous to the State, and the humanitarian religion; the belief in the higher value of man and his duty to human love is adopted as state and ONLY acceptable religion; it then is unavoidable that the anti-Christian religion of the Slavonic nations will reveal itself more in the Deistic form, the Latin nations in Atheism and the Germanic nations in Pantheistic form.

Thus will the great city be divided in three parts.

"And the cities of the nations fell." The great city is the whole of Christendom collectively named Babylon, while the cities of the nations are the non-Christian religions of the world that also are destroyed by the great earthquake.

THE SENTENCE OVER BABYLON

<u>Rev 18:8-12</u>

The execution of the sentence over Babylon is extensively described in the seventh vial, (Rev 18) which we left at (verse 8).

In (verse 1), we found the Apostolic church as the angel of spirituality with great power and clarity performed in (verses 2 and 3) in her manifest and preaching the conditions and the future lot of the Christian churches.

In (Verse 4), we heard the New Testament edicts of God over these churches begin, or the prophecies of the Holy Spirit, as this happened in the Apostolic church, wherein it admonishes God's people *to come out of the apostate Christian churches*, and wherein as from (verse 8) her sentence is predicted. This prophecy, starting with (verse 4), goes right through to (verse 20). We have interpreted it up to and with (verse 7), because it was already fulfilled up to then, and still continues in our days.

We must notice, that this prophecy, from (verses 4 to 20), or the voice of the Lord Himself in our century to His people, does not contain the comforting, the admonitions, etc. of the Lord to His people, as it is preached in the Apostolic church. Here in (Rev 18), it concerns Babylon only, the relationship of the Lord's people with her (verses 4–7) and her imminent judgement (verses 8–19).

It is remarkable to notice how in these 17 verses (verses 4–20), the tenses of the verbs change. With (verse 4) the prophecy begins in the <u>imperative</u>, as an order; this remains up to (verse 7). With (verse 8) the prophecy changes to the <u>future tense</u>, as the coming judgement over Babylon. The description thereof suddenly jumps, with (verse 11), over in the descriptive tone of the <u>present tense</u> and ends with (verse 14) in <u>the past tense</u>. With (verse 15) a new section of the prophecy starts in the <u>future tense</u>. Another starts with (verses 17–19) in the <u>past tense</u> and the whole prophecy ends with (verse 20), again as with (verse 4), in an <u>imperative tense</u>. This is not unusual with prophecies. See the prophecy of Jacob over his sons, especially over Judah, (Gen 49:8–12); the prophecies about Christ, (Isaiah 9:1, 5, 6, etc.)

The reason for this is as follows. Whenever the prophets of God were shown the future in vision and prophecy, they started by speaking in the future tense. By the power of the Holy Spirit, the future becomes so actual that they live in it, and they change over to the present tense. That which is already present in their feelings goes over into the past and they speak in the past tense.

This prophecy starts in the future tense predicting the judgement over Babylon.

Verse 8. **"Therefore <u>shall</u> her plagues come in one day, death, and mourning, and famine."** The meaning of "one day" we find in (Isaiah 47:9) is the sudden outburst of judgement and visitations. It is the hour spoken of in (verse 10), that the judgement is come over Babylon through the spiritual death, through spiritual hunger and through mourning over all she has lost.

This mourning is described in (Verses 11–16) as her lost treasures.

"And she <u>shall</u> be utterly burned with fire; for strong is the Lord who judgeth her." Therefore the destructive judgement of God (burning), will be the fire out of the bottomless pit, or the lusts of the godless, in the service of Satan, who will destroy all Christian churches and state ordinances.

Verse 9. **"And the kings of the earth, who have committed fornication and liveth deliciously with her, shall bewail her, and lament for her when they shall see the smoke of her burning."** The earth is the existing Christian and state society up to that time, and the kings of the earth are the rulers of church and state, with whom the church committed fornication and profited, instead of remaining pure and chaste for the heavenly bridegroom, and walking like Him in humbleness on the earth, in order to, like Him, be glorified. These church and state rulers will bewail her when they see the great destruction (smoke) of the judgement of the Lord (burning) over her.

Verse 10. **"Standing afar off for the fear of her torment, saying, Alas, alas, that great city Babylon, that mighty city! For in one hour is thy judgement come."**

Standing afar indicates that these rulers had already left Babylon. They find themselves subjected to the anti-Christian church and state, yet lament the destruction of this order, which they enjoyed so much, like the wife of Lot, they longingly look back to the burning Sodom.

Here the prophecy changes into a VISION and goes on in the present tense:

Verse 11. **"And the merchants of the earth shall weep and mourn over her, for no man buyeth their merchandise anymore."** The Lord compares Himself to a merchant, who sells wine, milk and bread (Isaiah 55:1, 2); He also names those who long for Salvation, believing souls, merchants (Matt 13:44–46), those who buy the truth, wisdom, instruction and wisdom (Prov 23:23). He even advises the believers of our present time to buy of Him gold and white raiment (Rev 3:18). The merchants of the earth are thus the ordinary clergy and teachers of the anti-Christian churches of this time, in contrast to the aforementioned kings of the earth or rulers in state and church. These false teachers had merchandise to sell, which no one now buys anymore. This is the reason for their mourning and weeping over the destruction of the church.

In verses 12 and 13, there now follows a description of all the merchandise, which these merchants offered for sale.

Verse 12.

1.) Merchandise of Christian faith and Salvation.
Gold: The truth of God.

Silver: Christian purity and love

Gold and Silver: (2 Tim 2:20) strong Christian life of faith.

Precious Stones: (1 Cor 3:9, 12. 1 Pet 2:4, 5, 9). Christians walking righteously.

Pearls: Men of faith, knowledge and upright walk of faith.

Fine Linen: (Rev 19:8). The righteousness of the Saints.

Purple: (Dan 5:7, 16,29. Matt 27:28, 29). High position in the kingdom of God.

Merchandise of Unchristian nature
Gold and Silver: (Psalm 115:4. Isaiah 1:22, 1 Pet 1:18, 19). The idolatry and the merits of the Saints in the Roman and Greek churches, virtue and good works in the Protestant churches.

Purple and fine linen: (Luke 16:19). Earthly honour and greatness.

Silk: (Ezek 16:10, 13. Ezek 27:16). Riches in all state churches.

Scarlet: Highest sinful condition.

2.) Personal Qualities of Christians.
Scented Wood: (Isaiah 44:19. 2 Cor 2:14, 15). Highly honoured and venerated departed Christians.

Vessels: (Jer 18:1–6. 2 Tim 2:20, 21). Higher or lower placed men in the Kingdom of God.

Ivory: (Ecc 5:14. Ecc 7:4. 1 Kings 10:18, 22). Excelling in purity, and costly.

Most precious Wood: (Psalm 92:12, 13. Luke 23:31. 1 Cor 3:12). Mighty witnesses of Christ.

Marble: (1 Chron 29: 2. Song of Songs 5:15. 1 Peter 2:5). Christians as costly living stones in the temple of God.

Unchristian Qualities
Wood: (Hosea 4:12. Isaiah 44:19). Idolatry with departed saints in Protestant, Roman and Greek churches. (Page 262. Vol 1)

Copper and Iron: (Jer 6:28–30. Dan 2:40, 42). Apostate destruction of Godliness and lack of love in all churches.

3.) Christian Works Verse 13.
Cinamon: (Prov 7: 17.) Christian charity.

Odours (spices): (Eph 5:2). (Phil 4:18). Christian love and sacrifice.

Ointments: (Exod 30:22–30. Exod 29:7. Matt 26:7, 12). The anointing of the Royal or priestly Ministry.

Incence: (Exod 30:34. Rev 8:3, 4). The prayers and supplications of the believers.

Unchristian Works
Incense: Intercessions of the departed Saints in the Roman church.

4.) Church Matters
Wine: (Page 124. Vol 1). The joy in the Holy Spirit.

Oil: (page 124. Vol 1) The sanctification by the Holy Spirit.

Wheat: (page 123. Vol 1) The belief in Jesus Christ, the believers.

Flour: (Lev 2:1–16. 1 Cor 5:8. Heb 5:12–14.) The teaching, ground from the wheat or the confessions of faith of the councils and Synods.

Beasts of burden: (page 124. Vol 1. Luke 10:34). The Shepherd and Teacher Ministry.

Sheep: (Matt 10:16. Matt 25:33. Luke 15:6. John 10). Scattered believers.

Unchristian Matters.
Oil: The futile Salving in the Roman and Greek churches.

Flour: All manner of confessions, deviating from God's Word and contradicting each other.

Beasts of burden: (Luke 11:46). Consecrated ones in all churches, but also (Isaiah 13:1–4. Isaiah 21:2) warlords and (Rev 17:3) state powers serving the church, to oppress those who disagree with them.

5.) Congregation Matters.
Horses: Congregations.

Chariots: (Ezek 1). Congregations or church clergy.

Slaves: (Rom 8:11, 13, 23. 1 Cor 6:15, 20. 1 Thess 5:23). Walk of life of the members of the congregation.

Souls of men: (Acts 15:26. James 1:21. Heb 10:39). Striving to convert sinners.

Unchristian Matters.
Slaves: Slavery in the Protestant and Roman States. Trading of relics in the Roman and Greek churches.

Souls of Men: Mass held for the departed and sales of Salvation in the Roman and Greek churches, but also, the loss of souls through the modern Protestant doctrine.

6.) Christian Striving of the Clergy. (Verse 14)
And the fruits that thy souls lusted after: (Prov 27:18. Matt 3:8. Matt 13:23. Luke 6:43–45. Luke 13:6. John 15:2–8. Rom 7:4. Col 1:10). The fruit of conversion and Salvation.

What was dainty: (What was fat, etc.), (Isaiah 25:6. Psalm 36:8. Psalm 45: 11. Isaiah 55:2. Rom 11:17). The knowledge of, the faith in, and the fellowship with Christ.

What was goodly: (Phil 4:8. Eph 5:27). All Christian virtues.

Unchristian Striving of the Clergy.
The fruit that thy soul lusted after: (Isaiah 10:12. Rom 7:5. 1 John 2:16). Greatness of life and sinful lusts.

What was Dainty: (Fat), (Ezek 34:2–4). The goodness of the earth in riches and lust.

What was goodly: (Luke 7:25) "Are departed from thee and thou shalt find them no more." The prophecy sees the future events as already fulfilled, and here speaks in the past tense.

All the above-mentioned merchandise will be destroyed in a storm of destruction unleashed after the ascension of the two witnesses, as soon as the Christians of the various churches realize that they have been lied to. How great will their anger be at the states, which carried them and now cease to support them any further? Babylon truly became the habitation of devils and a cage of unclean spirits, who fornicated with the kings of the earth, intoxicated the nations, and enriched themselves as a queen, instead of being a humble and chaste bride of Christ. **"Therefore"** (verse 8) – and in this "therefore", the righteous judgement of God is indicated, - therefore these plagues shall come over her.

Once more changing to the future tense, the prophecy continues:

Verse 15. **"The merchants of these things, which were made rich by her, shall stand afar off for the fear of her torment, weeping and wailing."**

Verse 16. **"And saying, Alas, alas, that great city, that was clothed in fine linen, and purple, and scarlet, and decked with gold, and precious stones, and pearls!"**

Verse 17. **"For in one hour, so great riches is come to naught."** And again reverting to the past tense it goes on:

"And every shipmaster, and all the company ships, and sailors, and as many as trade by sea, stood afar off." We know the ships as the image of missionary work or the ships of fishers of men on the sea of nations (Luke 5:10). When the Christian religion and churches are destroyed, all missionary work also ceases. When the anti-Christian states impound the assets and riches of the various church and Bible institutions, the whole missionary effort crumbles, and the missionaries are left prey to despair.

Verse 18. **"And cried when they saw the smoke of her burning, saying, What city is like unto this Great City!"** What religion can ever replace this Christian city?

Verse 19. **"And they cast dust on their heads, and cried, weeping and wailing, saying; Alas, Alas, that great city, wherein were made rich all that had ships in the sea by reason of her costliness! For in one hour is she made desolate."**

To cast dust on one's head is the image of remorse (Jos 7:6. Job 2:12. Lam 2:10) over the destruction of Christian churches and missions.

Dust is (Num 23:10) also the image of nations and (Isaiah 40:15) of islands and peoples. They cast the guilt, that the sea of nations will not receive the gospel of Salvation anymore, squarely upon their "heads" (or their rulers), because they did not guard against the pollution of the church.

For the third time in this chapter, it speaks of "in one hour", clearly indicating a point in time rather than a period of time. We know today, with all the high-tech communication, that any upheaval or event is almost immediately seen by the whole world and this predicted news will have a tremendous impact.

Now the predictions take on a present tense with:

Verse 20. **"Rejoice over her, thou heaven! And ye saints and apostles and prophets! For God hath avenged you on her."**

A better translation reads "For God has given judgment for you against her!" The Saints cannot be any other than the sealed ones, and the apostles and prophets those given since 1830, for they spoke out judgement against Babylon. Their judgement was God's judgement, which they had to proclaim. The execution of this judgement is proof that it was of God, and their righteousness before heaven and earth.

In confirmation of the fact that the prophecy over Babylon is truly fulfilled, John is shown the whole event in a new vision;

Verse 21. **"And a mighty angel took up a stone like a great millstone and cast it into the sea, saying. Thus with violence shall that great city Babylon be thrown down, and shall be found no more."**

Through the many different confessions of the Babylonian churches she became a great millstone, grinding all these different doctrines all claiming to be the truth, and this factory of all sorts of winds of doctrines, is thrown in the sea of nations and will not be found anymore.

That this is the meaning of flour and millstone, is apparent from the next two verses, wherein all forms of religion and worship, such as could be found in Babylon, are summarized in a few images.

Verse 22. **"And the voice of harpers, and musicians, and of pipers, and trumpets, shall be heard no more at all in thee, and no craftsmen, of whatsoever, craft he be, shall be found anymore in thee, and the sound of a millstone shall be heard no more at all in thee."**

Harpers: (Psalm 150:4. Psalm 77:6. 1 Cron 15:16, 20).
Musicians: (1 Chron 15:16, 19. Jer 7:34. Psalm 87:7).
Pipers; (Psalm 150:4)
Trumpeters: (Psalm 150:3).
Craftsmen: (Exod 31:1 – 11. Heb 11:10).
Millstone: (Jer 25:10).

Verse 23. **"And the light of a candle shall shine no more at all in thee; and the voice of the bridegroom and of the bride shall be heard no more at all in thee, for thy merchants were the great men of the earth, for by thy sorceries were all nations deceived."**

Verse 24. **"And in her was found the blood of the prophets, and of saints, and of all that were slain upon the earth."**

THE SECOND HARVEST

The Son of man shall send forth His angels,
and they shall gather out of His
kingdom all things that offend,
Matt 13:41.

Rev 14:17–20. Rev 16:16, 21. Rev 17:14. Rev 19:11–21.

Verse 17. "And another angel came out of the temple which is in heaven, he also having a sharp sickle."

These words contrast sharply with (verse 15). There the fifth angel or clergy came out of the temple or the Apostolic church on earth and pleaded with the Son of man who sat on the cloud, to thrust in His sickle on earth. This fifth angel however had no sickles but received it from the Lord.

Here the sixth angel in (verse 17), having a sharp sickle Himself, or a testimony from the Lord, now comes out of the temple. But this temple in heaven, or the glorified congregation, is the white cloud of the resurrected saints of (verse 14), who return to earth with Christ to judge the anti-Christian earth. Not only does John see this, but also the believers on earth will see this at that time. To them also will the resurrected saints appear, to proclaim unto them, that the time of the judgement is come. This is apparent from:

Verse 18. "And another angel came out from the altar, which had power over fire; and cried with a loud cry to Him that had the sharp sickle, saying. "Thrust in Thy sharp sickle, and gather the clusters of the vine of the earth; for her grapes are fully ripe."

This other angel is again a clergy, having power over the fire of the Holy Spirit, therefore apostles, having the power to dispense the Holy Spirit with His gifts, and to rule over these gifts (1 Cor 14), but who, with their fellow servants, have power over evil spirits (fire), just as the first Christians did.

The church of Christ is the vineyard of the Lord, (Matt 21:33--43. Matt 20:1–6). Jesus is the true vine, and His Father is the landowner. All branches, bearing no fruit in Him, he cuts away.

The unbelievers, therefore, who have not received the seal of God, but the mark of the beast, are the vineyard of the anti-Christian earth, and their fruit of unbelief, their grapes, full of the wine of fornication, are ripe, ripe to be thrown in the winepress of the wrath of the Great God.

The Lord asked the High Priest and Elders (Matt 21:36–40) "What will He do unto those husbandmen?" who killed His Son and took His vineyard, and their answer was: "He will miserably destroy those wicked men, and will let out His vineyard unto other husbandmen, which shall render Him the fruits in their seasons." This answer, in short, describes what is predicted in Revelation. (Rev 14:19, 20, etc.)

Verse 19. **"And the angel thrust in his sickle into the earth, and gathered the vine of the earth, and cast it into the great winepress of the wrath of God."** This is the war of the Lamb against the beast and the kings of the earth.

Verse 20. **"And the winepress was trodden without the city, and blood came out of the winepress, even unto the horse bridles, by the space of a thousand and six hundred furlongs."**

These few words, at the end of the seventh trumpet, describe the judgement of the Lord over the anti-Christ.

Which is the city mentioned here? We know that Babylon is already destroyed and her smoke goes up for eternity. In (Rev 11:2) we find the city, the Holy City, which is given to the Gentiles to tread underfoot for forty and two months. This was the forecourt of the temple (the Apostolic church) see (page 189. Vol 1)

Just as in former days the winepresses were built outside the city, the judgement will also take place only over the believers, who do not belong to the Holy City.

Outside Jerusalem was the Holy Land, which again is the image of the whole New Covenant people of the former Christian states of Europe. Revelation even indicates the size of the battlefield: *"a thousand and six hundred furlongs."*

This number does not appear anywhere else in the Scriptures. 1,600 furlong, however, according to Geographers, and Rabbinical sources is the length of the Holy Land. Revelation therefore here thereby describes the whole area of the New Testament Holy Land, that is: all the former Christian states of Europe. The judgement will be effected in this whole area, but will only affect the unbelievers, who live outside the city on the anti-Christian earth and in her institutions.

The horses we know as the congregations, here the anti-Christian congregations.

Bridles and bits in the mouth of the horses are in (Psalm 32:8, 9. 2 Kings 19:28. Isaiah 30:28. Isaiah 37:29. James 3:2, 3) the image of the rule and restraint over the people and godless nations fallen away from God, and thus here the image of the anti-Christian state power (the beast) over the nations of the anti-Christian Europe.

That the blood reached the bridles of the horse, means that all the sinful lusts (blood) of the godless will rise against the anti-Christian powers, causing uproar and revolution across 1,600 furlongs; over the whole of Europe.

The sum of all the images in this verse predicts that the judgement of God over the anti-Christian Europe will consist therein, that all devils in her will be let lose over all the states of Europe, that each hand will be lifted against that of his neighbour's (Zech 14:13), and Europe will be the scene of unheard of revolutions, plunderings, arson, war and destruction. (Isaiah 34) and (Zech 14. exp verses 12–15).

THE RIDER ON THE WHITE HORSE

<u>Rev 19:11–16.</u>

Verse 11. **"And I saw heaven opened, and behold a white horse, and He that sat upon him was called Faithful and True, and in righteousness, he doth judge and make war."** This is the appearance of the Lord in his future, all his enemies will see Him come with His resurrected Saints. The heaven which John saw, is the white cloud of (Rev 14:14), upon which the Son of man already sat and from which He now appears. From this, firstly emerges a white horse, or a congregation of glorified Saints, of which the Lord Himself is the rider who sat on it. This white horse or congregation is the clergy, New Testament Judah. "His proud horse in battle" (Zech 10:3–5), for Judah shall be the first (Gen 49:4, 8. Rev 7:5).

He who sits on the horse in His majesty, which carries Him in Triumph towards His enemies, was called Faithful and True, because He who is described as the Faithful witness in (Rev 1:5) and names Himself at the beginning of the seventh period (Rev 3:14) "the Faithful and true witness," now shows, by fulfilling all the promises concerning His Return, that He is the Faithful, who keeps His promise, and the True, of whom the prophecies of the Old and New Covenants testified, that He after humility would also come in Glory.

Verse 12. **"His eyes** (servants) **were as a flame of fire** (of the Holy Spirit), **and on His head were many crowns;** (the crowns of the seven great and ten smaller kingdoms of Europe, which He takes over and rules.) **and He had a name written, that no man knew, but He Himself."** (In total opposition to the names of Blasphemy of (Rev 13:1 and Rev 17:3).

Verse 13. **"And He was clothed with a vesture dipped in blood,** His vesture is His righteousness, dipped in the blood of our sinful natural life, (Isaiah 63:1–3) and His name is called the Word of God." (John 1:1–3).

Verse 14. **"And the armies which were in heaven followed Him upon white horses, clothed in fine linen, white and clean."**

The white horses or congregations consist of all the resurrected and transformed elect, called and faithful, who had part in the supper of the marriage of the Lamb, and now return to the earth with the Bridegroom and King, to take over His Kingdom with Him, as priests and kings. The riders are the faithful servants of the Lord who guided His congregation, taught them, comforted them, admonished and preserved them. They also are triumphantly carried by their congregations against the enemy.

Verse 15. **"And out of His mouth goeth a sharp sword, that with it he should smite the nations, the two-edged sword** (Rev 1:16) **of God's Word.** (Heb 4:12). This word is spoken during His walk on earth, "Rise from the dead! Be ye healed!" But will now utter words like: "Be ye cursed in Eternity! Wither and die!" (Zech 14:12).

"And He shall rule them with a rod of iron." Already in (Rev 12:5) it says that *the man-child* will rule all nations with a rod of iron. "And He trod the winepress of the fierceness and wrath of Almighty God." This again refers to the anti-Christian nations of Europe, the ripe grapes of the earth, being utterly destroyed. (Rev 14:20).

Verse 16. **"And he hath on His vesture and on His thigh a name written, KING OF KINGS, AND LORD OF LORDS."** Now Christ is revealed in His glory, in royal attire, to rule on earth with His elect. An active and actual battle cannot be expected, just as no battle took place between the Israelites and the Egyptian army, for here also the word applies: "The Lord shall fight for you, and ye shall hold your peace." (Exod 14:14).

The waters (sea of nations) will part (Armageddon) that is: they will be divided by anger and frustration and allow free passage to Christ and His army. Then the waters will collide in the winepress. (Rev 14:20), with blood flowing to the Bridle of the horses.

THE SUPPER OF THE GREAT GOD

<u>Rev 19:17–21.</u>

In (Rev 14:18) we found that the seventh angel pleaded with the angel of (verse 17), the resurrected saints, but no actual announcement was made. Now in

Verse 17. **"And I saw an angel standing in the sun;"** that is: a clergy (angel) standing in Christ (the Sun), (page 155. Vol.1) **"and he cried with a loud voice, saying to all the fowls that fly in the midst of heaven, Come and gather yourselves together unto the supper of the Great God."**

Who are the fowls? Not the unclean spirits of (Rev 18:2), neither people driven by evil spirits. Satan and his angels have previously been thrown out of heaven and can therefore not fly in it anymore. These birds fly in the midst of the heaven of the church and obediently accept the angels' invitation. They must therefore be believers, invited to eat the flesh of the anti-Christian horses and riders, which constitutes the supper of the Great God.

Indeed we again find the connection in (Matt 19:4, 19) the evil spirits or birds, or evil people, who ate the good seed of God's word out of the heart of people, but also in an opposed sense in (Matt 13:31, 32. Mark 4:31, 32 and Luk 13:18, 19.) In the parable of the mustard seed as the Kingdom of God, at the same time, the believers of that kingdom are described as the birds, but also particularly, as in (Rev 17:17), the foals of heaven. In (Matt 5:5) the Lord said, *"Blessed are the meek, for they will inherit the earth."* These blessed meek ones, in the heaven of the church in the white cloud of witnesses, are invited to come down to the earth and inherit all the assets of the anti-Christian nations.

Verse 18. **"That ye may eat the flesh of Kings, and the flesh of captains, and the flesh of mighty men, and the flesh of horses, and them that sit on them, and the flesh of all men, both free and bound, both small and great."** To eat of someone's flesh we already know to be the acquisition of all assets and property, and on God's command, the blessed meek ones, will divide the spoils of the anti-Christian nations, of the rulers of cities (kings), captains (ruler over thousand), the church possessions (flesh of horses), etc., after all the anti-Christians are destroyed by the Lord.

Verse 19. **"And I saw the beast, and the kings of the earth, and their armies, gathered together to make war against Him that sat on the horse, and against His army."**

Verse 20. **"And the beast was taken, and with him the false prophet that wrought miracles before him, with which he deceived them that had received the mark of the beast, and them that worshipped his image. These both were cast alive into a lake of fire burning with Brimstone."**

The anti-Christian state powers (the beast) and the false prophet (the blasphemous church leaders and teachers), and all those who had accepted the mark of the beast (who accepted the signs and lies of the prophet as their own) and worshipped his image (anti-Christian religion) are all thrown in the fire of hell. Just like the 144,000 sealed with the mark of the Lamb are the Bride of the Lamb, so are they who accepted the mark of the beast, the bride of Satan.

Where the Bride of Christ was taken up to heaven, so will the bride of Satan be thrown in the fire of hell. Just like the elect, they will also receive their incorruptible body and descend into hell, where their worm of eternal pain and fruitless self-condemnation does not die, and their fire of unfulfilled, devilish, sinful lusts and desires are never quenched or satisfied, (Mark 9:44), but the smoke of their torment will go up in all eternity, and they have no rest day or night, (Rev 14:11) while those, who accepted the seal of God, and ascended alive to heaven, are kings and priests upon the earth, reigning with Christ a thousand years.

Verse 21. **"And the remnant were slain with the sword,** those who accepted the mark of the beast, they are not taken and thrown alive in hell, but are killed with the sword **of He who sat on the white horse, which sword proceeded out of His mouth:"** as a result of the mighty words of the Lord, their flesh shall consume away while they stand upon their feet, and their eyes shall consume away in their holes, and their tongues shall consume away in their mouth. And it shall come to pass in that day, that a great tumult from the Lord shall be among them, and they shall lay hold every one on the hand of his neighbour, and his hand shall rise up against the hand of his neighbour. (Zech 14:12, 13).

So will the divided waters of the sea of nations fall upon each other, mutually destroying one another.

"And all the fowls were filled with their flesh."

THE TRIUMPHANT SONG OF MOSES

Rev 15:2-4.

Verse 2: **"And I saw as it were a sea of glass mingled with fire: and them that had gotten the victory over the beast, and over his image, and over his mark, and over the number of his name, stand on the sea of glass, having the harps of God."** The glorified Saints, the Holy City, is likened unto pure Glass. (Rev 21:18, 21), the sea of the glorified nations. Just as in (Ezek.1) the fire of the Holy Spirit also radiates from the sea of glass. The glorified Saints now stand around the Crystal sea as the saved souls, just like the Israelites, saved from the Egyptians, also stood at the Red Sea, when Pharaoh with his army were destroyed.

Verse 3. **"And they sing the song of Moses the servant of God, and the song of the Lamb, saying Great and Marvelous are Thy works, Lord God Almighty; just and true are thy ways, thou king of saints."** The song of Moses was (Exod 15:1, 4, 19, 21): a repetition of the refrain: *"I will sing unto the Lord. The horse and his rider hath he thrown into the sea."* The Saints sing that the anti-Christian horse with his rider is destroyed.

Verse 4. **"Who shall not fear Thee, O Lord, and glorify Thy Name? For Thou only art Holy: for all nations shall come and worship before Thee: for Thy judgements are made manifest."**

With this triumphant song, the history of the struggling church comes to an end.

THE KINGDOM OF GLORY

Rev 4:1-8

The reader will remember that during the first period, John was transported in Spirit to the day of the Lord to see the glory of the congregation of the resurrected Saints. Immediately after the completion of the seven candlesticks (Rev. 2 and 3) the following occurred in (Rev 4:1).

Verse 1. **"After this I looked, and, behold, a door was opened in heaven: and the first voice which I heard was as it were of a trumpet talking with me; which said, Come up hither, and I will shew thee things which must be hereafter."**

John again sees the first seal being opened and on completion of the seventh seal, he finds himself back on the day of the Lord. Similarly, he again experiences finding himself in the Kingdom of Glory, followed by the description of the victorious church. (Rev 20, 21 and 22).

The first voice, which John heard (Rev 1:10) is the voice of the angel who was commissioned to explain everything to him. (Rev 1:11).

In (Rev 1:17), the Lord, as the second voice, spoke to John explaining the seven letters he had to write.

Verse 2. **"And immediately I was in the Spirit; and behold, a throne was set in heaven, and one sat on the throne."**

Verse 3. **"And he that sat was to look upon like jasper and a sardine stone."** He who sits on the throne is not named, His name is unspeakable. His appearance is also not described, for God is a Spirit, He is invisible, and covers Himself with light and glory. (Psalm 104:1, 2).

This is why His appearance is as a costly stone, the brilliant diamond (*Jasper*) and the fiery red ruby (*Sardius*), as images of His *Holiness* and *righteousness*, for God is a light, but also a consuming fire for the sinner!

"And there was a rainbow round about the throne, in sight like unto an emerald." This is the brilliance and radiance of the glory of the Lord, a glory of light, as a smart coloured (Sea green) rainbow. (Exek 1:27, 28), the sign of a Covenant of His Grace and Mercy. (Gen 9:12–17).

Verse 4. **"And round about the throne were four and twenty seats; and upon the seats, I saw four and twenty elders sitting, clothed in white raiment; and they had on their heads crowns of gold."**

Daniel also saw these thrones (Dan 7:9), they are the heavenly governing council of the Lord, of which (Isaiah 24:23) already spoke: **"the Lord of**

hosts shall reign in Mount Zion, and in Jerusalem, and before His ancients gloriously."

Who are the twenty-four elders? As a result of previous reference to the four and twenty elders, one could assume them to be the glorified twenty-four apostles. Indeed! This explanation would have been inevitable had it not been that Revelation took away this solution by allocating these apostles to another and higher position in the Kingdom of Glory.

The four and twenty elders must consist of other glorified believers, who in their glorified condition became kings and priests. (Rev 20:4, 6. 1 Pet 2:9). In (Rev 5:8–10) the elders describe themselves as kings and priests, and cannot be the twenty-four apostles, but the high-ranking overcomers from the seventh candlestick (Rev 3:21), who partook in the First Resurrection. They all form a heavenly temple guard in the temple or congregation in the Kingdom of (1 Chron 23:24, 25). The twenty-four classes of Priests and Levites, described as *governors of the Sanctuary* and *governors of the house of God*, (1 Chron 24:5), consisted of thousands of persons as described in (1 Chron 24:7–18) as groups who took turns in the service of the temple. The four and twenty elders of (verse 4) also consist of groups of overcomers, taking turns reigning with Christ. They wear *golden crowns*, as the image *of their Royal power*, (Rev 4:4. Rev 5:10), they also have *harps and golden vials* full of odours, (the prayers of the Saints), over and above the *white raiment*, (a sign of their *priesthood*).

Verse 5. **"And out of the throne proceeded lightnings and thunderings and voices:"** In the Kingdom of Glory, the thousand years of peace on earth, the voice of the Lord will again be heard through His appointed servants to teach all nations the will of God.

"And there were seven lamps of fire, burning before the throne, which are the Seven spirits of God," and at the same time the seven horns or powers and the seven eyes or helpers of the Lamb, which we already know as the seven powers of the Holy Spirit, are sent into all lands. When John in (Rev 1:4, 5) greets the Asian congregations: *"Grace be unto you, and peace, from Him which is, and which was, and which is to come; and from the Seven Spirits which are before His throne,"* these seven spirits cannot be anyone else but the Holy Spirit.

Verse 6. **"And before the throne, there was a sea of glass, like unto crystal,"** the congregation, with no fault or guilt, the perfect righteous out of the sea of nations, the nations in the Kingdom of Glory are at peace, no more waves of tumult and upset.

"And in the midst of the throne, and round about the throne, were four living creatures full of eyes before and behind." The twenty-four elders sit around the throne and in the midst stood the four living creatures; these are actually four spiritual living beings, which have the life of God. They must however consist of human beings, since, together with the twenty-four elders they sing a new song (Rev 5:8, 9), "Thou art worthy to take the book, and to open the seals thereof, for of every kindred, and tongues, and people, and nation." They are therefore similar to the elders, previously sinners, but now redeemed and glorified people, who manifested the different human characters, active in the Lord's service. The four human spiritual gifts are the will, the feeling, the understanding and the power of imagination[58].

All four are present in each person but in different measures. The individuality of each person is determined by the dominant characteristic. For this reason in (Ezek 1:6, 10) the four living creatures each had four faces, while in (Rev 4) each living creature has only one of the four images.

Verse 7. **"And the first living creature was like a lion, and the second living creature like a calf, and the third living creature had a face like a man, and the fourth living creature like a flying eagle."** These four images are known by now, as the four ministries of the Lord, as He revealed Himself through human beings here on earth in His congregation, His will-power or courage in the Apostle ministry (lion), His love in the Shepherd ministry (calf), His understanding or clear understanding of God's counsel in the Evangelist ministry (man) and his imagination power or sanctified fantasy in the prophet ministry (eagle). See (page 51. Vol.1).

The high meaning of these four images in the kingdom of God dates back to (Num 2:3, 10, 18, 25) according to ancient history writers who described the 4 major tribes of Israel having these four symbols on their banners, Nahshon the captain of the tribe of Judah, having a lion in his blue banner, according to the prophecy of Jacob (Gen 49:9); the captain of the tribe of Ruben, Elizur, with a man in his red banner, Elishana, captain of the tribe of Ephriam, a calf in his golden banner (Deut 33:17) and Ahiezer, captain of the tribe of Dan with an eagle in a blue banner.

The four living creatures are in the midst of the throne and simultaneously around the throne. The Lord Himself, who sits on the throne, in unity with His Father, is the Great Apostle, Prophet, Evangelist and Shepherd; and after becoming man, He has these four characters and ministries within himself and thus sits in the midst of the throne. But He performs through his servants (eyes), who stand around His throne and are described with

---

[58] We use this word to describe the capacity of the soul, partially freed from the earthly, under higher influence, to be transported in times and circumstances; the peculiarity whereby the prophets could be driven by the Holy Spirit revealing the Prophetic character.

these four images. He himself is the Apostle in the apostles, the Shepherd in the shepherds, the Evangelist in the evangelists, and the Prophet in the prophets.

Verse 8. **"And the four living creatures had each of them six wings about him, and they were full of eyes all around and inside. (N.R.S).**

Wings we already know as the image of the protective powers of the Lord over people and nations. They are therefore six protective powers given to these four Christian characters.

The whole description of these four living creatures is the same in (Ezek 1), (Isaiah 6), and (Rev 4:8).

In Ezekiel, the Lord is shown as reigning over the cloud of His witnesses in the New Testament dispensation and being victoriously carried forward. This is an image of the struggling church on earth. The Cherubim or carriers of Salvation there have <u>four</u> wings.

To Isaiah, as also to John in Revelation, the Lord in the Kingdom of Glory, when the earth is full of His Glory (Rev 6:3) and "Holy, holy, holy is the Lord!" resounds before His throne, the Seraphim, or most important angels of the Kingdom have <u>six</u> wings. The animal images in the language of the Holy Spirit represent the characters, the wings or protection powers are the ministries. These wings or ministries are full of eyes, or servants of the Lord, the carriers of these ministries.

The Cherubim of Ezekiel represent the four ministries of Jesus, as they were present in the struggling church of the first century; the Seraphim of Isaiah, and the living creatures of John are the same ministries in the victorious church in the Kingdom of Glory.

If these Cherubim in the Kingdom of Glory in the victorious church now have <u>six</u> wings, they then must have received two more ministries, in addition to what they had before. On the question, "which two ministries did they acquire", they themselves answer in Revelation: *"what we were not on earth, we have now become kings and priests"* (Rev 5:10. Rev 16:12. Rev 20:4, 6. Rev 22:5). The Lord Himself, in the Kingdom of Glory, has become King of Kings and the High Priest among all priests.

The eyes, which these six wings have all around and inside, are all the servants of the Lord, who will be active in the Kingdom of Peace.

"They rest not day and night, saying: Holy, Holy, Holy, Lord God Almighty, which was, and is, and is to come."

This worship and glorification will be uttered once the Kingdom of Glory has been established on earth (and is to come).

SATAN IS BOUND FOR A THOUSAND YEARS

<u>Rev 20:1–6.</u>

Verse 1. **"And I saw an angel come down from heaven, having the key of the bottomless pit and a great chain in his hand."** This angel is described in the plural '**They**" in (verse 4), just as the sealing angel in (Rev 7:2, 3) named himself **"We"**. He is thus not Christ personally, but again Christ in and with His Ministries, apostles, prophets, evangelists and shepherds, or the glorified clergy of the first and last apostolic times, with whom He again comes on earth, as the angel of this new period. To come down from heaven indicated that Christ, just as in (Rev 11:1) and in (Rev 10:4) comes to earth to establish a new kingdom. Now, however, as the victorious church, as the undisputed dominion of Christ over the hearts of men, and over the institutions in state and society. For this purpose, He had the key of the bottomless pit, which, from the fifth trumpet, we know to be the power of superstition and unbelief in the hearts of the people. There the bottomless pit was opened whereas here it will be shut with the key.

The angel has a great chain in his hand. This is not a natural chain, and neither will it serve to bind Satan. On the contrary, we will soon learn that he will be cast into the pit and this pit will be shut and sealed.

This chain must have another meaning. Only one text in the Holy Scriptures alludes to a chain. In (Ezek 7:23), the Lord says to the prophet: make the decision. The prophet could not make a chain[59] to bind the whole of Israel. The chain was, in the Lord's word, as it is still in use in the East, the symbol of a linking together.

The chain that this angel carries is therefore the *long list of accusations,* which will be brought against Satan. Our sins, which we committed through his influence, and wherein the great seducer so often made us fall, are the chain of accusations wherewith he still accuses us before God.

But on the day, when all our sins will be forgotten, the accusations, which he earlier as our accuser brought before God (Zech 3), are now cast down upon him.

"Not My servant did the sin of own volition." The Lord will say in this judgement over the accuser, "But you seduced him to it. For him I paid the ransom, but all his sins are upon your head."

---

[59] The chain and not a chain, as is wrongly translated.

Each sin is a link in the chain. All the sins and accusations will form the great chain in the hand of the angel.

Satan now receives his judgement together with all his angels from the glorified servants of the Lord. Because "Know ye not that we shall judge angels" asks Paul in (1 Cor 6:3).

Verse 2."**And he laid hold on the Dragon, that old serpent, which is the Devil, and Satan, and bound him a thousand years."**

Satan will be bound and his power to deceive shall be taken away from him. He was always active in misleading the church and is still very active today, and nowhere can we find a period where he was not active and which could be construed as a thousand years of peace, which had already commenced, but one which is still to come in the future.

Verse 3. **"And cast him in the bottomless pit, and shut him up, and set a seal upon him, that he should deceive the nations no more, till the thousand years should be fulfilled: and after that, he must be loosed a little season."**

He is cast in the pit (the habitation of devils) and, Christ who had been bound by Satan and his servants in death and imprisonment, overcame death and the seal of Satan. Now in His return, He exercises the same judgement upon Satan, He imprisons him and seals the pit above him, and Satan will not be able to escape.

Verse 4. **"And I saw thrones, and they sat upon them, and judgement was given unto them."**

The glorified Saints here receive the power to judge, according to Jesus' promise (Matt 19:28).

"And I saw the souls of them that were beheaded for the witnesses of Jesus, and for the word of God, and which had not worshipped the beast, neither his image, neither had received his mark upon their foreheads, nor in their hands, and they lived and reigned with Christ a thousand years."

The angel or priesthood of (verse 1) speaks out the judgement over the martyrs and those who died during the 3 ½ years without receiving the mark of the beast. These all according to (Rev 14:13) are already sanctified; and being resurrected and alive, now receive their reward, (Luke 19:17, 19).

Verse 5. **"But the rest of the dead lived not again until the thousand years were finished. This is the First Resurrection."** Paul teaches us that two resurrections will take place in (1 Cor 15:23–26), "But every man in his own order, Christ the first fruits, afterwards they that are Christ's at His coming, then commeth the end."

Verse 6. **"Blessed and Holy is He that hath part in the First Resurrection; on such the Second death hath no power, but they shall be priests of God and of Christ and shall reign with Him a thousand years."** They have become like Christ, eternally glorified, and reign with him on the earth. The number thousand has no symbolic meaning in Scripture and must thus be taken literally.

A thousand earthly years must again represent one day in the Kingdom of God, as representing the Day of the Lord, the Great Sabbath day of rest, the Restitution of all things at the return of Christ, as Peter described in (Act 3:21). It is remarkable, how the old, strict Protestant theology, which is so hostile to Chilianism (doctrine of the thousand year kingdom), falls into the greatest inconsequent explanations of Revelation. While they categorically deny any imagery in the previous nineteen chapters, and take everything literally, suddenly with Chapter 20, take a different approach, and declare everything to be of a Spiritual meaning. The thousand-year kingdom is not only described in Revelation. The Old Testament as well as the New Testament cannot be understood without this doctrine.

The Kingdom of God, preached by Christ, did not yet reveal itself in His days on earth (John 18:36).

Daniel and the old prophets described the Kingdom of Glory in its external form, and the New Testament in its inward or spiritual form. Revelation combines both in their mutual relation and clarifies it as the completed Kingdom of Christ on Earth.

With the seventh trumpet, the Kingdom of Glory in all humbleness began to emerge on earth. Now it is revealed in its total splendour.

THE NEW JERUSALEM

THE CANDLESTICK IN THE KINGDOM OF GLORY

Rev 21:1-8.

Verse 1. **"And I saw a new heaven and a new earth: for the first heaven and the first earth were passed away, and there was no more sea."**

This *new heaven* and *new earth* are not eternity, such as after the last judgement of (Rev 20:11–15) which will follow.

We find ourselves in the Kingdom of Glory, before the last judgement, as a new order in the church (*heaven*) and in the state institutions (*earth*) has taken the place of the former ones, for the first heaven of the Christian church, struggling here on earth, has passed away; also the first state institutions on earth, which stood under the rule of Satan, the Prince of the world, are destroyed, and also the ever roaring waves of evil lusts, unbelief and religious disputes of the sea of nations are no more. There is rest and peace over the waters.

Verse 2. **"And I John saw Holy city, New Jerusalem, coming down from God out of Heaven, prepared as a bride adorned for her husband."**

In verses (2–8), this bride is described as the congregation, the heavenly Jerusalem, of which Paul already speaks (Gal 4:25, 26). Verses (2–8) thus forming the candlestick in the Kingdom of Glory, again containing a closing promise (verses 7–8).

The bride of the Lord, now His wife or congregation is found on earth again, as glorified people, walking and preaching and admonishing the people of the earth, just as Christ, the Lord did, after His Resurrection, remaining with His Disciples for forty days.

Verse 3. **"And I heard a great voice out of heaven saying, behold, the Tabernacle of God is with men, and He will dwell with them, and they shall be His people, and God Himself shall be with them, and be their God."**

This great voice cannot be that of the Lord, as He begins speaking in (Verse 5). It is the voice of the multitude of glorified Saints, who, as the New Jerusalem, came down from heaven, They themselves are the True

547

Tabernacle, the habitation of God. This voice comes out of the New Heaven. We know that we shall be like him (1 John 3:2).

Verse 4. **"And God shall wipe away all tears from their eyes; and there shall be no more death, neither sorrow, nor crying, neither shall there be any more pain: for the former things are passed away."** (Jes 65:17–25).

Verse 5. **"And He that sat upon the Throne said, behold, I make all things new,"** (and the angel goes on to say), **"And He said unto me, write: for these words are true and faithful."**

Verse 6. **"And he said unto me** (again the Lord Himself), **It is done,** (the struggle of the church has ended), **I am the Alpha and the Omega, the beginning and the end. I will give unto him that is athirst of the fountain of the water of life freely."** Also there, there will be a thirst for the water of life, proof that we here are not in eternity but in the Kingdom of Glory on earth.

Who will belong to the New Jerusalem?

Verse 7. **"He that overcometh shall inherit all things, and I will be his God, and he shall be my son."**

Verse 8. **"But the fearful, and unbelieving, and the abominable, and murderers, and whoremongers, and sorcerers, and idolaters, and all liars, shall have their part in the lake which burneth with fire and brimstone, which is the second death."** All those who feared to strive against the kingdom of darkness, who did not believe, who did not recognize Him in His Word and servants, the abominable who drank of the abomination out of the cup of Babylon, and not the pure water of life, and the murderers, who did not love their brothers in Christ, and the whoremongers who fornicated with the Great Whore, and the sorcerers who poisoned the wine which came from the vine (Christ), and the idolaters, who worshipped men and human institutions and statues instead of God and His Word, and all the liars, who seduced to unbelief (the false prophet), or to superstition (Roman and Greek churches), for all these the reward is the Second death. This is the final judgement reserved for the end of the Kingdom of Glory.

Verse 9. **"And there came unto me one of the seven angels which had the seven vials full of the seven last plagues, and talked with me, saying, Come hither, I will shew Thee the Bride, the Lamb's wife."**

The angel in (Rev 17:1) was the clergy of the Apostolic church, who revealed through their manifest and preaching, how the woman (congregation) had become a whore, a Babylon. This same clergy is also the angel, who will show to the believers, that the bride, the Lamb's wife, has come down to earth in His glorified and resurrected Saints.

Verse 10. **"And he carried me away in the Spirit to a Great and High Mountain, the Mountain of the Kingdom of the Lord, which in the last day will be exalted above all previous mountains"** (Isaiah 2:2–4. Mica 4:1. Dan 2:35, 44).

"And shewed me that Great City, the Holy Jerusalem, descending out of heaven from God." The coming down from heaven of the city of God is the return of Christ with his many resurrected and transformed Saints. It is important for the reader to note that the New Jerusalem is not the earth or Europe, but the glorified congregation, who, responsible for the *New* Church and *New* State ordinances, come down to earth with the Lord, to expand these ordinances over Europe and under their rule, make Europe the Kingdom of Glory.

Verse 11. **"Having the glory of God and her light was like unto a stone most precious, even like a Jasper stone, clear as crystal."** This glorified congregation or city of God, has the Glory of God, for she has become like Him, and the Lord lives in her.

Now follows a description of this Spiritual Jerusalem, or the glorified congregation, wherein the Lord lives. Remember that this forms part of the *seal* in the Kingdom of Glory, and thus describes the powers in church and state.

Verse 12. **"And has a wall great and high, and has twelve gates, and at the gates twelve angels, and names written thereon, which are the names of the twelve tribes of the children of Israel."** The city is a Spiritual city, the wall is a Spiritual wall against unbelief and superstition and consists of the fourfold ministries of Christ in the congregation. The inhabitants of the city are the twelve sealed tribes of Israel.

For each of the tribes there is one gate, giving access to this spiritual city, from which also flows the everlasting gospel for all the nations, and languages and tongues.

Verse 13. **"On the East, three gates, on the North, three gates, on the South, three gates, and on the West, three gates."** The elect of this spiritual city is gathered from the four winds (Matt 24:31), but also out of this Jerusalem the law will go out to the four corners of the earth. The Godly threesome of the gates and the earthly foursome of the sides of the city are the symbol: 1st. of the access to this heavenly Jerusalem appointed by God, 2nd. of the expansion of the Kingdom of God over the earth.

Verse 14. **"And the wall of the city had twelve foundations, and in them the names of the twelve Apostles of the Lamb."** The wall, or church ordinances and ministries, is built upon the twelve-fold apostle ministry, (Eph 2:20), of which Jesus is the cornerstone. He calls Himself the First and the Last. In the beginning, the Spiritual Jerusalem, the church, had twelve apostles with their fellow servants as gates and walls. The Apostolic church of the last period had, after coming out of Babylon, this wall and these gates, and kept them until their ascension at the First Resurrection. But also in the Kingdom of Glory, the believers on earth again receive the same twelve-fold Apostle Ministry with other ministries.

In the foundations, the names of the twelve apostles of the Lamb were written. These twelve names have a special significance, and the qualities, which are ascribed to them, are the different characteristics of these foundations, which not only refer to the original twelve but was also required and found in the later apostles.

John:	Lovable, also: the gift of Grace from Jehovah.
Peter:	A Rock. Simon: who hears with acceptance.
James:	A supplanter
Andrew:	Manly, Strong.
Phillip:	Who loves the Horse (congregation).
Bartholomew:	A son who stems the waters (nations or teaching) Nathanael: Given by God.
Thomas:	A twin brother. Didymus: the same.
Matthew:	A gift from Jehovah.
Alfeus:	A leader or teacher
Judas:	Worshipper of God.
Simon:	Who hears with acceptance.
Matthias:	The Lord's gift.

With the names of the twelve apostles of the Lamb, it is not implied to mean twelve persons, but the twelve-fold apostolate in the spiritual city of God.

Verse 15. **"And he that talked to me had a golden reed to measure the city, and the gates thereof, and the wall thereof."** The angel speaking to John is the Angel of (verse 9), representing the apostles in the Kingdom of Glory. A reed, a Jewish measure, is approximately 10 feet long, or 2.943 yards. The gold is the image of the truth of God, and to measure is to investigate. In total this means an investigation of the expanse of the Spiritual Kingdom of God and the extent of the truth of God over Europe. It is a repeat of the investigation that the apostles of the Apostolic church conducted in 1835 to 1839, as predicted in (Rev 11:1, 2a). Europe was then the great city, the spiritual Sodom and Gomorra, and the forecourt of the Gentiles. The believers in Europe made out the temple of God in the Great City, and the altar, where God was praised and worshipped. Now, in the Kingdom of Glory the temple has expanded to the whole of Europe, and the whole city has become a temple, and there is no more temple in the city, for the Lord, the Almighty God, is her temple (verse 22). For this reason, the temple must not be measured alone as in (Rev 11:1), but the whole city, the whole of Christian Europe with her apostles and ministries. The new clergy in the Kingdom of Glory will be commissioned to investigate the whole Kingdom and report to the Lord in order to establish this Kingdom on solid foundations of Apostles, Prophets, Evangelists and Shepherds, for this Kingdom must last 1,000 years. The results of this investigation are described in the following verses.

Verse 16. **"And the city lieth foursquare and the length is as large as the breadth, and he measured the city with the reed, twelve thousand furlongs. The length and the breath and the height of it are equal."** The big question is here: do we have to take this verse literally or symbolically? In (Rev 14:20), it seemed to be the literal interpretation. The similarity would lead us to believe that the measurement of the city in furlong is to be understood. The Holy City, as we know, the New City and church institution, is situated on the area which Babylon occupied during the activities of the beast, over the whole of Europe. And indeed, if we draw a square over Europe, with each of the sides toward one of the four winds, each 12,000 furlongs or 2413 km in length, it would clearly encompass the most populated areas of the Christian population of Europe. It has become the Kingdom of the Lord, which is higher than the former mountains and is the image of the foreshadowing of the Holy of Holies of the temple, a cube.

For its symbolic meaning, we have to notice that:

1st. The number twelve consists of three, the number of God, multiplied by four, the number of the earth, and in the Holy Scriptures is the symbolic number of the ordinances of the Lord in His Covenant people. We find twelve tribes of Israel, in the Old Testament, but also twelve spiritual tribes of Israel in the New Testament. For the twelve fathers of the first, we also have the twelve apostles of the second.

2nd. 1,000 is the volume of a cube, formed by 10, the number of the Kingdom of God, as length, breadth and height, multiplied with each other; 1,000 cubic yards was the volume of the cube forming the Holy of Holiest, wherein the Lord lived. The Kingdom of Glory wherein the Lord will live, will also last 1,000 years.

3rd. The length, breadth, and height find their perfect explanation in (Eph 3:18). The length, breadth and height of verse 18 convey the fullness of God, (verse 19). That is, on the external visible form and measurement of the temple, which is His Body, His Congregation, the fullness of Him that filleth all in all. (Eph 1:22, 23).

When we now consider that, in the thousand-year Kingdom there is no temple in the Heavenly Jerusalem, but the whole city is a Temple, filled with the fullness of God, or a congregation, wherein the Lord lives and reigns, then the summary of the symbols in our text become these:

The whole of Christian Europe lies foursquare, because in it, from the four corners of the earth, the elect and glorified assemble there, but also the Word and the law of the Lord will go out of this continent to the four corners of the earth, to the unbelievers in the four other continents. The length, breadth and height describe the temple city or the congregation, as the fullness of God, who lives in her, and the measurement of 12,000 furlongs, the ordinances of the Lord amongst His Covenant people, in the Kingdom of Glory, during the 1,000 years. Since the golden reed of (verse 15) is not expressed in reeds of 10 feet, but their number is converted to geographic measurements of furlong, we believe that the expanse of Europe must also be taken into account, and the meaning is, therefore, both literal and symbolical. That Europe, with the Holy land in Asia Minor, is the ground, on which the Holy City, the congregation of the Lord, the New Jerusalem, will be erected, will still become clearer.

Verse 17. **"And he measured the wall thereof, a hundred and forty and four cubits, according to the measure of a man, that is, of the angel."** This verse is, so far, badly translated and misunderstood. Some understand it in connection with the reading 144 cubits (yards), as length, another as the height, and a third (Luther) as the thickness of the wall.

The text does not indicate this. The verse exists in three different versions. 1st. 144 Furlong, 2nd. 144 cubits, 3rd.144, without adjective. The last reading, 144, seems to be the right translation. But, because it was incomprehensive, we suspect, that one translator of the previous verse's "furlong", added furlong to our text, understanding, that it was so intended, while another, considering it too big, added cubits (yards) to it, thinking, that this was intended here, but was somehow forgotten. If the word: cubits (yards) also appeared in the original text, it is incomprehensible, how it could have been left out of one transcription, and in another, the word furlong was changed to cubit.

Similarly, the second article of this verse was not properly accepted. The one understood, that THE angel of (verse 9) here not with His golden reed, but with a human yardstick did the measuring. Yet it here states in the original not "of THE Angel", but "of AN Angel". Others again supposed that here it was to be taken, that human and angel measurements are the same. We consider Revelation too Holy, to expect such senseless and pointless measuring systems from it. We conclude, that the word: measurement, here does not mean; the *measuring rod*, wherewith it is measured, but the *resulting size*.

This is grammatically correct. The original word for "measurement" used means, not only the measurement as measuring-rod, but also the resulting size, the number of the measurement, and this last is meant here.

The second part of the verse is difficult to understand and translate. Literally, it states "the size (or number) of men, which is of angels." While the number of men, is at the same time as that of angels, then those men and angels must be the same persons, and the wall consists of 144 men, who are the angels (clergy) of the city.

We consider the twelve angels of (verse 12), who belong to the wall, to be meant here. A spiritual city also has a spiritual wall. A wall is the image of Godly protection in many places in the Holy Scriptures. In (Zech 2:5), the Lord names Himself a wall of fire around Jerusalem.   In (1 Sam 25:16) men are described as a wall, and in (Jer 15:20) *the prophet Jeremiah* is made as a fenced brazen *wall* against the attacks of the enemies. The wall is therefore the Lord in His servants, who form the wall of this Spiritual city, numbering 144. If however the word: cubits (yards), belongs to the correct text, it cannot be meant in the Spiritual sense for the Spiritual city but must be a metaphor. As such the word "cubits" occurs only twice in the Holy Scriptures. In the foreshadowing Tabernacle, of the Old Covenant, the image of a cubit must be of men in the service of the Lord; the half cubit that of their help. (Exod 26:15, 16).

In the New Testament cubit occurs in (Matt 6:27 and Luke 12:25) as an addition, which no man, but only God can give. Both interpretations concur with the already given explanations. The wall of 144 men was an addition given by the Lord to the city, or the church, in the Kingdom of Glory. The 144 men were however angels of the congregation (Bishops), who therefore, as a temple guard for the protection of the city had to see that nothing unclean enters the city, (verse 27). This is proven by the following.

Verse 18. **"And the building of the wall of it was of Jasper: and the city was pure gold, like unto clear glass."** This wall or angel guard as like unto Christ, the Jasper stone, or Christ in His servants; the city, or the other believers, was of the pure gold of Godly truth, clear and pure as a glass of the crystal sea, without ripple or fault.

Verses 19, 20. **"And the foundations of the wall of the city were garnished with all manner of precious stones. The first foundation was Jasper, the Second, Sapphire; the third, a Chalcedony, the fourth, an Emerald.:**

"The fifth, Sardonyx, the sixth, Sardius; the seventh, Chrysolite; the eighth, Beryl; the ninth, a Topaz; the tenth, a Chrysoprasus; the eleventh, a Jacinth; the twelfth, an Amethyst."

The New Testament foundations of the congregation are once and for all the unchanging apostles and prophets (Eph 2:20. Eph 3:5. 1 Cor 12:28. Eph 4:11). They are like costly stones of all sorts of colours.

Precious stones dissolve the light rays, absorb some of the colours, and radiate the unabsorbed colours in the eye of the beholder. These radiated colours form the individual characteristic colour of each different stone. Similarly, the great men of God receive their light from the Lord (verse 23), and radiate, each according to his own character, a quality, which distinguishes one from the other. Therefore, precious stones and jewels are images of the gifts of the Holy Spirit, which reveal themselves in different persons in different ways. Revelation clearly indicates the connection of each stone to a corresponding foundation and shows a remarkable resemblance between a foundation and its corresponding precious stone. They are typically pictured in, and presumably, the same precious stones, imbedded in the breast-cloth of the High Priests, upon which the names of the twelve tribes were inscribed. It would be futile to try and unravel the connection of the meaning of each stone since we do not know which stones were known and described by the Jews or Greeks of old, and also that the character of half of the apostles of the Lord is unknown to us. The meaning of the names of the twelve tribes and that of the apostles (verse 14) will probably correspond with that of the precious stones.

Verse 21. **"And the twelve gates were twelve pearls; every several gate was of one pearl."** Pearls we know to be men excelling in Christian faith, knowledge, and walk of life.

In (Eph 4:11) the four ministries together form a unit, as the gate, giving access to the congregation. The twelve gates, each of the four ministries, form therefore 48 persons, as the servants of Christ, through whom He reigns in His church. Each four together form a pearl and are the gate, through which one can find the only access to this state of perfection of Christian life in the Kingdom of Glory. (Eph 2:19–21. Eph 4:11–13). There are twelve such gates.

"And the street of the city was pure gold, as it were transparent glass." The street is already known as the image of the judicial office, but also of the showcase of Christian merchandise. The civil justice which is practised in the Kingdom of Christ as the Gospel teaching, is proclaimed, will both be Godly and true, as the purest gold, but also recognizable to everyone as transparent glass.

Verse 22. **"And I saw no Temple therein, for the Lord Almighty and the Lamb are the Temple of it."**

The whole city is a temple, for the Lord lives in its inhabitants (verses 3, 11), and they in the Lord (Verse 9), filled with the Holy Spirit, (1 Cor 6:19. 2 Cor 6:16).

Verse 23. **"And the city had no need of the sun, neither the moon, to shine in it: for the Glory of God did lighten it, and the Lamb is the light thereof."** The Lamb is the candlestick, the light of the congregation.

Verse 24. **"And the nations of them which are saved shall walk in the light of it, and the Kings of the earth do bring their glory and honour into it."** A strong Gospel will be brought to all unbelieving nations. That there still are heathens and unbelievers is proved by (verses 8, 26, 27 - Rev 20:8 and Rev 22:15). The kings of the earth in the other continents do not seek to augment their own power and glory anymore, but, admit that the True God has established His Kingdom and throne in Europe, they come and bring their glory and honour in the city.

Verse 25. **"And the gates of it shall not be shut at all by day: for there shall be no night there."**

During the first period, the gate of the fourfold ministry was shut through the indifference of the believers. Now these ministries of Christ, and those called by Him and fully equipped ministries, remain, and uphold his light and Spirit in the congregation, for there will be no more night of spiritual darkness anymore.

Verse 26. **"And they shall bring the glory and honour of the nations into it."** All the glorious inventions which will still be discovered, as well as the existing ones, will be sanctified to the service of God. Commerce and shipping, railways, air traffic, radio, television, satellite communication, and computer technology, will continue to exist and blossom, even livelier amongst nations; yet all these earthly inventions will not stand in the service of sin, but to the honour and glorification of God.

Verse 27. **"And there shall in no wise enter into it anything that defileth, neither whatsoever worketh abomination or maketh a lie; but they which are written in the Lamb's book of life."** During the Kingdom of Glory, there will still be sinners, although of their own will and they cannot partake of Christ. After His Resurrection, Jesus appeared to His own and not to the heathen.

THE TRUMPET IN THE KINGDOM OF GLORY

<u>Rev 22:1–5.</u>

Verse 1. **"And he showed me a pure river of water of life, clear as crystal, proceeding out of the throne of God and the Lamb."** The angel, the same as in (verse 9) is the Apostolic clergy of the seventh period now in the Kingdom of Glory.

The river of waters of life, clear as crystal *is the Holy Spirit, in doctrine, preaching and prophecy*, which immediately comes forth from God the Father and the Son. It was already described in (Gen 2:10) in a natural image of the river, which parted into four streams representing the fourfold ministry of Christ.

Verse 2. **"In the midst of the street of it, and on either side of the river, was there the tree of life, which bare twelve manners of fruits, and yielded her fruit every month."** The tree of life is Christ (John 15:1), and the twelve fruits are the twelve apostles (John 15:5), who will in monthly shifts bring forth the gospel to all nations.

"And the leaves of the three were for the healing of the nations." These leaves are people, sent out to convert the Heathen. Job compares himself to a leaf, (Job 13:25) also in (Prov. 11:28 and Isaiah 64:6).

Verse 3. **"And there shall be no more curse: but the throne of God and of the Lamb shall be in it, and His servants shall serve Him."** The curse caused by Adam's fall is rescinded. There will be peace in political, religious and social circles. Satan is bound and cannot incite disorder anymore.

Verse 4. **"And they shall see His face, and His name shall be in their foreheads."** They shall be like him and see Him as He is. (1 John 3:2), they are sealed on their foreheads.

Verse 5. **"And there shall be no night there, and they need no candle, neither light of the sun; for the Lord God giveth them light; and they shall reign forever and ever."** The candlesticks are in their midst. They will reign as Kings and Priests in eternity.

THE VIAL IN THE KINGDOM OF GLORY

THE LAST FALLING AWAY

<u>Rev 20:7–10.</u>

It may seem strange to the reader, that Revelation, which predicts the history of the Christian church, gives no history of the thousand-year Kingdom; but of its establishing in (Rev 20:1–6), its ordinances (Rev 21 and Rev 22:1–5), and immediately goes over to the end of it (verse 7). It is however quite simple to imagine. A kingdom, where only peace reigns has no history. Only revolutions, wars, changes and exchanges of great joy and great sorrows in a kingdom form its history. Since Christ and His glorified Saints reign as Kings and Priests, the Kingdom of Glory is stable and blissful.

Verse 7. **"And when the thousand years are expired, Satan shall be loosed out of his prison."** Before the last judgement, it must first be ascertained which of the living on earth truly love God and fear him. Therefore, the seducer of men must be released for a short period, to test them.

Verse 8. **"And shall go out to deceive the nations which are in the four quarters of the earth, God and Magog, to gather them together to battle: the number of whom is as the sand of the sea."** It is frightening to realize that, after having experienced Christ's personal teaching, guidance and ruling for a thousand years, the inhabitants of the earth will again have to make a choice for or against Christ. Satan, after millenniums of experience with mankind, will proclaim a clever and appealing doctrine and a great last lie. He will convince uncountable people (*like the sand of the sea*) that if they stand together and destroy the Spiritual New Jerusalem, he will become the King of Kings and he will reward all those who participate in the last battle.

Verse 9. **"And they went up on the breadth of the earth, and compassed the camp of the Saints about, and the beloved city: and fire came down from God out of heaven and devoured them."** We are reminded of the fire from heaven consuming the altar of Sacrifice in the presence of the priests of Baal.

Verse 10. **"And the Devil that deceived them was cast into the lake of fire and brimstone, where the Beast and the False Prophet are, and shall be tormented day and night forever and ever."** Together with the Devil, all his fallen angels and evil spirits receive their eternal condemnation. This marks the end of the 1,000 years and is immediately followed by the Great Judgment Day.

THE LAST JUDGEMENT

Rev 20:11–14.

The last enemies of the Lord are destroyed, and no more rebellions against Him will disturb His Kingdom anymore. He can now give over His Kingdom to God the Father, that He may be all in all.

Verse 11. **"And I saw a Great White throne, and Him that sat on it, from whose face the earth and the Heaven fled away; and there was found no place for them."** The Son of man is the one who will judge and will do so as King, still in the Kingdom of Glory. The earth and the heaven therefore do not have to pass by; but the earthly social ordinances, and the heaven, the church and church institutions of the Lord, as they existed in the Kingdom of Glory, are ended, and must make way to even more perfect blissful conditions in eternity.

Men also cease to exist in the flesh; they are, just like the resurrected Saints of a thousand years before, changed and received their ascension body. The corruptible is changed to the incorruptible. Therefore, no church ordinances of Christ are needed anymore. There are no more souls on earth which must be converted or preserved for Eternity.

Verse 12. **"And I saw the dead, small and great, stand before God, and the books were opened: and another book was opened, which is the book of life, and the dead were judged out of those things which were written in the books, according to their works."**

All men, whoever lived upon the earth, now appear before the judgement seat of the Lord. (2 Cor 5:10. 2 Tim 4:1). The books represent the Remembrance of the Lord, wherein not only the greater or smaller sins of all mankind but also each idle word, spoken by them, are recorded (Matt 12:36), as also the cup of water (Mark 9:41), given in the name of Christ. Indeed, there are five books.

1st. The book of the people who lived from Adam to Moses, for those who lived without the law, they will be judged without the law. (Rom 2:12a)

2nd. The book of those, who lived from Moses under the law, they will be judged by the law. (Rom 2:12b)

3rd. The book of those, who lived under the Gospel, and will be judged by the Gospel. (John 12:48. John 3:18)

4th. The book of the Gentiles, who did not know the law or the Gospel, will be judged by their conscience. (Rom 2:14–16)

5th. The book of God's Kingdom of Glory. Those who lived under this full dispensation of Grace, and yet did not want to believe in Christ, or fell away from Him, will be judged by the glorified Saints. (1 Cor 6:2). These do not appear in the Book of Life of the merits of Christ.

From those whose names are written in the Book of Life, the sins, the shortcomings, and the evil are not recorded, but only their good works are remembered, because their sins have been forgiven.

Veres 13. **"And the sea gave up the dead which were in it; and death and hell delivered up the dead which were in them; and they were judged every man according to their works."**

The sea is the sea of nations over the whole earth. Her dead are the spiritually dead, who do not have the life of God in them, and although not experiencing the natural (first) death, receive the second death. The seas and oceans will also give up the thousands or thousands of dead who found their grave in them, in their resurrected bodies, just as those who found a grave, in Mother Earth.

All will resurrect to an incorruptible body. All those who had no part in the first resurrection, are still in Hades, the realm of the departed.

How they will be judged by Jesus, is described in (Matt 25:31–46). We will all appear before the judgement seat of Christ (Rom 14:10), when "the hail has come", when all who are in the grave, will hear his voice, and will come out, those who have done good, to the resurrection to life, and those who were evil, to the resurrection of damnation. (John 5:28, 29). The glorified Saints, who had part in the First Resurrection, will also stand before the judgement throne of Christ (2 Cor 5:10), not to be judged, for they were redeemed and glorified a thousand years ago, but now, to be presented by their Lord and King before all men and angels as a spectacle of Glory. (Heb 10:33. 1 Cor 4:9). The Lord is not only righteous in all His ways, but gladly shows His righteousness to all His creatures. If on Judgement Day one of his creatures tries to excuse himself by saying: "Lord! Your ways with me were too obscure, my life and tribulations too dark, and made it impossible to believe you," the Lord can refer to His Saints of the First Resurrection, and say: **"and what about these?** They have suffered mockery and stripes, bonds and prisons, were stoned, cut asunder, tempted, killed by the sword, roamed in sheepskins, abandoned, oppressed, etc., but they have believed, believed in Me, that I was their God. The world was not worthy of them, therefore I prepared a city for them." (Heb 11. Rev 21:2).

Verse 14. **"And death and hell (Hades) were cast into the lake of fire. This is the second death."** This occurs after all the dead in them are judged, for the last enemy, which is destroyed, is death (1 Cor 15:26). When men cease to be born, and the living changed to incorruptible bodies, death ceases to exist. And when all the dead are resurrected, the realm of the departed (Hades) also ceases to exist.

The natural death is the first death, which is not decisive for eternity. Then follows the Resurrection of the dead and the judgement, those who have spiritually died for God are lost forever. Those who do not partake of this second death obtain life eternal.

Verse 15. **"And whosoever was not found written in the book of life was cast into the lake of fire."** For all those who were saved now starts the eternal Salvation. What happens then is not mentioned by Revelation, because John was only transported to the judgement day to show him the final scenes.

About eternity Revelation does not say anything, and the Holy Scripture does not enlighten us either.

The Lord Jesus said, concerning eternity; *"For in the Resurrection they neither marry, nor are given in marriage, but are as the angels of God in heaven,"* (Matt 22:30), and Paul says (from Isaiah 44: 4),: *"Eye hath not seen, nor ear heard, neither have entered into the heart of man, the things which God hath prepared for them that love Him."* (1 Cor 2:9).

THE END OF REVELATION

Verse 6. **"And he said unto me, these sayings are faithful and true: and the Lord God of the holy prophets sent His angels to shew unto His servants the things which must shortly be done."** This angel is the same Apostolic clergy of (Rev 17:1. Rev 21:9), they do fulfil the task of declaring the return of Christ in our days, warning us that the judgement is at hand. The addition, that the Lord, who sent this angel, is the God of the Spirits of the prophets, who inspires the angel (clergy) to prophecy about all the things which will occur, indicates that this angel is one of the old prophets.

Verse 7. **"Behold I come quickly: blessed is he that keepeth the sayings of the prophecy of this book."**

Verse 8. **"And I, John saw these things and heard them. And when I had heard and seen, I fell down to worship before the feet of the angel which showed me these things."** Here again, it was the Lord who spoke through his angels (the Apostolic clergy) and this is confirmed in the following verse.

Verse 9. **"Then saith he unto me, see thou do it not: for I am thy fellow servant, and of thy brethren the prophets and of them which keep the sayings of this book: worship God."** The angel describes himself as a fellow servant (an apostle and prophet) and urges John to worship God.

We named the Revelation: "The Book for our Time".

In "the present", we explained that Revelation itself shows how it is given for our time, now that the return of the Lord is at hand. The last verses (10–17) of (Rev 22) contain a prophecy, a Godly decree of the Lord Jesus himself, totally and exclusively for our time.

Verse 10. **"And he saith unto me, seal not the sayings of the prophecy of this book: for the time is at hand."** The Lord now speaks Himself and contrary to what was commanded Daniel, to "seal up the prophecies until the end time, John is told not to seal it. This is proof that the Lord directs his sayings in the last times to His congregation in the seventh period. _It becomes apparent that only a substitute of John, an apostle of our Lord Jesus, can unseal the words for the prophecy of this book, and explain it for all to understand_. And when this unsealing of Revelation is completed, and its contents can clearly be read by everyone, the time is then also near, that the Lord shall come! We trust that with this work Revelation is unsealed.

Verse 11. **"He that is unjust, let him be unjust still: and he which is filthy, let him be filthy still, and he that is righteous, let him be righteous still, and he that is Holy, let him be Holy still."**

Continue in your ways, as if the time is too short to make any changes.

Verse 12. **"And behold, I come quickly; and my reward is with me, to give every man according as His works shall be."** Each one will be rewarded according to whether they were wise or foolish.

Verse 13. **"I am the Alpha and Omega, the beginning and the end, the first and the last."**

Verse 14. **"Blessed are they that do His commandments that they may have right to the tree of life, and may enter in through the gates of the city."**

The gates of the New Jerusalem are open and Christ urges the believers to make use of His offered Grace before it is too late.

Verse 15. **"For without are dogs, and sorcerers, and whoremongers, and murderers, and idolaters, and whosoever loveth and maketh a lie."** Dogs are impure (Matt 7:6. Phil 3:2), the sorcerers who poison the wine of the Vine Christ, (page 265. Vol.1), the whoremongers who fornicated with the state churches of Babylon, and the murderers, who do not love their brethren, (page 265. Vol.1), and those who lie and do not stand in God's truth. They are all excluded from the New Jerusalem.

Verse 16. **"I Jesus have sent mine angel to testify unto you these things in the churches. I am the root and the offspring of David, and the bright and morning star."** All these things were proclaimed by the apostles and prophets of Jesus in all Apostolic churches. The Elder of (Rev 5:5) names Jesus Christ the root of David. The morning star announces the day of the Lord, just as the apostles do in our time.

Verse 17. **"And the Spirit and the bride say, Come. And let him that heareth say Come. And let him that is athirst come. And whosoever will, let him take the water of life freely."** Here the Lord speaks in the present tense, therefore in our time.

Everyone is invited to partake of the water of life. The Holy Spirit and the bride both long for the day of the Lord. The elect cry day and night: Come Lord Jesus! Come!

Verse 18. **"For I testify unto every man, that heareth the words of the prophecy of this book, if any man shall add unto these things, God shall add unto him the plagues that are written in this book."**

Verse 19. **"And if any man shall take away from the words of the book of this prophecy, God shall take away his part out of the book of life, and out of the Holy City, and from the things which are written in this book."** These two verses contain a warning, that nothing shall be added or taken away from that which is written in Revelation. This warning concerns Revelation for it states "<u>from the words of the book of this prophecy</u>" and does not refer to the rest of the Holy Scriptures as some take this warning out of context.

Verse 20. **"He which testifieth these things saith, surely, I come quickly, Amen. Even so, come Lord Jesus."** Whosoever attentively followed the fulfilment of Revelation up to now, and learned to know the signs of the times, must agree: the threatening judgements are at hand, and the Lord comes.

He comes to judge the earth, but comes before that, to gather His bride to himself and to protect her from the time of tribulation. Yes, only in our days the Lord, through His reinstated gifts of prophecy, sounds the trumpet:

"I COME QUICKLY!"

John answers, Amen! Let it be so! And may this longing be loudly expressed by us all, by all our readers, and all Christians, equally warm, equally deep, equally fiery rise before the Lord: **"Amen! Come, Lord Jesus!"**

We now have said what we had to say about Revelation and thus make John's blessing our own, and commit the reader to the Lord:

Verse 21. **"The Grace of our Lord Jesus Christ be with you all. Amen."**

THE END.

CONTENTS
Volume one: The Past

First Period: The Longing

Second Period - Smyrna: The Bitterness

Third Period-Pergamos: Building The Tower

Fourth Period: The Unbridled Run-Away

Fifth Period- Sardis: The Remnant

Sixth Period-Philadelphia: Brotherly Love

Volume Two